Treating
Trauma-Related Dissociation

Treating
Trauma-Related Dissociation

A Practical, Integrative Approach

KATHY STEELE

SUZETTE BOON

ONNO VAN DER HART

W. W. NORTON & COMPANY
Independent Publishers Since 1923
New York • London

Note to Readers: Standards of clinical practice and protocol change over time, and no technique or recommendation is guaranteed to be safe or effective in all circumstances. This volume is intended as a general information resource for professionals practicing in the field of psychotherapy and mental health; it is not a substitute for appropriate training, peer review, and/or clinical supervision. Neither the publisher nor the author(s) can guarantee the complete accuracy, efficacy, or appropriateness of any particular recommendation in every respect.

Copyright © 2017 by Kathy Steele, Suzette Boon, and Onno van der Hart

All rights reserved
Printed in the United States of America
First Edition

For information about permission to reproduce selections from this book, write to Permissions, W. W. Norton & Company, Inc., 500 Fifth Avenue, New York, NY 10110

For information about special discounts for bulk purchases, please contact W. W. Norton Special Sales at specialsales@wwnorton.com or 800-233-4830

Manufacturing by Edwards Brothers Malloy
Production manager: Christine Critelli

Library of Congress Cataloging-in-Publication Data

Names: Steele, Kathy, author. | Boon, Suzette, author. | Hart, Onno van der, 1941 - author.
Title: Treating trauma-related dissociation : a practical, integrative approach / Kathy Steele, Suzette Boon, and Onno van der Hart.
Description: New York : W. W. Norton & Company, [2017] | "A Norton Professional Book." | Includes bibliographical references and index.
Identifiers: LCCN 2016012923 | ISBN 9780393707595 (pbk.)
Subjects: LCSH: Dissociative disorders—Treatment. | Psychic trauma—Complications. | Psychic trauma—Treatment.
Classification: LCC RC553.D5 S72 2017 | DDC 616.85/23—dc23 LC record available at http://lccn.loc.gov/2016012923

W. W. Norton & Company, Inc.
500 Fifth Avenue, New York, N.Y. 10110
www.wwnorton.com

W. W. Norton & Company Ltd.
15 Carlisle Street, London W1D 3BS

1 2 3 4 5 6 7 8 9 0

To all patients and therapists around the world who choose this challenging journey, who are willing to risk and persevere together in an imperfect but wholly "good enough" psychotherapy. To each of you, an abundance of compassion, courage, and clarity.

CONTENTS

This book was born not only out of countless hours of treating patients with dissociative disorders, but also out of the crucible of supervision and consultation, where therapists bring their most urgent questions, needs, and vulnerabilities. For many years we have heard therapists around the world ask similar questions and struggle with similar challenges with dissociative patients. In addition to an overview of phase-oriented treatment, it is this set of issues we have tried to bring to this volume: what to focus on first in a complex therapy, and how to do it; how to establish safety for a patient engaging in unsafe behaviors without rescuing; how to work with dissociative parts in ways that facilitate integration rather than further dissociation; how to set and maintain helpful boundaries; how to deal compassionately and effectively with dependency on the therapist; how to help patients integrate traumatic memories; what to do when the patient is enraged, chronically ashamed, avoidant, or unable to experience the therapist as having any good intentions; and how to compassionately understand and work with resistances. Most importantly, we have focused not only on how to conceptualize and treat dissociation but on how to *be* with patients who experience themselves as many instead of one.

Doing Versus Being

Most therapists who are just becoming familiar with working with dissociative patients are seeking techniques. When one is faced with complexity and unfamiliar territory, it is the most natural thing in the world to seek out what to *do*. These therapists will find that treatment of patients with dissociative disorders includes some very practical techniques that support gradual integration. Nevertheless, relational ways of being with the patient are the backbone of treatment, and are themselves essentialtherapeutic interventions.

The task of every good therapist is to seamlessly interweave a coherent combination of cognitive, emotional, and somatic interventions (things to do) with the relational experience in the moment between two human beings in a two-person psychology (ways to be). In fact, there is nothing more practical and integrative than making the therapeutic relationship an integral part of working with patients who have been so wounded by others. The findings of interpersonal neurobiology point more and more to the centrality and transforming power of implicit relational interactions in therapy (e.g., Cozolino, 2010; Schore, 2012; Siegel, 2010b, 2015). The effect size of the impact of the therapeutic relationship is even greater in patients with dissociative disorders than in many other clinical populations (Cronin, Brand, & Mattanah, 2014), so relational processes with these patients deserve extra attention and care. Yet, despite recommendations by experts to the contrary, therapists generally underutilize the relationship as a therapeutic process (Brand et al., 2013). Thus, we have set out to embed in a relational context a practical and integrative approach with as many and as varied techniques as possible for what often is a challenging and complex therapy.

When faced with urgency, crisis, and confusion, it is especially hard to follow the wise adage *Don't just do something; stand there.* Words may fail or are misinterpreted in therapy; interventions fall flat or are rejected out of hand; good intentions fall short; and issues emerge that are beyond any directive action to change or fix. Interventions then become invisible, transmuting into nonverbal, implicit, unconscious, intersubjective ways of being. Thus, we offer a slight twist on that old truism: *Don't just do something; be there.* Such relational interchanges are the hardest for therapists to recognize and participate in effectively. But they are so very important. We have tried to include ways for the therapist to communicate what is not communicable with words. This is essential for highly traumatized patients who are often living in an overwhelming inner world in which words have lost their meaning and language is not possible. To this end, we have also tried to include somatic interventions that are helpful when words fail or are not sufficient.

The common factors theory of psychotherapy suggests that particular theoretical approaches play little overall role in whether patients improve or not. Common factors that do make a significant contribution to the patient's improvement include collaboration on shared goals, therapeutic alliance, empathy of the therapist, positive regard and affirmation, congruence and genuineness of the therapist, and other therapist factors (Laska, Gurman, & Wampold, 2014; Wampold, 2001). These findings do not imply that therapists should abandon theory and technique in the treatment of patients with dissociative disorders—or any other disorder, for that matter. We believe an organized and thoughtful approach to treatment—regardless of what it is—is necessary for common factors to be effective. Even with sound relational approaches that include a solid treatment frame and boundaries, therapists still need special techniques to work with dissociative parts, at least in patients who have severe dissociative disorders. Such techniques are central to the effective treatment of these patients (e.g., Boon, Steele, & Van der Hart, 2011; Brand et al., 2011; Kluft, 1991, 1993a, 1995; Van der Hart, Nijenhuis, & Steele, 2006).

The Humbling Experience of Treating Patients With Dissociative Disorders

We offer the contents of this book with a large dose of humility, realizing that no single clinician has all the right or best answers. Even though the three of us have over 120 years of experience in treating patients with dissociative disorders between us, we are nevertheless acutely aware of so much that we do not know, that we cannot know, that others know so much more clearly than we do; and of the mistakes we so often make. However, we offer you what we do know, and what we are reasonably certain will add to your skills in treating patients with dissociative disorders.

We also acknowledge that evidence-based treatment of patients with dissociative disorders is still in its infancy, so the approaches in this book are based primarily on clinical wisdom and experience (a legitimate form of evidence), not randomized controlled research. Fortunately, there is a healthy and burgeoning body of empirical literature on the effectiveness of these time-honored, anecdotal approaches to working with dissociative patients (Brand, Classen, Lanius, et al., 2009; Brand & Loewenstein, 2014; Brand, Loewenstein, & Spiegel, 2014; Myrick, Chasson, Lanius, Leventhal, & Brand, 2015). What we—and others—have found successful in clinical practice is finally being validated by research. But we caution readers to stay abreast of current research and treatment recommendations.

In some ways we may seem to be trying to impose linear order on what is a very complex and messy process in the therapy room. We are perhaps guilty of making it seem easier than it is. However, we truly know from our own experiences that there is perhaps no other therapy that challenges the therapist's sense of competence so profoundly as work with chronically traumatized individuals. The humbling reality for all of us is that therapy can be uneven and uncertain, challenging and confusing. We, like other therapists, find ourselves sometimes lost for a moment, not knowing what to do or how to be, making unintentional mistakes, missing important cues, caught by transference and countertransference. Some of the lessons we share in this book evolved not only from our successes but also from our failures and mistakes. We hope you, the reader, will benefit from our mishaps as much as from our triumphs. We also hope that you can embrace your own mistakes and learn from them, knowing that you are not required to be perfect for this work, and every therapist would do best to eventually shed the heavy and unrealistic burden of perfection.

The Organization of the Book

In this book, we discuss treatment for patients who are appropriate for private practice or outpatient clinics. There is certainly a subgroup of more greatly disturbed patients who need to be accurately assessed in order to determine whether they are best treated in settings that offer crisis and supportive care, case management, and ready access to psychiatric hospitalization. Chu (2011) has referred to these patients as "chronically disempowered." They may have profound personality disorder comorbidity and may exhibit suicidality, self-harm, and other extreme acting-out behaviors. We have found that therapists are sometimes so focused on dissociative symptoms and the challenging presentations of dissociative patients that they may not readily distinguish between patients who are appropriate for outpatient settings and those who are not, or between those who need supportive care versus those who can eventually tolerate and thrive in a depth psychotherapy. To this end, we have spent time in the book describing the characteristics of patients with varying needs and prognoses, so the therapist can make wise choices about whom best to treat in which setting and what kind of treatment might be most useful. And as always, we encourage therapists to consult with others when in doubt, a practice that each of us continues to follow in our own work.

This book is divided into six sections. In the Introduction, the first chapter serves as an overview of the neuropsychological aspects of dissociation as a disorder of non-realization. Part I (Chapters 2–4) focuses on the therapeutic relationship and the person of the therapist. Part II (Chapters 5–9) is dedicated to assessment and planning. These chapters discuss assessment of dissociative disorders; case formulation; prognosis; treatment planning; principles of treating dissociative disorders; and an overview of the three phases of treatment, each with a set of goals. Part III covers Phase 1 treatment in Chapters 10–18, emphasizing specific issues and how to include dissociative parts in the work. Topics in this section include understanding and working with resistance, which is seen as a co-creation of the patient and therapist; managing dependency in therapy; and integrative approaches to understanding and working with chronic shame. Chapter 19 includes several selected topics, including helping patients deal with their current relationships and parenting, sexual issues, family of origin dilemmas, ongoing victimization; and managing treatment team splitting and conflicts. Part IV (Chapters 20 and 21) focuses on Phase 2 treatment of traumatic memories. Part V (Chapters 22 and 23) includes a discussion of integrating dissociative parts into a coherent whole and other Phase 3 issues.

We have included two additional features in the book that we hope will be helpful. The first is Core Concepts—fundamental ideas that are highlighted in the text in bold so they can be seen at a glance. These serve as guiding principles in treatment as well as a summing-up of many of the most important notions in each chapter. The second is a section titled Further Explorations at the end of each chapter, intended to capitalize on the fact that as a rule, therapists are eager and lifelong learners. These sections include additional ideas and questions, exercises for practicing skills, and suggestions for peer discussions based on topics in a particular chapter, meant to inspire further curiosity, discovery, and growth.

Finally, we are acutely aware that we have not included all that is relevant in this book. Our hope is that we have included enough and, most importantly, have provided sufficient guiding principles to help therapists find their way a little better through chaos and complications.

A Word About Terminology

We struggled a bit in deciding what terminology to use, as we wanted this book to be highly practical and as jargon-free as is reasonable. We found this particularly challenging when it came to a few of our own theoretical terms. The fact that we developed them in the first place means we found them to have great clinical utility. In the past, we have used two terms that especially deserve a brief note here, as we have chosen not to use them in this particular book.

In an attempt to define prototypes of dissociative parts of the personality, we have used the term *Apparently Normal Part of the Personality* (ANP) to describe parts that function primarily in daily life, are mediated by action or motivational systems of daily life, and avoid traumatic memories; and the term *Emotional Part of the Personality* (EP) to describe parts that are primarily fixed in action systems of defense against danger and life threat, and stuck in trauma. There are some pros and cons to using this language. For example, the term *ANP* does not indicate the quality of functioning in daily life (apparent normality) but rather the lack of integration vis-à-vis other parts, maintained by the ANP's phobia of these other parts and associated traumatic memories. Although one of us (Onno) remains attached to this term; the other authors (Kathy and Suzette) think the concept may be a bit too narrow to convey adequately the full range of experiences of dissociative parts of the patient that function in daily life, which have innumerable expressions. In this book we will therefore refer to ANP as *parts that function in daily life*, regardless of their appearance of normality or dysfunction.

Likewise, the term *EP* is useful, as it describes the vehement emotion common to parts stuck in trauma-time that accompanies defense against real or perceived extreme threat, even though some of these parts may be numb or may have developed some daily life functions. One of the authors (Onno) prefers this term, while the others (Kathy and Suzette) think the term is too restrictive, focusing on emotion rather than on the fact that these parts are fixed in trauma-time in defensive actions, with emotion as an outgrowth of defense. And some ANPs may also have the qualities of vehement emotions. In this book we will refer to EPs as *parts fixed in trauma-time*. One of the many things we value about our gratifying collaboration with each other for the better part of half a century is that we embrace these kinds of disagreements, which are merely fodder for more vibrant and enriching discussions.

A Note About Case Examples

While cases in this book reflect actual clinical issues, they are composites of patients and include reconstructions of clinical dialogues. Specifics have been carefully altered in order to protect the privacy of patients.

ACKNOWLEDGMENTS

Books are not written in isolation, and our years of experience reflected here did not occur in a vacuum. Indeed, our acknowledgments in this section are a testament to the fact that behind our writing and clinical experiences stand many dozens of individuals with wise minds and compassionate hearts who have taught us, challenged us, and supported us. We are fortunate to have colleagues literally around the world with whom we have exchanged ideas. Each of us has been richly influenced by masters of the field, by our peers, and by workshop participants from whom we have learned even as we taught them. We owe all of them our gratitude for their support, their willingness to share what they have learned, their incisive questions that challenge us, and their courage in treating patients who have extremely complex issues.

We are especially thankful for 20th-century pioneers in the field of complex trauma and dissociation who particularly inspired us, notably Elizabeth Bowman, Bennett Braun, David Caul (1921–1988), James Chu, Philip Coons, Catherine Fine, Jean Goodwin, Richard Kluft, Richard Loewenstein, Frank Putnam, and Colin Ross.

Our gratitude goes to our many contemporaries—too many to name, but no less deserving of praise—who have made major written and clinical contributions to the understanding and treatment of patients with dissociative disorders, from which we have learned much. We thank you, and we have been honored to travel these roads with you. For their phenomenal clinical contributions, research, and published works, we are especially indebted to Trine Anstorp, Peter Barach, Kirsten Benum, Bethany Brand, Philip Bromberg, Laura Brown, Richard Chefetz, Catherine Classen, Christine Courtois, Constance Dalenberg, Martin Dorahy, Paul Dell, Nel Draijer, Janina Fisher, Julian Ford, Claire Frederick (1932–2015), Steve Frankel, Jennifer Freyd, Denise Gelinas, Steve Gold, Anna Gerge, Michaela Huber, Anabel Gonzalez, Elizabeth Howell, Phil Kinsler, Jim Knipe, Giovanni Liotti, Willie Langeland, Ruth Lanius, Warwick Middleton, Andrew Moskowitz, Dolores Mosquera, Russell Meares, Ellert Nijenhuis, John O'Neil, Pat Ogden, Clare Pain, Maggie Phillips, Luisa Reddemann, Vedat Şar, Eli Somer, David Spiegel, Joan Turkus, Bessel van der Kolk, and Eric Vermetten.

On both a more personal level and a professional level, we extend our deepest appreciation and gratitude to those who have offered emotional support and opportunities for growth, case consultation, and lively discussions and debates. We are especially grateful to Pat Ogden for our many fruitful conversations on trauma, attachment, dissociation, and somatic experience, and for her unfailing support and her contributions on the body in this book. She has been central to our learning how to incorporate somatic experience into treatment, which has exponentially enhanced our therapy with traumatized patients.

Others to whom we wish to acknowledge our gratitude include, from the United States: colleagues at Metropolitan Psychotherapy Associates, Amanda Savage Brown for her insightful comments on acceptance and commitment therapy in working with shame, Heather McCormack Moon for her helpful comments on dialectical behavior therapy, Roger Solomon, and Marty Wakeland. From Belgium: Erik de Soir and Manoëlle Hopchet. From China: Ellen Ma. From Finland, our esteemed and cherished colleague and friend Anne Suokas-Cunliffe. From Germany: Helga Matthess and Bettina Overcamp. From Israel: Danny Brom and Eliezer Witztum. From Italy: Giovanni Tagliavinni and Alessandro Carmelita. From the Netherlands: Mariëtte Groenendijk, Desiree Tijdink, Annemieke van Dijke, and all colleagues from the Top Referent Trauma Center (TRTC) in Zeist. From Norway: Harold Baekkelund, Ingunn Holbaek, Ellen Jepsen, and Katinka Salvesen. From Sweden: Ann Wilkens. And from the UK: Remy Aquarone and Orit Badouk Epstein. It does indeed take a village to raise (and support) a therapist.

We have done our best to give credit where credit is rightly due in the book. If we have failed in this regard, it is entirely unintentional. The greater the body of literature, the more challenging this task is. And fortunately, the literature on treatment of dissociative disorders has grown exponentially. It is especially difficult sometimes to track down the original creator of a particular technique that may have been taught in workshops long before it was published. Again, we have done our best in this regard, which, alas, we know will not be perfect.

An abundance of thanks to our fantastic copy editor Virginia ("the Stickler") Wood, PsyD. Your knowledge of grammar and APA formatting and style apparently knows no bounds, and somehow here and there you helped us say clearly what we could not seem to articulate coherently.

Many thanks to our Norton editors, Deborah Malmud, Elizabeth Baird and Benjamin Yarling, who have patiently endured our delays and been incredibly responsive and helpful.

Above all, a warm and humble thank-you to our patients. You are the ones who have taught us the most, and have tolerated with grace our fumbling mistakes and human imperfections. Thank you for believing in us and sharing part of your journey with us. Be well and live well, with the compassion, care, and liveliness you so richly deserve.

Treating
Trauma-Related Dissociation

Introduction

CHAPTER 1

Dissociation as Non-Realization

Dissociation is the essence of trauma.
—Bessel van der Kolk (2015, p. 66)

When the realization is deep, your whole being is dancing.
—Zen saying

Helen is a bright, witty, resourceful middle-aged woman at the height of a successful career in human resources. From the outside, it looks as though she has everything going for her. But Helen is depressed, and she constantly fears she will be fired despite all evidence to the contrary. Indeed, she is highly respected and liked by her colleagues, but she cannot accept it. She is emotionally numb much of the time but also suffers from insomnia and violent nightmares, panic attacks, and fragmented flashbacks of childhood abuse full of terror, pain, and helplessness. Helen hears several frightening inner voices, one of which screams at her in rage and disgust and another that sounds like a small child inside crying out in pain. When she hears one of these voices, her eyes dart back and forth and she appears frightened. Her body is tense, her chest is caved in, and she keeps her head pulled into shoulders that hunch upward toward her ears. She is on the verge of breakdown by the time she decides to begin therapy.

Helen reports a history of severe abuse and neglect from an early age, though she only recalls fragments of her childhood. The rest she has pieced together from disturbing stories her siblings and other family members have shared, but which she does not actually remember. Some of the memories Helen does have of her difficult childhood seem dreamlike and foggy, as though they were not real or had happened to someone else. She recalls experiences in childhood of floating above her bed, watching "another little girl who was wearing my pajamas and had hair just like mine" be violently sexually abused by a family member. She painfully struggles with whether her unclear images are true and whether her siblings are exaggerating the horror of what happened. On the other hand, she is plagued with flashbacks that seem too real, blurring and blotting out her present reality with their sensorial vividness. Helen berates herself, believing she has no reason to be depressed, saying she is being weak and childish for complaining, and if only she tried harder, everything would be all right. She bears enormous emotional suffering every day, to the point of having trouble functioning.

A Continuum of Non-Realization: Not Real, Not True, Not Mine, Not Me

There are many issues that can be highlighted in Helen's story, but we begin with her startling difficulties with realization—that is, with accepting her life as it is and adapting to it. Realization is a powerful concept, relevant to everyone in their daily lives. It is a central component of integration. *Integration* involves ongoing actions that help us both differentiate and link experiences over time within a personality that is both flexible and stable. It thus promotes the best functioning possible in the present and in the anticipated future (Van der Hart, Nijenhuis, & Steele, 2006). Realization is not only pivotal to the resolution of trauma but necessary to successful coping with everyday life—from the mundane to the catastrophic, from the pleasurable to the painful, from the simplest to the most complex of experiences. We can best realize what others around us also realize; we tend to live in a shared social reality. When children are abused by a caretaker who is supposed to love them, when people and organizations do not protect like they should, it is intolerable for the children to realize. Betrayal inhibits realization and promotes dissociation (Freyd, 1996, 2013).

CORE CONCEPT

Realization is the ongoing action of being aware of reality as it is, accepting it, and then adapting to it effectively (Janet, 1935, 1945; Van der Hart et al., 2006).

Non-realization is the inability to grasp essential aspects of external experience that rightly and factually belong to our past, present, and future; our self; and our inner experiences, such as thoughts, physical actions, sensations, memories, and emotions. It comes in many shapes and sizes for all of us. It can be mild, moderate, or extreme, and related to simple daily experiences or catastrophic events. It can manifest in some areas of life and not others. It can range from minor momentary lapses to major amnesia—complete non-realization (Janet, 1945).

Non-realization can also pertain to some aspects of an experience and not others, and this applies to good experiences as well as to bad ones. For example, Helen was proud of being the first in her family to complete college but could not realize that it was her own intellectual capacities that made it possible; instead, she believed she was stupid in spite of clear evidence to the contrary. She realized that she was constantly fearful, reflected in her darting eyes and hunched shoulders, but she could not yet realize the root of her fear.

Trauma survivors have a mix of the normal, daily non-realizations that are common to everyone compounded by major non-realizatons: *I don't really have any issues; I'm only coming to therapy because my husband wants me to. I am not the problem; everyone else is the problem! My childhood was fine. I have no idea how those burns got on my arm—they don't hurt at all. I don't remember anything before high school. That little boy is not me; that face I see in the mirror is not mine.* The more entrenched and pervasive the non-realization, the more likely therapy will probably be long and challenging. In these cases, much work must be done to help the patients increase realization and integration.

Somatic Experience in Realization and Non-Realization

By blind omission, traditional psychotherapy has not supported therapists in realizing the central role of somatic experience—sensation, movement, posture—as necessary or even important to address. A few clinicians have complained that some therapists tend to treat dissociative parts as though they were "things" separate from the person as a whole. Yet therapy itself has somehow reified the mind as a "thing" to be treated without consideration that the contents of the mind are embodied. In reality, we are both mind *and* body; our minds are embodied. We sense and move in reaction to what is in our minds, and simultaneously our minds reflect what we are sensing in our bodies. They are truly inseparable, influencing each other in a constant implicit feedback loop. Even in the most profound non-realization, dissociative parts display themselves somatically, each with their own physical characteristics, even while they remain unknown or unacknowledged by the patient. In dissociative patients, aspects of the trauma as well as avoidance of the trauma are held in various dissociative parts. For example, one part of the patient may be fixed in fear, with tense muscles and a frozen facial expression or with severe physical pain; another may be slumped and shut down, curled in on herself, avoiding any acknowledgment of the trauma—both physically and emotionally numb. Each dissociative part has its own corresponding physiology, sensations, and movements that reflect their respective mental contents.

Habitual sensory experiences, gestures, movements, and postures play a pivotal role in supporting either realization or non-realization. Patients and therapists need to able to recognize, for example, the sweaty, sharp sensations; the jittery movements; and the tense posture of fear in order to intervene early to support regulation, to shift fear into a more adaptive emotion in the present. Emotions have affective somatic precursors and include sensations, gestures, and movements. The patient's posture collapses in depression; muscles tense with anxiety and fear; hands tighten into fists, the chest thrusts out, and shoulders are thrown back with anger; facial expression changes according to perceived safety or threat. The felt experience of relational support from another is necessary for secure attachment, and can be expressed in a warmth and expansion in the chest, a relaxation of tenseness, a straightening of posture, a seeking of eye contact. These and countless more somatic experiences are essential not only to notice but to utilize therapeutically.

A therapist's implicit avoidance of somatic experience can collude with the traumatized patient's avoidance, which may unknowingly maintain ongoing non-realization. Though patients may talk as if they have insight and have integrated trauma, often this superficial and unemotional narrative is an avoidance accompanied by dissociation and depersonalization. If the therapist only listens to the patient's words in this case, and does not attend to the patient's arousal level and somatic experience, an opportunity for further realization will be missed.

There is a painful awareness among therapists that words, the mainstay of talk therapies, often fail traumatized individuals; they are unable to understand, to speak, or to formulate thoughts when traumatic memories are activated, especially when these experiences were preverbal. Memory is not only emotional and cognitive; it has somatic components. In particular, traumatic memories are primarily somatosensory, often without (much of) a cognitive component, and the nonverbal experience of the trauma lives on in the body, held within particular dissociative parts (Brewin, Dalgleish, & Joseph, 1996; Ogden, Minton, & Pain, 2006; Van der Kolk, 1994; Van der Kolk & Fisler, 1995; Van der Kolk & Van der Hart, 1991). As Bessel van der Kolk noted, "The body keeps the score," even when the patient cannot recall a traumatic experience or has only fragmentary recall. (1994,, 2014). Patients often say, "I know I am safe and present, but I don't *feel* safe, and I *feel* like I am back there when [the trauma] was happening." Thus, repetitive and unfinished somatic actions of the trauma can continue, and can be held in various dissociative parts of the patient.

While realization and integration may implicitly include somatic shifts, such that the therapist does not always need to address them directly, other times it can be essential to work explicitly with somatic experience. Therefore, we believe it is imperative that the therapist incorporate somatic awareness and interventions with more traditional psychotherapy approaches with chronically traumatized individuals to facilitate realization and integration (Ogden et al., 2006; Ogden & Fisher, 2015).

Dissociation as a Problem of Non-Realization

Dissociation is perhaps the most profound type of non-realization. In fact, dissociative disorders have been called "syndromes of non-realization" (Janet, 1935, p. 349) and "multiple reality disorders" (Kluft, 1993a, p. 36). Dissociation involves a division of the patient's personality into parts that each have their own sense of self and some degree of first-person perspective (Nijenhuis & Van der Hart, 2011), with specific emotions, thoughts, beliefs, sensations, perceptions, predictions, physical actions, and behaviors. Each dissociative part of the patient's personality encompasses a unique perception of reality that can contradict the reality of other parts, with an amazing attitude of indifference toward profound inconsistencies.

CORE CONCEPT

Dissociation is a division of the patient's personality into parts that each have their own sense of self and experience too little or too much as a consequence of non-realization. These paradoxical experiences are the hallmark of the inability to realize trauma.

CASE EXAMPLE OF NON-REALIZATION: JOE

Joe's sister recalled that they had both been sexually and physically abused by their sadistic older brother. There was concrete evidence of the abuse, including the fact that the older brother was removed from the home and placed in juvenile detention at age 16. However, Joe could not fully realize his traumatic history. Over the course of one session, various dissociative parts of Joe said, *My brother abused me; I was never abused. I love my brother; I don't have a brother; a scary giant lived in the closet in my room and came out to hurt me whenever I went to sleep.*

The uninitiated therapist is understandably completely confused by such contradictions: *What is real, and what do I do with these incompatible statements?* However, the therapist can make sense of these contradictions by understanding that the division of self is a solution to unbearable and irreconcilable realities.

In the inner dissociative world of a patient, contradictory statements can coexist and each be experienced as true by some part of the patient, but not by others. Joe does not (yet) fully realize that he was abused by his brother. The adult part of Joe that is most often present in therapy completely denies that his brother hurt him. Another part of Joe has even more profound non-realization—this part denies he even has a brother, and has no memories related to having one. A child part of Joe accepts he was hurt but is unable to realize it was his brother, believing he was abused by a "scary giant." Another part of Joe wants to tell the therapist the story of the abuse but is viciously censored internally by a part that screams, *Liar!* The adult part of Joe engages in further non-realization by denying that these dissociative parts even belong to him at all: *Those are just crazy voices that don't belong to me. I am afraid I am insane!*

Of course, the therapist does not know for sure that Joe's brother abused him, but it is not the therapist's job to sort out "the truth." The patient will make his own meaning of what happened with the neutral and compassionate support of the therapist, who gently points out inconsistencies and helps all parts of Joe to learn to reconcile them over time. However, the therapist can be certain that Joe is terribly conflicted about his brother, that he is suffering greatly, and that some major realizations are being avoided. Becoming aware of and reconciling these conflicts and avoidances becomes the focus of treatment.

Too Much and Too Little: The Dynamic Duo of Dissociation

Dissociative patients tend to experience a confusing mix of "too little" or "too much" as a consequence of non-realization. For example, on the one hand, Helen avoids her traumatic past and tries to go on with daily life. This adult part of Helen is what we have referred to as the Apparently Normal Part of the Personality or ANP (Nijenhuis, Van der Hart, & Steele, 2002; Steele, Van der Hart, & Nijenhuis, 2005; Van der Hart et al., 2006). In this book we will refer to ANP as *parts that function in daily life.* As the adult part that functions in daily life, Helen experiences too little, such as emotional and physical numbing, amnesia, the inability to feel pleasure, and a growing avoidance of triggers and exposure to new experiences, which increasingly constricts her life. She easily becomes spacey, not grounded in the present, thinking of nothing at all. She does not feel her own skin and has scalded herself in the shower on more than one occasion because she does not completely feel the heat. She often feels so emotionally numb that she describes herself as being like "a piece of cardboard." The adult part of Helen does not realize she has been abused, and in this sense, realizes too little.

On the other hand, the part of Helen that she calls "Ellen" continuously experiences being abused. This part of Helen experiences too much. We have previously termed this type of part as the Emotional Part of the Personality or EP (Steele et al., 2005; Van der Hart et al., 2006). In this volume, we will refer to EPs as *parts stuck in trauma-time*. Ellen is forever a child stuck in trauma-time, in defense against real or perceived danger or life threats. In this part of herself, Helen is highly dysregulated, experiencing too much; overwhelmed with fear or shame or rage, sexual feelings, and body memories. Sometimes Ellen is completely shut down, to the degree that it is hard for her to recognize the present. So in this way, Ellen also experiences too little of the present.

As "the Watcher," a critical, observing part of herself, Helen experienced her abuse from a great distance, with no emotions except for anger and disgust for "the little girl who didn't stop it." This part of Helen is aware of the trauma but feels too little of the emotion, as though the experience did not happen to her. Even though she remembers the abuse, the Watcher part of Helen is still unable to put it in a realistic context, blaming Ellen for causing the abuse. Thus, each part of Helen has unique forms of non-realization that contribute to ongoing inner conflicts and must be addressed in treatment.

These poles of too much and too little are manifestations of the highly contradictory experience of trauma survivors who simultaneously know (in some parts of themselves) and do not know (in other parts of themselves) what has happened to them (Laub & Auerhahn, 1993). Knowing and not knowing are important experiences that coexist and create extreme conflicts in dissociative patients. The contradiction between the two implies that full realization has not been achieved. The therapist should notice the conflict and bring it to the awareness of the patient in a way that invites safe curiosity, without taking sides.

CORE CONCEPT

Dissociative parts are mesmerizing sleights of hand that cleverly hold and conceal what cannot yet be realized by the patient. Therapists must keep their eye on the prize of missing and needed realizations rather than on the fascinating features of dissociative parts themselves.

Dissociative Parts as Phenomena of Non-Realization

Janet (1945) noted that *substitute beliefs*, the alternate realities that help a patient avoid realization, include dissociative parts. The phenomena of dissociative parts—their ages, genders, preferences, activities, and so on—are a kind of psychobiological deception that cleverly holds and conceals what cannot be realized by the patient. Like the Wizard of Oz (LeRoy & Fleming, 1939), dissociative parts reflect wounded and vulnerable people essentially telling themselves and the therapist, "Pay no attention to that man behind the curtain," in an effort to distract from terrible realities that have yet to be fully realized.

Simultaneously, parts stuck in traumatic experiences desperately experience the trauma as happening *now*. But even these parts are unable to realize that the past is over and the present is different. They are so fixed in horror, rage, fear, or shame that the therapist may become overwhelmed and distracted by the intensity, as can the patient. The resilience and strengths of the adult part of the patient may be forgotten. Child parts stuck in trauma-time can pull the therapist to caretake instead of treating patients like adults whose therapeutic task is to realize that the child parts belong to them as adults.

The problem of psychic equivalence. The therapist must remain focused on discovering the non-realizations of the patient rather than on the fascinating features of dissociative parts themselves. Dissociative patients often have what is called *psychic equivalence*—that is, they experience internal reality (dissociative parts, flashbacks, even thoughts or emotions) as real and powerful external realities (Fonagy, Gergely, Jurist, & Target, 2005; Target & Fonagy, 1996). While Fonagy et al. (2005) have described psychic equivalence as a failure to mentalize, it is also due to the extreme hypnotic *trance logic* common in dissociative patients, in which critical thinking and logic are suspended (e.g., Orne, 1959; Kluft, 1982; see Chapter 8). Thus, they may view parts as real people instead of disowned parts of the self. They experience flashbacks as real events in the present instead of as memories of the past. They may literally perceive the therapist as the abuser because they *feel* abused. They may take their strong feeling of being bad as unbearable evidence that they *are* bad. Therapists must not engage in psychic equivalence in regard to dissociative parts—that is, they must not confuse the patient's dissociative parts that are manifestations of extreme non-realization with actual people who should be treated separately and differently from each other. The antidote for psychic equivalence is first to be present and mindful, then to mentalize—to step back and reflect on what is happening—which leads to realization.

For example, therapists must understand that needy child parts hold yearnings for closeness, which the adult self that functions in daily life typically denies, is disgusted by, or finds threatening. They are not actual children but psychobiological representations of what cannot yet be realized. As these young parts, the patient avoids the realization that she is now grown up and must grieve what she did not receive in childhood. An adolescent part may act out or hold anger or sexuality that is disowned by the adult part, which protects the adult part from what are perceived to be unacceptable feelings and irresponsible impulses. The adolescent part avoids the realization that she is now grown up and must find a balance between freedom and responsibility. A tough, aggressive part may be stuck in a fight defense and does not realize that there is no longer a need to fight. Such a part might also avoid the realization that she was indeed vulnerable and helpless during the abuse. The therapist must recognize and help the patient accept these realizations in a paced manner in the successful treatment of dissociation.

The Evolutionary Foundations of Dissociation and Non-Realization

Dissociation is both a psychological and a physiological problem. In the section above we discussed the psychological aspects of non-realization. Now we turn to the important physiological underpinning of dissociation and the somatic aspects of non-realization.

Evolutionary Action Systems

Humans have inborn tendencies that organize our physiology, attention, and behavior to help us survive and function in daily life and to defend ourselves against danger and life threat. These tendencies have been called *action systems* (Nijenhuis, 2015; Van der Hart et al., 2006), *motivational systems* (Cortina & Liotti, 2007, 2014; Lichtenberg & Kindler, 1994), or *emotional operating systems* (Panksepp, 1998, 2012). Action systems each involve their own neural networks and are organized by primary affects and physiological needs. They involve evolutionary "memory" for what is positive (to be approached) and what is negative (to be avoided). We have proposed that action systems are primary organizers of dissociative parts, and as such, are essential to recognize and understand (Van der Hart et al., 2006). Some of these include:

- *Exploration*, so we can be curious and learn about ourselves, others, and our world
- *Attachment*, so we can seek connection that offers a sense of security and safety

- *Caregiving*, in response to attachment seeking by others
- *Sociability*, so we can function in groups, which includes
  - *Collaboration*, so we can understand each other, communicate, and work toward shared goals
- *Ranking or competition*, so we can maintain a place in a social hierarchy through dominance, submission, and competition for resources
- *Play*, which supports learning and competence and connection with others
- *Energy management*, the ability to manage adequate rest and food intake and conserve or expend energy as needed, and
- *Sexuality*, so we can reproduce.

There are also action systems of defense that organize our behavior when we are in danger or under life threat. These will be discussed further below and throughout the book.

In order for various action systems to be activated appropriately, humans need some way to determine whether we are safe or not. Thus, we all have a natural, innate capacity to assess safety, danger, and life threat at a neural and preconscious level before conscious awareness. Porges has called this *neuroception* (1995, 2001, 2004, 2011). Unfortunately, dissociative patients (or parts of themselves) are often unable to accurately assess whether they are safe or in danger in the present moment. That is, they engage in faulty neuroception. They typically inaccurately detect danger and threat where there is none, but sometimes they also do not detect threat when it is actually there. This lack of a very basic, instinctive, misperception leads to further psychological non-realization. Patients cannot realize they are safe because their body signals tell them they are still in danger. They cannot experience safe attachment that supports integration, so their non-realization is maintained. Conversely, patients who are unable to assess when they are not safe are so disconnected from their body signals that they cannot accurately detect cues for danger. These patients are often victimized time and again.

The Integrative Functions of Safe Attachment
Humans have an inborn psychophysiological organization called the *social engagement system* (Porges, 1995, 2004, 2011) that helps us regulate ourselves, so we can explore our world and connect well with others. The social engagement system is online at birth, and it is our psychophysiological foundation for exploration and secure attachment, contributing greatly to our regulation. Via the myelinated branch of the vagal nerve, our neural pathways are organized to support behaviors that facilitate exploration, bonding, and attachment. The myelinated branch of the vagal nerve also

helps control heart rate and thus our arousal level. The social engagement system helps us maintain a calm state of being that promotes growth, integration, and a sense of well-being. It is what allows us to connect with others so that we experience the foundational relational regulation that is necessary for mental health (e.g., Siegel, 2010b, 2015).

Activation of action systems of daily life. Exploration, secure attachment, and the social engagement system support activation of other inborn motivational or action systems necessary for adaptive functioning in life (Cortina & Liotti, 2007, 2014; Lichtenberg & Kindler, 1994; Panksepp, 1998; Van der Hart et al., 2006). It is clear that patients who suffer chronic trauma have difficulties with many of the functions of these inborn systems because they are not well integrated. Their daily life action systems are constantly interrupted when defenses against threat emerge. For example, many patients lack curiosity about themselves or the world because they are fearful; fear inhibits exploration. Many are unable to maintain eye contact, an important signal of connection to others. Thus, they are unable to read other people, making it much easier to continue being stuck in defense and feeling unsafe. They cannot use relational regulation to calm themselves. Many are unable to play or have fun because they feel inhibited in some way, shameful, or fearful. Others are unable to grieve successfully, being chronically stuck in despair and unable to draw upon positive relational experiences for support to process their grief. Others struggle with hyper- or hypo-sexuality, viewing sex either as a threat or as a substitute for intimacy. Many traumatized patients struggle to maintain regular rhythms of eating, sleeping, and resting. Some have a hyper-activated caregiving system, which is commonly referred to as *codependence*.

Inhibition of defense against danger and life threat. The social engagement system not only activates behaviors that support adaptive functioning in daily life; it also inhibits unnecessary defense. For example, a child might be frightened by thunder, but the parent reassures and supports the child in slowly learning about thunder, encourages the child to make loud noises with her own voice that mimic thunder, and models excitement and curiosity. The child sees that the adult is not afraid, which is calming and reassuring. Social engagement deactivates the child's defense, and once she is regulated and her attachment-seeking needs are fulfilled, the exploration system is again activated and off the child goes to explore the world.

Defense Against Danger and Life Threat

From an evolutionary standpoint, staying connected with others is our first-line defense against danger, since the social group is our most powerful protection. However, assessment of serious threat automatically activates defense and inhibits all action systems of daily life. While attachment is a first line of defense in mild threat, it does become deactivated when threat becomes more severe. For example, when a young child feels discomfort or distress, especially the panic that is evoked when the caregiver is out of sight, the child will call out. This is a natural defense called the separation cry, attachment cry, or cry for help. It involves panic, rather than fear, and frantic searching and crying and clinging behaviors (Nijenhuis, 2015; Ogden et al., 2006; Steele, Van der Hart, & Nijenhuis, 2001; Van der Hart et al., 2006; Van der Kolk, 1987). It is attachment seeking at its most intense. Its purpose is to engage the caregiver for safety and survival.

However, when threat becomes too great, the child no longer searches for an attachment figure but instead reacts with evolutionary prepared defenses. *Flight* and *fight* result in extreme hyperarousal accompanied by a readiness for action—tension in the shoulders, arms, and hands (fight) or legs and feet (flight). *Freeze* also involves high sympathetic arousal in which muscles are tense and heart rate is high, but in addition, speech is inhibited and movement impeded by tonic immobility (rigid or high muscular tone). When threat is severe enough to be assessed as life-threatening, the child may often collapse in a kind of death feignt or *hypoarousal feignt* (Porges, 2004, 2011). While fainting is the most extreme manifestation of dorsal vagal shutdown, a gradual slowing down, referred to as *flag* (Schauer & Elbert, 2010), is more commonly seen in sessions. While patients in flag may not be completely unresponsive, as is true in faint, they may be considerably spaced out, slow to think and speak, tired, or sleepy. Both flag and faint are mediated by the parasympathetic system (specifically, the unmyelinated dorsal branch of the vagus nerve) and are characterized by an extreme shutdown in which muscles lose their tone and become flaccid. For infants and young children, severe attachment disruptions such as neglect or abandonment can be assessed as life-threatening, evoking chronic defense (Barach, 1991; Bowlby, 1969/1982, 1980; Liotti, 2009; Schore, 2003). Table 1.1 summarizes these defenses. It is important for therapists to be able to distinguish each defense based on its psychophysiological aspects, as treatment approaches to each will differ.

In addition to being stuck in animal defenses, patients may also be caught in other unhelpful strategies based on evolutionary action systems. For example, one part of Helen can be extremely submissive and appeasing at work, communicated by a habit of ducking her head, assuming a collapsed posture, and speaking in a soft, compliant way. On the one hand, her appeasement is a kind of dorsal vagal shutdown in an attempt to survive, as she feels highly threatened by people due to faulty neuroception.

TABLE 1.1
Innate Defenses

Defense	Type	Physiological Control	Arousal Level	Physical Cues
Social Engagement	Connection to others for safety; Most evolved defense	Ventral vagal; Parasympathetic	Regulation and sense of well-being; normal HR & BP*	Relaxed, open posture with others; smiling or relaxed face; good eye contact
Attachment Cry/ Cry for Help	Cry for help to mobilize a stronger, wiser other for survival	Sympathetic; Panic rather than fear system of the brain	High level of distress and panic; urgent seeking and clinging to caregiver	Pleading eyes that seek the eyes of the other; increased proximity seeking; tendencies to lean forward, reach with eyes, face, and body
Flight	Mobilizing defense	Sympathetic	Hyperarousal; increased HR & BP, muscle tension, and movement; fear	Tension and/or increased movement, sometimes jittery, especially in legs; tendency to lean away, turn away, look at the door or for other escape routes
Fight	Mobilizing defense	Sympathetic	Hyperarousal; increased HR & BP, muscle tension, and movement; anger	Tension in arms, hands, and shoulders; preparatory movement precipitating a fight action, such as lifting of the palms or closing of the hands; may display pushing or clenching motions with arms or hands
Freeze / Frozen with Fear	Immobilizing defense; Tonic immobility	High sympathetic	Extreme hypercrousal; increased HR & BP, rigid muscle tone; loss of speech and coherent thinking; fear	High level of overall tension and rigid muscle tone coupled with immobility; feeling "paralyzed"; eyes may dart around the room or remain frozen
Flag	Immobilizing defense	Increased dorsal vagal; Parasympathetic tone	Hypoarousal; decreasing HR & BP, vasodilation; cognitive, emotional, verbal, sensory, and motoric shutdown	Slow motor responses and responsiveness; orienting to the environment and sensory alertness are inhibited; blank facial expression and stare; flaccid muscle tone
Faint / Collapse / Shutdown	Immobilizing defense; Flaccid immobility; Most primitive defense	Dorsal vagal; Parasympathetic dominance	"Playing dead" or death feint; large and rapid drop in HR & BP; loss of awareness and consciousness	Flaccid muscle tone; blank stare; unable to speak or move; cannot orient to the environment; often cannot hear, smell, or taste; may exhibit robotic movements that are not remembered

*HR = heart rate; BP = blood pressure

On the other hand, she learned as a child that she was best able to maintain connection by being appeasing and submissive, as is fitting within the ranking or competition system. So her behavior is both a defense against threat and a way to maintain attachment within a social ranking system. Helen also has a highly sexualized adolescent part as a strategy to stay safe (*I can survive if I am sexual*) and to get what she needs in terms of connection (*If I have sex, somebody will love me*). Having a sexual part also allows Helen to avoid dealing with her own sexuality, as it feels threatening to her.

CORE CONCEPT

Natural physical defenses are activated during potentially traumatizing events and include attachment cry, flight, fight, freeze, flag, and faint. Dissociative patients have parts of themselves that are stuck in these defenses, unable to realize there is no longer any danger, and unable to accurately assess safety.

Helen experiences a central dilemma common to all patients with dissociative disorders: the need to defend because of chronically faulty neuroception in which she assesses constant threat, and the simultaneous need to be connected to others and feel safe. We will return to this dilemma throughout the book, and particularly in Chapter 3, where we discuss how this conflict affects the therapeutic relationship.

Pathways to Chronic Dissociation and Non-Realization

Why is it that Helen—like other severely traumatized individuals—continues to maintain serious non-realization and dissociation as an adult, long after the traumatizing event is over? Why did she not integrate once she left her abusive situation? The answers to these questions can be found in a description of how dissociation develops in the first place.

As a child, Helen had traumatic experiences that she was not able to integrate at the time, metaphorical "breaking points" (T. A. Ross, 1941, p. 66). Overwhelming negative emotions (e.g., terror, shame, and rage, along with shut-down reactions), physical pain, and negative thoughts (e.g., *I am unlovable*) precipitate a breaking point, a sort of psychological and physiological circuit breaker that has been tripped.

CORE CONCEPT

Dissociation of the personality is maintained over time by (a) chronic breaking points—that is, experiences that overwhelm integrative capacity; (b) the inability to expand integrative capacity; (c) the necessity of relating to caretakers who are simultaneously needed and dangerous or frightening; (d) lack of social support, attachment repair, and regulatory skills; and (e) conditioned phobic avoidance of inner experiences.

Breaking points can happen to anyone—children or adults. However, children reach breaking points more easily due to the immature regulatory structures in their brains and developmentally limited integrative capacity. Conditions in which breaking points are severe or enduring can give rise to dissociation, a division of personality. The integrative or regulatory structures of Helen's young brain (for example, the hippocampus and prefrontal cortices) simply were not mature enough, nor did she have the cognitive or emotional skills, to integrate her abuse (Siegel, 2015). In addition, she lacked adequate social support for integration. Helen lived in a chronic state of overwhelm, alternating between hyper- and hypoarousal. In a hyperaroused state, she experienced high anxiety and extreme sensory alertness and had tense, quick movements. In a hypoaroused state, her muscles were flaccid, her movements slowed, and her senses dulled. These physiological states are barren ground from which thinking, reflecting, and integrating cannot grow and bear the fruits of realization. As a child, Helen did not have the breadth of life experience available to adults to make sense out of what happened, nor enough relational support to provide her with soothing, reassurance, and safety. She could not comprehend the major betrayal of those whom she loved and relied upon for survival (Freyd, 1996, 2013).

An accumulation of breaking points resulted in discrepant and incompatible senses of self that were organized around certain perceptions, emotions, thoughts, and physical actions that Helen could not integrate over time (cf. Nijenhuis, 2015). For example, there was Helen, a child who was smart and competent in school and functioned in daily life, but who avoided thinking or knowing about the abuse. Later, Helen only has the most fragmentary recall of childhood. There was the shut-down child part to whom the abuse happened, and whom Helen—as the part that functioned in daily life—refers to as "Ellen." This part of Helen is forever stuck in fear. Helen says to her therapist, *Those nasty things have happened to Ellen, not to me. I wasn't there.* There is the Watcher, who "observed" the abuse "from the ceiling" and who blames "the stupid little girl" (Ellen), and subsequently criticizes Helen as an adult for never being good enough. The Watcher is judgmental, shaming, and chronically angry; always observing, but never helping.

What about after Helen left home and was safe? Could she not integrate her experience then? For many patients, there remains the insoluble conflict between realizing what happened and needing to maintain contact with their families, including perpetrators. The dilemma is to accept what happened and lose your family, or maintain dissociation and have your family. Thus, Helen, like most trauma patients, became a habitual avoider, especially of her own thoughts, feelings, sensations, and memories that were related to her abusive past.

CORE CONCEPT

Trauma survivors are stuck in a pain paradox (Briere & Scott, 2012)—the more they avoid the pain of the past, the greater their suffering in the present.

Pain and discomfort are signals. That is, they have an important role in alerting us to the fact that something is not right. Ideally, one learns to confront and deal with whatever might cause some pain or discomfort in order to avoid greater pain. For example, hard study is preferable to failure; dealing with a painful past is better than being sucked into a vortex of continual avoidance that constrains or destroys current quality of life. Unfortunately, patients often do not learn this lesson of tolerating a degree of discomfort and pain for a greater purpose. They are stuck in a *pain paradox* (Briere & Scott, 2012). The paradox is that the more they avoid the pain of the past, the more the suffering of the past is sustained in the present. The more suffering is sustained, the more patients avoid the pain and retreat into non-realization. The solution is to accept compassionately, that is, *realize* pain—be it physical or emotional—which ultimately can lead to a reduction in suffering. This is one of the central tenets of acceptance and commitment therapy (ACT; Hayes, Strosahl, & Wilson, 2011) and dialectical behavior therapy (DBT; Linehan, 1993, 2014) and is a particularly essential concept for chronically traumatized patients to grasp.

Trauma-Related Phobias That Maintain Dissociation
The adult part of Helen has developed a phobia of inner experience, a core problem that needed to be confronted and resolved in therapy (Boon et al., 2011; Nijenhius, Van der Hart & Steele, 2002; Steele et al., 2005; Van der Hart et al., 2006). Over time, even the hint of any emotion or traumatic memory, any sensation of fear or anger, sends Helen into a flurry of dissociation and other

avoidance strategies. The other dissociative parts of Helen avoid each other, feeling afraid, ashamed of, or angry toward each other. In this way, the dissociation of Helen's personality and sense of self becomes self-perpetuating and does not resolve over time.

CORE CONCEPT

Patients with complex dissociative disorders have developed a series of inner-directed phobias related to trauma, which support avoidance and non-realization: the phobia of inner experience (thoughts, emotions, sensations, predictions, wishes, needs); the phobia of dissociative parts of self; the phobia of attachment and attachment loss; the phobia of traumatic memory; and the phobia of adaptive change.

In fact, the phobia of inner experience is part of a much broader set of trauma-related phobias, which also include the *phobia of dissociative parts*; the *phobia of traumatic memory* (Janet, 1904, 1925b); the *phobia of attachment and attachment loss*; and the *phobia of adaptive risk-taking and change* (Steele et al., 2005; Nijenhuis et al., 2002; Van der Hart et al., 2006). Each dissociative part is relatively isolated from other parts by these phobias, which are maintained by painful conflicts and memories that cannot yet be realized, and by avoidance strategies. For example, an angry part might have tense arms and a hostile facial expression, and feel disgusted by a needy part and punish the patient when needs are expressed. The needy part, which has a sunken posture and clingy actions, feels overwhelmed, criticized, and afraid of the angry part. The underlying reason for avoiding the needy part is that Helen's basic human need for care was unacceptable and even dangerous as a child. The angry part attempts to ensure survival by disowning these needs. The more the parts avoid each other, the more likely amnesia occurs and is ongoing, further perpetuating dissociation.

Trauma-related phobias develop because we all naturally avoid pain when we can—it is a hardwired tendency that has a survival function and plays an important role in making life safer and less painful in the long run. This innate avoidance of serious pain helps us learn to keep our hands away from fire, or understand that cruel or volatile individuals do not make great friends or partners. So it comes as no surprise that traumatized individuals avoid realizing or connecting with the painful past in order to try to go on with daily life, making survival possible. This is normal for a time. Short-term avoidance in order to get safe and gather resources to cope with traumatic experiences is healthy and often necessary. However, chronic avoidance and non-realization become substitute actions that replace realization, and they lead to serious difficulties.

Disorganized/Disoriented Attachment in Dissociative Disorders

Dissociation related to childhood abuse and neglect can perhaps best be understood as developing in the context of unsafe relationships (Barach, 1991). Dissociative patients invariably have a particular type of insecure attachment pattern called disorganized/disoriented or D-attachment (Blizard, 2003; Chu, 2011; Herman, 2011; Howell, 2011; Liotti, 1992, 1999, 2009; Lyons-Ruth, 2007; Steele et al., 2001; Van der Hart et al., 2006). D-attachment involves an insoluble conflict between the simultaneous need for defense and attachment with the same significant person (Main & Hesse, 1990). It is strongly correlated with chronic dissociation and dissociative disorders (Lyons-Ruth, Dutra, Schuder, & Bianchi, 2006; Ogawa, Sroufe, Weinfield, Carlson, & Egeland, 1997). Disorganized attachment involves a failure in adaptive regulation and in interactive repair leading to physiological, behavioral, and emotional dysregulation, and to problems with accurate mental representations of self and others (Schore, 2003, 2009, 2012; Siegel, 2010a, 2010b, 2015; Solomon & George, 2011).

As a child, Helen was caught in a dilemma between needing her abusive father and mother while also needing to defend against danger from them. Dissociation thus occurs between engagement in daily life, which includes attachment strategies, and rigid, innate animal defenses against threat (attachment cry, freeze, flight, fight, flag, and faint). As Liotti noted, chronic threat from a needed caregiver "exceeds the limited capacity of the infant's mind for organizing coherent conscious experiences or unitary memory structures" (2009, p. 55). Helen thus developed attachment-seeking and defensive strategies that contradicted each other. She had to seek out her caregivers for essential needs while avoiding the fact that they may be dangerous. She had to defend against danger and mortal threat while having the natural drive to connect and get essential needs met. Once a child becomes dissociative, one part (or more) of the child avoids connection in favor of defending against threat, while other parts frantically seek connection, and still others simply go on with daily life as though there is no danger. Each part thus has its own physiology when activated. Each part has its own mental representations, emotions, thoughts, predictions, and movement and body postures based on which defense is activated.

Dissociation, Defense, and Non-Realization

Avoidance of pain is complicated in trauma by chronic guilt and shame and by the habituation of inborn defenses against threat: flight, fight, freeze, flag (slowing down), and faint (collapse). As noted above, various dissociative parts can be fixed in these defenses.

Lack of realization is implicit when these defenses are habituated in trauma survivors, resulting in a cascade of integrative failures that perpetuate traumatic reactions over time. When humans are fearful, one or more of these defenses is activated, and we are primed to look for danger cues, even when they are not there. The ability to realize we are safe is inhibited at a primitive, instinctive level, and rational logic does not quiet the fear. For example, the child who is afraid of monsters in the closet is not at all helped with words *Don't worry, there are no monsters in there.* The child's body both reflects and contributes to the fear through tension that might indicate a readiness to run, fight, or freeze in fear—perhaps pulling in, curling up, or widening eyes and exhibiting frantic seeking behaviors such as clinging. Instead, the child has to have a *felt* sense of safety to support realization, whether it is through the literal caring presence of the parent, or through some bedtime rituals that enfold the child in a sense of security and well-being. The child is then able to use (real or represented) secure attachment as a physiological regulator that dampens fear arousal, quiets the neuroception of danger, and deactivates innate defenses. Gradually over time, the child learns to distinguish between internally generated fears and external reality, and develops the capacity to calm and soothe alone when necessary.

When fear or shame are chronically activated in a dissociative part, these emotions are relatively inaccessible to change by the patient without outside help, partly because not only emotional but also physical and neural patterns have developed that sustain these dysregulated conditions. Chronic somatic patterns may ensue: the habitual tension and high arousal that can reflect fear; or the downcast eyes, lowered head, slack posture, and low arousal that typically reflect shame. Thus, defenses against threat continue to be internally generated, unabated. Although the adult may know he is safe from an adult perspective, this cognitive awareness has little impact on dissociative parts fixed in fear. These parts must be accessed by the patient, helped to discover the somatic and emotional patterns that contribute to these defenses, and allowed to experience a felt sense of safety in order to make adaptive changes. We will return many times to these defenses and how to work with them over the course of the book. But for now, we continue with the theme of non-realization, this time examining the therapist's own difficulties, because none of us is immune to ongoing struggles to realize.

Non-Realization in the Therapist

Sometimes it is therapists who have major non-realizations, and who suffer the vagaries of experiencing too much and too little. We are confronted with the task of needing to realize certain truths about ourselves as well as about our patients in order to move therapy along. Realization is the pathway to owning and resolving our own reactions and emotions in response to patient—that is, countertransference.

CORE CONCEPT

Major non-realizations of the therapist can contribute to therapeutic impasses. Therapists' capacity to realize accurately both their own experience and that of the patient is essential in keeping therapy on track.

CASE EXAMPLES OF NON-REALIZATION IN THE THERAPIST: JACOB AND HARRIETT

Jacob was a therapist who was highly skeptical of dissociative disorders, which precluded his ability to realize he was treating a dissociative patient. When his patient told Jacob that she had different "people" (that is, dissociative parts) inside that hurt her, Jacob dismissed it as an unwillingness of the patient to take responsibility for her self-harm; he viewed self-harm as something she had read about and was trying to imitate for attention. He even considered whether the patient was psychotic, though she had no other symptoms of psychosis. Jacob did not believe that the patient had been traumatized, but assumed she was making up abuse stories, again for attention, possibly based on books she had read. This belief was not the result of careful observations or inquiries of the patient, nor of empathic listening for the suffering that might lie beneath the content of her story, but rather on what little he had been taught about abuse in his training many years ago.

When the patient did not make progress and actually increased her self-harm and became suicidal, Jacob informed her that she had a personality disorder and was not ready for treatment. Jacob's fixed beliefs about dissociation and trauma, his lack of training in dissociative phenomena, and his inability to compassionately be with his patient in her experience led to a shutdown of his curiosity. Jacob was unable to realize his countertransference. He was unable to realize that he was being distancing and dismissive, or that his focus on blaming the patient activated panic and shame in her and increased her symptoms. He faulted the patient for her lack of improvement, without being accountable for his own harmful actions and inability to connect with and understand the subjective experience of his patient. He had too little empathy and curiosity and too much rigidity in his beliefs.

Harriet was a therapist who saw her dissociative patient for extended sessions three or four times weekly to work on traumatic memories, and offered phone calls of reassurance and support whenever the client felt the need, which was often. Harriet treated her patient's dissociative parts as separate people. She believed that sustained contact with young parts by a caring person was needed to repair the patient's insecure attachment and cope with her awful traumatic memories, in spite of much evidence to the contrary, as reported in the clinical literature (e.g., Chu, 2011; Courtois & Ford, 2013; International Society for the Study of Trauma and Dissociation [ISSTD], 2011; Kluft & Fine, 1993; Steele et al., 2001).

Harriet was unable to realize that excessive memory work was destabilizing her patient, and that her caretaking of child parts without encouraging the adult self of the patient to help these parts had created a dependency on her, about which the patient felt both shame and urgency. This resulted in an endless cycle of need, shame, and rage in the patient. Harriet felt that no one understood the patient quite like she did, and that she was the only one who could help. She was unable to realize that this belief in her own and her patient's "specialness" was a strong countertransference reaction based not in reality but rather in fantasies of rescue and omnipotence. It was also rooted in a fear that the patient would not survive without her. These beliefs, coupled with the patient's desperation, created a cycle in which Harriet's rescuing and caretaking evoked uncontained dependency in the patient, which increased the patient's distress, which then perpetuated and even increased Harriet's need to rescue and caretake. Harriet was too embroiled with the patient's suffering and her own urgency to rescue to be able to help, and she had too few boundaries to contain the patient's suffering or her own desperate need to save the client.

Jacob and Harriet represent unfortunate extremes along a continuum of countertransference that are all too common among therapists of highly traumatized patients. In part this is because clinical education typically does not provide comprehensive training in treatment of dissociative disorders. These extremes of countertransference represent the poles of too little and too much action and emotion that involve significant non-realizations and do not allow the therapist to be fully with the patient's whole experience or attend wisely to the complexity of dissociative parts. Neither of these therapists were attentive to relational process. Instead, they were focused on content.

Somewhere in the middle of this continuum, most therapists strive to maintain a highly nuanced but consistent therapeutic balance between feeling and doing too much and too little. They do their best to acknowledge countertransference before they do (much) harm, correcting their own inner course so patients can correct theirs in an interpersonal dance that is imperfect, but good enough. Over the course of this book we will return time and again to these most important difficulties of the therapist with realization, and how to recognize and correct them in order to keep therapy on track.

The Road of Realization

We have been discussing the many forms of non-realization. On the flip side, understanding the nature of realization is also important. Realization is the unspoken partner of the popular concept of radical acceptance (Brach, 2003; Linehan, 1993), the nonjudgmental acceptance of reality as it is. It takes radical acceptance to the next step: to engage in adaptation, based on our willingness and ability to take responsibility for acting on reality as it is now, not as we wish it to be or as it was in the past. It implies the ability to accept and make adaptive meaning out of our own experience—past and present—to know and own what happens to us and within us. It means we deeply know—cognitively, emotionally, and somatically—that the past is over but that it also influences us and remains part of our experience. We know the future is not yet here, though we can predict it to some degree. We know we are firmly rooted in the present, where we have the possibility and responsibility to make adaptive choices about our actions.

Realization means we engage in complex and flexible combinations of actions that involve assessing safety, danger, and life threat; and thinking, feeling, sensing, perceiving, predicting, being, and doing. We take responsibility for our own contributions to our suffering or contentment and to that of others. We can reflect on our actions, and we are accountable for them. We make meaning from our experience, and this meaning can change over time, as we reflect and continue to have more encounters with life. In other words, we learn from new experiences rather than being fixed in old patterns of behavior. Of course, this sounds easy in theory. The truth is that realization can be an extremely difficult and challenging journey, especially for trauma survivors who are so stuck in the past and are terrified or ashamed to face it.

There are two forms of realization on the road to integration: personification and presentification. The personal owning of our experience is called *personification* (Janet, 1929; Van der Hart et al., 2006; Van der Hart, Steele, Boon, & Brown, 1993). Patients eventually must accept or realize that whatever has happened in their lives has happened to *them*, for better or worse. This engraving of experience as one's own is an essential step toward integration: *That happened to* me! *That part is* me! *My uncle hurt* me! Personification is acceptance of one's own reality.

However, integration requires more than just owning experience. Many patients can say, *I know it happened to me, but I don't feel anything about it.* Realization must also include being in the present with a relatively integrated sense of both our past and future, something far more complex than mindfulness of the present moment (Janet, 1928). This is called *presentification* (Janet, 1928; Van der Hart et al., 2006), the ability to simultaneously be and act in the moment, influenced but not controlled by the past (or anticipated future). In presentification, one connects the past and future to the here and now, providing context and meaning for the present. Presentification helps people (re)organize how they are in the world as they grasp the reality of the present and act adaptively in response. For example, once patients realize a certain memory belongs to them (*That happened to me*), they are further able to understand their behavior (*So that's why I hate sex so much*), and then change their behavior (*I can enjoy sex in the present, where I am an adult and with a safe and loving partner*).

Realization is not only about acceptance of what is. Equally importantly, realization is about the capacity to achieve that for which we have hoped and worked. For example, *After many years of hard work, I am finally able to realize my dream of getting a graduate degree*; or *I have come to realize that my parents didn't have the capacity to raise me in a healthy way, but also that I can be OK in the world anyway.*

The Imperfect Nature of Realization in Daily Life

Complete realization is elusive, if not impossible. Because integration, and thus realization, is ongoing and not perfect, we all find ourselves continually working to achieve acceptance of reality in both minor and major ways: *I can't realize the deadline is already here; I just can't realize my friend has died and I won't see her again—I still start to pick up the phone to call her; I don't think I have yet fully realized what it means to be single again after my divorce.* These everyday, normal struggles in realization are markers along the way of our continued journey along the imperfect path of continual integration. How much more difficult, then, to realize extremely traumatic experiences of overwhelming pain and betrayal that have been avoided for decades because they are so overwhelming.

The degree of realization that can be achieved depends upon the individual's level of integrative capacity. Some have more and others have less capacity due to innate, developmental, and environmental factors. Some highly traumatized patients come to therapy with a limited capacity to accept what has happened and move on. This is reflected in their level of insight, motivation, defenses, and resistances. Thus, therapy must always take into account the degree to which a particular patient is likely able to build integrative capacity to resolve traumatic memories and live more adaptively in life. This is an important consideration in assessing the sequence and pace of therapy and in determining prognosis (see Chapters 6 and 7).

Realization: The Present Through the Lens of the Past and Future

In spite of a focus on the present, our here and now can never be completely separated from the rest of our experience, past and future. Rather, the present is a rich tapestry woven from the threads of what we have realized from our past and from the ways in which we have adapted, for better and worse, up to this moment in time. We always see the present through the lens of our past and anticipated future, even if only implicitly. It is to be hoped that we have a relatively balanced view of our lives most of time, able to see the present clearly enough so it is not completely obscured by the past or the anticipated future. Whether that vision is relatively accurate or terribly distorted depends upon how much realization we have achieved. We can be truly present only to the degree that we allow ourselves to accept and realize our past and incorporate it into the lived moment in the present, instead of trying to sweep it under the rug. This is an ongoing endeavor throughout our entire lives, not a series of discrete, one-time events.

Each of us is eventually touched by tragedy, loss, disappointment, betrayal, or other kinds of pain. These are inevitable ingredients of life, just as are joy, comfort, contentment, or success. So realization is about accepting all things that come our way: the good and the bad as we perceive them. Though not easy or pleasant, realization must include accepting the darker side of life, the pain and struggle, the lack of control and the uncertainty, the unfairness and vulnerability, and the defeat and despair we all encounter from time to time. In our acceptance, we make meaning that sustains us and helps us move forward. We are not stuck in bitter fantasies of how it should have been different, or in recriminations over what we did or failed to do to "cause" things to go awry, full of "if onlys" and "should haves" and regrets.

Sometimes, neither therapist nor patient fully appreciates how challenging it will be to make gains in realization in therapy. It requires hard work and strong, regulated mental energy. It involves aligning and sustaining mental and behavioral actions that require consistent integrative capacity.

Patients often feel they are taking one step forward and two steps back in the ability to realize. Sometimes, realization is impossible or premature, and patients fall into crisis when they try to accept what is (yet) too overwhelming, such as the patient who is overcome with ever more disturbing flashbacks. In fact, impasses in realization are a common cause of crisis in therapy, and therapists must help their patients slow down and integrate only what they are able in the moment. This requires a close collaboration between therapist and patient to determine the level of integrative capacity in the moment.

For example, Helen is not yet ready or able to make several major realizations that are key to her recovery: *My father abused me; I am a decent and capable human being, not a broken product of mistreatment; My parents were wrong in their mistreatment of me, and it does not mean that I am bad.* These realizations, and many others, will be hard-won, taking hundreds, if not thousands, of new and difficult mental and behavioral actions that must be practiced over time. Helen must learn to tolerate and accept emotions and their accompanying sensations instead of avoiding them: *I feel sad; my chest is tight. It's OK that I feel sad. That makes sense.* She must understand thoughts and wishes instead of acting on them impulsively: *I want to hurt myself. Let me take a moment and reflect on what is going on that is upsetting me.* She must be mindful in the moment instead of caught in the past or worried about the future: *I am focusing on work right now. I am not in danger of losing my job, so it doesn't help to be thinking of finding another job.* She must learn to reflect on her experience: *I wonder why those voices inside seem so upset?* Helen must change dysfunctional core beliefs: *I am not a bad person; I am a fallible and well-intentioned person who tries my best most of the time.* She must also learn she is capable of anger: *Sometimes I feel hate and rage. That is a normal part of being human. I am curious as to why I feel that sometimes.* She must learn to accept and accurately interpret body signals: *I feel like running away. That is an impulse from the past.* She must transform fragmented flashbacks into an autobiographical narrative story: *These intrusive images, sensations, and feelings are experiences of abuse that happened to me as a child.* She must accept dissociative parts as her own: *That little girl is me! That angry, hostile part holds my feelings of rage!*

Helen's ability to tolerate emotions must lead her to embodied actions of choosing different options in life, taking risks to develop new relationships, and trying new things that she had previously avoided out of fear. A newfound sense of competence and confidence must translate into concrete behavioral actions, such as going back to school or seeking a better job or promotion, taking enjoyment from the small pleasures of the day, getting out of the house more often, and finding activities and relationships that are meaningful. It will also change her body: Her posture will straighten, her shoulders will go back, her head will raise; she will make better eye contact. These physiological changes will, in turn, support an ongoing sense of competence and well-being (Ogden et al., 2006).

Therapy with chronically traumatized patients in general and dissociative patients in particular is a persistent and gradual endeavor to help them move from non-realization to realization. The therapist should be able to recognize statements and other indications that the patient is either stuck in non-realization or moving toward realization. To this end, we describe several indications of growing realization over the course of therapy in Table 1.2.

TABLE 1.2
Gradual Steps of Realization

Recognizing sensations and impulses to act
- I realize my chest is tight and I want to cry.
- I realize there is tension in my legs and I want to run.

Connections between past and present
- I realize my depression and anxiety have a lot to do with what happened when I was a child.

Developing empathy for dissociative parts
- I feel sorry for that little girl.
- I can understand why that part might be so angry all the time.

Developing inner "closeness" with dissociative parts, which implies gradual integration
- I am willing to listen to that voice and try to create a dialogue, even though it is scary.
- I can imagine holding and comforting that little girl; I am grown up and can take care of her.
- I would like to provide a safe and pleasant home for all parts of me.

Acknowledging what happened
- I now understand and know what happened to that little girl. No wonder she is so scared!

Placing an event in the past
- It's really over and won't happen again.
- That was just one day out of my life, and it happened a long time ago. It doesn't define who I am.

Changing a core schema or meaning
- It wasn't that little girl's fault; she did the best she could; she was only a child.

Personification of experience
- That little girl is *me*! That happened to *me*!

Grieving
- Those were awful things that hurt me a lot; I lost a lot of my childhood.
- It is OK to allow myself to grieve.

Anger
- It was wrong that I was hurt so much!
- It is OK to be angry, and I can learn not to act destructively when I am angry.

Shame and guilt
- I was just little; it wasn't my fault. And I can take responsibility for what belongs to me in the present.

Mentalizing
- My parents did the best they could; they didn't have good parents themselves.
- My father was sadistic and mentally ill—he seemed to enjoy hurting me and then blamed me. That was pretty crazy!
- That's not an excuse, but it helps me understand what was really going on with them, and to know it wasn't really about me.

Ending comparisons
- My experience was worse than some, not as bad as others. The important thing is that I realize the impact it has had on me and how I can overcome that in the present.

Full realization
- I am not afraid or ashamed or overwhelmed anymore. I have strengths in the present, and connections with others. I can make my own choices. I can be whole, sadder but wiser. I can cope with my losses.
- These are all parts of me; I can own them and bring them home to me.

Phase-Oriented Treatment and Realization

As discussed above, the long road to realization involves mental and physical actions that foster integration of the patient's personality, up to unification of the personality and beyond. Pierre Janet (1898/1911, 1919/1925a; cf. Van der Hart, Brown, & Van der Kolk, 1989) was the first to suggest that a phase-oriented treatment was necessary in order to gradually build the patient's integrative capacity. Since then, it has remained the standard of care for treatment of complex post-traumatic stress disorder (PTSD) and dissociative disorders (e.g., D. Brown & Fromm, 1986; D. Brown, Scheflin, & Hammond, 1998; Courtois, 1999, 2008; Courtois & Ford, 2012, 2013; Herman, 1997; Howell, 2011; Huber, 2003, 2013; ISSTD, 2011; Kluft, 1993a; Loewenstein & Welzant, 2010; McCann & Pearlman, 1990; Putnam, 1997; Phillips & Frederick, 1995; C. A. Ross, 1997; Steele et al., 2005; Van der Hart, 1991; Van der Hart et al., 2006). Most authors adhere to a three-phase model, consisting of (a) safety, stabilization, symptom reduction, and skills training; (b) treatment of traumatic memories; and (c) personality (re)integration and rehabilitation. In actual practice, and more so when the degree of non-realization is high, the application of this model takes the form of a spiral, in which different phases are alternated according to the needs of the patient.

As detailed in this book, treatment Phase 1—safety, stabilization, symptom reduction, and skills training—is geared toward strengthening the patient's realization of present-day reality; which, as Janet (1928) emphasized, should feel the most real and relevant, over and above the past or future. This does not negate the fact that the past is important, but it should be experienced as something that is indeed in the past, not in the present. Confrontation of the patient's non-realization of the past is delayed until the patient is able to engage in more realization. Thus, realization of traumatic memory mostly, but not completely, becomes the task of Phase 2, the treatment of traumatic memories. In Phase 3, personality (re)integration and rehabilitation, the focus is on facilitation of the fullest realization, with its twin components of personification and presentification of one's present life, past, and anticipated future. In Chapter 9, the specific goals of each of these phases are discussed.

Further Explorations

1.1 Spend some time reflecting on a couple of your own personal experiences that took some time and effort for you to realize (for example, accepting the loss of a relationship, coping with a difficult financial situation). What helped you and what hindered you on your road to realization? In what ways did realization make a difference in your life, if any? How does that realization affect you currently?

1.2 Make a list of non-realizations that one or two of your patients have. (It does not matter if they are dissociative or not; everyone has non-realizations.) Note what makes it hard for these patients to realize what they are avoiding, and what might help them move forward with realizations.

1.3 If you are currently working with a patient who has a dissociative disorder, make a list of non-realizations in various dissociative parts and what they serve to protect your patient from. (For example, a tough adolescent part might be protecting from the realization that the patient was helpless during the abuse, and might also contain anger that the adult self of the patient is unable to accept).

1.4 Identify a non-realization that has kept you from recognizing or working through your countertransference in the past. (For example, not realizing that you are caretaking a patient or that you have withdrawn in anger or frustration.) Are you aware of any non-realizations that might still be affecting your countertransference in the present? Your own therapy, consultation, and supervision can be of great help in resolving these. After all, we all have non-realizations and countertransference, and dealing with these is a lifelong journey.

1.5 Begin to practice identifying underlying non-realizations in each session.

PART I

The Therapeutic Relationship

CHAPTER 2

The Good Enough Therapist

*A good enough therapist is not perfect, but simply one dedicated
to ongoing self-discovery and lifelong learning.*
—Louis Cozolino (2004, p. 7)

Therapists do not always respond at their best when they are confronted
with a patient's humiliated fury, demands and needs, regression, entitlement, sadomasochism, unbearable suffering and loneliness, extreme avoidance and silence, or intense self-harm or suicidality. It is easy to become
confused when working with dissociative parts and to be unable to hold the
whole person in mind. Even seasoned therapists can become overwhelmed
by the basic question *How do I stay grounded and steady with my patients?*

In order to navigate successfully the many complexities and pressures
brought to treatment, therapists must have consistent ways to be aware of,
accept, and change our own unhelpful personal reactions, which we all
have. We are human and make mistakes; fail to adequately attune, understand, or empathize; get tired and frustrated; are too eager to fix and help
without setting important limits; are hurtful; and cross boundaries from
time to time. Often we have unrealistic expectations of ourselves as therapists. We may take extraordinary measures, or relentlessly twist ourselves
in knots to be better, be more, be different, in the hope that if we change,
our patients will change and get better. There may be some small truth in
this method when our countertransference or lack of knowledge is in the
way and we need to do something about it, but overall it is not an effective
strategy. We can only hope for and work toward being a "good enough" therapist for our patients.

The best place to begin therapy is with ourselves, the imperfect but good enough therapist. Who we are and how we are with our patients make a critical difference in helping them make progress. In this chapter we will focus on the person of the therapist, and in the next we will explore the therapeutic relationship—the shared medium in which both therapist and patient can grow and thrive; or conversely, in which they may unwittingly play out unresolved sadomasochistic enactments or rescue fantasies that typically do not end well.

The Good Enough Therapist

The idea of the good enough therapist (Cozolino, 2004) is based on Winnicott's concept of the good enough mother, who attends to her child in an ordinary, everyday way that does not require perfection, seamless attunement, or constant availability (Winnicott, 1968). Good enough parents are able to take in stride the rapidly shifting states of the infant, providing consistency and security across a wide array of experience. However, even good parents match and attune to their children only about one third of the time (Malatesta, Culver, Tesman, & Shepard, 1989; Tronick & Cohn, 1989).

CORE CONCEPT

A natural cycle of relational disruption and repair is even more important and predictive of secure attachment than attunement alone (Tronick & Cohn, 1989). The therapist's failures to understand or connect with a patient offer opportunities for this essential repair.

Thus, therapists' attunement to patients is by definition flawed and is only part of the story. The more complex and difficult part of therapy is often in limit setting and in repair and reattunement, without trying to make up for or protect patients from the harsh realities of their lives. Indeed, patients have the task, as do we all, of "mastering the disappointment and pain that comes with the recognition of just how limited, just how unreliable, and ultimately, just how separate, immutable, and unrelenting one's objects [relationships] (past and present) really are" (Stark, 2006, p. 2). It is avoidance of this realization that, in part, maintains dissociation in our patients and urges them to invite the therapist to relinquish the usual and essential boundaries and limits of psychotherapy. But at the same time, patients also need to experience a consistent and compassionate person who accepts them as they are, yet also supports them in making change.

Reenactments and the Good Enough Therapist

Reenactments are unconscious, somatically based relational interactions
in which both patient and therapist project onto the other unresolved experiences from the past (e.g., Bromberg, 1998; Davies, 1997; Frawley-O'Dea,
1997, 1999; Howell, 2005; Plakun, 1998). Along with others, we propose that
reenactments are dissociative in nature (Schore, 2012; Stern, 2010). The
enduring traumatic attachment patterns of our patients—and our own
attachment patterns, whatever they may be—are the filters through which
we see each other in the therapeutic relationship. The patients' living reenactments of abuse or neglect within dissociative parts of themselves have
not yet been fully integrated.

Reenactments are often felt experiences in the bodies of therapist and
patient, sensorimotor and emotional encounters that make reflection and
therapeutic change difficult, because they are typically not in conscious
awareness, or at least are difficult to put into words. Therapists and patients
may implicitly take on many unhelpful and interchangeable enactment
roles. These will be discussed in Chapter 3.

Patients—or particular dissociative parts—can experience the therapist
as being "too much": too punitive, pushing too hard, setting too many limits, asking too many questions, being too emotional or too cognitive, too
silent or too talkative, too fast or too slow, too smart or too uninformed.
Patients also may experience the therapist as "too little": not good enough,
not correct in our understanding of them, not responsive or available
enough, not kind enough, not helpful enough.

CASE EXAMPLE OF REENACTMENT: MARTHA

Martha experienced her therapist as cold and punitive, even though in reality she was a warm, vibrant, and highly competent therapist. During sessions the therapist would sometimes find herself feeling incompetent and a bit frozen, with a physical feeling like a cold stone in the pit of her stomach weighing her down and a vague sense of being disappointed in herself. She sometimes felt Martha was overwhelming and demanding and, in turn, Martha believed her therapist hated her and found her needs disgusting. Martha turned this disgust inward, and a critical dissociative part of her berated and punished the young parts of herself for being so needy. During these times, Martha was enraged, both toward her therapist for not meeting her needs and toward herself for having them. The reenactment from Martha's history was of herself as a child encountering her hostile, absent mother, while the reenactment from the therapist's history was based on an old pattern of believing she could not ever quite live up to her sister's stellar academic and social reputation.

The Experience of the Therapist in Reenactments. When we are pulled into reenactments with a patient, we may feel differently than usual: harsh, punitive, overwhelmed, too much in our heads when we should be connected with our emotions, too much in our emotions when we need to be reflecting. We may be enraged or humiliated, guilty or ashamed, unable to meet and match the patient's energy and capacities. We may feel superior in one moment and exceptionally stupid in the next. Sometimes we may feel like an all-embracing earth mother and other times cold and unfeeling as ice. We feel ourselves desperately caring and feeling utterly responsible for a patient's very life, and then drained and lacking in empathy. But sometimes we are easily caught in reenactments that are much harder to recognize because they are congruent with how we usually think and feel. For example, a very warm therapist may not recognize that a child part is pulling for caretaking, because the therapist normally feels so naturally attentive and giving. Or a somewhat avoidant therapist may not recognize that he is in a reenactment involving a neglectful, absent parent. Or we view our frustration and anger with the very real egregious behavior of a patient as a response to the present situation (which it is), but fail to recognize that we have also been pulled into a reenactment of the punitive, enraged parent.

Our bodies are the playing field for reenactments: We (and our patients) become hyper- or hypoaroused, tense, hot or cold; our gaze averts, our faces freeze, or we frown or smile even when we are tense around the eyes. We slump in our chair or lean forward aggressively, or cross our arms in defense. Our patients project these experiences onto us, and we unconsciously mirror dissociative parts of themselves that they cannot yet tolerate. Our role is to consciously take these experiences on, hoping to recognize and hold them, attenuate them, and hand them gently back to the patient to own at the right time.

As we see from the example of Martha's therapist above, these experiences are often not just projections from the patient but also come from our own personal experiences, triggered by the dynamics of the patient. They also are very real experiences born of actually dealing with individuals who are greatly suffering, enraged and humiliated, needy and clinging, avoidant and defensive, demanding and entitled, intense and relentless. Our experiences in real time with patients help us understand the difficulties other people have with them, as well as what struggles they themselves have in relationships. Most often, both the patient's and the therapist's histories are at play, interacting with the "real" relationship in the present, engendering a highly complex matrix of emotions and behaviors much like a three-dimensional chess game. Of course, we do not always know in the moment whether what we feel is from our own past experience, from the patient, or from the real relationship in the present. A willingness to stay curious and to accept any or all of these possibilities is important.

These byzantine experiences can be enormously challenging for us as therapists, whose best tool is ourselves. Of course, therapeutic success is not always complete or possible, and that is yet another reality we must come to accept. Or, at the least, our idealized version of success does not always happen. Some patients achieve stability, but not much meaning or contentment. Some are never able to fully trust, always remaining guarded. Some are unable to relinquish their fantasies of a magical cure that comes from outside themselves. A few patients will not get better despite our best efforts, and occasionally we ourselves are unable to sufficiently overcome our own personal challenges to be of help to a particular patient. Yet, there is reason for hope, because the majority of the time we are able to navigate ourselves and our patients through difficulties.

Painful reenactments must be acknowledged and shifted via consistent therapeutic boundaries and predictability, by talking about the felt experience in the moment with compassionate relational repair by the therapist, and by growing accountability and realization by the patient. We must remain as steady and nonreactive as possible in the face of our own and our patients' intense emotions, from euphoria to despair, from delight to rage, from grief to acceptance, from love to hate, from suffering to contented relief. It is the therapist's own relational capacities, emotional maturity, and high integrative level that can help pull the relationship time and again out of the mire of enactment and back onto the road of progress.

The rewards of being reflective and present in the moment, and offering patients a positive and new experience of being seen and heard—and of learning to see and hear the other—are well worth enduring these challenging times. Indeed, these are the fires in which the good enough therapist is forged.

What Makes a Good Enough Therapist?

Good enough therapists in general are characterized by collaboration, interest, and compassion rather than caretaking, and are able to reflect before they act. They are good at mentalizing and attunement (Schore, 2012; Siegel, 2010b). They regularly ask patients for feedback and closely monitor their progress (Norcross & Lambert, 2011; Norcross & Wampold, 2011). They are able to step into the patient's subjective world with its simultaneous and contradictory realities, and still "stand in the spaces between realities without losing any of them" (Bromberg, 1993, p. 166). They agree upon and work together with the patient on shared treatment goals. They are genuine, able to repair relational disruptions, can set firm yet flexible boundaries and limits, and have an ongoing awareness and management of countertransference. In addition, good enough therapists have a certain level of emotional maturity and self-awareness, and can realize (sometimes with supervisory help) the therapeutic needs of the patient in order to move forward in treatment. Good enough therapists do not know everything, but are aware of knowledge gaps and seek to fill them; are lifelong learners and innately curious; learn to be relatively comfortable with uncertainty and intensity; do not depend on the progress of the patient to sustain their professional self-worth; and are able to recognize when help is needed and to ask for it. Good enough therapists make plenty of mistakes, but are willing to acknowledge and continuously learn from them. They learn through experience and supervision how to set good boundaries and limits with patients. They have humility, no matter how skillful or mature they may be, acutely aware that our shared human condition both enriches and limits us all.

Good enough therapists keep in mind that it is much less about what they *do* for patients than how they *are* with them. Good enough therapists really do accept themselves as they are in the moment and know that aspirations for being a better therapist are not the same as expectations of being perfect.

Boundaries

In efforts to be good enough, to prove to their patients that they are not like the patients' abusers, therapists sometimes promise more than they can deliver, extending limits and crossing or even violating boundaries. Perfection, constant availability, assurances of never leaving, and golden fantasies of a second happy childhood are simply not within our human powers to promise (to anyone) and are unrealistic and unhelpful goals in therapy. Of course, therapists want to help—we are a decent and well-intentioned group of professionals in general—but our eagerness to relieve suffering or to avoid it sometimes gets in the way of our patients moving forward. We are not always able to easily handle our patients' rage, or demands, or suffering, or disappointment in us, or resolute silence, or verbal onslaughts, or clever end-runs around boundaries. Our limits can collapse, and we give in to a request or demand that is ultimately not helpful to the patient and highly burdensome to us, the therapists.

It is often easier to see our patients in all-or-nothing terms, as victims rather than as complex individuals who also—like all humans—have the capacity to hurt or to be sadistic, entitled, and enraged. Some therapists have never consciously encountered these emotions or behaviors before, and are baffled, frightened, and unable to respond. Others find them to be all-too-familiar repetitions of their own histories, and react by doing too much or not enough. Regardless, learning to be a good enough therapist involves reflecting on what boundaries and limits you do and do not set in therapy and why. Table 2.1 is a list of topics that can be explored to determine a therapist's boundaries. Some boundaries are set by licensing boards and should be strictly adhered to, such as abstinence from sexual contact, social media connections, dual relationships, bartering, and business transactions with patients. Every therapist needs to know the boundaries that are required by their specific code of ethics. Other boundaries are more flexible and vary from therapist to therapist.

Setting appropriate and therapeutic boundaries that are consistent yet flexible requires therapists to develop a certain comfort level with suffering, rage, shame, loneliness, terror, and dissociation. It also requires therapists to learn to set limits more comfortably, especially if they have little practice with that in their personal lives. Ideally, personal and professional limits and boundaries should be relatively congruent, so that it feels natural for therapists to set clear relational boundaries with patients. The more therapists are aware of their own limits, the more they will be able to recognize times when a patient might overstep boundaries, or when the therapist does. This allows the therapist to maintain consistent boundaries and to correct mistakes when they are made.

CORE CONCEPT

One of the most essential characteristics of the good enough therapist is the ability to learn, set, and keep therapeutic boundaries and limits.

TABLE 2.1
Exploring Therapeutic Boundaries and Limits

Explore with colleagues or a supervisor your professional boundaries and limits for the following:

- Ongoing serious self-injury or chronic suicide attempts
- Ongoing abuse of a patient by someone else, or the patient abusing another person (including the patient's own children)
- Physical contact with a patient during the session (including handshakes, hugs, reassuring or comforting touch, grounding touch, or restraining touch)
- Phone calls, texts, and e-mails from patients between sessions—whether any are OK, and if not, how much and for what reasons
- How, when, or if extra sessions are scheduled
- How, when, or if extended sessions are scheduled
- Starting and stopping sessions on time (within a couple of minutes)
- Criteria for voluntary or involuntary hospitalization, whether and when to hospitalize; what to do in crisis if hospitalization is not an option
- Disclosing personal information—what kind, for what reasons, when, how?
- Offering therapy outside the therapy room (for example, exposure therapy for agoraphobia, taking a walk to help ground the patient, home or hospital visits if the patient is extremely ill or unable to get to the office for a length of time)
- Attending events that are meaningful to patients (for example, graduations, concerts, marriage ceremonies, funerals, etc.)
- What to do when you unexpectedly see a patient in a social setting—do you acknowledge, and if so, what do you say?
- Verbal abuse and threats from a patient
- When and why to contact family or close friends of the patient
- Entitled or demanding behavior of a patient
- Childish behavior of a patient
- Amnesia in a patient for unacceptable behaviors
- Your reasons for unilaterally terminating with a patient
- Violence or threat of violence by a patient
- Stalking by a patient (of yourself or others)
- Gift-giving and receiving—none; small, symbolic gifts, such as stones; or slightly more expensive gifts
- Fees and fee collection policies
- Policies on running a balance with a patient—if any, for how much or how long, and with what sort of agreement in place for the patient to pay the balance
- Getting your own personal therapy
- Getting regular consultation
- Deciding whether you are the best person to work with a certain patient or how and when to make referrals

The most important thing about boundaries is not the specific parameters therapists set, as these will vary slightly from therapist to therapist. The key is whether the boundaries support the competence, growth, and responsibility of the patient, and whether therapists can keep their boundaries and limits respectfully, clearly, and consistently, yet can recognize when or if minor boundary crossings are necessary and helpful (Dalenberg, 2000). Peer support, consultation, and supervision are especially helpful for therapists who are unsure of particular boundaries, are struggling to maintain limits, or are considering temporarily flexing a boundary with a patient.

With a few exceptions, such as never being sexual with a patient, many boundaries are flexible within a small range. For example, different therapists have slightly varying policies regarding whether or how often they will accept e-mail or phone calls from patients. It is important that therapy boundaries are set such that therapists feel personally comfortable, although learning to set boundaries can certainly be uncomfortable at first. If the therapist's personal comfort level is at significant variance with recommended therapeutic boundaries, this should be discussed with peers and a supervisor or consultant. Hopefully, the therapist's personal and professional boundaries grow to feel relatively congruent. There are many guidelines for therapeutic boundaries that can be found elsewhere. A small sampling includes Epstein (1994); Gutheil and Brodsky (2011); Gutheil and Gabbard (1993, 1998); Harper and Steadman (2003); and Zur (2007).

The Good Enough Therapist and Dissociation

The good enough therapist is able to view dissociative parts as unintegrated aspects of a single person, not as things or entities in their own right. The focus is on helping the whole person resolve inner conflicts and integrate traumatic memories rather than on developing individual relationships with each part. Thus, the therapist is as consistent as possible in supporting parts to accept and cooperate with each other, since inner awareness, congruence, and self-compassion are foundations for integration in everyone. The good enough therapist keeps realization as a consistent major goal in the work toward integration. For example, patients must gradually come to realize that "parts" are indeed aspects of their own self, and each part must have the same realization from its own perspective.

Therapists who are accustomed to working with individuals who are relatively unified in mind and sense of self may feel quite off balance at first, trying to deal with what seems like more than one person at a time. The trancelike power of dissociation and non-realization, along with the patient's psychic equivalence, can compel the therapist to enter into an alternate reality without much reflection on what is actually occurring. Even when therapists truly grasp the concept of dissociation, it is still hard to learn how to effectively help a patient who experiences herself as a terrified or needy child one moment; then an infant; a raging, rebellious teenager; a dismissing, depressed, but competent workaholic who wants nothing to do with therapy; and then a sadistic male abuser who wants to kill the female child part.

Various theoretical models of how mental representations are formed and maintained—such as ego state theory, object relations, internal working models, and self psychology—are all helpful to the therapist in comprehending how the mind is structured, not necessarily in a completely unified manner. However, these abstract formulations of the mind do not entirely prepare the uninitiated therapist for the tangible manifestations of dissociative parts, in which the patient experiences him- or herself and may think, feel, and act like different people with convincing precision. Therapists must keep their feet grounded in the reality that a single individual can have multiple and contradictory experiences with multiple streams of consciousness. Although people without a dissociative disorder can also be changeable, the dissociative person can change so rapidly and profoundly—often without awareness or control—that it can be difficult to comprehend, especially for therapists new to the experience.

The very concept of working with parts of a person can be challenging. Inexperienced therapists often struggle with how to relate to so many different "personalities," or "identities," as dissociative parts are sometimes called. The most effective approach is to see the person as whole, with many inner conflicts and multiple realities (Kluft, 1991), which are not yet fully owned and realized.

One of the challenging aspects of working with dissociative individuals is the pull for therapists to feel and behave differently according to which part of the patient is dominant, and to subsequently loosen limits or boundaries for certain parts. Although we may modify our voice tone, eye contact, and posture from time to time to match our patients, they need us to remain a relative constant across all dissociative parts. Thus, therapists should be consistent in what they say and do with each part, and with the boundaries and limits they keep, and not shift their behavior and affect too drastically when working with certain parts.

For example, therapists might take a slightly softer tone when a child part is dominant, in the same way they might with any (nondissociative) patient who is overwhelmed, scared, or hurt. But if they begin to act as though a dissociative part is literally a child that they rock and hold, or play with, and so on, they are behaving as though they themselves are dissociative, forgetting (not realizing) that the patient is an adult and also has great ambivalence about dependency, and that the therapist is not a parent to the patient. Therapists then become "different" people, with different boundaries, corresponding to shifts in the patient. If, when a hostile part of the patient becomes angry with the therapist because she is paying too much attention to child parts, and the therapist becomes frozen or angry in return, the therapist has "switched" yet again. The same is true when therapists prefer to work with some parts of the patient (the nice ones, or the little ones, or the avoidant ones) and not others (the enraged or sadistic ones, the persistently suicidal ones, the overwhelmed ones).

The job of therapists is to hold the whole patient in mind. They must find ways to steady themselves when their patients abruptly shift from one emotion or thought to the next, from one dissociative part to the next. They learn to notice what came before the shift and to anticipate what might come after, and try to be as consistent and congruent as possible, no matter which part of the patient is present. In fact, we can think of the therapist as a bridge of realization and integration that crosses dissociative divides, until patients can also build their own bridges.

The Needs of the Therapist

Therapists are often so focused on what their patients need that they forget to ask themselves what they need in order to treat a particular individual, and by extension, what boundaries and limits are needed to protect both of them. Relationships are two-sided, even therapeutic ones. Therapists have a need to feel safe and not abused by patients. They have a need, as well as an ethical responsibility, to practice within the range of their competence. They have a need to conduct therapy within the limitations of their setting, particularly in outpatient private practice, where management of extreme crisis may be difficult. They need to know their own limitations regarding how much they are available to patients outside sessions. Thus, therapists need to have a stable and consistent therapy frame that protects them as well as their patients.

CORE CONCEPT

Therapeutic relationships are two-way streets. Therapists also have certain needs in a therapy relationship: to be compensated with a fee, to feel safe, to have boundaries respected, and to have patients collaborate on agreed-upon goals.

Therapists who wish to engage in psychodynamic oriented therapies need patients who are sufficiently motivated and responsible to be collaborative partners in therapy, at least to a degree. They must feel free to transfer or end therapy with patients who need increased levels of care beyond what can be reasonably provided, or who may need another type of therapy or a therapist with different skills. Of course, there are certain jobs that require therapists to work with all patients, regardless of their motivation or safety, so therapists in these situations need to seek out extra assistance. Therapists need the freedom to seek consultation, supervision, personal therapy, and other supports to help them in treating patients. They need to treat their patients without feeling trapped or under pressure of emotional blackmail—for example, *I will kill myself if you won't see me four times a week, because I can't function any other way.* Of course, therapists need to have their own meaningful personal lives and relationships outside the role of therapist. In other words, they need to not be overwhelmed regularly by emotions—their own or their patients'—so they have the mental space and energy for their personal lives.

Is Complex Trauma Work Right for Me?

Some therapists reading this book are generalists or specialize in other issues besides complex trauma. Some are well versed in the treatment of acute trauma and may not be aware that complex childhood trauma requires different approaches. Therapists do not have to specialize to be competent in the treatment of complex trauma and dissociative disorders. Our bias is that every therapist should be capable of assessment and treatment of complex trauma, because childhood and other types of trauma are endemic in mental health populations. The majority of mental health outpatients have a trauma history, somewhat depending on the particular population and setting (87%, Cusack, Grubaugh, Knapp, & Frueh, 2006; 81%, Davidson & Smith, 1990; 98%, Dominguez, Cohen, & Brom, 2004; 70%, Lipschitz et al., 1996; 65%, Muenzenmaier, Struening, Ferber, & Meyer, 1993; 84%, Rose, Peabody, & Stratigeas, 1991; 48% of males, Swett, Surrey, & Cohen, 1990). Of course, each of these studies defined trauma differently, and many did not distinguish between interpersonal and other types of events, nor determine whether it was a one-time episode or chronic. Nevertheless, these studies and others do show that it is inevitable that all therapists will encounter at least some patients who suffer from complex trauma-related symptoms and disorders, regardless of the areas of focus in their work or practice.

For those therapists who decide chronic trauma work is not for them, our suggestion is to learn the basics of complex trauma therapy so you know enough to assess and refer, and to contain and support your patient before referral (cf. Chu, 2011). One advantage of learning good assessment skills is that therapists can anticipate issues that may arise and with which they may choose not to work. It is helpful to learn who in the community does the work and to make referrals when needed. However, we strongly advise that therapists not continue to treat patients once they have been referred to another therapist for treatment of complex trauma and dissociation. After all, it is not the trauma that is being treated, but the whole person, and the trauma has affected most, if not all, of that person's life.

The Therapist's Personal History in the Therapy Room

Many therapists have their own trauma histories (Pope & Feldman-Summers, 1992), and everyone has less-than-perfect attachment histories. Whether or not a given therapist is a trauma survivor has no particular bearing on whether he or she is a good therapist. What is important is that regardless of personal history, therapists have been able to realize and integrate their history sufficiently so that it can inform them, yet not be a significant hindrance in their work. They are able to be present with their patients' issues and suffering the majority of the time and can reflect on their countertransference, set good boundaries and limits, be empathic, and be willing to seek out consultation as needed.

However, it is sometimes true that therapists have not completed their own personal work to a sufficient degree, such that their struggles impinge on their therapies, or on a particular therapy that especially triggers unresolved issues. Obviously, we cannot take our patients where we ourselves cannot go. Of course, all of us have our unique limitations in this regard. However, in cases where the therapist has an active complex trauma disorder, intensive supervision and therapy are highly recommended, with an emphasis on boundaries, management of countertransference, and good self-care. Some therapists may need to refrain from treating trauma patients, at least until they have better resolved their own histories. Otherwise, they may unconsciously use the patient "to achieve a vicarious mastery of their own unresolved issues," and subsequently become overwhelmed (Kluft, 1994a, p. 127). Such decisions should be made in consultation with a personal therapist and a supervisor or consultant.

The Toll of Trauma Work on the Therapist

There is much literature on the emotional toll of trauma therapy on therapists (e.g., Allen, 2001; Figley, 2013; Pearlman & Saakvitne, 1995; Rothschild, 2006; Wilson & Lindy, 1994). Sitting hour after hour, day after day with suffering most surely affects us, both emotionally and physically. We may experience one of the deadly traps of the therapist: When I get home after intense interactions all day, all I want is peace and quiet and not to talk to anyone. This can lead to isolation and a poorer quality of life. It is crucial for therapists to find ways to replenish themselves, and to take care not to become regularly drained by work.

CORE CONCEPT

Therapists are prone to burnout and vicarious traumatization. Regular self-care is essential to maintain a consistently replenished, open, and energetic personal and professional space.

Every therapist should know the early signs of burnout and vicarious traumatization. Some of these include hopelessness, a decrease in experiences of pleasure, irritability, constant stress and anxiety, hypervigilance and feeling unsafe, sleeplessness or nightmares, and a pervasive negative attitude. These can have detrimental effects on the therapist, both professionally and personally. They can lead to a diminishing effectiveness with patients, the inability to focus, and feelings of incompetence and self-doubt.

Therapists who are overly conscientious, perfectionistic, and self-giving without adequate boundaries are perhaps more likely to suffer from burnout or vicarious traumatization. Those who have poor or limited relationships or high levels of stress in their personal lives are more likely to develop these problems. The way in which therapists manage their emotions and stress levels is crucial to their well-being. Compassionate acceptance of inner experiences is as important for therapists as it is for patients. Those therapists who avoid their emotions, or who cannot keep their emotions at a tolerable level, are more likely to suffer and more likely to contribute to a derailed therapy. We will discuss practical susggestions for emotion regulation in Chapter 3.

Tolerating the Intolerable: Enduring Existential Crisis
Facing horrific trauma inevitably brings up existential issues, unanswerable but essential questions about existence and meaning, aloneness and isolation, suffering and pain, freedom and responsibility, death and mortality (Yalom, 1980). Therapists must be willing to grapple with these issues themselves and not be satisfied with oversimplified answers for their patients. Sometimes the answer is long and slow in coming, changing and evolving over time. Sometimes the answer is that there is no answer, and

the question becomes How, then, shall we live without an answer? Being able to sit with patients in deep existential crisis without having a quick, simple answer is a prerequisite for a good enough therapist (Steele, 1989, 2009; Yalom, 1980).

TABLE 2.2
Existential Issues for Patients and Therapists

Meaning
- What does my history mean?
- Is my life worth anything?
- What is my purpose in life?
- Why do terrible things happen?
- Why do terrible things happen to me?

Suffering
- Why do I have to suffer so much?
- What is the meaning of suffering and pain?
- Is there anything good I can get from my suffering and that of others?

Isolation
- I am alone in my own skin.
- No one can really know what it is like to be me.
- In moments of suffering, I have been completely alone, and it was intolerable.
- I am not seen and not heard by other people.

Freedom and responsibility
- I am ultimately responsible for myself, and that terrifies me.
- I am not sure I am free to make choices at all.
- I should be able to do what I want, because I was without freedom for so long.
- Being responsible is overwhelming.
- There are too many choices.
- I do not believe that I have any choices.
- I cannot lead my own life when others have needs and demands of me.

Death and mortality
- Life is finite, and that terrifies me.
- I am afraid to die.
- What is the point of making an effort if we all die anyway?
- I am too old; there is no point in trying to get better now.
- I feel dead already.

Self-Care of the Therapist

Therapists spend a lot of time in sessions supporting their patients to take better care of themselves. Do they practice the same for themselves? Often not. Yet physical, relational, and emotional self-care and the ability to maintain a relatively healthy balance and perspective in life are essential to being a good enough therapist. And, if it is important to a particular therapist, spiritual self-care may also be essential. Most certainly, it is necessary to explore and find ways to coexist with existential issues such as death, suffering, meaning, and aloneness, with or without a spiritual or religious structure. Those who do not or cannot adequately find some balance or take sufficient care of themselves are more prone to boundary violations, countertransference traps, burnout, and vicarious traumatization.

Lack of self-care makes us especially vulnerable because our job as therapists is highly stressful. In fact, being a therapist is considered one of the most stressful jobs by most measures of stress tolerance, consequences of errors, time pressures, and salary (Giang, 2013). Therapists listen to painful and sometimes devastating stories of human cruelty and injustice and intolerable suffering. They work with deeply troubled people and carry heavy responsibilities for their safety and well-being, while having no control over what they ultimately decide to do. Even though they have colleagues and supervisors, therapists work in complete isolation each therapy hour. They are constantly faced with highly complex and murky ethical, legal, confidentiality, and treatment issues. They must keep up with a staggering array of new research and evolving treatment recommendations. Therapists must generally hold themselves to a high standard, as their personhood is their most effective therapeutic tool. Finally, therapists are prone to the whims of physiological empathy, reflecting in their own bodies the uncomfortable somatic and affective experiences of their patients (Wilson & Thomas, 2004).

Self-care of the therapist is the foundation on which good boundaries and excellent therapeutic practices are built. From it flows the ability to return again and again to being present with patients without resentment, fear, guilt, or anxiety. The therapist's own self-care, though imperfect, can serve as an important model for the patient.

Further Explorations

2.1 Are you able to realize that you have many characteristics of a good enough therapist? List them. If you are not sure, ask colleagues to give you feedback.

2.2 Next, make a list of those qualities you would like to improve or attain. Include specific goals and a timeline.

    Example: I would like to recognize and set limits with a patient who is calling me all the time. In the next week, I will reflect and talk with my supervisor about the boundaries that are important for me to keep but hard for me to set. I will practice with a colleague exactly what to say to my patient and will practice keeping myself calm and compassionate, but firm. In my personal therapy I will explore what makes it hard for me to set these boundaries.

2.3 List five ways in which you regularly take care of yourself. Next, list five ways in which you could improve your self-care. How will you begin to implement these in your life?

2.4 Read through the list of boundaries in Table 2.1, Exploring Therapeutic Boundaries and Limits. Take some time to reflect on your boundaries and limits, perhaps looking at a few issues each week. Gather your colleagues and have a discussion, using Table 2.1 as a guide.

CHAPTER 3

The Therapeutic Relationship: Safety, Threat, and Conflict

Even if a therapist is able to get through the interpersonal defenses of a patient and to be seen as kind or helpful, the patient is thrown into more internal conflict, trying to juggle the fragile sense of the therapist as benevolent with the certainty that the therapist will use or abandon them.

—James Chu (2011, p. 161)

Most patients with dissociative disorders are conflicted about basic connection with the therapist from the first contact. They may appear overly compliant, ambivalent, highly anxious or fearful, distracted, aggressive, or depersonalized in early sessions. Their inner conflicts about the therapist may quickly escalate, since it is relationship itself that is both yearned for and threatening. In fact, relationships are primary triggers that evoke memories of interpersonal trauma, so patients can easily become flooded just by walking into the therapy room. Within the patient, some dissociative parts become activated to frantically connect and seek help, while others are simultaneously fearful of connection or punitive with those parts that seek help from the therapist. Thus, the ways in which therapists approach the patient from the first session can either support regulation or increase the internal war.

CORE CONCEPT

Relationships, including the therapeutic relationship, are major
triggers for the reactivation of traumatic memories. After all, patients'
traumatic experiences often occurred in the context of important
relationships, and some of their most severe traumatic wounds
include abuse, neglect, and betrayal in those relationships.

Attachment and defense are primary and contradictory motivators that influence the dynamics in the therapeutic relationship. Therapeutic approaches early in treatment should be aimed at reducing these conflicts so that neither the phobia of attachment nor of attachment loss is too intense or threatening for the patient. Relational patterns and transference reactions in the chronically traumatized are often founded on the basic animal defenses of flight, fight, freeze, flag, and faint and, on the other hand, on the need to safely attach, as described in Chapter 1. Therapists can support regulation in their patients as a whole and in particular in dissociative parts by working directly with these motivational or action systems.

CORE CONCEPT

Patients are caught in an impossible conflict of attachment, between
a strong wish for a therapeutic relationship and defense against this
same relationship. Therapists should avoid intentionally activating the
patient's attachment system until a reasonable degree of stabilization
and emotion regulation is possible.

Patients hope to be perfectly understood and have their needs met without distress, misattunement, or vulnerable risk. They fear, however, that the therapist can never truly understand them or be trusted, and thus the relationship should be avoided at all costs in order to avoid distress, misattunement, mistakes, or the vulnerable risk of being even more shamed. A particular type of insecure attachment strategy called disorganized/disoriented or D-attachment is developed under these conditions when children are seriously overwhelmed or threatened in unstable relationships with their caregivers.

D-Attachment and the Core Conflict of Safety Versus Danger

As noted in Chapter 1, D-attachment involves an insoluble conflict between the need for defense and attachment with the same person. Thus, most dissociative parts are organized to a large degree by different action systems and strategies that guide patients to either seek attachment or engage in defense against threat. Patients may further utilize caregiving and ranking (dominance/submission) strategies as means to maintain attachment.

Controlling-Punitive and Controlling-Caregiving Strategies

There are two major attachment strategies that emerge from disorganized attachment: controlling punitive and controlling caregiving (Liotti, 2011; Main & Cassidy, 1988). In the controlling-punitive strategy, the child, or at least one dissociative part, learns to defensively engage the caregiver in a power struggle of dominance. These patients, or dissociative parts, may be angry, obstinate, and highly demanding of the therapist and others around them. In the controlling-caregiving strategy, the child, or dissociative parts, takes an apparently submissive role, but is actually caring for the caregiver. Both strategies are intended to help the child receive what she or he needs.

Indeed, various dissociative parts can manifest one or the other of these strategies. They are typically two sides of one coin, with one being in the forefront and the other being more implicit. When one part is activated, conflict ensues internally. For example, when a controlling-caregiving part is solicitous to the caregiver, anger and resentment is often boiling underneath, and may eventually erupt outwardly or inwardly. And when an angry, punitive part is acting out toward the caregiver, a controlling-caregiving part becomes fearful that the caregiver will be pushed away and retaliate or abandon the child. Therapists must be aware of both types of strategies and how they sequence among dissociative parts. Otherwise they may be confused when a seemingly caretaking patient suddenly becomes angry, or vice versa. The therapist should explore the dynamics between the two positions instead of placating the patient or attending to one strategy but not the other.

Parts Fixed in Defense

Patients have become conditioned over time to react to others as though they are dangerous, often because certain dissociative parts and their respective traumatic memories have been reactivated, and their ability to assess threat accurately is impaired. Many (but not all) dissociative parts are fixed or stuck in particular defenses, each of which has its own limited set of emotions, behaviors, predictions, perceptions, beliefs, and decision-making patterns. Some parts implicitly misinterpret the presence of danger or life threat, and may not perceive cues for safety (faulty neuroception). They are unable to distinguish between the traumatic past and the safe present. For these parts of patients, the present moment is clouded or obliterated with implicit (or explicit) traumatic memories of events in which they needed to engage in defense. Thus, they continuously live in trauma-time. Each dissociative part of a person has a particular organization of threat and relational responses. Threat-related dissociative parts are typically activated in social or relational situations, regardless of how benign the situations may actually be, because as noted before, relationships themselves have been traumatizing.

Other parts of the patient are hostile, and engage in verbal (or occasionally physical) attacks on the therapist or patient (controlling-punitive strategies). Hostile parts predict that the therapist will be intrusive, untrustworthy, and unhelpful at best, and abusive and exploitive at worst. They disdain more vulnerable or needy parts, as they represent the helplessness the hostile parts cannot bear to feel. Some adult parts completely dismiss attachment as irrelevant and retreat into intellectual defenses and pursuits (e.g., work), insisting therapy is not within their domain of interest.

Parts Fixed in Attachment-Cry and Attachment-Seeking Behaviors

Dissociative child parts are often (but not always) organized around seeking attachment for protection or are terrified and engaged in freeze, flight, or collapse. They desperately seek help or attention, yet are often unable to truly accept help when it is offered. They may try to please or appease the therapist (controlling-caregiving strategies) and often react intensely to perceived rejection or abandonment.

The conflict between attachment and defense sets up further phobic avoidance between parts. For example, parts fixed in fight typically despise parts that are fixed in attachment cry and attachment seeking. They find child parts disgusting and weak. Child parts find that many parts of the patient lack compassion, and they feel neglected by them.

Some dissociative parts are unable to perceive threat at all, or perceive it and then completely shut down. Patients may seek attachment and are then vulnerable to exploitation and further victimization. This serves to reinforce the belief of other parts that no one can be trusted, and more importantly, patients come to believe that they cannot trust even themselves.

CORE CONCEPT

Dissociation is not just an inner experience. It is a response to what is happening in the relationship in the present moment. Thus, therapists should always consider what might be occurring in reaction to the therapeutic relationship in the moment when switching or increased conflict among parts occurs and when innate defenses are activated.

Dissociation is not only an intrapsychic phenomenon but an interpersonal one, being highly reactive to what is happening in relationships in the present (Allen, 2001; Liotti, 2009; Nijenhuis, 2015; Steele & Van der Hart, 2013; Steele et al., 2001). In fact, DID has been aptly described as a developmental attachment disorder (Barach, 1991). Allen has noted dissociation involves "switches in patterns of relatedness" (2001, p. 192). Activation of dissociative parts is also related to what patients, or parts of the patients, are perceiving, even though they may not have accurate representations of what is actually happening. For example, when a dissociative part is fixed in fight, the patient is angry and hyperaroused, expects the therapist to attack (verbally or physically), and is unwilling to connect with others. When a part is stuck in freeze, the patient is unable to move or speak and is terrified, expecting imminent danger. Obviously, dissociative patients engage in these defenses in relationships, from literal ways (e.g., becoming physically enraged or running out of session or getting sleepy or foggy) to subtler ways (e.g., masterfully avoiding topics that evoke distress). Therapists may also engage in these defenses when they feel overwhelmed, incompetent, threatened, or powerless with a patient.

Dissociative patients may experience panic when they feel alone or abandoned. Attachment-cry behavior is likely to be activated as the session is ending and the patient is leaving the office or after a (perceived) rupture in the relationship. The patient may frequently call or e-mail the therapist with crises and ask for extra sessions. Attachment cry may also be activated, for example, when the therapist is away from the office; when patients are alone, especially nights and on weekends, when others might be less available; or when patients are left with their overwhelming inner turmoil (Steele & Van der Hart, 2013; Steele et al., 2001).

Unfortunately, these behaviors are often labeled as manipulative. They actually represent efforts to attain safety via caretaking and attachment by the therapist, a legitimate and inborn tendency. Dissociative parts fixed in attachment cry are disconnected from adult inner resources that could be soothing and helpful, and the patient is often not well versed in using self-soothing. We will discuss much more about how to work with attachment cry in Chapters 13 and 14, as it is at the root of dependency issues in therapy and is a difficult and pervasive issue in many patients who have a dissociative disorder.

Treatment Implications of Attachment and Defense Conflicts in the Therapeutic Relationship

Defenses against danger, life threat, and loss of attachment are essential to understand, as they have important treatment implications. When patients or particular dissociative parts feel unsafe, they are not seeking attachment per se, but rather safety. Thus, it is essential that therapists provide safety before attachment and offer curiosity and collaboration instead of dependency. Of course, the patient's attachment system is already activated just by virtue of coming in to see the therapist, but so are defenses against attachment. The key is for therapists to avoid further intentional activation of either side (Steele, 2014). Patients who display D-attachment require a careful balance of consistent, predictable presence by therapists. They should strike a balance between being:

- too warm and close, or too clinical and distant;
- too inquisitive and probing, or so uninterested as to be unable to clarify the patient's experience and understand the patient's internal dissociative organization;
- too directive and rigidly structured, or too dedicated to following the avoidant wanderings of the patient in session; and
- too emotionally expressive, or too flat and nonresponsive.

CORE CONCEPT

Defenses against danger and life threat are important for therapists to understand, as they have many treatment implications and are often major organizers of dissociative parts. Dissociative parts are often in conflict with each other about whether attachment with the therapist is safe or not.

It is essential for therapists to understand why dissociative parts are stuck in habitual physical defenses and how they manifest (see Table 1.1 in

Chapter 1), so they can help the patient learn to engage differently. Therapists must know when to help patients increase or decrease their arousal level, and with what interventions. For example, when a fight part of the patient dominates, therapists should help create safety before relationship, backing off a bit and not being aggressive. The idea is to help this part of the patient move from a highly activated to a more modulated physiological state. Likewise, a patient (or dissociative part) in dorsal vagal faint will not benefit from cognitive interventions or relaxation techniques, because thinking is suppressed, and relaxation only increases the hypoarousal (Schauer & Elbert, 2010). Instead, the patient needs gradual movement and sensory orientation to the safe present. A patient (or dissociative part) in flight or fight mode will not benefit from attachment strategies and statements about caring about the patient, because the social engagement system is deactivated and the therapist is perceived as a threat. Thus, better to first give the patient some respectful distance to create safety and reduce activation, then become curious with the patient about what so evokes defense in the moment, once the patient can observe rather than be embedded in emotion. Then if the therapist needs to offer repair, it can be done when the patient is more regulated and can actually receive it.

One caveat to note: Switching, flashbacks, inner conflicts among parts, and daily crises can be caused by many factors. However, sometimes the content of these experiences serves as the vehicle for the patient to seek attachment from the therapist (via e-mail or phone or during sessions). Thus, the therapist sometimes must address the underlying dependency needs in addition to supporting the patient in learning to manage the content of these experiences.

Relationship is so fraught with conflict and threat for dissociative patients that therapists need to examine the paradigm of attachment that they typically use in therapy—that is, a parent–infant model of attachment. Instead, consider that it could be more helpful to establish a collaborative relationship between therapist and patient before attachment issues become an explicit focus (Cortina & Liotti, 2010, 2014; Steele, 2014; see Chapter 4). It provides a safer way eventually to work on deeply painful attachment issues without activating overwhelming emotions in the patient too quickly. In fact, mere contact with the therapist at the beginning of therapy can be overwhelming to dissociative patients, as both attachment and defense become activated at the prospect of working closely with someone else in order to get help. The next chapter is devoted to why a collaborative relational approach can be helpful.

Relational Reenactments

The nature of reenactments was discussed in the previous chapter. We can think of dissociative parts as being characters or roles in traumatic reenactments. For example, the needy child part is in the role of victim who seeks the rescuing therapist to help and protect. The hostile, punitive part is in the role of perpetrator and tries to emotionally hurt the therapist because of past experiences. This part's attitude is that it is better to hurt others before you get hurt by them. With these types of parts, the therapist might implicitly assume the role of a wounded child, or enact the role of perpetrator and fight back.

When one of the therapeutic dyad enacts a role, the other is implicitly pulled to act in a corresponding role (Bromberg, 2006, 2011; Chefetz, 2015; Davies & Frawley, 1994; Frank, 2002; Frawley-O'Dea, 1999; Howell, 2005, 2011; Schore, 2012). Therapists can reenact their own stories, or aspects of them that are not yet well integrated (Bromberg, 1998, 2006; Wallin, 2007). Therapists need to understand the past experiences that shape their own perceptions of patients, what shapes the patients' perceptions of them, and how the pasts of both intersect and entwine even as patient and therapist try to remain fully present in the room together. Figure 3.1 lists a number of dyadic reenactments for which the therapist should be alert.

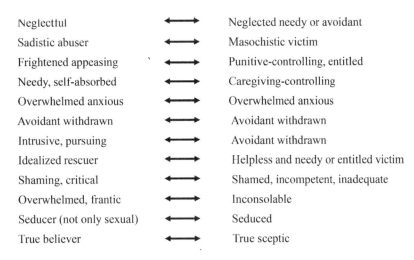

Figure 3.1. Common Relational Reenactments Between Therapist and Patient
From *Treating the Adult Survivor of Sexual Abuse: A Psychoanalytic Perspective*, by J. M. Davies and M. G. Frawley, 1994, New York, NY: Basic Books. Copyright 1994 by Basic Books. Adapted with permission.

Resolving Relational Reenactments

There are many ways to work with reenactments in a collaborative manner. The first step for therapists, which is often the hardest, is to realize a reenactment is occurring. Habitual attention to roles and relational patterns in which therapists find themselves with a patient is the best way to recognize reenactments. But it is a fact of therapy that often reenactments are not recognized until after therapists have been in a particular role for a period of time. Sometimes therapists feel that a reenactment is occurring, but they do not know the actual history from which it emerges. The use of regular consultation and supervision is essential to ensure that therapists are recognizing and working with implicit reenactments, which might be very subtle. In Table 3.1 you will find some ways to recognize and resolve reenactments.

TABLE 3.1
Resolving Relational Reenactments

- Track your own experience of the patient and your reactions in sessions, including your fantasies and daydreams.
- If you notice your experience is unusual for you, pay extra attention. For example, note if you begin having an unusual daydream of being angry with the patient, or if you start feeling suddenly sad during or after a session for no clear reason, or if you dread sessions or feel hopeless. Such experiences may be indications of a reenactment.
- Notice and be curious about the patient's experience. What is happening in the patient's body (muscle tone, unusual posture or movement, stereotypical movements, such as a fist lightly hitting the sofa repetitively)?
- Inquire about what the patient is thinking, perceiving, or predicting about you. What does the patient feel in the context of the relationship right now?
- Notice if dissociative parts are in conflict. For example, does the patient seem to be attending to voices of parts inside? Is the patient blocked internally when trying to talk in session? Has there been a switch or partial intrusion all of a sudden? Specific interactions among dissociative parts are often the first indication of what is being reenacted, even though the patient does not recall or cannot put into adequate words what happened.
- Help dissociative parts recognize and accept each other with compassion or, at least in the beginning, without overt avoidance or attack. Gradually help each part of the patient to understand the viewpoint of other parts.
- Support the patient in appropriately expressing concerns, feelings, or wishes about you, the therapist. Accept these with compassion and without judgment, while helping the patient and yourself not to act on them.
- Ask the patient if any part feels that the present experience is familiar in some way. If so, ask if the patient, or some part of the patient, would like to share something about what is so familiar, and if this would be acceptable to all parts. If it is not acceptable, the therapist can then explore this conflict among parts, asking for the concerns about sharing.
- Maintain awareness of your own experience: your thoughts, fantasies, emotions, sensations, posture.
- When you feel defensive, notice it but try not to act on it. It is a signal that may give more information about the reenactment.

CASE EXAMPLE OF MUTUAL REENACTMENT: MYRA AND JODY

Myra is a therapist who has a history of neglect by her mother. Early on, Myra leaned she had to be self-sufficient and never ask for help, and eventually she took pride in her ability to cope successfully with life on her own. Although Myra was highly functional, she had not yet fully owned her needs or her anger at not having important needs met as a child. She had developed a controlling-caregiving strategy, to some degree.

Her patient, Jody, had a history of more extreme neglect. A part of Jody reacted to being neglected in a highly entitled and regressed manner, often angrily insisting Myra meet many inappropriate demands, and was given to temper tantrums when she did not get what she wanted (a controlling-punitive strategy). Another part of Jody felt she deserved no help at all. Myra unwittingly aligned with the part of Jody who tried to never ask for help, and felt utter disgust toward the part of Jody that was demanding and needy, which was a controlling-punitive strategy for Myra.

Myra was embedded in a double reenactment: She played the role of her own neglectful mother who did not see her needs, and also the role of the patient's mother. She allied herself with the part of the patient that denied any needs, because it was a familiar and valued coping strategy in herself to deny her own needs. This alliance with one part of the patient served to help Myra and her patient continue to avoid accepting their own needs and grieving that these important emotional needs had never been met in childhood. In supervision, Myra was able to recognize what was happening: *I am rejecting the part of the patient that is enraged and needy, and I am siding with the part that insists she needs no support. And I am enacting the role of the neglectful mother—my own and my patient's!—and keeping the patient from accepting her own needs, anger, and grief. I realize that maybe I am avoiding my own shame, rage, and need by being disgusted by my patient's entitled demands. In disowning her needs and rage, I can continue to avoid my own.*

Fortunately, Myra was an excellent therapist with strong reflective capacities, and she quickly realized the reenactment and was able to work on further acceptance of her own needs, anger, and grief while also helping Jody to express needs in a more adaptive way. She helped Jody work with both the entitlement of one part and the feeling of not deserving help in the other part, which reduced the vehemence of Jody's entitlement and Jody's disgust at her need. Jody became more aware that she had an inner cycle of her own in which she enacted her own history.

Unfortunately, not all of us can be as insightful or as quick to recognize what is happening as Myra, so therapists must be compassionate with themselves and open to feedback from peers, consultants, supervisors, and their own therapists.

The Impact of Relational Dysregulation on the Therapist

Attachment theory emphasizes the important role therapists have in helping patients regulate themselves with a collaborative model of being in the moment together. But in turn, patients also influence the therapist's own regulation, often for the worse. Relational regulation—also known as dyadic, interactive, or co-regulation—is mutual, not just one-way (Fogel & Garvey, 2007). Relational regulation works well when therapists are at their best. A nonthreatened and nonthreatening response can downregulate an angry or anxious patient or upregulate a patient who is shut down. However, sometimes co-regulation can be decidedly unhelpful. As humans, therapists sometimes get tired, frustrated, defensive, angry, overwhelmed, scared, hopeless, or ashamed. They have lapses in understanding and compassion. In those moments they may struggle with their own self-regulation, and have difficulty managing the patient's activation, which only serves to further escalate the therapist. This dysregulation of both patient and therapist can result in "mutually escalating over-arousal," as when a mother and distressed infant become increasingly stimulated by each other (Beebe, 2000, p. 436).

CORE CONCEPT

The therapist has an important role in helping patients regulate themselves, and in turn, patients influence the therapist's regulation during sessions. The therapist's ability to maintain regulation in the face of the patient's dysregulation is essential.

Even while therapists seek to manage their countertransference feelings, their emotional regulation is further influenced on a somatic level by the patient's physiology. Wilson and Thomas (2004) have called this *physiological empathy*. The therapist implicitly simulates the patient's state of mind and body, as noted in Chapter 2. Thus, the therapist's body mirrors the patient's depression, sadness, hopelessness, rage, and frustration. When the patient suffers, the therapist's body responds as though the therapist is suffering. On one hand, this lends itself to compassion, which is essential in helping maintain the relationship regardless of the patient's state of mind (Wilson & Thomas, 2004). On the other hand, this leaves therapists with powerful physiological reactions that can profoundly affect them. This is a normal physiological process involved in social engagement and attachment that cannot be completely controlled. So how can therapists manage it?

First, therapists must learn to notice the effects on their body and state of mind that result from being with a patient. Once they recognize, for example, that they are holding their breath, slumping in their chair, sighing, feeling hopeless, or keeping a flat facial expression, they can take conscious steps to regulate and ground themselves. This means that therapists must pay close attention to their own somatic experience, even while they are focused on the patient's experience. In other words, they must be mindful and present with themselves, as well as with their patients (Cozolino, 2004, 2010; Siegel, 2010a, 2010b).

Second, therapists need to focus on activation of positive experiences in therapy. This does not mean they try to get patients to laugh when they are suffering, or distract them with something positive. It does not even mean patients should focus on the positive lessons of what has happened to them. The latter may be appropriate at some point, but only after the therapist has journeyed with patients through their suffering, and only if the patient finds meaning that way. Rather, therapists focus on helping the patient have a positive experience of being understood and being with their suffering, which itself changes suffering.

Third, therapists can help both themselves and their patients return time and again to the regulating shelter of social engagement. There, both can access the sense of physical and emotional well-being that good relational connection affords. Therapists cannot undo their patients' suffering, or rescue them from it. But they can give patients a different experience of tolerating and being with suffering in the presence of another compassionate human being in a way that gradually returns them to the present moment of positive connection and safety.

In order to support positive engagement, therapists must be able to regulate themselves. Table 3.2 lists some methods therapists have found helpful in consciously regulating themselves before, during, and after sessions.

TABLE 3.2
Tips for Therapists to Regulate Themselves in Session

Top-down interventions (using your mind to change your reactions)

- Change your cognitive frame with compassion: My patient is feeling misunderstood or rejected instead of My patient is angry with me.
- Take a mental step back and observe yourself with compassion: I am feeling afraid or angry right now. I need to take the time to calm myself down.
- Remind yourself that the patient has survived to this point, and having strong feelings is not an emergency.
- Remind yourself that your role is to remain nondefensive, not to meet every demand of the patient.
- Remind yourself that the patient's distress is not really about you.
- Find something about the patient that you genuinely like, and focus on it.
- Listen to what the patient is telling you beneath the intensity: I am hurt, I am afraid, I am ashamed, I am misunderstood, I have needs. Respond to these implicit statements rather than to the content.
- Recognize that you cannot actually keep the patient safe; this is up to the patient.
- If you are dealing with an emergency, get support. Call the patient's psychiatrist or other team members. Insist on calling the patient's emergency contact. Know the limits of your role as therapist. Do not be afraid to hospitalize as a last resort, even if you know the patient may not be kept for long. This helps the patient know you are serious about safety.

Use imagery to help support yourself

- Imagine stepping aside from the intensity directed toward you. Let it flow past you rather than into you, and imagine observing what is happening from that place of safety.
- Imagine being in an invisible, permeable bubble or other protective shield. Relational connection can easily flow back and forth, but the patient's intensity slides off and passes by, and does not reach you.
- Imagine being backed up by people who support you: your therapist, supervisor, consultant, colleagues, or other team members. Imagine them whispering in your ear how to handle the situation and expressing confidence in your abilities.
- Visualize yourself opening up to compassion and clarity and letting them flow through you, bathing you in a sense of well-being.
- Imagine, as you regulate yourself, projecting that capacity to your patient. Invite your patient to breathe along with you.

- When the patient is sharing difficult memories, do not focus on images of the patient as an actual child being abused in the past. These take you away from the present and can be overwhelming. Focus instead on the adult who has survived and is in your office, and concentrate on the present moment.

Bottom-up interventions (using your body to change your reactions)
- Relax your muscles.
- Sit up straight.
- Hold your chin up.
- Put your shoulders back.
- Move around in your chair a little.
- Feel your feet on the floor and scrunch your toes.
- Look around the room to remind yourself that you are safe.
- Make eye contact with your patient if appropriate (not aggressively!).
- Breathe deeply in to the count of three, hold for the count of three, and breathe out to the count of three several times.
- Let go of the tension in your belly.

Further Explorations

3.1 Review the innate defenses in Table 1.1 from Chapter 1. Notice your own reaction to each type of defense. Which are easier or more difficult for you to handle? Which type of patient, or what issues or emotions, tend to activate your own defenses?

3.2 Is there a defense in Table 1.1 that you most commonly experience as a therapist?

3.3 What is your own attachment style, if you know? How does it help and hinder you as a therapist?

3.4 Write down the issues or emotions with which you become the most dysregulated in sessions. What regulatory skills can you try for yourself next time you are dysregulated in session?
    Tip: Practice your skills daily for a while outside of sessions. Then they become second nature and more effective in sessions.

3.5 Ask your colleagues what skills and techniques they use to ground and regulate themselves during sessions, and compile a list, including those that you already use.

3.6 Review the relational reenactments in Figure 3.1. Write down the types of reenactments with which you do well and those with which you have the most difficulties. Which are familiar from your own history? Discuss with a colleague, supervisor, consultant, or your therapist those with which you struggle.

3.7 Take careful notice of your own subjective experience in session with your patients. Note your posture, sensations, movements, breathing, muscle tension, thoughts, fantasies, emotions, and perceptions. Think about what these experiences are telling you about your patient, about the relationship, and about your own experience with the patient.

CHAPTER 4

Beyond Attachment: A Collaborative Therapeutic Relationship

. . . at the beginning of treatment . . . complex trauma can best be dealt with by trying to maintain a dialogue that attempts to limit the activation of the attachment system by taking advantage of the natural tendency to want to cooperate and collaborate on an equal basis level. Optimally, people try to develop a secure base and a haven of safety in therapy to facilitate the exploration of the relational dilemmas and severe conflict brought by complex trauma and disorganized attachment. But in cases of severe trauma, this goal has to be reached through a circuitous route that tries to limit the premature activation of the attachment toward the therapist.
—Mauricio Cortina & Giovanni Liotti (2014, p. 892)

As mentioned in the last chapter, therapists may need a way to modify the paradigm of secure attachment meant for infants and young children into some type of therapeutic adult model that is more effective for complex trauma patients and manageable for therapists. A collaborative model likely provides the most effective paradigm for adult growth, change, and development.

The Challenges in Using a Parent–Infant Attachment Model in Trauma Therapy

The parent–infant model has many limitations when it is applied to adults in therapy, especially with highly traumatized individuals. First, when their attachment system is highly activated, patients are focused exclusively on the availability of the therapist, and are unable to explore their own inner experience. Attachment-seeking deactivates the exploration system.

Second, unlike personal relationships, the ultimate success of the therapeutic relationship naturally results in its end. Thus, the parent–infant bond is not apt in this regard. Some parts of the patient are often terrified that therapy will end and that the therapist will abandon them. Patients may withhold important details of experience in order to avoid upsetting the therapist, and may be fearful of adaptive change, as it will result in the end of therapy. These are deep conflicts that should be recognized and resolved over the course of treatment.

Third, therapists cannot possibly be there most of the time for their patients, as literal parents are for their very young infants. This is not a realistic adult model, and can quickly overwhelm and exhaust the therapist, who becomes increasingly resentful and taxed. Highly traumatized patients, like no other population, implicitly and often explicitly pull for more contact with the therapist, and understandably so. It is often hard for therapists—especially those who have hyper-activated caretaking action systems—to refuse the requests and demands of patients who are deeply suffering and have had such painful lives. At the very least, the parent–infant model implicitly encourages activation of caretaking.

Fourth, dependency needs are especially intense in trauma survivors (Hill, Gold, & Bornstein, 2000; Steele et al., 2001; see Chapter 13), so a nuanced and careful approach is required in order to help patients remain in their window of tolerance. Although a significant number of trauma patients are relationally avoidant, and dependency is not apparent, their insistence on a kind of hyper-independence hints at overwhelming dependency yearning on the other side of the coin, which they are avoiding.

Fifth, in dissociative patients, some parts may be dependent and attachment seeking, while others are ashamed of and avoid dependency and attachment. Thus, therapists need a model that takes into account the contradictions, conflicts, and confusions of multiple dissociative parts within one person, each in their own way approaching or avoiding relationships and dependency issues. We must simultaneously hold equal space for the young, needy dissociative parts of the patient and for those dissociative parts that are highly avoidant, disdainful, or fearful of closeness. These latter parts only respond with further distance when the therapist encourages them to become more attached (Muller, 2010; Steele & Van der Hart, 2013; Steele et al., 2001).

Sixth, patients are not children but adults, with adult developmental needs and responsibilities as well as unmet—and unintegrated—childhood needs. We need a model that helps us support the adult capacities, freedoms, and responsibilities of our patients as interdependent and whole human beings, while also working with the painful struggles of early attachment trauma, developmental deficits, and dissociation.

For example, a major goal in therapy is to help dissociative patients first accept child parts, develop understanding and compassion for them, and eventually realize they are aspects of themselves. They can learn to take care of child parts, and foster the child parts to "grow up" and learn to deal with dependency needs from an adult perspective. Most importantly, our patients must also grieve what has been lost in childhood—what cannot be undone or loved away no matter how much someone does, or cares, or is available in the present.

Finally, we need a relational model in which both patients and therapists are active participants, a model that is more collaborative than hierarchical. This invites the patient to be an active and willing team member and a participant rather than a passive recipient. The more our patients feel they make their own changes with our compassionate support, but without hoping for some magical wisdom or interventions from us, the more they are able to function in the world with a sense of competence and agency. So, whatever compassionate interventions therapists employ, the foundation is the knowledge that our patients must be the actual doers or actors in therapy, as in life.

The Foundation of Collaborative Relationships

The need to be understood, to share, and to collaborate with each other is a basic motivational or action system that partially directs our social behavior (Cortina & Liotti, 2007; 2010, 2014; Lichtenberg, 1989; Stern, 2004; Trevarthen, 1980; Trevarthen & Aitken, 1994). It is separate from, but strongly linked to, the attachment and care systems.

CORE CONCEPT

We all have an innate need to compassionately share with others, to understand them, and to be understood. As sentient beings, we have a need to understand ourselves. This essential communication is the basis for collaborating with others in a way that we can enjoy and respect our similarities and our differences.

As Cortina and Liotti (2007, 2010) have noted, attachment is directed toward safety, and caregiving is directed toward attachment-seeking behaviors; collaboration, on the other hand, is about understanding and sharing. As self-aware beings, we all have this inborn need to be understood by other people and to understand them—not only their words but their implied motivations and intentions. In the same way, we need to understand ourselves and our own minds—not only what we think and feel but how we came to think and feel that particular way. This is the solid relational foundation of *mentalizing* (Allen, 2001, 2012; Fonagy et al., 2005), or what Siegel has termed *mindsight* (2010a, 2010b, 2015). It prevents us from living in a perpetual Tower of Babel, where implicit as well as explicit communication is an insolvable enigma. This ability to mentalize, that is, to (relatively) accurately perceive the meaning of a person's verbal and implicit communications—and to be aware of our own—allows us to successfully navigate a relational world where we share and collaborate on common goals.

CORE CONCEPT

A collaborative relational model requires that we be present with what is happening right now, both internally and between therapist and patient. This is the ultimate experience of sharing and being understood and is what our dissociative patients most need from us.

Collaboration Versus Caregiving in Therapy

Therapists and patients often confuse attachment and caregiving. Caregiving is a motivational or action system, innately mediating behaviors of a caregiver to ensure the survival of the other through direct care (Britner, Marvin, & Pianta, 2005; George & Solomon, 1999; Solomon & George, 1996). It also becomes a particular strategy of controlling (perceived) caregivers in disorganized attachment, as noted in the previous chapter. Of course, attachment is also an inborn system, and its goal is to ensure a felt sense of security and safety so the child can explore and interact with the self, others, and the world. Caregiving is not attachment, though it is often accompanied by attachment. The child seeks care, and the caregiver gives it; this is an intrinsic part of the parent–infant attachment model.

The patient may view the therapist as a caregiver, whether or not the therapist is engaged in caretaking. The patient sometimes seeks to take care of the therapist through appeasement or solicitous behavior, denying the patient's own needs, or withholding painful issues to protect the therapist, engaging in controlling-caregiving strategies. Other times the patient is angry with the therapist for not providing what is wanted, pleads and demands, engaging in controlling-punitive strategies.

The role of the therapist is not that of caregiver; rather, it is much more like a compassionate and interested mentor or guide who ensures that the patient feels safe to explore and learn along with the therapist, and is thus able to work toward therapeutic goals. In fact, being in the role of caregiver with highly traumatized patients can be fraught with complications. When caregivers have been the source of pain and danger, and have had all the power and control, a parent–child paradigm is a potential reenactment from the beginning of therapy.

Often, therapists implicitly turn to a caregiving relational model in the hope of providing secure attachment. They may make superhuman efforts to be available and not make mistakes, so patients do not have to experience relational disruptions. These actions are based on the mistaken belief that secure attachment is grounded primarily in attunement and constant availability, rather than in repair, the acceptance of loss, the ability to have positive emotions and experiences with others as adults, and in de-activation of attachment seeking so the patient's exploration system can be activated in therapy.

How unprepared for the real world our patients might be if their expectation is that others will be available all the time, or that they will always be careful not to say or do anything that might be distressing to the patient! The caretaking therapist may place few, if any, demands on patients, who may be viewed as too fragile and incapable of doing much until the therapist provides sufficient care and nurturance to activate them. This paradigm already sets up the patients to be helpless, and it can only be taken so far in therapy with adults before it becomes highly problematic (Steele et al., 2001). Even when therapists do not take on a caregiving role, patients often view them as failed caregivers, and they respond with controlling-punitive or controlling-caregiving strategies, so these must still be addressed in therapy.

A collaborative model supports our patients in developing healthy interdependence. They are encouraged to understand themselves and others, including the therapist. Many of their relational problems stem from a lack of understanding and compassion not only for themselves but for other people, and from unrealistic expectations. Therapists help patients learn to take into consideration not only their own needs and desires but also those of others, to balance them fairly when possible, and to make reflective choices when balance is not possible or reasonable. They can help patients learn to recognize and compassionately shift controlling-punitive and controlling-caregiving strategies in various dissociative parts of themselves. This includes understanding the needs and desires of every part of the patient, which are often in great conflict. While the therapist may feel pressure to meet those needs and desires, the real work lies in compassionately and steadily helping the patient come to terms with inner conflicts and unmet needs from childhood instead of focusing on what the therapist does and does not provide in terms of care.

Often patients challenge therapists to "prove" their caring. The problem is actually that the patients are unable to take in a felt sense of being cared for, or parts reject or fear it. Put another way, the problem is the patients' inner conflicts about care, which they attempt to resolve by changing the behavior of the therapists via controlling-punitive or controlling-caregiving strategies.

A collaborative model helps us support the adult capacities, freedoms, and responsibilities of our patients as interdependent and whole human beings. At the same time, we are able to work together on the painful struggles of early attachment trauma, developmental deficits, and dissociation without becoming overinvolved caregivers or underinvolved, detached interventionists. We—patient and therapist—work as a team to help the patient realize inner conflicts and painful realities, including the fact that the therapist is not a caregiver. Often the therapist serves as "team leader," but as patients develop more reflective and integrative abilities, they will step into that role more often.

Table 4.1 compares three different models of relationship: dependent (caregiving), collaborative, and independent (dismissing). Though these are presented as distinct, often therapists may subtly shift between the three positions.

Dependent or dismissing relational models in therapy are generally

TABLE 4.1 Relational Models in Psychotherapy		
Collaborative Model	**Dependence Model**	**Independence Model**
Clear, consistent boundaries and treatment frame no matter what patient or therapist feels.	Unclear, reactive boundaries and treatment frame.	Rigid, inflexible, sometimes inconsistent and punitive boundaries.
Boundaries supported by understanding conflicts about dependence and autonomy.	Boundaries depend on what the client wants from the therapist.	Extreme boundaries discourage any relational regulation by therapist.
Offers predictable but limited availability outside of session.	Extensive contact outside session, subject to the demands of the patient; underestimates patient's competence.	Encourages complete independence; underestimates the patient's lack of skills and need for connection.
Encourages collaboration—the understanding of each other's minds.	Encourages dependency—chronic use of therapist as a "stronger and wiser" other, implicitly devalues competence of the adult.	Offers little to no discussion of patient's experience of dependence or fear of dependence.
Explicitly and implicitly acknowledges, accepts, and works with dependency wishes, emotions, and conflicts.	Offers little to no discussion of the patient's experience of dependence or fear of dependence.	Offers little attention to helping patient learn regulation.
The patient is viewed as the agent of change with support of therapist.	The therapist is viewed as the agent of change.	The patient is viewed as the agent of change without support of therapist.
Teaches appropriate balance between self-regulation and relational regulation.	Teaches overreliance on others to regulate, and not sufficient self-regulation.	Teaches overreliance on self-regulation.
Therapist and patient feel competent and collaborative.	Therapist vulnerable to burnout, caretaking, and boundary transgressions; patient vulnerable to decompensation and maladaptive dependence.	Therapist vulnerable to distancing countertransference; patient vulnerable to decompensation or premature ending of therapy.

maintained by particular approaches and behaviors of the therapist. We briefly discussed the tendency to caretake patients, which might lead to a dependent kind of relational model. Therapists who are excessive caregivers are typically overinvolved with their patients and highly distressed by their patients' distress. Therapists who are largely dismissive are underinvolved with patients, avoidant of their distress, and perhaps even disdainful toward patients. Of course, these are the more extreme ends of the continuum of the level of involvement with patients.

In truth, all therapists lean a little in one direction or another, depending on their own tendencies, the patient, and the situation. Some therapists tend to become more solicitous and caregiving when they feel tired or overwhelmed. Others withdraw, become irritable, and avoid. Some patients may evoke overinvolvement, while others may evoke underinvolvement. Take, for example, Sharon, a highly experienced therapist. Sharon felt a tendency to want to take more care of a young traumatized woman about the same age as her daughter. On the other hand, Sharon noticed that she felt rather cold and distant with a man who was highly narcissistic and who continually noted all of her shortcomings and faults as a therapist. Notice that Sharon had many countertransference feelings and impulses. However, she did not act on them, at least not explicitly.

Our patients need to be able to experience their need of us and be angry and dismiss us, without us becoming too close or too distant (Dalenberg, 2000). Chronic trauma survivors struggle with managing adequate regulation of closeness and distance, often swinging wildly between the extremes according to the defenses and needs of various parts of themselves that are dominant in the moment. When therapists allow dependency on them to develop to the degree that patients cannot tolerate their absence and call incessantly—or conversely, when they pull away and avoid contact because they are frustrated, tired, or angry—they pull their patients out of the moderated range of experience that offers the potential for social engagement. This is particularly true of patients with complex dissociative disorders, because various dissociative parts perceive (emotional or physical) movement toward or away from them as both needed and threatening, which sets up intolerable inner conflicts. These are then externalized and played out in the therapeutic relationship.

The therapist's job is to stand relatively still no matter which part of the patient is prominent, without pursuing or distancing much, without becoming too enmeshed or too detached, while being engaged and present to the greatest degree possible. This most difficult balancing act is almost never mentioned in training, and therapists are often unprepared for such a relational roller coaster. Table 4.2 describes the more extreme poles of the over- and underinvolved therapist.

TABLE 4.2	
The Over- and Underinvolved Therapist	
The Overinvolved Therapist	**The Underinvolved Therapist**
Feels helpless, hopeless, urgent.	Feels helpless, hopeless, but not urgent.
Unable to tolerate patient's suffering—has to do something; tends to appease patient.	Feels revulsion, disgust, fear, or anger at patient's needs.
Attempts to control own anxiety, guilt, shame, or pain by "fixing" patient's need.	Attempts to control own emotions by avoidance, dismissal, and denial of patient's needs.
Has difficulty viewing patient as an adult.	Intellectualizes therapy; overly focused on cognition; avoids emotion.
Reacts to patient's need or demand in the moment instead of helping patient reflect.	Shames or blames patient for expressing needs or is unable to respond.
Unable to take a healthy distance from patient's suffering.	Dismisses patient's needs or demands in the moment instead of helping patient reflect.
Engages in boundary violations or constant boundary crossings.	Has overly rigid and/or punitive boundaries.
Has inconsistent limits.	Unable to withstand intensity of patient's demands and withdraws and/or punishes.
Unable to help patient understand, accept, and work through dependency conflicts.	Fails to address significant attachment issues.
Unable to help patient understand, accept, and tolerate the fact that the therapist and others cannot meet all the patient's needs.	Does not provide adequate help for patient to function in daily life.
Underestimates patient's abilities and resilience.	Overestimates patient's abilities and resilience.
Potential sexual exploitation of patient.	Potential sexual exploitation of patient.
Involved in daily life of patient in concrete ways (e.g., loaning patient money).	
Has difficulty setting treatment goals and keeping patient on task in sessions.	Inability to set therapeutic goals due to avoidance or dismissal of particular issues.
Promotes excessive dependence.	Believes patient is not trying hard enough or is manipulative.
Believes that constant availability and caring for the patient will result in improvement.	Controls the therapy and topics discussed.
Feels burned out.	Feels burned out.

The Road to Collaboration in Therapy

How do therapists support the need to collaborate and understand in the context of building social engagement and competence in patients? Their way of being with the patients is the place to begin. Therapists try to be fully with their patients to the degree possible, seeking to understand the patients' experience in the moment, rather than focusing only on the content of what the patients are saying or trying to immediately fix the problem. They need to be present with themselves as well, not getting lost in the drama, the suffering, and the complexities of the patients. They imagine what it is like to be in shoes of the patients—that is, they mentally imitate the patients to build compassion and understanding, to mentalize accurately. They focus on process, on the relational experience in the moment, on how patients experience themselves and the therapist, and on how they experience themselves in the moment. They are not impatient with slow progress, but they do not let resistance and unwillingness to work in therapy go unaddressed, insisting that only shared goals are achievable. They contain and do their best to work through their own wishes to rescue, fix, berate, control, abandon, or re-parent patients. They hold the dialectical tension of accepting patients as they are while still supporting change.

They also accept themselves in the moment as they are. Good therapists know they can only do their best, even though they do not know everything. When they make mistakes, they notice, apologize, and repair. In this way, patients learn that even the best of relationships follow a rhythm of attunement, mis-attunement, reattunement, and repair, and that no one can or needs to be perfect. They are supported in accepting and grieving that no one can really rescue them from themselves or their histories, and they can then be empowered to direct their own lives to the degree possible. They can learn the difference between everyday mis-attunements or misunderstandings versus true betrayal and danger. To be sure, this is not an easy or obstacle-free journey, but it can be accomplished.

Therapists can support patients in recognizing ways in which patients themselves create ruptures with others, and how to handle their own relational mistakes, which often involve the inappropriate reactions of different dissociative parts. Patients learn to accept their inner experiences (including dissociative parts) without judgment, fear, or shame—a task modeled by the therapist.

Collaboration and Implicit Communication: The Felt Sense of You and Me

Collaboration begins long before verbal language develops, and continues at an implicit level to corroborate or contradict what we actually say. Collaboration thus involves not only verbal language but also body language, and at the most basic level, neuroception of safety and danger (Porges, 2001, 2003, 2004, 2011). Language and implicit communications must be relatively congruent with each other for us to accurately share and mentalize. Therapists and patients are always communicating implicitly with their bodies even while they are using words, and are responding or reacting to those implicit messages to and from each other.

In order for collaboration to be possible, social engagement must be activated. In a positive feedback loop, collaboration also supports and strengthens social engagement, which allows for the possibility of secure attachment. This has major treatment implications for work with dissociative patients. It offers a particular sequence of relating that fosters safety and curiosity rather than dependency and chronic attachment-seeking behaviors.

Collaboration involves what is termed a *felt sense*, which is "a special kind of internal bodily awareness . . . a body sense of meaning" (Gendlin, 1981, p. 10). A felt sense of the situation and the other person allows us to know what we know without consciously being aware. Felt sense begins with neuroception, detecting safety and threat, but then goes far beyond. Therapists and patients are always communicating implicitly even while they are using words, and are responding or reacting to those implicit messages to and from each other (Bromberg, 1998, 2006; Ogden & Fisher, 2015; Ogden et al., 2006; Lyons-Ruth, 2007; Trevarthan, 1980). Dissociative patients have overlapping and conflicting undertows that may be felt by the therapist. Dissociative parts often communicate implicitly when they are "behind the scenes"—that is, when they are not in complete executive control.

Therapists often feel these unspoken undercurrents, these persistent threads of feelings and urges. For example, therapists may feel confusion or fogginess, a strong pull to distance or caretake, lassitude or hopelessness, sexual tension, anger, dread, sadness, or a sense of not really knowing the patient even after many months. These each tell the therapist something about the patient and about what the patient cannot or dares not yet know or speak.

CORE CONCEPT

Patients need to learn when it is adaptive to use self-regulation and when to use relational regulation. But most importantly, it is *how* they use support from others that can either spiral them into unhelpful dependency or propel them further along the journey of self-discovery and change.

Relational regulation and self-regulation in a collaborative model. The social engagement and collaboration action systems support us in further learning both relational regulation and self-regulation. Empathy and compassion stem from these systems, creating a fertile and inviting relational space in which to grow and thrive, and to be with others safely. At its best, this is the sacred space that the good enough therapeutic relationship offers the patient.

However, relationships are not perfect. Even normal, healthy relationships involve hurt, misunderstanding, mis-attunement, and rejection from time to time, resulting in dysregulation. When social engagement is coupled with the ability to understand another's intentions and motivations, we are able to regularly repair and reconnect, which is what helps (re)regulate us. Through repair we can strengthen our trust that a good enough relationship can withstand the usual foibles and failures of a good enough person. We can also accept that not all relationships last for the length of our lives, and we do not have to negate the good parts of a relationship when it ends or changes. We come to realize that loss is forever a part of life and love, and that we can still take the risk to be vulnerable and open, and tolerate loss when it comes.

We all need to rely on others for emotional help and support at times. We also need to manage our own emotional regulation when support from others is not necessary, not available, or not sufficient. We need to learn the situations when it is appropriate to reach out for support and when it is not, or when a combination of both is important. We also learn that even while needing the support of another, we can be interdependent, aware of what the other person may also need, and able to reciprocate. All things being equal, we each have a tendency to prefer either relational regulation or self-regulation. Some people naturally tend to reach out to others first when distressed—to call a friend or talk to a partner. Others find it natural to want to self-regulate first—to take a walk, to reflect and sort out their feelings before talking with someone else. Either approach is fine, as long as we are also able and willing to use a nonpreferred type of regulation when it is needed and appropriate.

How patients use relational regulation. The effectiveness of relational support does not depend on the amount of time it is available but on how it is used by when it is accessible. Many patients are able to use relational support as a stepping stone to take the next steps in therapy and in life, while others use it to become ever more dependent and helpless, waiting for that "feel-good" moment of support, and collapsing or becoming enraged when it ends.

Take me with you. Our patients need to learn that instead of depending
on the therapist's constantly availability, they can learn to carry within
themselves the experience of being attuned to, grounded, and present with
the therapist (and supportive others). For example, the therapist can encourage all parts to *feel what it is like to be supported by me (or your friend or partner) right now. Take that support and wisdom with you, and carry it wherever
you go. It is yours whenever you need to call upon it.*

A focus on *how* the patient experiences positive moments of being with
the therapist (and others) gradually translates to a greater ability to call
upon positive mental images or memories of being with others. These tem-
plates gradually develop into more enduring and positive mental representations of the self and others that influence our patients' ability to collaborate
and share. Then they are better able to retain a felt sense of security even
when they are alone and no one is immediately available.

Sometimes patients are unable to conjure any image of the therapist nor
have a felt sense of support outside of session, or their image of the therapist is critical and punitive. Not only is the ability to hold a positive image
of others a developmental skill that must be learned over time, but there
may also be complicating dynamics of active opposition from some dissociative parts that prevent the experience. For example, hostile parts may
want to punish patients by denying them the therapist's support. Some
parts may feel that support is not deserved. Sad or terrified parts may be
living in trauma-time to the degree that they cannot hold the reality of the
presence of the therapist. Other parts that are avoidant and afraid of dependency may block a felt sense of support, believing it to mean that the patient
is needy and weak. Thus, the therapist should make a habit of having the
patient check in with all parts to begin to understand and work with what

is often a multilayered obstruction to internalizing positive supportive experiences.

CASE EXAMPLE OF HELPING A PATIENT DEVELOP A FELT EXPERIENCE OF THE THERAPIST'S SUPPORT: NATALIE

Natalie was a patient who had dissociative identity disorder (DID) and borderline personality disorder. She could not talk about painful subjects in sessions partly because she was focused on the fact that the therapist would not be there to help her with the difficult emotions between sessions. Overall, she had a controlling-punitive strategy, including many demands, complaints, and chronic insistence that the therapist was not helping her sufficiently. She stated, *You are never there when I really need you!* Yet when the therapist was available in session, Natalie could only focus on the fact that soon she would have to leave, and the therapist would disappear again. Thus, she was unable to use the positive experience of being with the therapist to explore her inner world. The therapist helped Natalie explore what happened in session.

Therapist: Natalie, can you notice and share with me what happens inside right now as we are together?

Natalie: What happens inside? It's miserable, that's what happens! The babies *[child parts of Natalie]* are crying. Everybody is yelling for them to shut up right now.

Therapist: So the baby parts of you are encouraged not to show their pain right now. Why do you suppose that might be important?

Natalie: Because! They just get started, and then we have to leave and be grown up. We just can't do that!

Therapist: Hmm, sounds like quite a dilemma. I wonder if we might find a way to work with that.

Natalie: I don't see how when we only have one hour a week together.

Therapist: Well, I imagine we will find our way together with it, even though it might be challenging. Shall we give it a try?

Natalie: I guess, but I don't see how unless you are willing to talk with me on the phone every day when they really need you.

Therapist: Well, let's see if we can take one step at a time, shall we? Let's start with here and now for the moment and not jump ahead too quickly. I have the feeling that we are missing something really important right now before we move ahead.

Natalie: I don't know what that is. I'm here, aren't I? I show up for every single session!

Therapist: Yes, you do, and you are very committed to showing up. That's wonderful and an important start. And can we be curious for a moment about other parts of you inside and what they are experiencing right now?

Natalie: I told you already! The babies are crying, and everybody is yelling for them to shut up.

Therapist: So it sounds like the babies are showing up, but other parts of you don't want them here?

Natalie: Of course, because they will just get hurt at the end of the session when we have to go home without you.

Therapist: Let's begin working with those parts of you that hold back in session. Could we allow, just for the moment, the baby parts of you to be in a safe space that is comforting to them, just for the short time that we are working with these other parts together? The baby parts are, of course, as important as every other part of you, and we will get to them.

Natalie: You want David and Sam here? *["David" and "Sam" are the parts of Natalie that protect her from disappointment and hurt by insisting she avoid relational closeness and trust.]*

Therapist: Yes—those parts, you, and all other parts of you that might find it helpful. Can David and Sam and other parts of you, along with you, focus on the room for a moment? Just look around and see very clearly where you are, what the sounds are, the feel of the chair that supports you, the sensations in your body of being in this room. *[The therapist takes time to help these parts of Natalie notice many details of being present in the room.]*

Natalie: OK, OK, we know this room. So what?

Therapist: It has occurred to me that these parts of you are skipping too quickly over experiences that might help them feel more safe. I am hoping that in slowing down these parts enough to really notice and feel the present moment, you will find another way to help with the dilemma of having to leave session and not being able to feel support. Can you stay with me, with your curiosity, so that we don't jump ahead too soon? Let's just take small steps right now.

Natalie: *(Sighing heavily)* All right. I don't see how this will help, though.

Therapist: Now that these parts of you are aware of the room, the safe present, of here and now, could they turn their attention to what it is like to be with me right now?

Natalie: I already told you, it's terrible!

Therapist: Yes, you did tell me earlier, and that's a really quick answer right now. Would you be willing to slow it down with me, the feeling of it being terrible? Again, I wonder if we might be missing something important here.

Natalie: What do you mean, "slow it down"?

Beyond Attachment: A Collaborative Therapeutic Relationship 81

Therapist: Well, let's just take this next 15 seconds and no more. Let parts of you notice what it is like to be here without going to what might happen after those 15 seconds. Is that something you can try?

Natalie: OK. Just 15 seconds and that's it?

Therapist: Yes, just focus on what it is like to be with me for 15 seconds.

Natalie: It's too short. It makes me panic.

Therapist: OK, tell me more about what happens.

Natalie: David started screaming that 15 seconds isn't enough time.

Therapist: Enough time for what?

Natalie: To feel better! It's not enough to feel better!

Therapist: Oh, I see. David is expecting that these 15 seconds are supposed to make him feel better. No wonder it's hard! Perhaps I wasn't clear in explaining. Let me try again, and I hope that David is listening. The only goal is to notice what it is like to be with me in this moment. The goal of feeling better is really important, but that isn't what we are doing for these few seconds. Could the David part of you just notice what it is like to be with me, to focus on that for a moment? Just let David, Sam, all parts of you look at me and notice what it is like to be here together. Just the two of us, just focused on exploring what is happening in the moment. No more, no further than the next few seconds.

Natalie: That is hard! I just think of what it will be like when I leave.

Therapist: Yes, it is hard! And like many hard things, it will take a good bit of practice. Remember when you really struggled with hurting yourself and how hard it was to stop, yet you learned how, even though it was really hard? And now you don't hurt yourself anymore! Can you remember what it felt like to be in charge of yourself and to stop hurting yourself? Just feel that experience right now for a moment. *[The therapist is taking the patient to a moment of competence, which is, in itself, a positive experience.]* How does that feel in your body?

Natalie: Strong, warm. I feel a little bit proud.

Therapist: Strong, warm, a little proud. Can David, Sam, and other parts of you feel that right now too?

Natalie: Kind of, I guess.

Therapist: Good. Let all parts of you really take notice of that. Strong, warm, proud. *[Here the therapist may use bilateral stimulation or some other way to further embed these positive sensations and cognitions.]* Now, let's come back to here and now with me. Can David and all other parts of you notice being here with me in the moment, when we are both completely focused on you and your experience right now? Try just to stay in the moment.

Natalie: Yeah, David is a little more relaxed. Sam is staying in the shadows, but he is pretty quiet. But when are you going to help the babies?

Therapist: We *are* helping the baby parts of you right now. Perhaps not in the direct way you expect. But helping the more grown-up parts of you will help the younger parts. Can you bear with me for another few minutes and continue with what we are doing? Good, so draw your full attention to being here in this moment with me. Neither of us has anywhere we need to go and nothing else to do right now except to be here together. What happens inside when you notice that?

Natalie: Feels good, safe. Kind of relaxed.

Therapist: Let all parts of you feel this moment. Good, safe, kind of relaxed. *[The therapist may reinforce this experience with bilateral stimulation, somatic work, or other approaches.]* Yes, take this in, especially the David and Sam parts of you. Just take the time you need.

Natalie: OK. Is that enough? Now what?

Therapist: I'm curious about what the hurry is?

Natalie: I want to feel better! This isn't doing anything!

Therapist: Really? I thought you were feeling good and safe and relaxed just now.

Natalie: Well, yes, but it won't stay that way.

Therapist: Perhaps, and it is also true that you are moving away from that experience so you don't get to have it while it is here.

Natalie: Oh, I guess I am.

Therapist: Let's just stay in this moment for a while longer. Is that OK?

Natalie: Yeah, I guess. It does feel kind of good. I'm just afraid it won't last.

Therapist: Yes, I understand that, and we will work on that fear. But right now just stay with what is actually happening.

Table 4.3 includes exploratory questions about how a patient experiences the felt sense of the therapist both in and between sessions.

Collaboration and Availability of the Therapist

A collaborative relational model includes being consistent in our availability, whatever it may be. We need to offer patients a regular appointment each week, show up (and end) on time, and give ample notice when we need to change an appointment or miss a session due to vacation or other reasons. We tell our patients when we are available outside sessions and for what reasons, how best to reach us, what to do when they cannot reach us, and give clear instructions on what to do in an emergency. And together we define "emergency." When a patient calls, we return the call as promptly as possible, within the parameters we have given the patient. There will be times when an unexpected illness or other problem necessitates the late cancelation of a session, or when a message somehow does not get through. We will inevitably find ourselves in a painful situation when we

TABLE 4.3
Exploring the Patient's Felt Sense of the Therapist

A felt sense during session
- What is your experience of me right now?
- Do all parts of you feel me here with you?
- If some parts do not: What do you suppose keeps those parts of you from feeling this moment with me?
- Is there any conflict about feeling my support here with you now? For example:
  - You (the therapist) won't be here later, so what's the point?
  - I can't rely on you all the time.
  - I don't deserve support.
  - How could you really be here with me? I am so disgusting.
  - You like the child parts but don't want the angry part of me around.
  - I will just get disappointed again.
  - Part of me says it will hurt me if I feel your support or care.
  - Asking for help always gets me in trouble.
  - Comfort from you isn't enough. I need comfort from my mother or my _____.
  - I pay you to be here, so it's not real.
  - Suffering is all I know; it's who I am. Who will I be if I don't suffer?
- The therapist might say, You say that some parts of you feel my support, but others do not. Can you help us both understand those parts of you? What is the objection or stumbling block for these parts of you?
- Can the parts of you that do feel my support connect with the parts that do not? Let them feel what it is like, just for a moment, and notice what happens.

A felt sense of care and support between sessions
- Do you ever take a sense of care and support with you from others or from myself when you are going about you daily life?
- If so, what does that feel like in your body?
- Are there times when you lose that sense of care and support?
  - Can you notice when that usually happens? *(e.g., as soon as the patient leaves the session, or when the patient is home alone)*
  - Can you notice if you have any particular thoughts or feelings that go along with the disappearance of that sense of care and support?
  - Perhaps we can explore whether some parts of you find it difficult to allow that care and support.
  - Is there anything that helps you get it back?

forget a session or double-book two patients for the hour or forget to call the patient back. However, we can apologize and be as consistent as humanly possible.

Often, at least some *occasional* extrasession contact during crisis or other temporary situations is helpful, but only to stabilize, not to provide therapy. The issue is not whether there is contact between sessions, but how it used by the patient and the therapist, that is,

- whether there are well-defined parameters that allow the therapist to have a life and patients to be focused on their lives rather than relying on constant contact with the therapist, and
- whether it supports patients to focus more in sessions on the work of therapy.

Therapists must engage in attunement *and* clear limit setting, compassion *and* strong boundaries, reasonable flexibility *and* predictable consistency, support for the patient to learn skills *and* insistence on regular practice of those skills. They must accept the patient's experience *and* respectfully confront unacceptable behaviors. Therapists must support the patient in grieving the painful reality that life does not provide perfectly all the time, but conversely, that it can also provide enough.

CORE CONCEPT

The patient needs at least one other support person in addition to the therapist. This may be a family member, friend, another member of a treatment team, or other professional.

Of course, certain patients display more dependence on the therapist, while others maintain such a distant and pseudo-independent stance that they cannot experience the therapist (or other people) as helpful or present at all. Patients who are extremely socially isolated may view the therapist as their only source of support, a trap for both therapist and patient. Our patients' needs are often broad and great, requiring a "village" or team approach. To this end, therapists should strongly encourage the patient to have at least one other support person. After all, a major goal is to help patients participate in life and relationships. If they remain in a safe cocoon with the therapist, some patients may be unwilling to ever risk the rough-and-tumble of the real world. Of course, we realize that some patients are so isolated, this may be next to impossible.

CASE EXAMPLE OF LEARNING TO SELF-REGULATE: ROGER

Roger was a patient with a dissociative disorder and a severe anxiety disorder. He constantly called his wife from work for reassurance when he was anxious. He would go to his boss time and again to clarify his directions, which irritated his boss to no end. Roger was afraid to make a mistake or displease his boss. Some dissociative parts were crying and insisting he go home, another yelled at Roger internally that his boss was too demanding and Roger ought to quit right now, and yet another was shouting that Roger was completely stupid.

Roger's therapist helped him learn to tolerate and manage his anxiety by helping him work with his dissociative parts, and through a variety of breathing and mindfulness techniques. Roger's therapist encouraged him to practice several techniques to regulate his emotions. Roger had a dissociative part that insisted he was a failure. The therapist worked with this part to understand its functions (to prevent Roger from having painful experiences and to defend against shame by attacking self). The therapist helped both Roger and this attacking part of himself to learn more about his shame (see Chapter 15) and to have more compassion for himself.

As Roger was able to successfully regulate emotions when not under stress, the therapist was able to highlight his successes, for which he began to have some pride. With a little more compassion among dissociative parts, they began to be more willing to cooperate at work and take small risks there. Roger was slowly learning to regulate himself without always needing someone else to do so.

Internal Collaboration Among Dissociative Parts

In a collaborative model, the therapist acknowledges the patient's inner experience, especially the conflicts, ambivalence, and unintegrated experiences among and within dissociative parts of themselves. Together with the patient, the therapist begins to understand how various dissociative parts do and do not collaborate with each other, both implicitly and explicitly. These internal dynamics are at the core of the distress and lack of coherence and congruity for dissociative patients.

Therapists might, for example, empathize with a young part of the patient that wants constant contact—an understandable wish, no matter how unrealistic. However, they also acknowledge the rage and shame this evokes in other parts whose intent is to protect from hurt and vulnerability, and how this dependency wish also undermines a sense of competence in the individual, who is an adult, not a child. They have compassion for the pain and distress of the conflict, the insistence on an idealized fantasy of caretaking, and the eventual grief of losing this fantasy and facing reality. They understand and accept the partial legitimacy of all the positions of each part of the person, holding the whole person in mind even when this is impossible for the patient to do. Then they offer ways the patient can learn to deal with these conflicts more adaptively, instead of taking one side or the other (Steele et al., 2001). This approach creates inner collaboration and cohesion among dissociative parts whose *raison d'être* is to avoid the internal connection, acceptance, and realization that leads to integration.

Using Countertransference as a Collaborative Intervention

Sharing countertransference directly or indirectly can be incredibly powerful in supporting relational collaboration, if done in the right way with the right timing. Depending on theoretical models, therapists are advised not to share anything, to share in careful moderation, or to share a lot. We believe that knowing a specific patient well and knowing the therapist's own motivations for disclosure are important first steps in deciding whether, when, and what to share. Disclosure is definitely not a one-size-fits-all endeavor, particularly with dissociative patients. And therapists need to know that different parts may have vastly different reactions to a disclosure, some of which may not be anticipated. However, when done well, self-disclosure can enhance the effectiveness of psychotherapy (M. S. Barrett & Berman, 2001).

CORE CONCEPT

Sharing our experience of the moment with patients can, when done appropriately, enhance the relationship, build trust, and help patients improve their capacity to share and relate. It is a way of saying, *You are part of the human race, as we all are.*

Some types of disclosures are more helpful, others less so. For example, a therapist who self-discloses that she suffers from severe depression is likely to evoke a negative or frightened reaction, whereas a therapist who talks about ways she deals with occasional "down times" that everyone experiences as part of the human condition is likely to evoke a positive reaction.

That is, disclosures that join with the patient in being human are more likely to be helpful than specific disclosures of content. If the therapist discloses too much, patients may perceive the therapist as less competent and effective, even fragile, and worry about their impact on the therapist's state of mind. But a collaborative disclosure puts both patient and therapist squarely in the realm of normal human experience and helps the patient have a felt sense of the therapist as "being with."

CORE CONCEPT

Personal disclosures about the therapist's experience in the moment with the patient, or those that join with the patient in being human, are generally more helpful than disclosures of facts about the therapist's life or history.

Another way to approach this type of disclosure is to say something like, *I don't completely know your experience of despair and depression, but there is something there that is a bit familiar to me. We humans have each found ourselves somewhere on that continuum from time to time. How important that you are beginning to share yours now so you don't have to feel so alone in it.*

The purpose of sharing the therapist's feelings or experiences with patients is to use it as a bridge to help them connect with their own unintegrated or disowned experiences and relational patterns. The therapist needs to find a careful balance between using countertransference feelings, sharing them with modulation when appropriate, and aiming for the patient's experience in the moment. Sometimes it is more therapeutic to simply notice and use inner experiences as silent guides in sessions without sharing them with the patient.

The choice as to whether or not the therapist should share countertransference emotions directly with the patient is based on many factors. The following questions might be helpful in making decisions.

- *Do I have strong feelings about what I want to disclose? Is it something that is still unresolved for me?* Unresolved issues are likely too vulnerable to share, and the therapist's judgment about disclosure may not be clear. Get consultation or supervision to discuss whether disclosure might be helpful; and if so, what, how, and when to share.
- *Is the patient likely to appreciate his or her impact on me as the therapist, and can the patient use my disclosure to reflect?*

- *Does the patient have a positive alliance with me?* Research indicates self-disclosure when the patient perceives the therapeutic relationship as negative only deepens the negative perception of the therapist (Myers & Hayes, 2006).
- *Is the patient likely to use my disclosure to further berate or humiliate me— that is, would the patient be sadistic toward me? If so, would it be helpful to share my curiosity about what happens for the patient when she or he hurts or humiliates me?*
- *Would a disclosure of my experience of the patient be too much for the patient to tolerate? Would it likely engender shame, guilt, rage, care-taking?*
- *Is there a way to share my experience without overwhelming the patient?*
- *Would the patient likely use my disclosure to deflect from her or his own experience? Would the patient ruminate about the disclosure and demand even more be shared?* Obsessional defenses might preclude much sharing until they are worked through more completely.
- *How will each part of the patient likely respond to my disclosure? Is it likely to create more cohesion or less among parts?*

How the therapist discloses is also important. Disclosures should be framed with the focus on compassionate understanding of the patient's experience. It is essential that countertransference reactions are shared in a nonthreatening and modulated way. Some examples of how to disclose in ways that foster collaboration are given in Table 4.4.

Summary

A parent–infant model of attachment can greatly inform the therapeutic relationship—yet there are difficulties with using the model without additional modifications. Our innate need to collaborate and share can also contribute to the structure of the therapeutic relationship. Collaboration is as much about implicit communication and sharing as it is about explicit words, and good collaboration results in a sense of competence and well-being. Countertransference disclosures can be a powerful way to promote collaboration in therapy.

TABLE 4.4
Disclosures by the Therapist That Support Collaboration

- I feel a sense of hopelessness strongly in the room, and I feel it inside myself as you are trying to share what it is like to feel so hopeless. Seems so dark and empty. Is that a little of what it is like?
  - Not: *I feel so hopeless with you right now. I have tried everything I know and it does not help you.*
  - Not: *You feel so hopeless. But there is a lot of hope! I am here and will help you feel better.*
- Somehow, I feel a bit of turmoil in myself, as though you are somehow sharing some ambivalence or confusion with me. I wonder if parts of you are in disagreement with each other. Does that fit? If so, what are the reactions of other parts of yourself regarding what you are saying?
  - Not: *I have no idea what you are talking about. I feel like you are trying to confuse me.*
- I notice you are holding your breath and your muscles are tensed while you are telling me this happy story about your sister. Can you notice that and be curious with me about what might be happening for you right now? Because I also find myself feeling quite tense along with you.
  - Not: *You are so tense. Just relax.*
- I find myself feeling sad as you tell me this story, yet you are laughing and smiling. I am curious that we have such different reactions. Could you share your experience of telling this story to me?
  - Not: *You are incongruent when you laugh about something that is clearly sad. You need to feel that sadness.*
- I just realized I have been holding my breath, and I notice you are doing it too. Let's both take in some deep breaths and be curious about what we both are trying to accomplish by not breathing.
  - Not: *I am holding my breath waiting for you to say something.*
- I notice a lot of frustration in the room. I feel it. I could imagine you do, too—is that right? Let's find a way to understand that.
  - Not: *I am really frustrated with you right now. I don't understand why you are so resistant to something that will clearly make you feel better.*
- When you shout at me, I feel a bit scared. It is hard to understand what you are really trying to say, and I want to hear you. So please lower your voice, and let's find a way to be together so I can get it.
  - Not: *Stop being so angry and calm down!*
- If a patient is being sadistic, instead of revealing fear and vulnerability, the therapist should immediately refocus on the patient's experience: *I'd like to stop for a moment, because I just realized that what is happening between us is very much like what you describe happening in other relationships. There is*

a sense that you take some enjoyment in the discomfort or fear that other peo-ple feel around you, which you have noted gives you a sense of power. I wonder if that is something that is happening now?

- o Not: *I feel really hurt. I am just trying to help you. Why do you treat me this way?*
- There seems to be some sexual energy in the room. Let's find a way to talk about that safely, with all parts of you being present.
  - o Not: *You are having sexual feelings for me.*
  - o Not: *I am having sexual feelings.*
- I find myself having a curious experience of feeling a bit incompetent right now. I wonder if that tells us something about what is going on with both of us in this session. I am guessing that is a familiar feeling for you. Let's take this important opportunity to understand more about your experience and our experience together.
  - o Not: *You came to me because I am an expert, and I really do know what I am doing. I want to help you, but you reject everything I suggest.*
- It's interesting that I find myself a bit sleepy even though I am very rested. Do you also find that it is difficult to stay present today? I wonder what might be going on that we are not very present with each other?
  - o Not: *You are so boring that I can hardly stay awake in sessions with you. You are not bringing into session what you really need to work on.*
- I notice that I am having the experience of feeling a bit like nothing is ever good enough, and it came to me that what is happening between us might be a helpful window into some of what it was like for you growing up. Am I get-ting it right that you never felt good enough, no matter how hard you tried? Can you tell me more about what that was like? I can also imagine that your experience was that your parents never could quite understand you in a way that was helpful enough for you. Is that right?
  - o Not: *You reject everything I do. You have a pattern in relationships of mak-ing people feel inferior to make yourself feel better. Let's look at that.*
- I find myself feeling torn right now about what to do, and I wonder if you also experience this with me. The young part of you wants me to soothe you, while the angry part of you wants me to have nothing to do with those longings, and in fact, does not even want to be in therapy. It seems that if I choose one over the other, something essential of yourself will be lost to us in this moment. I believe that both are very important. I wonder if the conflict between those parts of you is something we could both be aware of and think about together.
  - o Not: *I am not taking care of child parts. That's not my job. And the angry part of you needs to back off. You expect the impossible of me.*
  - o Not: *Yes, let's have the child here now. She needs so much care and sooth-ing. The angry part hurts her so much. That anger doesn't belong to you. That is your father's anger. Give it back to him.*

Further Explorations

4.1 Describe an example of how you shared countertransference with a patient that helped the two of you collaborate on what was going on in the moment.

4.2 Which do you tend to use most often for yourself—self-soothing or relational soothing? Your answer is neither good nor bad. Different people tend to lean one way or the other. Are you able to know when it is appropriate to ask for support and when it is appropriate to go for it on your own? If you have beliefs about whether one is better than the other, write them down.

   Example: People should be independent and able to manage on their own all the time. People should never have to be alone when they are having a hard time. I can't depend on people to help me, so I have to do it myself. I can't soothe myself, so I have to depend on someone else to help me.

4.3 In what ways do your beliefs about relational and self-regulation affect your tendency to influence your patients to emphasize either relational or self-regulation?

4.4 Practice focusing on process—that is, what is happening between you and the patient and what is happening within each of you during sessions this week. What makes it hard for you to notice process? What have you learned from focusing more on process?

   Tip: If you need help with recognizing and working with process, ask your consultant or supervisor. We recommend videotaping sessions as a great way to learn to work with process. Another way is to role-play with a colleague, each taking turns as patient and therapist. Practice in the role-play only focusing and commenting on process for 10 or 15 minutes.

4.5 Take careful notice of your own subjective experience in session with your patients. Note your posture, sensations, movements, breathing, muscle tension, thoughts, fantasies, emotions, and perceptions. Is some of your experience different with different patients or different dissociative parts?

PART II

Assessment, Case Formulation, and Treatment Planning

CHAPTER 5

Assessment of Dissociative Disorders

Screening for dissociative pathology should become an integral part of routine diagnostic assessment.

—Suzette Boon and Nel Draijer (1993a, p. 270)

Accurate diagnosis of dissociative disorders is essential because it structures the specific treatment approach that is most likely to help patients with complex dissociative problems improve. When dissociation is directly addressed in phase-oriented treatment, patients show progress in daily life functioning, decreased self-injury, lower PTSD and dissociative symptoms, less need for hospitalization, and lower treatment costs (Brand, Classen, Lanius, et al., 2009; Brand & Loewenstein, 2014). However, those whose dissociation is not attended to in treatment continue to have dissociative symptoms and other difficulties, as their underlying dissociative organization has not changed (Brand, Classen, McNary, & Zaveri, 2009).

CORE CONCEPT

Complex dissociative disorders require specific treatment approaches. Thus, assessment is of major importance.

There are many excellent sources for diagnosis of patients with dissociative disorders (see Appendix A for a list of assessment instruments). In this chapter we briefly describe the major symptoms of complex dissociative disorders. It is important for therapists—even those who do not specialize in dissociative disorders—to be able to do at least a basic screening for dissociative disorders. If needed, further consultation may help clarify diagnosis. Sometimes, because dissociation may remain hidden, the diagnosis may not be clear for quite some time. Therapists may suspect a dissociative disorder, but may have to wait until patients are safe enough to more fully express their inner experience.

Challenges in the Assessment of Dissociative Disorders

The therapist needs to ask both direct and subtle questions about dissociation without overwhelming the patient, but also without avoiding the subject. There are several major challenges in assessing dissociative disorders that need to be addressed so the therapist will be adequately prepared to understand dissociative symptoms and their varied presentations (see Boon & Draijer, 1993a,1993b, 2007; Dell, 2002, 2006a, 2006b, 2009a, 2009b; Draijer & Boon, 1999; ISSTD, 2011; C. A. Ross, 1997; Steinberg, 1994, 1995, 2004; Van der Hart et al., 2006).

Multiple Meanings of Dissociation

Dissociation has many definitions and descriptions in the literature, and thus it may be hard for the therapist to know exactly what to look for in the patient (Boon & Draijer, 2007). One major question is whether dissociation is on a continuum from "normal" to "pathological" (e.g., Bernstein & Putnam, 1986; Carlson & Putnam, 1993; Cardeña, 1994). Some theorists consider symptoms such as spaciness, imaginative involvement, and absorption as being on the "normal" end of this continuum, with dissociative parts of the personality and psychogenic amnesia being on the pathological end (Butler, 2006; Dalenberg & Paulson, 2009; Waller, Putnam, & Carlson, 1996). The symptoms on the normal end are quite ordinary in all populations and involve a narrowing or lowering of the level of conscious awareness. We prefer not to call these phenomena dissociation, as they do not involve dissociation of the personality, the original meaning of the term (Boon & Draijer, 1993a; Steele, Dorahy, Van der Hart, & Nijenhuis, 2009; Van der Hart, 1991; Van der Hart et al., 2006). They naturally occur when we are tired, ill, preoccupied, stressed, or so focused on one thing (for example, reading a book or working on a project) that we do not notice others. However, even these normal symptoms may be pathological when they are persistent and severe, such as in patients who are "spacey" to the point of dysfunction or who spend many hours in fantasy instead of living their lives, whether or not they also have dissociation of the personality (Somer, 2002).

We, along with others, question whether there is a continuum, given that the dissociative symptoms of those with Other Specified Dissociative Disorder (OSDD) and DID are qualitatively different than "dissociation" observed in other populations (Boon & Draijer 1993a; Nijenhuis, 2015; Rodewald, Dell, Wilhelm-Gößling, & Gast, 2011; Steele et al., 2009; Van der Hart & Dorahy, 2009; Van der Hart et al., 2006; Waller et al., 1996; Waller, Ohanian, Meyer, Everill, & Rouse, 2001). It is certainly likely that alterations in and narrowing of the level of consciousness are fertile ground for pathological dissociation, but they are not sufficient in themselves to cause dissociation of the personality.

CORE CONCEPT

Changes in attentional focus—what some authors call "normal" dissociation—are most certainly one component of dissociation of the personality, but they do not account for the separation in sense of self that occurs in complex dissociative disorders that makes the symptoms of these disorders qualitatively different than spaciness, daydreaming, or shutdown.

A few theorists describe dissociation as *hypoarousal* (e.g., Lanius et al., 2014; Porges, 2011; Lanius, Brand, Vermetten, Frewen, & Spiegel, 2012; Schore, 2009, 2012). For example, Schore notes that infants may engage in either hyperarousal in response to relational trauma or in dissociation, which he describes as a hypoaroused "parasympathetic dominant state of conservation/withdrawal" (2009, p. 120). This is a quite different description of dissociation than that which accounts for dissociation of the personality. Neither hypoarousal alone nor typical alterations in consciousness include the core symptoms that are unique to the complex dissociative disorders (DID and OSDD)—that is, dissociative parts of the personality (Nijenhuis, 2015; Steele et al., 2009). Dissociative parts of the personality may involve extreme hyperarousal as often as they do hypoarousal. In fact, many dissociative parts are chronically hyperaroused, and the patient alternates between hypoarousal and hyperarousal according to which part is in control.

For the purposes of assessing and treating DID and OSDD, we might understand dissociation as an underlying organization or structure of the patient's personality and self that involves unusual degrees of separation, including separate senses of self that each have their own first-person perspective (Nijenhuis, 2015; Nijenhuis & Van der Hart, 2011; Steele et al., 2009; Van der Hart et al., 2006).

CORE CONCEPT

Dissociation in OSDD and DID is best understood as a particular organization of the patient's personality and sense of self that is overly compartmentalized and rigid and includes separate senses of self. Symptoms emerge as manifestations of the activities of dissociative parts.

What is truly unique in OSDD and DID is not the presence of absorption or dorsal vagal shutdown, but of dissociative parts of the personality (even if rudimentary). It is likely that persistent and pervasive alterations in consciousness—what some call "normal" dissociation—are a necessary ingredient for the development of a dissociative organization of the personality, but they are not sufficient to cause and sustain it. It is significant that these symptoms are neither specific nor sensitive in assessing DID and OSDD, and are ubiquitous across many disorders—for example, panic disorder (Aderibigbe, Bloch, & Walker, 2001). What is unique to dissociative disorders is not arousal or attentional patterns but the fact that the patient has different senses of self and related first-person perspectives with which particular arousal and attentional patterns are associated.

Differences in Classification Systems

The therapist may also be confused by differences between the two major and widely used psychiatric classification systems, the Diagnostic and Statistical Manual of Mental Disorders (DSM-5) and the International Classification of Diseases (ICD-10), in the diagnostic categories of dissociative disorders. For example, most somatoform dissociative disorders, labeled dissociative disorders of movement and sensation, are included in ICD-10 but not in DSM-5. Many patients with a complex dissociative disorder have severe somatoform dissociative symptoms; they may present in the mental health system with paralysis, unexplained intrusive pain or other sensations, or pseudoseizures. However, in DSM-5 these are labeled as conversion symptoms or disorders and are not considered to be dissociative—a view criticized by many (e.g., Bowman, 2006; McDougall, 1926; Kihlstrom, 1992; Nemiah, 1991; Nijenhuis, 2004, 2015; Van der Hart et al., 2006). Therapists who depend on DSM-5 may easily overlook dissociation in cases where somatic symptoms predominate.

Lack of Training

A third challenge in assessment is that most therapists rarely receive adequate education in their training programs on how to recognize dissociative disorders (Boon & Draijer, 2007). This leads to problems of underdiagnosis by those who never consider dissociative disorders, and to overdiagnosis by those who do not know how to distinguish these disorders from other phenomena such as normal ego states, inner conflicts, or dramatic fluctuations in emotion or thoughts.

CORE CONCEPT

Most therapists have received little to no training on assessment of dissociation. This can lead to under- or overdiagnosis, both of which result in inadequate treatment of patients. Therapists who work with populations who have complex trauma have an ethical obligation to accurately assess for dissociative disorders.

While the clinical literature has been critical of overdiagnosis, it is highly likely that failure to diagnose is a much more pervasive problem, as many practitioners and centers never even consider the diagnosis. Many patients with a dissociative disorder have spent years in the mental health system before their dissociative disorder was accurately diagnosed (Şar, 2011).

Likewise, clinicians must be able to distinguish dissociative amnesia from failures to encode memory due to stress, absorption, fatigue, or illness. Many trauma survivors spent much of their childhood absorbed in fantasy, reading, watching TV, or playing video games and the like as an escape from painful realities. In addition to dissociative amnesia of traumatic experiences, they may also simply not recall much of childhood because they were absorbed or spacey so often. This distinction is essential to discern, otherwise the patient and therapist may make continued fruitless efforts to fill in the blanks of the patient's history.

The Hidden Nature of Dissociation

A fourth challenge to adequate diagnosis is that dissociation of the personality is a private, internal organization that is often not readily visible (Kluft, 1987a). Since complex dissociative disorders develop in early childhood, patients often have no reference point for whether their inner experience is common or usual—they report they have "always been this way." Thus, many have never conceptualized or verbalized their inner experience of dissociation, and it does not occur to them to do so without specific questioning by the therapist. Other patients are intensely ashamed of their symptoms and fear they are "crazy," and are therefore highly motivated to keep them hidden.

A common myth is that a major manifestation of dissociation involves blatant switching between parts that are vastly different from each another, as described in well-publicized cases in the media. Actually, this is an unusual clinical presentation (about 5–6% of cases of DID; Kluft, 1985a; Boon & Draijer, 1993a, 1993b). These few patients may have a comorbid histrionic personality disorder, leading to a dramatic or flamboyant presentation of genuine DID. Or they may be individuals under great stress so that their symptoms have temporarily flared to an unusual degree.

In general, patients with DID and OSDD are extremely avoidant of their dissociative parts and not likely to present them in public except under severe duress (see the case of Bob below). Most patients are fearful or ashamed of switching, as it is experienced as a frightening loss of control. Dissociative patients have usually become masterful at camouflage as a way to stay safe and unknown, and they tend to hide or explain away their symptoms (Kluft, 1987a). After all, abused children learn it is best not to be seen or really known. When symptoms are severe, it is an indication that the patient is under duress and is highly conflicted internally. Therapists often end up with such patients as their first case of DID because they are easier to spot. Unfortunately, highly symptomatic patients are usually more challenging to treat as they may be invested in keeping parts separate or have intense conflicts among dissociative parts of themselves.

CORE CONCEPT

Dissociative symptoms are often hidden from the therapist because the patient is unaware, ashamed, or does not know how to describe experiences. Therapists should ask specific questions about dissociation and request numerous examples of the patient's experiences, not only from the present but also from the past.

Dissociative symptoms are manifestations of a dynamic inner organization of the personality, a private and often terrifying world, operating under the surface. Some patients are so troubled by their dissociative symptoms they become convinced they are psychotic, since some of these symptoms—in particular, hearing voices—overlap with those of psychosis or schizophrenia (e.g., Kluft, 1987b; Moskowitz, Schäfer, & Dorahy, 2008; C. A. Ross et al., 1990). And sometimes they do suffer from a psychosis, in particular a dissociative psychosis (Van der Hart & Witztum, 2008). They have jarring intrusions of dissociative parts, puzzling lapses in awareness, and a deep sense of fragmentation or brokenness. Patients may be ashamed to share their dissociative experiences, as they are evidence of "not being strong enough" or being somehow defective. And, of course, acknowledging dissociation is akin to acknowledging the painful experiences that are dissociated. Non-realization thus may extend to avoiding awareness of having a dissociative disorder.

When a dissociative disorder is suspected, the therapist should be aware of the possibility of dissociative parts having some role in other clinical problems. Sometimes the first symptoms are puzzling variations in other problems. For example, some parts engage in eating-disordered behaviors while others do not, leading to abrupt onset and termination of eating problems. Some parts may be depressed while others are not, leading to a puzzling rapid cycling of depression that can occur in minutes or hours. Some parts have pain while others are numb, so it may seem to both therapist and physician that the patient is giving contradictory information.

CORE CONCEPT

Therapists should be aware that the activities of dissociative parts may mimic or exacerbate other symptoms and disorders, such as depression, self-harm, suicidality, eating problems, addictions, and panic.

Some patients may react with anxiety or anger when asked questions about dissociation, which can surprise the uninitiated therapist. In fact, these negative reactions of shame and fear further raise the index of suspicion for dissociation. Patients who are not dissociative usually simply say they do not endorse the symptoms, and they have no severe reaction to questions. Intense assessment that is premature may evoke a crisis and could end in a flight from treatment for some patients. Thus, a slower assessment pace that takes into account the patient's window of tolerance can be helpful and effective.

Distinguishing Ego States and Modes From Dissociative Parts

A fifth challenge is to distinguish normal ego states or self-states, or modes, from dissociative parts. Work in ego state therapy (EST; J. G. Watkins & Watkins, 1997), schema therapy (Young, Klosko, & Weishaar, 2003), and recent studies in neurobiology indicate that consciousness and self are never completely unitary. Everyone has multiple self-states or ego states. Yet only a small percentage of the population suffers from dissociative disorders—that is, has dissociative parts. Young et al. (2003) refer to different modes in borderline patients; these are comparable to ego states. We might think of dissociative parts as residing under a larger umbrella category of natural ego states. Metaphorically put, all tigers (dissociative parts) are mammals (ego states), but all mammals (ego states) are not tigers (dissociative parts) (see Kluft, 1988a, 2006).

CORE CONCEPT

Ego states are normal phenomena that we all experience, and they do not indicate the presence of a dissociative disorder. They differ from dissociative parts in their lack of autonomy and elaboration, personal experience and memory, and unique self-representation and first-person perspective. The patient readily acknowledges that ego states are part of the self, which is not the case for dissociative parts.

Theoretically, Watkins and Watkins (1993, 1997) originally intended the concept of ego states to include dissociative identities or parts. Kluft (1988a), however, proposed that dissociative parts, as opposed to ego states, have their own sense of identity, self-representation, autobiographical memory, and personal experiences. Dissociative parts have a distinct first-person perspective—that is, a sense of *I*, *me*, and *mine*—which can include any or all aspects of experiences, such as thoughts, feelings, memories, fantasies, perceptions, predictions, moods, sensations, decision making, and behavior (Nijenhuis & Van der Hart, 2011; Van der Hart et al., 2006). Ego states, on the other hand, seem to retain a shared sense of belonging to the person as a whole. They are usually less distinct, with less amnesia and autonomy, and without investment in being separate. They emerge clearly most often under (formal or informal) hypnosis rather than on a day-to-day basis, when they can have an influence but not gain complete control.

Unfortunately, in practice it is sometimes difficult, if not impossible, to distinguish the two in some patients. There is most certainly a wide gray area. Nevertheless, the major question still must be answered: *Does the patient have a dissociative disorder?* Confusing normal ego states or borderline modes for dissociative parts can result in overdiagnosis of dissociative disorders, while confusing dissociative parts for normal ego states or borderline modes can result in underdiagnosis. Distinctions between the two therefore need to be based not only on the characteristics of dissociative parts but, perhaps more importantly, on other symptoms that are consistent with the presence of dissociative parts and which are found only in dissociative disorders. These include, for example, amnesia for the present, passive-influence phenomena, switching, and jarring partial intrusions (see Table 5.1 for a list of symptoms of dissociative disorders).

Symptoms of Dissociation of the Personality

Symptoms of dissociation of the personality can be roughly divided into negative and positive dissociative symptoms, both psychoform (cognitive-emotional) and somatoform (sensorimotor) in nature (Nijenhuis, 2015; Nijenhuis & Van der Hart, 2011; Van der Hart et al., 2006; see Tables 5.1 and 5.2). Negative dissociative symptoms refer to the absence or loss of function that should be present in theory. Positive dissociative symptoms are transient and intrusive. Table 5.1 shows the most common dissociative symptoms, including those that are currently classified as somatization symptoms in DSM-5. The therapist should always ask for several examples of endorsed symptoms and try to determine how often symptoms occur, when they began, what helps, and what makes them worse. Many patients can give a history of dissociative symptoms dating back to childhood or adolescence. Since complex dissociative disorders almost always develop in childhood, patients may not realize their inner experiences are outside the norm, and thus may not report that, for example, they hear voices, lose time, or have out-of-body experiences. However, many patients are so phobic of inner experience that they have avoided acknowledging symptoms or have minimized or dismissed them.

CORE CONCEPT

Dissociative symptoms can be positive or negative. Positive symptoms are temporary intrusions such as voices, pain, thoughts, and emotions. Negative symptoms are losses of function that cannot be explained by other reasons, such as emotional numbness, analgesia or anesthesia, paralysis, and sudden loss of skills such as driving a car or cooking.

Therapists should be aware that patients with a complex dissociative disorder present a cluster of common dissociative symptoms and, in addition, may report many other trauma-related symptoms (Boon & Draijer, 1993a; Brand & Loewenstein, 2010; Carlson & Armstrong, 1994; Dell, 2009a, 2009b, Frankel, 2009; C. A. Ross, 1995; Steinberg, 1994, 1995, 2004; Steinberg, Cicchetti, Buchanan, & Hall, 1993). Again, what may seem at the surface a comorbid disorder may be due to or at least exacerbated by the actions of various dissociative parts. Often, a dissociative organization of the personality becomes clear when asking about trauma-related symptoms. Dissociative parts of the patient fixed in trauma-time endorse many of these symptoms, while parts functioning in daily life may have amnesia for symptoms endorsed by other parts or experience themselves as observers who cannot influence symptoms or behaviors.

Table 5.1 lists common symptoms of complex dissociative disorders.

Caveats About Diagnosis of Complex Dissociative Disorders

There are a number of important issues that therapists need to take into account during assessment. First, therapists should always screen for dissociation in patients with an extensive trauma history. However, they should not assume that a high score on a self-report measure of dissociation necessarily means that the person has a dissociative disorder. Instruments such as the Dissociative Experiences Scale (DES; Bernstein & Putnam, 1986; Carlson & Putnam,1993) include many items that ask about absorption, imagination, and mild depersonalization. These non-dissociative symptoms are not diagnostic of OSDD or DID. Thus, an individual may have a high score without having symptoms that indicate the presence of dissociative parts.

Therapists should never assume that a patient has a dissociative disorder based solely on one or two symptoms (e.g., the patient hearing a voice and reporting depersonalization). Diagnosis should be based on a constellation of symptoms that can be described over time. Therapists should refrain from talking with the patient about dissociative parts if there is no clear evidence of a cluster of dissociative symptoms that indicates a division of the personality.

The presence of ego states that appear rather separate during times when the patient is in an altered state, such as in hypnosis or with eye movement desensitization and reprocessing (EMDR), does not, in itself, indicate a dissociative disorder. Symptoms should be present not only within sessions but also outside sessions and over time as reported by the patient or others.

Comorbidity in Dissociative Disorders

Patients with DID and OSDD typically present with many different symptoms and several comorbid diagnoses, including personality disorders (Boon & Draijer, 1993a, 1993b; Mueller-Pfeiffer et al., 2012; Rodewald, Wilhelm-Gößling et al., 2011). Treatment is greatly complicated by coexisting disorders, and the therapist should be familiar with current standards of care for all of the disorders for which a patient qualifies.

However, multiple diagnoses may be deceptive for patients with a history of chronic traumatization, especially those with dissociative disorders.

TABLE 5.1
Common Symptoms of Dissociation

Amnesia

Amnesia is a hallmark of DID and may occur for both past and current experiences. It should be distinguished from absorption and spaciness (failures to encode). Amnesia must not be due to substance abuse (blackouts). Significant psychogenic or dissociative amnesia rarely exists by itself, but is most often a symptom of a more complex dissociative disorder (Loewenstein, 1991b)

- Large gaps in memory of the past.
- Gaps in memory for the present, including "micro-amnesia"—that is, very brief lapses in awareness during sessions due to covert switching. This can be observed when the patient frequently seems to lose track of what is being discussed. This must be distinguished from absorption and spaciness.
- Lack of memory for important events that goes beyond normal forgetfulness (e.g., patients cannot remember their own wedding, birth of a child, graduation, death of a loved one).
- Evidence of behaviors in the present that patients do not remember doing.
- Patients find themselves in a strange place and do not remember how they got there.
- Patients have a lack of awareness of dissociative parts and their behaviors, emotions, thoughts, and so forth.
- Patients report that others tell them of behaviors they do not recall.

Depersonalization and derealization symptoms referring to a division of the personality
- Patients experience themselves outside their bodies, as though they were watching someone else.
- Patients feel no control of what they are saying. They may know what they are saying, but cannot control it.
- Patients experience their bodies in a distorted way (e.g., smaller, larger), or as not belonging to themselves.
- Patients do not recognize family or good friends or their environment (e.g., their own home or the therapist's office).

Passive influence
- One or more dissociative parts influences the patient's behavior, thoughts, sensations, predictions, and perceptions internally (without overt switching). This may result in Schneiderian symptoms (see below).
- Two or more dissociative parts are (co)present at the same time. This may result in Schneiderian symptoms.

continues

- One part fully switches to another part and is observed by the therapist or by others close to the patient.

Somatoform dissociative symptoms

A wide variety of somatic symptoms occur in patients with complex dissociative disorders (Nijenhuis, 2000, 2004, 2010, 2015; Loewenstein & Goodwin, 1999; Ross, Heber, Norton, & Anderson, 1989; Van der Hart et al., 2006) While DSM-5 does not include somatoform symptoms in the diagnostic criteria for DID, they are included elsewhere under Conversion, Medically Unexplained Symptoms, and Somatic Symptom Disorders. ICD-10 includes specific somatoform dissociative disorders.

- Patient reports unexplained pain. or sensations (often related to trauma).
- Inability to feel pain (analgesia).
- Physical numbness (anesthesia).
- Paralysis or partial paralysis without medical cause.
- Loss of physical function without medical cause (movement, sight, hearing, smell, taste, sensation, not feeling hungry, not feeling temperature).
- Distorted somatic perceptions.
- Seizures or epilepsy that do not have a medical cause (pseudoseizures).

Schneiderian symptoms

Schneiderian symptoms of schizophrenia (also known as positive or first-ranked symptoms) are very common in dissociative disorders and are the result of the activities and influence of dissociative parts (Brand & Loewenstein, 2010; Kluft, 1987b; Dorahy et al., 2009; C. A. Ross et al., 1990; Steinberg & Spiegel, 2008). In patients who have a history of chronic trauma, the presence of any of these symptoms should raise the question of whether a dissociative disorder is present, and further assessment should be conducted.

- Auditory hallucinations, often of voices that comment on the patient, but may include inner dialogues that are not about the patient, crying, screaming, and berating. Dissociative voices may be distinguished from psychotic voices by the following criteria (Dorahy et al., 2009; Moskowitz et al., 2008):
  - Dissociative voices, as opposed to psychotic voices, usually begin in early childhood rather than late adolescence or early adulthood;
  - often include voices of children and adults;
  - often include voices of people from the patient's past;
  - are more often heard regularly or constantly instead of intermittently;
  - often comment about the patient or have conversations about the patient that the patient "overhears";

- can be engaged in dialogue with the therapist and the patient;
- have their own sense of self, even if very limited.
- Thought insertion—the experience of strange or unfamiliar thoughts that suddenly "pop up" in the patient's mind, typically experienced as ego dystonic or puzzling.
- Thought withdrawal (the patient's mind suddenly feels blank of thoughts, or even words are experienced as "taken away").
- Feelings, impulses, and actions that seem as though they are created or directed by someone or something else (partial intrusions of dissociative parts).
- A sense of the body being controlled or influenced by another force (may also be an intrusion of a dissociative part).
- Hallucinations, often related to trauma. Dissociative patients are often aware, with an exception for dissociative psychosis, that their hallucinations are not real, and may experience a dual reality: *I know it's not real, but it feels real.*
- Delusions (in dissociative disorders often related to trauma).
- Thought broadcasting—the sense that one's thoughts can be heard by others. This is actually the one Schneiderian symptom that is not common in dissociative disorders. However, many trauma patients are afraid others can read their minds, a function of the fear and shame of being known rather than a true psychotic symptom.

Other symptoms that cross diagnostic categories

The following symptoms may signal the presence of a dissociative disorder but are also endorsed by patients with other mental disorders, especially personality disorders. Thus, careful differential diagnosis is essential.

- Behavior
  - Patients report puzzling fluctuations in skills and abilities (e.g., driving a car, cooking a meal, doing math).
  - Patients are told by others that they act very differently in situations and seem almost like different people.
- Affect
  - Patients report unexplained and rapid fluctuations in mood and emotion.
  - Patients feel as though they are not in control of their emotions, as though they come "out of the blue."
- Verbal
  - Patients have a disorganized/disoriented attachment narrative that is not cohesive or coherent, and that involves lapses in attention and confusion of past and present.
- Depersonalization and derealization symptoms across psychiatric disorders
  - Patients report feeling as though they are in a dream or an actor on a stage.
  - Patients feel as though they are unreal, a robot.

continues

> - Patients feel alienated or disconnected from their surroundings or from their bodies.
> - Patients feel as though they are underwater, wrapped in cotton, or two-dimensional.
> - Patients experience tunnel vision.
> - Patients report difficulty hearing, as though they are down a long tunnel.

The impact of trauma can cause many mood, cognitive, executive-functioning, perceptual, and sleep changes. To name each symptom a separate disorder may not help the patient, and in fact may confound treatment. The therapist should understand that the dissociative disorder is the underlying disorder, involving dissociative parts that manifest different symptoms related to the traumatizing events, such as depression, sleep problems, eating problems, and struggles with emotion regulation (hypo- and hyperarousal). Moreover, many patients use drugs, alcohol, and engage in other behaviors other substances, which can be considered addiction disorders, but which also involve the activity of particular parts that must be addressed in addition to the standard addiction treatment approaches. Common comorbid disorders include:

- Mood disorders—depression, bipolar disorders (e.g., Allen, Coyne, & Huntoon, 1998; Brady, Killeen, Brewerton, & Lucerini, 2000; J. G. Johnson, Cohen, Kasen, & Brook, 2006; Şar, Tutkun, Alyanak, Bakim, & Baral, 2000)
- Anxiety disorders—panic disorder, obsessive-compulsive disorder, agoraphobia (Brady, 1997)
- Substance abuse (Brady, 1997; J. G. Johnson et al., 2006; McClellan, Adams, Douglas, McCurry, & Storck, 1995; McDowell, Levin, & Nunes, 1999)
- Eating disorders—anorexia, bulimia, binge eating, bulimarexia (Vanderlinden, 1993; Vanderlinden, Spinhoven, Vandereycken, & van Dyck, 1995)
- Psychosis, brief or enduring (Allen & Coyne, 1995; Allen, Coyne, & Console, 1996; Moskowitz et al., 2008; Van der Hart & Witztum, 2008)
- Sleep disorders (Van der Kloet et al., 2013)
- Personality disorders—DID patients have personality profiles that are similar to those with PTSD (avoidant, 76%; self-defeating, 68%; borderline, 53%; and passive-aggressive, 45%; Dell, 1998; J. G. Johnson et al., 2006)

False-Positive DID Diagnoses

While there is little research on the prevalence of false-positive (or feigned, malingered, or imitated) cases of DID, most experts in dissociative disorders have seen examples in their consultations (Boon & Draijer, 1995; Coons & Milstein, 1994; Draijer & Boon, 1999; ISSTD, 2011). The untrained therapist may easily confuse ego states or borderline modes with a dissociative disorder. But sometimes patients themselves may be confused about their symptoms or may feign the disorder. Feigning psychiatric disorders has been described for other disorders as well, including PTSD, borderline personality, and schizophrenia, so it is certainly not unique to the dissociative disorders. Detection of feigning or imitation of DID is often quite difficult (Brand, McNary, Loewenstein, Kolos, & Barr, 2006; Draijer & Boon, 1999), although it may be helpful to use additional instruments (Brand, Armstrong, & Loewenstein, 2006), such as the Minnesota Multiphasic Personality Inventory-2 (MMPI-2; Brand & Chasson, 2015), the Rorschach (Brand, Armstrong, Loewenstein, & McNary, 2009), or the Millon Clinical Multiaxial Inventory II (Ellason, Ross, & Fuchs, 1995).

Patients who have features suggestive of imitated DID have been described in the literature (Boon & Draijer, 1995; Brand et al., 2006 Brand & Chasson, 2015; Draijer & Boon, 1999; Thomas, 2001) and may include those who

- Offer "cookbook answers" during diagnostic assessment—that is, only symptoms that are widely described in the media, such as dramatic shifts between parts
- Become angry and defensive when asked for more examples, stating that the therapist does not believe them
- Are able to give a clear chronological history and can sequence events in time
- Are able to use the first-person "I" across a range of emotions and experiences or trauma-related symptoms
- Use second- or third-person language ("we" or "she") only when asked about dissociative symptoms
- Dramatically switch in the first session and during assessment
- Insist the therapist believe that they have DID
- Bring "proof" of DID to sessions, such as extensive maps of parts
- Reveal alleged abuse and diagnosis to many people without fear or shame
- Report alleged abuse that is inconsistent with their medical or psychiatric history
- Are heavily involved in online DID chat rooms
- Have obvious secondary gain from a diagnosis of DID.

Patients may have read about dissociation or participated in online chat groups or self-help groups and become convinced they have the disorder. They may have a trauma history and some dissociative symptoms such as depersonalization and PTSD symptoms, but not DID. And they may have symptoms of a personality disorder and are genuinely confused about who they are. For them, the idea of having DID provides an acceptable explanation for their fluctuating sense of identity.

A few patients prefer to have a dissociative disorder rather than a personality disorder or other psychiatric problems. These patients may exaggerate their symptoms and present with classic symptoms, especially amnesia and blatantly different "personalities." Their presentation is more dramatic; for example, it includes frequent and overt "switching" during an interview to offer evidence of the existence of dissociative parts. They lack the characteristic phobia for dissociative parts that is often found in genuine DID patients. On the contrary, they talk about their parts with ease and a certain eagerness, sometimes telling the therapist about many parts, each with its own complex history and preferences (of clothes, food, hobbies, etc.).

The therapist needs a great deal of expertise and experience to distinguish genuine DID from imitated DID in these few cases, especially in histrionic patients. Additional psychological testing and questions about trauma-related symptoms are sometimes quite helpful in making the distinction: These patients do not really know or realize how genuine DID patients present with subtler or unusual symptoms. In cases where the therapist is unsure of the diagnosis, the patient should be referred for an assessment by an expert diagnostician. Forensic cases present additional difficulties, as there may be secondary gain to having the diagnosis to avoid responsibility for a crime (Coons, 1991; Frankel & Dalenberg, 2006; Orne, Dinges, & Orne, 1984; Serban, 1992; Spitzer et al., 2003).

It is essential to remember that patients who imitate DID (or any other disorder) are deeply wounded and need the same compassion and good treatment accorded those with these actual diagnoses. Their core problem is typically identity confusion, but in a different way than patients with DID. Most of these patients have suffered serious emotional neglect as children and feel chronically ignored, unseen, and misunderstood. Often they have a strong wish to gain attention and to remain dependent and cared for, and thus often present with needy "child parts."

Assessing the Level of Dissociative Organization of the Personality

As noted in Chapter 1, a person with a complex dissociative disorder has a dissociative organization of personality comprising two or (almost always) more dissociative parts, each having its own first-person perspective and different responses, feelings, thoughts, perceptions, physical sensations, and behaviors (Nijenhuis & Van der Hart, 2011; Van der Hart et al., 2006). In clinical practice it helps to differentiate between two somewhat different dissociative organizations of the personality, as the treatment will be slightly different (see Boon et al., 2011; Van der Hart et al., 2006). In the first organization (as in our case example of Bob below), the patient has a single part of the personality that is functioning in daily life, while all other parts are fixed in trauma-time. Though these parts may intrude on the patient, they rarely take full control. When they do, they are usually in a flashback, not attempting functions of daily life.

In the second organization, there is more than one part that functions in daily life, while other parts are fixated in trauma-time. Though the DSM-5 does not make this distinction, it is important to determine in assessment, even though symptoms of dissociation may not necessarily differ between the two organizations. However, patients with more than one part that functions in daily life are far more likely to have amnesia in the present, and at least those parts will have a greater degree of elaboration and autonomy.

CORE CONCEPT

It is important to distinguish between patients who have only one dissociative part that functions in daily life and those who have more than one. In addition to helping make a correct dissociative disorder diagnosis, this distinction has important treatment implications.

One Dissociative Part Functioning in Daily Life
In OSDD, parts are primarily mediated by the action systems of defense, are stuck in traumatic memories, and do not engage in daily life to a significant degree. Patients with this personality organization may not report amnesia, or will report only minimal and transient amnesia. They also tend to report fewer Schneiderian symptoms (see Table 5.1) than patients with DID, but they may hear the voices of parts. Clearly, dissociative patients with only one part functioning in daily life are more difficult to differentiate from patients with PTSD or complex PTSD. In these cases, careful assessment may reveal more dissociation, as patients with OSDD often have additional issues in which passive influence and the presence of dissociative parts can be verified (e.g., eating problems, suicidality, self-injury, sleeping problems, and complex PTSD symptoms).

More Than One Dissociative Part Functioning in Daily Life

The presence of two or more parts functioning in daily life complicates treatment, because there is typically more amnesia for current experience and more inner conflicts about daily life, not only about trauma-related experiences. Patients with this organization can be considered as having "classic" DID, and they usually report more obvious dissociative symptoms (as described in Table 5.1). If phobic avoidance of their symptoms is not too severe, they may report amnesia for current daily life activities, passive-influence symptoms, different forms of depersonalization and derealization, and sometimes clear confusion about their identity. In addition to these symptoms, they usually also endorse a whole range of other trauma-related symptoms. In these cases, early therapy work will need to focus first on building communication and cooperation among parts that function in daily life.

Below we discuss two cases in terms of assessment. The first is a case of OSDD with one part that functions in daily life, and the second is a case of DID.

CASE EXAMPLE OF ASSESSMENT OF OSDD: BOB

Bob was a 40-year-old man who sought help for sexual problems. For the first time in his life he had a stable relationship with another man, John, but he experienced a lot of anxiety in their relationship, in particular when they were sexual. He was afraid that John would leave him, as he believed he let John down and that he was a failure in sex. He had known that he was gay for a long time, and had had several relationships in the past with different men, but none of these lasted longer than a few weeks. Most of the time, Bob ended these relationships.

He told the therapist that he had been abused by a neighbor from ages 7 to 12. He realized that his sexual problems were related to the abuse in some way. He reported that he had had therapy and EMDR for his trauma history, but he had stopped the EMDR sessions, as they seemed to make his problems worse. In fact, he had become totally overwhelmed and terrified. His solution had been to avoid both therapy and sexual relationships for the past 10 years.

Bob functioned quite well as an engineer and had many superficial social contacts as well as a couple of close female friends. It was one of these friends who had motivated Bob to seek help again. Bob told the therapist that as long as he stayed away from sex and relationships with men, everything went well in his life. When asked about somatic symptoms, Bob noted that in general he did not feel his body very much. He liked intense workouts in the gym, but said he never felt soreness or pain, even when he had injured himself.

Bob had previously told his partner about his trauma history, and John seemed quite empathetic, but this did not reduce Bob's fear or shame. John had observed that Bob was restless at night, as if he had constant nightmares. Several times during the night Bob did not seem to recognize John, and on several occasions when they were having sex Bob behaved strangely, almost like a much younger person, to a degree that disturbed John, who stopped the sexual encounter. The therapist asked if John was willing to come to a session, as she wanted to hear John's thoughts about what might be going on with Bob. Although Bob was a bit hesitant, he agreed.

During this meeting, John reported that Bob sometimes suddenly seemed afraid of him and at other times was angry for no discernible reason. In the evenings, he said, Bob sometimes seemed "very far away," staring at the wall, so that John was unable to make contact with him. John said that he had recently stopped sexual contact, as Bob seemed to get so upset during sex.

John wondered if Bob had PTSD, which in his opinion explained most of Bob's behavior. Bob was initially ashamed, but at the same time he was glad to be able to discuss his problems openly with John, who was quite loving and compassionate. The therapist decided to do an assessment for complex PTSD and dissociative symptoms over the course of the next few sessions.

During the next session, Bob told the therapist that he was having more flashbacks of his abuse since he had begun his relationship with John. They appeared during the day as well as at night. He saw what he described as "movies" of the abuse in his head, as though it were happening to another boy. During these flashbacks he heard an inner voice, like his abusive neighbor, which threatened him for talking about the abuse. Bob denied amnesia for daily life activities. He did say that he did not always remember having sex with John, or that his memories of it were sometimes vague. He told the therapist that since he had moved in with John several months ago, he had awakened in the morning several times and had not known where he was, not recognizing John or his surroundings for a few minutes. This frightened Bob. Only as John started to talk to him did he gradually realize where he was. He reported that his body sometimes felt strange, much smaller than normal. He added that years ago, when he had been sexually active with other men, these experiences had occurred frequently.

When the therapist asked about his previous therapy, Bob said he had been afraid he was going crazy, because he began to hear several voices during the EMDR sessions—not only the abuser's voice, but the voice of an angry adolescent, a frightened young boy, and a calming voice that was like his beloved grandmother, who had been a loving presence for him as a child. He was too afraid to admit these voices to the therapist at the time. He abruptly left therapy to avoid dealing with the fear that he was psychotic. Since he had begun living with John, the voices had returned. The therapist commented that she was glad that Bob had such a kind internal support, and that it did not seem strange that he could take comfort in his grandmother's voice. In fact, she thought it was a wonderful sign of strength that he had such a voice. This relieved Bob a great deal.

In the next session, when the therapist asked Bob about the possible existence of dissociative parts, Bob named several: an angry adolescent, fearful "Little Bobby," and the part he called "Granny." Bob did not believe the threatening voice was a part, describing it as a memory of his neighbor's voice, and did not want to elaborate on the voice any further, as it frightened him. However, the therapist noted that this voice also communicated to Bob and to other parts and made comments about the therapy. This implied that the voice belonged to a part, and was not merely a memory. It was only later in therapy, as Bob became more comfortable and safe, that he was able to acknowledge and work with this part of himself.

In Bob's case, there was no evidence for the existence of other dissociative parts with functions in daily life. While parts sometimes briefly intruded, they did so only in the context of being triggered by sex and the relationship with John, not for the purpose of dealing with Bob's everyday experiences. Bob did not report amnesia for daily life, except for these brief intrusive episodes. He functioned quite well at work and in a few relationships. He heard several internal voices related to his past, and he reported other dissociative symptoms such as episodic depersonalization and some derealization (not recognizing his surroundings or his partner—something that can happen when a dissociative part fixed in trauma-time is activated). Bob also reported somatic symptoms such as distorted perceptions of his body as being smaller (a passive-influence phenomenon when a younger part is copresent) and not feeling his body or noticing pain.

According to the *DSM-5*, Bob met criteria for OSDD. The case of Marianne, described below, differs greatly, as she had more parts with functions in daily life, serious amnesia, and other dissociative symptoms that indicated the presence of DID. In the next two chapters we will discuss how the differences in these cases may influence treatment planning.

CASE EXAMPLE OF ASSESSMENT OF DID: MARIANNE

Marianne was a 30-year-old woman with a treatment history dating back to the age of 20. At that age, she left home and began school in another city. She lived alone and was only able to work part-time for a software company, and she had few social contacts. She had been treated by multiple therapists for recurrent depressive episodes, anxiety (including social phobia and panic attacks), and bulimarexia. She had also received a diagnosis of unspecified personality disorder with mixed features. During her last treatment in an inpatient eating disorders program, Marianne reported memories of abuse by her father and also began to report more dissociative symptoms. Marianne was referred for assessment of a dissociative disorder by her primary care physician, who had learned about dissociation from another patient he was treating.

Marianne appeared younger than her actual age, was nervous, and laughed constantly. She also showed some tic-like behaviors, squinting her eyes often. She hardly made eye contact with the therapist. She was interviewed using the Trauma and Dissociation Symptoms Interview (TADS-I; see Appendix A for this and other screening and diagnostic instruments). She reported chronic and severe sleep problems—mainly that she always postponed going to bed and was afraid to go to sleep. Sometimes when she awakened, she did not recognize her bedroom and was confused as to where she was. These episodes would last much longer and were more consistent than in the case of Bob. She reported nightmares, but she also had the feeling that she was sleepwalking. When the therapist asked her to give an example, she said that when she woke up in the morning she sometimes found that her kitchen was a mess with leftovers, and that she apparently had been using her computer. Other times she found her messy house cleaned when she woke up in the morning. When the therapist commented that it was not likely that these complex behaviors could be explained by sleepwalking, Marianne stared at the wall for a few moments and then asked, *What was your question again?* During the interview, this occurred several times. Each time the therapist would ask Marianne, *Can you tell me the last thing you remember talking about?* This type of question helps the therapist track how much intra-session amnesia is occurring. Marianne's lapses were momentary, evidence of micro-amnesia; usually, she could not recall only the last question of the therapist. The therapist noted which topics tended to evoke this reaction in Marianne.

Marianne reported eating problems, mainly episodes of binge eating and purging, but seemed to have amnesia for some of these. She noted that she was often depressed and had suicidal thoughts but had never attempted to kill herself. She added that these thoughts could suddenly pop up even on days when she felt quite normal, and that she was often puzzled by their sudden appearance "out of the blue." She added that she was a "weird person" but could not elaborate. When asked about relationships with other people, she told the therapist that she did not have many friends and did not like social contact, but that she did sing in a choir and liked sports.

Marianne had a tendency to minimize her dissociative symptoms. When asked about gaps in her memory, she first told the therapist: *I think it is not so bad; I always have my knowledge, so I do not really lose time.*

Therapist: Can you tell me a bit more about what you mean when you say you "have your knowledge"?

Marianne: Well, I just know what I have done.

Therapist: Mmm, and how do you get this knowledge?

Marianne: Well, most of the time it is as if I get a report about what I have done, so I am not missing any time.

Therapist: And how do you get this report?

Marianne: As if somebody is talking to me, like someone is reporting on what has happened. It's just the way my mind works, that's all.

Therapist: Yes, everyone's mind works a bit differently, doesn't it? And I am glad you have these reports. When they come, how do you hear them—outside or inside your head?

Marianne: Well, it is probably my own thoughts, otherwise I would be really crazy.

Therapist: I do not think that you are crazy. In fact, many people hear voices, and it does not mean they are psychotic. A lot of trauma survivors hear them. Can you tell me a bit more about how you get these reports? Is this something that can happen every day?

Marianne: Yes, it happens very often, but I do not have gaps in my memory; I know what has happened.

Therapist: When does it happen?

Marianne: It can happen in any situation—at work, or when I am at choir practice or am shopping. Just normal things. I do not really pay much attention as long as nothing goes wrong.

Therapist: Marianne, I am sorry that I am so insistent, but I really want to understand this very well, and I am not quite yet clear. I apologize that sometimes I need more clarification. Is it that you do not know what has happened until you get the report, and then you get the knowledge?

Marianne: If you want to know if I always have a picture of the situation before the report, the answer is no. But as I said, I do not lose time. I know what I have done.

The therapist concluded that Marianne likely did have amnesia, even though she denied losing time. In fact, there were quite a few times during the interview that Marianne lost contact with the therapist and could not remember what had just happened. Moreover, the examples of her amnesia were about activities in daily life such as work, being in choir, and going shopping, indicating the possibility that more than one dissociative part might be functioning in daily life. The therapist also noted that Marianne was rather vague in her answers and was somewhat avoidant.

Later in the interview, Marianne hesitantly confirmed that she heard more than the reporter voice, and that these voices used different names, but then she began to dissociate again, staring and unable to hear the therapist. When she was oriented again to the present, she was unable to give further explanation. She confirmed chronic feelings of depersonalization, such as feeling outside of her body and watching herself from a distance, which often happened at work. Marianne told the therapist that out-of-body experiences had been commonplace her entire life. Sometimes, especially when she was alone at home, Marianne had the experience that her body seemed strange, as if her hands or legs were suddenly smaller. Marianne reported a number of Schneiderian symptoms in addition to hearing voices. These included made feelings and impulses, thought insertion and withdrawal, and terrifying pseudohallucinations of a man standing over her bed.

When asked about thought insertion and thought withdrawal, Marianne said: *You know, I never can choose; there are so many different and weird thoughts in my mind. It is hopeless sometimes! It is as if a group of people with totally different opinions are trying to force their ideas on me all at once. But at other times, my mind suddenly goes blank, as if my thoughts are stolen. Somehow, I become totally blank and don't have any idea of what I was talking about. I hate that; it is so stupid. I wonder if I am getting dementia?*

Marianne was unable to give any examples of dissociative parts of herself. During the interview it became clear that she was afraid and ashamed and made a huge effort to find alternative explanations for her dissociative symptoms. This is not uncommon in an early assessment for dissociative disorders (Boon & Draijer, 1993a,1993b). It is rare that a patient actually switches overtly during an initial interview. However, Marianne had already reported a cluster of severe dissociative symptoms: amnesia for daily life activities, behaviors she must have done but did not recall doing, several voices with different names, other Schneiderian symptoms such as passive-influence phenomena stemming from other parts, and out-of-body experiences while at work.

The therapist concluded that it was highly likely that Marianne had DID. She carefully explained to Marianne that these signs indicated the presence of a dissociative disorder. It was interesting that Marianne, who had been so avoidant and anxious in the interview, felt relief, as she had been so afraid she was crazy or schizophrenic.

In the next chapters we will describe some follow-up on Marianne's case, confirming the DID diagnosis later in her therapy.

Summary

Assessment of dissociative disorders is complex because symptoms may be hidden and involve an intrapsychic organization that does not always manifest overtly; because DSM-5 descriptions of dissociative disorders lack clear detail; and because some potential dissociative symptoms may be present in several different disorders. Thus, differential diagnosis is essential. Therapists should be aware that both over- and underdiagnosis can be problematic. Distinguishing between patients who have one dissociative part that functions in daily life and those who have more than one of these parts has important treatment implications. When in doubt about the diagnosis, therapists should refer patients to a consultant who is experienced in assessment.

Further Explorations

5.1 Have you ever assessed a patient for a dissociative disorder or received training in how to do so?

5.2 Looking back over your cases, do you think you might have been working with a patient with a dissociative disorder and you did not know it? How might you assess that person differently now?

5.3 If you are currently working with a patient who likely has a dissociative disorder, what comorbidity is present? Have you found that a dissociative part is central to another problem, such as addiction, an eating disorder, or depression? (That is, a dissociative part is engaged in those behaviors or has those feelings, but other parts do not?) If so, does this change the way you work with the problem with your patient?

CHAPTER 6

Beyond Diagnosis: Further Assessment, Prognosis, and Case Formulation

By predicting therapeutic outcome before treatment commences,
efficacy might be enhanced since patients with unfavorable
prognostic signs can be apprised of therapeutic limitations.
—John Curtis (1985, p. 11)

Case formulation is most useful when viewed as a dynamic,
iterative process that invites frequent revisiting of hypotheses as
new client data become available.
—Bethany Teachman and Elise Clerkin (2010, p. 7)

It is not nearly sufficient for treatment to assess for diagnosis and a history of trauma. In this chapter we explore specific areas of further assessment beyond diagnosis, as well as how to use assessment to determine an initial prognosis and then to develop a case formulation. The therapist uses case formulation to infer how the patient's problems developed and what maintains them, which then informs treatment (Eels, 2010, 2015; Ingram, 2011; McWilliams, 1999; PDM Task Force, 2006; Westen, 1998). This typically involves the patient's intrapsychic and relational processes.

Most dissociative patients have many complex symptoms that do not fit neatly into any one diagnostic category. At the same time, they typically fulfill the criteria for many additional diagnostic categories (Boon & Draijer, 1993a, 1993b; Rodewald, Wilhelm-Gößling, Emrich, Reddemann, & Gast, 2011). Therapists need to have a dual awareness of diagnosis *and* the overall pervasive developmental impact of cumulative trauma. They realize that diagnosis as such is necessary but insufficient to guide effective treatment. Diagnosis and trauma history tell therapists many things, but not everything—particularly not about the impact of the context of everyday life on the development of our patients (Gold, 2000). They do not inform therapists of the patient's inner organization and way of being in the world—key information in case formulation and in planning effective therapy. Because patients can be more different than alike, it is also essential to look at what is unique to a given patient.

Much of what follows in this chapter cannot be assessed immediately; rather, it evolves over the course of therapy. Gradually, therapists more fully understand their patients' general functioning and their responses to specific treatment interventions. Assessment is an ongoing process. Nevertheless, it is helpful to assess at least some of the strengths and deficits of a patient while in the early planning stages of therapy. A rating scale for prognosis and treatment progress is included in Appendix B. This checklist has not been validated, but we find it clinically useful. It can be used in the beginning of the assessment phase and repeated quarterly or once every six months to evaluate progress in therapy and aid in planning. Several domains are assessed, such as the patient's daily functioning; support systems; capacity for relationship with the therapist and others; trauma-related phobias; management of dissociation; and ability to cooperate in therapy, learn new skills, and profit from interventions. Finally, vulnerability for crises and resistance are assessed.

The Patient's Resources and Needs

Patients greatly benefit from a thorough exploration of their resources and deficits, both internally and externally, as a part of case formulation and understanding prognosis. Therapy can only progress as far as patients' own resources can take them. For example, insight-oriented therapy is not especially effective for individuals with moderate to severe cognitive deficits, and those who have few emotional skills cannot integrate the overwhelming emotions of trauma. Assessing skills and resources directs treatment to begin where the patient most needs to build a foundation for the complex and challenging work of therapy. Below we discuss some important resources, particularly those that will support the patient in therapy.

Financial Resources

One of the first things to determine, even before a thorough case formulation, is whether the patient has the financial resources to engage in a particular type of therapy in a particular setting, and whether those resources are relatively stable. Diving in to a complex treatment when the patient cannot sustain payment is likely to end badly for both patient and therapist. In a best-case scenario, the patient can be referred to a low-cost center that has the capacity to treat dissociative disorders, but this is rarely an option. Otherwise, the therapist can contract to do short-term stabilization work that will help the patient improve daily function and symptoms to the degree possible. Financial resources for therapy differ greatly from country to country. In some countries, insurance covers long-term therapy; in other countries it does so rarely or not at all.

Social Support and Sociocultural and Religious Resources and Deficits

The social context of the patient may provide substantial support or may be a source of distress. An important question is whether a patient has friends, a current family, or any other person who can be supportive outside of therapy. Many of our more challenging patients are quite isolated and need far more than a single therapist to help them move forward. Apart from providing emotional support during the therapy, it is also important for the therapist to know whether the patient has some friends or acquaintances with whom to be social.

The therapist should thus assess the following:

- Social supports and how the patient utilizes them
  - Does the patient have any other individuals (family, friends, neighbors) to whom she or he can turn for help?
  - Is the patient willing to ask for support?
  - Does the patient use support appropriately?
  - Does the patient need a psychiatrist, case manager, primary care physician, or other professional who can be part of a treatment team?
  - Does the patient have friends and acquaintances with whom to be social—for example, seeing a movie, walking, having dinner, spending holidays together?
- Community resources
  - Does the patient have resources—for example, for free classes, volunteer work, support groups, or other types of social or community supports?
- Cultural resources
  - Does the patient's cultural and ethnic background promote any type of emotional and social support, acknowledge trauma, or support therapy?
- Spiritual or religious resources
  - Is the patient interested in exploring and using spiritual or religious resources?

- If so, do the patient's spiritual or religious beliefs support healing or further entrench the patient in shame and self-blame?
- If the patient does not have spiritual or religious beliefs, what helps him or her find meaning and purpose?

Multicultural Factors

Our psychopathology models are based primarily on Western culture. When a client is from a different culture, the therapist should take care to explore the following and adjust therapy accordingly. The patient's culture may be a source of support or may be a detriment to treatment—for example, if it tends to foster the belief that therapy is not acceptable. A few important cultural considerations include whether

- the patient's symptoms have particular cultural expressions that would be helpful to understand;
- certain child-rearing practices within the patient's culture may be relevant to treatment (and attachment);
- the patient has specific cultural parameters for grieving and dealing with loss that are different from what the therapist expects;
- the patient's ways of expressing (or not expressing) emotions are a function of the patient's culture rather than being pathological; and whether
- different needs and expectations about dependency, individuation, and autonomy are part of the patient's culture.

Cognitive Resources and Deficits

The ability of the patient to think coherently and logically, to use memory to learn and grow, and to deploy intellectual abilities to gain insight and change is essential in therapy.

CORE CONCEPT

It is essential to assess for traumatic brain injury (TBI) in patients who have been chronically abused since childhood or who have a history of physical assault or accidents potentially resulting in head injury. Undiagnosed and untreated TBI can significantly interfere with therapy progress.

Traumatic brain injury. One important question is whether a patient may have an undiagnosed traumatic brain injury (TBI) that affects not only cognitive but also emotional and social functioning. Many symptoms of TBI may mimic psychological problems. They include difficulties thinking and problem-solving, difficulty learning new material and retaining new information, being easily confused, somatic complaints such as fatigue and headaches, mood changes, impulsivity, executive function problems such as inability to focus and concentrate, and relational disturbances (Stoler & Hill, 2013; Vasterling, Bryant, & Keane, 2012). Patients who have a known history of serious head injury, repeated blows to the head, prematurity, or birth trauma should have a neurocognitive assessment for TBI. If needed, therapy should be modified to accommodate concurrent neurocognitive treatment of brain injury.

It is helpful to understand the patient's capacities and deficits in the following cognitive domains:

- Intelligence
  - What is the patient's level of intelligence?
  - Is the patient able to access intelligence as a resource rather than a defense in therapy?
- Verbal skills
  - How well can the patient articulate her or his experience in therapy?
- Coherence of thought
  - What is the patient's usual capacity for coherent thinking, and what happens under moderate stress?
  - Do various dissociative parts have more or less coherence than others?
- Capacity for mindfulness
  - Is the patient able or willing to learn to be more present and mindful of what is going on internally and in the patient's surroundings?
  - Does mindfulness increase or decrease the patient's distress?
  - Does the patient have any meditation practices? Do they help, increase distress, or promote further dissociation?
  - What is the patient's level of executive functioning (planning, organizing, prioritizing, time management, setting and pursuing goals, completing activities, shifting between one activity and another)?
    - Can the patient concentrate and stay on track in therapy to a sufficient degree?
    - Can the patient get to therapy (or anywhere else) on time?
    - Can the patient follow through with homework or other tasks related to therapy?

Capacity to mentalize. Good treatment depends to some degree on the ability of patients to know their own minds, to reflect, and to infer accurately the motivations and intentions of others. While there may be significant resistances to realizing inner experience, the willingness and ability to do so, over time and with support, bodes well for therapy. Even patients who are quite concrete and cannot easily understand deep psychological meanings can still make progress if they are willing to accept their inner experience.

- Can the patient relatively accurately hypothesize about other people's motivations and intentions, including the therapist?
- Can the patient step back and recognize why he or she is thinking, feeling, or behaving in a certain way?

Schemas. Schemas are broad, pervasive themes or core beliefs about the self and others. They may be founded on basic, even implicit, assumptions about the self, others, and the world. Janoff-Bulman (1992) described three core assumptions: that (a) the world is (relatively) benevolent, (b) the world is (relatively) meaningful, and (c) I am worthy as a human being. Patients with early childhood abuse may have never developed these core assumptions at all, or the assumptions may have been destroyed by highly traumatic experiences. The failure to develop or loss of these core assumptions adds to chronic traumatic reactions and loss (Janoff-Bulman, 1992; J. Kaufman, 2014). In the wake of shattered assumptions, maladaptive schemas may develop.

Young et al. (2003) have expanded on core beliefs that are common in chronically traumatized individuals. These beliefs overlap to a significant degree with the core conflictual relational themes (CCRT) described in the psychoanalytic literature (Book, 1998; Drapeau & Perry, 2004; Luborsky & Crits-Cristoph, 1998). Using the CCRT method, the therapist examines the wishes patients have about a relationship, which involve schemas; the patient's response to self; and the other's response to the patient. These dynamics can be explored with patients. According to Young et al. (2003), schemas include beliefs about disconnection and rejection, autonomy (dependence) and performance (competence), impaired limits (entitlement and insufficient self-control), other-directedness (appeasement, self-sacrifice), and overvigilance and inhibition (negativity, hypercriticalness). Therapists can use a schema-focused questionnaire (Young & Brown, 2001) to assess predominant schema, or simply ask about them:

- What are the patient's predominant schemas?
- How do schemas differ among dissociative parts?
- How do the patient's schemas influence the patient's functioning, relationships, and therapy?

Insight

Insight is one of the common factors in psychotherapy that is known to help patients change, and it is a cognitive first step in realization. How insight is acquired and even whether it is completely accurate is not important. What is important is that the patient finds an explanation that supports an adaptive outcome—that is, one that helps the patient change and cope more effectively (Wampold, Imel, Bhati, & Johnson-Jennings, 2007). Insight without change is not especially helpful; it is merely an intellectual exercise that does not involve full realization and so does not support effective adaptation to reality as it is (Van der Hart et al., 2006). Thus, the therapist must determine whether patients have capacity for insight—that is, whether they have reflective functioning skills—and then whether they have the ability to use insight to effect change. Typically, those who have intellectual insight without change are stuck in some type of resistance that is, in principle, amenable to resolution. But the therapist must then focus on working with the resistance rather than on making further gains in insight.

One important note about insight in dissociative patients is that one part may have understanding while another does not. In other words, insight does not develop evenly across parts. Dissociative patients can seem to have great insight in (and memory for) one session and have completely lost it in another. Insight is thus often a slow evolution of realization rather than a series of major "Aha!" moments.

At first, highly dissociative (and resistant) patients may appear on the surface to be incapable of insight. However, once the therapist can help them develop a strong alliance, and understand their resistances with compassion, more capacity may develop over time (see Chapters 11 and 12 on working with resistance).

CASE EXAMPLE OF DELAYED INSIGHT: CORETTA

It was only in the sixth year of therapy that Coretta, a highly dissociative patient with DID and obsessive-compulsive personality disorder, could begin to develop an understanding of her self-punitive behavior of withholding any pleasurable experiences from herself and could make significant changes to accept more positive experiences in her life. She had believed for most of those years that she was only being pragmatic and doing without when she needed to, and that her behavior was normal and responsible. She would say things that on the surface seemed reasonable, but actually the way she used these beliefs was harmful to her: *You have to*

make do with what you have; You have to do things you don't want to do.
The insight that she was withholding from herself, in order to punish herself
for being abused, was long in coming. But once that insight took hold with
true realization, she made significant changes over the course of the next
two years, including getting a better paying job and a better place to live,
buying herself some new clothes for the first time in years, taking a vacation for the first time as an adult, and finding several healthy relationships.

It is also important to recognize that some behavioral change can occur
without any insight whatsoever.

CASE EXAMPLE OF BEHAVIORAL CHANGE WITHOUT INSIGHT: DONALD

A male patient, Donald, had been self-harming with cutting for many
years. He was unable to be aware of why it happened or what triggered
it because he had a severe phobia of his inner experience and of dissociative parts that were involved in the self-harm. The therapist helped Donald
learn behavioral skills to reduce and eliminate self-harm, such as replacing
cutting with a substitute action of using a red marker or holding ice in his
hand, as well as engaging in vigorous exercise when he felt the urge to
cut. He stopped cutting long before he could connect with dissociative
parts of himself that were involved.

These two cases are instructive in that some patients can effect behavioral change without first developing insight (Donald), while others must
develop insight first (Coretta). Needless to say, lack of insight likely leaves
patients vulnerable to returning to problematic behaviors under stress.

Motivations
One of the most important assessments for case formulation is to understand what motivates our patients to behave, think, feel, perceive, and predict in particular ways. Primary motivations come from the patient's
goals, wishes, values, schemas, or core beliefs, and from any conflicts
among these.

Resistance in therapy typically lies with unresolved conflicts among different dissociative parts of the patient and with the phobia of these parts
and other inner experiences. Typically, different motivations are held in
conflicted dissociative parts. For example, the part of the patient that functions in daily life may have a goal to feel better and be more independent
and competent; a child part has a wish to be taken care of; most parts have

schemas that they are unlovable; and a perpetrator-imitating part screams that no one deserves to get better. The more that therapists can identify these conflicting thoughts, wishes, goals, and schemas, the better they can help their patients find ways to accept and change them.

Emotional Resources

Skills to recognize, tolerate, and regulate emotions are essential to develop in the beginning of treatment, as dissociative disorders are partly disorders of regulation. Patients may have never learned these skills, resulting in inner-directed phobias (see section on trauma-related phobias below). Both dialectical behavior therapy (DBT; Linehan, 1993, 2014) and acceptance and commitment therapy (ACT; Hayes, Strosahl, & Wilson, 2011) offer helpful approaches, but both must be modified to include dissociative parts that have different emotions and different ways of avoiding them (see Boon et al., 2011). Emotional skills may vary widely among patients, and therapists must determine the degree to which an early focus on skills training is needed.

The following questions about emotional skills can be helpful in assessment:

- To what degree is the patient phobic of emotions, and of which emotions in particular?
- Does the patient already have some healthy ways to regulate emotions?
- Does the patient use self-hypnosis or imagery to regulate?
- Does the patient have the ability to enjoy positive experiences as a way to regulate?

Somatic Resources

Somatic resources are those that are derived from the body, from the patient's physical experience of sensation, movement, posture, gesture, and so on. They support a felt experience of well-being, safety, and competence. There are hundreds of ways to elicit and support somatic resources (e.g., Levine & Frederick,1997; Levine & Mate, 2010; Ogden et al., 2006; Ogden & Fisher, 2015). While patients may be phobic of their bodies, somatic resources are still important to develop early in therapy to the degree possible.

It can be helpful to assess the following:

- Is the patient able to feel his or her body in a pleasant way (for instance, feeling relaxed, enjoying a warm bath or massage, or simply liking good food)?

- Does the patient use physical activity in a balanced way to regulate emotions, to feel better (e.g., gardening, walking, cycling)? Note that many patients engage in physical activities in order not to feel their emotions.
- Is the patient able to use breathing as a resource to calm down?

Resources can include somatic experiences that accompany feeling safe, confident, strong, curious, boundaried, or supported. Sensorimotor psychotherapy (Ogden et al., 2006; Ogden & Fisher, 2015), somatic experiencing (Levine & Frederick, 1997; Levine & Mate, 2010), and EMDR (in particular, resource development and installation; e.g., Gonzalez & Mosquera, 2012; Knipe, 2014; Korn & Leeds, 2002) all place a strong emphasis on developing somatic resources.

Imaginal Resources

Dissociative patients often have a creative capacity for rich imagination, at least in part because of their tendency to be highly hypnotizable. Imaginal resources, such as a safe space and an ideal figure, among others, may be extremely helpful in offering regulation, comfort, and strength.

CASE EXAMPLE OF AN IMAGINAL RESOURCE: CARA

Cara was a patient who was just beginning to be able to approach some of her more painful emotions. The therapist decided to help Cara use resources for comfort and safety more consciously. Cara chose to use a resource figure with positive qualities. She developed an image of an older woman who was compassionate, just, loving, wise, and strong. She had long, flowing silver hair, was dressed in a billowing emerald-colored robe, and had the kindest face on earth. Cara imagined herself walking hand-in-hand with this figure on a path, feeling unafraid and solid.

Once Cara had practiced using this inner resource when calm, she was better able to conjure it when she felt stressed. She found this enormously helpful. Cara was able to use this resource not only when she needed to approach a frightening feeling but also afterward. She used the wise woman figure after a productive session to continue to reflect on the work, feel strengthened by it, and gain comfort when she needed to grieve. Thus, Cara used the wise figure not only to overcome her phobic avoidance but also to support her in continuing gains.

The therapist started by helping Cara experience the wise woman with her and notice what that felt like in her body, what emotions she felt, and what her thoughts were. After she had time to solidify this positive experience, the therapist directed her attention to a frightening, dark sensation, with the intent to pendulate between the positive and the negative experience. However, this was overwhelming to Cara, so the therapist directed her back to the positive image until she was regulated again. The therapist asked Cara what might help, and Cara suggested that she might feel safer if the wise woman figure could go with her to the frightening dark place. Cara tried this, and found it possible, letting the wise woman walk ahead of her. The wise woman looked inside the dark place for Cara. She turned to Cara with tears in her eyes, saying, *That person in there feels so besieged. She is exhausted and fighting with all her strength to stay safe. She has never realized she is safe. Let's help her.*

Cara was able to use the new perspective to understand her rage that was held in the dark place, and be more accepting of it. At that point, the therapist was able to help Cara feel the rage a little at a time, pendulating back and forth between the calm, solid feelings that helped her accept and integrate her intense rage.

Trauma-Related Phobias

Most trauma-related phobias (Boon et al., 2011; Nijenhuis, 2015; Nijenhuis, Van der Hart, & Steele, 2002; Steele et al., 2005; Van der Hart et al., 2006) are inner-directed. Dissociative patients have at least some phobic avoidance of inner experience, in particular traumatic memories (Janet, 1904, 1928), and from there flow the other phobias. The more phobic patients are, the more resistant they will be. Early treatment will be geared toward reducing these phobias, as patients must learn to tolerate inner experience to make progress. The therapist should note how patients developed these phobias and what maintains them, how chronic and intense each phobia is, and which parts are more and less phobically avoidant. There are several variations of phobias:

- phobia of inner experience (thoughts, emotions, sensations, memories, perceptions, predictions, fantasies, wishes);
- phobia of traumatic memory;
- phobia of dissociative parts;
- phobia of attachment (and intimacy) and attachment loss; and
- phobia of change.

Psychological Defenses

Recognizing and working with psychological defenses is a mainstay of psychodynamic approaches (Vaillant, 1977. However, it is important for therapists to recognize that psychological defenses are often intimately tied to the physiological animal defenses, which are responses to danger and life threat. The therapist should always be curious about why the patient has the need for a defense and what it helps the patient avoid (see Chapters 11 and 12 on resistance). Various dissociative parts may engage in different psychological defenses.

Previous Treatment History

Previous treatment history informs the therapist about the habitual problems the patient might have in therapy, and what inner and relational conflicts are manifested and remain unresolved. It is important for the current therapist not to engage in splitting with the patient about previous therapists, as some patients insist all their former therapists were unhelpful or actively harmful. Unfortunately, it is true that dissociative patients tend to be misunderstood, misdiagnosed, and mistreated by therapists who are overly skeptical, fascinated, or uninformed. Nevertheless, the current therapist needs to listen to process when patients talk about former therapists, rather than focusing on the content of what therapists allegedly did or did not do.

CORE CONCEPT

A careful history of the patient's previous therapy is helpful in revealing potential transference and countertransference problems that may arise in the current therapy, how endings are managed by the patient, expectations of therapy by the patient, and what should be similar and different in the current therapy.

Regardless of whether or not a former therapist has been perceived as helpful, patients are communicating about their habitual attachment patterns and perceptions, and their conflicts, wishes, and fears about therapy and therapists. Patients often have conflicted feelings about former therapists or treatment teams, for which they need a supportive person to listen and help them integrate discrepancies. The therapist should also be alert to the patient's unrealistic expectations for the current therapy and the danger that the patient will idealize or devalue the current therapist from the start.

The therapist will find it helpful to explore the following:

- Length of previous therapies—this may indicate the patient's willingness to engage in therapy, tolerance for the therapeutic process, and ability to remain connected with a therapist or not

- Therapy outcomes from the patient's perspective
- Reasons for termination from the patient's perspective
- Previous diagnoses, if known
- Medications, outcomes, and medication compliance
- Hospitalizations, dates, reasons, and length of stay—this helps the therapist determine how unstable the patient is over time and what the major issues are that lead to destabilization
- What was helpful and what was not in previous therapies from the patient's perspective
- Quality of previous therapeutic relationships from the patient's perspective. For example, the patient might say, *He didn't understand me or make efforts to do so; She was really cold and uncaring, just saying Hmm all the time; He didn't want me to talk about parts or about my abuse; She was never on time and forgot appointments; He kept telling me what to do; She wouldn't help me figure out what to do; She wanted to work on parts, but I don't believe in that stuff; We were fighting a lot and I got frustrated; He didn't want to have contact between sessions, and I need that!* Whether these are accurate or not, they reflect a sense that the relationship was not secure.
- Reported abuse or exploitation by previous therapists; when patients report abuse, the current therapy relationship will be greatly affected, and mistrust should be expected (Pope, 1994)
- Are any other therapists or other practitioners currently involved with the patient?
- Is the patient is willing to sign a release for the therapist to speak with previous therapists or other practitioners, or obtain treatment records (unless the former therapist was abusive)?

Attachment Patterns

Research has shown that children may have a secure attachment with one caregiver and an insecure one with another (Bretherton & Mulholland, 1999). Thus, patients may display different attachment patterns with different people in their lives; perhaps they have even had a secure attachment with someone. This is useful to know, as it can be a wonderful resource, and can provide the patient with a model for how to be in healthy relationships.

However, insecure attachment patterns that are more fixed and pervasive will cause patients and those around them (including the therapist) difficulties. Insecure attachment patterns are helpful to understand (Crittenden, 2006; Crittenden & Landini, 2011; George, Kaplan, & Main, 1996; Main & Goldwyn, 1984). For example, habitually avoidant patients seek to minimize experiences that might evoke attachment-related emotions, and they avoid relational connection because doing so prevents dysregulation. On the other hand, patients who are highly anxious seek excessive and exhausting contact with others and may be highly preoccupied with what others are thinking and feeling.

Each dissociative part may have a different attachment style. For example, a child part stuck in attachment cry may have an anxious attachment pattern, while a worker part that functions in daily life may have an avoidant style. Overall, then, the patient exhibits a disorganized pattern, alternating between approach and avoidance, attachment seeking and defense (Liotti, 1992, 1999, 2011; Steele et al., 2001). The therapist should note the attachment dynamics of each part of the patient at one level, and at another should determine how these patterns (and the parts involved) interact and conflict in relationships.

Assessing the Patient's Reactions to Dissociation

Once a diagnosis of a dissociative disorder is made, it is important to explore how the patient reacts to being dissociative, the functions of each dissociative part, and what conflicts maintain dissociation.

CORE CONCEPT

How the patient reacts to being dissociative, how dissociative parts (and the patient as a whole) deal with conflict, and which conflicts are intense among parts are all essential to assess.

Reactions of the patient to being dissociative. One of the first things to notice is how various parts of the patient accept a dissociative disorder diagnosis. Some dissociative parts may be more accepting, while others are more avoidant. Often the major part functioning in daily life is reluctant to deal with dissociation. However, some patients are tremendously relieved to understand what is going on with them. Bob, from the case example in Chapter 5, was one of these patients. As the adult part functioning in daily life, he started to communicate with his dissociative parts almost immediately, and he accepted his young traumatized parts and could comfort them. Others, like Marianne, also discussed in Chapter 5, are frightened or ashamed, and deny or avoid any attempts of the therapist to work with dissociation. These attitudes affect the progress of therapy and should inform how the therapist might approach the subject of dissociation. The more patients as a whole are fearful, ashamed, or phobically avoidant of their dissociative parts, the slower therapy may progress, and the more stabilization and emotional skills development they may need.

It is also essential to understand areas of both explicit and implicit cooperation and conflict among dissociative parts, as phobic avoidance among parts results in strong resistance and must therefore be approached carefully. The therapist must try to find ways to decrease patients' phobic fears and increase their curiosity about their internal experience. It is much less important that patients accept a diagnosis and certain terminology than it is to find ways to help patients accept their inner experience.

A few patients embrace their dissociative disorder as a lifestyle and identity. This, too, informs treatment. These patients often have little else to turn to in their lives for meaning and purpose. Often, their life is organized around their disorder.

Assessing precipitants of switching. Switching from one part to another may not be obvious to the therapist in the beginning, particularly those therapists who have not had much experience with dissociative patients. However, if and when switching is observed, it is essential to understand what is most likely to precipitate switches from one part of the patient to another or the strong intrusion of certain parts (see Chapter 10). Switches and passive influence are essentially symptoms of some type of stress. They are often evoked in the context of relationship, so the therapist should carefully explore what happens internally within the patient when a switch occurs in the presence of another person. Traumatic memories are also strong triggers for switching or passive influence. The therapist can be curious about inner experiences, such as certain emotions, thoughts, or wishes that might evoke switching. For example, one patient switched to a frightened, frozen child part each time she might have more appropriately been angry. The fear helped her avoid her anger, which felt far more dangerous and intolerable to her.

The therapist can also explore whether there is any voluntary control over a complete switch. For example, a patient switched to a funny, flippant part whenever she was in the presence of men. She was able to control when she switched and did so intentionally to protect herself from being close and vulnerable. The patient and this part of herself had an explicit agreement that this specific part would "handle all the men."

Finally, it can be helpful to notice whether there is a particular sequence of parts involved in switching. This helps the therapist with patterns that can be predicted. For example, a patient would first switch to a needy part that was unusually demanding. When her demands were not completely met, she switched to a highly aggressive part. If that resulted in her getting what she wanted, she switched back to a reasonable adult. If it was not successful, she switched to a part that was collapsed and hurt and would not leave the office. While these parts could be mistaken for mere changes in behavioral tactics, they were actually quite separate and not fully aware of each other, even though they were part of an entrenched pattern present since childhood. When the therapist could help the patient notice the sequence, she was eventually able to understand and have more control over it.

Relationships and conflicts among dissociative parts. As noted throughout the book, the relationships among parts and their conflicts inform the course of treatment and are a core aspect of the patient's intrapsychic functioning. The more therapists can understand the dynamics among parts, the better they can help patients accept and change them. Of course, in the beginning of treatment this may not be obvious, and so it involves ongoing assessment. However, the therapist can make some educated hypotheses about conflicts when the patient is dissociative. For example, common conflicts include those between attachment and defense, knowing and not knowing, maintaining the status quo and changing, and feeling safe and being vulnerable or genuine. The following questions can help both the therapist and patients learn more about these internal dynamics:

- What is the level of awareness of one part for others?
- What are the typical reactions of one part toward others? For example, does the patient freeze upon hearing a punitive voice, or feel disgust upon noticing a small child part of herself? Do parts hate each other? Fear each other? Are they ashamed of each other?
- What is the function of each dissociative part? For example, does a part engage in daily life activities, hold a particular emotion or memory, or serve to defend against a particular realization?
- What are the areas of cooperation among parts (implicit or explicit)? For example, conscious or unconscious agreements about not interfering with parenting or working.
- What are the major non-realizations held in each part? These will be treatment targets over the course of therapy (see Chapter 1 for examples of non-realization).
- What are the major conflicts among dissociative parts? Dissociative patients hold their conflicts in dissociative parts of themselves, so that they often do not recognize that they have a conflict. When the therapist is only interacting with one part of the patient, only one side of a conflict may be apparent. Some conflicts may not manifest clearly until later in therapy.

Assessing Trauma History

Trauma-informed care highlights the importance of asking patients whether they have experienced past trauma. This is an essential component of assessment; otherwise, the therapist may be blind to the pervasive effects of trauma. There are a number of instruments that assess exposure to traumatizing events. One of the simplest is the Adverse Childhood Experiences Questionnaire (ACE; Felitti et al., 1998). It asks 10 questions about childhood exposure to various stressful experiences, and it is easily accessible online. Others include the Traumatic Experiences Checklist (TEC; Nijenhuis, Van der Hart, & Kruger, 2002) and the Trauma History Screen (THS; Carlson et al., 2011), which ask more detailed questions—for example, number of times an event occurred, the ages at which it occurred, and the emotional impact of the event.

While these instruments may be useful in helping the therapist understand the extent of the patient's trauma history, there are important caveats to note, especially early in therapy. Patients, especially dissociative patients, may be easily triggered when they think or talk about traumatic events. The therapist must carefully assess whether a given patient can tolerate even the most gentle exploration.

How the therapist asks about trauma sets the stage for pacing. For example, the therapist might preface questions by asking the patient to just give a brief statement without going into detail: a "bird's-eye view" or "just the headlines." The therapist might ask, *How was discipline handled in your family? How was anger expressed in your family? Did you ever feel physically hurt by someone? Have you ever had any especially painful or scary experiences? Did anyone ever say or do something sexual that made you feel uncomfortable or frightened? Was there anyone in your life when you were growing up whom you could go to if you needed to talk about something that was upsetting you?*

The therapist should pay close attention to the patient's response to the questions, particularly noting any evidence of freezing, hyperarousal, fogginess, or blanking out that might indicate dissociation and the possibility that the patient is outside the window of tolerance. Noting changes in posture or movement can be helpful in determining the level of activation.

If the patient becomes activated, the therapist should stop inquiries and draw the patient's attention back to here and now by saying something like, *It sounds like you really had a hard time as a child, and that is something important for us to consider in our work. I notice that when you talk about it, you are tensing up and spacing out. So for right now, can you put your feet on the floor and take some deep breaths? We will return to this important topic, but first let's find a way for you to feel more present.*

If a conflict about the reality of events is already in evidence during assessment, the therapist can accept any parts of the patient that acknowledge trauma, as well as parts that might contradict the claim, without taking sides in these inner conflicts of "truth." Thus, some compassionate connection is made so the patient feels heard and understood. But details are not discussed much, and the therapist ensures the patient is grounded and present, staying somewhat at the surface of consciousness, to the degree possible.

Assessing Prognosis

In many respects, assessing prognosis in patients with dissociative disorders is the same as with any other patient. However, how patients react to and manage their dissociation adds another dimension to prognosis. Some dissociative patients have been in the mental health system for years without a proper diagnosis. Much like patients with borderline personality disorder in years past, they may come to a new therapy having been labeled as "untreatable." Yet many of these patients do well and make improvements over time with adequate treatment, so the fact that they have been in treatment for a long time does not necessarily imply a poor prognosis (Brand et al., 2013; Brand & Loewenstein, 2014).

Nevertheless, while most patients improve, a few do not, and quite a number have a slow, uneven course of improvement that can take years (Horevitz & Loewenstein, 1994; Kluft, 1994c, 1994d). To a large degree, progress depends upon prognosis, and prognosis informs treatment planning. Ongoing assessment as described in this chapter helps therapists assess the strengths and deficits of a patient and the patient's degree of resistance.

The following factors, some of which were discussed above in the patient's resources and needs, are important in determining the prognosis.

- Highest level of functioning achieved
- Degree of comorbidity, including personality disorders
- Degree and flexibility of psychological defenses
- Willingness to share personal thoughts and feelings
- Degree of trauma-related phobias
- Severity of trauma history, including early age of onset and chronicity
- Capacity for mentalizing
- Level of motivation and insight
- Level of self-compassion
- Ability and willingness to learn to regulate and tolerate inner experience

- Severity of attachment problems that undermine and complicate the therapeutic relationship (severe dependency, avoidance, entitlement, etc.)
- Acceptance of dissociation and willingness to work with dissociative parts
- Degree of conflict between dissociative parts
- Ongoing victimization or abuse of others

Of course, prognosis can change over time. Thus, some patients who initially have a poor prognosis can potentially make progress if given enough time and good treatment, while others cannot make use of therapy.

Prognosis is useful in guiding treatment in that it helps the therapist have a realistic perspective that lends itself to patience and informs pragmatic therapy goals. For example, a patient with a poor prognosis is not ready to engage in working with traumatic memories. Whether this patient can ever do so is something that can only be determined with time and patience. But the therapist must walk a tightrope between holding out hope and not having unrealistic expectations that will make the patient feel like a failure.

Highest Level of Functioning Achieved

An assessment of prognosis can begin with the therapist exploring the highest level of functioning of patients. Higher levels of functioning and longer periods of maintaining it bode well for prognosis.

- Have patients had any periods of better function and subsequently decompensated, or has functioning always been at a low level? For example, a patient who has struggled with severe depression and anxiety since childhood and has multiple treatment failures is likely to be chronic and may not respond well to treatment. Thus, treatment planning must include helping the patient focus on coping with this condition rather than completely eliminating it.
- How long have patients been able to maintain their highest level of functioning?
- What support and resources helped patients achieve or maintain a certain level?
- When was the last time they were able to function at that level?
- Is there evidence that dissociative parts contribute to better adaptive function?
- Are patients able to work; do they have a job?
- Do patients study or have any volunteer work?
- Do patients take care of current family? Are they able to do so and also engage in good self-care?

- Are patients able to structure their days and establish routines?
- Are patients able to use leisure time constructively?

CASE EXAMPLE OF HIGHEST LEVEL OF FUNCTIONING: MARIANNE

Marianne (see case from Chapter 5) had been able to maintain a part-time job for quite a few years and received feedback that she was good at her work, even though she had amnesia or reported being out of her body sometimes while at work. The therapist concluded that there was sufficient cooperation among dissociative parts to work and that Marianne had considerable ego strength that allowed her to function well at work, even though she reported significant other difficulties.

Severe Comorbidity

Most patients who have a dissociative disorder also have significant comorbidity that needs attention in treatment and may influence prognosis. Early in treatment, the therapist can address some of these issues, including depression, anxiety, and panic attacks. Generally, the more severe and enduring the comorbidity, the poorer the prognosis. On the other hand, a dissociative organization may sometimes underlie these symptoms or disorders, which can improve if dissociative parts are directly addressed. For example, there may be extremely depressed or anxious parts, suicidal parts, parts that engage in substance abuse, or parts that obsess and ruminate.

It is prudent to attempt to address specific comorbid problems with treatments that have been shown to be effective—for example, treating depression with interpersonal therapy or cognitive behavior therapy (CBT) and perhaps medication. The one exception is that comorbid PTSD should not be treated with exposure or EMDR unless the patient has been deemed stable enough (see Chapters 20 and 21). If standard treatments are not successful, the therapist should explore the possibility of an underlying dissociative disorganization and work with the parts that are entrenched in these behaviors. Some persistent comorbid problems such as alcohol or drug dependency, severe and recurrent self-harm, and suicidal attempts may have a negative influence on the overall prognosis even though they can be seen as substitute actions—that is, coping strategies that are maladaptive.

Finally, prognosis is influenced by the presence of personality disorders. The more severe the disorder, the poorer the prognosis in general, though many patients do well with long-term therapy with a well-boundaried and experienced therapist.

Level of Self-Compassion

Self-compassion is a major factor in making progress for traumatized patients. The faster they learn to be compassionate toward themselves and their parts (and toward others), the better treatment gains they can make. Those lacking in self-compassion are often self-destructive and have profound shame and self-hatred that slows progress. Thus, treatment planning includes as many ways as possible to increase the self-compassion of patients.

Willingness to Share Personal Thoughts and Feelings

Dissociative patients are often reluctant to share their innermost thoughts and feelings. They may feel deep fear and shame or be unaware of thoughts and feelings that are sequestered in various dissociative parts. However, with careful and compassionate encouragement to disclose in a paced manner, most patients are able to slowly open up to the therapist. Those who cannot are not likely to do well. Some patients have such inner conflicts about therapy that dissociative parts interfere with sharing; some have limited ability to verbalize inner experiences; and a few have a kind of psychotic thought blocking that goes beyond the interference of dissociative parts.

CASE EXAMPLE OF INABILITY TO SHARE THOUGHTS AND FEELINGS: MOIRA

Moira was a 42-year-old patient with DID who sat in terrified silence in spite of everything the therapist did to try to create some regulation and safety. She was extremely paranoid that the therapist would use any information against her and reported that several previous therapies had not helped at all. She refused for almost a year to allow her partner to even know she was in therapy and shared nothing with the partner about what was going on with her. She refused medication and would not give consent for the therapist to talk with her previous therapists. She was unable to allow the therapist to work with any dissociative parts. Moira was also unable to work on stabilization skills at home and could not write down her thoughts or use any other creative adjunct modalities. In spite of 24 months of good stabilization treatment and 9 months in intensive residential inpatient treatment, she remained silent, frozen, highly guarded, and paranoid. A trial of antipsychotic medication was unhelpful. Her prognosis remains poor.

Enmeshment With Family of Origin and Ongoing Victimization

Patients who are not safe in the present are unable to make much good use of therapy. Those who are unwilling or unable to leave abusive situations after receiving support are unlikely to show much improvement. Dealing with patients who continue to be victimized in the present is addressed in Chapter 19.

CASE EXAMPLES OF DETERMINING PROGNOSIS: BOB AND MARIANNE

Based on the information and initial assessment, it was clear that Bob (described in Chapter 5) seemed to have many resources and good social support, no severe comorbidity, no severe attachment problems, excellent executive functioning skills, and little phobia of his dissociative parts after he overcame his initial shame. He quickly developed a solid working relationship with the therapist and diligently practiced emotion-regulation skills. While he often felt shame about his sexual abuse, he had a reasonably accurate appraisal of himself in other domains, and he was able to develop self-compassion. His level of functioning was high, even though his PTSD and dissociative symptoms had increased when he began his relationship with his partner. Bob had an excellent prognosis, provided the therapist could help pace therapy so that Bob could stay functional in daily life (Kluft, 1986a).

Marianne's case was much more complicated and her prognosis less clear, although she had never been treated for a dissociative disorder, and her phobia and social isolation were not uncommon for a patient with DID. There was more comorbidity, such as eating problems and self-harm, and she had less compassion for herself. She had more difficulty mentalizing across situations than did Bob, whose challenges in reflection were mostly restricted to his sexual relationships. The most difficult obstacles in her treatment was her severe phobia for her dissociative parts and a lack of compassion. Her initial prognosis would be moderate.

Tracking Treatment Progress

There are currently three measures that examine treatment progress over time in dissociative patients, which can inform prognosis. The first is the Dimensions of Therapeutic Movement Instrument (DTMI; Kluft 1994c, 1994d), the second is the Checklist for Evaluation of DID Treatment (Boon,

1997; see a revised version in Appendix B), and the third is the Progress in Treatment Questionnaire (PITQ; Brand, Classen et al., 2009). At the time of writing, only the PITQ has been validated. The therapist can use these checklists as an informal way of estimating initial prognosis and treatment planning. Over time, these factors can be reexamined to see whether the goals of treatment should change or efforts should be redoubled. The scale in Appendix B integrates usual prognostic factors with those specific to dissociative disorders.

Case Formulation: Using the Patient's Process to Guide Treatment

Diagnosis is focused on the outward manifestations of the patient's problems—that is, on symptoms. Psychosocial assessment is broader in scope and helps the therapist understand how patients got to this point by examining their history and current situation. However, it is essential also to conceptualize the patients' struggles based on the ways they are organized and function intrapsychically and interpersonally—that is, to develop a case formulation. For dissociative patients, this includes how dissociative parts are organized (Van der Hart et al., 2006).

Case formulation helps the therapist understand what precipitates and perpetuates the patient's difficulties. For example, the patient may engage in self-harm. The therapist may determine that the patient's attachment style is disorganized, and thus involves particular negative mental representations of the self and others, as well as beliefs and schemas that others cannot be trusted. These lead to intense aloneness, yearning, and shame, but also fear and anger: One dissociative part punishes and berates another internally when the patient attempts to connect with others, which then evokes intense self-hatred and shame. The angry part is defending against yearning and shame and attempts to prevent connection because it is viewed as dangerous. The patient as a whole has limited regulatory and reflective skills and engages in self-harm as a coping strategy to regulate these relational dilemmas, emotions, and internal conflicts. Thus, the therapist has a conceptual formulation of the patient's inner process that evokes self-harm, and can devise a treatment plan to address these issues.

The treatment plan would therefore include improving emotion regulation; resolving shame defenses; changing maladaptive schemas; helping the patient develop more flexible and realistic mental representations of self and others; understanding the functions of dissociative parts; promoting inner communication and resolving conflicts among parts, especially the conflict between attachment and defense that perpetuates disorganized attachment patterns; and focusing on what happens in the therapeutic relationship as a particular way to address many of these issues.

CORE CONCEPT

Diagnosis is focused on symptoms and disorders. Case formulation employs assessment toward understanding the *process* of patients, how they are organized and relate to self, others, and the world. Case formulation then informs treatment.

Case formulation is focused primarily on the emotional, relational, and somatic process of patients. For example, how do patients experience themselves and others, and what are their persistent ways of relating? How do they experience emotions somatically and make sense of them? Which emotions are commonly avoided, and which are typically experienced? What wishes, goals, and values motivate patients? What are their major inner conflicts, and how do these manifest in various dissociative parts? What psychological (and physical) defenses do patients use on a regular basis in response to trauma-related phobias, and how do these defenses affect functioning? How do dissociative parts interact or not, and what conflicts among them maintain dissociation? What are the major non-realizations of the patient and of each dissociative part that maintain dissociation?

CASE EXAMPLE OF FURTHER ASSESSMENT AND CASE FORMULATION: MARIANNE

In assessing Marianne, the therapist found that she had a stable living situation and housing, sufficient finances to engage in treatment, and was not involved in any current dangerous relationships. Even though she seemed to have amnesia in the present and she dissociated in sessions, Marianne appeared to have sufficient inner cooperation among parts so that she could manage in daily life. She had good executive functioning. She found comfort in her dog and enjoyed playing the piano and singing in a choir, where she had some superficial acquaintances. She admitted that she had a tendency to isolate herself, had no close friends, and never told anyone about her problems. She also said she did not "need close friends" and was content being alone. However, this contradicted a young part of her that felt extremely lonely. She had one younger brother but did not see him often, as she minimized contact with her family of origin. As a young child she had two teachers who were supportive of her, whom the therapist believed could be used as resources.

Marianne was intelligent but seemed to have great difficulty talking about her problems and dissociated often in the beginning of treatment. She showed motivation and some insight, but at the same time, she was afraid of her inner experience, and she had a strong phobia of her diagnosis and dissociative parts. There was clearly an enormous internal conflict among parts, noted by the therapist, but Marianne could hardly comment on what she experienced and was dismissive of her parts. However, she kept herself well within the therapeutic frame, never missed a session, was always on time, and did not call or e-mail the therapist in between sessions inappropriately.

Based on this and other information during the assessment period, her therapist developed a case formulation. Marianne had some ego strength, intelligence, insight, and motivation to engage in treatment. However, the following would have a major impact on her treatment: (a) her ongoing inability to realize, which resulted in a phobia of inner experience and dissociative parts to the degree that she could not accept her diagnosis; (b) serious internal conflicts among parts, which resulted in frequent switching during sessions and inability to recall what was discussed; (c) severe attachment conflicts and difficulties, indicating rigid schemas and resulting in social isolation and chronic defense when she perceived the therapist as caring and close; (d) use of projection as a defense such that the therapist often felt ashamed and incompetent with her, which protected the patient against these feelings; (e) transference that involved a complex combination of approach and neediness by parts fixed in attachment cry, rapidly followed by excoriating rage by parts that needed to defend against attachment, or by dismissing and avoidant behaviors by parts that functioned in daily life; and (f) competing and conflicting motivations to connect and disconnect, to maintain the status quo and to change, to punish herself and to feel better, to feel and to avoid sensation and emotion, and to remember and to avoid remembering traumatic events.

Summary

Assessment, prognosis, and case formulation are integral in informing treatment planning and progress. Therapists should make ongoing assessments and change treatment plans accordingly. They should also regularly—quarterly, every six months, or annually—discuss treatment progress and goals with patients to determine whether therapy is effective and what might need to be adjusted or improved.

Further Explorations

6.1 Do you regularly assess treatment progress in your patients and discuss it with them? If not, how might you begin to incorporate that into your practice?

6.2 Have you treated patients whose prognosis ended up better or worse than you anticipated? In hindsight, was there something you missed that might have helped you determine a more accurate prognosis?

6.3 How do you define and set a treatment frame? How is your frame similar to or different from your colleagues', and why?

6.4 Write up a brief case formulation for one of your patients, focusing on the patient's process and capacities, and discuss it with colleagues.

CHAPTER 7

Treatment Planning

The treatment plan designed for patients with dissociative disorders (DD) is vital since this patient population is a financial burden as utilizers of the highest number of psychotherapy sessions compared to those with all other psychiatric disorders.

—Julie Gentile, Kristy Dillon, and Paulette Gillig (2013, p. 26)

Once initial assessment and case formulation are complete, a coherent treatment plan must be developed. The context for treatment planning is a phase-oriented approach, with safety, stabilization, skills building, and development of a collaborative therapeutic relationship being the major priorities in the first phase. Treatment planning organizes therapy and helps therapists choose appropriate approaches (Groth-Marnat, Gottheil, Liu, Clinton, & Beutler, 2008; Horowitz, 1997; Woody, Detweiler-Bedell, Teachman, & O'Hearn, 2003).

CORE CONCEPT

Treatment plans depend upon diagnosis, case formulation, and prognosis. The majority of dissociative patients need at least a short period of stabilization, while some may need prolonged support to become stable.

While a treatment plan is essential for every patient, its use with dissociative patients is particularly invaluable because therapists can use it to stay on track in a complex and often disorienting therapy. Although treatment plans depend on the prognosis of a patient, most will start with a stabilization phase, and all need clarity on the treatment frame and boundaries. For these and other reasons, it is important to make a shared treatment plan with a patient after assessment. It must contain (a) an agreement on the treatment frame, including frequency of sessions and boundaries; (b) short-term and long-term goals; and (c) what to do in case of crisis or emergency.

Treatment Frame and Boundaries as a Foundation for Treatment Planning

An important part of the early phase of a therapy with a patient with a dissociative disorder is to set and give a clear explanation about the treatment frame, boundaries, and limits. What can a patient expect from the therapist? What does the therapist expect from the patient? Topics to discuss include:

- Length and frequency of sessions
- Guidelines regarding contact outside of sessions such as phone calls, texting, or e-mailing
- Crisis and emergency protocols
- The expected availability of the therapist
- Whether a backup therapist will be needed
- Policies on lateness or missed sessions
- Reasons for immediate termination of therapy (e.g., violence in the session)
- Informed consent for treatment
- Contact with other treating professionals
- Whether or how physical touch might be used as part of a treatment plan
- Protocols in case of sudden incapacitation or death of the therapist

In Chapter 2, therapists were encouraged to explore their boundaries and to know ahead of time what is generally appropriate. Boundaries are meant to help both patients and therapists. They are intended to provide a focused space for treatment in sessions; prevent undue dependency from developing; maximize the competence and responsibility of the patient; and keep therapists from overextending themselves with too much availability, or conversely, from not being sufficiently available.

Patients need to know what to expect and what is expected of them, and
what will happen if they violate boundaries. They should be instructed as
to what to do should a therapist or other professional violate boundaries
with them. We recommend giving guidelines to patients in writing and
having a discussion about them in the first session. Agencies usually have
set policies on these issues, while therapists in private practice may need
to make their own.

Two aspects of the treatment frame are commonly challenging for many
therapists: deciding on the frequency of sessions, and whether or how to
use e-mail with patients.

Determining Frequency and Length of Sessions

The treatment guidelines for dissociative disorders recommend one or two
sessions per week, ranging from 45 minutes to 120 minutes (ISSTD, 2011).
However, how does the therapist determine what will be most effective and
helpful for a given patient? More therapy is not always more helpful or
faster, and can actually overwhelm a patient who may not have the integrative capacity to deal with the intensity. Greater frequency also leads to a
deepening of transference, which may not be desired in extremely dependent or avoidant patients.

The first two issues to determine are whether the therapist has the time
to commit to longer or more frequent sessions on a regular basis, and
whether the patient has the financial resources to afford it. If so, the next

step is to begin with a routine weekly session of normal length, and further assess the patient for whether longer or more frequent sessions make sense. Beginning with more than that may overwhelm the patient or create a dependency that neither therapist nor patient is ready to handle. The therapist should determine if the patient can abide by a standard treatment frame, stay motivated, take responsibility for treatment, and use sessions profitably. Although patients may ask for more time, the therapist must make a careful, reflective decision about whether this will be in the patients' best interest rather than reactively agreeing.

A major factor is how patients are using sessions. Are they engaged and focused on work that is consistent with the treatment plan? Are they willing to contain traumatic memories until later? Are they able to bring dissociative parts of themselves into treatment gradually? Do they have a good working alliance with the therapist? Are they able to leave the session grounded and on time? If so, the patient is working well in therapy.

The next question is whether twice a week might speed stabilization. If the patient is working well in therapy but is having trouble maintaining stability in between sessions, twice a week might be considered. The purpose is not to dig up more content but to help the patient gain greater capacities to manage and reflect on emotions, challenge maladaptive beliefs, work with dissociative parts more compassionately and consistently, and decrease serious symptoms of distress. The therapist should carefully note if crisis calls or distress increases when frequency increases, as this may indicate that therapy is becoming overwhelming. A dependent transference must also be carefully monitored and contained (see Chapter 13).

During Phase 2 work with traumatic memories, an additional session each week can be helpful to foster further realization, and to focus on daily life issues in one session and traumatic memories in the other.

CORE CONCEPT

Sessions should always start and stop on time. Extended sessions should be planned ahead of time, not be spontaneous. The therapist should ensure enough time before the end of session for the patient to be grounded and contained and able to leave without undue distress.

Ending sessions on time. Each session should start and stop on time as part of a basic therapy frame, and the therapist is responsible for making this happen. However, this is not always easy. Toward the end of the session, the avoidant patient may feel increasing pressure—often from other parts—to talk about what the patient has not yet been able to bring up. This inner desperation may snowball, resulting in switching, flashbacks, or major revelations in the last few minutes of the session. The looming separation from the therapist may evoke an attachment cry, with panic, tears, pleading, and other strategies to prolong the session. Often this is in the form of child parts that switch and refuse to leave or seem overwhelmed. The therapist should provide psychoeducation about the necessity of ending on time, help pace the session so the patient has ample time to ground at the end, and enlist the help of all dissociative parts internally.

Extended sessions. Another issue is whether the duration of a session should be extended. First, extensions of sessions should be planned with forethought. Some patients are slow in being able to get started with therapy work, and also need more time at the end to ground and be ready to leave the session. There may be a lot of conflict and chaos internally, and it can take time each session to calm it down enough for the patient to work. Longer sessions may allow some patients sufficient time and regulation to engage. The therapist must be cautious, however, in ensuring that more time does not result in more wasted time, or in more content that overwhelms the patient, or in fostering greater need of and dependency on the therapist. Anything beyond the time of a double session is not recommended without careful consultation, as it usually exceeds the integrative capacity of both patient and therapist.

E-Mail and Texts

Communication with patients through e-mail and texting has become a hot topic, with guidelines still being developed. Therapists must use caution with these modes of communication, because they are not confidential and take place outside the therapy hour. However, specific approaches may allow for special use of texts or e-mail. For example, some DBT therapists coach patients in the use of their skills via texts or e-mail. If therapists do utilize texts or e-mail, they must be aware of and abide by existing jurisdictional and professional codes, and inform patients that texts and e-mails are not secure or confidential. Many therapists are moving to more secure and encrypted data services, but even this is not a guarantee of the patient's privacy.

If therapists decide that texts and e-mails are something they want to include in practice, the question remains of how to use e-mail or text therapeutically with informed consent. Guidelines should be set that maintain effective boundaries and ensure that patients continue to bring relevant issues to sessions.

The four major issues with which therapists struggle include: (a) how to avoid dependency and boundary issues; (b) whether various dissociative parts of the patient should use texting or e-mail to communicate with the therapist, and with or without the knowledge of other parts; (c) whether or how much of therapy issues should be shared by the patient in texts or e-mails; and (d) whether or how the therapist should respond to the patient's texts or e-mails. Additional contact outside sessions may potentially precipitate dependency that is difficult to contain. The therapist must be on the alert for excessive texts or e-mails and must address dependency issues immediately, firmly, and compassionately.

That said, the use of e-mail or texting to "check in" with the therapist can provide important holding and containment for some patients in between sessions during occasional times when extra support may be needed. Such communications should be relatively short.

Therapists should be clear from the beginning what kind of e-mails or texts are appropriate, when the patient should use them, and how the therapist may respond. The therapist should be consistent with these guidelines, perhaps merely acknowledging reception of the communication with a brief message supporting the patient. For example, the therapist might write, *I received your e-mail today. I'm sorry you are having a hard time and hope reaching out has been helpful in reminding you that you have support. Please practice those skills we have been working on together—you did a great job with them last week. I look forward to talking with you about it when we meet on Friday.*

A major issue with dissociative patients is the use of e-mail or texts by specific parts. The therapist must beware of becoming embroiled in inner conflicts, in which parts are writing secrets to the therapist that they do not want other parts to know, or will only reveal themselves via telecommunication rather than in therapy. This sets up an impossible dilemma in which the therapist becomes a part of the dissociative system. In these cases, therapists might note that parts must not share secrets with them, and that parts are expected to engage during sessions. Therapy time is taken to explore why parts feel the need to keep secrets from each other and what might help parts participate during sessions.

On the positive side, sometimes a reluctant or ashamed part of the patient can begin to engage in treatment via e-mail, as it is less relationally intense than face-to-face sessions. As long as it leads to these parts eventually engaging in sessions, this can be helpful. Sometimes angry parts take the first risk to express anger with the therapist via this more indirect way, but it should not be abusive. The therapist should respond to the underlying process rather than the content of the e-mail and direct the response to the person as a whole to the degree possible.

If the patient has amnesia for sending a text or e-mail, the therapist should bring a copy of the communication to session and help the patient explore what is difficult about being aware that some part of herself is communicating with the therapist this way. Regardless of whether the patient as a whole or a dissociative part is communicating, the therapist insists that the patient as a whole—that is, all parts—must abide by the same boundaries.

CASE EXAMPLE OF RESPONDING TO E-MAIL FROM A PLEADING PART OF THE PATIENT: JOAN

Patient's e-mail: You don't know me. My name is Joanie and I am 6 years old. Sometimes I see you, but you can't see me. Big Joan doesn't want me to talk to you. She keeps me locked up. My bottom hurts all the time! My brother hurt my bottom, and Big Joan doesn't believe me. She says I am a liar. But he did too hurt me! Please help!

Therapist's e-mail response: Thank you for letting me know about this painful inner conflict. We will address it together in our next session. I can see how this is really hard for all of you. I am confident we will be able to find our way with it so that you as a whole person feel heard and helped.

CASE EXAMPLE OF RESPONDING TO AN E-MAIL FROM AN ANGRY PART OF THE PATIENT: SHARON

Patient's e-mail: You are such an idiot! Why do you try to help Sharon? She's hopeless and doesn't deserve help. She's just a loser. What is it with you? I guess you just want her money. Well, don't try that crap with me. I don't want anything to do with you, and I am not going to talk to you!

Therapist's e-mail response: I appreciate your honesty in letting me know you are angry with me and have strong feelings. Even though I hear that you don't want to talk with me, I am hopeful that we can deal with this more in session, as I am interested in learning more about what you think.

In the next session, the therapist learns that Sharon was initially unaware of having sent the e-mail, but received the therapist's response and was frightened by it. The therapist helped Sharon talk about her fear of her angry part and what it meant to express overt anger to the therapist. Sharon was reluctant to deal with her angry part, but the therapist reframed the intent of the part to be protective of Sharon, not wanting the therapist to take advantage of her and not wanting Sharon to be disappointed if therapy did not help. The therapist reassured all parts of Sharon that being angry was normal and healthy and that it would be all right to express it directly in session. The following session, the angry part was able to be present and was willing to talk with the therapist for a few minutes.

Text or e-mail should never be used to try to contact the therapist in an emergency. The patient should first try to reach the therapist by phone. If the therapist does not respond in a reasonable amount of time, the patient should contact emergency services, as indicated in a safety plan that has already been put in place.

CASE EXAMPLE OF SETTING NEW BOUNDARIES: LOUISA

Louisa was 35-year-old DID patient referred to a special treatment center for complex trauma-related disorders, as her former therapist had moved to another city. Although she had functioned as a social worker for several years in the past, she had a long history in the mental health system, had not had a job for many years, and received disability. She also had problems with substance abuse and self-harm and met criteria for borderline personality disorder (BPD). She was prone to crises. She had been treated for DID and BPD for a number of years. She had had several conflicts in the mental health system but was fond of her previous therapist. This therapist, however, reported in her referring letter that she had felt stuck in the therapy, having seen the patient more and more often in an effort to deal with many dysregulated child parts. She had felt isolated, unable to find local consultation. Louisa had become accustomed to at least two sessions a week and many crisis interventions. This therapist had also allowed child parts to come forward for lengthy parts of the sessions, as Louisa convinced her that this was the best way to regulate herself and calm her down.

When Louisa came for assessment, the DID diagnosis was confirmed with testing. Further assessment and case formulation made it clear that Louisa's previous treatment had caused many problems, fostering dependency. Louisa idealized her previous therapist but at the same time felt abandoned by her. She was convinced that she needed a continuation of the kind of treatment she had received earlier. Thus a major challenge, and a first goal in itself, was making a treatment plan with Louisa with different boundaries than she was used to in her previous therapy. She had to accept only one session a week, without "playtime" for her child parts. She had to learn to take responsibility for herself and to deal with crises in a different way. In the first half year, every session was a fight over the therapy frame and the boundaries that had been set. The therapist remained compassionate and explained to Louisa that she understood how hard it must be to make such big changes. Louisa gradually adjusted, and over the course of several years learned to regulate herself much better and was able to be seen weekly with minimal crisis intervention. She learned to accept and work with her child parts in constructive ways.

CORE CONCEPT

The therapist should discuss short- and long-term treatment goals and progress on a regular basis with patients and adjust treatment as needed.

In Louisa's case, the following short-term goals were set in her initial treatment plan. These goals were evaluated every three months:

1. Establish a therapeutic relationship with healthy boundaries.
2. Develop a better understanding of why a new treatment frame would be helpful.
3. Learn to take responsibility for herself and her child parts.
4. Learn to regulate herself when she felt she was in crisis.

Whose Goal Is It?

It is easy to lose sight of whether a goal is one to which the patient has actually agreed, or whether the therapist alone has decided to direct therapy toward a certain goal. Therapy works best when goals, however limited they may be, are collaboratively shared by patient and therapist.

Therapists must respect the goals of the patient as long as they are within a therapeutic range. Of course, goals are continually renegotiated, on both a macro and micro level. On a micro level, for example, we may agree with the patient temporarily in a session not to directly work with a certain part of which they are intensely afraid or ashamed, as in the case of Anna below. We shift the focus to the intense resistances to that part, helping the patient understand the functions of the part and become less phobically avoidant. On a macro level, for example, many dissociative patients do not have a goal of integration of their parts in mind when they come to treatment. Nevertheless, we are always working toward greater integration within the patient, which will indirectly support parts in becoming more integrated over time.

CASE EXAMPLE OF COLLABORATIVE GOAL SETTING: ANNA

Anna was a patient with DID who was extremely avoidant of her parts. She stated, *I want to sleep better and get rid of these nightmares, but I do not want to deal with the parts.* Her therapist agreed that they would work with sleep and her nightmares with standard approaches first. After several weeks of intervention, not only had Anna's sleep not improved, it had gotten much worse. The therapist then explained that in order to improve her sleep, Anna would need to be willing to understand a little more about her parts and in what ways they contributed to her sleep problems, as she suspected they had a major role, because Anna frequently reported amnesia for many different behaviors during the night. The therapist spent time with Anna, reassuring her that her fears were understandable and that she could take the time she needed to take small steps forward. This helped Anna decide together with the therapist that she could set a goal of exploring her fears of dissociative parts. Once the fear was decreased, an additional goal was set for greater communication and cooperation about sleeping at night.

Once a therapeutic goal is established, the next challenge for the therapist and patient is to determine what the patient needs in order to reach the goal, and what steps are manageable enough within the window of tolerance. This careful step-by-step approach paces therapy according to what the patient can tolerate, and gives the patient small experiences of mastery upon which competence and confidence can be built. If the patient is consistently unable to reach a goal, the therapist must consider if perhaps it has not been broken down into manageable steps, or whether the patient possesses the skills and motivation to take the next step.

In Anna's case (above), she and her therapist agreed that she would first take time to discuss her fears without having to make contact with any parts. Anna also wanted more explanation from her therapist about the way parts could influence her sleep (cf. Boon et al., 2011, for sleep issues in dissociative patients).

The Patient, Not the Therapist, Is Responsible for Meeting Goals
One countertransference pull for therapists is feeling the need to rescue and "do for" the patient. It is imperative to continually help patients take responsibility for their own treatment, in each session and outside of session, with the support and guidance of the therapist. This includes maintaining safety and practicing skills, inner communication, and functioning in daily life. It is crucial to convey to the patient that all parts are equally

responsible for each other, and that the person as a whole is responsible for her or his behavior.

Prioritizing Treatment Goals

In Anna's case, one of the first concrete goals in her treatment plan was improving sleep problems. These concrete goals, however, have to be part of some overarching, more general goals that we will discuss below.

The first goals of treatment are twofold: (a) establishing a therapeutic alliance and engaging with patients in ways that help them commit to at least a short-term treatment, and (b) establishing safety to the degree possible. The therapist should be open, flexible, and interested, but neither too probing and enthusiastic nor too uninvolved and silent. A modicum of compassion and active participation by the therapist may prevent a rush to dependency or a flight from connection. It can create the possibility of collaboration from the beginning.

Establish Safety

Safety is a major stumbling block for many dissociative patients. They often do not even understand the concept, having never had a felt sense of safety before. As noted in earlier chapters, therapists should not expect highly traumatized patients to trust them. So one initial goal for patients may be to start to feel safer (or less unsafe!) from session to session. This is often difficult, as many dissociative patients experience a lot of inner conflicts about whether therapy or a therapist is safe. In fact, it is not uncommon that there is an increase in "unsafe behaviors" in the beginning of therapy, caused by these inner conflicts about being in therapy. So feeling safe in session may take a long time, and the focus is on giving the therapist the benefit of the doubt in the moment and checking afterward to see how things went.

Safety needs are both internal and external. In fact, patients do not have safe lives because they feel unsafe internally. A common reason for feeling unsafe is the phobia of inner experience and inner reenactments of abuse among dissociative parts. Most patients are overwhelmed, frightened, ashamed, or disgusted by their inner experiences. They develop a phobia of their inner experiences—emotions, physical sensations or movements, impulses, behaviors, thoughts, wishes, fantasies, and needs. Many unsafe behaviors such as addictions, self-harm, and abusive relationships occur because patients are engaging in behaviors to avoid their intolerable inner experience and because they do not believe that they deserve safety. The phobia of inner experience compels patients strenuously to avoid internal discomfort, uncertainty, or conflict, and to feel unsafe within themselves.

A subset of the phobia of inner experiences includes the phobia of dissociative parts (see the case example of Anna above), because parts not only contain these avoided inner experiences but create additional symptoms of intrusion that can be quite frightening in themselves (Van der Hart et al., 2006). For example, many patients are terrified and ashamed of hearing the voices of dissociative parts, especially the angry or threatening ones and the crying or screaming child voices. The experience of being controlled by another force or of "coming to" and realizing they have done something they do not remember doing is terrifying. Patients fear they are crazy and feel out of control. Overwhelming emotions seem to come out of the blue. They cannot trust themselves, and they already do not trust others, so they may feel completely without safe harbor. Therapy initially focuses on building internal safety through careful pacing and psychoeducation, helping patients become curious about their inner experience. Understanding reluctance and resistance to exploring inner experience is thus an important topic early on the agenda for therapy (see Chapters 11 and 12 for more on resistance).

CORE CONCEPT

The therapist should return on a regular basis to case formulation, prognosis, and treatment planning in order to determine if therapy is on target and the patient is gaining safety and emotional skills.

Thus, while it is a laudable goal to create safety immediately for patients, this is not always possible. Some patients, or parts of them, remain in abusive relationships; others have parts that are chronically suicidal or continue to engage in high-risk behaviors for long periods of time. Many patients need a long time to reduce the intensity of conflict and reenactments of dissociative parts, so inner safety may be tenuous. The therapist should consider what is "safe enough" for treatment to proceed for each patient. Therapists may find it helpful to return from time to time to case formulation, prognosis, and pacing of the therapy to determine whether the patient is becoming safer in increments over time and what more might be done to support greater development of safety.

Balance Functioning in Daily Life With Therapy
The next goal in the early phase of treatment is stabilization and improving the quality of daily life by helping patients learn skills to regulate emotions and deal with PTSD and dissociative symptoms. Challenging dissociative patients present a conundrum. They have little capacity to deal with their

overwhelming traumatic experiences, but those unresolved experiences create ongoing difficulties in their everyday functioning. They want to feel better, but they need to realize many negative, painful feelings in order to do so. The therapist walks a fine line between helping the patient function better in the world and attending to difficult therapeutic work that can add to stress, depression, anxiety, and being overwhelmed. Ample research and a preponderance of clinical wisdom suggest the therapist should help stabilize patients and support function in daily life prior to working on traumatic memories (for example, see Courtois, 2008; Courtois & Ford, 2012, 2013; ISSTD, 2011; Van der Hart et al., 2006). Stabilization includes a focus on helping the patient understand and accept parts, develop compassion for parts, and learn to work effectively with parts to improve functioning, but not yet share traumatic memories (Boon et al., 2011; Van der Hart et al., 2006). However, as noted in Chapter 21, sometimes circumscribed integration of a traumatic memory may improve stabilization in carefully selected patients (Kluft, 2013; Boon & Van der Hart, 2003).

Set Major and Minor Goals

Within the context of establishing a therapeutic relationship and gaining more internal and external safety—challenging and quite big goals—it is often helpful to formulate smaller goals and ways to reach them with a patient. Marianne, the patient we described in the earlier chapters about assessment, acknowledged that she was terrified of her DID diagnosis and dissociative parts. She agreed that she should overcome this fear and it was an important goal early in her therapy. But as soon as the topic of having dissociative parts arose, she shut down and was not responsive. It was much easier for Marianne to talk about her daily life. Therefore, although she agreed to an overall treatment goal of overcoming fear, her therapist suggested that they also work on a more practical goal in daily life. This was done as a strategy both to improve her life and to help Marianne learn some skills to help her approach her fear. Marianne felt relieved, as she felt that she could achieve more in daily life and would not feel like such a failure all the time. She proposed to set herself a goal to learn to become more social and overcome some of her fears in social situations. With her therapist she made a step-by-step plan, spanning several months, which felt feasible for her. The plan consisted of (a) exploring her fears of social contacts, (b) analyzing her successes and failures in social contacts, (c) analyzing triggers in the past that had caused her to start to avoid even superficial social contact, and (d) working on cognitive correction of her fears and catastrophic predictions. After several months of working on this goal, Marianne was invited by a member of her choir to have dinner together before going to their evening choir practice. She decided to accept and proudly reported to her therapist that it has been quite nice. Marianne thus learned to gain mastery over her fear in a situation that felt more manageable than addressing parts. Once she learned she could confront her social fears, she was more amenable to working with parts of herself.

Stay on Track

It can be a difficult task to stay on track in the psychotherapy of dissociative disorders. On the one hand, patients can be highly avoidant and masterful at getting the therapist off topic. On the other hand, they may be crisis prone, so that the therapist jumps from one crisis to the next, or from one dissociative part to the next, without time to actually deal with the underlying causes of chronic urgency and switching. The therapist new to work with patients with dissociative disorders may also feel overwhelmed and try one technique after another to try to gain some stability in the therapy.

It is essential to stay on task with treatment goals, and to help all parts of the patient focus on the goals. The therapist should be firm but respectful, perhaps using gentle humor when appropriate to remind patients to come back to the topic at hand. Remember, phobic avoidance is a major defense in dissociative patients, so dissociative parts, by their very nature, will try to avoid what is painful. Therapists may need to guide the therapy more than usual, which can be a challenge if their training has instructed them to always follow the patient rather than lead. Even then, there is the question of what the patient can tolerate, and whether leading results in the patient being overwhelmed or prevents issues from emerging that might come up if the patient had more quiet space. It is a tightrope walk to keep therapy on target, to respect the patient's own pace, and to direct attention to what is being avoided. Again, thinking about the relationship as collaborative and about the work as focused on particular collaborative goals can be helpful in this regard.

With some highly dissociative patients, or with those who tend to meander aimlessly in sessions, it can be helpful to take notes during the session, so therapists can refer to them when they get lost.

CORE CONCEPT

Short-term goals that include small steps toward long-term goals can help keep therapy on track, so that overarching goals that need more time do not get lost.

One helpful way to maintain focus is to have concrete short-term goals for therapy written down for both the therapist and patient. The therapist can refer to these in each session, helping to redirect if needed. The dissociative ambience in the room may render the therapist foggy or sleepy, making it difficult to think clearly (Loewenstein, 1991a). It is not uncommon for both therapist and patient to be confused about what was just talked about.

CASE EXAMPLE OF STAYING ON TRACK IN THERAPY: JANE

Jane had many parts that switched frequently in session, and she changed the topic every time she switched. The therapist was overwhelmed with labyrinthine topics that seemed to go everywhere and nowhere all at once. Finally, the therapist encouraged Jane to pick one goal, that of helping a young part feel more present and safe, to which all parts of her could agree. Each time Jane switched topics, the therapist would remind all parts of the goal they were working toward at the moment and asked that each part hold whatever they wanted to talk about until another time. The therapist promised that all parts would be heard in good time. He also asked parts about their concerns about working with the child part. It became clear that some parts were afraid the child part would tell "stories of bad things that happened." The therapist reassured the patient as a whole that the goal at this time was to help the child part feel more safe and present, not to "tell." Sharing traumatic events could occur only when all parts were in greater agreement that it was appropriate to do so. Though the therapist had to work hard to keep Jane on topic, he was able to help the child part and enlist other parts to take care of her internally. Jane's switching diminished significantly as parts felt that therapy was respectful to Jane's overall need for pacing.

CASE EXAMPLE OF STAYING ON TRACK IN THERAPY: MARIANNE

Marianne would become nonresponsive and could not remember what was being discussed in therapy sometimes. Even her therapist found it difficult to remember what they were talking about when Marianne had one of these episodes. Marianne dissociated often during the session, especially when the subject was about her diagnosis and dissociative parts. It was hard for Marianne to focus on this for more than a couple of minutes. Thus, the therapist had to address Marianne's underlying conflicts. She did so by "talking through" to all parts inside (Kluft, 1982), without actually mentioning the word *part*, as she guessed the term would only increase the conflicts: *Marianne, I see that you struggle to stay present especially when we talk about your dissociative symptoms. I wonder if there might be many thoughts and ideas in your mind and perhaps some concerns about talking about dissociation?* Marianne was able to nod in affirmation but could not to answer; she seemed frozen.

The therapist continued: *Even now I see that it is so difficult for you, and I am sorry. I just want to say that I am interested in these different thoughts and worries about being here and that all of them need our attention in due time. I wonder if perhaps you might be able to write down some of them; then, when you feel ready, we could talk about them one at a time.* Marianne nodded yes, and the therapist continued, *Great. I hope that your thoughts and feelings are willing to become a little quieter. Maybe they could just step back for a moment or temporarily find a quiet space in your mind so that you can concentrate on just one at a time. I wonder if that might be possible right now, because we are finding a way for you to express them in writing. I want to reiterate that every thought and feeling is equally important and needs to be heard and understood, and we will do that in your own time and your own way, which I am sure we will find together. Feel free to write at home when you feel less pressured. If it doesn't feel right, feel free to stop, and we will sort it out. I want to thank you, Marianne, to thank all corners of your mind for listening and participating so we can find our way together. Now, would you be willing to stand up with me and walk around the room so you can feel more grounded?*

Marianne and her therapist got up and walked around together, and even laughed a bit. Marianne became much more present and was able to say that indeed there was a voice that was constantly telling her that she should not come to therapy and she was not allowed to talk about the other voices. The therapist thanked Marianne and all corners of her mind for allowing that to be shared, and promised that the next session they would find a way to deal with it that was acceptable to Marianne and her whole mind.

During the next session, the therapist was able to negotiate spending 10 minutes each session exploring one of these "thoughts," and the rest of the session discussing topics about daily life, such as trying to become a bit more social. The part that was most adamant that Marianne not deal with her dissociation was attended to first, and the therapist made strong efforts to create a working alliance with this part (see Chapter 17). In the course of the following months, Marianne gradually was more present, and this voice became quieter, as she shared different thoughts and feelings about accepting her dissociation. At the same time, the therapist began to make contact with some of the most critical voices that were so against Marianne being in therapy.

Work With Dissociative Parts of the Patient

Treatment planning with patients who are dissociative is quite similar to treatment planning for all patients in psychotherapy, with one major difference: it must accommodate all parts of the patients. Chapter 10 is focused on the specifics of working with dissociative parts. Briefly, work with parts requires that the patient is at least willing to accept the existence of parts, so there has to be some realization about the diagnosis. So, often early treatment may need to focus on helping the patient gradually accept these parts (overcoming the phobia of dissociative parts) before any direct work with parts can begin. The therapist cannot push, but rather needs to be with the patient. Most important in Phase 1 is establishing a working alliance with parts that are against therapy or seem to be unwilling to participate in therapy (see Chapter 10 for a general description on working with parts).

There are times when it is not appropriate to work with dissociative parts, and this must also be considered in planning treatment. According to Kluft (1996a), the therapist should not work with dissociative parts when (a) all parts are living in trauma-time and are overwhelmed—that is, when a patient's entire system is disrupted; (b) patients need all their energies directed to a stressful period in daily life; (c) patients are overwhelmed with other (daily life, physical, or mental) problems and do not have the capacity to tolerate work with parts; (d) therapy is short-term or supportive rather than uncovering; and (e) the therapist is unprepared (and without adequate consultation or supervision) to work with parts.

CASE EXAMPLE OF DEVELOPING A TREATMENT PLAN: BOB

In the previous two chapters, we described the assessment information on Bob. He clearly had a good prognosis. He accepted his diagnosis and was willing to make contact with his dissociative parts once he had overcome his initial shame. Moreover, Bob was supported by his partner and some good friends. In Bob's case, both short-term and long-term goals could be set early in treatment. It was clear that Bob had enough ego strength and support to be able to proceed to Phase 2. So his short-term goals all had a focus on improving inner collaboration, learning more techniques to regulate his emotions, and preparing for Phase 2 work.

Bob and the therapist agreed on the following short-term goals: (a) to learn more grounding techniques to stay in the present, (b) to create inner safe places for parts stuck in trauma-time, and (c) to understand and gain some collaboration with all of his dissociative parts, including the angry voice he heard. For Bob, the greatest challenge was to understand that the angry voice of the perpetrator was in fact a dissociative part of himself, and that he had to develop some compassion and then cooperation with this part. He was afraid to communicate directly with this part and feared its anger. So in the end, the therapist, with Bob's agreement, made contact with this part first and established a working alliance. Once this part felt acknowledged by the therapist, Bob could gradually accept and work with this part more easily. Bob was then able to proceed rapidly to Phase 2.

Summary

The therapist can plan treatment in a reasonable, sequenced, and paced way, and be flexible in revising the plan as needed. A collaborative approach that focuses on shared goals is necessary. The therapist can plan accordingly how best to achieve those goals given the patient's strengths and deficits.

Once the patient has come to a reasonable acceptance of the diagnosis (which may still vacillate from time to time), the next step is to plan how and when to work with dissociative parts. Treatment planning involves knowing which approaches to take and when to take them. General principles of when and how to work with parts are primarily based on the patient's window of tolerance and complexity of dissociation of the personality, which are discussed in Chapter 10.

Further Explorations

7.1 Do you make a formal written treatment plan with your patients?
7.2 What might be some challenges in sharing a treatment plan with a particular patient?
7.3 What are your policies regarding texts and e-mails from patients? What are the pros and cons of your policy? Take time to discuss colleagues' policies with them.

CHAPTER 8

Principles of Treatment

I now declare myself a practitioner of "plain old therapy."

—Jon G. Allen (2013, p. xxi)

The treatment of dissociative disorders may seem very different than other psychotherapies, as it concerns work with a divided personality and sense of self. However, the best approach is simply good, solid psychotherapy, with the addition of an understanding of and ability to work with trauma and dissociation. While techniques are helpful, it is the ability to follow the essential principles of psychotherapy and to maintain a working relationship with the patient as a whole that truly makes treatment effective with dissociative patients.

Many sources address treatment principles for complex trauma patients (e.g., Briere & Scott, 2012; D. Brown et al., 1998; Chu, 2011; Courtois & Ford, 2012, 2013; Herman, 1997). Others offer specific principles for working with dissociative disorders (e.g., ISSTD, 2011; Kluft & Fine, 1993; Putnam, 1997; Steele et al., 2005; Van der Hart et al., 2006). Below we discuss these major treatment principles that support a rational, sequenced treatment of complex dissociative disorders.

Good Psychotherapy Is the Foundation for Effective Treatment of Dissociative Disorders

Effective therapy for patients with complex dissociative disorders begins and ends with the principles and approaches of good psychotherapy in general, with the ability to foster mentalizing, regulatory capacities, and self-compassion (e.g., Allen, 2001, 2012). Without this essential foundation, treatment of dissociation at best falls short, and at worst can be disastrous.

Focus on Process, Not Content

Throughout this volume we highlight how essential it is to focus on and work with the process of the patient and the therapeutic relationship. We highly recommend that therapists first become trained in some type of psychotherapy approach that addresses process, and which offers a frame for understanding the inner conflicts and defenses in the patient, both internally and in relationships. Therapy can easily get bogged down in content: what happened at home last week, what happened in the traumatic past, the many crises of daily life, what is expected to happen in the future, and all the differences between and characteristics of dissociative parts that can become so fascinating to both patient and therapist. The more therapists can help the patient stay in the moment with what is happening internally and in the relationship right now, the more effective therapy will be.

CORE CONCEPT

Therapists should have a good grasp of how to understand and work with process with dissociative patients. Simply learning techniques and skills is insufficient.

Concentrating on the subjective experience of the patient during sessions, and staying with the moment-to-moment changes in the therapeutic relationship, are profoundly important in facilitating change and integration. The therapist must often reflect on what patients are trying to communicate about their experience and about the therapeutic relationship.

What happened in the traumatic past is important for context, but *how* the patient is affected by what happened is really the focus of treatment, as well as how the patient may be enacting this in the relationship with the therapist. Of course, traumatic experiences are essential to integrate and should not be ignored, but they are dealt with in the context of the patient's intrapsychic and relational experiences in the present.

For example, Mara was a patient with DID who would often tell long stories about the many times she felt hurt in her family interactions, often focused on the problems with the other person. The therapist would make occasional comments about how painful it must be for Mara not to be heard or respected. Gradually she was able to help Mara notice that she was fearful that the therapist would not hear or respect her. The work could then shift to Mara's experience in the moment rather than telling repetitive stories in which she avoided her own dynamics in relationships.

CORE CONCEPT

The content of traumatic memories should not be ignored, but therapists should understand and work with the dynamics of the patient's inner system and relationships when traumatic memories emerge or are avoided. What happens within the patient and what happens in relationship when traumatic memories are evoked is an essential focus of treatment.

Content focuses on:

- what the patient says and does,
- the content of traumatic memories and crises, and
- the overt manifestations of dissociative parts.

Process focuses on:

- underlying meanings and core beliefs;
- defenses and resistances;
- the function of and relationships between dissociative parts, rather than on the parts themselves;
- the reasons why dissociation of the personality is maintained;
- emotions and how they are experienced;
- felt experiences in the moment;
- implicit communications between patient and therapist;
- transference and countertransference;
- how the patient talks about a topic;
- how the patient experiences relationships; and
- what happens for the patient when he or she talks about a topic—for example, changes in voice, muscle tension, and posture.

Below are some examples of helping the patient focus on process:

- As you are talking, what is happening for you, and for parts of you?
- I notice you are looking away more and more, and your body is

slumping. Can you notice that with me and be curious about what is happening?

- I notice there seems to be tension in the room, perhaps a kind of anger or irritation. Are you aware of it too?
- What is your experience of sharing that very private and vulnerable experience with another person—with me—right now?
- There seems to be a lot of conflict about remembering. I wonder if we might help all parts of you understand that conflict a bit more.
- When you experience that conflict, what do you notice inside (or in your body)?
- Let's explore what happens for you in those moments just before you leave session, when you get really distressed. Let's find a way to help you with that.
- When you hear that critical voice, what happens for you?
- I wonder if we could explore what parts of you experienced last week when you felt I didn't take you seriously enough, even though you say you completely understand. I don't know for sure, but perhaps there is something more that could be important.

Provide Treatment Within the Window of Tolerance for Both Patient and Therapist

Treatment must be provided according to what both patient and therapist can tolerate. This treatment principle is closely aligned with the principle of "safety first." Whenever the therapy is outside the range of tolerance, the relationship and therapy no longer feel safe, and defense is evoked in patient and therapist. Learning can only occur effectively within a moderated range of emotional arousal. Thus, therapists need to be alert to when therapy might move faster, or when, as is often the case, it should move slower or in a different direction.

CORE CONCEPT

Pacing requires that therapists determine how much time and what kind of support the patient needs to contain and ground in order to leave sessions on time and be safe and modulated.

Effective pacing involves managing the session so that there is sufficient time at the end for the patient to be contained enough to leave. Kluft (1991) suggested a *rule of thirds*, in which sessions are roughly divided into three segments. The first third, which may be quite brief, involves checking in and preparing for the work of the session. This checking in is usually done with the part that functions in daily life. The second third is the major work of the session, often involving emotional experiences, such as talking with parts or addressing a certain symptom. The last third may be longer or shorter, depending on the need of the patient, and is focused on helping the patient (or part functioning in daily life) to become fully oriented in the present, contain those feelings that the patient has been working on in the session, and prepare for the week.

Patients Who Need Small Steps

Therapists tend to expect too much change too quickly in patients who have long histories of developmental disruptions and trauma. Imagine changing all of your eating, sleeping, and exercise habits, your inner dynamics and relational patterns, and your coping strategies in a couple of weeks and learning how to manage emotions for the first time after a few times of practice! In an era of short-term therapy, the therapist (and patient) may feel tremendous pressure to see rapid improvement in many arenas when it may not be realistic. Many patients improve, but only slowly over long periods of time. Small steps are often needed, rather than giant leaps. With each small step patients take toward mastery, the therapist should help patients reward themselves in some way to continue on: At least I tried to do it, even though I didn't quite get it right. I was able to figure out what to do after the fact; next time I will try to think ahead of time. This time I knew what to do but couldn't quite stay with it, but at least I stopped to think about it first. I do it sometimes, not always—but at least I am doing it!

An early determination of the general treatment trajectory and prognosis of the patient (poor, fair, good) will help both therapist and patient accept a reasonable pace of improvement. Some patients are robust. Regardless of their level of functioning, they are motivated and persevere through thick and thin. Other patients are extremely and chronically phobic of dissociative parts or are highly invested in remaining separate, lack any self-compassion, and feel helpless and hopeless. These latter patients need a slower pace and a more supportive approach that focuses on a greater degree of functioning in daily life. The poorer the prognosis for a patient, the slower therapy likely needs to go.

The old adage "slower is faster" is a good model for the treatment of dissociative disorders. Both patient and therapist often feel an urgent need to make the patient better, to work on traumatic memories, and to integrate parts. The therapist can best think of therapy with these patients as a marathon, not a sprint. There may be pressure to take giant leaps in a given session—for example, to have the patient accept and have compassion for an especially challenging part of herself. However, taking such a large integrative action and breaking it down into small and manageable steps is often much more effective and prevents further resistance.

To that end, therapists might first establish cooperation, even if there is little trust, in order to take one small step at a time: *Do you think you would be able to give me and you the benefit of the doubt as we take this next step* [which is described in detail to the patient]? *At any moment if something feels amiss, I want you to let me know immediately and we will stop. It is important for all parts of you to feel comfortable enough to experiment with taking this step, and to know how important it is to stop when something doesn't feel right to you. If you or any part of you finds it hard to speak up, you can even use a nonverbal signal, such as raising your hand. What sort of signal would you prefer? Let's practice having you stop me now.* . . .

Next, the therapist might go back over the next step (for example, having two parts communicate or work on a traumatic memory) and explore any concerns, hesitations, or fears that any part of the patient might have. Each of these should be addressed sufficiently before moving forward. Then the therapist must be willing to stop when the patient so asks in order to build trust consistently and for the patient to feel like a collaborative partner. It is also important to remember that stopping and addressing a concern does not at all mean the intervention or topic is abandoned. Often just the respectful act of pausing and listening to concerns is all that is needed is for patients to feel heard and to be convinced they can indeed stop. This builds confidence, and the patients are more likely able to then move forward again.

Pacing also means taking the time to stay with a positive experience to ensure the patient is able to actually take it in. All too often, both therapist and patient are quickly off to the next thing. The idea is to savor the moment, so that it can become more a part of familiar experience (Ogden et al., 2006). In following sessions, the therapist can check in about how the patient has experienced a change, and whether anxiety has emerged or not. Often, small experiences of positive change must be reiterated again and again to become more a part of the patient's ongoing experience.

Changing the focus of therapy as a pacing strategy. Often, the pace of therapy is not the problem; rather, the *focus* of therapy needs to be different. For example, a common problem is for therapists to jump into work with traumatic memories with dissociative patients before they have the regulatory skills and cooperation among parts to manage. Therapy may be able proceed at the same pace, but with a focus on skills building, containment of traumatic memories, and acceptance and cooperation among dissociative parts as preparation for work on traumatic memories. The patient will become more stable simply through this shift in treatment.

Once regulatory skills are in place, treatment of traumatic memories can commence.

Another example of an effective shift in focus pertains to premature grief work. Sometimes when therapists try to support a patient to grieve and experience loss, despair and self-destructive behaviors only deepen. This typically happens because the patient is still unable to experience positive emotion and a sense of competence and positive experiences in daily life that serve as a foundation and container for grieving. The patient may be unable to experience the present moment and becomes lost in the past. Helping the patient learn to be in the present and have positive emotions and experiences must precede a focus on grief and loss.

Dependency and pacing. Therapists must be able to tolerate the intense dependency and need of the patient without rescuing or withdrawing, as we discuss in Chapter 13. The treatment frame helps contain the patient's dependency behaviors. The overly fast pace of therapy sometimes implicitly encourages a chronic crisis mode, so slowing therapy down may decrease crisis. For example, if the therapist continues with an intensely emotional or otherwise difficult subject right up to the end of session, and the patient does not have time to become grounded and stable, it is likely that the patient will have a crisis after session. Or perhaps crisis is induced because the therapist insists on having the patient confront dissociative parts without first addressing the phobia of dissociative parts.

The Therapist's Own Pace

Therapy can only go as far as a given therapist has the capacity to take it. When the therapist is overwhelmed by the patient's emotions or story, the therapy is then outside the window of tolerance of the therapist. Immediate consultation and perhaps personal therapy are necessary, or else the decision to transfer the patient to another therapist may be made with consultation. The therapist should not be the one for whom therapy must slow down, at least over the long term. Of course, if a therapist does not feel well and an intense session has been planned, it is certainly acceptable to let the patient know you are not at your best and give the patient the choice of continuing the work or postponing and doing something less intense for this session. But this is a temporary relational process, not a countertransference per se.

Sometimes therapists can use their feeling of being overwhelmed as a barometer for whether therapy may be too overwhelming for the patient. Some patients are so chronically intense or produce such vast quantities of information—verbal stories, journals, e-mails, artwork, and so on—that the therapist is unable to integrate it all. This can be a clear indication that a patient may also be unable to integrate. In this case, more is not better. It can be helpful to have a discussion about this with the patients, exploring their experience of sharing all this information and what they hope to accomplish by it.

Recognize and Utilize the Patient's Somatic Experience

As we noted in Chapter 1, being able to notice and work with patients' somatic experiences and physical actions can be an additional strategy in treating dissociative disorders. It is important to note that somatic work does not need to include touch. The therapist can comment on patients' gestures, posture, and muscle tension, explore sensations and felt experience, and encourage patients to practice new patterns or try experiments of movement and awareness without ever touching them.

Some approaches are already incorporating more work with somatic awareness, experience, and actions, such as EMDR and some CBT mindfulness approaches. Pat Ogden has developed the most comprehensive and theoretically integrated sensorimotor approach, helpful for traditional and body therapists who work with complex trauma and dissociation (sensorimotor psychotherapy; Ogden et al., 2006; Ogden & Fisher, 2015). But others have also made important contributions to practical clinical interventions (Levine., 2008; Levine & Mate, 2010; Rothschild, 2000).

Therapists first need to simply become more comfortable with noticing their own somatic experiences. This can provide a kind of inner map for understanding and exploring a patient's somatic experiences. Indeed, the therapist's body is the locale of countertransference and projective identification. We know reenactments are happening because we first sense something different in our bodies, even if only implicitly. Next, the therapist can practice getting comfortable noticing the patient's experience, and then sharing that awareness with the patient, inviting curiosity.

While it is relatively simple to notice somatic experience, the real challenge is in what to do with it. Below we list several possibilities, but these are far from comprehensive.

- Explore what happens next once a sensation or movement is identified.
  - And as you notice that, what happens next?
  - So you want to run. Can you make slow movements with your legs, like running in slow motion, and see what happens?
  - As you notice that sensation, can you also be aware of that child part of you? What happens with that sensation now?

- Use somatic experience as a positive resource.
  - Notice the feeling in your body when you feel connected.
  - Notice what it feels like to sit up straight and put your shoulders back. Can you take a body picture of that so that you have that feeling available to you whenever you need it?
  - Can you share that feeling with other parts of you, so they can also have this resource?
- Explore relational and physical boundaries.
  - (After carefully setting up an experiment) So just notice what happens in your body when I move this pillow toward you. Notice how each part reacts. Is there any part of you that would like to push the pillow away? What does that feel like? Would you be willing to experiment by pushing the pillow away from you?
- Use somatic awareness as a tool to regulate.
  - So, that cold feeling in your belly you describe seems to signal that you feel really alone, and usually you feel it before you hurt yourself. Let's brainstorm about what you can do besides hurting yourself when you first notice that cold feeling.
- Reduce the phobia of dissociative parts.
  - (Following a lot of psychoeducation) When you think of that angry part or have a picture of it in your mind, what happens? You feel tight and afraid. Could you imagine that maybe that part of you is trying to protect you, and has been doing so since you were young? When you think of that, what do you notice inside (or in your body)? So your body is more relaxed. Good, just stay with that and notice that when you realize this part of you is trying to help, you can relax a bit more.

Somatic work can easily be paired with imaginal work—for example, helping a patient get a felt sense of a safe space, not merely a visual representation of one. In several chapters we have discussed the utility of helping patients focus on their felt experience. While somatic work is not always necessary with every patient, it truly enhances treatment and improves the skill set of the therapist.

Use Level of Functioning in Daily Life as a Major Signpost of Progress

Ideally, patients would feel better early in therapy. However, because dissociative patients have avoided realizing so many painful experiences, it is likely that they may have more negative feelings as they begin to realize more about their lives. Of course, realization has to be paced so the patient does not decompensate. However, even when they may feel more genuine emotions that are painful, they may suffer less because they are learning to accept and tolerate inner experience instead of avoid it. At the same time, patients may need help in functioning more effectively in daily life, even though they continue to struggle with negative emotions. One of the major signposts of progress is for the patient's functioning in daily life to at least be maintained, and hopefully improved. If the patient's functioning declines, the pacing and work of therapy should be considered as a one possible contribution.

CORE CONCEPT

The patient's general level of functioning should be maintained or improved by treatment, with any regressions being short-lived. If the patient has increasing difficulty in dealing with daily life, the intensity and pacing of therapy must be examined as a potential contributor.

Therapy is about quality, not quantity. Just because a patient brings reams of journal pages to session, or has a lot to talk about, has intense emotions, switches among parts in session, or spends hours each day mapping parts and writing up extensive descriptions of all of their preferences does not mean the patient is moving in a positive direction in therapy. The question is whether working with that material helps the patient function better over time and contributes to further internal integration. The ability to balance an inward focus on painful emotions and experiences and continue with daily life is important for long-term functioning.

For example, when a patient is producing hundreds of pages of journaling every week, at what price are these writings produced, and what is being neglected in daily life? What is happening with the patient's children, partner, friends, work, study, household chores, and bills? What is the purpose of the writing? Is it perhaps an avoidance of dealing with daily life, which feels overwhelming or boring? Does the patient feel unheard and unseen unless mass quantities of information are given? Does the patient feel the therapist cannot possibly understand unless he knows every detail and nuance? Is the writing actually an avoidance of fully accepting what happened? Is the patient suffering from obsessive-compulsive disorder, and is the writing a symptom of that particular problem? The function of the writing becomes the focus, rather than the content of the writing.

Some of the best markers of progress are often small positive changes in daily life. For example, a patient might call a friend after months of isolation, pay bills on time, feel safe for a few moments with a partner, enjoy time with another person, function better at work because parts are more cooperative, or see a medical doctor after years of procrastination.

Communicate Clearly and Clarify What the Patient Means

Language matters. It can be subjective and vague, so we need to help our patients clarify as needed and make sure we are also clear about what we mean. We should be sure we are both talking about the same thing in essentially the same way. For example, when patients say, *I am upset*, therapists should understand that what a particular patient means is that he is angry, not anxious or sad. What do patients actually experience when they inform the therapist that they are "dissociating" or "stressed"? What do they mean when they say a family visit "went OK"? What do patients mean when they say they "had a bad day"? What is happening internally; what are their thoughts, feelings, and somatic experiences?

Set and Keep Good Boundaries and a Clear Treatment Frame

As noted in previous chapters, and in every publication on treating complex PTSD and dissociative disorders, it is essential to set consistent and clear boundaries with patients whose boundaries have been terribly violated and who may have little sense of other people's needs and limits (e.g., Chu, 2011; Courtois & Ford, 2012, 2013; ISSTD, 2011; Kluft & Fine, 1993; Van der Hart et al., 2006). Good boundaries and treatment frame also reduce the possibility of therapists acting out their rescue fantasies or becoming drawn in by the patient in other ways. Finally, boundaries protect therapists by ensuring therapy is contained and not intruding into personal life outside of therapy too much. Specific boundaries were discussed earlier in Chapters 2 and 6.

CORE CONCEPT

Boundaries are essential. While they should be somewhat flexible within a limited range, they should not change merely because a patient wants or demands something, or because the therapist is feeling intensely.

A general guideline is that boundaries need to be kept in the face of a patient's desires, demands, or crises in the moment, as well as when the therapist has intense feelings or wishes to rescue or to avoid. Boundaries should be relatively, though perhaps not exactly, similar for all the patients of a given therapist. If a therapist has markedly different boundaries and limits with one patient (for example, running sessions over consistently, having extended sessions or frequent phone calls or e-mails, or some personal involvement in the patient's work or personal life), this can serve as a red flag that countertransference issues need to be addressed and boundaries reset. Remember that it is much more painful and dysregulating for patients when therapists have to set firmer boundaries after being lax. This is typically perceived as withholding, punitive, and rejecting. So it is better to begin with firmer boundaries and occasionally flex them as needed.

Understand the Role of Hypnosis, Trance, and Trance Logic in Dissociative Parts

Therapists need to be aware of the hypnotic bedrock on which dissociative disorders are built. Most patients with OSDD or DID are highly hypnotizable, engaging in spontaneous self- or autohypnosis (ISSTD, 2011; Dale, Berg, Elden, Ødegård, & Holte, 2009; Janet, 1898/1911; Kluft, 1982, 1983, 1985b, 1988a, 1989, 1994b, 1994c, 1994d, 2012, 2013; Spiegel, 1990). From the late 19th century to the present, clinicians have acknowledged the central role of hypnosis and hypnotic techniques in the treatment of dissociative disorders. Many techniques used today have their origins in hypnosis (Kluft, 2013), and in ego state therapy (D. Brown & Fromm, 1986; Phillips & Frederick, 1995; J. G. Watkins & Watkins, 1991, 1997), which is a special hypnotherapeutic approach. For example, safe space, dissociative table or meeting spaces, and containment imagery all emerged from the clinical hypnosis traditions.

Hypnotic trance often occurs regularly in dissociative patients. All dissociative parts are characterized by a certain degree of *trance logic*. This term, coined by Orne (1959), indicates a special type of concrete thinking that is often paired with strong imaginative components, in which there is a decrease in critical judgment and an increased tolerance of logical incongruity. It inhibits the ability to reflect and take perspective, and it involves very concrete thinking and psychic equivalence (confusion between internal and external reality). In trance, dissociative patients more easily think in terms of images than words. For example, a patient can say with no sense of incongruence that her mother lives in her head, or that a part is sitting on the sofa next to her, or that there is a hallway inside with many doors, some of which are sealed shut. A "dead" part may talk with the therapist, and a part that is a "tree" can also has a lively conversation with the therapist or comfort a small child part. The perpetrator may be experienced as living internally, even though the actual person is dead or old and infirm. A deaf part somehow knows what is being said in session. Patients may see their hands as those of a small child, or a child part may see the adult hands as not belonging to her. One part tries to kill the body, so she can live on without the irritation of other parts. Patients may say they do not lose time, but give many examples of serious time loss with no explanation.

Each of these examples indicates the presence of hypnotic trance and trance logic, in which logic is suspended and some salient information is not noticed—such as that brains do not have hallways, hands do not change size, and there is only one body. Patients do not sense that anything is amiss with their perceptions.

Dissociative patients are more often in trance than not, so the therapist who is trained in hypnosis can make use of trance to further integrative work (e.g., D. Brown & Fromm, 1986; Fine, 1993, 1999; ISSTD, 2011; Janet, 1898/1911; Kluft, 1982, 1983, 1985b, 1988a, 1989, 1990a, 1990b, 1992a, 1992b, 1994b, 1996a, 2001, 2013; Phillips & Frederick, 1995; Spiegel, 1990; Van der Hart, 1991). However, the therapist must also help the patient to get *out* of trance and live in the present as much as possible (Kluft, 2013). Therapists are encouraged to learn classical hypnosis, as they will have a much greater understanding of the phenomenon of hypnosis in dissociative patients and will gain many effective tools. Many of the case examples in this book include hypnotic languaging by the therapist.

There are some caveats regarding the use of hypnosis with trauma survivors in general, particularly around recovering dissociative memories (e.g., Allen, 2001; D. Brown et al., 1998; ISSTD, 2011; Kluft, 1996b). Trance can enhance emotional intensity and blur the boundaries between fantasy and reality. Thus, the veracity of memories recalled under hypnosis has been called into question. However, there are examples of both accurate and false memories retrieved with these techniques. All memory is a representation, not an exact reconstruction of events, whether it is recalled under hypnosis or not. And as Allen has noted, "An individual with a complex history of childhood maltreatment has memories spanning all levels of accuracy" (2001, p. 134). It is not the modality of hypnosis itself that is problematic in the treatment of dissociative disorders but rather its application by those who have insufficient understanding of the nature of memory, trance phenomena, and suggestibility (ISSTD, 2011). In the hands of a careful and well-trained therapist, hypnosis is a wonderful and powerful adjunct in the treatment of dissociative disorders, and often underappreciated.

Treat All Dissociative Parts Equally and as Aspects of One Person

The literature is unanimous in insisting that therapists view dissociative parts as aspects of a single individual, not as separate entities. Even when the patient does not share this view, the therapist's experience stays in the room: *Even though I know you experience being very separate, I still view you as one person.* Otherwise, therapists can collude with patients' insistence in disowning important aspects of their experience, and focus on fascination with different parts rather than on the true work of therapy.

Therapists are also encouraged to treat all parts with the same acceptance and openness, not favoring one over another (Chu, 2011; Kluft, 1993a; Kluft & Foote, 1999; Van der Hart et al., 2006). In general, it is easy to like certain aspects of a person and not others. For example, we enjoy the humor of a colleague but dislike his controlling and berating behaviors when he is stressed. In complex dissociative disorders, this tendency is magnified, in part by patients who disown aspects of the self that are not acceptable and who do their best to keep those parts out of therapy so that the therapist cannot even access them. The therapist is implicitly directed not to notice certain parts of the patient, or to be extremely fearful or disgusted by them, much as the patient is. If the therapist finds certain parts charming or repellent, the odds of treating those parts differently increases. Instead, these reactions should be acknowledged and explored as important information about the patient's intrapsychic organization and ways of being in relationships.

Never Try to "Get Rid of" Dissociative Parts

Dissociative parts are not entities that can be killed off or exiled from existence. They can be transformed and they can be integrated, but they cannot simply be ignored or told to go away because they present a problem. Of course, patients wish it could be so easy, and they might try to convince therapists to try it if they do not know better. But disowned parts must be accepted and changed. Thus, the long-term goal is to help all parts of the patient understand and accept each part, even though certain behaviors are not acceptable. In this way every part begins to have more in common with the others, sharing similar skills, emotions, and beliefs, to the point that there is no longer the need for parts to be separate. After all, healthy development of self involves being creative, adaptable, and flexible enough that we can cope with whatever comes.

CORE CONCEPT

One long-term goal of treatment is to help patients accept with compassion all parts of themselves, and to separate disapproval of behaviors from disapproval of parts of self.

Constantly Monitor and Manage Transference and Countertransference

As we have noted in previous chapters and will continue to emphasize throughout the book, therapists' reactions to patients are essential to understand. If therapists do not pay close attention, they will miss interchanges rich with the possibility for intervention and change. Awareness of countertransference, honest discussion of it with colleagues and supervisors or consultants, and regular self-reflection are necessary components of treatment.

When the Therapist Becomes Defensive or Makes a Mistake, Repair With the Patient

Every therapist will have countertransference reactions, will be defensive, or will behave inadequately in some way with every patient. This can be predicted early in therapy for patients by saying something like, *When I make a mistake or misunderstand you, what is the best way for us to handle that together?* This models humanness, humility, and a willingness to repair from the very beginning of therapy. As discussed in Chapter 4, repair is essential to the health of relationships in general, and especially to the therapeutic relationship. It is the responsibility of therapists to get themselves grounded and clear, and go to the patient to repair the misunderstanding, misattunement, or hurt.

CORE CONCEPT

Therapists must learn to repair relational ruptures with humility, even when they have done nothing wrong.

View Resistance as Protection

One of the most helpful approaches in the treatment of complex trauma patients is to take a compassionate and pragmatic view of what the literature calls resistance. This is the patient's seeming unwillingness, for example, to feel, to remember, to practice a skill, to communicate with a dissociative part, to stop self-harm behaviors, or to collaborate as part of the treatment team. Our task is to understand the function of resistance as a protection against something the patient is not yet able or ready to experience (Messer, 2002). These actions are attempts to solve a problem. Even if they are effective (for example, to help a patient avoid something that is intolerable), they still come at great cost. When therapists approach the resistance indirectly by being curious about its protective function, they are already helping the patient have a different conversation about change. Thus, therapists can take themselves out of a potential power struggle, which they would always lose anyway. In this way, therapists can hand back to the patient the possibility of taking smaller steps toward a goal instead of continuing to shore up resistance. Many ways to recognize and work with resistance are discussed in Chapters 11 and 12.

Further Explorations

8.1 What principles currently guide your treatment of patients? Did any of the principles discussed in this chapter surprise you? Do you disagree with any of them or have additional ones that you might add?

8.2 Take one of your current cases and review it to see if you are applying principles of treatment.

8.3 Practice breaking down larger goals into smaller steps for a patient. For example, try to list steps in learning how to regulate emotions or communicating with a dissociative part. With what steps would you start? If you have difficulties, enlist your colleagues to help you.

CHAPTER 9

Phase-Oriented Treatment: An Overview

Phase-oriented treatment may be rather straightforward for relatively simple cases of traumatization. However, it may be much more complex, with more alterations among phases, and need to address multifaceted and chronic issues.
—Onno van der Hart, Ellert Nijenhuis, and Kathy Steele (2006, p. 15)

The standard of care for the treatment of dissociative disorders is a tripartite phase-oriented treatment (e.g., D. Brown et al., 1998; Chu, 2011; Courtois & Ford, 2013; Herman, 1997; Howell, 2011; ISSTD, 2011; Loewenstein & Welzant, 2010; Van der Hart et al., 2006). This approach has been shown to decrease dissociation and other symptoms (Brand & Loewenstein, 2014). Therapy begins with stabilization, then treatment of traumatic memory, and finally integration of dissociative parts and more standard therapy issues. Almost all patients need to start with at least some development of greater emotional skills, and Phase 1 can be prolonged for some. Phased treatment is not actually linear; rather, it is recursive, returning as needed to earlier issues according to the needs of the patient. For example, when the patient is working in Phase 2 on the integration of traumatic memories, it may be helpful to return to stabilization work from time to time. It is not unusual for patients in Phase 3 to return to the need to integrate further traumatic memories, a Phase 2 goal. Therapists should be able to flex with the needs of the patient, as long as basic principles and goals of treatment remain the focus, especially helping the patient generally remain within a window of tolerance.

CORE CONCEPT

Treatment for dissociative disordered patients is phased in order to
help build necessary cognitive, emotional, somatic, and relationship
skills early in treatment.

The treatment of most patients with a complex dissociative disorder,
even when it follows a relatively steady road, is not without difficulties.
Therapists will normally face resistance, rage, intense shame, suicidality
and other self-destructive behaviors, powerlessness, and vulnerability.
Therefore, a "normal" therapy scenario is a good place to begin to conceptualize more complex treatment issues, and serves as a beacon that helps
therapists correct course when they become stuck or confused with a
patient.

Phase 1: Safety, Stabilization, Symptom Reduction, and Skills Building

Treatment for patients with complex PTSD or dissociative disorders begins
with creating safety, skills building, relationship building with the therapist and safe others, and symptom reduction (e.g., Boon et al., 2011; D.
Brown et al., 1998; Courtois, 2008; Courtois & Ford, 2012; Herman, 1997;
Howell, 2011; Kluft & Fine, 1993; Van der Hart et al., 2006). This is quite
different from the first-line treatment for PTSD, which generally involves
some type of exposure to traumatic memories with relapse prevention
(Foa, Keane, Friedman, & Cohen, 2009). In Phase 1, traumatic memories
are primarily contained to the degree possible until the patient can develop
the capacity to remain within a window of emotional tolerance. Although
patients may certainly talk about what happened to them to some degree,
the therapist does not generally encourage talking about details so that further triggering does not occur. One possible metaphor to offer the patient is
the idea of preparing for a sports event: You must be in condition to be successful, so practice and preparation are important. Patients must practice
skills to regulate arousal before addressing memories directly in order to
maximize the chance of success. In this first phase, a relational approach
takes into account that chronically traumatized patients have been injured
in the attachment arena, and thus safety should precede attachment, and
consistent relational repair is an essential component of treatment (D.
Brown et al., 1998; Chu, 2011; Courtois, 2008; Courtois & Ford, 2012; Ford,
Courtois, Steele, Van der Hart, & Nijenhuis, 2005; Howell, 2011; Loewenstein & Welzant, 2010; Schore, 2012; Siegel, 2010b).

Table 9.1 provides an overview of the goals in Phase 1.

Stabilization skills include how to establish and maintain inner and external safety, use self and relational skills and regulation effectively, reflect on experience, use energy more wisely, and accept and work with dissociative parts, among others. These have been described extensively elsewhere (Boon et al., 2011; Cloitre, Cohen, & Koenen, 2006; Cloitre, Koenen, Cohen, & Han, 2002; Courtois, 2008; Courtois & Ford, 2012; Ford et al., 2005; Howell, 2011; Kluft, 1993a; Steele et al., 2005; Van der Hart et al., 2006). Stabilization skills are listed in Table 9.2.

Managing and Working With Traumatic Memories in Phase 1

Many problems of dissociative patients have underlying traumatic antecedents. Thus, therapists often believe it is logical to resolve traumatic memories first, as when treating PTSD, and everything else will fall into place. However, exposure treatments for PTSD are not completely effective for the long-term and pervasive effects of complex developmental trauma. Since a major consequence of chronic trauma is a deficient integrative capacity, patients often do not yet have the foundation to tolerate exposure to traumatic memory early in therapy (Boon et al., 2011; Gold, 2000; Kluft, 2013; Steele et al., 2005; Van der Hart et al., 2006). In addition, many problems of dissociative patients are developmental—that is, they lack capacities that are learned over the course of normal development. No amount of work on traumatic memories will provide these capacities.

Many patients present either with a complete aversion to traumatic memories or an aggressive push to talking about them that overrides the

TABLE 9.1
Phase 1 Treatment Goals

- Make initial and ongoing assessments.
- Develop case formulation and treatment planning.
- Set a clear treatment frame and boundaries.
- Develop a crisis protocol.
- Address initial fears about therapy.
- Develop safe contact with the therapist.
- Develop a collaborative working relationship.
- Offer referrals for medication and physical assessment and care.
- Share diagnosis with the patient, if helpful.
- Maintain therapy within a window of emotional tolerance.
- Provide psychoeducation on trauma, dissociation, treatment boundaries, the need for emotional skills, and the therapeutic relationship.
- Help patients establish external and internal safety.
- Develop awareness of somatic precursors to dysregulation.
- Teach somatic resources to regulate.
- Reduce symptoms (depression, anxiety, dissociation, PTSD symptoms, substance abuse, eating disorders, psychosis, etc.).
- Support patients in maintaining and improving functioning in daily life.
- Help patients acquire stabilization skills: regulatory and daily life functioning skills (see Table 9.2).
- Coordinate with other treatment team members and family, as appropriate.
- Contain traumatic memories to the degree possible.
- Help patients accept and explore the functions of dissociative parts.
- Support increasing communication, compassion, and collaboration among dissociative parts as tolerated.
- Make referrals for therapy with partners and children or adjunctive treatment as needed.

fears and concerns of some dissociative parts of themselves. In Phase 1, the therapist must be mindful of this inner conflict and ensure that it is fully addressed so that therapy is neither too stagnant nor too fast-paced (Van der Hart & Steele, 1999).

The fact that developmental skills and capacities need to be addressed in the first phase of treatment does not mean that traumatic memories are never addressed during this time. Trauma-informed care includes regular acknowledgment of the effects of trauma. However, this does not mean the patient should share the details to the point of becoming overwhelmed in

TABLE 9.2
Stabilization Skills for Patients

- Overcome the stigma of needing help and therapy.
- Establish and maintain internal and external safety.
- Reduce life crisis and chaos.
- Improve self and relational regulation skills.
- Enjoy positive experiences and emotions in the present.
- Learn to be more mindful and present.
- Identify, tolerate, and regulate emotions.
- Tolerate the normal distresses of daily life.
- Accept and effectively work with dissociative parts.
- Gradually confront and overcome the phobia of inner experiences.
- Develop and increase use of reflection and mentalization.
- Improve daily life skills.
  - Learn adequate eating and sleep routines.
  - Balance recreation, rest, and work.
  - Manage finances, parenting, maintaining a household, etc.
- Improve relational skills, including assertiveness and setting relational boundaries.
- Improve executive functioning.
  - Maintain focus and attention, planning, organizing, prioritizing, time management.
  - Improve problem-solving and decision-making abilities.
  - Sustain concentration when necessary, and change the focus of attention when necessary.
- Take ownership of responsibility for behaviors and treatment.
- Improve physical self-care.
- Improve somatic awareness and learn how to use somatic resources and signals.
- Increase compassion for self and others.
- Contain traumatic memories.
- Reduce switching among dissociative parts.
- Learn how to be safely vulnerable in the therapeutic relationship.
- Recognize the difference between internal "reality" (dreams, emotions, activities of dissociative parts, etc.) and external reality (psychic equivalence).
- Learn how to make adaptive meaning out of experience.

early treatment. The purpose in Phase 1 is primarily helping patients learn to regulate, and this includes regulation in regard to traumatic memories. Thus, patients may create a metaphor for what happened, such as "the black box tied up with pretty ribbon," or "the event," or "the blue bedroom." These representations provide simultaneous distance and acknowledgment, with the purpose of containing full processing of memories until the patient and the therapist agree that the time is right. The patient can already try containment imagery for traumatic memories in Phase 1, some examples of which are given below. Acknowledgment of traumatic memories in Phase 1 and explorations of how they affect the patient in the present already provide some initial steps toward integration.

Some patients may be able to engage in carefully titrated work on traumatic memory, that is, in very small increments, if they have enough integrative capacity (see Chapter 5). However, virtually all dissociative patients need to learn containment strategies and emotional regulation skills (e.g., Boon et al., 2011; D. Brown & Fromm, 1986; Chu, 2011; Howell, 2011; ISSTD, 2011; Kluft, 1982, 2013; Van der Hart et al., 2006).

CORE CONCEPT

Patients may present with complete denial of traumatizing events, extreme phobic avoidance, or a tendency to immediately talk about every detail. The therapist should be aware that the patient usually has intense conflicts among dissociative parts about facing traumatic memories, and that what is presented to the therapist is often only one side of the conflict of knowing and not knowing. This conflict itself must be addressed in treatment in a paced manner.

For patients who tend to forge ahead without regulation, the therapist might gently recommend that they not talk about details yet, but speak in more general terms. Therapists should be careful to convey this is not because they do not want to hear about it, but rather the patient as a whole needs to find the right time and pace. The therapist might ask the patient, *How would you know if your sharing with me was too much right now?* Many patients would not be able to give an answer, which indicates that they are yet unable to recognize their own somatic signals of distress very well. In fact, some patients are so numb and depersonalized that they can recount trauma without emotion. The therapist should beware that this does not indicate the presence of integration and regulation, but rather dissociation and hypoarousal.

Containment of Flashbacks

Prior to the successful treatment of traumatic memory, the patient must be able to contain flashbacks, at least to some degree. This type of containment demonstrates that the patient has some regulatory skills necessary for the integration of traumatic memory. Virtually all dissociative patients experience some type of flashbacks. These are reactivated somatosensory relivings that involve some or all of the components of a traumatic memory.

CORE CONCEPT

Flashbacks should be contained and the patient grounded in the present. These are overwhelming experiences in which the patient is outside the window of tolerance, and thus not a good place to begin work on a traumatic memory.

Flashbacks are terrifying, fragmentary, and overwhelming experiences. Patients often are not very present or able to be fully aware of what is happening. Integrative capacity during flashbacks is low, and patients are outside their window of tolerance. Thus, this is not the time to work on traumatic memory, even though the memory has presented itself. Instead, the therapist should help patients contain the memory and reorient to the present. If the patient is not stable enough, containment will need to continue over time. Once the patient ready and grounded and oriented to the present, and if there is sufficient time in the session, the therapist can prepare the patient for a specific segment of work.

The presence of dissociative parts adds an additional complexity to managing flashbacks. Sometimes the presenting adult part of the patient reports that other parts are highly distressed and having flashbacks that the adult part does not experience. Or the adult part may have a vague sense of distress or unease. Thus, the therapist needs to work with the specific parts that are involved in the flashback. Sometimes patients have the experience of a perpetrator-imitating part evoking flashbacks intentionally as a punishment, perhaps as a reminder not to tell, or as a way to control other parts through fear. In these cases the therapist must work directly with the perpetrator-imitating part in order to explore the reasons for the flashbacks and to find cooperative ways to stop them (see Chapter 17).

Table 9.3 gives a small sampling of ways to help patients ground, orient, and contain during a flashback.

When patients become dysregulated as they share something in early treatment about traumatic memories, an excellent opportunity presents

TABLE 9.3
How to Contain Flashbacks

- Act calm, even if you, the therapist, do not feel calm. Flashbacks and dissociative episodes are usual for trauma survivors. They are intense but are usually limited.
- Do not touch the patient without permission (always ask first). Unexpected touch during a flashback can be perceived as dangerous, even when the therapist is trying to comfort or ground the patient.
- Speak slowly and calmly, use a few simple words, and repeat them, e.g., *You are in a safe place. You are having a flashback. Even though you are feeling intense, everything here and now is just as it should be. You are in my office and you are safe.*
- During flashbacks, patients often close their eyes. Ask them to open their eyes and look around the room, naming three or four things that remind them they are in the present (e.g., sofa, clock, picture on the wall, chair).
- Encourage all parts to look out through the adult's eyes and listen with the adult's ears so that all parts of the patient can see where they are and hear the sound of the therapist's voice and know that they are here and it is safe.
- Help the patient use perceptual grounding: *Name three things in the room that you see, that you hear, that you feel (touch); and name one or two things that you smell.* (The therapist can keep pleasant but intense-smelling material in the office such as peppermint, citrus, or cinnamon).
- Ask the patient to move: to stretch, get up and walk around, or change position.
- Help the patient use relaxing breathing or progressive muscle relaxation.
- Ask if parts inside can help contain the flashback and help calm and ground parts that are triggered.
- Use the sound of your voice: *Let all parts listen to the sound of my voice. My voice reminds you that you are here and now, because I am here, not there. You are here with me, and you can hear my voice. Here. Now. Like breadcrumbs that show the trail, follow my words back to here and now.*
- Do not ask about what is being remembered. This may only serve to increase the flashback, as it keeps the patient focused on content.
- Compassionately remind the patient that it is very important to be in a safe place with adequate help and preparation when remembering.
- Help the patient contain the memory, perhaps by using imagery. Containment imagery such as bank vaults; chests; storage bins; boxes; jars; closets; or computer metaphors such as storing the memory in the cloud, on a disk, or putting it in an encrypted folder may be useful. This imagery should come from the patient to the extent possible.

> - Ensure that the patient is oriented and grounded before leaving session. Some-times it takes a few minutes for a person to get fully oriented again, and there is a tendency to re-dissociate, so the therapist should continue to interact until the person is fully aware. Kluft (2013) has emphasized that patients may still be in trance even though they appear relatively grounded and present.

itself to help the patient begin to be more attuned to somatic symptoms of distress and regulation. The therapist can also inquire about whether there are other parts of the patient that may not be ready to talk, gently helping the patient realize more about the inner conflict between knowing and not knowing. The somatic correlates of knowing and not knowing can be help-ful in working with this conflict. For example, the therapist might ask, *What happens inside when you think about "knowing what happened" or "it's true"? And what happens when you think about "not knowing" or "not true"? What happens in your body when you feel this conflict? Could you imagine there might be a place in between for now, a place of accepting both knowing and not knowing, true and not true, a place where you do not need to decide for now? What does that feel like in your body? Let's try to find that place and use it as a resource for you. You have plenty of time to sort out these dilemmas.*

CORE CONCEPT

Patients generally have strong inner conflicts among dissociative
parts between knowing and not knowing, telling and not telling.
These are essential to acknowledge and resolve.

CASE EXAMPLE OF WORKING WITH TRAUMATIC MEMORY IN PHASE 1: MEGAN

Megan was a 52-year-old patient with major depression and OSDD. She grew up with an extremely violent brother with a severe mental illness. Though Megan saw a psychiatrist for a dozen years, she never talked about what had happened other than to acknowledge that it had been difficult. She noted to her current therapist that her parents had made no efforts to have the brother treated, trying to manage him at home. When her brother would hurt Megan, the parents would blame her, asking, *What did you do to upset him?* Megan shared few details beyond these facts at this point in her treatment, as she became overwhelmed each time she did.

She also hinted that maybe she had been sexually abuse by her brother, but that she did not "want to know" if it was true. The therapist understood not to push Megan to confront her traumatic memories without much more exploration of her avoidance and a time of regulatory skills building. Instead, the therapist offered some education about family violence and how victims often believe they are to blame as a way to feel more in control of the situation, which Megan did not know. In just the first three sessions, Megan began to realize she was not to blame and found great relief in this fact.

Gradually Building a Better Life

If the patient is not active in creating a better life or maintaining a good one in the present, no matter how slowly, therapy is on the road to failure. Overall functioning cannot be abandoned in order to invest energy in inner work. Of course, temporary and short-term regressions may occur. These should, to the degree possible, be minimized and carefully planned. For example, one patient planned to take off four weeks from work in order to deal with some specific and difficult traumatic memories. The therapist helped him pace during that time, so he was ready to return to work and was able to function better than before.

Many patients come to therapy with the idea that if they can "get over" their childhood and "get the trauma out," they will have a better life. So some practically abandon their lives and jump headfirst into their inner world. Others are so depressed or overwhelmed that they find the idea of coping with life unappealing and exhausting. But in reality, our patients need a better life, which makes it worth their while to be in the present and do the hard work of therapy. A life lived to the fullest extent possible should be the ultimate goal of therapy. Otherwise there is only despair and emptiness when patients are finally able to be present. It is in getting out there in the world, relating to others and not just hiding under the wings of the ever-supportive and warm therapist, taking control of what they can in their lives, that helps patients develop a sense of competence and confidence.

As one patient said, *I am realizing I need to take ownership of my life, because I am really sick of spending all my time living like I was still in the past.* Making improvements in life involves constant effort, both internally and externally. So therapy must help patients not only explore their inner world and overcome their past but improve the quality of their lives now. This involves a complex balance of being present with an inner *and* outer focus, or at least the ability to effectively alternate the two.

Of course, many patients continue to have profound difficulties in the present, either because of the inexorable erosion of functioning over time or through terrible life circumstances beyond their control. Therapists cannot always honestly say to their patients that their lives are good or even better in the present; sometimes this simply is not true. For example, because chronic trauma has an impact on the body, some older patients find they have seriously limiting physical conditions that affect their quality of life (e.g., Fisher & Gunnar, 2010). Others find themselves late in life without a partner or children, alone at a time when they most need connection. Some have experienced so much hardship and loss that they have little resilience to cope with the small indignities of life, much less the major blows that come along. But still, therapists can only help their patients play the hand they were dealt as best they can, and be proactive in changing their lives for the better when the opportunity arises, if even in small ways.

The Central Role of Trauma-Related Phobias in Phase-Oriented Treatment

One way to organize the therapy of dissociative patients—at least in part—is to address trauma-related phobias across the different phases of treatment (Steele et al., 2005; Van der Hart et al., 2006). Avoidance and lack of realization must be continually assessed and approached within the tolerance of the patient. These phobias are discussed throughout this volume.

Trauma-related phobias in Phase 1. In Phase 1, the first phobia that needs to be addressed is the overarching one: the phobia of inner experience. Of course, when patients are phobic of external stimuli, such as situations or people, the real avoidance is of their inner experience. In this sense, all phobias are inner-directed. A central problem for dissociative patients is their ongoing avoidance of various aspects of their inner experience, including memories, thoughts, emotions, sensations, reactions to relationships, and dissociative parts. A phobia of the body is a major challenge in the treatment of patients with dissociative disorders. Many patients are extremely avoidant and fearful (and sometimes ashamed) of their sensations. Many, if not most, regulation skills have sensory components, and being present requires bodily awareness, so this phobia is particularly essential to overcome.

The more phobic the patient, the more resistance to progress exists. The phobia of attachment and attachment loss will also be addressed, particularly in relation to the therapist. The phobia of dissociative parts becomes a central focus in the beginning, when the therapist has made a diagnosis of a dissociative disorder but the patient cannot accept it. The dilemmas between knowing versus not knowing and true versus not true are conflicts that reflect the phobia of traumatic memory in Phase 1. Throughout therapy the phobia of change may be evident, but it may be particularly strong in Phase 1 before the patient has gained sufficient insight, self-compassion, and sense of competence and agency.

Trauma-related phobias in Phase 2. The treatment of traumatic memory brings the patient into direct confrontation with fears of remembering or reliving. Thus, the phobia of traumatic memory is a major treatment target in this phase. The phobia of physical sensations related to the trauma and to animal defenses may be particularly strong in this phase, and needs careful attention. In addition, the phobia of attachment and attachment loss will be addressed in regard to the patient's relationship with the perpetrators.

Trauma-related phobias in Phase 3. Phase 3 involves successful grieving and more change and growth. The phobia of inner experience may reemerge during this time as a defense against sadness and loss. The phobia of change can reflect the patient's fears of getting better because it may mean the loss of the therapist when therapy is successfully completed. In this phase, patients may be challenged to take adaptive risks that they have never been willing to take before. They must risk vulnerability if they wish to have more and better relationships, which may again evoke the phobia of attachment and attachment loss. The phobia of the body emerges again in Phase 3, with issues around sexuality and coming to terms with the body one owns. The therapist should ensure that patients are able to overcome these inner-directed phobias to the degree possible for each one.

General approaches to resolve trauma-related phobias. It is typically helpful to spiral in to a particular phobia, using these general approaches:

- Educate about trauma-related phobias, using analogies of fear of flying, bugs, heights, etc.
- Reassure the patient that you will work together to approach the phobia within the patient's tolerance level.
- Explore how avoidance helps the patient. For example, a patient might say, *I can't listen to parts or else my mind would be too chaotic. They all want to talk at once;* or *Not having feelings allows me to work. Otherwise I would fall apart.*
- Explore concerns: *What are you most worried about or afraid will happen if you approach that feeling, that memory, that part of yourself, that sense of abandonment?*
- Explore the experience of "thinking about": *What happens for you as you think about the idea of approaching what is fearful for you?*
- Help the patient stay in the window of tolerance, taking one step at a time.
- Explore the felt sense of the phobia. Have the patient notice the sen-

sations and movements that increase or decrease the sensations, supporting regulation.

- Help the patient learn regulation skills: mindfulness, tolerance and acceptance of inner experiences as normal and important, distress tolerance, using self-soothing and relational soothing and support, distraction, and titration, that is, addressing a small component or percentage of a trauma or an emotion, e.g., *Imagine being able to notice that feeling just for 10 seconds.*

The patient must first develop skills to cope with and accept discomfort, pain, uncertainty, ambivalence, and conflict. These skills are the foundation for overcoming the overarching phobia of inner experience and are a major focus of Phase 1 treatment. Thereafter, all phobias will be addressed throughout treatment, as appropriate for the individual.

Working With Dissociative Parts Throughout Phase-Oriented Treatment

Phase 1 treatment involves helping the patient learn to acknowledge and accept dissociative parts. Some patients are able to accomplish this more rapidly and smoothly than others. The degree to which patients can learn to work effectively with their parts determines to a large degree the duration of Phase 1. This phase of treatment is focused on establishing and improving communication, cooperation, and compassion among dissociative parts, and helping the patient as a whole be accountable for the actions of each part. As a general rule, the part (or parts) of the patient that functions in daily life should be immediately engaged in therapy. The therapist must beware of waiting too long to engage parts in treatment, which may lead to greater instability and conflict, and conversely, of working with parts too quickly, which may overwhelm the patient.

In some patients, child parts may emerge quickly to seek attachment, rescue, and support, and to "tell the story" of traumatic events. The most effective approach is to help adult or higher functioning parts be responsible for the care of child parts, not the therapist. The more the therapist works intensively with child parts, the more hostile parts can be activated, creating a systemic imbalance that can destabilize the patient. It is not recommended to play with child parts or treat them as literal children (See Chapter 14).

Many patients are afraid and ashamed of angry, self-destructive parts, including parts that imitate the perpetrator (see Chapters 16 and 17). Therapists can also fear these parts. It is imperative for both patient and therapist to gradually understand these parts and their functions and learn to communicate and collaborate. Therapy easily becomes stuck if these parts are not included, as they create ongoing inner turmoil. Much more about the process of working with dissociative parts is discussed in Chapter 10.

Phase 2: Integrating Traumatic Memories

Phase 1 is designed to address many trauma-related issues and self-regulation deficits prior to focusing on specific traumatic memories. When Phase 2 interventions directed toward exposure to and integration (also known as processing) of traumatic memories are initiated, it is with several caveats. First, the therapist needs to understand that not all dissociative parts have access to a given traumatic memory, and that additional steps need to be taken in order to ensure that all parts have eventually resolved a particular memory. Second, confrontation of a traumatic memory does not necessarily address the integration of dissociative parts, which can remain even after memories are resolved. Third, the patient's integrative capacity typically varies among dissociative parts, so exposure that seems tolerable to one dissociative part may not be to another. For these reasons, dissociative patients can become more easily dysregulated than other individuals. The treatment of traumatic memory is discussed extensively in Chapters 20 and 21.

Table 9.4 lists the goals of Phase 2 treatment.

TABLE 9.4
Phase 2 Treatment Goals

Integrating traumatic memories
- Ensure that the patient has sufficient integrative capacity and stabilization.
- Work through phobias and resistances to approaching traumatic memories.
- Prepare the patient to work with traumatic memories.
- Engage in the treatment of traumatic memories.
- Engage in realization and further integration.
- Complete actions related to the trauma, e.g., animal defenses.

Resolving traumatic attachment bonds with perpetrators
- Learn to mentalize and reflect on perpetrator's state of mind.
- Accept any positives as well as negatives about connection with perpetrator—i.e., resolve conflicts of loyalty and fear, love and hate, etc.
- Increase capacity to hold ambivalent feelings of hate and love.

Resolving traumatic transference
- Help dissociative parts be oriented to the present.
- Help all parts of the patient notice not only what is similar between the past and present but what is different.
- Collaborate and share about relational experiences in the moment between patient and therapist.

Major contraindications to Phase 2 work include lack of adequate motivation or resources. These issues may be enduring and thus related to poor prognosis (e.g., Boon, 1997; Kluft, 1997b), or may be temporary, due to transient crises or the need to give full attention to other issues. The major phobia addressed in Phase 2 is that of traumatic memories. However, disorganized attachment to abusive and neglectful family members must also be addressed, since these unresolved relational experiences, often sequestered in various parts outside of the patient's conscious awareness, interfere with the integration of traumatic memories.

Treatment of Insecure Attachment to the Perpetrator

The inner conflict between attachment to and defense against perpetrators becomes heightened when traumatic memories are reactivated, hindering integration. Some patients may be enmeshed with their families in the present, unable to set healthy boundaries and limits. Simultaneously, other dissociative parts of the individual may hold strong feelings of hatred, anger, shame, neediness, or terror toward family perpetrators and others (Steele et al., 2001). The therapist must empathically explore all the patient's conflicted feelings and beliefs related to perpetrators and not scapegoat them, remembering that one part of the patient can hold one view of the perpetrator (e.g., *I hate my mother! Every time I'm around her I want to kill myself! I hate my aunt because she abused me!*), while another part espouses a completely different view (*I love my mom! She always bakes my favorite cookies when I visit! My aunt was fantastic. She always took me on such fun trips!*). The more the therapist takes one side, particularly in encouraging the patient to diminish or cut off contact, the more the patient may be compelled to protect perpetrators and even strengthen the traumatic bond (Kramer, 1983). Thus, the therapist should remain neutral and help the patients explore their inner conflicts about loyalty to the perpetrator. A major challenge with many dissociative patients is to help them realize that internal parts that imitate the perpetrator are different from the actual perpetrators. This is a common confusion and one that creates much fear, as patients (or a least some parts) experience the perpetrator as being ever present.

Treatment of the Phobia of Traumatic Memory

This is one of the most difficult phobias to overcome, requiring high and sustained integrative capacity. Particular dissociative parts may be especially reluctant to realize these memories, in spite of growing recognition and awareness among other parts of the personality. For example, one part may continue to have a "golden fantasy" of having perfectly loving parents, even as other parts become more aware and accepting of past abuse. Thus, the individual as a whole continues to have significant lack of realization. Sadness and grief over past and current losses must be supported in order to support growing realization. However, grief must always be counterbalanced by the ability to gain satisfaction, contentment, pleasure, and joy from positive experiences in the present.

The sharing of traumatic memories among dissociative parts, or what we have termed *guided synthesis* (Van der Hart et al., 1993, 2006), requires several steps to ensure full realization of traumatic memories. Exposure is a technique that helps the patient face traumatic memories while preventing avoidance strategies. When the patient is dissociative, memories are often quite fragmented, and thus are not available as a whole. Synthesis involves the bringing together fragments of memory into a coherent whole, which is then shared among dissociative parts—a more complex process.

First, the therapist and patient collaboratively plan, deciding on a specific memory or group of memories to address, and whether all parts will participate or only some. Some dissociative disorder patients have sufficient integrative capacity to tolerate sharing a traumatic experience as a whole person at once. With other patients it is necessary to work with smaller groups of parts in a graduated manner, or work with specific elements of the trauma, a technique referred to as *titration* or *fractionation* (e.g., Kluft, 1990c, 2013; Van der Hart et al., 2006).

Certainly, not every detail or every memory of trauma need be synthesized; rather, it is essential for patients to realize their reactions surrounding the event, the most threatening aspects of the memory, and the maladaptive core beliefs and behavior that evolved from the memory. Synthesis is the necessary beginning of a difficult and longer course of realization that involves accepting, owning, and adapting to what was and what is. Realization continues throughout Phase 2 and long into Phase 3.

Phase 3: Integration of the Personality and Rehabilitation

This final phase of treatment resembles a more typical psychotherapy. And it also requires some of the most difficult integrative work yet: painful grieving that paves the way for deepening realization, confrontation of existential crises, relinquishing maladaptive beliefs and behaviors, learning to live with a (more) unified personality, and ongoing struggles to engage in the world in new and unfamiliar ways. Chapters 22 and 23 focus on Phase 3.

Table 9.5 describes the major goals of Phase 3 work.

In large part, Phase 3 involves grieving, as the patient increasingly realizes the cumulative losses suffered as a result of being traumatized and the

TABLE 9.5
Phase 3 Treatment Goals

- Accept and grieve losses of the past, present, and future.
- Overcome the phobia of intimacy, including sexuality and the body.
- Adjust to a more normal daily life and routine, learning to live more fully in the present.
- Take adaptive risks to improve life and relationships.
- Accept change as inevitable and adapt to the degree possible.
- Establish enduring, healthy relationships.
- Integrate personality and establish a unified self, to the degree possible.
- Build capacities to enjoy daily life.
- Develop meaning and purpose in life.
- Continue to improve daily life situation.

fact that life at times can continue to be very difficult and painful (Van der Hart et al., 1993, 2006). Yet this integrative grief work can eventually support the patient in making adaptive changes that can bring greater meaning, balance, and perhaps even pleasure to current life. The therapist must ensure that grieving is coupled with experiences of success and joy in the present.

Patients often have the fantasy that all will be well when they have reconciled with their histories. In fact, although Phase 3 may indeed include pleasure, relief, and newfound enthusiasm for life, it also involves the ongoing need to reconcile serious losses of the past, present, and future. The therapist has an obligation to educate the patient regarding this painful dichotomy and to support healthy grieving.

Phase 3 also requires a return to the phobia of attachment and attachment loss in the form of developing new and healthy relationships and risking intimacy. Patients who cannot successfully complete Phase 3 often continue to have difficulty with normal life, despite significant relief from traumatic intrusions (Kluft, 1993b). However, it is also common for additional traumatic memories and dissociative parts to emerge in Phase 3 in response to a growing capacity to integrate. During such times, Phase 1 and Phase 2 issues need to be revisited.

Over the course of Phase 3, patients see incremental gains in the ability to experience themselves as whole, relatively unified individuals. As personal ownership broadens, dissociative parts become successively merged or integrated into a more coherent and cohesive personality. This process mostly occurs in a gradual fashion as the reasons for ongoing dissociation are eliminated, although some integration of parts occurs spontaneously, and some through formal therapy techniques (Kluft, 1993b; see Chapter 20).

Termination

The process of termination should be carefully planned as it often needs to be undertaken gradually over time, and may include an invitation to return to therapy, if needed (see Chapter 23). Termination can be very emotional, as it involves change and loss due to separation from the therapist, who has become a central attachment figure for the patient. Follow-up is considered essential to monitor full integration—that is, unification of the patient's personality.

Case Management Versus Psychotherapy

Therapy is concerned with the intrapsychic and interpersonal functioning of the individual. However, many serious problems that arise for chronically traumatized individuals are outside the usual scope of therapy, such as housing, transportation, financial, legal, occupational, medical, and social service needs. Therapists should do their best to view patients holistically and avoid reenactments of neglect in the therapeutic relationship, so these issues are legitimate topics of concern. They can also derail the focus of therapy. Thus, therapists must make decisions about when and how they will support patients in receiving holistic care. Many patients with poorer prognoses need some degree of help with coordination of care and advocacy—that is, case management. Case management is defined as

> a collaborative process of assessment, planning, facilitation, care coordination, evaluation, and advocacy for options and services to meet an individual's and family's comprehensive health needs through communication and available resources to promote quality, cost-effective outcomes. (Case Management Society of America, 2008)

Therapists must beware of fundamental survival problems that are so urgent, especially in very chaotic patients, that their entire energy is taken in just managing to get through the day, keep a roof over their heads, and obtain food to eat.

A recurring fantasy and need of trauma therapists is to have a treatment team that can offer adequate resources in all areas of life for patients who have so many needs and so few skills. Unfortunately, this fantasy rarely translates into reality. Instead, therapists are confronted with very limited or even completely absent support systems and resources for patients. Thus, they sometimes must find creative ways to support patients in living daily life, but without rescuing or "doing for."

There are many online resources to which therapists can direct their patients, and which have incredibly helpful advice and skills: resources for managing money, help with job searches and job training, and so forth. Therapists may decide to do some research first and offer specific websites, or direct patients to do their own searches, depending on their level of functioning. Some patients need to be referred to appropriate social agencies for basic services before therapy can begin. Patients should be assessed on intake to ensure that basic needs are covered before starting therapy.

Many other problems and issues may fall within the scope of treatment, yet are not considered to be therapy per se, but rather case management and support. Although some therapists do not normally think of therapy as addressing basic life skills, many survivors of chronic abuse and neglect have never learned them, and they are a necessary part of the first phase of therapy, the foundation upon which an integrative life is built. In fact, these skill deficits often contribute to ongoing depression, a sense of failure and hopelessness, and even a poor physical condition that adds to mood dysregulation and other problems. Insight and understanding are inadequate without skills to facilitate change and gains.

Further Explorations

9.1 What criteria do you use to determine when to shift with a patient from phase to phase?

9.2 Would you have additional goals in each phase that you think might be important for patients?

9.3 There is currently some debate about whether patients with childhood histories of abuse and neglect need phase-oriented treatment—that is, require a period of stabilization prior to integration of traumatic memories (e.g., Van Minnen, Arntz, & Keijsers, 2006; Van Minnen, Harned, Zoellner, & Mills, 2012). What are your thoughts about this? What experiences have you had with patients that might sway you toward one side or the other of the controversy?

PART III

Phase 1 Treatment and Beyond

CHAPTER 10

Working With Dissociative Parts: An Integrative Systems Perspective

My experience has taught me again and again that either approaching DID as if the alters were completely separate persons or as if the patient was a person whose subjective experience of having separate selves can be discounted is counterproductive. These approaches deny, dismiss, and disavow both the nature of DID phenomenology and the subjective world of the DID patient.

—Richard P. Kluft (2006, p. 293)

The unique challenge in the treatment of dissociative disorders is in working successfully with dissociative parts in ways that support patients to stabilize, mentalize, and achieve further integration, while still acknowledging they are single individuals with a fragmented sense of self. There are a number of major publications that address the treatment of complex dissociative disorders in adults, with various approaches (e.g., Boon et al., 2011; Chefetz, 2015; Chu, 2011; Fraser, 1991, 2003; Frewen & Lanius, 2015; Howell, 2011; Kluft & Fine, 1993; Kluft, 2006, 2013; Krakauer, 2001; Paulsen & Lanius, 2014; Putnam, 1989, 1997; C. A. Ross, 1997; Van der Hart et al., 2006). This chapter will offer an overview of practical ways to work directly and indirectly with dissociative parts of the patient while approaching the individual as a whole person.

While many standard clinical approaches seem to be helpful in the treatment of patients with dissociative disorders (e.g., psychodynamic, object relations, self psychology, cognitive behavioral therapy, EMDR, ego state therapy, internal family systems, acceptance and commitment therapy, dialectical behavior therapy), the therapist must also include specific approaches to working with dissociative parts in a paced, systematic, and integrative manner. Those who use ego state work must recognize the special issues in treatment that arise due to the differences between ego states and dissociative parts (Kluft, 1988a, 2006; Phillips & Frederick, 1995). Emerging clinical outcome research indicates that a direct focus on the patient's dissociation with careful stabilization leads to increased functioning and decreased symptoms (Brand, Classen, Lanius, et al., 2009; Brand, Classen, McNary, et al., 2009).

Regardless of diagnosis, psychotherapy is directed toward helping every patient maintain and improve functioning while changing enduring ways of being that are not adaptive. This basic principle must be applied to chronically traumatized patients as well. Thus, first and foremost, effective therapy for patients with a complex dissociative disorder involves "plain old" psychotherapy (Allen, 2012), but with the addition of interventions and approaches that specifically address the dissociative organization of the personality.

Therapists new to working with dissociative disorders often are concerned with how many parts a patient has. Can someone have hundreds or even thousands of "personalities"? This question is really not a useful one to ask, as it tells us little about a patient or what the patient needs in therapy. Each individual has only one personality, however divided it may be. There is no logical or natural limit to how fragmented a dissociative patient can become. The more helpful question is *What is the integrative capacity of the patient?* The lower the capacity for the challenges the patient faced as a child and still faces in the present, the more dissociation will occur as an ongoing coping strategy. If patients have many parts, this merely tells us that they have less ability to stay present, to tolerate and regulate emotions, and to accept and realize a wide range of experiences as their own. However, there are patients who only have a few dissociative parts, but their parts are strongly separate. One therapeutic approach to treating a patient who is highly fragmented with many parts is for parts to be "grouped" together in various configurations (Kluft, 1996b, 2013).

Patients who are not dissociative typically uncover experiences as therapy progresses: previously hidden memories, feelings, wishes, and so on. Neither patient nor therapist knows everything that may emerge in the beginning. The therapist does not know the entire patient, nor does the patient, in the beginning of treatment. So, too, with dissociative patients, but in more complex ways. Parts may be dormant or hidden until late in therapy.

Understanding the Nature of Dissociative Parts

Many psychological and social theories and recent studies in neurobiology indicate that consciousness and self are never completely unitary constructs. We need some way to organize and understand our many different tendencies: emotions, behaviors, movements, postures, sensations, and thoughts. A fundamental organization occurs along the lines of action systems, which were discussed in Chapter 1. These enduring tendencies and patterns make up our personality, and our personality includes a sense of self. The terms self and personality merely represent our inner organization of attitudes, expectations, feelings, and meanings (Sroufe, 1990). Personality can be thought of as a dynamic biopsychosocial system of these enduring traits, and of the ways in which we interact with others under various circumstances (Van der Hart et al., 2006). It is the umbrella under which sense of self resides.

CORE CONCEPT

Personality, identity, and self are not actual things. They are terms that give a broad and condensed impression of who we are to others and to ourselves. We do not have a self like we have a brain or a heart. Instead, our minds construct a continually evolving story about who we are; this is what we call our "self." Patients with dissociative disorders subjectively experience their selves and personalities as fragmented, and often as outside of their voluntary control and awareness.

We all construct a "self" out of multiple selves, each with its own characteristic postures, gestures, and expressions. John and Helen Watkins, the founders of ego state therapy, noted that all people have normal ego states that are "covertly segmented personality structures" that exist on a continuum of less to more discrete (1997, p. ix). We can easily understand dissociative parts in terms of this underlying structure or organization of the personality (Van der Hart et al., 2006). In a healthy person, ego states are normally connected and cohesive (i.e., they do not have their own separate sense of self), and the movements of the body are also cohesive and in alignment with thoughts and emotions. In trauma-related dissociation, dissociative parts are much less connected, and each takes on a life of its own to some extent, having some degree of first-person perspective that include a sense of *I*, *me*, and *mine*, along with characteristic physical postures and movements. Of course, we reiterate that neither personality nor self are actual things or beings.

One's personality, and thus one's sense of self, involves an ongoing developmental and perceptual journey across one's entire life (Boon et al., 2011; Damasio, 1999, 2012; Hood, 2013; Janet, 1929; Schore, 2003). In some ways self is an illusion constructed by the mind as a shorthand way to understand oneself and others (Hood, 2013). It is never a complete representation of who someone is, but like one's personality, it is constantly being organized, disorganized, and reorganized in a continual update based on integration of present experience with the past and expected future (Damasio, 1999; Gallagher, 2000; Janet, 1929; Schore, 2003; Van der Hart et al., 2006). A person's movement vocabulary also develops with each reorganization of the personality: Old movement patterns are relinquished, and new possibilities are developed. For example, an increase in self-esteem precipitates a more erect posture. The problem with people who have dissociative parts is that this natural and necessary revision and updating does not occur sufficiently over time as it normally should.

CORE CONCEPT

Normally, our sense of self is continually updated as we learn from and reflect upon both new and old experiences. Dissociative patients seem unable to sufficiently engage in this natural revision, leaving them with relatively rigid and divided selves.

Many dissociative parts become fixed and relatively impervious to change and learning from new experiences, at least in regard to overcoming traumatic experiences. When dissociative patients become overwhelmed in one part of their personality, they may shift to another instead of updating and modifying the first.

Each part has a separate sense of self that is experienced as "me," while other parts are experienced as "not me," or are not even recognized as existing at all. Each part is reflected and sustained in particular physical patterns that can often be observed by the therapist. Dissociative patients thus involve a personality organization of multiple senses of self that are divergent. That is, they have a dynamic system of dissociative parts, rather than a seemingly unified, coherent, and continually renovated organization. Each dissociative part experiences itself in a particular way, and also experiences the world in a particular way based on specific perceptions supported by physical patterns. For example, a part experiencing herself as a victim might be supported by a collapsed posture, downcast eyes, and rounded shoulders.

In trauma-related dissociation, the patient develops multiple (and often contradictory) senses of self over time. Each dissociative part of the patient is organized around relatively inflexible and usually narrow ways of thinking, feeling, and behaving that are almost impervious to change. As noted in Chapters 1 and 2, many dissociative parts are stuck in trauma-time and in animal defenses of freeze, flight, fight, flag, and faint, accompanied by the action tendencies characteristic of the particular defense, while others are focused on functioning in daily life (Boon et al., 2011; Van der Hart et al., 2006). This fixation results, for example, in scared parts that are always collapsed and scared; in angry parts that are tense and chronically enraged and ready to fight; in developmentally young parts with childlike actions that constantly need reassurance but never seem to get enough, and so on. Thus, dissociative patients are often unable to respond to the present situation in the most flexible and adaptive way.

CASE EXAMPLES OF SEPARATE SENSE OF SELF IN DISSOCIATIVE PARTS: HELEN AND DERRICK

Helen, the patient first discussed in Chapter 1, had a part she called "Ellen." Ellen experienced herself as a child, with a posture that seemed childlike, vulnerable, and frightened, still stuck in the trauma of Helen's past. She viewed Helen as a separate adult who neglected her, and was unsure of her relationship to Helen. In fact, she gave little thought to Helen, an example of the narrowing of attention and non-realization that are hallmarks of most dissociative parts. She had a vague sense of being at Helen's work, but she was not aware of what Helen did there, and did not view it as relevant to her own experience.

Derrick a patient with DID, mentioned that he was frightened because he often did not know what had happened at work or whether he had been there at all. He recalled leaving his house and driving in his car, but then he would lose track of time. He worked as a technician in a lab. Derrick, the part who presented in therapy, did not experience himself as doing most of this work. Instead, two other parts that referred to themselves as "Stephen and "Joel" were the main parts of Derrick that went to work. Stephen and Joel believed that Derrick was too weak to be able to work; and indeed, Derrick was highly anxious and depressed, often unable to function at home, with a burdened, downtrodden physical appearance and slow, plodding movements. But when Stephen and Joel emerged, both displayed subtle physical changes: Stephen was more erect, with a determined lift to his chin, and Joel had quicker movements and was mobilized for action. These two parts of Derrick were not keen to participate in therapy or communicate with Derrick, insisting that they did not have DID and that therapy was a waste of valuable time. Later in therapy, they could share their true fears with the therapist: the fear that if they got closer to Derrick they would be flooded with feelings of anxiety and depression, which they currently did not experience. They worried they would not be able to continue to work.

Autonomy of Dissociative Parts

Dissociative parts come in all varieties and degrees of separation. Autonomy refers to the degree to which a given part functions outside conscious control of the patient. Greater autonomy implies lower realization. Autonomy implies that a part experiences itself as more separate and can act alone, like in the example of Derrick, who had several separate worker parts with different postures and movements, and thoughts and feelings, that enabled accomplishing work-related tasks. Of course, dissociative parts are a patient's particular ways of being, but outside the awareness or control of the patient as a whole, to varying degrees.

Some parts never directly interact with the outside world but still experience themselves as separate and autonomous internally. For example, it is not uncommon for parts that imitate the perpetrator to firmly believe they *are* the original abuser, and yet the patient may never overtly switch to these parts, which exert their influence internally (see Chapter 17). In DID, some parts have such a strong belief of separateness as to insist that they do not inhabit the body of the patient, or have no children when the patient has several, or do not work or have a partner even though the patient does. A few parts even believe they can kill or hurt other parts without killing or hurting themselves. This is a phenomenon that may accompany self-harm and suicidality in highly dissociative patients, and a most important one to address in treatment. Special approaches to self-harm and suicidality in dissociative patients are discussed in Chapter 18. The degree of non-realization in such cases is profound, which implies that the patient's integrative capacity is low and treatment may take longer.

In other cases, parts may have lesser perceived degrees of separation. Parts may note, *I feel like me, not like a part of her. But I know I am a part of her.* There may be a wide range of autonomy among parts in one person, with perhaps one or two parts having more extreme autonomy and others having much less.

Elaboration of Dissociative Parts

Elaboration refers to the defining sense of self of a dissociative part. While the degree of elaboration is not a criterion for diagnosis, parts with more defined senses of self are often seen in DID rather than in OSDD, with some exceptions. Usually the more autonomous a part is, the more elaborated it becomes, developing unique "personal" characteristics and preferences. These parts may interact more in the outside world, with overt switching, rather than primarily being internal phenomena, though not always. A dissociative part may have a particular age or age range; gender; sexual orientation; preference in clothes, music, and food; and capacities, skills, and deficits; as well as postures and movement vocabularies, all of which may be different from other parts.

Sometimes differences in preferences become so extreme as to create inner conflicts about the most minor issues—for example, what to wear or what flavor of ice cream to buy. When this is the case, the patient is often avoiding much more serious conflicts by focusing on the clashing preferences of parts. These minor issues may offer a great opportunity to help the parts learn how to cooperate with each other if the therapist spends a short time on them and helps the patient move on. However, it is essential for the therapist not to spend endless time helping the patient make agreements among parts about minor issues such as what to buy at the grocery, but rather help all parts of the patient communicate with one another and learn strategies to manage inner conflicts more effectively. It is vital for the therapist to recognize the avoidance inherent in insignificant conflicts and to help the patient begin to accept and address the major conflicts that are the real reason parts remain separate.

Understanding the Functions of Dissociative Parts

It is important for therapists to understand why patients remain divided—that is, the reasons for ongoing non-realization. Why do they continue to need dissociative parts, instead of experiencing themselves as a single self? The phobia of inner experience is often a major factor that maintains dissociation. The patient is avoidant not only of thoughts, feelings, and sensations related to traumatic memories and dissociative parts but also of other inner experiences that also can extend well beyond the trauma.

CORE CONCEPT

The therapist must understand the reasons why the patient continues to have dissociative parts—that is, continues to have profound non-realization. These reasons are the targets of treatment and include the phobia of inner experience, of dissociative parts, and of traumatic memories.

The phobia of unresolved traumatic memories is another major reason why parts remain separate. One part may hold a memory that is intolerable to another part that seems to have no memory of what happened. One part may hold a particularly intolerable aspect of a memory—an emotion such as guilt or shame, a physical sensation such as sexual arousal or unbearable pain, a movement such as ducking the head and avoiding eye contact, a threat by the perpetrator, or a moment when the patient believed she was going to die—while other parts retain the rest of the memory. However, there are other, equally powerful conflicts that maintain dissociation, which may be directly or indirectly related to trauma.

A particular dissociative part must always be understood in the context of the person as a whole—the dynamic system of which the part is a subsystem. That is, it is important to grasp the functions of a given part within the whole person. As Janet (1945) noted, dissociative parts represent certain non-realizations. The functions of parts are closely tied to the non-realizations they uphold. For example, a child part functions to contain dependency yearnings—with wide eyes and a helpless, collapsed body posture—that the adult part of the patient, who has a more upright posture, is yet unable to realize, while the child parts are unable to realize they are now adult. An angry part, with extreme tension in the jaw and shoulders, functions to defend against threat and is unable to realize that the threat may not exist or is not so severe, and that there may be other ways to deal with relational conflicts. The patient, who cannot realize anger, relegates it to this angry part, which the patient then avoids out of shame.

Organization of the Dynamic System of Dissociative Parts

Although each part may have some unique features on the surface, there are some typical underlying similarities in the basic functions of parts and in the way they are organized. At their most basic level, parts are likely organized by action systems (Van der Hart et al., 2006). This is a dual organization based on defense against threat and on functioning in daily life, as we have noted.

The complexity of the patient's personality system can have many levels; the simplest is one major part that functions in daily life and one or more parts fixated in trauma-time. Some parts may take on greater autonomy and elaboration over time, but not all. For example, in the case of Helen, presented in Chapter 1, her system consisted of one part (Helen) functioning in daily life and several parts stuck in defense against danger or life threat. These dissociative parts, such as the child part called Ellen, hold memories, emotions, and so on that Helen cannot yet realize. Most cases of OSDD have this level of dissociative organization.

At a more complex level, which we consider to be the case in DID, patients have more than one part that functions in daily life in addition to more than one part fixed in trauma-time. Derrick's dynamic system of dissociative parts was at this level of complexity (see his case earlier in this chapter). He had several different parts involved in tasks and functions in daily life, including the two parts that dealt with work, each with particular physical and emotional characteristics that were adaptive in the context of work. Derrick also had a part that was very active in sports, as well as a part that dealt with tasks such as taxes, shopping, and paying bills. Derrick was aware of a trauma history of sexual abuse by several men, starting at a very young age. He talked about "children that are locked in the basement" inside of him, and wanted nothing to do with these parts, which were all fixed in trauma-time.

Parts that function in daily life most often present to therapy and are typically avoidant of other parts, though not always. Often parts stuck in trauma-time are organized around certain traumatizing experiences; there may be several of these subsystems in some patients. In David's case, there were two systems of parts stuck in trauma-time that were connected in some ways, but also separate. One subsystem of parts kept most of the memories of abuse that happened at home, and another subsystem kept memories of abuse by a group of pedophiles in his neighborhood.

Practical Approaches to Working With Dissociative Parts

Given that dissociative parts are subsystems of one person with one personality, the ways in which therapists work with the person as a whole can greatly influence the outcome of treatment. When therapists are fascinated by differences among parts—their number, styles, preferences, and characteristics—and work with them as though they are actual individuals, therapy can easily become derailed and dissociative tendencies can be exacerbated. In this case, the therapist is colluding with the non-realization of the patient, acting as though the patient is not a single person.

CORE CONCEPT

The therapist must work with dissociative parts as subsystems of a whole person, not as individuals.

On the other hand, some therapists may ignore the central importance of working with parts, treating the patient as usual in the hope that parts will somehow disappear or their conflicts will be resolved. Without adequate training and a conceptual frame to make sense out of dissociative parts, some therapists report feeling overwhelmed and confused about how to deal with parts. These therapists might avoid working with parts because they simply do not know how or are afraid to do so.

Some therapists avoid working with parts because they are concerned that the patient is creating them for some type of secondary gain, or are worried that paying attention to parts will increase the patient's sense of separateness. Unfortunately, dissociative patients do not tend to integrate on their own because of the extreme phobic avoidance and lack of realization inherent in dissociation. Recent research has demonstrated that highly dissociative patients do not improve without specific treatment that addresses dissociative parts (Brand, Loewenstein, & Spiegel, 2014). Brand et al. (2014) also noted that dissociation (and other major symptoms) actually decreased when therapists acknowledged and worked with parts.

CORE CONCEPT

The question is not "Should I work with parts?" The question is *"How should I work with parts in ways that facilitate integration?"*

The question is *how* to work with parts in ways that decrease dissociation and facilitate integration. Interventions that decrease dissociation include those that

- have a systems theory perspective (dissociative parts are subsystems within the dynamic biopsychosocial system of the whole personality);
- have a relational approach;
- include all dissociative parts in therapy;
- treat all dissociative parts respectfully and as belonging to one person;
- help the patient confront what is keeping dissociative parts separate, as the patient can tolerate;
- keep treatment within a window of tolerance for all parts; and
- work systemically no matter which parts are or are not present in the moment.

A Graduated and Systemic Approach

The most effective way to work with parts is to view them as subsystems within a dynamic system of the whole individual, with each part having relevance and importance to all other parts, and with each part needing to learn to understand, be compassionate toward, and be responsible for all other parts. Whether the therapist works with one, two, groups of parts, or all parts at once depends on the integrative capacity and motivation of the patient. Below, we will discuss how to determine whether and when to work with one, several, or all parts.

CORE CONCEPT

The therapist needs to assess (with the patient when possible) in a given moment whether it may be more effective to work with the patient as a whole via "talking through," with two or more parts to facilitate awareness and cooperation, or with only one single part. Simply interacting with whatever part "shows up" in therapy is not sufficient to facilitate integration. The therapist's interactions with parts should have the purpose of meeting specific goals in therapy.

Explicit interactions among parts can sometimes be heard, seen, or felt by the patient. Helen could sometimes see the young part of her that she called Ellen, and could sense Ellen in her body. At times, Helen would see Ellen in her mind's eye as a bereft orphan in tattered and dirty clothing, and at other times she would see Ellen outside of herself, curled up in the corner of her bedroom. Ellen would cry and ask for Helen to hold her, and expressed great fear of "the Watcher," a punitive part. The Watcher often appeared as a looming, shadowlike, dark figure that called Ellen terrible names and threatened to kill her.

We can think of these parts of Helen as fragmented representations of her childhood—the victim and the persecutor—with Helen often in the role of a neglectful bystander, ignoring what is going on with these parts of herself, or helpless to do anything about it.

A family systems approach to working with internal parts is one way that offers a systemic perspective (e.g., Chu, 2011; R. Schwartz, 1997; Van der Hart et al., 2006). In family systems therapy, there is no identified individual patient; rather, the entire family system is the treatment target. Changing the family system—how individuals interact with and relate to each other—is the focus of treatment. In the same way, the focus of treatment for dissociative disorders is to adaptively change ways in which dissociative parts do and do not relate to each other and to the world.

A sensorimotor psychotherapy approach (Ogden et al., 2006; Ogden & Fisher, 2015) offers theory and interventions that help therapists and their patients become aware of the somatic organization of parts, and how the body itself can become an asset to support realization and integration. The movements, sensations, and postures of the patient are viewed as reflecting and sustaining various parts; and therapeutic interventions that change and integrate physical actions, such as finding postures and actions acceptable to more than one part, are used to help them communicate and cooperate with one another.

The importance of the therapeutic relationship as an interpersonal and integrative container that invites and holds all dissociative parts cannot be overstated. As the therapist accepts and relates to the subjective experience of each part of the patient while embracing the reality of the patient as a whole, "each part of the self becomes increasingly able to coexist with the rest, and in that sense is linked to the others. It is an experience of coherence, cohesiveness, and continuity, that comes about through human relatedness" (Bromberg, 2003, p. 704).

The more complex the dynamic system of dissociative parts of the patient, the slower and more careful the therapist usually should be—as integrative capacity is limited, at least in terms of dealing with inner experiences. The therapist must be able to distinguish brittle functioning in daily life in DID patients that is based on extreme avoidance from adaptive functioning in which the patient is able to deal with inner experiences, no matter how slowly. Otherwise, work may proceed too quickly and overwhelm the patient.

Where to Start?

A sequential approach to working with parts is often helpful. The first step, then, is to determine how tolerant the patient is of the idea of parts, and how much the patient as the main part functioning in daily life already knows about other parts and is able to communicate with them.

Psychoeducation. Next, the therapist offers psychoeducation to help the presenting part of the patient accept the importance of working with other dissociative parts. Because many patients are fearful or ashamed of their parts, they are often extremely reluctant to accept that they are dissociative. The therapist needs to help patients understand how the body responds to trauma, the animal defenses that are evoked, and how the posture and movement of the body contributes to maintaining dissociative parts as well as particular emotions and beliefs. The therapist's attitude and language can be helpful in decreasing the stigma of having parts. Therapists should find the way that is right for their patients, using their own language and ways of understanding.

Normalize the experience of parts. Therapists can explain that trauma, by definition, evokes instinctive animal defenses accompanied by characteristic physical actions and emotions and involves the inability to completely integrate the experience. A child cannot integrate a sense of who she is during abuse—when animal defenses, such as freeze or death feint, come into play—with who she is during daily life, when these defenses are not needed. In the former "self," the child is frozen and immobilized, unable to think. In the latter, she may be highly active, with a wide range of emotions and thoughts. The felt sense of her body and mind is vastly different in these different experiences. It is thus completely understandable that not only emotions, sensations, movements, and so on would be dissociated, but also a sense of one's own identity. Once the diagnosis has been made, some patients find it helpful for the therapist to explain that we all have different aspects of ourselves. We are different when we are at work, at home with our family, or enjoying a holiday. However, not everyone experiences these sides of ourselves as *not me*—that is, as having their own first-person perspective and sense of self; not everyone has dissociative barriers between parts and can shift easily from one mode to another. The therapist can explain that these barriers were necessary to help the patient survive very difficult times during childhood. The intrusive symptoms of parts can be explained so the patient does not feel crazy.

Explain and reframe the behaviors of dissociative parts. Most patients describe having dissociative parts that are haunting, threatening, terrorizing, or shameful. Some parts may appear as the perpetrator, others just as very angry and threatening voices. Patients may hear or experience inside themselves a grievously injured child, crying all the time and in excruciating pain, or other young parts that have temper tantrums or shake in fear. They may describe parts outside of their control that hurt their body, engage in promiscuous sex or prostitution, or drink or use drugs. From the start of therapy, it is helpful to explain the original functions of the behaviors of these parts and to reframe them as behaviors that attempt to solve a problem (see examples in Chapters 16 and 17).

Use language that helps the patient. Therapists tend to have their own favorite terminology for parts. Yet what is most important is to match the patient's experience. For example, one patient found the term *parts* frightening: *It makes me feel like I really* am *crazy!* The therapist asked what the patient would call these inner experiences and she replied, *My little fragments.* In her mind, this term was much less stigmatizing, so this was how the therapist referred to her dissociative parts. Another patient could not relate to having parts but did relate to animal defenses and physical patterns that reflected his "instincts." He referred to his instinct to get tense and puff up (angry part) and the instinct to freeze (immobile part). The therapist should inquire about how patients would like to talk about their experiences. Above all, the therapist must be flexible and use descriptors that patients prefer.

However, some patients simply refuse to acknowledge dissociation in any way. Sometimes a compromise needs to be found—for example, talking about *different ways of being* or *different moods*. Other patients are so convinced that parts are separate people that the therapist must tread carefully. For example, Marta, a patient who had DID, referred to her parts as *my inner people*. The therapist sometimes referred to Marta's parts as *what you call your inner people and I call parts of you*. If the patient has no particular preference, one of these terms could be used:

- parts of me or dissociative parts of myself;
- alters;
- parts of my personality;
- different ways of being me;
- modes;
- moods;
- aspects of myself or aspects of me;
- the angry part of me; or
- the little me, or the adult me.

Some patients do not have names for their parts, especially those with OSDD. Therapists should *not* name parts, nor encourage the patient to do so if it has not already been done prior to therapy, except to identify them in a broad way, such as *the angry part* or *the young part of you*. The exception is perhaps to rename a part as a component of helping the patient accept the part more fully or emphasize their original protective or helping function. For example, renaming "the Bitch" to "the Protector," or "the Monster" to "the Little Child," or "Dad" to "Harry" can be helpful. This sort of reframing through renaming can only happen if the part agrees to another name, as it should not be forced. Usually, reviled parts are eventually eager to be accepted and often choose their own new name.

CASE EXAMPLES OF RENAMING A PART AS A THERAPEUTIC STRATEGY: TERRI AND PATRICIA

Terri had a part she called "Slut." Eventually, as they were working through Terri's shame at being sexually promiscuous, the therapist commented on what a harsh name that was. As Terri developed more compassion, she renamed that part of her "Cassidy," which means "clever" in Gaelic. She understood that Cassidy was the part of her that had learned to use sex as way to get attention and love under difficult circumstances. As Terri was better able to own her sexuality, Cassidy became less and less active and eventually integrated with Terri after an additional few years of treatment.

Another patient, Patricia, had two dissociative parts that she called "Mom" and "Dad." These parts terrified her, reenacting sadistic abuse from both parents. As part of an overall strategy to help Patricia become better able to mentalize effectively, the therapist focused on the differences between "inside" Mom and Dad and "outside" Mom and Dad. Patricia sensed that the internal parts were "younger versions" of her now-aging parents. The therapist suggested several ways to help Patricia distinguish between her internal parts and her actual parents. One suggestion included renaming the parts. Patricia liked that idea and renamed them "Edith" and "Archie" (from the sitcom *All in the Family*). This made her giggle and feel much less threatened.

Patients with DID often do have parts that they have named earlier in life. A common question is whether or not the therapist should refer to parts by name. There is no hard-and-fast rule other than that, regardless of how the therapist refers to parts, it should always be clear that the parts are seen as subsystems of one person.

Most therapists will use a specific name for a part if that part has already been named by the patient. For example, Helen called the young part of her Ellen. Sometimes the therapist referred to Ellen by name, but also often would say *the little part of you*, or *Ellen, the young part of you*. Interweaving this kind of clarifying language with a name is a helpful reminder to the patient that the therapist is holding both the patient's subjective reality and the reality that the patient is one person.

In general, using names should not become a power struggle. The therapist can use the above approach described with Helen if the patient insists on different names. The goal is to develop a working alliance with all parts of the patient. Therapists must risk entering the inner world of the patient with one foot, keeping the other foot grounded in the shared common reality of the present.

Begin work with the adult part(s) of the patient. The most stabilizing way to begin working with dissociative parts is with the adult part of the patient that presents to therapy and is usually phobic of other parts. In patients with DID, this may be more than one part, as there may be several parts that function in daily life and are phobic of parts stuck in trauma-time. A therapeutic contract must, by definition, include the adult part (or parts) of the patient so that the capacity to function in everyday life is maintained and improved. In addition, the adult part of the patient is held responsible for the actions of other dissociative parts.

Some patients come to therapy because their traumatic memories have become activated, and thus dissociative parts living in trauma-time have become more active. These patients may be switching during session, and the therapist must make a decision about which parts to work with first. Conversely, some patients may hide switching and the fact of dissociative parts, and it may be extremely difficult for the therapist to work knowingly with any parts. It is easy in these cases to act as though they do not exist, just like the patient as the adult part does. Some patients, as adult parts, may seek to have the therapist deal with other dissociative parts, so they will not have to. Others may have a strong wish to receive what they did not get in childhood and thus hope that the therapist will take care of young parts of themselves. The problem of switching will be discussed later in this chapter.

Some therapists are concerned with whether they must work with what has sometimes been called the "host"—that is, the part that is in control most of the time—or with the "birth personality" or "original personality or self." The host is simply the part of the patient that seems to be active in daily life most often, accompanied by postures, movements, and expressions that reflect that the patient is responding to current reality rather than being stuck in trauma-time. This may change over time, or may be a conglomerate of parts that have a (relatively) cooperative relationship regarding functioning in day-to-day life, so there may be no single part that is present most of the time. Because of the psychobiological nature of the development of dissociative parts in childhood, there may not be an "original" or "birth" personality. Personality is a developmental achievement: We are not born with a fully developed personality. Highly traumatized children may never have developed a cohesive personality in the first place. The therapist helps the patient as a whole be responsible for the actions of all parts, regardless of which part is "up front." This means that each part is eventually responsible to and for every other part.

Explicitly clarify that all parts have some common goals. Virtually all parts want relief or to feel better, even the ones that seem to have fierce objections to therapy, including parts that want to die to end the pain or believe they deserve to be punished. Therapists should help their patients understand that, no matter how much resistance and conflict they are experiencing, there are common goals for the person as a whole. The therapist may try explain it like this: *It's true, isn't it, that all parts of you do not wish to suffer? And it is true, isn't it, that even though you can hardly imagine it, all parts would like to feel better, even if only secretly? And all parts have agreed to allow you to come to therapy, even if reluctantly, otherwise I think you would not be here in my office. So somehow, without your awareness, all parts of you have somehow agreed that you do not want to suffer any longer, even though some think you should suffer and some feel you cannot stop suffering. It seems that all parts of you want to eliminate suffering. Would you agree with that? So there are some things that all parts have in common, and these are truly essential and good things, and we can start with these goals to which all parts can agree.*

Contacting Dissociative Parts

Before direct attempts at contact are made, the therapist needs to be clear about what is most helpful to discuss. Dissociative parts may have an endless array of topics they want to talk about. Each part has its own agenda and set of interests. Many of these are avoidance strategies. Some topics are important, but are presented at an inappropriate time, such as traumatic memories early in Phase 1. The therapist must remain a guide to keeping therapy on track, following coherent threads without getting sidetracked (see Chapter 8).

CORE CONCEPT

Initial attempts to facilitate communication among parts should focus on stabilization and helping the patient function in daily life, not on sharing traumatic memories.

In general, therapists should begin promoting communication, cooperation and, when possible, compassion among parts as soon as is feasible. Initial inner communication should focus on daily life function and stabilization, not on traumatic memory. To the degree possible, the work should remain at a somewhat cognitive level until dissociative parts are able to regulate emotion. For example, the therapist can encourage parts to work out conflicts about going to work or caring for the patient's children, or ways to decrease self-harm or other unsafe behaviors. Those parts that want to share traumatic memories can be asked respectfully to hold those memories in a safe container until the time is right. Below, we share several possible ways to make contact with dissociative parts.

- ***Talking through*** (Kluft, 1982). Speaking to the patient, the therapist can say something like, *As we are talking, you can allow all parts of you* *(or all corners of your mind; all aspects of you; your whole being or self) to listen and participate.* Talking through is a regular part of most sessions, and can be encouraged even when the therapist is only working with one or two parts. Talking through is often effective in beginning to address perpetrator-imitating parts and other parts that object to being in therapy or to working on certain issues. Above we described how important it is to explain and reframe the functions of parts. This can first be accomplished via talking through. Some patients find it frightening when the therapist talks through to other parts, in particular to perpetrator-imitating parts or other very ashamed parts, because they begin to experience these parts, of which they are phobic. In the beginning of therapy these reactions may be fierce and overwhelming. As always, pacing is essential, so for some patients with very intense reactions, talking through must come in small doses.

- The adult part of the patient as mediator. Another way of communicating with parts is through the adult part presenting in therapy. This adult part of the patient can listen internally and communicate to the therapist on behalf of other parts. This method is effective when the phobia of dissociative parts is not so extreme, usually in cases where there is just one adult part functioning in daily life.

- Other parts as mediator (inner observer parts). Some patients have one or more parts that serve as "communicators" for inside parts. These may not be the same as the adult part that is present most of the time. These inner observer parts may be helpful in starting a communication between the therapist and other parts (with or without the adult part present initially), as they usually are aware of parts. Commonly, these parts are relatively free of emotion, making them helpful objective observers. (The ability to avoid affect is useful in the short run, but in the long term these parts also need to learn to feel.)

- Asking a part to come forward in the session. The most direct way of communicating with a part is to ask the part to come forward in session and talk to the therapist. Of course, this is best when the adult part presenting in therapy is "listening in." However, if dissociative barriers are still rigid and the phobia for each other is strong, the therapist may talk with a part without the adult part present. In this case, the therapist acts as a "go-between" or mediator, as a main goal of therapy is to help parts understand each other and promote constructive inner communication. In general, it is best to share as much between parts as can be tolerated, and patient and therapist together should determine how much at a time is helpful. If the therapist pushes and shares too much, this will only result in more adverse reactions. Working directly with parts through switching should be done early in a session, with plenty of time to have the adult part of the patient grounded and present before the session ends.

- Asking a part to communicate through writing or art. If parts are still too phobic to communicate directly with the therapist in the session or the presenting adult is too terrified, the therapist may ask the patient to allow parts to write in a journal. In some cases, e-mails can be helpful, but the therapist should receive consultation on whether this is appropriate and how it should be structured, due to the danger of dependency and having too much material coming from outside the sessions. Some parts communicate well through art. It is wise to negotiate with all parts to agree not to destroy the work or communications of any part, as this happens often when there is minimal collaboration and maximum conflict. For most patients, this may take time, and it is not uncommon for them to consistently "forget" to bring a journal to session, or be unable to find it, or discover pages are torn out.

- Ideomotor finger signals. Ideomotor finger signals are an advanced hypnotic technique. They involve the elicitation of automatic and often minute muscle reactions in the fingers (lifting the finger) when the therapist asks the patient a question (Cheek & LeCron, 1968; Cheek & Rossi, 1994; Ewin & Eimer, 2006). This technique should not be used without training in hypnosis, specifically in using ideomotor signaling. Ideomotor signaling has been used quite effectively in the treatment of dissociative disorders, especially in contacting parts that are reluctant to participate in therapy or in eliciting information not known to available parts (e.g., Fine, 1993; Kluft, 1982, 2001; Loewenstein, 1991a). The therapist sets up a set of signals with the patient's fingers indicating *Yes, No, I don't know,* and *Stop!* The stop signal should be a big signal with the whole hand, so that the therapist can never miss it. The therapist then assures the patient as a whole that he or she is in control and can always use the stop signal when needed. Some patients have different systems of parts that want to use different hands to answer, especially patients with more complex inner systems. The therapist then asks non-open-ended questions. For example, *I wonder if perhaps the part that is cutting you has a concern that we do not yet understand?* or *Could it be that some part of you knows more about what is making you so suicidal?*

A Rational Sequence of Working With Parts

Although every patient's dissociative organization is different, an effective general sequence of working with parts involves the following:

- Strengthen and stabilize parts that function in daily life and help these parts to develop some inner collaboration.
- Simultaneously contain parts stuck in trauma-time (for instance, by helping these parts to create safe places to which they can retreat or have containers for their traumatic memories) and identify somatic characteristics of these parts.
- Work with all parts of the patient via talking through or other means to the degree possible in every session.
- When work with all parts is not possible, work with two or more parts to facilitate communication, cooperation, and compassion. For example, if two parts that function in daily life are in conflict, work with those parts to increase their cooperation.
- When it is not possible to work with two or more parts simultaneously, work with a single part to decrease arousal, orient to the present, and then foster inner communication with other parts.
- Engage parts early in therapy that are opposed to therapy, highly defensive, self-destructive, or undermining of the therapeutic relationship, such as parts that imitate the perpetrator(s).
- Gradually expose parts to each other first, without sharing traumatic memories. Keep the focus on present-day life and problems until it becomes clear that traumatic memories can be resolved (see Chapters 19 and 20).
- Help parts develop ongoing awareness (co-consciousness) and cooperation regarding functioning in daily life and the postures and actions that support this functioning.
- Help all parts develop self-compassion as expressed to various parts, and find physical actions that demonstrate compassion.
- As needed, work with intrusive parts that cannot be contained.
  - Ground and orient parts to the present.
  - Engage other parts to help each other by comforting, orienting, etc.

By working with adult parts that function in daily life first, and identifying and practicing the physical organization associated with these parts, there is a greater chance to improve the patient's coping skills. The therapist focuses on those issues that are destabilizing the patient—that is, the adult part presenting in the therapy room. The following questions might be helpful:

- What are your concerns and feelings about parts of yourself?
- What are you afraid might happen if you know more about these parts of yourself?

- Are you aware of different opinions inside yourself with regard to being in therapy?
- What posture or movement can you embody to help you remain present and not switch to other parts?

CASE EXAMPLE OF WORKING WITH DISSOCIATIVE PARTS: PERRY

Perry, a patient with DID, told his therapist after the first few months of therapy that he was often very confused and sometimes totally paralyzed after a session. He said that inner voices would become loud, and the fights inside were increasing to such an extent that he really wondered if he should continue therapy. He described being pulled in many different directions: (a) wishing to stay in the office of the therapist because he felt safe there, (b) running away terrified because it felt like something terrible was going to happen, (c) imagining himself shouting at the therapist that she was stupid and didn't know what she was getting herself into, (d) being really interested in what was being discussed although it felt that it was not relevant to him at all, and (e) feeling stupid and ridiculous about himself and all these reactions.

His therapist validated his fears and told Perry that he was courageous to share his different thoughts and feelings. Gradually, Perry understood that these different reactions to therapy stemmed from his inner parts and were based on their past experiences in relationships. Each part was invited to let both Perry and the therapist know their concerns about therapist that led to the inner chaos Perry experienced. Each part was validated as having an important function, and the therapist helped Perry learn to fear these parts less and acknowledge them with compassion more often. Perry and his therapist slowly learned to identify the emotions, thoughts, and the physical characteristics of each part and associate the movements and postures with the particular function of each part, which also supported understanding, cooperation, and compassion.

Dealing With Switching Among Dissociative Parts

The therapist should always be curious about why the patient is switching at a given moment, as it is not random but has both function and meaning. The therapist should remember that switching can have more than one function, one of which is often in reaction to something in the therapeutic relationship. As noted earlier, switching may occur for the following reasons:

- to manage closeness or distance in a relationship in the present;
- in response to internal conflicts about being in therapy, or about different opinions with regard to therapist and attachment to him or her;
- in response to inner conflict about the topic that is being discussed at that moment;
- to receive something from the therapist that is not otherwise acceptable to the person (e.g., patient switches to a child part to receive nurturing);
- to express what might otherwise be unacceptable to the person (e.g., patient switches to an angry part to express anger toward the therapist);
- to avoid confrontation by the therapist about inappropriate behavior (e.g., patient switches to a scared child part in order to avoid dealing with an episode of cutting or shoplifting);
- for one part to assert control over others (usually for the other reasons listed here);
- to avoid the current work of therapy, including to distract the therapist;
- in response to particular sensations, movements, and postures that "pull" the patient into a particular part;
- in response to reactivated traumatic memories or to a trigger related to traumatic memories; and
- in response to the activity of parts internally—for instance, threats against talking about a certain subject.

The goal is to notice what precipitates switches in a patient, to support all parts in being more present and focused on one topic at a time, and to increase the capacity of the patient as a whole to tolerate distress with more adaptive skills than switching. Often, helping a patient become aware of the somatic precursors to switching, such as a particular sensation, tension, movement, or posture, can help the patient exert a measure of control over switching by executing a different action or purposefully creating a different sensation.

CORE CONCEPT

Overt switching between parts is not random. It always has a function—often of avoidance, getting unacceptable needs met, or coping with threat—and typically occurs when the patient is under some duress.

TABLE 10.1
Managing Switching During Sessions

- When you notice a switch, immediately stop and ask the patient what just happened.

Example: *Mary, what just happened? Something has shifted, and I am not sure why. Let's help you get more present.*

- Ask if the part can "return" to the present.

Example: *I'd like to ask if Mary can be present again, because we were not finished with our conversation. I'm glad to help if you need.*

You can also identify the somatic change and ask for a different posture: *Let's both try sitting up tall in the chair right now.* Or, if a patient has become very still: *Let's get up and walk around for a minute.*

- If not, encourage the part to listen.

Example: *Mary, it is important that you continue to listen and participate. I have confidence that you will be able to do that in your own time and at your own pace.*

- One option is to stay on the original subject with a different part in the forefront.

Example: *Are you aware of what we were just talking about? I'd like to understand your thoughts and feelings about what we are discussing.*

- If the part was not aware, be curious about why not.

Example: *I wonder what is making it difficult for you to be aware? I wonder what prompted you to be here all of a sudden? Would parts of you inside be willing to share with you what we were talking about?*

- Or ask if that part is aware of the part that "went away."

Example: *Could you check inside and see what is happening with Mary? Let's find a way to help her. Or, Can you notice what it is like for you to be aware of Mary, even if at a distance?*

- Or inquire about why the part switched.

Example: *Could you help me understand why it is important for you to be here right now and not the adult part of you?*

The first questions to ask when a sudden switch occurs are geared to understanding what might have precipitated the switch.

- What just happened?
- What changed in your body that precipitated the switch?
- Is the part of you that was just here still able to listen right now?
- Are you aware of what we were just talking about? No? Then can you check inside and see if a part of you will help you?

In Derrick's case, he became uneasy because he did not remember being at work, and he switched. One of the work parts (the dissociative part that had a social function to deal with colleagues) came forward when the therapist explored the work situation. This part started talking about Derrick to the therapist: *Well, he can't work anymore. He's just such a weak, fearful character. He can't concentrate and makes stupid mistakes. We are going to get fired because of him. What is he going to do then?* The therapist responded that she understood that this part came to help Derrick because he was feeling uneasy about losing time. However, she also asked whether this part was willing to start some communication with Derrick—that is, the main part functioning in daily life—in the coming week.

Sometimes one part may be pushed forward by other dissociative parts; for instance, to divert attention from an inner conflict or emotion that is too overwhelming. This is often the case when younger parts suddenly come forward without apparent reason. If switching is clearly a protective action, the therapist should always ask the part of the patient that "disappeared" to return and continue the conversation, or to at least explore the reasons why that is not feasible.

The therapist should continue to talk through to all parts, focused on the reason for switching and, to the degree possible, on the original conversation, unless it is clearly outside the window of tolerance of the patient. Inner parts are encouraged to care for a part that may be overwhelmed. The therapist might remark that it is not fair to a small child part to be sent to deal with things that adult parts are not willing to deal with. In this way, the therapist continually focuses on the need for parts to care for each other and find more adaptive ways to cope with the present.

Further Explorations

10.1 Can you accurately describe the reasons for dissociation to your patients? If not, go back and review, and practice until you feel confident.

10.2 Make a list of the functions of parts of one of your patients. Can you identify the actions involved, as well as the non-realizations?

10.3 Practice "talking through" to all parts with a dissociative patient. If you do not feel comfortable, ask a colleague to role-play with you.

10.4 Do you have a sense of when you should work with all parts, when with some parts, and when with only one part at a time?

10.5 How do you feel when a patient switches? Use role-playing with your colleagues to practice handling patients' switching, so you can gain confidence.

10.6 Can you identify the subtle or not-so-subtle changes in the body that indicate the emergence of a part of your patient? Can you think of ways that you could use the body to help parts of the patient communicate, develop compassion, or understand one another?

CHAPTER 11

Resistance as Phobic Avoidance: An Introduction

"Resistances" in therapy can be understood as the maladaptive avoidance and escape strategies of a traumatized patient.
—Onno van der Hart, Ellert Nijenhuis, and Kathy Steele (2006, p. 234)

When therapy does not progress, it is usually a function of both the client's resistance and the therapist's counterresistance. Therapeutic stalemates, in effect, are a mutual creation of client and therapist.

—Howard Strean (1993, p. 2)

Challenging patients are typically portrayed as those who avoid or oppose the work of therapy. The literature has long described such individuals as "resistant." Unfortunately, the term resistance has become a pejorative judgment of patient behaviors or attitudes that therapists experience as thwarting their efforts (Messer, 2002). This completely discounts the fact that the therapist also has resistances (Schoenewolf, 1993; Strean, 1993). Chronic trauma survivors in particular often have been labeled as resistant, in large part because many therapists simply do not fully understand their needs and issues in treatment and how to approach them. In fact, resistance is often a very understandable phobic avoidance of what the patient deems intolerable. Ultimately, resistance is a phobia of realization.

Problems With the Term Resistance

There are several difficulties with the term resistance that make it a potential impediment for the therapist to understand and help the patient. First, as noted above, resistance is often used as a pejorative, and inappropriately so. A resistant patient is often overtly or implicitly considered to be a "bad," "untreatable," or "refractory" patient who obstructs the therapist and the therapy. This view leads to increasing frustration, hopelessness, and disdain from the therapist, and to a rupture in the therapeutic relationship, which then leads to intractable impasses. This does not discount that patients can be challenging and that some may not benefit from therapy.

Second, resistance implies there is an obstruction interjected by the patient that disrupts an otherwise natural trajectory of treatment. In fact, our patients come to treatment *because* they cannot make certain changes and because they are phobically avoidant of what is painful, which they cannot overcome themselves. Resolving resistance *is* the major and essential work of psychotherapy (Messer, 2002).

Third, the therapist often focuses on resistance as a problem rather than as a symptom of underlying distress that needs to be directly addressed. Patients are described as resistant, for example, because they do not come to sessions consistently or leave sessions on time, do not stay on topic, refuse to accept dissociative parts, are constantly self-harming or suicidal, make unreasonable demands in therapy, or are in constant conflict with the therapist. But *why?* What purpose do these behaviors serve? And, as importantly, how can the therapist join with the patient to explore and gradually erode the resistance in a collaborative and compassionate way? These are essential questions to answer, as they lead to understanding and the ability to help the patient gain competence in a stepwise fashion to overcome avoidance.

Last, but certainly not least, resistance may actually lie not with the patient but with the therapist. As we will discuss further in this chapter, therapists often create or co-create impasses in treatment (e.g., Schoenewolf, 1993; Strean, 1993). Thus, when patients are labeled as resistant, therapists must also look at their contribution to the situation. For example, therapists may not understand the patient or the issues. They may fail to attend to the therapeutic relationship. Perhaps they do not formulate a coherent treatment plan or revise it as needed. They may not keep adequate boundaries, or maybe they are overly rigid and unavailable. They may find the patient's behavior irritating or frightening on a personal level and be unable to resolve their irritation or fear. They may focus too much on content instead of process; neglect to pace treatment; or feel chronically anxious, frustrated, angry, ashamed, or overwhelmed by the patient. Therapists may also automatically engage in their own animal defenses—for example, freezing in the face of an angry or demanding patent, shutting down when a patient is needy, or reacting aggressively to a patient who is provocative in some way.

CORE CONCEPT

Resistance is perhaps best conceptualized as phobic avoidance of what the patient believes is too overwhelming to realize. Phobic avoidance can develop for certain thoughts, emotions, sensations, predictions about the future, behaviors, dissociative parts, memories, current or past situations, relationship disruptions, and change in general (Janet, 1904, 1925b; Steele et al., 2005; Van der Hart et al., 2006).

Resistance as Physiology

Resistance is not only a psychological problem. Certain behaviors, such as silence, shutdown, extreme avoidance, or anger, are embedded in the body's chronic reactions to danger and life threat. When our patients are fixed in animal defenses of attachment cry, fight, flight, flag, freeze, or faint, they respond in maladaptive ways to the usual verbal and psychological nuances of psychotherapy.

Therapists may misinterpret the psychological and relational symptoms of these physiological conditions as resistance. For example, silent patients are often labeled as resistant. Withholding from the therapist may be one reason for silence, but it is certainly not the only one, and perhaps not even the most common one. Understanding that resistance is a way to solve a problem is crucial. Patients fixed in a freeze or shutdown reaction are overwhelmed with emotion and literally unable to speak—although they might desperately want to—as the speech center of the brain is not functioning. This is not a resistance at all, but a physiological condition.

The therapist should be able to

- recognize physiological signs of animal defense,
- help the patient feel safe first by orienting to the present and reducing hyper- or hypoarousal, and
- then be curious with the patient about the reasons for the defense in the moment.

Resistance as Phobic Avoidance

Resistance can be understood as phobic avoidance of what is perceived as overwhelming or otherwise beyond the capacity of the patient to realize. Addressing resistance as phobic avoidance places the therapeutic focus squarely on what the patient is avoiding and why, rather than on the behaviors that serve as the avoidance strategy. Phobic avoidance, which is often implicit and which may be compartmentalized in various dissociative parts of the patient, is intended as protection against traumatic and other painful experiences that are difficult or impossible for the patient to accept and integrate (Steele et al., 2005; Van der Hart et al., 2006). Some patients may have the potential to deal with what is avoided, but the avoidance has become such a habit that it is very difficult to stop. Either way, avoidance keeps intolerable experiences out of the foreground so that patients do not have to feel, think, sense, or know what they fear will lead to decompensation, rejection, or shaming by others: *If I remember, I will go crazy,* or *If you really knew what I thought, you would hate me.*

During and immediately after traumatic experiences, dissociation involves an *inability* to integrate experience sufficiently. But thereafter, even if patients develop better capacities and skills, they may still become increasingly avoidant of certain experiences, resulting in a cascade of trauma-related phobias (Steele et al., 2005; Van der Hart et al., 2006). As mentioned before, these include the phobia of inner experience, the phobia of attachment and attachment loss, the phobia of dissociative parts, the phobia of traumatic memory, and the phobia of adaptive change.

Trauma-related phobias have been discussed in earlier chapters, and their resolution is central to the successful treatment of dissociation. These phobias typically underlie resistance in the patient. The therapist needs to assess whether the patient has the capacities and skills needed to overcome these phobias, and if not, must first help the patient develop these skills in the early phase of treatment. Otherwise, resistance may be inevitable. If the patient has skills and is still phobic, the therapist can explore the avoidant resistance with the patient. Often fear, shame, or unrealistic beliefs remain about facing what is avoided. Particular dissociative parts remain stuck in trauma-time and thus unable to realize that there is now adequate safety and support to deal with painful issues. Instead of blaming the patient and feeling frustrated, the therapist can remain with the patient's experience and explore it with compassion and interest.

CORE CONCEPT

The therapist's attitudes toward and beliefs about resistance expand
or diminish the possibilities of helping patients effectively work
through their phobic avoidance.

Dissociative patients typically have an inherent conflict among their dissociative parts in almost all phobic avoidance: *I want to change because it will be better for me; I do not want to change because it will be worse for me.* It is this kind of conflict that needs to be held in the forefront of the therapist's mind, in a compassionate way, so that the patient can be supported in accepting various sides of the conflict that may be dissociated into different parts.

CASE EXAMPLE OF RESISTANCE AS PHOBIC AVOIDANCE: TALLY

Tally was a 33-year-old gay male patient with diagnoses of DID, major depression, and significant relationship problems with his partner. The partner periodically became violent when under the influence of alcohol, and several parts of Tally that functioned in daily life were eager to separate from him. But every time Tally began talking about leaving, he felt an intense nausea and paralysis, in which his thinking became foggy and he felt suicidal. Gradually, with the help of the therapist, an adult part of Tally was able to recognize that a child part was frozen, terrified at the prospect of being alone, and desperately did not want to leave the partner, as that would trigger unbearable abandonment issues. The child part's phobia of attachment loss fueled "resistance" to moving forward with leaving a violent partner. The therapist helped the adult parts of Tally accept and be more compassionate toward the child part. Tally could then make a safety plan that involved leaving his abusive partner.

Resistance as a Co-Creation of Patient and Therapist

Therapists have their own counterresistance, which often implicitly intertwines with the patient's phobic avoidance to create an impasse in treatment (Boesky, 1990; Schoenewolf, 1993; Strean, 1993). Any time therapists become defensive, they increase the possibility of resistance on the part of the patient. Any time we avoid; dread; feel ashamed; act out of anger, frustration, hopelessness, or fear; or fail to maintain adequate boundaries, we increase patient resistance through our own counterresistance. In this way, patient and therapist both contribute to lack of progress. There is certainly no other therapy that unearths more unresolved issues, evoking counterresistances in the therapist, than work with highly dissociative individuals. Dissociative patients struggle with profound attachment, trauma, identity, regulatory, and existential problems, and have intense resistance of their own. It is little wonder that therapists develop resistances as well. We offer a partial list of counterresistances in Table 11.1.

TABLE 11.1

Indications of Counterresistance in the Therapist

- Talking too much or not enough during sessions
- Self-disclosing too much or too frequently
- Patient and therapist both avoiding difficult issues while enjoying their relationship
- Becoming friends or becoming sexual with the patient
- Idealizing the patient
- Devaluing and talking badly about the patient to colleagues
- Feeling sorry for the patient
- Needing to fix or cure the patient
- Being enthralled by the patient
- Having chronic negative feelings about the patient (frustration, anger, shame, guilt, disgust, boredom) without resolution
- Feeling that the patient is special and thus needs special treatment
- Experiencing fascination with dissociation and dissociative parts
- Treating dissociative parts as different people
- Dreading sessions
- Seeing a particular patient at odd hours, in places other than the office; having sessions without a set beginning or end time
- Violating boundaries; being inconsistent with boundaries and the therapy frame
- Increasing contact with a chronically suicidal patient out of fear
- Being chronically late to sessions or not ending sessions on time
- Forgetting sessions
- Chronic overscheduling or double-booking
- Not setting a regular schedule with a patient
- Being overly reassuring, appeasing, caretaking, judgmental, or critical of the patient
- Being unable or unwilling to talk about important subjects with the patient (e.g., sex, fees, fantasies, shame, boundaries)
- Being unable or unwilling to deal with certain parts of the patient (e.g., perpetrator-imitating part, angry or hostile part, sexualized part, child part)

continues

Resistance as Phobic Avoidance: An Introduction   **231**

- Favoring certain parts over others
- Denying problems with the therapy
- Experiencing inability or unwillingness to act due to shame, fear, or rage; or acting impulsively or in reaction to the patient
- Demonstrating inability or unwillingness to abide by reasonable suggestions given in supervision and consultation
- Failing to seek supervision or consultation
- Remaining unwilling to terminate an unworkable therapy after extensive consultation and recommendations to do so
- Needing the patient to be successful as a reflection of being a good therapist
- Needing to "save" the patient at all costs
- Needing to be needed
- Avoiding discussing or dealing with dependency issues in treatment
- Trying to work in emotional "blackmail" scenarios without addressing them directly (e.g., *If you don't call me every day I will kill myself; If you stop the therapy I will kill myself—you are the only one that can help me*)
- Splitting with a treatment team; talking badly about other team members to the patient, or talking badly about the patient to team members
- Overfocusing on the content of traumatic memories or exhibiting a counterphobic attitude to trauma
- Completely avoiding traumatic content
- Having uncritical belief (or disbelief) of the patient; being unable to reflect on what the patient needs instead of what is "true" or "not true"
- Sadistic acting out toward the patient with punitive interpretations, withholding, scorn, etc

---

CORE CONCEPT

Resistance involves interactional patterns between the patient and therapist that block effective therapeutic work in the moment (Van Denburg & Kiesler, 2002).

CASE EXAMPLE OF RESISTANCE AND COUNTERRESISTANCE: MIA AND BEVERLY

Mia, a very competent therapist, sought consultation for a challenging case. Her patient, Beverly, was engaging in self-harm after sessions several times a month. Mia expressed frustration, saying she had tried to teach

Beverly every self-regulating skill she knew, but this had not been effective. She kept excellent boundaries with the patient and worked in a systemic way that did not foster further dissociation. She could not understand why Beverly continued to engage in self-destructive behavior. The consultant asked about what was being worked on currently in the sessions, what happened at the end of sessions, and what the therapeutic relationship felt like to the therapist. Mia noted that session content was focused on stabilization skills, which was appropriate for this phase of early therapy. She also noted that Beverly seemed to switch to a kind of calm but flat affect before leaving session. *To be honest,* she told the consultant, *I feel a little relief when she leaves like that, because it's not such a struggle to end the session like it used to be. But I wonder if maybe she is a bit depersonalized. I haven't addressed it because I had such a hard time getting her contained before this.*

The consultant pointed out that perhaps the patient was engaging in a controlling caregiving strategy (Hesse, Main, Abrams, & Rifkin, 2003; Liotti, 2011), making sure she did not display any needs that might bother Mia at the end of session. And perhaps Mia was colluding with that caretaking by feeling relief, giving the implicit message to Beverly that suppression of part of her experience was welcome. Mia recognized this in herself immediately and after reflecting more, discussed the end of sessions with Beverly. Indeed, there were child parts that were being punished internally for trying to "show up" in session. Beverly desperately did not want to push Mia away with her neediness, yet she could not contain it once she got home. A very angry adolescent part would cut her as a punishment for what she believed were the unacceptable needs of the child part.

Once Mia was able to acknowledge and resolve her own avoidance by recognizing it, talking with the consultant, and confronting her discomfort, she could help Beverly find more effective ways to bring her neediness into session without being overwhelmed, and to contain with compassion at the end of session rather than use forceful suppression. Beverly felt more connected to Mia, and could thus use sessions as a more effective container. Together they developed a collaborative strategy to pace the therapy and make the end of sessions tolerable, effective, and timely. Mia worked with the adolescent part to deal with her anger both at child parts and at Mia (for not helping). And Mia helped Beverly connect more to the adolescent part of herself. The self-harm completely abated over the course of several weeks.

Temporary Versus Enduring Phobic Avoidance

Therapists should assume that patients come to therapy intending to make positive changes for themselves. The very act of coming for help is already a step in the right direction. Yet who among us is not sometimes hesitant, or even phobically afraid, of the changes we need to make or of the realizations we need to accept? We all experience transitory resistance from time to time. This has been referred to as state resistance—a temporary condition that can be due to a variety of factors, such as timing or lack of skills, awareness, or support (Beutler, Rocco, Moleiro, & Talebi, 2001; Van Denburg & Kiesler, 2002). But once we have sufficient support and skills, we are usually able to move forward relatively effectively. Kluft (1995, 2007) has more aptly referred to this as reluctance rather than resistance.

It can be helpful to know if a patient's phobic avoidance is due to a temporary problem—such as a recent rupture in the relationship, fear of a particular emotion or memory, or the emergence of a new part—or whether the patient's resistance to change is more enduring. Temporary or state resistance (reluctance) is generally resolved within the context of the therapeutic relationship, with trust, education, reassurance, and collaboration. However, these direct interventions rarely work with phobic avoidance that has become a part of the way the patient deals with life in general.

CORE CONCEPT

Resistance can be temporary—based on reluctance due to lack of knowledge, fear, or shame—or it can be enduring. The latter is an expression of persistent and pervasive phobia of realization and change. Those patients with phobic avoidance as part of their enduring way of being are the most challenging to treat. However, when success is achieved, it is when the therapist has been able to remain consistently patient, persistent, curious, engaged, and nondefensive, and has kept healthy boundaries.

As stated above, some patients have developed an enduring way of being that is strongly avoidant of—and sometimes aggressively opposed to—change, realization, or any interpersonal influence from the therapist (Beutler et al., 2001; Van Denburg & Kiesler, 2002). Their phobic avoidance spills over in their daily lives and contributes to chronic relationship problems at home and at work. These patients typically have severe attachment and regulatory problems, with high levels of reactivity and rigidity, and little capacity to mentalize. Patients with enduring resistance have multiple layers of phobic avoidance that stand like a series of walls between them and what they fear. Thus, they may eschew almost any attempts at connection with what they avoid, no matter how innocuous.

This leaves the therapist feeling hopelessly de-skilled and incompetent, and sometimes frustrated and enraged. Which, in turn, leads to counterresistance. A vicious cycle ensues that cements and prolongs the impasse.

Change in these patients is a "hard work miracle," as one therapist described it (S. M. Johnson, 1985). Therapy is often slow and arduous for patient and therapist, and uneven over many years. Such patients need much more room to be self-directed, feel in control, and come up with their own therapeutic goals (Beutler, Harwood, Michelson, Song, & Holman, 2010).

Working With Enduring Resistance

Enduring resistance takes many forms, but it is mostly experienced via difficulties in the therapy relationship and various forms of acting out. There is little conflict internally about the resistance, and it feels ego-syntonic to the patient. The therapist may experience the patient as extremely demanding, entitled, aggressive, avoidant, fearful, controlling, sadistic, withdrawn, silent, enraged, or intensely suffering. The patient may experience the therapist as not doing or saying the right thing, not understanding, wanting the patient to suffer or not caring if the patient suffers, being cold and callous, withholding, punitive, or controlling. The patient believes that if only the therapist would be different, do something different, say something different, feel something different, he or she could get better (Stark, 2002). No matter what the therapist suggests, it is experienced as unhelpful, stupid, condescending, insufficient, or just plain wrong, at least by dominant parts. There is always at least one reason, and often several, why the patient believes a given suggestion will not work or an interpretation is not accurate.

Guidance must be implicit rather than explicit in enduring resistance. Often, the more creative and clever therapists try to be in offering interventions and suggestions, the harder they work to be helpful, the greater the resistance. Power struggles must be avoided at all costs; therapists must not take on the patient's changes as their own goals. The goal of the therapist in these situations is to be compassionate with the patient's phobic avoidance without trying to force change, and to keep therapy focused on resolving reasons for the resistance.

Enduring resistance related to ongoing victimization. In some patients, enduring resistance may be a sign that continuing abuse is occurring. As shocking as it may seem to the uninitiated therapist, abuse by perpetrators from childhood can be carried on into the adulthood of the patient. For example, Middleton (2013, 2014) has noted the hidden problem of ongoing incest. There is also now much information on the enormous problem of ongoing victimization in sex trafficking, for example.

Severe enmeshment with and loyalties among specific dissociative parts to the perpetrators make it extremely difficult for the patient to stop contact and make progress in therapy. Patients who are still being abused may appear extremely resistant. Even the most basic and helpful interventions to regulate may be unsuccessful. If a patient does not improve in spite of good care, the therapist should at least consider the possibility that the patient may be in an ongoing abusive relationship. We will further discuss the complex issues of ongoing abuse in Chapter 19.

Table 11.2 offers suggestions for working with resistance.

TABLE 11.2
Tips for Working With Enduring Resistance

- The best place to start with patients who have enduring phobic avoidance is with assessment. The earlier in therapy these entrenched patterns are recognized, the less likely the therapist will be caught in impasses and power struggles.
- Try to understand everything about the phobic avoidance: the beliefs that reinforce it, the somatic experience of it, how it helps, any costs to it, the emotions related to it (e.g., fear, shame, rage).
- Give highly resistant patients plenty of room to direct themselves, to develop their own goals in therapy, and to feel in control of what happens (Beutler et al., 2010). It is generally very helpful to go back again and again to a patient's stated goals: Let's return for a moment to the goals you have set for yourself in therapy and that we have agreed upon. How can we best address some of those in the session today?
- Even though the patients are directing their therapy, the therapist must be firm in keeping the basic frame and boundaries of therapy despite patients' intense demands to do otherwise.
- Point out double binds in an empathic way, metacommunicating the problem: I notice that when I try to help or understand that I am not really being of much help or am not understanding clearly, even though I would like to. On the other hand, if I sit back and say or do nothing, that also isn't experienced as helpful, of course. I would like for us to find our way together, so I wonder if there might be some inner conflicts among parts of you that might be helpful

---

for us to explore. Also I wonder if various parts of you have some better ideas of how I might best be with you right now.

- Always have the patient experiment with a new skill or experience without any expectation of success or failure: Let's just notice together what happens (Ogden et al., 2006).
- Help all parts explore conflicts about change, so that the therapist becomes less triangulated as the only one promoting change. Are there any parts of the patient that feel more open and curious than others? Could those parts share their interest with more avoidant parts?

CASE EXAMPLE OF ENDURING RESISTANCE: RORY

Rory was a 46-year-old woman with DID and borderline personality disorder who had been relatively functional until her father died when she was 33 years old. At that point she decompensated and was flooded with traumatic memories. She became severely depressed and anxious, cut herself regularly, and was chronically suicidal and unable to work. However, she did not enter therapy for another 10 years. By the time she came to therapy, Rory was thoroughly entrenched in chronic dysregulation, instability, and crisis. She was lonely and hated herself. She had unbearable and nearly constant flashbacks of abandonment and of sexual and physical abuse by several perpetrators. She sometimes bordered on abuse and neglect with her own children and partner, often cut herself, and made numerous suicide attempts. She stopped eating and lost 30 pounds. She was very wedded to the idea of being victimized—sometimes she drove to dangerous areas of the city in the middle of the night and walked around; she explained to her therapist that *It is my fate to be raped.* Over and over she said, *I am nothing. I am just pain.*

She was hospitalized several times to prevent a suicide attempt or following one. Stabilization was painfully slow to develop, but gradually she became less suicidal, and the self-harm stopped. However, she remained highly dysregulated, in much conflict with the therapist, and unable to enjoy anything about life. She was so wrapped up in her suffering that nothing seemed to make a difference.

The therapist asked Rory about her experience of making changes in therapy and she replied, *Change means everything will be gone. Everything will change, just like it did when I was a kid. Someone was always making "a change," and it was always hurting me. My mother left me when I was a month old because she wanted "a change." My father abandoned me when I was six because he wanted "a change."* Rory asked that the word *change* not be used anymore, as it held so much terror and uncertainty for her, and suggested instead that they use the word *heal.* The therapist then asked if Rory could think about *wanting to want* to heal, and she could, even though she believed she did not deserve it.

From this small foothold, Rory and the therapist began to explore what it was like for Rory to want to want to heal, which gave her the safety of exploring change without having to make a change. The therapist focused on positive experiences in which Rory could experience a small moment of positive emotion or sensation. She gave Rory as much control and as little direction as possible, offering support and relational regulation. Rory developed small goals toward healing that she could gradually meet. The therapeutic relationship improved considerably: There was less conflict and more trust. The therapist was careful not to highlight to Rory the fact that she was slowly making progress, as she knew that Rory was so afraid of getting better.

The therapist worked diligently to access a very difficult sadistic per-petrator-imitating part. Over the course of three more years of the thera-pist falling into and getting out of power struggles and double binds, this part gradually engaged in therapy and became cooperative. Rory allowed her extreme dependency needs to surface, which took tremendous trust in herself and the therapist. She imagined an infant without skin being cared for by both her and the therapist. She imagined the infant gradually developing skin, and then growing into a healthy child and then becoming an adult. One day in therapy while working with this part, she suddenly looked up and said, *That is me! That's me!* Slowly but surely, she turned the corner, after many years of a crisis-prone and difficult therapy. Rory could finally use the word *change* in a positive way. She integrated all of her parts and completed therapy. Sixteen years later, Rory is still doing well. She went back to work, though she has serious health problems as a consequence of a lifetime of stress. She and her partner have a stable, if not perfect, relationship; she reconnected with her birth father, who had abandoned her; and she was able to make amends with her children and continues to enjoy them as adults.

Cognitive Resistance

Some patients with enduring resistance may be less overtly focused on the therapist as problematic, but may have profound cognitive resistance, even while maintaining a pleasant demeanor. That is, they may have a sense of humor and express appreciation of the therapist, but are unable to think coherently because of the interference of parts, or use all sorts of indirect and convoluted narratives, focus on trivia, or tell meandering tales. Unable to stay on topic, they are difficult to follow in conversation. They are unable to remember sessions or insights, as switching and conflicts about change are strong among dissociative parts. In short, they make no changes. Various parts may be involved in different ways; for example, one part may think quite well, but another part is foggy and confused. Tangential thinking may also be a consequence of rapid switching between parts, each of which follows a different thread.

This style can be understood as the type of incoherent narrative so commonly found in disorganized attachment, which can be easily activated with the therapist. One should compassionately understand that these patients have profound phobias of attachment and loss, and of inner experience, underneath their obfuscation and cognitive disorganization.

CASE EXAMPLE OF EXTREME COGNITIVE RESISTANCE: MARIE

Marie was a 62-year-old woman who had been in a number of long-term therapies since her early 30s. None of these therapies had been especially effective. She had DID, severe executive dysfunction, depression, and panic. She also had a very high IQ, did well in her profession as a teacher, and had a wonderful sense of humor. She was referred by a retiring therapist who specialized in DID to a therapist also known for treating dissociation. The new therapist could not piece together what Marie was talking about in the first two sessions. She believed the patient was switching, but was unable to confirm that in early sessions.

Despite her high IQ, the patient jumped from one story to another, not completing any one account, and never clearly identified people or herself. She constantly used indirect pronouns and mixed the past, present, and future tenses: *We would have a fantastic time. Fantastic times now. Next week is going to be fantastic. We have so much fun! She keeps me laughing. My father taught me to have fun. He was so great in that way, even when he was trying to kill me. So much fun he was! We had tea parties. Little cups and play dress up. Yes, he was the much better parent. Just had to be a little careful around him, not let him get too close. Next week we are going to dress up and go out on the town, all of us! Though last time, last years, the last times, I couldn't quite manage to go. It's just so fantastic! I am going to start walking every day! I'm riding my bike, too—I feel so free when I ride! Got to get it fixed. I bought it with my own money in 1962! It's a beautiful shiny green! Just dazzling! I can scrape that stuff off when I get some time—uh, a little rust. And get some new tires. Maybe a new seat and brakes? Well, I have to get it out of storage. I think it's there somewhere. Maybe my mother sold it. She did. Can't wait to ride again!*

Marie could not remember any of her sessions, no matter how mundane and devoid of emotion the content was, and thus asked to audiotape them. She listened over and over to the tapes, but still could not retain what she and the therapist had said. There were times when she literally could not hear the therapist if the content was too emotionally challenging.

Marie was highly resistant to any suggestions or ideas, but in an unusual way. She readily accepted them and then promptly forgot them. She would have "great" insights and forget them within seconds or minutes. Over the course of some time, the therapist came to the conclusion that the client simply was not capable of doing more than she was doing. The fact was that Marie explicitly pushed herself to work hard in therapy, and then implicitly stopped herself by forgetting everything. She had little to no awareness of this inner conflict. No parts of Marie could be engaged to work on this enduring problem.

Marie had extensive neuropsychological testing twice during the therapy, as the therapist was concerned about cognitive impairment, but she scored mostly within normal ranges. However, she readily admitted with glee to her therapist that she had been at least somewhat dishonest, especially on the psychological testing. Because she administered this type of testing in her work, she was able to cover some of her difficulties, and was quite pleased with herself that she had been very clever and had outsmarted those testers. She was deeply paranoid about anyone discovering more about her, and could acknowledge that to the therapist.

Marie was able to develop a little more coherence in her narratives when the therapist prompted her to clarify over time, as her trust in the therapist grew a bit. She did not integrate, and was rarely able to acknowledge her parts, though they were clearly quite active. It was simply all too terrifying and overwhelming for her. Therapy focused on stabilization, life skills, and support, with no insight-oriented work. In the last years of this supportive therapy, Marie developed dementia. She eventually became unable to drive and had to discontinue treatment. She was referred to geriatric psychiatry, which she refused. She continued to refuse any help in her daily life, insisting she was doing fine, in spite of obvious difficulty managing on her own.

Resistance in the patient can take almost any form. Below in Table 11.3 we list a number of common resistances, and of course, this list is not exhaustive.

TABLE 11.3
Common Phobic Avoidances (Resistances) in the Patient

- Not keeping boundaries that have been clearly set by the therapist
- Showing up late
- Refusing to leave session on time or having a crisis at the end of session (assuming the therapist is adequately wrapping up the session with time to spare)
- E-mailing or calling beyond set limits
- Stalking the therapist or being preoccupied with the therapist's personal life
- Trying to engage in extreme and literal dependence on the therapist
- Being unwilling to form a therapeutic relationship
- Threatening violence or becoming violent or sexual in session
- Being violent to others outside of session
- Unable to think, feeling of fogginess and "blankness," or chronically answering *I don't know* in therapy
- Being unable to stay grounded in sessions or at home
- Remaining unwilling to accept the existence of dissociative parts
- Switching uncontrollably and chronically having flashbacks
- Being unwilling to allow certain parts into sessions (e.g., sexualized parts, perpetrator-imitating parts, adult parts that function in daily life)
- Presenting only as child parts in therapy
- Maintaining an investment in remaining DID
- Coercing belief or disbelief: *You must believe me; You must not trust anything I say.*
- Not collaborating with the therapist to keep therapy at a tolerable but progressive level
- Demanding that the relationship with the therapist become sexual; masturbation in session (extreme erotic transference)
- Insisting on sharing extremely graphic details of abuse over and over, and drawing them incessantly (exhibitionistic and voyeuristic behaviors in session)
- Behaving sadistically toward the therapist and taking enjoyment in this—e.g., saying cruel things
- Insisting that the therapist meet unmet needs; persistent fantasy that the therapist can fix everything
- Talking too much; producing overwhelming amounts of content in written form (often regarding traumatic memories, dissociative parts, or feelings about the therapist)
- Using too much small talk or sharing too many funny stories
- Meandering, incoherent, disorganized, tangential speech
- Chronically going into trance or spacing out

continues

- Remaining invested in a rich inner fantasy life instead of becoming willing to accept and deal with external reality
- Remaining unwilling as a whole person to take responsibility for various dissociative parts
- Splitting between the therapist and others—family members, friends, other mental health professionals (e.g., *My husband says you are pushing me too hard and that he is needing to protect the child [part of me]; My psychiatrist thinks you should see me more often—he is very concerned about how unstable I am and wonders if you know what you are doing.*)
- Remaining in ongoing abusive relationships (as victim or perpetrator)
- Engaging in chronic approach-avoidance behaviors, e.g., *I hate you; don't leave me.*
- Avoiding, clinging, or becoming aggressive in relationships
- Using destructive coping strategies (drugs, alcohol, self-harm, relational turmoil, etc.)
- Inconsistently attending therapy
- Chronically responding from a *Yes, but . . .* or *No, you're wrong . . .* mind-set
- Externalizing problems to others: inability to reflect about self
- Obsessive preoccupation with revenge or unfairness
- Attempting to subjugate the therapist to the patient's needs and demands, disregarding any subjective experience or needs of the therapist—traumatic narcissism (Shaw, 2013)
- Viewing the therapist as abusive or sadistic if the therapist does not meet the demands of the patient (T. Ogden, 1992)
- Being extremely jealous of the therapist's "perfect" life, or the lives of others
- Feeling extremely bitter about life, sometimes referred to as post-traumatic embitterment disorder (Linden, Rotter, & Baumann, 2007)
- Engaging in chronic fantasies or maladaptive daydreaming (Somer, 2002) or relating mostly to "the third reality"—that is, the inner world of parts (Kluft, 1998)
- Chronically and unremittingly preoccupied with suicide

Additional Case Examples of Resistance

Below we give a number of case examples of resistance and counterresistance. These are meant to familiarize the reader with the wide variety of phobic avoidance strategies. The more therapists can identify these themes and work directly with them, the more effective they can be in helping patients make progress.

CASE EXAMPLE OF DEPENDENCY AS RESISTANCE: SERENA

Serena begged her therapist, *I need to see you four times a week, and an hour just isn't enough! I hardly get started and then I have to leave, and my parts don't get to even talk to you. You don't understand how much I am suffering every minute. I can't take it anymore. It helps to see you—it's the only thing that helps! How could you not help me?! I guess you don't want to see me because I can't afford your full fee. I knew you didn't really care about me. Fine! I don't know if I will be around for any more sessions anyway.* Serena left the office crying and slammed the door, leaving the therapist feeling incompetent and overwhelmed, wondering what she should do, and fearing for her patient's safety.

Serena is phobically avoidant of her needs. Her hope is that if she can demand the therapist be there and soothe her, she will not have to feel discomfort or pain, or deal with needs that do not get met in life. She also has a phobia of attachment loss, frantically seeking the therapist and feeling ashamed of her need at the same time.

CASE EXAMPLE OF USING ANGER AS RESISTANCE: TIM

Tim had an angry part that tended to become violent with others. When he suddenly threw a pillow toward his therapist in session, the therapist told him to stop and sit down and talk instead of throwing things. Tim reacted angrily: *You want to brainwash me to be one of those submissive and quiet robots, just like everybody else in society. You want me to get rid of my anger. I have a right to be angry! You're the one who can't take my anger. So what if I throw something in your office? It didn't hit you, and I had no intention of hitting you! You're making a big deal out of nothing. I thought you were supposed to accept my feelings. I feel totally betrayed.*

Tim resisted realizing that the way he expressed anger was inappropriate and frightening to others. It was easier for him to act out his anger and blame the therapist, because he was phobically avoidant of actually reflecting on his anger and uncovering what might be beneath it: pain, shame, and helplessness. He also felt shame about impulsively throwing the pillow, and attacking the therapist allowed him to avoid his shame.

Tim's therapist was intimidated by him. Although she was outwardly calm, inwardly she felt afraid to set further limits for fear he would be violent. Tim reminded her of her father, who was prone to rage. She could not meet the energy of Tim's anger with firm, compassionate limits. Instead she tried to convince him that she did accept his anger and that maybe she had overreacted a bit. She ended up apologizing to Tim. Her counter-resistance was in not setting appropriate limits, not helping Tim accept his anger and shame, and not teaching him the distinction between having an emotion and acting it out. Both therapist and patient left the session feeling overwhelmed and frustrated.

CASE EXAMPLE OF A POWER STRUGGLE AS RESISTANCE: LUNETTE

Lunette had extremely demanding and unreasonable child and adult parts. In one session she learned the therapist was going out of town. Usually the therapist told her the general location of where she was going, as this helped the patient maintain some object constancy, and it was something the therapist did with most of her patients. But this time Lunette switched to a child part that began incessantly asking the therapist more and more specific questions about what she was going to do and where she was going. The therapist felt coerced and invaded, and decided it would be better not to tell Lunette anything at all about where she was going. The child part of Lunette had a temper tantrum, lying on the floor of the office, kicking and screaming. The more the therapist asked her to calm down, the louder Lunette screamed, cried, and demanded to know where the therapist was going. The therapist was finally exhausted and relented: *If you will stop yelling and sit up and get grounded, I will tell you where I am going.* Lunette promptly sat up and quieted, though she was still angry with the therapist.

Lunette was resistant to basic limits and to containing child parts of herself. She had a controlling-punitive style of interacting with others, especially the therapist, and felt entitled to get what she wanted or needed from the therapist. The therapist was counterresistant to setting consistent limits when she felt overwhelmed; she also acted out the wish to punish the patient by withholding information that she normally shared. Over many episodes like this, the therapist gradually learned to be less reactive to the patient's tantrums and to insist on different behavior from her, while still remaining connected.

CASE EXAMPLE OF INNER CONFLICT AMONG PARTS AS RESISTANCE: MANDY

Mandy, and several parts of her that functioned in daily life, appeared highly motivated to change. But other parts of Mandy appeared highly phobic of change. One part, called "Party Girl," only wanted to have fun and stayed out all night so that Mandy could not get to work on time the next morning. Mandy, as Party Girl, was developmentally fixated in avoiding responsibility. The therapist suspected that being responsible was overwhelming and frightening to this part of Mandy. Party Girl felt entitled to have a good time because of her painful childhood and believed she should be taken care of by others. She found drinking and partying an effective escape from the painful realities of her drab and lonely life and was furious at any negative consequences, labeling them as "unfair." Party Girl experienced any encounter with an authority figure, including the therapist, as a threat to her freedom and control.

The responsible parts of Mandy found Party Girl disgusting and immature, had no compassion for her, and certainly did not accept the major conflicts that Party Girl represented. For example, Party Girl wanted freedom without responsibility, while the worker parts of Mandy focused only on work and chores, with no time for relaxation and fun. Party Girl was enthralled with the excitement of partying and drinking, while other parts of Mandy were terrified of excitement, as it too closely matched the feeling of fear. Party Girl felt the world owed her for her suffering, while Mandy as an adult believed she did not deserve anything good at all and denied any needs or wants.

Neither Party Girl nor the worker parts of Mandy had sufficient emotional regulation skills. The former was underregulated and the latter were overregulated, representing both sides of the coin of dysregulation (Van Dijke et al., 2010a, b). Mandy as Party Girl struggled for control and domination over Mandy as worker, and vice versa. Between these two major parts of Mandy, collaboration was far from a reality. The worker parts of Mandy bitterly complained about how Party Girl was unwilling to cooperate, but did nothing to try to improve the situation. The worker parts were thus implicitly colluding with the resistance even while stating loud and clear that resistance was a painful problem.

Another part of Mandy believed that getting better meant that she could never ask for help again, as she "should" be completely self-sufficient once she was better. Another was too hopeless to try for any positive change.

CASE EXAMPLE OF SUFFERING AS RESISTANCE: NANCY

Nancy, a patient in her mid-sixties with DID, seemed to make great strides in many sessions, having what appeared to be breakthrough realizations about how she failed to take care of herself, and felt pleased and optimistic when she left these sessions. However, she would invariably revert back to severe depression, self-deprivation, and intense suffering, experiencing a kind of inner backlash. The session following a "good" one would be exceptionally painful, and both therapist and patient would feel frustrated and disconnected. Their experience was of one step forward, two steps back.

Repeated exploration of this pattern over the course of many years was not very successful, though Nancy still made incremental progress overall. Finally, after years in treatment, Nancy was able to share a specific memory of being terribly abused by someone who had enjoyed her pain. She had then begun to turn the rage at her abuser onto herself because it was too dangerous to be angry at him. She was also attacking herself out of deep shame. She had developed a perpetrator-imitating child part that she called "It."

This part of Nancy would kick and punch her internally, resulting in intense pain; cause her to "accidentally" burn herself on the stove or with the iron; deprive her of food and liquids; or make her fall down the stairs. This very strong, intense, angry child part developed a mantra to protect itself from the pain that the perpetrator inflicted. It would cause her own masochistic suffering: *You want me to suffer? I will show you how much I can suffer! You can hurt me, take away everything I love; and I can hurt myself more than you can. I can take away from myself until nothing is left and I can still survive. I won't let myself have anything good ever. I am stronger than you!*

This was the only way It could control the horrific suffering, helplessness, and shame in the face of sadistic abuse, while simultaneously punishing herself out of phobic avoidance of these experiences. Nancy had avoided dealing with this part of herself for so many years because of profound shame and rage, which she did not want to accept as her own. After many years of patient and slow work in therapy, Nancy finally was able to realize she had internalized her abuser's sadism in the form of It. She had a further realization of how ashamed of It she was. She did not want the therapist to know that part of her, which had been hiding in plain sight for many years in therapy despite repeated attempts to acknowledge and work with it.

Only after years of building trust, being mindful time and again of the pattern of progress followed by regression, building skills, working successfully with less intense memories, and having many small positive experiences in present life was Nancy finally able to acknowledge to herself and the therapist the root of her long-standing self-sabotage. This marked the beginning of a major turning point in therapy, in which It was finally able to become more aware of the present, work through its anger, and grieve. Both It and the adult part of Nancy became much more compassionate with each other.

Within a few months, they were blending together much of the time, and It became much less distinct. Though Nancy continued to have occasional minor regressions after that, her progress became much more consistent and rapid, and her self-harm abated. This part was invited to participate actively in therapy, and Nancy expressed much gratefulness and compassion toward It, which she temporarily renamed "Valerie," which means *strong* and *valiant*. At this point Nancy was able to begin in earnest Phase 2 work on traumatic memories, which was interspersed with other integrative work among parts and continued improvement of her daily life.

Further Explorations

11.1 What did you learn in your training about resistance and counterresistance? How does it help or hinder your approach to yourself as therapist and to your patients?

11.2 Make a list of resistances or inner-directed phobias that are most difficult for you to handle. What makes them difficult?

11.3 Make a list of your own typical counterresistances or phobias toward a patient. How are you able to recognize them? Talk with a trusted colleague or supervisor to explore your counterresistances further.

11.4 Choose one of your cases and explore the resistances. Next, for each resistance, look for your counterresistance that either comes from your own history or from your reaction to the patient.

CHAPTER 12

Resistance as Phobic Avoidance: Practical Approaches

*By accepting resistance as an inevitable, even desirable, feature
of our work, we are equipped better to be truly accepting of our
clients and therapeutic in interacting with them. Therefore, I
say, vive la résistance.*

—Stanley Messer (2002, p. 163)

Although there is never one single right way to approach resistance, the
more respectful and understanding the therapist is of why the patient
is avoidant, the better the beginning of a careful and effective approach. In
addition, the more therapists are aware of their contributions—for better
and worse—to the therapy, the more counterresistance can be addressed
quickly and effectively. Of course, the main tenet is to work within the
window of tolerance of all parts of the patient, often going as slow as the
slowest part, one small step at a time.

As noted in the previous chapter, the phobia of inner experience is the
overarching reason for resistance, followed by phobias of dissociative parts,
attachment and loss, traumatic memory, and change. Unfortunately, therapists do not assess often enough for avoidance of inner experience and why
it might exist. It will help therapy considerably for therapists to be aware of
the degree of resistance patients have to their own experience.

One of the first and most important steps in resolving phobic avoidance
in dissociative patients is for the therapist to recognize that resistance is
often held in dissociative parts that are not in the forefront in sessions and,
simultaneously, that resistance is a systemic issue not contained in a single
dissociative part.

CORE CONCEPT

Resistant behavior often occurs in parts that are not easily accessed
in therapy and that the patient can easily blame for the problem,
when resistance is actually an issue for the patient as a whole
system. All parts have a role in maintaining resistance, even if only
by avoiding and blaming resistant parts.

Below we describe some practical approaches that are often helpful in
resolving resistance.

Practical Approaches to Working With Phobia Avoidance

The first step in working successfully with resistance, as noted in the previous chapter, is to thoroughly assess patients and their strengths and deficits in therapy. This will include determining the extent of enduring
resistance that is present and whether it is held in certain parts or is a sys-
tem-wide issue. The more enduring and entrenched the resistance, the
more methodical and slow the pace will be, and the more patience is
required of the therapist. Second, therapists must be aware of and open to
their own counterresistances, which have the potential to interfere with
therapy. The therapist's counterresistance changes depending upon the
issues and resistances of a particular patient, so this awareness needs to be
ongoing. Third, the therapist should obtain consultation on resistance and
counterresistance. Such consultation should feel effective and supportive.

Stay Compassionately Curious About the Function of the Resistance

Phobic avoidance is protection. Thus, the first step in resolving resistance
is to explore with the patient how the avoidance helps. For example, what
does self-harm accomplish for the patient? Does it make the patient feel
more real, relieve distress, punish a crying part into silence, or avoid traumatic memories? The very act of asking these kinds of questions helps the
patient feel more heard and understood. Once the function of the avoidance is understood, other ways to achieve relief can be explored. For example, if a patient feels more real when he sees blood during self-harm, then
the therapist can help find adaptive grounding approaches, such as smelling a strong pleasant scent, touching a transitional object like a stone, or
helping inner parts feel more calm.

Build Inner Resources to Overcome Phobic Avoidance

In order for patients to have the confidence to address chronic phobic avoidance, they must have some type of psychological resources available. Resources include anything positive and adaptive that helps patients stay within their window of tolerance. There are thousands of resources, and dozens of ways to access them, including hypnosis and imagery (e.g., Hammond & Cheek, 1988), EMDR (e.g., Gonzalez & Mosquera, 2012; Korn & Leeds, 2002), and somatic approaches (e.g., Ogden et al., 2006; Ogden & Fisher, 2015). Below we discuss a few that are often helpful to dissociative patients.

CORE CONCEPT

Skills and resource building are essential for the patient as a whole
to feel able to move beyond phobic avoidance.

Resources can be any positive, comforting, supporting, safe, calm, or good experience, no matter how small. They can involve another person (real or imagined), an animal (real or imagined), nature, a somatic sensation, an image of a safe or healing place, a "spirit guide" or religious symbol, or a simple moment such as having a steaming cup of tea or feeling the sun on your face. Patients are asked to remember or imagine the experience and notice what that experience is like in their body. It can be helpful to ask for specific sensations; for example, *It's warm in my chest, My muscles feel relaxed*, or *Everything in my head gets quiet.* Therapists who practice EMDR often use bilateral stimulation for resource installation (e.g., Korn & Leeds, 2002). Those who use hypnosis can use hypnotic imagery and suggestions to develop resources. Hypnosis and bilateral stimulation can quite easily be combined (e.g., Fine & Berkowitz, 2001).

Once the patients are able to access the resource, the therapist should ensure patients stay with the positive experience in order to really take it in and make it meaningful. All too often, both therapist and patient are quickly off to the next thing before the positive experience is solidified. The idea is to savor the moment, so that it can become a more familiar experience (Ogden et al., 2006).

The therapist can encourage the patient to practice the resource every day. In follow-up sessions, the therapist should check in about whether the patient and various dissociative parts were able to use the resource to feel more calm and competent. If not, explore what happened and return to further interventions. Often, small experiences of positive change must be reiterated to become a part of the patient's ongoing experience.

Use Socratic Questioning

There are times, as long as it is not overused, when Socratic questioning can be helpful in challenging the maladaptive beliefs of dissociative patients and the conflicts among parts. By asking a series of questions, the therapist leads patients to discover maladaptive beliefs and logical contradictions on their own, without being told directly by the therapist. However, such intellectual questioning of the patient should not substitute for relational ways of being with the patient, listening to the patient's own words, or attending to the patient's nonverbal feelings (without trying to first change them). It should not, of course, be done in a condescending or sarcastic manner. Moreover, when any part of the patient is fixed in a highly emotionally charged defense such as fight, flight, freeze, flag, faint, or attachment cry, regulation and safety are the first interventions, not cognitive questioning. Socratic questioning ideally should lead the patient to examine avoided emotions, memories, or other inner experiences. It should not merely direct the patient to a cognitive level but should be interwoven with relational connection, compassion, and interest in the patient's experience.

These types of questions are open-ended and meant to help the patient reflect upon strongly held beliefs or behaviors that perhaps have never been examined before. For example, the therapist might respectfully ask the patient:

- You are suffering so much. I wonder what led you to believe that your purpose in life is to suffer.
  - Is this a new belief, or have you always had it? How did you come to this conclusion?
  - Hmm, you've had this belief for so long. That must be terrible, to believe that your lot in life is to suffer. Can you tell me more about it?
  - Do you think that others believe this is your purpose, too?
  - Could you help me to understand how injuring your body helps you?
  - Do you have other ways in addition to hurting yourself to help you feel less suffering?
  - I wonder if hurting yourself helps all parts of you or only some? Could you check inside about that?
  - Is there anything about hurting yourself that is not helpful to you?
  - How do you manage the conflict between those parts that find it helpful and those parts that suffer from it? That must be quite a difficult balance to find.
  - Can you help me get more clear? Are you saying that drinking is the only option available to you to relieve your pain?

- How did you manage this emotional pain before you started drinking?
- What do you imagine might happen if you were to feel your sadness or anger?
- What do you imagine it might be like if we faced it together and only a little tiny bit of it, not the whole big feeling?
- What is the worst thing you could imagine happening if you acknowledged that crying voice inside of you?
- Have you ever heard anyone express a different opinion about dissociation than your belief that it means you are crazy? What do you think about those other opinions?
- If you were talking about another child, would you recommend that he or she be punished in the same way you punish that little child part of you inside? If not, what is different about the other child?
- You [a perpetrator-imitating part] say that your only job or function is to hurt the [inner] children. How did you come to get that job? Have you always had that job?
- Were there other jobs that might have been available to you that you chose not to take?
  - What do you do for yourself on your time off your job [of hurting or frightening parts inside]?
  - You never take time off? You must be exhausted! Would you be interested in taking a break?
  - I wonder what you might do with yourself if those child parts were no longer there?
- You experience yourself as separate from that other part of you. Yet, I see the same person when I see you and when I see that other part of you. That's a real mind-bending thing, isn't it? Can you help me understand that?
- You tell me you are 3 years old. Can you look at your hands for a moment and notice that wedding ring? Where did you get that? And when? If it is not yours, how do you explain how it got there?
- How do you know that the angry part of you would be violent if it was present in session? Has it ever happened that the angry part of you has been violent with others?
- What tells you that I am disgusted or angry with you? What do you notice about me that indicates that?
- How does the belief that you have to be perfect affect your everyday life? Your therapy? Do you believe that others must be perfect? If not, why is it different for them than for you?
- Do you suppose there might be alternative ways of thinking about

these parts of yourself other than they are dangerous and have to be destroyed?

- What would happen, or what would it mean, if you were to accept what happened to you as a child?

Work With the Felt Experience of Resistance

Conversation is often woefully insufficient to address resistance. In fact, some patients can talk about resistance endlessly and with insight, but still not change. Working with the felt (somatic) experience of resistance can be extremely effective to actually help the patient take steps forward. Somatic work, as with all therapeutic approaches, requires training and experience. Readers are encouraged to do further study and practice (e.g., Levine & Frederick,1997; Ogden et al., 2006; Ogden & Fisher, 2015).

CORE CONCEPT

Working with the somatic experience of resistance or phobic avoidance can be a powerful way to help the patient access change.

The therapist might ask, *What does the avoidance feel like inside? Where do you notice it most?* The patient might describe, for example, tension in the chest that is cold or hot, a shaking that centers in the stomach, a sense of being armored all over, a feeling of shutting down, of being enclosed in a glass box, of being surrounded by blackness through which light cannot penetrate, of being at a great distance from the therapist, or a sense of a shield or wall coming between the patient and the therapist.

The therapist can encourage the patient to notice the experience with curiosity rather than fear. *What is it like to notice the experience? Do all parts have the same experience?* As the patient stays with the experience, what happens? *Does the experience change in any way? Is there a physical movement that goes with the experience?* The patient might imagine making the movement, or actually make it very slowly (to prevent dysregulation).

Work With the Imagery of Resistance

Since dissociative patients are generally highly hypnotizable, the use of hypnotic imagery and positive hypnotic suggestions can be invaluable (e.g., Kluft, 1992a, 1992b; Van der Hart, 2012). However, patients are only able to use imagery of resistance when they can recognize that resistance exists. Often this is not until later in therapy.

The therapist utilizes the patient's imagery to support gradual shifts in the capacity to reflect upon and change resistance. For example, if the patient (or a part of the patient) imagines a wall, the first step might be to encourage the patient, or this part, to just notice the qualities of the wall: how high it is, how thick, how long, what it is constructed of. *You have constructed an excellent wall for your protection. It is your wall, it is extremely strong, and that strength comes from you.* After exploring and admiring the wall, the therapist might encourage the patient to imagine touching it, and even leaning up against the wall to feel its support and strength. *Can you lean up against the wall to feel how strong it is, how strong you are in making that wall? That strength of that wall is available for you to use in many ways, in ways that you can hardly yet imagine, ways that will help you and make you feel better able to cope, to feel competent and calm.* This kind of intervention begins to harness the strength of the resistance as a resource that supports therapy instead of hindering it.

Other imagery approaches include, for example, exploring small steps of change in relation to the wall. Can a small peephole or intercom be placed in the wall? Is there a door? Can the patient climb up a ladder and look over to the other side, using binoculars the wrong way so that whatever is near seems very far away? The therapist explores with the patient what a more effective approach might be. For example, *So, looking over the wall and making a small hole in it doesn't seem possible at the moment. That is fine. Let's be curious about what the next step might be. So many options, endless options, are always there. There is always a way forward, even though we may not see it just at this moment. The wisdom of our minds working together will show us the way when it is time.* If the patient is unable or reluctant to try a step, the therapist simply acknowledges it, collaboratively exploring what is difficult about it so a potential resolution can be found.

CASE EXAMPLE OF WORKING WITH IMAGERY OF RESISTANCE

Therapist: That's a wonderful wall you have there. It is strong and tough. I wonder what it might be like, don't you, to allow yourself to lean up against your wall and just notice what that is like.

Patient: I feel relaxed, like I am letting go of a heavy burden. I feel supported. I can rest.

Therapist: Good, let yourself let go of that burden and feel supported. The strength of that wall is your strength. Take that in. *(The therapist waits; if using EMDR, may use bilateral stimulation here.)*

Patient: Yes, I feel good.

Therapist: You feel good. Just notice and accept that. How it feels in your body. And now notice your wall again, the wall that supports you and carries your burdens.

Patient: I rather like it. It doesn't feel so formidable. More like a resting place where I am supported. I feel glad for it. I can actually see the top of it now.

Therapist: Not so formidable. Now it's a resting place of support. *(Waits)* Would you be interested in taking a look over the top?

Patient: Maybe just a little. *(Becomes tearful)* It's so beautiful over there. So incredibly beautiful. I didn't know.

Therapist: Hmm, beauty you did not know. That's really something, isn't it. Just take all the time you need to know that beauty.

Patient: I *realize* the wall is not keeping me safe anymore. The wall *is* my pain: It is made up of everything that has hurt me that I don't want to know about. It holds my pain for me, but it is keeping me away from that beautiful life. I think I can start to let that be mine now. *(More tears of relief, sadness, and realization)*

Therapist: Yes, you could, couldn't you, start to let that be yours. . . . Could you check and see what happens with you and the wall now?

Patient: The wall feels very different. Very relaxed, almost like the stones are becoming lighter, flexible. *(Laughing in delight)* Like they are becoming bubbles that are floating in the air. Beautiful bubbles. Yes, little bubbles that are very alive! They are floating over this beautiful scene, in awe of what is there. They feel like they have finally come home. *I* have finally come home. *(More tears)*

Reexamine Shared Therapy Goals and Therapy Progress

When phobic avoidance is preventing the patient from working on agreed-upon goals, the therapist should return to treatment goals and ask patients what they want and feel able to work on. This should be done in a curious and compassionate way, rather than in a punitive manner that implies the patients are not working on what they should be doing.

CORE CONCEPT

A review of therapy goals with the patient can be helpful when phobic avoidance is strong.

This review of goals is not only for the patient but also for the therapist. Sometimes it is the therapists who implicitly develop their own goals for the patient, such as working on traumatic memories or accessing disso-ciative parts before the patient has made those a personal goal. Motivational interviewing can be helpful when it seems the patient is stuck and cannot move forward (Miller & Rollnick, 2012). All parts should be included in this process (see Chapters 7–9 for more on setting appropriate treatment goals).

Special Issues of Working With Resistance in Dissociative Patients

Working with resistance in dissociative patients can be complex, as parts often function together in implicit ways to maintain resistance, and may do so in ways that are not completely clear to the therapist. Below we discuss several common issues.

Resistance in One Dissociative Part but Not Another

Resistance can appear to be present in one part but not in another. Some parts recognize resistance in other parts and do not experience it as their own. This, of course, is just another manifestation of the core non-realization in dissociation: *That is not mine; that is not me.* Thus, some parts of the dissociative patient may seem completely willing and ready to change, but other parts appear intensely resistant. The entire system—that is, the individual—has quarantined resistance within certain parts, thus disowning the resistance: *I want to get better, but that part does not. That other part is the problem.* Of course, that part is expressing something the patient as a whole cannot yet own, but which nonetheless comes from the patient. What the patient is often unable to realize is how the rest of the system tacitly supports the ongoing resistance of other parts by disowning and being helpless in the face of the conflict or resistance. Often only when the patient as a whole can compassionately own responsibility for all sides of the conflict can resistance be fully resolved.

CORE CONCEPT

Resistance is a systemic problem. That is, although one or more parts may be labeled as the resistant ones, while other parts appear to want to make progress, *all* parts of the patient serve to maintain the status quo of the whole person. Thus, the therapist should compassionately address the role of each part in explicitly or implicitly maintaining phobic avoidance.

Resistance in Inaccessible Dissociative Parts

Dissociation is a disorder of hiddenness and dissimulation. Thus it is quite common that some hostile, sadistic, or extremely fearful or shameful parts remain hidden "behind the scenes," sometimes unknown to the patient, and often unknown (or only suspected) by the therapist. It can take much patience and compassionate persistence from the therapist for the patient to gather the courage to allow these parts to be more present in treatment. In the meantime, these parts remain highly phobic of change and often to the therapeutic relationship. The patient does not understand his or her resistance, as it is held in various parts (at least partially) outside of awareness.

The Complexity of Inner Conflict in Dissociative Patients

Conflict is often much more complex than a two-sided coin, particularly in dissociative patients. For example, one part of the patient may love and idealize her mother, who was sometimes nurturing and attentive, and be strongly loyal to her mother; another part hates her mother and never wants to speak to her again; another denies she ever had a mother; while yet another part believes she is the mother. This complexity may be confusing to the therapist. However, each facet of the conflict begins to make sense in the context of the chaotic, painful world of the abused child. Of course a child would both love and hate her abusive mother. Of course the child might wish she never had a mother, and in deep absorption and trance, she could come to believe this. And of course the child introjects the bad self of her mother, which takes on a life of its own. So abhorrent, confusing, and terrifying is her mother that the child cannot integrate her as a whole person. Neither can the child integrate her own various insoluble conflicts about her mother, and her own discrepant senses of self in relation to the mother. Thus, each dissociative part has limited realizations about the patient's own experience and about her mother.

Often one or more sides of a conflict are hidden from the patient, and thus also from the therapist, as noted above. Therapists must learn to recognize and look for typical conflicts and make inquiries and hypotheses about what conflicts might be operating underneath phobic avoidance. They should compassionately insist that all parts learn to participate in understanding and resolving these conflicts instead of acting them out. Of course, this can be long and arduous work, but the understanding that hidden conflicts abound can be helpful to keep in mind.

The therapist needs a mind-set, regarding dissociative parts, that if you are not a part of the solution, you are part of the problem. For example, some critical parts are always complaining about other parts of the patient, often the one or ones that function in daily life: *She is lazy, stupid, eating too much, a loser.* The therapist can help these hostile, critical parts of the patient learn to reflect more effectively: *So, you are really concerned that she isn't getting her work around the house done. It sounds to me as if you are paying very careful attention, so I can see that you are not lazy at all. You want her to be able to accomplish what she needs to do. Tell me about what you are doing to help her be more motivated, because it seems like you are really wanting her to change. I'm guessing that she doesn't want to be lazy or stupid or a loser either. Let's explore this together, shall we?* At some point when the patient is ready, the therapist can add a little more confrontation about avoiding integration: *Well, it is also your house, so I can see why it is important to you for it to be clean and cared for. But something confuses me. Precisely because it is your house, I am wondering why you do not participate, as though these daily responsibilities do not also belong to you?*

The more communication and collaboration among parts seemingly on opposite sides of a conflict, the more integrative capacity the patient gains. This approach also helps keep the conflict about resistance from being externalized between the patient and therapist. Resistance is ultimately a conflict within the patient that must be resolved internally.

The Complexity of Avoidance in Dissociative Patients

Phobic avoidance typically becomes multilayered in dissociative patients, making it more complex than in those who do not have dissociative disorders. For example, there is the initial phobia of an experience itself (e.g., shame, anger, pain, rejection), then of the dissociative parts that contain that experience, of memories that involve the experience, of the potential for relational loss if the therapist "discovers" the experience and judges the patient for it, and of any change that requires realizing the experience. Thus, phobic avoidance can be complex and enduring, and the therapist should not assume because one phobia is overcome that others are resolved.

"Relay" Resistance Between Dissociative Parts

The therapist can experience a kind of confusing "relay" resistance in dissociative patients, in which one part appears dominant in the resistance and then suddenly the resistance is handed off like a baton in a relay race to another part that continues to maintain phobic avoidance. For example, an angry part may switch to a scared part that feels crushed when the therapist sets limits on the angry behavior. Thus, when the therapist changes approaches or shifts emotionally, the patient responds by shifting accordingly. The therapist is perhaps able to handle the patient's anger about limit setting, but wavers in the face of a child part's pleas. Often there is a particular sequence of switching that is highly instructive to observe, as it implies relationships among parts and emotional patterns that can be productively addressed. In the above example, the therapist learned to ask the scared part to allow the angry part to be present again. Then the therapist, who had been working on his ability to tolerate pleading and hurt from the patient, was able to work with both child parts and angry parts of the patient more effectively.

One part may seem resistant while another part is not, and then all parts appear to reverse roles. The next session, or even later in the same session, the resistant part begins to ally with the therapist, while the formerly cooperative part disappears or rejects the newly cooperative part, thus maintaining the resistance. This is a common dynamic between adult parts and child parts. The adult part of the patient insists she wants the child part to feel better, but in reality is disgusted by it and rejects its needs, taking no time during the week to reflect and accept the child part of herself. The child part appeals to the therapist for help, feeling rejected and abandoned by the adult part. At some point, the patient switches from the child part back to the adult part, who then insists she really does want to help, but now the child part torments her and then refuses to talk to her: *How can I help her when she won't come to therapy or give me any information?* The therapist needs to understand that both parts are equally avoiding each other, and this "team" approach, although not conscious, is an effective strategy to prevent either part from having to change and realize painful issues.

Preferences Among Dissociative Parts as Resistance

Some DID patients who are highly invested in separateness bring many conflicts among parts to therapy. The therapist must discern whether these conflicts serve to maintain avoidance of therapy or whether they are central to treatment.

For example, a patient had a number of parts that constantly fought over what food to buy. The client would subsequently come home with junk food or several types of ice cream, or sometimes with nothing at all. Parts bitterly complained in therapy that they did not get their preference of food, and they could not come to a compromise. The therapist wondered aloud if this fighting was helping the patient as a whole to somehow avoid something that was much more painful and difficult. The patient vehemently denied this. However, a few weeks later during session, he switched to a child part and said he was plagued by traumatic memories of severe neglect and food deprivation, and that fighting over the food was both a way to avoid dealing with that very painful subject and a reenactment for some parts of not getting food they needed. The adult part of the client was unaware of these memories, and the function of the fighting served to be a great distraction from realizing this painful history.

Shame, Dissociation, and Resistance

Shame maintains dissociation (J. A. Talbot, Talbot, & Tu, 2005) and is a central issue to resolve in the treatment of the resistant dissociative patient (Chefetz, 2015; Herman, 2011; Kluft, 2007). As one patient said after successfully working through her shame, *I came to therapy to get better and deal with everything except what I felt most ashamed of. I was going to never speak of those things and take them to my grave. But that is exactly what kept me from getting better.* Specific approaches to working with shame will be addressed in Chapter 15. It is often missed, or avoided or minimized by the therapist, who may feel incompetent to deal with such a painful and entrenched dynamic.

Steps to Solidify Change in Dissociative Patients

Because change can be so frightening and feels so permanent for patients with enduring resistance, it can be useful to help them (and their various parts) notice the differences between the experience of phobic avoidance and its resolution. What is different afterward, both internally and in daily life? Are any differences better or worse? The goal is to solidify in the patient's mind and felt experience that realization not only is more adaptive but feels better than phobic avoidance.

To this end, the therapist can direct the patient to go back and forth between a positive experience of change and a negative or uncomfortable experience of resistance. This is called *pendulation*, which is a somatic technique that helps the patient move back and forth between dysregulation and regulation, using resources (Levine, P. & Frederick, 1997; Miller-Karas, 2015). The gentle pendulating movement between feelings and sensations of regulation and controlled dysregulation, coupled with titration of sensations and emotions in small increments, helps decrease arousal. Additionally, a focus on present experience prevents the patient from spiraling into negative thoughts, memories, or emotions.

Further Explorations

12.1 What are the most challenging resistances that you face with your dissociative clients?

12.2 Do any of your patients complain that parts of themselves are resistant? If so, can you help them accept that all parts have a role in this protection?

12.3 Find a colleague and role-play resistances with each other to become more effective. Share with each other what you struggle with most regarding resistance. Every therapist struggles with coping with resistance.

12.4 Notice your own reactions when you encounter strong phobic avoidance in a patient. Do you tend to work harder than the patient? Give up? Become angry or frustrated?

CHAPTER 13

Dependency in Therapy: Always, Sometimes, Never?

*An empathic acceptance and understanding of the sometimes
intense, desperate, and painful nature of the patient's
dependency, or conversely, the shame and vehement disavowal
of dependency, is essential, as it is the basis for resolving
insecure attachment and dependency.*
—Kathy Steele, Onno van der Hart, and Ellert Nijenhuis (2001, p. 96)

Dependency is a natural component of any long-term psychotherapy. There is nothing wrong with dependency per se; however, it can range from adaptive and helpful to destructive. We will examine some of the challenges dependency may entail with dissociative patients.

How can the therapist effectively deal with the patient who calls for help late at night for the third time in a week, or who leaves a dozen voice-mail messages threatening self-harm or suicide in a day, or sends incessant e-mails with volumes of material and questions that beg an immediate response? What should the therapist do when a child part asks to be held in session, or the patient switches to a nonverbal baby part, or the patient insists she cannot function unless therapy is increased to four times a week and that contact is necessary over the weekends? What response should the therapist offer when adult parts of the patient ask how could they be expected to care for (inner) children when they never received care themselves? The solutions to these and other difficult therapeutic dilemmas lie in how therapists understand and work with dependency.

We are all dependent on each other to some degree, some of the time, for various needs (and desires). We can certainly understand how neglect and abuse foment a profoundly deep and powerful wish to be cared for in our patients. The wish and the need are not problems, but the patient's manifestations of dependency and the therapist's responses can combine in problematic ways. The question, then, becomes not whether dependency is good or bad, but whether it provides a greater sense of security and competence for the patient and serves as a springboard toward more interest in exploring the self and the world. This question is often especially hard to answer when considering patients who have severely insecure attachment, since they may seek constant attachment (or completely avoid it) rather than use it to develop a secure base from which to go forth in their lives. A constant need for literal connection with the therapist is a dependency gone awry and does not lead to secure attachment (see Chapter 4; Steele et al., 2001).

In order to be effective with dependency issues, it is helpful for therapists to understand

- the ways in which secure attachment, dependency, and caretaking are and are not related;
- how to assess patients for their capacity to tolerate and work through dependency issues;
- the central importance of understanding and managing one's own countertransference, in particular one's counterresistance about dependence (and independence), which may become entwined with the patient's issues;
- appropriate forms of dependency in therapy;
- the clinical differences between adaptive and maladaptive dependency in treatment, and how to support the former without encouraging the latter; and
- how to work with inner conflicts in dissociative patients between parts that are deeply ashamed and avoidant of dependency on the one hand and parts that frantically seek out the therapist to be a substitute parent or comfort object on the other hand.

These pivotal issues will be discussed below.

Secure Attachment Versus Dependency

Secure attachment is one of the major goals of therapy for our patients. For this reason, therapists are encouraged to develop a strong therapeutic relationship. Sometimes secure attachment involves elements of dependence, but they are two quite different concepts.

CORE CONCEPT

Dependency and secure attachment are two different concepts.
Dependency is reliance on a competent other for help, care, and
attention. The end goal is to have needs met by another person.
Secure attachment is an inner felt sense of security. The end goal is
to feel safe enough in order to explore, learn, and develop a sense
of competence and interdependence.

Dependency

Dependency involves reliance on another person for care, attention, and assistance (Sroufe, Fox, & Pancake, 1983). The goal of dependency is to receive care and help from a stronger, wiser other, not necessarily to develop secure attachment. Dependency involves strategizing to have one's needs met, rather than using the therapist's availability to build an inner sense of security. A patient stuck in dependency will feel highly distressed when the therapist is not available, and energy will be directed either toward further attempts to contact the therapist or toward behaviors that numb the distress—for example, drinking or self-harm. The patient may feel panic, rage, or despair. This most often happens between sessions. However, it may also occur during a session when the patient does not explicitly share dependency feelings and the therapist does not recognize or attend to them directly.

CASE EXAMPLE OF DEPENDENCY: JOSIE

Josie frequently requested extra sessions, had difficulty leaving sessions, and often called her therapist for crises. She made strong attempts to stay on the phone with him for long periods of time when he called her back. She insisted she could not function without these calls. When the therapist did not call her within what she considered to be a reasonable time frame, she would become enraged and leave him verbally aggressive voice mails, then panic and cut herself (precipitating even more crisis), and leave him pleading voice mails. The therapist responded to the content of the crises, but did not understand Josie's dependency on him. Thus, his responses further escalated her behaviors.

A Felt Sense of Security

Secure attachment is not based on the need to be dependent, on the strength or intensity of the relationship (Sroufe, 1977), or on the physical availability of another person (i.e., the therapist). Rather, it is founded on an inner felt sense of security (Bowlby, 1988). Secure attachment is a state of being, not the presence of another person (Bowlby, 1969/1982). Thus, the development of secure attachment in our patients depends upon a reorganization of the ways in which they deal with their inner experiences of attachment and their relationships with others, rather than upon an unusually available therapist.

The Quality of Relationship

In fact, as noted in Chapters 2 and 4, the quantity of time one is available is less important than the quality of the time that focuses on attunement in the moment and reattunement and repair when needed (Lyons-Ruth, 2007; Trevarthen & Aitken, 1994; Tronick & Cohn, 1989). Research shows that these qualities of relationship are more essential in developing secure attachment than relatively constant proximity and availability (Lyons-Ruth, 2007; Trevarthen, 1980; Tronick & Cohn, 1989). The sense of being understood and the ability to understand themselves and others is perhaps what our patients most require us to provide. Thus, the therapist helps patients focus on their inner experience (for example, having a need, struggling with an emotion, or being ashamed of a dissociative part), rather than fixing the problem or eliminating the issue for them. The therapeutic resolution lies in helping the patients notice and change how they deal with the experience of dependency, and especially in changing the rigid interactions between dissociative parts of the patient that feel helpless and seek dependency and parts that are ashamed of it.

CORE CONCEPT

A secure base is a means to the end of being able to explore one's world with confidence.

A Secure Base for Exploring

Security may be inferred not from generalized proximity seeking but rather from the ability of the infant to use the caregiver as a base from which to explore the environment. Indeed, the inability to find comfort in contact with an attachment figure is an important sign that the attachment behavioral system is not serving the adaptive function that it does for most infants (Ainsworth, Blehar, Waters, & Wall, 1978). Insecurely or maladaptively attached children may need contact even when environmental stress is minimal, may be unable to regain security or resume exploration upon reunion, or may actively avoid contact or interaction upon reunion.

Bowlby (1988) has stressed that a secure base with another person is essential for healthy development and is the means by which children feel supported and competent to explore the world (both internal and external). One of therapy's main goals is collaborative exploration and the fostering of more adaptive and fulfilling functioning in daily life, not caregiving from the therapist. Of course, some caregiving is not entirely without merit in therapy, but it should have the aim of increasing the patient's competence rather than promoting further helplessness. For example, soothing a highly dysregulated patient can be extremely helpful if the intervention does not end there. The objective is to calm patients sufficiently so that then they can return to an issue in measured doses to resolve it with support. This soothing eventually teaches patients how to engage in self-soothing, including with inner dissociative parts.

CORE CONCEPT

Our main goal as therapists is not to take care of the patient but to provide for the possibility of collaborative exploration and improved functioning in the patient's life.

As Bowlby (1988) noted, our main task as therapists is to be

a secure base from which patients can explore the various unhappy and painful aspects of life, past and present, many of which are difficult or perhaps impossible to think about or even consider without a trusted companion to provide support, encouragement, sympathy, and, on occasion, guidance. (p. 138)

CORE CONCEPT

The purpose of secure attachment—of a felt sense of security—is a capacity to explore one's world from a secure base. Thus, the therapist supports patients in examining their experience in the moment with compassion, curiosity, and confidence, rather than seeking to be immediately available or to rescue patients from distress.

Secure attachment actually leads to a *decrease* in attachment-seeking behaviors and an *increase* in exploration of both inner and outer worlds. Conversely, activation of attachment needs leads to deactivation of exploration. Translated into clinical practice, the patient who is stuck in dependency on the therapist is focused on procuring the comfort and presence of the therapist, not on accepting and changing inner patterns. Conversely, the relatively securely attached patient does not often frantically seek out the therapist for comfort and care. Rather, this patient uses whatever felt sense of security exists to explore what is happening in the moment, to understand, to compassionately accept and tolerate, to experience what is positive in life, and to grieve losses. This exploration and acceptance is a major goal in therapy. The road to such realization via a felt sense of security may be long and arduous for some patients, but it is essential for the therapist not to lose sight of what needs to be accomplished.

CORE CONCEPT

Activation of attachment needs results in deactivation of exploration, and vice versa. Thus, a patient who is frantically seeking the therapist cannot explore inner experience, and thus cannot engage in the work of therapy.

The patient's capacity to use the therapist's support in session to explore gradually increases risk-taking outside of session in working more adaptively with inner experiences, including dissociative parts. Conversely, the dependent patient is focused externally on the availability of the therapist, and internally on distress. Most typically, dependent patients have difficulties in using positive experiences of soothing by the therapist to move forward. Rather, they are in a continual feedback loop of distress and attachment seeking. We discussed ways to help patients take in the therapist's support to develop a consistent felt sense of security in Table 4.3 in Chapter 4.

CORE CONCEPT

Attachment-seeking behaviors are not only a strategy to reduce experiences of attachment loss; they are also sometimes a strategy to prevent contact with painful inner experiences, such as dependency, yearnings, anger, shame, or fear.

Phobia of inner experience and dependency. One of the most difficult aspects of treating highly traumatized individuals is that they perceive danger not only externally but also internally: Their own inner experiences (thoughts, sensations, emotions, needs, dissociative parts, etc.) feel overwhelming or dangerous. Attachment-cry behaviors are triggered when a phobia of attachment loss is reactivated in the patient. But attachment-seeking behaviors in our patients can also be evoked because they are seeking to avoid contact with frightening or shameful inner experiences, including dependency yearnings. In fact, our patients may most frantically seek us out when dependency yearnings arise, precisely because they are so painful and overwhelming in themselves. Momentary retreat back to the safe haven of the therapeutic relationship may give the patient the support to deal with painful experiences. But some patients try to ensconce themselves in a cocoon of comfort and support with the therapist that protects them from confrontation of painful realities, both past and present. The former is adaptive, while the latter perpetuates insecure dependency and leads to impasse.

CORE CONCEPT

The development of secure attachment in therapy involves changes in the patient's inner organization that are supported by a compassionate therapist, not one who offers increased contact and caregiving.

Of course, secure attachment does involve *some* availability of the therapist, but more importantly, it involves stability, predictability, repair, and a safe focus on consistently exploring the patients' experience within their window of tolerance. And as we discussed in Chapter 4, it includes careful attunement to the felt experience of the patient in the moment, a *being with* the patient. Thus, the therapist helps the patient share the experience of feeling needy, and is *with* the patient in collaboratively understanding and working with it, rather than merely acting to relieve it. It is being with the patient in those most painful moments in session—where the therapist is fully present and focused, and can assure that the patient is feeling the therapist's presence in a positive way—that is infinitely more healing and helpful than regular contact outside of session. Of course, there is a stepwise progression to the (often slow) development of the capacity to use the therapist in this way to explore, and some experiences are much more difficult to explore and resolve than others.

CASE EXAMPLE OF WORKING WITH DEPENDENCY: ARTHUR

Arthur was a 45-year-old man with a long history of childhood sexual, physical, and emotional abuse by his severely alcoholic mother. His father abandoned the family when Arthur was 3 years old. His mother frequently disappeared for several days at a time or went on drunken binges, leaving Arthur alone with his sister, who was only two years older. The sister was highly anxious and cried for hours on end for their mother. The sister overdosed on methamphetamine at age 26 and died. Arthur was able to get through a master's program, but had been unable to hold a job for more than a few months at a time due to severe anxiety, flashbacks, and depression. Arthur had been in six different therapies, and had completed two rounds of DBT. His dissociative disorder remained undiagnosed, while treatment focused on borderline personality disorder with dependent features and major depressive episodes. He had been on disability since the age of 35.

Arthur showed up hours early for his sessions, hanging out in the waiting room, and lingered long afterward, either in the waiting room or parking lot, feeling afraid to be too far away from his therapist. He called or e-mailed many times each week with crises and anxieties, both large and small. Arthur never quit therapy; rather, his various therapists grew increasingly frustrated with his constant needs and lack of progress, and they referred him on. Finally, he reached a therapist who diagnosed DID, and perhaps as importantly, understood the dynamics of his dependency. Arthur was highly fragmented, with many child parts, most of which were fixated in attachment cry. His adult functioning involved several parts, all passive and anxious. He described his inner experience as a school full of crying children in his head, locked in dozens of classrooms without a teacher, able to see out of small windows in the doors but not able to get help. These child parts had little to no awareness of the present, living as they did in trauma-time. This description immediately helped the therapist understand more about why Arthur was not able to develop a felt sense of a supportive other internally. The parts of Arthur that needed the most had access to the least, and were so focused on distress that they were unable to perceive the therapist's presence. A bit later Arthur described a vicious perpetrator-imitating part modeled on his mother that stalked the halls of the school with a baseball bat, slamming it against the doors, telling the children to shut up. He also had a kind but ineffective inner caretaker that resembled a very elderly, frail grandmother and had the helpless, overwhelmed qualities of his sister. This grandmother part wrung her hands and often cried, *I don't know what to do, I don't know what to do.* She wanted to help and protect the children, but felt unable to do so, much like his sister, and like Arthur in the present.

Understanding these inner dynamics opened the door to specific interventions that helped Arthur deal with his anxiety and dependency by working with his dissociative parts and inner landscape, as discussed below.

Dependency in Therapy: Always, Sometimes, Never?   **269**

Of course, Arthur's patterns were extremely entrenched, so therapy was neither easy nor fast, even after a proper diagnosis was made, especially regarding setting a new treatment frame and boundaries. But over the course of seven years, the therapist was able to help Arthur slowly change his inner world for the better.

The therapist immediately started by setting firm limits on contact outside of session, reinforcing a strong therapy frame that held Arthur securely if not happily. Arthur was expected to come to his appointments no more than 15 minutes early, and to leave the premises within 15 minutes of ending sessions. This was extremely difficult for Arthur at first, resulting in many tears, entreaties, threats of suicide, and rages. But the therapist held fast with compassion, tolerating Arthur's railing and anxiety. The therapist worked hard to help Arthur find some activities he could enjoy in daily life, encouraging him to get out of the house on at least some days, and out for a short walk almost every day. Arthur was encouraged to journal, not about his needs or painful history, which was overwhelming to him, but about his goals each day and how he accomplished them. In session, the therapist very gradually was able to work with the abusive mother part of Arthur. She gave up her baseball bat and took on the job of a strict but distant principal sitting in her office: a vague, lingering threat in the background, but one that allowed work to progress. The therapist helped Arthur find new models for caretaking internally: "good people who are competent and compassionate." The doors to the classrooms were gradually opened, with images of these good caretakers—some were book or television characters, and some were animals—entering and offering the children comfort, food, and care.

As he and the therapist worked with the child parts, Arthur became better able to talk about his dependency needs without becoming overwhelmed. He had the idea that the grandmother part could receive a special tonic that enlivened her. With the therapist's support, he was able to recall some experiences when he felt competent, and could transfer these to the inner grandmother, as well as to the other caretaker figures, and let it seep under the cracks of the principal's office, so the mother part could also feel competence. Slowly, very slowly, Arthur began to feel a little less needy; his rage at the therapist's lack of constant availability calmed. His reflexive tendency to call the therapist diminished, though he still complained about the rigidity of the "rules." The child parts became more curious about school and learning, opening the possibility of inner growth and development. Arthur still wanted to spend all his time with the therapist, but nevertheless was able and willing to participate in treatment.

After several years, Arthur began to foster an abused dog, and he took great pride in his ability to bring the dog out of its shell. He realized that the dog needed love, but also needed play, rest, and quiet time without contact, and most importantly, it needed time to explore and adjust to its environment and to a nonthreatening person. The metaphor was not lost on him, though it was hard to hold on to for more than short periods. Still, that he could hold on to a new paradigm of secure attachment that was not only about comfort was real progress. Arthur still had few social contacts—and was highly resistant to making them due to his extreme social anxiety—but already he had been able to improve the quality of his inner world, with which he began to feel more safe and comfortable. The dog offered essential companionship in a way he had never experienced before.

Although Arthur has needed to continue on disability, he remains an active participant in therapy, and his dependency behaviors are much diminished. His therapist was able to create a therapy frame that works over the long haul for both of them. Recently Arthur has been able to address some traumatic memories successfully.

Dependency and chronic crisis. Chronic crisis—such as ongoing self-harm or relational disruptions even after the patient has learned skills—requires a different approach rather than regular availability of the therapist outside sessions. When the patient is first learning skills, it may be appropriate to have contact between sessions for the purpose of coaching the patient to practice skills; for example, as recommended in DBT (Linehan, 1993, 2014). And indeed, therapy is not conducted during these contacts, which are limited to specific skills practice and grounding. Thus, phone calls are limited to a few minutes, exploring what the patient has tried, why it did not work, and what the patient can try next. Any therapeutic work that comes up during the call can be contained and addressed in the next session.

CASE EXAMPLE OF CONTAINING CRISIS CALLS IN ORDER TO MANAGE DEPENDENCY: GAIL

Gail frequently called her therapist after fights with her boyfriend. She would be hysterically crying and nearly incoherent. In sessions, the therapist worked to help Gail learn several grounding and calming techniques, which she practiced at home. Then, when Gail called with a crisis, the therapist would instruct her over the phone to use the techniques: *Gail, as we are together on the phone, remember the breathing technique that you learned? Let's take several deep breaths together at the count of three. Good. Now let's do it again together once more. OK. I know you want to talk about what happened, but that really deserves time when we are together. Right now I want to help you get grounded and make sure you are safe. What else might be helpful to get you grounded and present right now?* If the patient cannot come up with a suggestion, the therapist can suggest something. *OK, how about you put your feet firmly on the floor and feel the chair you are sitting in. Let all parts of you listen to the sound of my voice. You are safe. You are having some strong feelings, and that is OK. We will sort them out together when you come in for your session. Right now, could you imagine letting those feelings be in a safe container, not to disturb you until you arrive in my office next time? In the meantime, please practice your skills, the breathing and the calming ones. You've been doing great with those, so keep it up! I will see you when you come for your session.*

Once the patient knows the skills to regulate and titrate, but still continues to make chronic crisis calls, the therapist needs to reassess whether extrasession contact is serving a helpful purpose (see the case example of Marjorie and Pam at the end of the chapter). Chronic crisis may require a reassessment of therapeutic boundaries and of the patient's capacities for psychotherapy, and perhaps a referral to a higher level of care (for example, an outpatient or inpatient program, or a center that has a crisis team available). It might be important to further assess whether the patient is continuing to be abused in the present, as this can result in a puzzling decompensation and crisis when the therapist does not know. The therapist should carefully explore whether inadequate pacing of therapy may be contributing the patient's dysregulation (Van Dijke, 2008). The therapist should also explore the meaning and function of the crisis in the therapeutic relationship and whether the therapist may be unconsciously encouraging or perpetuating crisis.

Distress as a relational strategy. Some patients seem able to connect with the therapist only through distress. The more the therapist seeks to soothe, the more these patients return with distress. It is as though they are buckets with holes in the bottom. They have an overwhelming phobia of both contact and loss of contact. The more the therapist tries to fill them up with positive connection, the more they are unable to use it to their advantage. Instead, for example, during the (presumably positive) experience of receiving support from the therapist in session, they are already focused on the end of the session when they have to leave, the next distressing memory, fear or shame about their needs, or the fact that what is being offered isn't enough. It seems that positive experiences only painfully remind them of what they did not get as children or are missing now. They must be helped to stay focused on the present moment, on the positive experience. Thus, a considerable amount of time must be spent exploring the felt sense of being with the therapist and what happens internally when the patient has a positive experience.

Patients unconsciously fear they are in peril of losing the one sure way they have learned to maintain connection with the therapist—that is, via their distress. In addition, some patients have a severe phobia of their dependency feelings, no matter how titrated they are, at least early in therapy. These incredibly painful and urgent feelings result in frantic clinging and seeking behaviors. Such behaviors are motivated by panic and fear of loss, which the therapist needs to explore and understand rather than reacting to the behaviors.

Dependency as reenactment. Dependency feelings and behaviors are often an enactment of unresolved yearning and panic from the past, and can be considered as emotional flashbacks, a possibility often overlooked by therapists. Various dissociative parts of the patient—especially child parts—are fixated in desperate loneliness, need, and yearning for care. When therapists understand that intense dependency needs are reenactments, similar to fear or shame or sexual feelings in the therapy relationship, they can take an approach to either contain the whole traumatic memory until a better time or help the patient integrate the memory. Of course, dependency is virtually never limited to a single memory, but rather is part and parcel of the individual's entire childhood. Nevertheless, it can be helpful to work on some specific memories in which unmet dependency needs were central.

CORE CONCEPT

Unmet dependency needs involve overwhelming panic and distress, and may be a component of a flashback, as they are often a central part of early traumatic experiences.

When dependency leads to more dependency. Of course, the patient often experiences relief when the therapist is available to help calm, encourage, offer options for skills, and educate. Some patients are able to use these positive experiences to gain a greater sense of competence and confidence. But others become ever more dependent on the therapist, with the absence of contact always evoking the need to seek out the therapist again and again. For them, the presence of the therapist becomes like a drug that numbs pain, prevents realization and grieving, and reduces the patient's efforts to become more effective in living. We discuss below the differences in the capacities of these patients. It may be counterintuitive, but the therapist needs to realize that the neediest, most desperate patients are typically the least likely to make effective use of the therapist's presence between sessions, at least at first.

These patients typically view dependency as literal, expecting the therapist to take care of them and be available when they need. They require careful skills building, development of a sense of competence, containment of dependency needs and affects, and support in having positive affects and experiences with the therapist first. However, no matter how little or how much the patient can tolerate, it is the therapist's capacity to maintain a stable therapy frame and boundaries as illustrated above, and to manage countertransference and counterresistances to dependency, that is paramount to successful therapy.

Assessing Patients for Tolerance of Dependency Feelings in Therapy

How can the therapist distinguish between patients who can tolerate the emergence of intense dependency feelings and those who will be overwhelmed by them; between patients who make positive use of contact outside session and those who do not? This is an essential question to ask because treatment approaches differ, at least at first. The therapist can titrate or contain dependency needs in the patient once it is clear what the patient can tolerate.

Below are some questions that help the therapist determine whether a patient may be able to tolerate the emergence of dependency yearning in therapy. If many of these questions are answered in the affirmative, the therapist must be extremely careful not to evoke dependency unless and until the patient has greater integrative capacity.

- Does the patient have a history of strong and panicked attachment-seeking behaviors, such as frequent calling or e-mails between sessions, chronic demands for more time, or difficulty ending sessions or leaving the office?
  - If so, is the patient unable to notice, accept, and shift these behaviors?
  - Is the patient as a whole unwilling to curtail the behaviors of dependent dissociative parts with some compassion?
- Does the patient chronically present with child parts in therapy and seem unable or unwilling to have adult parts present in sessions?
- Does the patient present with child parts at the end of the session that are unwilling to have an adult part return home? This is a classic reenactment, as the therapist has to send away the child part, and

inside often adult parts then say to the child parts, *See, she sends you away just like your mother did,* or *See, she doesn't want you.*

- Does the patient, or do parts of the patient, have implicit or explicit expectations and demands that the therapist and others will give, and perhaps even owe, the patient the love and care that was absent in childhood?
- Is the patient, or are parts of the patient, fixated on times when the therapist is not available?
- Is the patient unable to take the felt sense of the therapist's presence with him or her after session?
- Do parts of the patient sabotage the therapy relationship or the felt sense of security that the patient gains from being with the therapist?
- Does the patient lack healthy relationships apart from that with the therapist?
- Is the patient highly dependent on others outside therapy?
- Is the patient unable to understand dependency as an experience— like other experiences—that must be worked through; but rather, expects the therapist to relieve or fix it?
- Is the patient unable to acknowledge dependency without excessive shame, guilt, rage, entitlement, or severe inner conflict?
- Is the patient unable to tolerate and regulate the intense emotion and loss that are activated with dependency yearnings?

The Therapist's Issues With Dependency: Countertransference

Therapists must assess themselves carefully, because sometimes a patient's dependency yearnings are workable in therapy in principle, but the therapist is unable to provide the frame that supports the work. To this end, therapists might reflect on the following questions:

- What are my experiences with and beliefs about dependence and independence in adults?
- How do I feel when a patient is dependent upon me?
- Do I enjoy, detest, fear, or simply accept feeling needed by a patient?
- Do I feel compelled to give in to or withhold from a patient who is being demanding or needy?
- Do I feel sorry for or pity my patient, and feel pulled to offer comfort?
- Do I feel strong urges to take care of my patient and do something to relieve her suffering?

- Can I tolerate my patient's suffering without confusing it with my own feelings?
- Am I clear about the difference between caring about (being with) and caretaking (doing for) a patient?
- Does my patient's self-harm, chronic suicidality, or intense suffering scare or overwhelm me to the degree that I have constant or very regular contact with the patient over long periods of time?
- Do I feel the need to rescue my client from poor decisions, difficult or unfair life circumstances, or from other treatment team members who may disagree with my approach?
- Am I treating this particular patient differently than other patients? If so, do I have a sound clinical rationale for doing so? Do I have support from my supervisor, consultant, or treatment team to do so?
- Do I often feel preoccupied with the patient outside of sessions?
- Do I initiate contact with the patient between sessions when I feel worried about him, or do I wait and allow him to contact me?

All therapists have their own unique countertransference and counter-resistance to patients who have dependency yearnings.

Avoidant therapist, avoidant patient. An avoidant therapist coupled with a predominantly avoidant patient results in a collusion to keep therapy at the surface, with little to no focus on transference and countertransference. The patient is implicitly rewarded for not bringing dependency issues to treatment. The therapist is unlikely to seek consultation, often unaware of underlying and profound insecure attachment issues. Avoidant therapists may be quick to terminate with the patient and refer elsewhere, and may find it quite difficult to challenge their beliefs about dependency.

Avoidant therapists may fail to notice or deal with the patient's dependence, or they may feel disgust, aversion, or overwhelmed at the very idea of a patient needing them. They are sometimes intolerant of emotional intensity or of another person's needs. Often, avoidant therapists are avoiding their own unresolved attachment needs as well as the patient's. The avoidance of dependency issues serves to modulate the emotions of both therapist and patient within a narrow band of the therapist's tolerance, at least regarding dependency issues. The avoidant therapist usually has a mistaken belief that dependence is bad, and values self-sufficiency to the exclusion of adaptive interdependence.

On the avoidant spectrum, patients—or parts of the patient—will eschew even the remotest hint of dependence. These parts are driven by shame and disgust, often with punishing rage toward dependent parts, and sometimes toward the therapist. Usually the main adult parts of the patient are disgusted by or dismissive of child parts and wish to get rid of them.

Avoidant therapist, anxious patient. Unfortunately, when avoidant therapists respond, they may do so with frustration, anger, or disgust rather than with compassion and patience. This results in further panic, shame, rage, and despair in the patient. The patient may engage in increasing self-harm or suicide attempts, may become enraged or hopeless, and may leave therapy because there is little to no attunement. Avoidant therapists may not seek consultation except to deal with the "problem" of the patient's dependency, and may view the patient as "impossible."

The anxious patient is one who is desperately seeking connection, feels panic at separation, fears abandonment and rejection, and is often preoccupied with having contact with the therapist. Many child parts have these qualities, but often so do some adult parts of the patient. When the adult parts collude with or abdicate to the child parts, very intense dependency results. This can lead to increasing acting out on the part of the patient to gain the attention of the avoidant therapist.

Anxious therapist, avoidant patient. Anxious therapists may overfocus on caretaking activities and worry about the patient excessively. They may confuse secure attachment and dependency; pursue the patient, perhaps telling patients that they have to rely on the therapist in order to heal; or call the patient when worried. Anxious therapists are focused on the need to caretake, rescue, and help.

The predominantly avoidant patient will react with fear or disgust and withdraw further. The avoidant suicidal patient is especially problematic for the anxious therapist, who makes ever greater efforts to get the patient to talk about suicidal thoughts, plans, or intentions and to reassure the therapist that the patient will be safe. The patient becomes ever more reluctant to share, out of fear the therapist will make interventions that are overwhelming, creating an impasse. Often the patient leaves treatment.

CASE EXAMPLE OF ANXIOUS THERAPIST AND AVOIDANT PATIENT: ANN AND STEPHEN

Ann was treating Colin, a male patient who was using cocaine on a regular basis and engaging in binge drinking that interfered with his ability to function at work. He eventually lost his job and became chronically suicidal. Colin refused to go to AA or to an emotional skills group, take medication for depression and anxiety, or stop using drugs and alcohol.

He often canceled appointments, and Ann—worried about his suicidality—would pursue him and try to have therapy sessions on the phone. Stephen suffered from DID but was unwilling to acknowledge or work with parts and would not allow the therapist to access parts. However, parts of the patient were constantly switching in session, and e-mailing Ann about various issues which then could not be discussed in therapy. Therapy sessions devolved into Ann pleading for Colin to engage in some—any—therapeutic action, and Colin refusing. After consultation Ann was able to realize that she needed support to be less caretaking and more curious with the patient about his experience and what kept him from making changes. She needed to explore his motivation to make changes. She became clearer about what she required to continue treatment. As importantly, she realized that she and the patient needed to find at least one shared treatment goal that could be worked on consistently in therapy.

Anxious therapist, anxious patient. The anxious therapy dyad is the one most likely to end up with more serious boundary violations. Anxious therapists typically feel overwhelmed by the needs and suffering of the patient, and may feel guilty, overly responsible, and preoccupied with the patient's well-being. They seek ways to actively take care of or help the patient. The caretaking serves to temporarily relieve the anxiety of both the therapist and the patient, and circumvents difficult work with the inner experience of either party. Anxious therapists have much more difficulty setting appropriate boundaries out of inability to tolerate discomfort and pain in either themselves or their patients. Such therapists often have learned to cope with relationships via controlling-caregiving strategies.

The anxious patient escalates in reaction to the anxiety of the therapist, becoming ever more dysregulated and distressed, in a spiral of mutually escalating arousal (Beebe, 2000; also cf. Chapter 4). The goal for the anxious patient and therapist is soothing of intense distress, rather than exploration of why they might be responding to each other this way and what could change. Anxious therapists often seek consultation after they are exhausted from contact and crisis, but feel the only option is to do still more. They may be highly reluctant to transfer the patient or change their patterns of response to the patient.

For What Do Patients Really Need to Depend Upon the Therapist?

Patients are dependent upon therapists to some degree. But the major question is, For what? They need the therapist to serve as a guide in a safe passage through chaotic and intense transferences and reenactments, through challenges in daily life, and through phobic avoidance as they try to acknowledge and accept painful memories, emotions, and dissociative parts of themselves. They depend on the therapist to respond humanly in the moment, as a compassionate witness and active participant in a relationship that offers shared honesty, curiosity, compassion, clarity, regulation, repair, and sense of competence. They need the therapist to value their competence as adults, while shoring up their deficits. Patients must learn to provide all this for themselves when they are alone, as does everyone else, so that as a whole person they can engage in healthy and meaningful relationships.

Patients depend on the therapist to be present for the session, to start and end on time, to give ample notice of planned absences or vacations. They depend on the therapist to minimize personal defensive reactions as much as possible, and to monitor and control countertransference behaviors. They depend upon the therapist to engage in repair as needed and pay close attention not only to patient's experience but to the therapist's own subjective experience, which can inform the patient's experience.

Patients slowly come to realize that although the therapist is not always physically available, the therapist is as consistent and predictable as humanly possible, and is present in the moment with them during sessions. Although they may not be able to reach the therapist at 3 a.m. when they are having a flashback, if the therapist has helped them learn skills to ground and calm (Boon et al., 2011), they know the therapist will be there to help them in the next session. They learn to wait, to soothe themselves, and to introject the good self of the therapist, along with other positive figures, as an intrapsychic comfort and guide.

Patients learn an essential life lesson: Sometimes we all have to wait to get help, but in general, help is available. We all have to learn to tolerate distress until we can get help. Even children must learn to help themselves in the temporary absence of outside support. Real life does not consist of constant availability and soothing; rather, it is an endless dance of ever-changing closeness and distance, both planned and unexpected. Thus, patients must develop mental representations of supportive others on which they can rely. They must not only intellectually know but must *feel* these experiences in their bodies.

CORE CONCEPT

Patients depend on us to help them learn to tolerate measured vacillations of connection, separation, disruption, reconnection, and repair in the therapeutic relationship.

One unique problem with dissociative patients is that only some parts are able to have these positive experiences at first. It is thus important for the therapist to realize that the experiences of one part do not automatically transfer to other parts. The therapist, therefore, must encourage those parts that do have a greater sense of felt security to share it with other parts. Our patients need us to help them build bridges of awareness and empathy between dissociative parts of themselves in ways that support growth, maturity, and competence.

Patients depend on the therapist to help them accept and cope with separation and loss as normal and inevitable life experiences. We help them realize the losses of the past, present, and future, as tolerated and appropriate, and only after they are capable of having positive experiences and emotions as a foundation of support. Thus, we compassionately acknowledge the patient's distress over the fact that we are not always there, cannot be the patient's parent, partner, friend, or other "real-life" attachment figure, and cannot magically make the patient better.

The Dissociative Patient's Conflicts About Dependence

Dissociative patients tend to have different parts that express various sides of the dependency conflict. For example, a patient may have a child part that desperately seeks literal care from the therapist; a numb, detached adult who finds relationships irrelevant or uninteresting and wants nothing to do with the inner child part; a perpetrator-imitating part who finds the dependency in the child part abhorrent, and thus punishes the child internally; and so on.

The greater this conflict among parts of the patient, the greater the pressure on the therapist to choose sides, which further serves to increase the internal divide of the patient. A perpetual inner war between these parts ensues, heightened by the very fact of being in therapy. Parts that want—or even demand—caretaking will be activated by the attunement and compassion of the therapist. In turn, this activation triggers parts that find dependency frightening, shaming, or otherwise aversive. Therapists are all too often pulled to take one side or the other. The more we do so, the more the dependency is evoked in certain parts, the greater the internal threat for other parts, creating a vicious cycle.

The Dependency–Threat Cycle
The patient and therapist may become caught in a vicious cycle of dependency and threat. The patient (typically one or more dissociative child parts) feels unsafe due to an external or internal trigger, often both simul-

taneously. Attachment cry is activated and results in frantic seeking and clinging to the therapist. The patient, or some parts of the patient, feel shame and fear due to the vulnerability of this need and helplessness. Typically, some parts of the patient become enraged as a defense against the shame: *You are bad and disgusting because you are so needy*, or lash out externally toward the therapist: *You aren't there when I need you! You don't care about me; you just want my money!* These enraged parts of the patient further activate fear of abandonment and rejection in child or other dependent parts, which exacerbates dependency, incompetence, and helplessness.

The patient's inner experience is now chaotic and disorganized, leading to ever more frantic pursuit of relief from the therapist and ever more internal rage, shame, and disorganization. The more the therapist caretakes or withdraws instead of building competency and helping the patient understand and stop the cycle, the worse the cycle becomes.

CASE EXAMPLE OF WORKING WITH THE DEPENDENCY–THREAT CYCLE: CAROLINE

Caroline was a patient who was extremely phobic of a child part that cried all the time, calling out for help internally, and also of an inner critical part that was always telling the child part to shut up. This inner conflict was so intense she began calling her therapist, Susan, frequently between sessions to get help with her anxiety. Susan first helped Caroline understand and verbalize more about her conflict about dependency on the therapist, and addressed her concerns. Then she asked for permission to speak to the hostile part of Caroline, and determined that the function of this part was to maintain safety by keeping the "crybaby" quiet so the child part would not cry too much and get in trouble. This hostile part was living in trauma-time, unaware of the present, and was well defended against dependency needs by rage.

Susan helped Caroline orient the critical part to the present and agreed with this part that she also did not want the child part (or any part of Caroline) to be in such a painful state. The therapist then encouraged Caroline to understand the functions of the critical part, as well as the dependency yearnings of the child part. Caroline gradually became less phobic and more compassionate toward these parts of herself and could accept their functions. The therapist supported an alliance between the critical part and the adult part of Caroline, which in turn supported the child part in being acknowledged and helped in appropriate ways. This significantly calmed the inner conflict.

We end this chapter with a case example that examines the challenging therapeutic task of setting appropriate boundaries with a dependent patient once the therapist realizes they have been overextended.

CASE EXAMPLE OF BOUNDARY REPAIR: MARJORIE AND PAM

Marjorie took on a patient as a referral from a day treatment program. Pam, a 42-year-old single woman on disability, was chronically suicidal and intensely suffering, with a diagnosis of major depressive disorder, DID, and borderline personality disorder. She had been through more than three years of DBT training without improvement. Marjorie began the standard DBT protocol by being available for skills coaching outside sessions and also began working with Pam's dissociative parts to stabilize her. However, Pam only increased her suicidal calls and e-mails over time, until Marjorie was receiving several calls a day and multiple e-mails. No matter how much she coached Pam and tried to help her analyze why the skills did not work, Pam did not improve.

Marjorie felt overwhelmed, resentful, and exhausted, so she sought consultation. She knew she could not continue this way and needed to shift something in therapy. She began reflecting on the underlying phobia of attachment and attachment loss in Pam, and how the contact in this case was serving to increase Pam's insecure dependency rather than support skills building. She felt some relief and knew she would be able to continue treatment when she had the option to reset boundaries. The next session she began the hard task of reestablishing therapeutic boundaries.

Marjorie: I want to share something that may be hard for you to hear, but I want to be clear that what I am going to say is in no way meant to shame or chastise you; this is something that is my responsibility, not yours. I have done a disservice to you with our e-mail and phone contact between sessions in the last year. Although we both have been hopeful that this additional contact would help you develop more skills and decrease your suicidality, in fact, the opposite has happened. We need to rethink how we are approaching your distress. I think I understand what is happening and would like to share more about it, but first I want to check in and see what is happening with you right now.

Pam: You're going to cut off all contact between sessions! You know I can't tolerate that!

Marjorie: I hear that this is very hard, and I have confidence that we will be able to work through it together. We've just started talking about it, so it's only natural that you would feel panic. I want to assure you that I am not suggesting we stop therapy. To the contrary, I want us to continue so we can meet the goals you have set and are working so hard to achieve.

Pam: I can't tolerate not having contact. I can't make it!

Marjorie: You are feeling a lot of panic right now. Let's slow down and take this one step at a time. As we always do together, if something isn't working, we will revisit it. I am aware that you have tried this way with several other therapists and now with me for quite a while, and it isn't helping you reach your goals. In fact, your suicidality and distress between sessions have been increasing. I respect and value our work together and hope you will continue with me, as I am confident that we can find a more effective way to help you. Would you be interested in hearing more?

Pam: I don't have a choice, do I? You are in total control, and I have no say in it.

Marjorie: That's a painful place to be in, to experience yourself as helpless and at the mercy of someone else. I know that is a familiar place for you, and I can empathize with how frightening that must be, and it must bring up anger as well. Yet, some parts of you know me pretty well. Can those parts help you to hang in with me even while you are having those strong emotions, so we can work our way through this? You and I know it is my job, however difficult for both of us, to direct therapy in a way that is effective and helpful. I'm doing my best right now to do that.

Pam: Taking away something important is not helpful!

Marjorie: Hmm, perhaps, and I am sure it doesn't feel helpful right now. But there might be a different way to look at this. For example, you decided last year not to drink anymore; you took alcohol away from yourself, even though parts of you found it very helpful and you craved it. It had an important purpose to numb your suffering. Remember how hard it was to let that go? Maybe there is something for us to look at with that analogy.

Pam: But drinking was hurting me! This is totally different.

Marjorie: Of course there are differences, and there are also some similarities too. I have a hunch about how this might be hurting you. Would you like to hear more?

Pam: I guess, but I think you are doing this because you are sick of me.

Marjorie: I am doing this because I see it isn't working for you or for me. You are exhausted in your suffering. I am tired too. This level of intensity and distress is not something either one of us can sustain. We are both tired right now. That's OK; it's just a signal that we need to look at what is happening so we can do something more helpful. Instead of running away, I really want to be here with you and make this work for both of us, so that we have focus and energy together to help you move forward.

Dependency in Therapy: Always, Sometimes, Never?   **283**

Pam: You are tired of me! I knew it! I knew that I was bothering you too much. I would try not to call and beat myself up when I did because I knew you would get sick of me.

Marjorie: Right, this is exactly my hunch! We are on the same track. I do feel tired when I get so many calls from you between sessions. In order to be at my best, I have to feel rested. Even though it may be scary for you to know that I get tired, I think it's really important for both of us to acknowledge. You have talked about how everyone gets sick of you and leaves. I don't want to do that. It's our job to take a look at what happens in our relationship and in relationships with others where they feel exhausted and pull away and you feel desperate and afraid. I think that is the last thing in the world you want them to do! At the same time, I realize that you are feeling so very desperate for help. That's a terrible dilemma for you, to feel desperate and to worry you are exhausting people.

Pam: Yeah, happens all the time. I am just such a loser. If I killed myself, you wouldn't have to feel tired anymore. I'm just a burden to you.

Marjorie: I hear you, and I hear that you don't want to be a burden and that you need help. That must seem like a real double bind to you. I know you turn to the thought of suicide when things feel desperate, but I do have some ideas about how to help. I am really hoping that you choose to work this out with me.

Pam: Just seems like there is no other way out.

Marjorie: Well, could we try first to see if we can find a way out together?

Pam: Whatever.

Marjorie: OK. Thank you for being willing. So, some part of you feels panic and desperation and then calls me. But other parts are very worried about how that will affect me and our relationship. And the same goes for your relationships with others, too. So far in therapy, we have only focused on the parts that feel the need, but not those parts that feel so protective of our relationship. They are important too, and perhaps hold the solution. Do you suppose those parts of you feel ashamed of your need?

Pam: Yeah, like it's disgusting. I hate myself when I have to call you.

Marjorie: Yeah. This is what we have been missing. You have the need and call me, but then feel ashamed.

Pam: Well, I don't feel anything at all.

Marjorie: So other parts of you are feeling the need and the shame?

Pam: I think so, yeah.

Marjorie: How do you suppose your numbness helps you?

Pam: I guess I just don't want to deal with any of it.

Marjorie: That's understandable. It would be great if I dealt with it for you, wouldn't it? I would get to feel so helpful, like Super Therapist, and you would be able to feel fine without having to do anything at all, like magic! What a great deal for both of us! *(Smiling)*

Pam: *(Smiling too)* Yes, exactly!

Marjorie: Yes, exactly! Well, let's have Ms. Super Therapist and Ms. Magic Patient sit on the sidelines for a while—they have been working hard and deserve a rest. It's a wonderful fairy tale for both of us to enjoy, but I have to admit those two are not helping us figure this out very much! So parts of you feel a need and call to relieve their distress. Other parts feel shame and disgust and lash out at those parts. How do you imagine the parts with the need feel when the other parts of you lash out? Could you check with them?

Pam: I guess maybe they feel bad—there is a lot of screaming and crying inside after I call you.

Marjorie: They—you—feel bad. So there is a need, a call to me, some relief, an immediate backlash, and then parts are right back to feeling bad, and you are numb to it all. This is exactly what I think is going on that isn't helpful for you. If you agree, I'd like for us to spend some time looking at this cycle. Now let's check and see how you are doing and what you think about this idea.

Pam: Calmer. Still scared. Mad. I don't know what to expect—like you are going to pull the rug out from under me.

Marjorie: Yes, a lot of emotions right now, and uncertainty. I also feel a little uncertain. I want us to work this out, and I feel a little unsure that you might not hang in with me and that I might not say it exactly right the first time. I guess we share that together, huh? This is hard and kind of risky for both of us. Still, I am confident we can do hard things together—we have before.

Pam: Maybe.

Marjorie: So, I am going to offer some new guidelines that help us work with this inner cycle. I have written them down for both of us because I've given it a lot of thought and it is so important to me that I get it right. We are not going to have contact between sessions, and I want to help you set up other supports in your life. We are going to work in sessions with the parts that feel the need and with the parts that are ashamed of the need, and help all of you work together more effectively. You can journal and bring in your thoughts to session, and then we can deal with anything at that time. You can call if you need to change or request an appointment, but that is the only reason to call me between sessions. If you are imminently suicidal, you can call the emergency numbers for a crisis team, and they can then call me. If you feel distress, you can call a support person in your life. Who would that be?

Dependency in Therapy: Always, Sometimes, Never?   **285**

Pam: *(Tearful and angry)* I wouldn't call anyone. I don't want to bother them.

Marjorie: Hmm, this is also part of our dilemma. You feel ashamed to reach out, so your need of me increases. You don't want to "bother" others, but it's OK to then call me? Help me understand that.

Pam: It's your job to be there when I need help.

Marjorie: Oh, now I begin to see how I have not helped you understand my role very well. I am really sorry about that. My job is to help you notice what happens inside you and for you to learn to do something about it, whether that is working internally yourself or reaching out to others in your life in ways that don't exhaust them. Together, we are working on understanding what happens and what might help. OK, let's proceed with making a safety plan for you between sessions.

Pam was able to go a week without contacting the therapist. She remained angry, hurt, and unsure if she wanted to continue therapy, yet was engaged in session and had no crises during the week. The second week, she e-mailed a question to Marjorie about whether she should bring in her journals to next session, since she had done a lot of journaling about her progress. Marjorie was delighted that Pam was willing to journal, and was quite tempted to respond to this legitimate question. After consultation, she decided to hold the boundary of no contact, as she felt this was a first testing of the limits. Once in session again, Pam was angry that Marjorie had not responded to her e-mail.

Pam: You could have just responded with a yes or no. That's all I was asking! I was trying to figure out what would be helpful in session—I'm trying hard! You are so rigid.

Marjorie: It's OK to be angry with me. Yes, you are indeed trying hard. It's also important that you can count on me to be consistent. The guideline was that we would not have any e-mail contact. I didn't want to disrespect all the hard work you have done in the past two weeks by going back to something that wasn't working. I also trust that you will make good decisions about what to bring to sessions, and know that even if you bring something, it is still your choice as to whether you share it.

Several months later, Marjorie and Pam were working well together, and the crises between sessions had almost completely stopped. Pam had identified a child part, which she called "Pammie," that held dependency yearnings. She had also identified an adolescent part she called "Angry Girl," which felt both yearning and disgust for the yearning. This part tried to care for Pammie, but was also frustrated and exhausted by her and by her own needs. The adult part of Pam continued to be disengaged and numb in relation to Pammie and Angry Girl. Finally, Pam also described a part she called "Queen," which imitated her mother, who was emotionally and physically abusive and neglectful, and cold like "an ice queen." Pam and Marjorie were able to map out the conflict cycle as follows:

- Pammie would become activated because of inner interactions with Queen, in which Queen would scream at her and slap her face. Queen, like Angry Girl, could not tolerate the child part's needs and yearnings.
- Pammie would feel terrified and want comfort, pushing Pam to call Marjorie.
- Angry Girl attempted to protect Pammie from Queen by berating the child part's neediness and telling her to be quiet. She would lock Pammie in a closet (which further increased Pammie's fear and isolation), and Angry Girl herself would become the object of Queen's rage.
- Angry Girl would then become enraged, afraid, and helpless, leading her to feel intensely suicidal. Pam, a combination of numb and distressed by this point, would inexplicably feel suicidal and have an urgent need to call Marjorie because of so much inner chaos that she did not understand and could not control.
- Once Pam called the therapist, Queen was further activated to punish Angry Girl and Pammie for their "disgusting neediness that is worse than any baby I raised." Shame served to increase the suicidality, which in turn increased the calls to the therapist.

Marjorie began working with these various parts of Pam in session to notice and interrupt this inner dynamic between dissociative parts. She chose to work with Queen first, as this was the part that was most avoidant of need. Working with other parts on dependency at this point would only serve to further activate Queen and increase self-destructiveness. Marjorie began by simply talking through to Queen and noting that she thought she had some understanding of Queen's concerns, and would she be willing to talk further about them? (Working with perpetrator-imitating parts is discussed in Chapter 17, so we will not now focus on that work with Queen.) At first Queen refused to respond, but still allowed Marjorie to talk to her. Gradually Queen began to respond as a hostile inner voice that Pam could relay to Marjorie. Over the course of a couple of months of regular work, Queen began to soften as she realized Marjorie did not vilify her as other parts of Pam did, but actually understood her. She became willing to participate more actively in therapy, although she remained disgusted with Pammie and Angry Girl, but in a less intense and malevolent way.

Further Explorations

13.1 How do you feel about patients who exhibit dependent behaviors?

13.2 What messages did you get about being dependent in your life? How do these affect your being with patients who struggle with dependency?

13.3 How easily do you set limits with your patients for whom dependency is an issue? Practice with a colleague specific ways of talking to patients about limits with compassion.

13.4 Do you have a tendency to want to rescue or take care of some of your patients? What would help you tolerate this wish without acting on it?

13.5 Can you describe for yourself the difference between secure attachment and dependency, and how that manifests in your patient?

CHAPTER 14

Working With Child Parts of the Patient

Working with personalities that present as young children often brings a different kind of vulnerability to making errors in psychotherapy. . . . These child identities are personifications of the patient as a child—not actual children.

—James Chu (2011, p. 222)

I had to find a way to integrate the night child. . . . Until the night child had been fully heard, honored and integrated, I, the adult would continue to fear the night and clutch to my clenched body.

—Marilyn Van Derbur (2003, p. 546)

Dissociative child (and adolescent) parts are representations of the many developmental injuries and deficiencies endured by the patient. They are often stuck in particular action systems of defense such as attachment cry, flight, fight, freeze, flag, or faint. Child parts are often needy or terrified, while adolescent parts tend to be angry, rebellious, and not interested in responsibility. Of course, this varies widely. In Chapter 13, we gave examples of how to work with highly dependent child parts, and in Chapter 15, we will give case examples of working with angry child parts. But there are other presentations as well, such as the playful child part, the sexualized child part, the child part stuck in trauma-time, the frozen or shutdown child, and the entitled or shamed child. There may be infant and toddler parts that are preverbal, parts that are physically injured or ill, or even "dead" child parts that are perceived to have died during abuse. Some of these dissociative parts appear to be deaf or mute. Child parts are sometimes depicted by the patient as naked or dirty, as not having mouths or eyes or hands.

These images, of course, represent the terror and helplessness of the patient as a child, the fear of telling, the shame of being seen or known, the profound neglect that was part of their existence. Often these parts are experienced as being in original scenes of trauma; for example, in a bed or basement, beaten, or abused. They are often stuck in trauma-time and in defenses against danger or life threat. Some continue to be abused internally by parts that imitate the perpetrator, in an ongoing inner reenactment (see Chapter 17).

CORE CONCEPT

Dissociative child parts typically represent the most vulnerable, painful, helpless, and disowned experiences of the patient. However, they may also contain disowned rage, entitlement, sexual feelings, and a strong need to control others.

Some child parts are quite active in daily life, some are only active internally, and still others are completely isolated from other parts and unknown—kept internally in dark holes, behind walls, or otherwise hidden deeply. The therapist must remember that the inner dissociative world does not follow linear thinking and logic. So, for example, so-called dead parts may not be actually dead, but only appear to be so for a time; and deaf parts can understand without hearing.

As always, the therapist and patient must begin to understand the meaning of these presentations, and specifically, the non-realizations that they contain. For example, a dead child may have developed when the patient lost or nearly lost consciousness during abuse and believed she had died. Thus, neither this part nor other parts of the patient realize she survived. A dead child might represent the feeling that the abuse "killed my soul," or may represent another child who is not the patient. Some child parts function in daily life or heavily influence the adult part of the patient.

CASE EXAMPLE OF CHILD PART THAT PARTICIPATES IN DAILY LIFE: DANIEL

Daniel, a 40-year-old man, had a child part called "Danny." This was an intelligent and playful child part whose function was to go school when

Daniel was a boy, unaware of the abuse at home. Danny stopped growing up at the age of 11 because he could not realize that his grandmother, a major attachment figure in his life, had died and was no longer there to protect him from his abusive parents. Danny was convinced his grandmother was still alive and talked to an internal part that he experienced as his grandmother. This part of Daniel would often surface when Daniel was depressed, to influence his mood (to make him happier).

CORE CONCEPT

Child parts are not actually children. They are representations and should not be treated by the therapist as children but as aspects of an adult patient.

Inner Reaction to Child Parts

Child parts are most often reviled by other parts of the patient, especially by adult parts, as they represent much of what the patient wishes to avoid: intolerable feelings of fear, disgust, dread, horror, shame, need, rage, helplessness, and dependence, and intolerable sensations, thoughts, or beliefs. As Marilyn Van Derbur (2003), a survivor who wrote about her experience, noted:

> My night child kept her part of the deal. She had "taken it" [the abuse] until I [the adult] was strong and secure enough to come back and rescue her. Now, instead of gratitude for her sacrificing herself, I loathed, despised and blamed her. (p. 191)

Sometimes these parts are experienced as screaming, crying, or moaning incessantly, which further frightens and overwhelms the presenting part of the patient.

Some patients have at least some compassion toward their child parts, which typically bodes well for treatment. Internally there may be caretakers of child parts; for example, nurturing older children, adolescents, kindly grandmother figures, or other adult parts of the patient that can be of help in therapy. Other times, the care is perfunctory at best and conducted with a surly and resentful attitude that perhaps reflects the way the patient was cared for as a child, as well as the exhaustion and distaste of the adult patient in the present. Some patients find child parts completely disgusting or frightening and are highly phobic of them.

Parts that imitate the perpetrator are most often abusive to child parts, internally calling them names, humiliating them, withholding food and water, hitting or slapping them, using self-harm to injure them, and even torturing them. Working with these parts, which originally had a protective function, is discussed in depth in Chapter 17. The adult part of the patient often ignores and neglects child parts in a reenactment of old patterns. The adult part may bitterly complain about the weakness and neediness of child parts while refusing to attend to those needs to mitigate them. The therapist must be careful to help the adults part realize their role in maintaining child parts that remain stuck in need or fear.

Practical Approaches to Working With Dissociative Child Parts

Perhaps the most important concept in working with child parts is to ensure these parts remain the responsibility of the patient, not the therapist. To this end, it is helpful and necessary to have an adult part that functions in daily life present in session the majority of the time when the therapist is working with child parts. It may help protect the patient from expecting the therapist to re-parent child parts while the adult part of the patient continues to disown dependency needs. However, there are a few exceptions to this guideline, which will be discussed below.

CORE CONCEPT

Dissociative child parts should always be the responsibility of the patient as a whole, not the therapist. Although the therapist may help the part(s) functioning in daily life learn to understand and have compassion for these parts, the adult parts of the patient must be the ones to care for them and ultimately to integrate them as part of the patient's experience.

Understanding the Functions of Child Parts

It is important to understand the role of dissociative child parts in maintaining the status quo of the system as a whole, and their individual functions in maintaining inner phobias. Child parts may represent the following functions in the person as a whole:

- to hold defensive actions, such as attachment cry, flight, fight, freeze, flag, faint, or even play;

- to hold traumatic memories;
- to avoid responsibility as an adult;
- to preserve an idealized version of abusive parents;
- to hold attachment and dependency needs;
- to hold anger, rage, shame, fear, and other intense emotions or sensations; or
- to hold a sense of joy and play.

Many child parts hold intolerable traumatic memories and dependency feelings so that other parts of the patient can continue to avoid these experiences. Thus, the efforts of (parts of) the patient to keep child parts hidden or quiet inside protects the patient from having to accept painful realities. Keeping these parts quiet often involves abusive tactics from the patient's childhood—internal enactments that tell the story without a narrative.

On the other hand, some child parts are intent on telling the story, feeling oppressed and ignored if they are not heard. Sometimes they interrupt in session, stuck in flashbacks, unable to be grounded. They may be easily triggered in daily life and in therapy. The more these parts intrude and the more other parts attempt to suppress them, the greater the disruption internally for the patient. They may resent the adult part of the patient that despises and ignores them, and be angry with the therapist for attempts to contain talking about the trauma prematurely. Nevertheless, the therapist always holds both sides of the conflict, aware that other parts of the patient may not yet be ready and would find it overwhelming to know the whole story.

Thus, the therapist can ask the child part to check inside and see whether all parts agree that the story can be told. Sometimes the child part ignores inner warnings or is unwilling to acknowledge them. At this point, if therapists know that sharing traumatic memories is not appropriate yet, they must insist gently but firmly that the child part stop, with the compassionate support of the patient as a whole.

Understanding the Dynamics of Child Parts Within the Patient's Dissociative System

The therapist can begin to explore internal dynamics related to child parts. For example:

- What is difficult for other parts of the patient to accept about child parts?
- What would it mean for other parts of the patient to accept child parts?
- What emotions, beliefs, sensations, thoughts, wishes, and needs do

child parts contain that are disowned by other dissociative parts of the patient?

- How much awareness of child parts does the patient as an adult have?
- How active are child parts both in the inner world of the patient and in the external world? Are they helpful with daily life functioning or a hindrance?
- Does the adult part of the patient (and perhaps also the therapist) have difficulty setting limits with some child parts—for example, those that want to play at night, or act out at work, or take over therapy sessions?
- Are there other parts that already take care of child parts or are willing to do so?
- Are there other parts that are hurting or frightening or even torturing child parts?
- Do child parts continue to live in trauma-time, unaware of the present? If so, are they responsive to time orientation?
- What might be reasons that prevent child parts from continuing to develop and grow up?
- What dynamic patterns are noticed that involve the child parts? (For example, the patient consistently switches to a child to get dependency needs met or to avoid a painful topic in therapy.)
- What are the primary non-realizations held by child parts? (For example, traumatizing events, dependency needs, rage, feelings of sexual arousal or pleasure during abuse, or the possibilities of play and joy.)

Once these dynamics are mapped, the therapist has an easier time of planning the next steps. For example, if a particularly intrusive child part primarily holds dependency needs, the therapist can begin to support other parts in learning to accept and tolerate these needs as normal, and help them build skills to deal more effectively with dependent feelings and wishes. This allows the patient as a whole to have more compassion for a child part and offer internal help. If a child part is stuck in trauma-time and the usual interventions to orient to the present are not effective, the therapist can consider whether the child part has reasons to remain stuck. For example, a child part may be stuck in traumatic memory because other parts refuse to realize what happened, a perpetrator-imitating part is continually punishing the child part, the adult part of the patient does not want to accept that the child parts exist, or there are significant unresolved conflicts between the child part and other parts of the patient. Next, the therapist can help the patient as a whole begin to deal with reasons why the child part wishes to remain a child, and learn to more effectively support that part. Or the therapist can actively elicit the perpetrator-imitating part to help that part begin to slowly resolve rage and become more compassionate over time toward the child part.

Working With Hostile and Perpetrator-Imitating Parts Before Working With Child Parts

It is often helpful to work with hostile or perpetrator-imitating parts before working with child parts. This follows the general rule in psychotherapy of working through resistance before dealing with a particular issue. Hostile parts, such as angry adolescent parts that are not mimicking perpetrators, are often protective of child parts, and fear that the therapist will interfere and hurt these parts. Their anger toward the therapist is a way to protect child parts. Thus, a working alliance needs to be built with these parts first, which are often gatekeepers to child parts. They can be encouraged to watch and listen, to participate in therapy, and to learn that the therapist will stop if they so ask. They can learn that the therapist has similar goals of protecting vulnerable parts of the patient, only with different methods than hostility and punishment. Chapter 16 discusses ways to work with hostile or angry parts of the patient.

While angry parts are typically protecting child parts from being hurt by others, those that imitate the perpetrator are avoiding awareness of vulnerability held in the child parts. They have completely disowned the pain that child parts carry. When a child part is persistently reliving traumatic events, and grounding and orientation to the present is not successful, the therapist should consider whether a hidden perpetrator-imitating part is punishing the child part internally. Examples of working with perpetrator-imitating parts can be found in Chapter 17.

Resolving Problems With Dissociative Child Parts in Daily Life

Child parts often interfere with effective functioning in daily life. For example, they prefer to play instead of work; become panicked if the patient has a doctor's visit; or have their traumatic memories easily triggered, leaving the patient overwhelmed. They may partially intrude, for example, leaving the patient with puzzling feelings of terror or uncontrollable urges to eat unhealthy food or hide in bed. The following interventions may be helpful in improving cooperation in daily life.

- First and foremost, the therapist should encourage adult parts that function in daily life to accept and be responsible for and responsive to child parts. Often, child parts act out because the adult part ignores their needs. The more they feel understood and attended to by the patient and the therapist, the more cooperative they become.

- Help the adult parts of the patient set reasonable guidelines in daily life: routine bedtime, proper nutrition, a balance of work and leisure time, and the possibility of enjoyment in life. For example, the patient as a whole can share internally that all parts must sleep at the same time, that getting up to play during the night makes it hard to be functional in the daytime, and that the adult needs support to provide for and take care of all parts. In return, the patient as a whole should provide attention to child parts, as the absence of care is often what causes them to be active at night. This simply follows the principle of tending to all of one's needs with compassion and acceptance, particularly emotional needs.

- Help the adult part of the patient learn to orient these parts to the present. Examples of approaches are included below in the section on working with parts stuck in trauma-time.

- Provide inner safe or calm spaces for vulnerable child parts when the patient must engage in an activity that might be especially triggering (e.g., having sex, dealing with a difficult boss, going for a gynecological or dental exam, or parenting actual children). During the event, child parts may sleep or play or whatever makes the most sense for the patient.

- Gradually, as safety and time orientation are established, child parts can be encouraged to observe daily life and therapy from their safe places, with adult parts reassuring them that these situations are not dangerous, even though they may be uncomfortable or painful. Eventually, the patient should be able to approach these life events with child parts being fully present, with the adult part of the patient co-conscious with them and in charge. After all, the goal is not to protect parts of the patient from the realities and discomforts of daily life forever but to provide a stepwise approach that first helps them distinguish the present from past danger, and then to build their tolerance for these necessary activities as an adult person.

Resolving Problems With Dissociative Child Parts in Session

Sometimes the patient fully switches to a child part during session. In this case, the therapist may follow suggestions on how to deal effectively with switching (see Chapter 10). The therapist should explore the reasons for the switch in general, and the reasons for the switch to this specific part in particular (i.e., why now, and why the switch to this particular part). Patients usually switch to child parts (a) because they have become triggered, (b) as a way to express disowned dependency needs, (c) as a way to avoid a painful topic, or (d) in response to inner conflict or chaos. Of course, there may be other reasons; the therapist must simply explore with the patient until they both understand what has happened.

The Dissociative Child Part Stuck in Trauma-Time

Some child parts are very oriented to the present, although they continue to be unable to realize they have grown up. However, many child parts, like other dissociative parts, are often not oriented to the present, or only partially so. In these cases, the therapist must first use grounding and orientation to the present before relational connection, as safety needs are the foundation for attachment. The therapist can use many methods to support grounding, orientation, and better awareness of the present. A few approaches follow.

- Support other dissociative parts internally to help orient the child part to the present.
- Have the child part "look out with the adult's eyes" and "listen with the adult's ears" to experience the present.
- Use perceptual grounding such as smell, taste, touch, sound, and sight.
- Ask the disoriented child part to notice what is different in the present, as opposed to what is similar to the past (for example, there is a sofa that is like one in the past, but it is a different color; the therapist is a person who was not in the patient's past; or the therapist may have the same eye color as the perpetrator, but has different hair, clothes, and voice).
- Have the child part notice her hand, and any rings, watch, or bracelet. The therapist might ask something like, When did you get that? How big is your hand? Whose hand is that? Can parts inside help you know something about that hand? (The same can be done with the patient's clothes, shoes, and other possessions.)
- When a child part is stuck in the moment of abuse, it is sometimes possible to help the child part connect with a different part that knows the abuse has ended. Or the therapist might encourage the child part to *listen to the sound of my voice and follow it from the middle to the end, noticing that it is over, it is all over, and that you are now safe in my office in the present.*

Many of these techniques can be integrated with specific approaches, such as somatic work or EMDR (e.g., Gonzalez & Mosquera, 2012).

Playful Dissociative Child Parts

Playful parts can have several different functions and meanings, and are fixed in the action system of play. Most simply, playful child parts may hold joy and playfulness remembered from childhood as a way to preserve it in the face of overwhelming trauma. These parts are often unaware of trauma. They do not feel the sadness, rage, fear, and shame that other child parts do. They may hold hopeful childhood dreams that will be helpful for the patient as a whole.

Helping other parts of the patient connect with the positive feelings of playful parts is important prior to helping the playful part become more aware of the full range of childhood experiences. The child part can be asked to share positive experiences with all parts, if possible. Sometimes the patient fears that highly traumatized parts will "contaminate" the playful part, so directly sharing the positive experience is not always possible at first. It may still be possible to work with bilateral stimulation or somatically to help other parts of patients feel the experience in their bodies, without direct contact with the playful child part.

Other playful parts, however, are more complex. Their purpose is not to preserve joy and play but rather to distract from painful experiences. These parts often have a driven quality to their play and are not especially responsive to interaction with the therapist.

CASE EXAMPLE OF A PLAYFUL CHILD PART: DENISE

Denise had a dissociative child part who experienced herself as 5 years old, and she only danced. She felt happy and free when she danced and dreamed of being a ballerina one day. Of course, that dream was no longer possible, but she was able to share with the adult part of Denise the sense of happiness and freedom, which all parts could enjoy when Denise incorporated dance lessons in her life. Denise could gradually integrate a sense of joy and freedom in more and more of her daily life.

CASE EXAMPLE OF AN AVOIDANT PLAYFUL CHILD PART: JARED

Jared was a 28-year-old male with a diagnosis of DID. A young adolescent part of Jared would interrupt therapy when painful material emerged. This part of the patient would pretend to play drums at a frenzied pace, making sounds to replicate the drums, shaking his head wildly to the beat, seemingly unaware of his surroundings. The more the therapist tried to engage this part, the louder and more frenetic he became. It was quite difficult for the therapist to get the adult part of the patient grounded in the room again. Gradually the therapist helped other dissociative parts of Jared come to know "the Drummer" and helped that part become more oriented to the present. He helped all parts learn to tolerate distress a little better as skills were practiced over the course of therapy. Gradually, Jared had less need for the Drummer to interrupt therapy. Jared became better able to tell the therapist he was getting activated, so together they could slow down before the Drummer became triggered. The patient came to understand the Drummer as a part of himself that, as an older child and young adolescent, could get lost in music as a way to avoid his painful abuse at home.

Some dissociative parts may begin with play and quickly devolve into traumatic memories. Play may have been a prelude to abuse as a child, or the physical activation of play in the present may be a trigger for or simply an avenue to hyperarousal related to trauma.

CASE EXAMPLE OF CHILD PART EXPRESSING TRAUMA THROUGH PLAY: MONIQUE

At home, Monique, a patient with DID, allowed her 8-year-old part to draw. At first the childlike pictures were simple, happy depictions of trees and sunshine and so on. However, this part would soon take dark crayons and begin to vigorously color all over the page in a chaotic manner, until the whole page was covered. The more this part of Monique colored, the more agitated and frightened or enraged the child part became. Time and again, the pictures would become graphic representations of abuse. Even when Monique stopped allowing the behavior during the day, she would often wake up to paper torn by intense scribbling with a pencil or pen.

The therapist supported all parts of the patient to help this young part be more aware of the present. Over time, Monique came to understand that this part of her represented threats from her father not to speak of the abuse. As a child, she resented having to act as though everything was normal and happy when her home life was, in fact, dreadful. The beginnings of happy pictures were destroyed as a way to tell the story. Eventually the adult Monique was able to help this young part become more verbal, and the destructive behaviors gradually became more of a narrative. The young dissociative part learned to tolerate her emotions and share them along with the adult part of Monique.

Entitled Dissociative Child Parts

Entitlement often accompanies dependency on the one hand and narcissism on the other hand. The highly dependent child (or other) part who feels entitled to get needs met by others often has a fragile, narcissistic core. The patient as a whole feels unworthy and insecure and builds strong narcissistic defenses against this vulnerability. Entitlement involves a failure to grieve and accept that one cannot always get everything one wants or needs. It involves a failure to accept the basic unfairness of life, in which a childhood of abuse cannot be undone. Being a survivor does not mean one gets a free ride to compensate for it—as one patient insisted, *I have suffered enough; I shouldn't have to work. I should be able to relax and do what I want now.*

A sense of entitlement can wear on the therapist, who feels constant pressure to give more and do more for the patient. Demands can be quite intense, and when needs are not met, the therapist can be faced with humiliated fury from the patient or part of the patient. Other dissociative parts are entitled in subtler ways, with entitled beliefs implicit rather than conscious.

The therapist should first determine whether entitlement is part of a larger, whole-person narcissistic wound, or whether it is contained in one part or several parts of the patients. If it is more of a characterological issue, the therapist can best follow guidelines to treat narcissism, while including work with dissociative parts. Some recommended readings on understanding and treating narcissism include the works of Gabbard (1989); Jallema (2000); S. M. Johnson (1987); Kohut (1971); Stark (2000, 2002); and Wurmser (1987).

Resistance in Dissociative Child Parts

Of course, interventions with child parts are not always effective. It is important to assess for resistances, including phobias (see Chapters 11 and 12). Why, for example, would child parts continue to interrupt daily life, or remain stuck in trauma-time? The therapist might wonder what keeps child parts from growing up. There may be many reasons, mostly related to lack of realization and the failure to grieve.

CORE CONCEPT

It is helpful to explore why child parts have failed to "grow up."
Various non-realizations are at the heart of this stuckness. Once the
therapist and patient can acknowledge the non-realizations, work
can commence on resolving them.

Child parts have a vested interest in non-realization, avoiding grieving what was and what cannot be. For example, a part may not grow up because becoming an adult involves acknowledging the trauma happened, or means patients must now be responsible for their own decisions. Some parts may wish to remain a child in order to be taken care of by others (including the therapist). The adult part of the patient may not know how to integrate childlike needs or play into an adult framework. Adult parts may not want to deal with what child parts hold, which keeps these parts fixed developmentally. Some child parts have a fantasy that as long as they stay young there is still a chance that their parents will change and they will be loved.

Infant and Toddler Dissociative Parts

It is not uncommon for patients to report they have infant dissociative parts. Often, very young behaviors are associated with activity of these parts, such as thumb sucking, rocking, and bed-wetting. The therapist can support the patient in taking care of these parts and understanding their functions over time. Since these parts are typically nonverbal and the trauma they hold is preverbal, somatic work or EMDR may help resolve their issues and help them integrate with the patient.

CASE EXAMPLE OF INFANT DISSOCIATIVE PART: VICKY

Vicky, a patient with DID, reported chronic nightmares and episodes of bedwetting which were very shameful to her. At the behest of her therapist, Vicky saw her primary care physician, who determined there was no medical cause for the bedwetting. The therapist and Vicky then could explore other possibilities. A young child part that Vicky called "Reggie" admitted that there was a "baby in the dumpster" inside. The baby was cold, hungry, wet, and unattended. Through imaginal work, the therapist helped Reggie and Vicky retrieve the baby and care for her. Vicky was shocked to find this inner infant, but easily began to care for her, and was pleasantly surprised when the infant started growing after a few weeks. She said, *I guess that is the part of me that was so neglected as a baby. I used to be left in the crib. I feel so sad for her, and for me.* Once this realization occurred, Vicky never wet the bed again.

Summary

Child parts most typically are organized by defense action systems, but some are involved with functions in daily life. The therapist should not treat child parts as actual children, but as one of many aspects of the adult patient. It is essential to encourage the patient as a whole to accept and care for these parts so the therapist does not take on a caregiving role. There are many inner conflicts about child parts, who often have disowned yearnings for care and love, and hold traumatic memories. These conflicts should be resolved carefully and thoroughly so there is less and less need for child parts within the personality of the patient.

Further Explorations

14.1 Is it harder for you to keep boundaries with child parts? Why or why not?

14.2 Do you have a tendency to work more with or favor child parts over adult parts?

14.3 Do you think some limited re-parenting is helpful with child parts since the patient as a whole has missed so much in childhood? Discuss the pros and cons with colleagues.

14.4 Are you able to identify inner conflicts in the patient about child parts, and work with parts that despise, punish, or avoid child parts?

14.5 Is your caretaking system activated with child parts? How might you manage that tendency without acting on it?

CHAPTER 15

Integrative Approaches to Shame

Shame is felt as an inner torment, a sickness of the soul.
—Sylvan Tomkins (1963, p. 118)

From the beginning to the end of our therapeutic relationships with chronically shamed clients, we have to be there, emotional self to emotional self.
—Patricia DeYoung (2015, p. 78)

Joanne is a patient who is kind and compassionate with others, engaging in a lot of caretaking in her relationships. She is often concerned about whether her therapist feels all right or is tired. Once her therapist was very late to a session and Joanne reassured her that it was not a problem at all, because she was sure the therapist had other patients who needed her much more than she did. Yet she had a collapsed posture, did not make eye contact, and smiled during the entire conversation. Dean, another patient, was not kind at all. By all accounts from others, he was selfish and irritable, often saying things like *You have to take what's yours because people won't give it to you.* He has a tense posture, often leaning forward and jabbing his finger aggressively at others to make his point. Jody had severe social anxiety. Whenever he went out, he was convinced that people were talking about him and laughing, though he showed no other signs of paranoia or psychosis. He had a perpetual frown, was tense, and looked around incessantly. Prior to being sexually abused from ages 8 to 12 by an aunt, he had been an outgoing little boy. Now he avoided people as much as possible and spent his time at home playing video games and sleeping. Nell sat silently in session most of the time, hunched and obviously anguished. She never made eye contact with the therapist and often could not put her experience into words. She often felt foggy and confused.

As different as their presentations were, each of these patients shared a pervasive and profoundly embedded chronic shame. Joanne covered her shame with a controlling-caregiving strategy, viewing others as more in need than she was. Her own needs could not be important, as they were so shameful. Dean was ashamed that he was not good enough, and defended against his shame by attacking others and making sure he always had what he needed. Like Joanne, Dean was secretly ashamed of his needs, and so he tried to make sure he would never have to experience need. Jody avoided people and his own inner experience in order to avoid his shame. Nell was paralyzed by shame, with a vicious internal voice attacking her, screaming loudly, *Nobody cares about you. You're a total loser, bitch!*

In this chapter we will describe shame; examine some of the research that informs us about it; and share ways to identify, understand, and work with it effectively. Every major publication on complex trauma and dissociation notes the problem of shame. It is endemic and deeply embedded in our patients' experience. It lurks beneath many symptoms and is often unspoken and implicit. Therapists often underestimate the effect of shame in psychotherapy (Nouri, 2013) and are unclear how to work with it beyond acknowledging that it exists. The first step is to understand the functions of shame.

Understanding Shame

It is no surprise that childhood abuse is a risk factor for shame (Karan, Niesten, Frankenburg, Fitzmaurice, & Zanarini, 2014), and that shame is a mediator between child abuse and adult psychopathology (N. L. Talbot, 1996), including dissociation (Andrews, Brewin, Rose, & Kirk, 2000). In fact, shame is pervasive in dissociative patients (Dorahy, Gorgas, Hanna, & Wiingaard, 2015) and is hypothesized to evoke and maintain dissociation (DeYoung, 2015; Irwin, 1998; Kluft, 2006; Van der Hart et al., 2006). Shame has a negative impact on interpersonal relationships (Dorahy, 2010; Dorahy et al., 2013, 2015; Middleton, Seager, McGurrin, Williams, & Chambers, 2015), including the therapeutic alliance (Black, Curran, & Dyer, 2013; Dalenberg, 2000). It is correlated with PTSD (Leskela, Dieperink, & Thuras, 2002) and with less willingness to seek treatment for PTSD (Bratton, 2011). An important clinical feature of shame is that it is hidden from others, including the therapist, and by its very nature is often avoided in treatment by both therapist and patient alike (DeYoung, 2015; Hultberg,

1988; G. Kaufman, 1989; Kluft, 2013; Lewis, 1992; Nathanson, 1989; Nouri, 2013; Wurmser, 1987).

CORE CONCEPT

Shame is an important signal that there is a misattunement or more serious threat in our relationships, and thus has important functions. Before chronic shame can be resolved, its functions must be fully understood, and the profound disconnection and hiddenness of shame must be compassionately experienced by patient and therapist together.

While our tendency is to try to get rid of shame because it is so dysphoric, the fact is that it is one of the primary emotions and has important functions (Nathanson, 1992; Tomkins, 1963). Thus, it will forever be a part of our experience. Rather than completely being eradicated, chronic shame needs to be attenuated, put in its proper place, and compassionately understood. We must learn how to accept and regulate shame as an occasional part of the human condition. As a signal, shame has important functions, which we describe below.

The Physiology of Shame

One reason shame is so very powerful is that it involves intense physiological activation, which takes us outside our window of tolerance. Some theorists believe shame is fundamentally hypoarousing and mediated by the parasympathetic system (Hill, 2015; Nathanson, 1989; Schore, 2003), while others see it as classically hyperarousing and mediated by the sympathetic system (DeYoung, 2015). It may be hard to distinguish defenses against shame that are hyperarousing, such an anger, from the physiology of shame itself. It may involve an immediate hyperarousal (flushing, rapid heart rate) quickly followed by hypoarousal. The physical sensations of shame often compare to those of freeze, flag, or faint and involve collapse and hiding, all involving hypoarousal. Based on anecdotal accounts of our patients, it may be possible that shame is experienced differently under diverse circumstances. Defenses against shame are so instantaneous that it may be difficult to sort out the shame physiological response from the defensive response. Regardless, shame is definitely a physiologically taxing experience, raising cortisol and adrenocorticotropic hormone (ACTH) levels, indicating a stress response (Dickerson & Kemeny, 2004).

Either way, social engagement is immediately deactivated to varying degrees. When we feel shame we want to disappear, hide, camouflage ourselves, or shut down. These impulses generally involve hypoarousal and are typically accompanied by a lowering of the head, loss of eye contact, and curling of the spine. But we also may want to defend, run away, or attack, which involve hyperarousal. In any case, we do not want to be seen or known. Shame may dissolve all relational connection in the moment, and leaves us with a sense of emotional, cognitive, and physical disintegration. This feeling can be so dysphoric and catastrophic that almost any strategy will be employed to avoid it (DeYoung, 2015). Why would we have such a negative experience as an innate tendency?

Shame as an Inhibitor

Shame has a function to decrease or inhibit other emotions, thoughts, and behaviors, especially positive ones, a bit like an off switch. Shame was originally understood as a more general inhibitor of interest and excitement (Tomkins, 1963; Demos, 1995). Schore (1991, 1994) later noted its function in making a rapid shift from a positive affective hyperarousal to a more energy-conserving but negative affective hypoarousal that subsequently cannot be regulated by the patient.

CORE CONCEPT

Shame inhibits positive emotion, especially interest, excitement, and joy in the context of relationships. It can also inhibit experiences that the patient believes are unacceptable to others, such as anger, need of others, or sexual feelings and urges.

In clinical practice we observe that shame not only puts the brakes on excitement and joy but can inhibit any emotion, thought, sensation, belief, or behavior that is perceived as unreciprocated by or unacceptable to others, such as anger or sexual arousal. When shame is chronic, it becomes entwined with the phobia of inner experience. Emotions that stem from shameful experiences are inhibited or sequestered in dissociative parts, which are then also disowned, as in the case of Ted below.

CASE EXAMPLE OF SHAME AS AN INHIBITOR: TED

Ted was a 38-year-old professional with a dissociative disorder who came to therapy in search of help with his romantic relationships. He went on many first dates, but never on a second date. Before each date he would feel excited and hopeful. Yet when he actually met the woman, he felt acute shame and could barely speak. His body was tense and pulled inward and away from his date. A child part of him would become activated and reenact experiences from his childhood. Ted learned as a child that excitement and connection were not only unacceptable, they were dangerous. For example, when his depressed and angry mother came home from work and he ran to greet her, she would push him down hard and walk away. When he expressed any enjoyment, she would yell at him to shut up and bemoan the fact that she had ever had children. His excitement in relationships was met with hostility and outright rejection. The child part of Ted learned to inhibit his excitement with shame, accompanied by tension that truncated his needs and kept his emotions from being expressed. Ted himself was ashamed of the child part that had needs that were unacceptable to Ted as a whole person. Ted also felt shame about who he was, which seriously limited any possibility of intimacy.

Shame as an Evolutionary Social Function

Shame as an inhibitor of hyperarousal makes sense in the context of relationship with others. Some authors have postulated that shame evolved as a component of a submission tendency within the ranking or competition action system that guides us in finding our social place (Boehm, 2012; Gilbert, 1989). We have an inborn tendency shared with mammals to prove ourselves to our group and to be aware of behaviors that might be socially unacceptable or displeasing.

CORE CONCEPT

Shame helps us learn the boundaries of socially acceptable behavior so that we can be a part of our group, with the optimal level of closeness and distance. Thus, it has important social functions.

Shame may serve as a social threat detector, alerting us to correct behaviors that will result in social rejection. By the second year of life, children exhibit signs of shame in reaction to misattunement or disapproval (Schore 1991). This is crucial to our survival as social beings, and to our need for social safety. We need to evoke positive experiences in others in order to be attractive to them (Gilbert, 1997). Shame is a signal that we are not pleasing and that others are not pleased with us. This makes us feel unsafe, and safety is essential for social engagement and relationships. But when we feel shame that is not due to our own inappropriate behavior, it inhibits our ability to be with others. Chronic shame alters the ability to accurately distinguish safety and threat in relationships, resulting in a persistent sense of rejection and relational danger and activation of defense instead of social engagement.

DeYoung (2015) noted that a young child learns what is and is not acceptable to caregivers, and develops a self-concept based on "a certain self she wants other people to see; a good self that is, by definition, not certain kinds of bad self" (p. 47). Children develop certain coping strategies to deal with chronic shame, most typically caregiving or controlling-punitive approaches to their caregivers (Lyons-Ruth & Jacobvitz, 1999), which may become part of their enduring attachment patterns. These children develop a major inner conflict about their needs, both necessary and shameful, and these painful needs are inextricably part of the developing sense of self.

Several clinicians have noted that shame is not only a reaction to interpersonal trauma but is also evoked in children when aspects of themselves are unacceptable to or unacknowledged by their caregivers over the course of relatively normal relationships (Bromberg, 2011; Ogden & Fisher, 2015). Thus, we all have some shame about what we perceive as unacceptable aspects of ourselves. This is heightened in trauma, and shame is doubly disowned in dissociation: Patients not only avoid shame, but they are ashamed of parts of themselves.

Shame is a regulator of the extremes of interpersonal distance and closeness (Herman, 2011). We may feel shame if we are ostracized on the one hand, or if our personal boundaries are violated on the other hand. Patients typically withdraw, collapse, or tighten up and move away when they feel ashamed, or they may evoke shame in the therapist to induce the the therapist to move away.

CASE EXAMPLE OF SHAME AS A RELATIONAL REGULATOR: SABINE

Sabine: I don't understand, but I always feel shame when Dana [*patient's friend*] hugs me or is really warm with me. I actually turn my body away. Maybe because I don't deserve it?

Therapist: Is that something you believe?

Sabine: Not really. Just a thought. I really am beginning to accept that I am an OK person.

Therapist: Hmm, I wonder if maybe your shame keeps you from letting Dana get too close? You describe her as the most accepting and warm person you know. Maybe it's scary to let her get close because you would be vulnerable.

Sabine: Well, that's for sure! As much as I want her to be close, it still doesn't feel safe.

Therapist: So, maybe shame is trying to help you stay safe by shutting down your wish for her to be close?

Sabine: I hadn't thought of it that way, but that fits. Maybe I can try something else the next time.

Shame as a Self-Conscious Emotion

Shame is a response to (real or perceived) abandonment, rejection, or criticism, and is thus deeply embedded in the attachment system and attachment cry, especially for those who have experienced relational trauma. It is one of the self-conscious emotions, an affect-laden judgment we make about who we are (Mitmansgruber, Beck, Höfer, & Schüßler, 2009; Tangney & Fischer, 1995). This self-judgment begins around the time the child develops an explicit sense of self—that is, an awareness of "I" and "me," and the felt sense of whether that self is acceptable in the eyes of others.

CORE CONCEPT

Shame is not only a feeling about what we feel, think, sense, and do.
It is a judgment about who we are from the perspective of a critical,
rejecting other, directed from ourselves to ourselves.

Shame is a view of ourselves from the perspective of the rejecting other: When we feel ashamed, we are always looking out through the eyes of another at ourselves. Chronic shame does not require the actual presence of another, as it is fueled by internal shaming representations of others that may be based on past experiences and may not reflect current reality. Thus, shame can be felt just as acutely in private as in public.

Dissociative patients have parts of themselves that are locked in perpetual cycles of shaming and being shamed by each other. They often hear inner critical voices that tell them they are stupid or ugly or a total loser, and they are afraid that other people might find out. Thus, they may make strenuous efforts to hide these voices from the therapist. Chronically ashamed people believe themselves to be fundamentally flawed, bad, disgusting, or evil. They condemn not only what they do (or fail to do) but how they appear physically (e.g., ugly, too fat, too disproportionate in some part of their body), what they feel (e.g., anger, sadness, sexual arousal, fear), and, fundamentally, who they are. Ultimately, chronically ashamed patients lack compassion for themselves and for dissociative parts of themselves and find it impossible to believe that anyone could care for them. Yet at the same time, they yearn to be seen, heard, and accepted.

Shame and Animal Defenses in Trauma

Patients often feel shame because they have been abused, believing either they should have stopped it or they deserved it. They feel shame because they fought or froze or submitted, or because they did none of those things and "should" have done them. Thus, they feel shame for inhibited or expressed animal defenses that were involuntary (Nathanson, 1989; Ogden et al., 2006; Ogden & Fisher, 2015).

CORE CONCEPT

Patients often feel shame about what they did or did not do during relational trauma to contribute to or stop what was happening. In other words, they become ashamed of the animal defenses that were naturally activated, such as freeze, fight, or faint, even though these were not within their control.

CASE EXAMPLE OF SHAME ABOUT DEFENSE: MARGO

Margo frequently froze in situations of flirtation or any kind of sexual advance. Her shoulders tightened, her posture slumped, and she became very still. She had done the same when her aunt sexually abused her from ages 3 to 11. Margo felt incredible shame for shutting down and being unable to move during the abuse, and she believed it meant that she wanted the abuse. Yet, the more she was ashamed of her automatic shutdown, the more it happened in her present-day life. Shame had itself become a trigger for her defense of collapse. Margo and her therapist discovered that a young part was frozen, and would become activated when Margo was confronted with something sexual. The child part was not ashamed, but rather afraid, while Margo was the one who was ashamed of the behavior of the child, and of the fear.

Hidden Shame

The nature of shame is to hide, to protect oneself from the vulnerability of exposure. Unfortunately, this is antithetical to therapy, which by its very nature is focused on relational connection and on exposing what is hidden. This hiding may be conscious, but much more often shame is simply outside the awareness of patients, who have managed to hide it so thoroughly from themselves that they cannot recall the memories that sustain it. Experiences that evoke chronic shame are dissociated and not accessible to the patient (e.g., DeYoung, 2015; Hill, 2015; Kluft 2013). Even when dissociative parts are known to the patient, these experiences may still be sequestered and unavailable. The therapist must be extremely careful to recognize shame so that these experiences can be uncovered and resolved—otherwise they will continue to exert a toxic influence on patients.

CORE CONCEPT

The nature of shame is to be hidden. It may not be obvious to the therapist that the patient is ashamed, and even the patient may not know. The therapist must become adept at recognizing the verbal and body language of shame, its cognitive correlates, and the relational disconnections that signal shame.

Shame Triggered by Therapy

Shame can be evoked by seemingly innocuous and normal occurrences in therapy. For example, when the therapist is a couple of minutes late to session or perhaps is tired, the patient may not only feel angry but interpret the lateness as meaning that the patient is not worthy of the therapist's time and attention, and feel ashamed. The patient's basic need of help or support from the therapist may evoke shame. In fact, Dalenberg (2000) noted in her research that patients reported feeling shame in therapy most often in response to their dependence on the therapist. Dependence leaves the patient in a lower status than the therapist, vulnerable to the therapist's whims.

Some shame triggers in therapy include:

- Feeling rejected or criticized by the therapist (real or perceived)
- Not knowing the answer to a question or being unable to do a skill or activity recommended by the therapist
- Feeling abandoned or neglected by a tired or inattentive therapist
- Experiencing mis-attunement, perceived or real
- Being unable to find words or to speak in session; being unable to think clearly
- Having emotions, thoughts, sensations, and fantasies in session that the patient believes are unacceptable or believes the therapist thinks are unacceptable
- Remembering a shameful experience in the presence of the therapist
- Sharing a shameful experience with the therapist
- Making a mistake or believing a mistake was made

- Needing help from the therapist (may imply the patient is incompetent or inadequate, and sets up a possible situation of criticism or rejection)
- Feeling judged (implicitly or explicitly) by the therapist, or negative feedback
- Feeling disregarded when the therapist denies a request by the patient, such as for physical contact or extra sessions
- Having to wait for the therapist, as it evokes powerlessness and a feeling of rejection (e.g., the therapist is late to session or does not immediately return a phone call from the patient)

When patients tell the therapist they "cannot" do something, and implicitly feel ashamed about it, the therapist is often pulled to reassure them, *Yes, you can. I have faith in you.* But on an emotional level, this can discount their deep feeling of inadequacy and ineffectiveness, leaving them alone with these overwhelming feelings. Instead, the therapist might inquire, *How have you learned, or how do you know that you can't?* Or, *Yes, you can't right now because you haven't learned how quite yet. Let's work on that so you will feel like you can.*

The therapist should learn patients' unique shame reactions and be able to recognize them in session. For example, when patients engage in the defenses against shame (cf. Nathanson, 1992), therapists can notice that something has shifted. Therapists can then ask if perhaps they have done something to evoke disconnection in the patient (DeYoung, 2015). This approach places no blame on the patient and offers an open and curious approach to what might have happened. It is important initially that therapists not be too direct in naming shame, as this may overwhelm the patient (Dorahy et al., 2015). Instead, therapists can talk about feeling disconnected, mortified, shut down, and so on.

CASE EXAMPLE OF SHAME EVOKED BY THERAPY: SHERRY

Sherry was speaking with her therapist about her mother, and how she rarely offered Sherry a compliment or said anything good about her. As Sherry was telling the story, she suddenly stopped and broke off eye contact with the therapist. She said, *Some part of me wants to you know I went shopping yesterday.* The therapist believed this to be an avoidance of the topic, so she gently suggested that she and Sherry continue to talk about her experiences of her mother. Sherry seemed to shut down and became silent. She put her head down and was very still. The therapist recognized some kind of rupture had occurred. She asked Sherry, *I notice that something happened that seemed to disconnect us. I wonder if there was something I said or did that you felt you needed to disconnect?* Sherry eventually looked up and replied, *Little Sherry is upset that you don't want to hear about her shopping trip.*

The therapist started to explain why she had stopped the conversation about shopping, but decided she would follow the relational dynamics a bit more. *So when I said we needed to return to talking about your mother, that part of you felt really invalidated and unheard, is that right?* Sherry nodded yes, with tears dripping down her face. The therapist said, *So can that part of you that is Little Sherry notice both of us realizing that she felt so discounted? Can she hear that I am very sorry, because I realize I must have missed something important? I am imagining just how painful that must be for her.* Sherry again nodded yes. And in a quiet voice, she said, *And for me too.* The therapist said, *Yes, for you too. How painful to feel so unseen by me. And how painful that must have been with your mother.* More tears came for Sherry as she began to sob. The therapist sat with her, letting Sherry know she was present with her pain. Eventually Sherry looked up and quietly said, *You get it.* Sherry's shame was beginning to be repaired by reconnection with the therapist, who could acknowledge the shame with her without ever naming it verbally.

The next session Sherry and her therapist were able to revisit the last session and Sherry was able to explain that the shopping trip was actually related to talking about her mother in Little Sherry's mind. Sherry had bought a beautiful dress as a step forward in treating herself with kindness, and Little Sherry wanted to share that with the therapist as a source of pride in her progress. The therapist's unknowing discounting of her pride and competence evoked shame. It might have been more effective to first ask Sherry's help in understanding how going shopping was connected with talking about her mother. Instead, the therapist jumped to a conclusion that shamed her patient. Fortunately, the therapist repaired the rupture so that Sherry and Little Sherry were able to continue to be more compassionate with each other as they more fully realized their mother's inability to express care for Sherry. Note that shame was addressed without confronting or naming it directly, by working with the felt experience of the therapeutic relationship.

Defenses Against Shame

We all engage in defense against shame some of the time. However, when these defenses become chronic, they create problems. Nathanson's compass of shame is enormously helpful in understanding how we react to shame (DeYoung, 2015; Kluft, 2006; Nathanson, 1992, 1997). He describes four defensive scripts that help avoid shame: attack self, attack other, isolate from others, and avoid inner experiences. These were at play in the case examples at the beginning of the chapter.

Each dissociative part may have its own approach to shame. A perpetrator-imitating part attacks other parts internally, or other people externally. A traumatized child part may believe she is to blame for her sexual abuse, attacking herself. Some parts avoid other people, being more involved in work, or have a dismissing attachment style in order to avoid shame. Dissociation is an integrative failure that subsequently can be used as a major avoidance strategy to evade shame. All parts avoid at least some inner experiences because they feel ashamed of them. The therapist will find it useful to map how each part of the patient deals with shame by attacking self, attacking others (including other parts), avoiding inner experience, or isolating from others (including other parts internally).

CORE CONCEPT

We defend against shame with four basic strategies: (a) attacking ourselves as bad, incompetent, or inadequate; (b) attacking others as bad, incompetent, or inadequate; (c) avoiding inner experiences that evoke shame, or avoiding the feelings of shame itself; and (d) avoiding contact with others to prevent shaming experiences from occurring (Nathanson, 1987). The therapist must be able to recognize and address these defenses.

The Therapist's Own Shame

Therapists are caught in a bit of a dilemma when working with shame. On the one hand, they are supposed to help patients with shame; that is, the therapist should be competent. On the other hand, it is almost universal for therapists to feel, at some time or another, deeply inadequate to address the needs of patients who have so many and complex difficulties. More specifically, it can be extraordinarily challenging to address shame with patients. Furthermore, patients may project shame onto the therapist, and indeed, shame may be the medium in which therapist and patient are unknowingly immersed, unseen but smothering.

Therapists will have their own reactions to the patient's shame defenses and to the patient's shame, and may feel ashamed of these reactions. Finally, therapists may not have worked on their own shame to a sufficient degree. Thus it is inevitable that the therapist will feel shame at some points in the treatment of complex trauma (Dalenberg, 2000; DeYoung,

2015). We need to do our best to acknowledge and work with our shame, becoming more willing and able to own it in sessions (DeYoung, 2015).

How to Work With Shame

In the movie *Good Will Hunting* (Bender & Van Sant, 1997), Sean McGuire is an unorthodox therapist who takes on an underachieving, dismissive, tough, and brilliant young man, Will Hunting. Will is deeply ashamed and highly defended against his shame. In one scene, the therapist confronts Will (not a recommended treatment intervention) about his terrible abuse history, which Will has always avoided. Sean begins repeating over and over, *It's not your fault.* Will responds at first by saying, *I know, I know.* But Sean keeps repeating it. Will backs up, as though avoiding his emotions, and McGuire continues to say, *It's not your fault.* He understands that Will's acknowledgment that it is not his fault rings hollow and is merely a cognitive statement, not a true belief. Finally, Will becomes angry and then collapses into tears, accepting at last that, indeed, his abuse was not his fault. This is a major turning point for him in the movie and opens the door to his risking relationships.

If only the resolution of shame were that quick and easy. Unfortunately, it is not. Many a therapist has tried this cognitive approach, trying to convince patients that they are not at fault and have no reason to be ashamed. Not only is this approach mostly ineffective by itself, it leaves patients completely alone and unseen in their experience of shame. Patients feel they are wrong for feeling ashamed, which only heightens their sense of incompetence and inadequacy. In addition, the patient who feels shame is experiencing a cognitive slowdown or shutdown, so cognitively based interventions are often not helpful. Exposure-based treatments that may be helpful with fear may only further entrench and exacerbate shame, which may be more effectively approached somewhat indirectly (Dorahy et al., 2015) or in a titrated manner (Kluft, 2013). This has many important treatment implications.

There are many entry points to work with shame. They can be cognitive, emotional, sensory, imaginal, or relational. Several approaches are discussed below.

General Principles of Working With Shame

Because shame is such an overwhelmingly powerful and isolating emotion, it is very hard to take a realistic perspective on it. Clinically, then, the therapist must create the safest possible relational environment before shame can be addressed in therapy. At any moment of feeling ashamed, humiliated, embarrassed, or vulnerable, patients may disconnect from themselves and from the therapist. Thus, the therapist must be highly attuned to both implicit and explicit signs of shame and other self-conscious emotions that may lead to relational rupture.

Recognizing shame. The classic signs of shame are downward gaze and loss of eye contact, head dropped or turned away, flushing of the skin, hunching or other efforts to make one's body smaller and less visible, covering the eyes or face with the hands, flushing, rigid or collapsed muscle tone and posture, a slowing or absence of speech, and nausea. Some describe the experience of having ice or ice water in their veins, with a cold, freezing sensation. Others describe a sinking or fluttering in their belly, something often associated with fear or intense anxiety. Some describe a depersonalized experience with tunnel vision or being out of body. Patients may appear either more hypo- or hyperaroused. They may suddenly engage in one of the defenses against shame: attack on self or others, including the therapist; withdrawal; or avoidance of inner experience. When the therapist believes that shame has been evoked in session, the therapist should immediately turn the attention to the relational disconnection.

Slowing down when shame is evoked. When patients feel ashamed, they are in a state of heightened sensitivity and have a degree of cognitive shutdown. In order to really be with the patient, therapists need to slow everything down. They should speak more slowly, with only a few considered sentences at a time. Questions can be altered to be less open-ended, requiring less talking from patients at a time when they may be unable to speak much or think clearly. The goal is first to help the patient return to the window of tolerance and keep the interaction within that window, neither hyper-activating shame nor ignoring it, while allowing the patient and therapist together to track what is happening.

CORE CONCEPT

Shame creates a cognitive shutdown. The therapist should take a slow pace when addressing it, with slower and more simple speech, pauses, careful tracking of the patient's reactions and adjusting accordingly, and respectful pacing.

Linking shame to past experience. If patients are ready and able, the therapist can gently link their present-day shame to experiences from the past.

If the patient is not yet ready, the therapist can ask if the feeling is familiar to the patient, a gentler approach. It is not helpful to directly evoke shame memories until the patient can tolerate it and both therapist and patient are prepared for it. Shame memories are experienced in the same way as other traumatic memories (Matos & Pinto-Gouveia, 2010; Pinto-Gouveia, & Matos, 2011), and premature evocation can lead to the patient being overwhelmed. However, the awareness that the patient is feeling something familiar from the past helps the patient ground and take a perspective on shame rather than be deeply embedded in the experience: *I am feeling something familiar from my past* versus *I am a horrible person who is unlovable.*

CORE CONCEPT

Shame is experienced as a traumatic memory, with intrusion, avoidance, and arousal (Matos & Pinto-Gouveia, 2010). Thus, the therapist must be careful not to evoke it without careful preparation and, when needed, adequate titration.

Working with shame in dissociative parts. Shame is a major reason parts remain phobically avoidant of each other. Thus, shame is a barrier to internal communication, cooperation and, ultimately, integration. The therapist should carefully explore the role of shame in keeping parts separate. For example, a man who had a child part that cried at night was mortified that he woke up in tears. He found it emasculating and was furious with the child part. He was thus engaged in the "attack other" defense against shame. It took a long time in therapy for him to even begin to tolerate this child part of himself.

Shame is a dynamic that maintains maladaptive interactions among dissociative parts. There are almost always shaming parts and shamed parts that interact beneath the dissociative surface, creating intense dysphoria. As DeYoung (2015) has noted, this is going on all the time for patients. Interrupt this cycle by helping patients be curious about parts and how they interact, and by encouraging patients (or parts of themselves) to learn to accept and work with ashamed and shaming parts. Shaming parts are often hostile parts, especially parts that imitate the perpetrator. Chapter 17 focuses on how to work with these types of parts.

Being With Shame: A Relational Approach

Shame is resolved as it is held up to the compassion and safety of relational connection, as patients feels attunement, acceptance, and compassion for the darkest, most disowned parts of themselves (B. Brown, 2009, 2012, 2015; DeYoung, 2015). First and foremost, therapists must be willing to fully enter the dark world of shame with their patients, to hear and be with what it is like for them to feel so very ashamed (without trying to talk them out of their shame), and to have compassion and empathy. Shame cannot be banished with words, but must be invited to be a part of our own and our patients' whole human experience. We must be with our patients, with their experience of shame, and with our own experience of shame, and accept it, which is a tremendous challenge (DeYoung, 2015). However, the profoundly ashamed patient is one who cannot tolerate connection in the moment. Note that as illustrated in the examples in this chapter, shame does not always need to be named explicitly.

CORE CONCEPT

Direct connection with the profoundly ashamed patient may be overwhelming, and requesting eye contact may prove to further alienate the patient. Initial relational interventions may be more indirect, such as empathizing with the effects of shame, or exploring how the patient manages shame, rather than focusing on the emotion itself.

While mild shame responds to direct relational interventions, profound shame may need more circumspect and indirect approaches. The therapist needs to find the optimal degree of closeness and distance that the patient can tolerate at the moment. For example, sometimes asking an acutely ashamed patient to make direct eye contact with the therapist may be far too painful, evoking defense instead of social engagement.

The therapist can invite patients to share more about the conflict between needing to stay hidden and isolated while yearning to connect and be accepted. Empathy for the incredible loneliness and pain of shame can be helpful, as it focuses on the results of shame rather than shame itself, while still fully acknowledging the emotion.

Psychoeducation

Psychoeducation can be helpful to provide a useful cognitive frame for understanding why patients might feel shame and for understanding behaviors or feelings they might fear are unacceptable. However, timing is important. In the early part of therapy, some therapists can give some education as part of broader instruction about emotions and their functions, and about how relational trauma evokes so much shame. Normalizing the experience of shame is essential, as many patients feel ashamed that they are ashamed.

The therapist might hint at the possibility that shame may arise in therapy, and when it does, the patient should know it is normal, expected, and something with which the therapist can help. To support this, the therapist might share an anecdote (actual or made up) of someone who experienced shame, all the while tracking the patient's nonverbal response and adjusting the intervention. Many patients feel a little relief just knowing that others, including the therapist, find shame challenging too. Some patients may not have ever considered they are feeling shame, labeling it as something else, or only as part of an array of dysphoric feelings.

It might help patients to know that animal defenses are not choices but automatic reactions to danger, and that sexual arousal is natural when the body is stimulated, whether a person wants that arousal or not. Patients also need to know that shame is a natural reaction to powerlessness, helplessness, and injury. A bit later in therapy, explaining the compass of shame (Nathanson, 1992, 1997) can also help patients begin to recognize their reactions to shame and see them in others as well. This may help them have more compassion toward dissociative parts that are engaging in defenses, such as attacking the patient internally or dismissing the therapeutic relationship.

Cognitive Approaches

Cognitive approaches to shame target related specific beliefs and schemas. These might include statements such as *I am worthless; I don't deserve anything good; If you really knew me, you would be so disgusted; I was born bad*. Once these statements are clear to the therapist, there are myriad ways to work with them. Challenging all-or-nothing beliefs and overgeneralizations are the first obvious step. However, patients often do not find that very useful, as it is the felt sense of the belief that is entrenched and feels true. It may be more helpful to support patients in observing from a distance their beliefs, so that they observe them as beliefs rather than experience them as truths. The felt sense of the belief in the body can be an entrée into resolution. Unexpected questions can sometimes be helpful to help patients get more perspective, when they are timed carefully so as to be tolerated and when they are asked respectfully. For example, the therapist might say, *You tell me that you don't deserve anything good. I'm curious, who has decided that you don't deserve anything good? Not anything at all, or just certain things? How do you suppose it gets decided about what good thing you might or might not have?* These questions may confuse the patient, which is the initial experience of cognitive dissonance. As patients begins to wonder about their rigid beliefs based on shame, the therapist may find other entrées into working with shame, as we discuss below.

Various third-generation CBT approaches that go beyond exposure techniques have been used to diminish shame. These include DBT (Linehan, 1993, 2014), functional analytic psychotherapy (FAP; Kohlenberg & Tsai, 2012; Tsai & Kohlenberg, 2009), and ACT (Hayes, Strosahl, & Wilson, 2011). It is likely that the compassion and acceptance that underlie all these approaches is what most helps patients reduce shame (Luoma & Platt, 2015). Of course, these approaches are not strictly cognitive, even though they are labeled as cognitive approaches. They involve mindfulness, which is very much a sensory activity, and compassion, which is a relational approach.

Dialectical behavior therapy. Some work has been done on helping patients use the DBT skill of *opposite action* in managing shame (Rizvi & Linehan, 2005). The goal is to help patients engage in less defense against shame, such as isolating or attacking self or other. Patients might be encouraged to engage in an opposite action instead. For example, they can express compassion for a dissociative part of themselves even if they do not feel it, just trying it as an experiment to see how it feels. They can seek out connection with a trusted other or with another dissociative part, even though they may want to avoid contact. The therapist can help the patient explore what happens when an opposite action is contemplated or taken, and whether it helps diminish the shame or not. While this may be helpful, it is critical that the experience of shame not be discounted in the process. Close attention should be paid to the patient's felt sense when the action is tried; otherwise, it can be invalidating. Suggestions for opposite action, like all interventions, should be offered in a compassionate and curious spirit, with the therapist inviting patients to simply explore without judgment what happens.

Functional analytic psychotherapy. Functional analytic psychotherapy focuses on patients' behaviors in session, particularly in the therapeutic relationship. The antecedents of shame in the relationship—that is, what triggers shame in relation to the therapist—are closely examined. Patients are supported in engaging in compassionate behaviors that reduce their shame (Koerner, Tsai, & Simpson, 2011).

Acceptance and commitment therapy. ACT has been shown to improve shame (Luoma & Platt, 2015). ACT emphasizes self-compassion and *defusion*, which involves observing one's own experience without judgment and with reflective thinking. It also emphasizes *self as context*. This is the *observing self*, which is separate from that which is observed. For example, when a patient observes her emotions, she can notice that she is observing her feelings instead of "being" her feelings.

Self-as-context interventions involve mindful observations that increase patients' adaptive and compassionate ways of relating to self (including dissociative parts), while also emphasizing their relationships with others, or at least with the therapist. The therapist also helps the patient focus on relational values; that is, what is important to patients in relationships. Values might include safety, caring, or listening. Patients are encouraged to apply those values to the ways they treat and view themselves (Luoma & Platt, 2015).

Compassion-focused therapy. Although compassion-focused therapy is considered to a CBT approach, it is actually far more. Compassion-focused therapy evolved not only from cognitive theory but also from social, developmental, evolutionary, and Buddhist psychology, and from neuroscience (Gilbert, 2009). In this approach, the therapist helps patients experience safety in therapeutic interactions, learn to tolerate and feel safe with whatever emerges in therapy, and learn to replace self-criticism with self-compassion (Gilbert, 2009, 2011). The therapist begins working with shame by consistently expressing attributes of compassion, including:

- motivation to care about the well-being of the patient;
- sympathy—being emotionally moved by the suffering and experiences of the patient;
- empathy, which involves mentalizing—understanding what underlies the patient's behaviors and distress;
- distress tolerance—being able to tolerate and be with the patient's experiences rather than avoiding them;
- sensitivity to the patient's distress and needs; and
- nonjudgment of the patient's experiences, even when the therapist has different preferences or perspectives (Gilbert, 2009, 2011).

The therapist, by example and by teaching, helps patients learn these attributes, as well as specific compassion skills. Below we have adapted compassion-focused skills for use with dissociative patients.

- **Compassion attention**—noticing strengths or positive resources.
  - *Can you notice that the angry part of you is trying to protect you and thus must care about your safety very much? Can you notice that perhaps that part of you does not feel safe at all, and how frightened that part must feel?*
  - *As you try to connect with that little child part of you, can you offer yourself some encouragement and compassion for how hard it is to do, for the feelings it brings up for you?*

- Can *other parts notice the courage you have in trying to work on your shame?*
- Can *you feel me with you, encouraging and supporting you as you try to get to know this part of you that feels so very ashamed?*

- **Compassion reasoning**—being able to have more balanced reasoning, tempered with kindness and compassion, which implies that what has been learned can be unlearned.
  - You *tell me you are bad. That is so painful. Can you help me understand how you learned that you are so bad?*
  - Even *though you hate that sexual part for what she does, I wonder if you might also be able to consider with compassion how she might have come to learn those ways of relating?*

- **Compassion behavior**—using warmth, compassion, and gentleness to engage in difficult activities (confronting a painful traumatic memory or going for a job interview), or engaging in positive experiences that support safety and compassion.
  - As *you begin to think about how to approach this very frozen part of you that feels so hopeless and terrified, let us create together a place of warmth, compassion, and respect for yourself, a space of safety and courage. Can you take the next small step to just notice this part as you experience such a compassionate space?*
  - Can *parts of you take care and compassion to that frozen part of you? Can she feel their kind intentions, along with yours and mine, so that she is bathed in kind and safe intentions?*

- **Compassion sensation**—exploring the sensations of being compassionate.
  - As *you feel my compassion now, what is that like for you inside?*
  - As *you are feeling compassion toward that part of yourself, just notice what that feels like in your body; the sensations, your muscles, your posture.*
  - *Just notice now, as you feel compassion for how much shame you have felt your whole life, for how hard that has been, how isolating. Just notice your compassion for your suffering.*

- **Compassion feeling**
  - Can *you allow yourself to feel compassion for all that you experience? For your thoughts? For what you sense in your body? For parts of you? For your struggles?*
  - Can *you experience compassion when you think of other parts of you, even though you might also be scared or hesitant? How important to realize that each part of you has a special role in helping you survive!*

Note that these approaches involving compassion might evoke emotions or dissociative parts so the patient becomes overwhelmed, adding to the shame. Or it might stimulate attachment needs that the patient cannot yet integrate, so careful tracking and adjusting is critical.

Imagery Approaches

Compassion-focused therapy also uses imagery of a compassionate figure as a resource for the patient. Patients are encouraged to add all the attributes that are ideal for them, such as compassion, wisdom, strength, courage, love, understanding, and perspective. All parts can be invited to participate. In some cases, certain dissociative parts may need their own unique ideal figure. The figure need not be human. Some patients prefer an animal, a spirit guide, an angel, God, a fairy godmother or good witch, or even an object like a tree or stone. Whatever that patient can conjure as compassionate, wise, and helpful should be used. The more these images come from the patient and not from a therapist who is overeager to be creative, the more effective they are. However, if the patient cannot come up with any image, the therapist might suggest examples. Below are questions to support patients in using an ideal figure.

- *Can you imagine an ideal figure that has all the attributes of compassion, of safety and dignity, of kindness and respect? What would that figure look like? What might that figure say to you? What might that figure say to other parts of you?*
- *Can you imagine your ideal figure of compassion going to that frightened little child inside? What might that figure do? What would that figure say? How would that figure be able to help that child?*
- *And can that small child inside notice that figure, full of compassion, safety, warmth, gentleness, with no intent to harm in any way?*
- *Can you imagine a compassionate figure being with you as we begin to deal with your shame? What would that figure say to you now? How would that figure encourage you now, offering support and warmth, caring and compassion? Can you feel all of that from your figure?*

Imagery can be used in other ways, as well. The felt sense of shame can be combined with imagery to help patients concretize their experience, distance themselves from shame, and find new pathways to resolution. Patients can describe their shame in terms of shape, size, color, texture, and so on. They can dialogue with it, and just notice if or how it changes as they stay with it

CASE EXAMPLE OF WORKING WITH SHAME IMAGERY: CONNIE

Connie: The shame is a wall made if ice. It keeps me locked in, away from everybody. It's cold, slick; I can't climb it. I think it smells bad, like something rotten is encased in the ice. Pain, rejection, hopelessness, all the bad things I have done, all the bad that I am. The very idea of being born and taking up space. That is what is in the ice. It's so tall I cannot see the sky, and so long that I cannot see the end. There is no way around it, no way out.

Therapist: Hmm, cold, slick, smelling rotten. Let's just be with that for a moment. Is that all right? Just to notice it and accept it is there?

Connie: I hate it. It keeps me away from living. I feel like shivering.

Therapist: Yes, go ahead and shiver and notice what happens. Let's not make any judgments right now and stay focused with our compassion.

Connie: It's cold, like a lonely cold, you know? Like being left out in the cold.

Therapist: Absolutely, like being left out in the cold, terribly alone. I am right with you in that. Just notice the shivering and the wall.

Connie: *(Hugging herself as though trying to warm up)* I just wanted love. Just to be let into someone's heart. So ashamed that no one loves me.

Therapist: Just to be let in. Those words are so powerful: just to be let in. Notice your arms hugging you as you have the feeling of just wanting to be let in. Notice what happens next.

Connie: I feel so sad for that little girl that I was. *(Tearful and silent for a while)* I'm just hugging her now. *I* can let her in to *my* heart now! *(Tears and a long pause)* I'm feeling warmer, like an ember is glowing inside.

Therapist: So feel that ember glowing, the warmth of letting yourself in, of being let in, no longer feeling left out in the cold.

Connie: *(Smiling)* Yes! I can let her in now!

This is a joyful statement, what Pierre Janet called an *act of triumph* (1925b), an action of completion and integration that is full of pride, competence, and compassion.

If not in this session, then in another, the therapist would eventually return to the image of the wall and its other characteristics (slick, smelling terrible) and work in the same way with those. The bad smell indicates the emotion of *dissmell* is active (Kluft, 2007, 2013; Tomkins, 1963). Dissmell is closely related to shame, as is disgust. Dissmell and disgust originated as an evolutionary protection against noxious food. Dissmell is about noxious smell and is translated as *You stink!* at a relational level. Disgust is about noxious taste and is translated as *You make me sick!*

A few patients, having trouble with any kind of visualization, are unable to use their imaginations. In these cases, the therapist can help the patient in more concrete ways; for example, aiding the patient in drawing or constructing a figure, making a collage of ideal attributes, writing down ideal characteristics and putting them in a box, or using a stone or other transitional object.

Somatic and Nonverbal Approaches

Because shame is a whole-body experience that involves catastrophic emotion and disconnection, cognitive interventions are rarely, if ever, sufficient by themselves. Work with implicit process, both in the therapeutic relationship and somatically, can be highly effective, as it reaches what the mind is unable or unwilling to grasp.

Working with the felt sense of shame. One helpful way to approach shame is to focus on the felt body sense of shame. Patients can be supported in attending to body sensation, posture, and movement rather than on the cognitive meanings of shame, which may be further activating. Since the physical components themselves both reflect and sustain shame, these somatic elements "pull" a patient into shame. Without a patient noticing and changing these somatic correlates, shame can become ubiquitous and be much more difficult to address and resolve.

Identifying the somatic precursors to shame can help patients recognize the beginning of feeling shame before it "takes over." They can learn to intervene somatically by executing an alternative action or implementing a somatic resource, which can mitigate the effects of shame (P. Ogden, personal communication, October 15, 2015). The therapist can ask patients to describe sensations associated with shame, such as *I feel sick to my stomach*; *My heart is thudding*; *I feel like I am in a tunnel and feel far away.* Movement tendencies can be explored, for example, *I want to curl up*; *I want to fall through the floor*; *I want to run away and never come back.* Patients can be supported in exploring movements in extreme slow motion, noticing what happens with micromovements rather than trying to complete the motion quickly (Ogden & Fisher, 2015). Often there is a realization or resource that can be found in slowing down the movement. For example, a patient can realize that she wanted to push her abuser away, but her arms were held down. She then further realizes that she did indeed want him to stop, but that she was prevented, instead of believing she wanted it to happen or was just too passive to do anything about it.

Working with the felt sense of compassion, pride, and competence as resources. Some propose that the antidote to shame is pride and competence (Nathanson, 1992, 1997), while others say it is empathy and compassion (B. Brown, 2009, 2012, 2015; Gilbert, 2009, 2011). Actually, these two remedies may not be very different, in that competence and pride in the child arise in the context of compassionate attunement of the parent. Pride and competence are feelings that are not isolated to what we do or accomplish, but are experienced as we feel ourselves as lovable though the eyes of the compassionate other. This is the paradoxical human condition—that we fail, are vulnerable, and have no control, yet we are still lovable and competent as human beings. The antidote to shame, then, is compassion, self-compassion, pride, and competence in being a human being—a sense of being acceptable and capable.

The therapist can help patients focus on the experience of having previously felt competent or proud for a successful behavior (for example, learning to ride a bicycle, feeling good about learning an emotional skill, accomplishing a project at work). The therapist instructs the patient to focus on the felt body sense of the pride, competence, or adequacy, emphasizing the positive feelings and sensations, posture and movements. A major sense of competence should come from relational experiences in therapy. Patients can be encouraged to focus on the felt sense, for example, of being able to feel more comfortable with the therapist, or being able to talk about a difficult subject, or having compassion and understanding for a dissociative part. Therapists can support feelings of competency and adequacy by tracking their physical indicators, such as a slight lift of the chin, a deep breath, a more upright posture or direct eye contact.

However, the therapist is also with patients in their shame and vulnerability in ways that help them feel safely seen and accepted. This helps the patient learn to accept with compassion the rampant failings and vulnerability that all human beings share. Therapists automatically mirror patients' physical organization (and vice versa) and may find themselves in a collapsed or hunched posture themselves, which implicitly can indicate to the patient that the therapist is "with" them in their shame, without ever verbalizing it.

One of the challenges in helping patients have these positive experiences is that they may be too afraid or ashamed to allow themselves to feel something positive. They may believe that an experience of competence only foreshadows yet another failure. They may implicitly fear losing the therapist if they have too many positive experiences. These resistances are understandable and can be addressed compassionately (see Chapters 11 and 12 for suggestions).

Exploring and completing animal defenses. It was noted earlier that patients may feel ashamed of either engaging in animal defenses or of not doing so when they believe they should have (Nathanson, 1987; Ogden &

Fisher, 2015). Completion of defenses, again in very slow motion, with mindful awareness of "what happens," may give the patient a sense of relief and resource. For example, a patient might be ashamed of not having run away from a perpetrator. This tendency had to be inhibited because the perpetrator would have punished the patient as a child for doing so. Supporting patients to allow their bodies to slowly engage in the movements of running, for example, by just slightly moving the legs, may offer a realization that the patients could not have run away, or relief in feeling like they could run now if necessary. The patients are encouraged to just notice what happens without judgment or expectations (Ogden et al., 2006; Ogden & Fisher, 2015). When the felt sense of being unable to execute an active defensive response is a potent source of shame, executing these defenses in the present moment can mitigate the shame associated with not having been able to do so in the past.

EMDR

Approaches to resolving shame with EMDR have been described by several clinicians (e.g., Balcom, Call, & Pearlman, 2000; Gonzalez & Mosquera, 2012; Knipe, 2009a, 2014; Leeds, 1998). One of the great values of EMDR is that it can help patients access and resolve issues that are nonverbal or too overwhelming to verbalize, as long as the therapist knows how to work within the window of tolerance of the patient. EMDR has been shown to decrease the experience of shame in some patients (Balcom, Call, & Pearlman, 2000). Leeds (1998) stressed using resource installation as a precursor to directly approaching distressing emotions like shame. While the standard protocol of EMDR may be too triggering to use directly with profound relational shame, modified approaches can be used. For example, Knipe (2009a) targets phobic avoidance (resistance) to changing a belief (e.g., *I am bad to the core*) or of feeling shame by asking *What's good about or how does it help you to . . . believe you are bad, or avoid the shame?* Then bilateral stimulation is used. Subjective Units of Distress (SUDS) can be used to track the diminishment of intensity of negative beliefs and the growth of positive beliefs: *On a scale of 1 to 10, how much do you believe you are bad to the core? How much do you believe that you were not at fault?* Again, bilateral stimulation is utilized with each statement.

Several authors have proposed targeting positive emotions and experiences, as they sometimes involve phobic avoidance or important realizations (Gonzalez & Mosquera, 2012; Knipe, 2009a, 2014). For example, EMDR can target defensive idealization of a parent that maintains shame in patients, who must conversely see themselves as bad objects.

Developing Shame Resilience

Bréne Brown (2009) developed a curriculum for helping people learn to be more resilient to shame. She notes there are four major steps of shame resiliency. These are very useful for the therapist to employ with patients on a regular basis. Indeed, therapists will need to learn their own shame resilience skills.

1. The first step is to accept and tolerate personal vulnerability, including recognizing shame triggers and shame reactions. It is essential to acknowledge and accept that we are all fallible and imperfect.
2. The second step is to contextualize shame within social, cultural, or religious expectations. Patients can see how certain expectations (e.g., being thin, having money, appearing as though you have a perfect life with no problems, or experiencing yourself as a unified individual) lead to shame and are not, in themselves, reasonable or realistic to attain all of the time. It can be helpful to step out of the awfulness of shame and realize there are social pressures that shape our shame, and that we can change our attitudes toward those expectations.
3. The third step is to reach out to others with our own vulnerability and compassionately accept the vulnerability of others. In this way, we learn we are not alone and that another's compassion can relieve our shame. Therapists must be willing to share to an appropriate degree that shame is also hard for them, that indeed they feel shame and vulnerability at times.
4. The last step is speaking shame—that is, being able to talk about it openly with trusted others; distinguish it from guilt, embarrassment, and humiliation; and separate it from other emotions, such as anger or fear.

These approaches to dealing with shame can provide a relational context that prevents activation of unnecessary shame. All parts of the patient can be encouraged to take these steps with each other internally, and with the therapist. The patient as a whole can try small experiments with these approaches in relation to others in the patient's life, when it is safe enough to risk.

Further Explorations

15.1 Describe what is most challenging for you in working with profoundly ashamed patients.

15.2 Describe an event or situation in therapy with a patient in which you, the therapist, felt shame. List your thoughts, feelings, sensations.

15.3 Describe how you use any or all of the shame scripts to protect yourself against shame you are feeling with a patient (attack self, attack other, isolate from others, avoid your inner experience). How do these affect you when you are with a patient?

15.4 Describe a situation in a session where you felt a sense of pride when working with a patient. Notice your felt sense of the memory, your thoughts, feelings, and sensations.

15.5 Imagine your own ideal figure, who compassionately supports you in your work. Imagine this figure standing behind your chair, offering quiet wisdom and compassion to you, the therapist.

15.6 Practice being compassionate with yourself as a therapist. All therapists—even seasoned experts—sometimes feel uncertain or confused, make mistakes or don't know what to do, and have awkward moments and strong countertransference. These are normal human experiences that are best compassionately accepted as part of being a therapist.

15.7 Find a peer, supervisor, or consultant with whom you can safely share your shameful experiences as a therapist.

CHAPTER 16

Working With Angry and Hostile Parts of the Patient

The spontaneous appearance of a hostile alter is a major landmark, because usually these alters exert their impact within the world of the alters and are loath to acknowledge or to commit themselves to the therapy process.

—Richard P. Kluft (1993b, p. 113)

Anger, rage, and hostility toward self, other dissociative parts, and other people is a common core of work with dissociative patients. There are several reasons that anger and hostility become chronic in dissociative patients. First, patients typically have been severely invalidated, ignored, hurt, betrayed, and sometimes even tortured over extended periods of time, while being helpless to stop it. In itself, this is enough to generate enormous rage in anyone as part of the naturally occurring fight defense. Second, as children, patients often had little to no help in learning how to regulate and appropriately express normal anger, much less how to cope with it. Often it was unacceptable for many patients to express any kind of anger as children, while the adults around them were uncontained and highly destructive with their anger. Others had no limits set on their angry behaviors.

CORE CONCEPT

The therapist's compassionate acceptance of angry parts of the patient creates an avenue for them to engage in therapy and resolve their anger. The therapist can be compassionate while still setting limits on inappropriate behavior.

Angry dissociative parts are feared and avoided internally by most other parts, particularly those that function in daily life. After all, angry behaviors toward self and others may interfere with functioning in a variety of personal and social ways. An ongoing vicious circle of rage and shame ensues internally: The more patients avoid their angry and destructive dissociative parts, the angrier these parts become, and the more they shame other parts and are shamed by them.

Angry parts can be highly threatening to the patient, which reinforces ongoing avoidance not only in many parts of the patient but sometimes also in the therapist. Chronic anger that is embedded in the patient's general way of being can overwhelm and exhaust the therapist, who may feel frightened, intimidated, humiliated, paralyzed, frustrated, and ashamed, or who may engage in reciprocal fight or shaming responses. Therapy can quickly become derailed if these parts of the patient are not dealt with early in therapy. When therapists feel hesitant to work with angry and hostile parts, they should immediately seek supportive consultation.

Angry, hostile parts are often major impediments to engaging in therapy, participating in relationships, reducing self-harm and suicidality, and resolving traumatic memories. Therefore, it is an important goal for therapists to obtain a working alliance with these parts—the earlier in therapy, the better.

CORE CONCEPT

The earlier in treatment the angry parts of the patient can be engaged in a therapeutic alliance, the more likely the patient as a whole learns to cope with anger in appropriate ways.

However, angry parts have a deep shame and are highly defended against a strong belief that they are very bad. Their defense is reinforced by the shame of patients that such parts of themselves even exist. These parts of the patient are terrified of attachment to the therapist and view the relationship as dangerous, mainly because they are afraid that the therapist will never accept them. So it is often a challenge to help these parts over-come their shame and convince them that they are welcome as important participants in the therapy. Once a working alliance can be developed, the patient's compassionate acceptance of these parts allows them to become important collaborators in treatment and can dramatically change the course of therapy. This is particularly true for perpetrator-imitating parts, which will be discussed in the next chapter.

The Functions of Anger

Anger has a number of functions. These include the affect that directs the fight defense, an attachment strategy, and a secondary emotion that pro-tects from vulnerability.

Anger and the Fight Defense

Anger is, of course, a natural emotional component of the fight defensive system, in which particular dissociative parts of the patient are commonly fixated. Anger is an affect derived from activation of the sympathetic ner-vous system, geared to energize the body for maximum effort to fend off perceived danger. Psychologically, it protects from awareness of vulnera-bility and lack of control, and, therefore, from shame. In fight mode, we are all primed to perceive cues of danger rather than cues of safety and relational connection. In such a heightened state of arousal it is easy to misunderstand the intentions of others. When patients (or parts) remain fixated in fight mode, they are not able to distinguish the difference between minor relational mistakes and major betrayals, since they are primed to expect danger.

CORE CONCEPT

Anger is the primary emotion of the "fight" defense. When (parts of) the patient become stuck in this defense, anger becomes chronic. Thus, the first intervention is to create safety.

As long as a fight reaction remains unresolved, anger will remain chronic. However, it is good to realize that not all angry parts are always hostile toward the patient or therapist. Sometimes, these parts actually want help to deal with their anger more effectively and are willing to coop-erate in therapy. Such parts can easily become great allies in therapy, and the internal phobia for these parts can resolve relatively quickly. This is particularly true when the therapist is not afraid and can accept these parts compassionately, leading the way for the patient to do so.

Anger in Controlling-Punitive and Caregiving Attachment Strategies

As noted earlier, patients may develop particular attachment strategies for managing relationships (Liotti, 2011; Main & Cassidy, 1988). Patients (or parts) who develop controlling-punitive attachment strategies are prone to acting out their anger as a way to get what they want and need from others. Those who have controlling-caregiving strategies tend to direct anger toward themselves. Thus, patients learned that anger is a method to get what is needed in relationships, or that it should be completely suppressed because it is overwhelming or dangerous to feel. Most often, different dissociative parts within the patient have different strategies for dealing with anger, creating much inner conflict. Whether the anger is part of a fight response or not, it is often a secondary emotion that protects the patient from feelings of sadness, extreme powerlessness, shame, guilt, and loss.

CORE CONCEPT

Parts of the patient that developed controlling-punitive strategies will be angry with others to get what they need, while those that have controlling-caregiving strategies will punish themselves for being angry or having needs.

Anger as a Secondary Emotion

Anger can serve as a defensive emotion that protects against shame, grief, vulnerability, helplessness, and powerlessness. This is often the case in hostile parts such as those that self-injure or encourage other parts to self-harm, prostitute themselves, abuse drugs or alcohol, or engage in other self-destructive behaviors. They are often stuck in destructive and harmful behaviors that are an "attack self" defense against shame (see Chapter 15, on shame, and Chapter 18, on unsafe behaviors).

Introjection of the Perpetrator's Rage

Finally, the rage of the perpetrator is often an embodied experience from which patients cannot yet escape without sufficient realization and further integration. Some dissociative parts imitate perpetrators internally, repeating the family dynamics from the past with other parts in a rather literal way (see chapter 17). This type of dissociative part is discussed extensively in the following chapter, as these situations involve complex relational dynamics that do not necessarily include the fight defense per se.

The Treatment of Angry Parts

There are countless interventions to help patients deal with anger, ranging from cognitive to behavioral, psychodynamic, EMDR, and hypnosis. It is helpful for therapists to have a wide array of these at their disposal. The challenge is to help the patient as a whole learn to cope with anger, which means that these interventions must be learned by each part of the patient.

Managing the Expression of Anger

Therapists often wonder when it is helpful to allow the patient to express anger and when to interrupt and stop it because it is destructive. The mere expression of anger, or any other emotion for that matter, is not helpful in and of itself. "Getting anger out" is rarely useful, as the problem is that the patient needs to learn how to effectively express anger verbally rather than physically, and in socially appropriate and contained ways, so the patient can be heard by others. It is less the fact that patients express anger, but how they do so, and whether that expression allows them to remain grounded in the present, to retain important relationships, and to avoid being self-destructive.

The ongoing expression of vehement anger may be a strategy to avoid more painful experiences such as shame, vulnerability, or powerlessness, which need to be realized. If the patient (or dissociative part) is able to remain grounded and present, maintain relational connection, and regulate at least to a degree, then it can be useful to hear the patient's anger out in a nonjudgmental and compassionate way.

CORE CONCEPT

Expression of anger is not necessarily therapeutic in itself. It is *how* (parts of) the patient experience and express it that is important; whether it is within a window of tolerance and is socially appropriate and safe. Therapists must learn when expression of anger is therapeutic and when containment of anger is more helpful.

When a dissociative part is clearly escalating, is unable or unwilling to remain grounded, or is screaming and shouting, it is best to stop the behavior immediately and help the patient get grounded. Then the therapist can help the patient find a different way to deal with the anger. Often, escalating anger is due to the fact that the patient does not feel safe. The therapist's withdrawal, escalating anxiety or fear, or excessive appeasement and solicitous ministrations may evoke further anger. The therapist should, to the degree possible, remain unruffled, calm, and clear, setting necessary limits while remaining empathically connected to the patient's explicit and implicit communications. When the therapist cannot do so, some metacommunication with the patient about the need for both to calm down and get safe is in order.

For example, the therapist might say, *You know, right now it's difficult for us to hear each other. Let's find a way to calm ourselves and start over. Let's stop what we are doing and practice one of those grounding and mindful exercises together. Or, if you like, we can take a short break and walk around outside for a couple of minutes and then come back and see if that helps us.* The key is for the therapist to intervene to break the impasse of defenses in both parties.

Therapists need compassion for sadness, shame, and negative sense of self behind the patient's anger. Parts fixated in fight mode are afraid that others, both inside and outside, will condemn their behavior and will never listen to or accept them. Thus they feel chronically alienated and isolated both internally and externally.

Below we offer suggestions on how to integrate standard approaches to anger with the needs of the dissociative parts of the patient:

- Therapists need to strive to maintain a calm, nondefensive stance.
- Take the time to educate the patient as a whole about the functions of anger and angry parts. Although they may seem like "troublemakers," they can be understood as attempting to solve problems with ineffective or insufficient tools.
- Encourage all parts of the patient to understand, accept, and listen to angry parts, instead of avoiding them.
- When the patient becomes hostile or angry in session, therapists should immediately stop and check in about what is happening: *You seem angry right now. Can we stop and try to understand what just happened?*
- Make efforts to understand what provokes angry parts. There are many potential triggers. Examples might include:
  ○ The therapist said or did something that was perceived as rejecting or critical to another part of the patient.
  ○ An angry part of the patient is concerned about too much vulnerability, for example, because child parts are feeling strong dependency needs with the therapist, or traumatic memories are accessed prematurely.

- An angry part feels attacked, rejected, or misunderstood by the therapist or by other parts of the patient.
- Validate the patient's angry feelings, even if there is a need to set limits on angry behaviors: *I can understand why you—or that part of you—might feel so angry about that, and I would very much like to hear more about your experience.*

Therapists should apologize if they have made a therapeutic error or were mis-attuned. Even when no mistake has been made, therapists can still empathize with the felt experience of the patient: *I'm sorry that you feel so hurt (or misunderstood). That certainly was not my intention, but I can see that you feel very hurt by me.*

- Interrupt abusive or unacceptable behaviors.
  - *Your anger is understandable and I want to hear more about it. However, I am going to ask you to stop shouting. I want to sort this out with you, and when you are shouting it is hard to focus on how we can resolve this together. In addition, your shouting is disruptive to others in the office who have also come to get help.*
  - *Please stay in your chair. It is important for both of us to feel safe. When you move toward me like you are going to hit me, I don't feel safe, and neither do other parts of you. We must keep this a safe and respectful place for both of us.*
  - *I am glad to move my chair farther away if that would help you feel more safe.*
  - *Do not hit the sofa or yourself. We will find a way to work this out, but physical violence is not OK. Let's get you grounded and then I promise we will sort it out together. I'm going to ask that other parts inside help contain you until you can be more calm.*
  - *It's not OK to threaten me and call me names. I am glad to talk with you, but we must treat each other with respect even when we have difficult feelings.*
  - *Let's take a five-minute break to help you calm down a bit. Would you like to stand up and walk around the room, or go outside for a minute and take some breaths? Then we can continue our conversation, because I want to work this out with you.*
- Check if other dissociative parts are aware of the issue and whether there are different perspectives on what is happening.
  - Do all parts feel the same way as the angry part?
  - If not, can those parts listen to and accept the angry part's perspective?

- Would the angry part be willing to listen to other internal perspectives?
- Once the patient is calmer, invite other parts of the patient to "watch and listen" if possible.
- If this is too overwhelming for the patient, work only with the angry part. The goal is to decrease threat, promote safety, and then gradually introduce a sense of connection with the therapist and among dissociative parts. It is paramount to help the angry part feel safety before relational connection.
- Encourage the patient to set limits on inappropriate behaviors of the angry part. However, containment must be coupled with the patient's compassionate understanding of the angry part: Limit setting must not be punitive.
- Enlist the help of other parts to orient the angry part to the present time. As is true for many other parts, angry parts often do not recognize they are in the present.
- The patient as a whole (and the angry part) needs to learn that healthy relationships do not include punishment, humiliation, or force.
- Enlist angry parts in the service of therapy:
  - *I appreciate that you are trying to protect other parts of you from danger or failure. I agree with you that it is important to be safe and feel competent in your life. I would like to help you find some additional ways that might be more effective. Are you interested in exploring them with me?*
  - *I agree with you that no part of you should tell what happened unless it is safe to do so. You seem to believe it is not safe right now. I'd like to know more about that, and I would like your help to know how to better pace therapy so that all parts of you feel safe.*
  - *I can understand your concern about the child parts of yourself getting too close to me. You are worried that they might get hurt or disappointed. I am in agreement with you that we need to make sure they are safe. Would you be willing to work with me to find a good balance where all parts feel OK about what is happening?*
  - *Yes, you view the adult part of you as being a wimp and a loser because she won't stand up for herself and is too passive. That results in her getting hurt sometimes, so it is very understandable that you are upset. You have a lot of strength and seem to know when your boundaries are crossed. She can learn so much from you. Would you be willing to work with me to help her become more assertive?*
- Use titration. Help parts of the patient experience just a small amount of anger while still remaining grounded in the present; for example,

for just a few seconds, a 1 or 2 on a scale of 1 to 10, a teaspoon, a tiny drop, etc.

- Help more grounded parts share the felt experience of calmness or safety with angry parts. This can be accomplished via hypnotic imagery, EMDR, and somatosensory approaches (see the case of an enraged child part below).
- Allow patients to swaddle or cover with a blanket or fortify their bodies with pillows to feel more protected and contained in sessions, which may reduce angry reactions to vulnerability.
- Using calming sensory input such as music or pleasant smells and tastes (an orange or cookie).
- Focus on slow, mindful breathing.
- Use safe, calming, beautiful, or healing-space imagery.

Working With Angry Child Parts

Angry or enraged child parts are common, sometimes manifesting in what looks like temper tantrums or affect storms. These parts are often a source of major emotional dysregulation, quite active in the inner dissociative world of the patient—screaming, hurting other parts or even other people. They typically have little impulse control and little to no verbal and cognitive capacities, perhaps holding preverbal rage that is primarily somatosensory. Sometimes they are experienced as being like feral children or wild animals by the patient (and also by the therapist).

Often child parts are angry not only with therapist but with adult parts of the patient for not protecting or taking care of them. Their trance logic is that the patient was somehow an adult who was present at the time of abuse and thus could have "saved" the young parts. A realization that the patient was a child with no inner adult, and that she did the best she could to survive, is often a turning point for these parts. This opens the door to grieving the helplessness and vulnerability that is endemic to trauma.

CASE EXAMPLE OF AN ENRAGED DISSOCIATIVE CHILD PART: CARL

Carl was a 33-year-old patient who had previously been labeled as schizophrenic because he heard voices and would act like he was shadowboxing in public situations, which frightened those around him. Sometimes he would suddenly hit the wall with his fist, bang his head repeatedly, or punch himself in the stomach. Hospital records confirmed that he had suffered numerous broken bones and other serious injuries from severe physical abuse before being removed from his home at age 10. Carl was put in a strict religious foster home where expression of anger was not allowed and was seriously punished. The only recourse was for Carl to turn the anger onto himself.

After a thorough assessment, it became clear to his new therapist that Carl was highly dissociative. He had a 2-year-old child part he called "Bobby" that would punch Carl in the stomach internally, and he would suddenly double over as though he had been hit. Bobby was angry all the time, though he could not articulate why. He punched internal dissociative parts randomly and just screamed. Bobby had a very primitive anger without words or coherent thoughts, and would blindly strike out and scream at the top of his lungs internally. His anger also manifested in the external behaviors of fighting that had previously been labeled as psychotic.

The therapist first worked with the adult part of Carl to begin making very short contacts with Bobby. Carl was encouraged to watch Bobby on a very small TV screen and turn down the sound. He was instructed just to observe and see what he noticed. Carl remarked that Bobby was like "a wild wounded animal that doesn't understand what is happening to him." Carl could not see on the screen what was happening to Bobby, but he did have a sense that it was terrifying and painful. That gave him a much more compassionate perspective on Bobby. On the screen, Bobby was encouraged to open his eyes for brief moments and become more oriented to the present for a few seconds at a time. Both Carl as an adult and the therapist reassured Bobby that he was safe and that he was no longer being hurt. They empathized with his vehement anger. Gradually, Carl and the therapist could invite Bobby to step out of the screen and into the room to become even more oriented.

The therapist tried several approaches to help Bobby become calmer. The therapist found that Bobby responded to tightly wrapping himself in a blanket and barricading himself with pillows on the sofa during sessions. An ice pack to his face was calming. Certain music helped. He could peel and eat an orange, which calmed him. Carl created an imaginary safe space internally for Bobby that included all the things that helped to calm him, and practiced these interventions at home. The therapist encouraged Carl to remind Bobby that the past was over and to use anchors in the present to help reinforce that fact.

Bobby began to have brief times of feeling much calmer. He stopped screaming and striking out as often, though he continued to be mute. During one session, the therapist offered some puppets to Bobby, with the adult part of the patient watching from a distance internally. Bobby began to reenact abuse from his father in which the father puppet punched the child puppet in the stomach and face repeatedly. The child puppet fought back and received an even more severe beating.

The therapist used an additional puppet to reach out to Bobby and help him move away from the father puppet. With the help of the adult part of Carl, Bobby took the father puppet, opened the therapy room door, and dropped it outside. After that he was calm and began to talk in halting sentences. The therapist encouraged the adult part of Carl to come closer and support Bobby, who felt very relaxed and safe for the first time. Internally, Bobby reached out his hands to Carl and apologized for hurting him. Carl reached back and hugged Bobby, telling him that he accepted and understood his anger, and even shared it. After that session Bobby was able to actively participate in therapy and did not strike out in blind anger anymore.

What to Do When the Patient Becomes Abusive

Angry parts of the patient may be extremely hostile to therapists, at least initially. This raises the question of when therapists should set limits on aggressive behaviors. They first need to be able to recognize what is abusive or disrespectful. Of course, this can be quite subjective. Therapists have their unique tolerance levels, based on their own histories with verbal and physical aggression, and on their capacity to stay present. Mostly, however, we know unacceptable behavior when we experience it.

But whatever their tolerance levels, therapists who are either afraid or aggressive in certain situations in therapy are not effective in that moment. Neither are therapists who have a cavalier and dismissive attitude toward aggression, as they may tolerate behaviors that the patient would do better to control. Patient and therapist can devolve into a condition of mutually escalating arousal (Beebe, 2000; cf. Chapters 4 and 13), in which the combined fear of the therapist and the patient provokes ever-increasing aggression by the patient. Often patients are coming to therapy precisely because they have lost relationships due to their difficult behaviors, so therapists have an obligation not to collude with them. Therapists also have a responsibility to take care of themselves. Abusing the therapist will in no way help the patient heal.

There is a certain degree of trust therapists need to have in knowing themselves and the patient as a whole as they determine when to set limits. Limits that are too rigid will alienate and shame these parts, while too few limits will embolden them. Issues of power, control, and vulnerability are potentially explosive. The patient as whole needs to feel the therapist is both strong and accepting. Patients need to feel they are safely contained within reasonable limits, even though they may protest those limits, because they feel unable to provide containment for themselves. Consultation may be very helpful in finding the right balance for a particular patient.

Some therapists have the mind-set that therapy is an opportunity for the patient finally to express long-suppressed anger, no matter how aggressive or disrespectful. However, it is not expression of anger per se that is helpful to the patient. The key is to help the patient learn to express anger while maintaining a respectful relationship, staying grounded in the present, and reflecting on what is happening. The ability to mentalize while angry is essential.

In general, unacceptable behaviors include name-calling; harassing or threatening e-mails, phone calls, letters, or texts; presence or use of weapons of any kind in session; prolonged yelling, screaming, or cursing; behaviors that interfere with other patients receiving treatment in the office or that feel unsafe to the therapist, staff or other patients, such as throwing objects, destruction of property on the premises (including parking lots), or self-harm or suicide attempts on the premises; threats directed at the therapist, the therapist's colleagues, or the therapist's family; or stalking the therapist or the therapist's family members.

Of course, aggression does not occur in a vacuum. Therapists must be very aware of ways in which they might be provoking the patient. A few behaviors that are likely to evoke aggression include:

- getting into a power struggle (the therapist always loses);
- failing to set an appropriate pace in therapy;
- engaging in premature memory work (i.e., before stabilization);
- working with angry or sadistic parts without sufficient preparation or in a directly challenging way;
- working with child parts in a way that evokes too much dependency;
- not including the adult part(s) of the patient in sessions;
- failing to recognize and attend to defenses against shame; and
- being defensive with the patient.

Some therapists may excuse abusive behavior because it only involves one particular dissociative part and not others. Patients may insist they have no control over that part, and therapists might believe that the only way to engage with the part is to accept the behavior. However, this is a trap that only reinforces maladaptive patterns for the patient. Instead, the therapist might say something like,

- *It is important for all parts of you to participate in therapy. Some parts of you know quite well how to manage your behavior. Let's explore how those parts can help the parts of you that have so much trouble with their behavior.*
- *If that part cannot be here without maintaining control, maybe another part of you would be willing to be a spokesperson for that part.*

- *The adult part of you must also be here with this part so that you can maintain control.*

In general, it is necessary to discuss a clear treatment frame at the start of therapy and tell the patient which behaviors are unacceptable. Therapists should also mention what will happen in case these guidelines are defied. When a patient violates guidelines that were made sufficiently clear, therapists must immediately follow through with the consequences. Depending on the severity of the behavior, consequences may mean stopping the session until the next one; taking a brief break and returning to session to see if the patient can shift behavior; skipping a session or two; taking a longer break from therapy, or sometimes even ending the therapy (this last in the case of egregious violence or repeated dangerous acting out).

Most patients will not violate the basic ground rules of therapy, but a few do, and therapists should be prepared to deal with these patients firmly, though, as always, respectfully. If the patient has no history of acting out, there can be a greater sense of trust that the bark of angry parts is worse than their bite, which is much more often the case than not.

CORE CONCEPT

The best predictor of violence by angry parts is a past history of violence. Extra precautions should be taken with dissociative patients who have a history of uncontained violent behavior.

The best indicator of violent acting out is a history of acting out by the patient in the past. Nevertheless, verbal threats may not be acceptable to the therapist, and limits will need to be set. The therapist might say something like: *I understand you are angry and want me to back off. That is fine, and I will do so. But it is not OK to threaten me (or the staff, my family, etc.). You were threatened as a child and it really hurt you. All you need to do is let me know what you are angry about and I will respond to it. I will never threaten you. Threats are not necessary or acceptable here. I am confident we can find a way to be respectful toward each other as we begin to understand each other and learn each other's boundaries.*

Summary

Anger is a difficult emotion for both patients and therapists. The earlier in treatment therapists can engage angry parts of the patient with a combination of compassion and limit setting on inappropriate behavior, the more effective therapy can be. As patients as a whole begin to understand the functions of these parts, they are better able to accept anger as a natural human emotion, and they can help these parts of themselves move beyond the fight defense and develop greater relational capacities.

Further Explorations

16.1 Describe the family rules about the expression of anger in your own family of origin. Were you allowed to express anger, and if so, in what ways, and in what ways not? How does your experience of anger help or inhibit you in your work with patients?

16.2 What do you experience in your body when a patient is angry with you?

16.3 How do you tend to respond to an angry or hostile patient (for example, appeasement, confusion, fear, shame)?

16.4 If you have a hard time tolerating the anger of a patient, could you imagine what support you might need (imaginal and otherwise) to become less afraid?

CHAPTER 17

Working With Perpetrator-Imitating Parts of the Patient

This predator of the interior is not at all what it seems. A closer look reveals an embodied survival guide written by a child, a scaly armor that protects soft and vulnerable underbelly. It is assembled from a patchwork of painful lessons reaped from the grim world of . . . childhood.

—Kathy Steele (2009, p. 10)

We all naturally develop mental representations (also called objects in object relations theory or internal working models in attachment theory) of our early caretakers, for better and worse. These serve as models for our own self-representations as well as for those of others. Ideally, over time we are able to integrate more fully their positive qualities into who we are and sift out their more negative qualities to a reasonable degree. The resulting positive inner representations of caretakers are mirrors that help us build and sustain a healthy sense of self. But we also often retain at least some of our primary caregivers' negative habits and ways of being in the world. Negative inner representations of others remain our worst inner critics when they are not yet integrated effectively.

In cases of severe abuse and neglect, negative representations (*bad objects*, in terms of object relations) serve as the foundation for dissociative parts of the patient that imitate the perpetrators to a greater or lesser degree. But dissociative parts are also embedded in deep hypnotic processes, so they experience themselves to be real, and are experienced by other parts of the person as real. In this psychic equivalence, some parts believe themselves to be the actual perpetrators, impervious to reality and the passage of time in which the actual abusers grow old and infirm and eventually die. In their hypnotic world of non-realization, these inner parts remain forever young, strong, in control, and invincible in their own minds as well as appearing to be so to other parts internally. They believe they have never been hurt or vulnerable; instead, they dole pain out to other parts, an inner projection that helps them retain a sense of power. Unfortunately, these dynamics ensure the ongoing cycle of abuse continues internally for the patient.

CORE CONCEPT

Parts that imitate a perpetrator often literally experience themselves and are experienced by other parts as the actual perpetrator. Thus, they understandably induce fear and shame within the patient as a whole, and sometimes fear in the therapist.

It is essential for therapists to understand the role of perpetrator-imitating parts in the development of the patient's overall personality and self. They are not something to "get rid of," as the patient so often wants. They are *not* the actual perpetrator, nor do their feelings and thoughts belong solely to the perpetrator. They contain some of the most difficult experiences for patients to integrate, including their *own* sadistic feelings and tendencies. The therapist's acceptance of these parts and emotions, while not tolerating abusive behavior, can lead these highly defensive parts to be some of the best allies in treatment (Blizard, 1997; Boon et al., 2011; Howell, 2011; Kluft, 2006; Schwartz, 2013; Van der Hart et al., 2006). Indeed, a major turning point occurs in therapy once these parts have developed an alliance with other parts of the patient and the therapist, even though this may take an extended period of time to accomplish.

Understanding the Functions of Perpetrator-Imitating Parts

Perpetrator-imitating parts seem to take delight in meting out punishment internally, at least on the surface. But this is a façade, albeit a strong one. It is a defense that the therapist must recognize, an original attempt by the patient to prevent abuse by being one step ahead of the perpetrator. The logic of these parts leads them to engage in behaviors that are like the perpetrators, yet which have a protective function that is implicit, outside the awareness of the patient as a whole.

We can understand the functions of perpetrator-imitating parts as being similar to angry parts in some ways. They are protective in that they resist any movement toward unbearable realizations about the patient's experience as a child. They protect the patient in that they often hold the most sadistic and unbearable abuse. They also hold the patient's own sadism, which is a natural reaction to being abused, and yet which is intolerable to the patient and sometimes to the therapist (Boon et al., 2011; Schwartz, 2013; Van der Hart et al., 2006). They do not realize the abuse has happened to them, though they may often remember the abuse from the perspective of the perpetrator.

For example, they may re-enact abuse scenarios internally with other parts, leaving the patient with a chronic sense of unremitting terror and helplessness. They help patients avoid additional pain and shame by paradoxically immersing them in an internal world of chronic pain and shame. Through the use of fear, trance logic, and shaming, these parts seek to maintain the fragile status quo of the patient's inner system as a whole, remembering through reenactment while not explicitly remembering because they maintain non-realization.

Perpetrator-imitating parts ensure that patients retain a negative view of self, blaming themselves for whatever happened. When the patient has persistent critical self-beliefs, therapists can be curious about whether a perpetrator-imitating part is acting behind the scenes. At the very least, everyone has negative internal working models or introjects; whether or not they are actual dissociative parts should be determined through assessment.

CORE CONCEPT

Therapists should work actively to accept and include perpetrator-imitating parts in therapy as soon as is safely possible. Premature work with these parts can frighten the patient, who then flees therapy or decompensates. On the other hand, avoidance of work with these parts leaves the patient vulnerable to continued inner chaos, punishment, fear, and shame, and the therapy vulnerable to impasse.

Of course, these behaviors are not effective in the long run, in the same way that self-harm or substance abuse may be effective momentarily but is not adaptive in addressing problems over time. But it is essential that the therapist understand the protective *intent* of these parts. And most importantly, the therapist should work actively to include these parts in therapy. As Kluft (2006) has noted, these parts

> often cause chaos and instigate self-injury behind the scenes but are more likely to become amenable when regularly accessed and brought into therapy. Their defensive narcissistic constellations often preclude their feeling included in approaches that do not address them directly. (p. 293)

Perhaps not all patients have parts of themselves that imitate the perpetrator, but they are certainly extremely common. They are a central issue to resolve in the vast majority of patients, a core of resistance that must be gradually understood and transformed. They may not be identified for a long time in therapy, because the patient is ashamed and terrified of them, and these defenses cannot be resolved as long as they are not fully engaged in therapy. Table 17.1 described the several functions of perpetrator-imitating parts.

Countertransference With Perpetrator-Imitating Parts

There is nothing like the patient's rage and sadism to unsettle and overwhelm therapists, particularly those who are having a first encounter with this kind of intensity. Therapists new to this work are often hesitant or even afraid to engage these parts. They find their intensity and sadism disconcerting, to say the least. They may feel as though the actual perpetrator is in the room, reflecting the projection of the fearful patient, who cannot distinguish internal from external experience when it comes to these parts.

<table>
<tr><td colspan="1">

TABLE 17.1
Functions of Perpetrator-Imitating Parts

- To protect the patient against the threats of the original perpetrator, which may serve as malignant posthypnotic suggestions, with the patient reflexively believing them to still be true in the present. The perpetrator-imitating part repeats the threats internally to keep the patient from telling (e.g *" If you ever speak of this to anyone I will hurt your sister;" "If you don't do exactly what I say, your mother will disappear and you will never see her again;" "This is your fault and you will go to prison if anyone ever finds out."*)
- To defend against vulnerable feelings, such as shame, guilt, fear, loneliness, sadness, helplessness, powerlessness
- To contain the patient's own wishes for and sense of power and control that were unacceptable or dangerous in the past
- To contain the patient's own sadistic tendencies and wishes that the patient cannot yet accept or tolerate
- To protect the patient through criticism and punishment
- To internally reenact past trauma in literal ways internally, which ultimately prevents realization
- To prevent the patient from feeling connected to the therapist (or other people) in order to avoid rejection, loss, or unbearable dependency feelings; that is, these parts have a phobia of attachment

</td></tr>
</table>

It helps always to remember these are aspects of the patient and have defensive functions.

Perhaps one of our most powerful tools as therapists is in being able to accept our own "bad self" or "shadow self," the part of our own self that we experience as hateful, invalidating, critical, hostile, shaming. When we can accept these human tendencies as part of our overall experience, we need neither disown them nor act on them. They can simply become part of our felt experience that informs us. Our capacity to do this integrative work within ourselves opens the door for patients to do the same. It is much easier to accept negative aspects of our patients when we realize we are not immune to the same experiences.

It is true that in most cases patients experience perpetrator imitating, as well as most angry parts as much more dangerous and violent internally than they actually are in therapy. And while some parts of the patient can be quite verbally aggressive, they are typically not physically so. *The best predictor of whether these parts will actually act out in therapy physically is whether the patient has a history of violence.* In some cases, the more the therapist expects acting out, the more it occurs. Patients with a long history of violence may not be appropriate for treatment in private practice settings, unless the therapist has experience in working with potentially violent populations and has adequate backup and agency support to do so.

Nevertheless, even with the patient who has no history of violence, it is wise to move forward carefully when the patient is very fearful that a part might be violent or verbally abusive. The key is to find a path of respect and interest rather than to avoid perpetrator-imitating or angry parts or unduly provoke them. The therapist should neither strongly challenge these parts nor appease them. Rather, a straightforward, honest, and clear approach is effective. Unfortunately, some therapists tend to be even more fearful than the patient, while others might move too quickly, without pacing.

Bearing the brunt of the patient's rage is not easy. It helps for therapists to realize the patient's anger is not really about the therapist, but is a reenactment of how the patient has learned to cope with perceived danger, suffering, rejection, and humiliation. Some therapists find it helpful to imagine stepping aside from the anger of the patient and just observing (a kind of imagined out-of-body experience that involves reflection rather than dissociation). Just noticing your own reactions can be helpful in understanding more about what the patient might be avoiding by being the aggressor and projecting vulnerable feelings onto the therapist. That is, often the therapist feels overwhelmed, afraid, frozen, misunderstood, and rejected. These are the very experiences from the patient's history that are projected onto the therapist because the patient cannot yet tolerate them. When the therapist can hold these experiences without becoming embedded in them, there is the opportunity to gradually hand them back to the patient.

CORE CONCEPT

Therapists need to recognize reenactments in which perpetrator-imitating parts play a central role. Therapists may be pulled into these reenactments, and may feel similarly to the patient as a child or as the perpetrator. These experiences within the therapist must be recognized instead of acted out to the degree possible.

Some perpetrator-imitating parts are quite sadistic, which is overwhelming for the patient and often for the therapist, who may have never encountered blatant sadistic behavior before. Such parts can seem to take enormous pleasure in hurting other parts, and may enjoy toying with the therapist. Therapists may have the uncanny feeling that they are with the actual perpetrator. It is essential to remember that this is not so, that these are defenses and partial experiences of the patient, not people. But still, these experiences sometimes can be quite unsettling and even frightening.

Countertransference ranges from disgust to rage to fear. Therapists may withdraw and avoid dealing with angry or perpetrator-imitating parts, which only serves to heighten the inner conflicts of patients and the sense that they are unacceptable. Or therapists may be disgusted by the behavior of these parts and harshly judge the patient, a shaming experience that may derail the therapy. It is natural for therapists, like any other people, to become angry when unreasonably provoked, so they may respond to these parts with anger. In fact, it is common for therapists to have sadistic fantasies and feelings toward the patient. These must be accepted and used as important information, rather than avoided or acted upon.

CORE CONCEPT

Therapists need a reasonable balance between compassionate acceptance of perpetrator-imitating parts and limit setting on aggressive or sadistic behaviors, both internally for the patient and externally with the therapist or other people in the patient's life.

Even while being compassionate and respectful to the angry patient, the therapist should always also set appropriate limits on aggressive or sadistic behaviors (see the previous chapter on dealing with abusive behavior by a patient). Of course, the more the therapist can learn not to take these provocations personally, the better. And the more clear and firm boundaries the therapist can set, the less acting out toward the therapist will occur. Relational repair is always essential when the therapist does become angry and defensive.

How to Work With Perpetrator-Imitating Parts

It is often easier to develop a working alliance with angry parts fixated in defense than with perpetrator-imitating parts, although the same approaches discussed in Chapter 16 on working with angry parts of the patient are still helpful. Perpetrator-imitating parts are often the linchpin that holds non-realization together and thus are sometimes the last parts willing to engage with the therapist. Typically, once these parts become accepted and learn to be compassionate themselves, a difficult therapy will turn the corner. However, this can take a long time, and much patience is required.

Even though these parts may be difficult to engage, it is imperative to do so as early and consistently in therapy as possible. After offering initial psychoeducation about the functions of perpetrator-imitating parts (see below), the therapist should stay with the resistance of these parts with compassion and curiosity, giving them space in therapy to explain their rationales and accept very small and incremental challenges to their trance logic.

CORE CONCEPT

The more vulnerable parts (such as child parts) become activated in therapy, the more perpetrator-imitating parts will resist the vulnerability and act out by punishing these parts. The therapist must typically work with perpetrator-imitating parts prior to working with vulnerable, needy parts.

The more vulnerable parts become active in the therapy, the greater the inner conflict about safety and shame about needs, and the more perpetrator-imitating parts will become active in their resistance to therapy. Thus, although it may seem counterintuitive to therapists, work with perpetrator-imitating parts often comes before work with child parts, or at least simultaneously in a back-and-forth manner, using something akin to shuttle diplomacy. Therapists (ideally with the assistance of more objective parts of the patient) go back and forth between parts to help acknowledge and resolve conflicts. In this way the wildly divergent needs and goals of each side are gradually understood, and acceptable compromises are made. However, because patients are so afraid and ashamed of these parts, it is often (but not always) necessary to work with these parts individually before bringing in other parts to develop more inner collaboration. As noted in Chapter 10, the therapist should choose the level of systemic interventions with parts that best fit the patient's highest integrative capacity. If the patient as a whole can tolerate being with a perpetrator-imitating part, there is then no need to work with that part separately.

Once there is some initial contact, therapists can explain the vicious loops of experiences and ways to interrupt these ongoing inner processes—for instance, by having the patient create and allow safe or calm inner spaces for parts. When an alliance with perpetrator-imitating parts is more solid, therapists may gradually confront the rigid behaviors in which these parts get stuck, such as punishing child parts or giving constant negative comments to the adult parts that are trying to function in daily life.

- *OK, so you do not want her to fail at her new job. That is great! How are you going to help her succeed? What can you do to help instead of standing on the sidelines and pointing your finger and predicting she will fail?*

- *I understand you want the child parts to stop crying. And yes, it is temporarily effective to yell and hit them inside—it does make them be quiet. However, in the long run that only makes them more afraid, more ashamed, and more overwhelmed, which only makes them more prone to crying the next time. After all, you have been doing it that way for 40 years, and they still cry every day. Would you be willing to learn a different way that helps them actually feel better?*

- *May I ask where you learned to yell and hit children that way? Did anyone teach you other ways of helping children?*

- *I understand that you want Mary [the adult part that functions in daily life] dead because then all this suffering would come to an end. But do you realize that you share the same body? What you do to her body, you do to yours. And there are many, many ways to reduce suffering. I am glad to help you discover more of them. It's pretty limiting to have just one option on hand.*

Psychoeducation About the Functions of Perpetrator-Imitating Parts

The therapist initially begins with educating the patient as a whole about the roles and functions of perpetrator-imitating parts. Perpetrator-imitating parts are especially encouraged to listen.

- *These parts of you are completely understandable and natural. They are as important as all other parts of yourself. They developed to help you in the most difficult situations in the past and managed for you when pain, fear, or shame was unbearable. (Here it might be helpful to give some examples from the patient's history: The part of you that seems like your uncle likely developed in this way: Your uncle was hurting you, and you felt so vulnerable, so powerless, that this part came to believe he is your uncle, who did have all the power and was not vulnerable or hurt. In such a way, this part could protect you from the threats that your uncle would make it worse for you if you told, and from more pain and helplessness.) Although I understand that their behaviors are often threatening or hurting you or other people, and you certainly do not consider their behavior helpful, these parts of you are trying to protect you, just not in a very effective way. For example, they do not want you to tell what happened, because telling seems too painful and overwhelming right now, and might have been very dangerous in the past. These parts are actually helping you pace yourself so you do not go too quickly, until we can make sure that all parts know that it is now safe. They tell you that you are going to fail, that you are a loser, because they do not want you to try things and fail and then feel disappointment and hurt. They tell you therapy is useless because they do not want you to get your hopes up and then be disappointed, and perhaps they are worried that changing anything might make your life worse instead of better. They believe in preemptive strikes: Prevent it before it happens. Since they could not control what happened outside of you, they try to control you. Can you understand, as backwards as their ways are, that the intention is to protect you?*

After helping the patient gain greater cognitive understanding of the function of these parts, the therapist can continue to "talk through" the patient directly to perpetrator-imitating parts, offering understanding for their stance. However, too much empathy, softness, or acknowledgment of vulnerability are not helpful with these parts in the beginning, as this is a frontal attack on their primary defensive strategies against shame and connection. Instead, the therapist can appreciate their strength and toughness, noting that the patient needs these qualities as well. The therapist must genuinely appreciate the functions of these parts, and view them as part of the patient as a whole, even while perhaps loathing their behaviors. This kind of psychoeducation should be repeated in different ways over time. The idea is to acknowledge the presence and power of these parts as essential in the overall collaboration in therapy. Therapists can loosely follow this sequence:

- Acknowledge these parts and their power internally and their original protective functions without challenging their defenses against vulnerability.
  - *You have had a hard job of protecting Mary in very difficult situations. You have incredible endurance and strength. You are able to notice Mary's smallest transgressions, so I know that you are very vigilant and pay attention to detail. I know you must feel very frustrated with other parts, and I can understand that. You see them as weak, and I think I also understand that. You have a right to exist and are important. I really would like to understand your position and point of view better.*
- Next, appreciate how these parts help the patient (for example, they attempt to ensure the patient never makes a mistake, or force the patient to avoid social situations to prevent humiliation or rejection, or keep child parts quiet internally by screaming at them to shut up or beating them).

- Gradually and respectfully offer facts that confront these parts' beliefs that they are the perpetrator (for example, the perpetrator is actually dead, or is very old, or lives in another city, or is in prison; the patient is now grown up and has a family of her own; the therapist was not there when the patient was young, and being in the office is an indication that time has passed; the part shares the same body as the patient).

  o *Even though you may believe that you are Mary's father, there are important differences. For example, you say you are 35 years old, but Mary's father is now a very old man, and has Alzheimer's. Did you know that? You are a part of Mary, even though it does not seem like that at all to you right now.*

  o *Even though Mary says that she wants to get rid of you, and you want to get rid of Mary, that really isn't possible. If you kill Mary, you kill yourself, and vice versa. You cannot get rid of each other, as much as you would like to right now. Although I could certainly be wrong, I wonder if deep down, you don't really want to get rid of each other, but rather you want your life to work better, and you don't have much hope that can happen. The truth is that you are all in the same boat. Right now there is a storm, and in your boat some are paddling, some are rocking the boat to tip it over, some are plotting mutiny, some are punching holes in the bottom, some are bailing water out, some are trying to hoist the sails, and some are just sitting around, waiting for someone to rescue them, and no one at all is minding the rudder and wheel. But it is up to all of you together to sail this one boat, even if you don't especially care for some of your shipmates. I believe you can be successful in helping this boat sail.*

  o *Working together with all parts of Mary and with me does not mean that you will lose control. You play a very important role as an advisor and as a discussion partner in therapy, and I am relying on you to warn me when I go too fast or make a mistake or ask Mary to do something with which you disagree. I very much value and need your input.*

Help the Patient Distinguish Between the Internal and External Perpetrator

Early in the work with perpetrator-imitating parts, the therapist can not only gently confront these parts with differences between them and actual perpetrators, but can also help the patient as a whole notice these differences. For example, often perpetrator-imitating parts are experienced as having the age of the perpetrator when the patient was a child, or as saying things related to the present, but in the same voice as the perpetrator. The therapist should introduce the beginnings of cognitive dissonance and encourage all parts of the patient to stop reacting to these parts and engage in reflecting on their inner experience more.

- *Do you have an image of this part? Does he look like your brother? Can you notice any differences between how that part looks inside and how your actual brother looks now in the present?*
- *Does this part seem to have an age? Does that fit the age of your perpetrator in the present? That part seems to be the age of your mother when you were little, and your mother is very old now. Do you think that part of you knows your mother is old?*
- *I wonder if there is some way to help you distinguish this inner part from your real uncle who hurt you as a child. Perhaps you might notice that "inside uncle" wears a different shirt or hat than your real uncle. Is that something you could notice? Can other parts of you help you tell the difference?*

Value the Goals but Not the Means of Perpetrator-Imitating Parts

The therapist can respectfully note that however much these parts work toward a goal (for example, keeping the child parts quiet to prevent them from telling because these parts believe that original threats not to tell are still enforced, or preventing the patient from trying anything that might lead to failure), somehow they are never able to achieve a goal for more than a temporary time, and that the problem returns.

- *I understand that you are doing your very best to protect Mary. Yet somehow, in spite of your best efforts, Mary continues to have difficulties in daily life, the child parts continue to cry, things continue to go wrong, you continue to threaten parts to self-harm or kill themselves most of the time. I wonder if you might be interested in learning some new ways that might work in addition to what you already know.*
- *I can hardly imagine how difficult for you it must be that those child parts are crying all the time inside. It's no wonder you want them to be quiet! And I also wonder if perhaps you have some concern that if they are not quiet, something terrible might happen, like it did in the past? It is important for you to remember, even though it may be hard, that you are safe now, and my office is a quiet place where all parts of you are accepted and are welcome. Still, would you be willing to try something different with those upset child parts in the office with me now? Would you allow them to go to a place inside that is calm and quiet, perhaps where they could rest or play? This is an experiment you could try here to see if it helps them to be more quiet.*
- *I know you have a lot of concerns about Mary's ability to function at work,*

and I share your concern. We both want her to be successful and keep her job. I can't help but wonder if it were more quiet inside, then Mary could focus better on her work. You know how much those child parts bother you when they cry? I wonder if your yelling at Mary all day feels like that to her? I know you don't trust her much, but could we try another experiment, like having the child parts go to a special place inside? Could you try allowing Mary to have a morning at work without yelling at her? I am pretty sure if she makes a mistake, she will figure it out. Let's just see if that makes a difference.

Help the Patient Recognize Internal Reenactments

The therapist can also help the patient as a whole understand the ongoing vicious cycle of reenactment by all parts internally (Boon et al., 2011.

- *These* [perpetrator-imitating] *parts may seem to you similar in many ways to the people who hurt you. They appear on the surface to have the same emotions, thoughts, and behaviors as did those people. They are essentially telling the story of what happened by acting it out instead of talking about it. In fact, internally, all parts are triggering (or activating) each other constantly. Fear, sadness, and pain can trigger feelings of powerlessness, shame, and anger. This can result in overwhelming experiences inside so that you hurt yourself to try and stop it. But self-harm, while it works for the moment, triggers further shame and bad feelings about yourself. This evokes even more vulnerability and pain, self-criticism, and so on. If we take a bird's-eye view, we can see that every part of you is telling a part of the story by the ways each one acts, feels, and perceives. While it may seem that the parts that are like the perpetrator are causing the problem, in fact, all parts have a role in this cycle. There are many ways to change this ongoing vicious cycle. One way would be to find safe or calm places for parts that are crying or in pain.*

Help the Patient Recognize and Change Reactions to Perpetrator-Imitating Parts

Each patient and each dissociative part has particular habituated somatic, emotional, and cognitive reactions to other parts. It is helpful for the therapist to encourage the patient to notice, work with, and change these reactions.

- *I notice that every time you hear that part scream at you, you freeze and your mind goes blank, and you look around as though you are very afraid. Have you noticed that? Let's find a way to help you respond in a different way.*

- *I wonder if instead of believing everything that part says, you can take a step back and see that maybe at least some of what that part of you says is not accurate?*
- *What if you expressed that you are beginning to understand and feel a little compassion toward that part of yourself, even if you do not feel it so strongly? I am sure that part of you has not experienced that before, and I believe it might help.*
- *What if you began to reassure this part of you that you are now safe?*
- *Would it be possible for you to start a dialogue with this part instead of just being afraid?*
- *I wonder if perhaps you and that part have some important values in common? For example, you do not want to fail. That part is calling you a loser because, I believe, she does not want you fail either. So you both do not want to fail. Is that something you could agree on?*

Help Perpetrator-Imitating Parts Accent Their Own Vulnerabilities and Strengths

As an alliance is slowly developed, the therapist gradually helps the perpetrator-imitating parts accept and realize their own vulnerabilities. This may take a long period of time, and perhaps it will not happen until much later in therapy. It should not be the first interventions with these parts. Because these parts have a narcissistic investment in remaining powerful and in control, the therapist must not challenge their status or try at first to uncover their vulnerabilities (e.g., Kluft, 1996a).

- *I could imagine that you have a difficult position inside, because the other parts of Mary are afraid of you, angry with you, misunderstand and avoid you. I could fully understand if you would not like other parts to know, so you could just nod your head yes or no if perhaps you feel a bit lonely sometimes, perhaps like Mary was lonely as child?*
- *You are not bad even though you sometimes may act in an aggressive or sadistic way to other parts inside or people outside. Behaving badly is not the same as being bad. Behaving badly is a way of expressing your anger and other feelings, since you have not learned how to deal with unbearable feelings in other ways. I am sure you can learn to deal with these feelings in a different way that works better for you, in ways that keep these feelings from constantly returning and plaguing you. Would you be interested in that?*
- *Your anger is a source of strength and vitality. You can learn to use this strength in different ways, not against yourself or other parts inside, but for yourself and each other inside.*
- *I am guessing that you do not in any way want to be weak and vulnera-*

Working With Perpetrator-Imitating Parts of the Patient 357 *ble if you participate in therapy and start talking about your feelings, like other parts inside. But are you aware that accepting all your feelings is not a weakness, but rather a great strength? It takes a lot of courage and fortitude to accept difficult feelings, to not be afraid of them, and manage them in a helpful way. In fact, it is often one of the hardest things people learn to do.*

- *I wonder how you came to protect Mary? What is the first thing you remember?*
- *Mary must have felt so helpless and vulnerable and afraid when her father was hurting her. I can't help but wonder if you learned to take on his sense of control and power so you didn't have to feel those awful feelings Mary had?*
- *Please take your time to think about these things, and we can continue to discuss your thoughts and concerns at your pace.*

Gradual Cooperation

Therapists should not expect perpetrator-imitating parts to collaborate right away. Often they may surface and just as quickly submerge again, or remain more present only to castigate the therapist and say in no uncertain terms that therapy is useless, the patient is hopeless, and the therapist is incompetent. Therapists must simply take this in stride and continue gently moving forward when the time is right.

Sometimes when talking through the patient to perpetrator-imitating parts, a switch will occur or the therapist can suddenly see an angry or scornful gaze, which can be disconcerting. Many therapists experience this as a uncanny sense of "someone else looking out of the eyes of the patient." This is a normal occurrence in patients with dissociative disorders. When it happens, the therapist can continue, taking it as a good sign that these parts are willing to listen, if not engage in dialogue quite yet.

The therapist might say something like, *It's very good for these parts of you to check me out thoroughly when we are together, and I very much appreciate that these parts of you are willing to listen. I invite these parts of you to be present as they are ready, and I am very open to anything they wish to share with me.*

Psychoeducation and gentle relational forays must be offered over and over. Understanding, let alone cooperation, will certainly not come after one session, or even after many. The therapist must be patient, content with the slow erosion of defenses. In fact, when working with these parts it is a good sign if nothing too dramatic is occurring other than the occasional castigation and protestations of these parts.

- The therapist takes time to validate, understand, and work with the perpetrator-imitating part, commiserating with what a hard and exhausting job it is to be continually angry and punishing to keep things in line.

- These parts also have intense fear of what might happen if they are not in control and cannot prevent other parts of the patient from talking about traumatic experiences, as they often have retained threats by the original perpetrator about what will happen if they talk. They can be valued for their strength.
- Therapists should work with other parts of the patient, compassionately validating the experience of being treated so badly by these parts, and how it must be to have such vicious inner voices active much of the time, while also sharing the protective functions of these parts.
- Next, the therapist searches with the patient for commonly held goals between the perpetrator-imitating part and other parts.
  - *I'm wondering if it is true that neither of you want suffering and pain in your life, that you both would like some relief?*
  - *It seems that neither one of you wants you to be a loser, a slut, fat, lazy, etc.*
  - *Perhaps all parts of you are hoping in some smaller or larger way that therapy can help you.*
  - *Even though this part says he won't come to therapy, he allows you to show up every week. I am guessing that there is some hope somewhere that you share, even though he may not be aware of it.*

Perpetrator-imitating parts can greatly benefit from much-needed, consistent attention by therapists. They feel heard and respected for the first time. They realize the therapist is not trying to "get rid of them," and is even helping other parts be more accepting of them. They become more curious about therapy and how it might help them. Gradually their acceptance by both patient and therapist leads to patients being much better able to own their own anger and sadism, and therefore, to transform it.

CASE EXAMPLE OF WORKING WITH A PERPETRATOR-IMITATING PART: SAMANTHA

Samantha had a vicious inner "Mom" and "Dad" that berated and beat her internally, threatened her with punishments, and told her to kill herself. She also had a very young 4-year-old part named "Dolores" that was loyal to inside Mom and Dad and was bitterly angry all the time. This part of Samantha often kicked her in the stomach internally, causing intense pain, and would not allow Samantha to eat enough or buy any clothes.

Dolores was furious with the therapist because she would not change Samantha's history so that she had good parents; but at the same time, sometimes Dolores insisted her parents were wonderful. She stayed hidden and refused to be present in therapy, so the therapist continued to talk through Samantha to this part. The therapist recognized that Samantha and Dolores sometimes worked in tandem to punish each other as a way to avoid realization of the past. At other times, Dolores was aligned with inside Mom and Dad, punishing Samantha.

After some years of an arduous treatment plagued by self-harm and suicidality, Dolores came to realize her loyalty to inside Mom and Dad protected her, as she would be hurt by them if she was disobedient. Further, she realized her attempts to deprive Samantha of food and clothing were not only reenactments of real experiences of deprivation, but also a test of strength. As long as Samantha could tolerate doing without necessities, Dolores believed she was strong enough to survive whatever came her way. Very slowly, over the course of years of therapy, Dolores, as well as inside Mom and Dad, became more amenable to accepting Samantha, and vice versa. The more compassion these parts expressed toward each other, the better Samantha's life became, the more she could engage in healthy self-care, and her self-harm and suicidality completely abated.

CASE EXAMPLE OF WORKING WITH A PERPETRATOR-IMITATING PART: MARY

Mary was a 45-year-old woman with recurrent depressive episodes and a history of sexual and physical abuse by her father and other family members. After several years in the mental health system, she was diagnosed with DID, and treatment for her dissociative disorder began. After some initial stabilization interventions, Mary reported with hesitation that she was hearing constant child voices crying in her head and often the voice of a man, who sounded like her father and was shouting at her and crying child parts internally. She was terrified that this part would take over and hurt her or the therapist. The therapist provided her with psychoeducation (as described above) about the functions of this part and talked through Mary to this father part of herself.

In response to this session, the therapist received a voice mail from the patient, who in an angry voice said: *Why are you interfering? You are useless and spewing all kind of lies. Leave us alone! It is dangerous for her [Mary] to listen to you, and now those stupid crying children are upset, and worst of all, you suggest there is hope. How could you even think it would help her to have hope? What the hell is hope, anyway? There is no such thing! I will never take part in this ridiculous therapy, which is really about how much money you can get from her. I know about people like you.*

You seem nice, and then you use people. I am going to make Mary stop coming to see you, and if she doesn't, I will make her regret it. It's her fault we are in this mess, and now you make it worse—all these crying babies wanting you to save them! I will teach them how to shut up and be tough. We do not need you to be meddling in our affairs, so stop, and don't you dare talk to me again!

This kind of message (which may also be received directly in therapy or perhaps via e-mail or letter) is a rather typical and often expected reaction of a perpetrator-imitating part after being addressed by the therapist for the first time. Of course, these parts cannot and will not let down their defenses immediately, as they are too afraid that the therapist will hurt them or "get rid of" them. The key is for the therapist to back off just enough, yet continue to gently be curious and attempt contact over time. For example, the therapist might say it is important to have the feedback of this part on some issue, and would this part be willing to offer an opinion? In some cases, very hostile communication will continue for quite a while, and the therapist should remain patient and stick to trying to understand what is driving the intensity of these parts.

The next session, Mary told the therapist that she had had a dreadful week and lost time during the days. She had also found herself alone at night walking in the woods, terrified, wet, and cold. She was threatened all the time by her father's voice in her head saying she had to stop therapy or he would kill her. However, there were also other voices that told her it was OK to continue, and she had resisted the urge to cancel her next appointment.

Therapist: I am very sorry to hear this. It seems that there is lot of conflict inside, and the father part of you felt in some way that I was not safe. I wonder if perhaps I went too fast or did something that was upsetting? But I also wonder if perhaps that part of you might have felt shock and confusion about being recognized so directly. What do you think? I wonder if any other parts of you have some ideas about this?

If communication from a part occurs outside sessions, the therapist should always bring it up, as the patient may be amnestic.

Therapist: Can we check in about the voice mail you left me after last session? You sounded pretty angry and upset.
Mary: What? I left you a voice mail? What are you talking about?
Therapist: Well, yes, that part of you did. [*Therapist repeats the gist of the message, and offers to play the message, which the patient vehemently declines.*] That part of you does not want me to interfere, but other parts

want help. That is quite a conflict within you, isn't it? But how good that we now understand and can talk about this conflict a bit more. I am so glad that angry part of you decided to communicate, even though you may not like the way it happened. We are on our way, and this is a very good beginning. I am grateful that part of you was willing to be heard. Certainly, though, I did not intend to make things worse for you. This part of you thinks I have done so, and I am truly interested to understand that part's point of view. The fact that you are here today means that part did allow you to come, even though a lot of doubts about therapy are being expressed.

Mary: Well, he is the main cause of this mess. I was terrified in the woods! Why did he make me go there? Why does he hurt me? I do not want anything to do with him. I want him to go away.

Therapist: I understand how frightened you must have been, and I agree that going to the woods in the middle of the night is dangerous. But maybe we can find out why this part felt that was important. It is something we can be curious about, as all your behavior has important meanings that we can begin to understand. In the voice mail, this part of you said that you are in a big mess because of you and other parts. Apparently, you are blaming each other, and the fighting inside gets worse. What do you think?

Mary: This has been going on as long as I remember, but it is far worse now. Maybe he is right and I should stop coming here?

Therapist: Well, do you think that will solve this terrible conflict and help you feel better?

Mary: I don't know . . . no, it won't. I have felt better since I am seeing you some of the time, and I finally do not think that I am crazy. A lot of what you have explained makes sense and has helped me. I am starting to understand these stupid child and baby parts and tried to follow your ideas to make a safe place for them. But then he became furious and destroyed their safe place. I am so afraid he is really going to do something destructive, like kill you or me. Can't you make him go away?

Therapist: Although I understand you are afraid, it won't work to have this part of you go away. And though you may not yet fully understand, this part of you is essential. You developed this part to protect yourself in the past, and I think that this part still wants to help you. This part of you has reasons to think that therapy is bad for you. I want us to understand those reasons. So maybe, deep down, he also wants to get out of this mess, because he has allowed you to come to therapy all this time.

Mary: I don't want him here. That terrifies me. He is listening and is starting to yell at me again. (*Patient puts hands over her ears as though to shut out the shouting.*)

Therapist: Well, I am glad that he is listening, and I understand that maybe it is not yet time for him to be in session directly. But perhaps this part might be willing to write to me in your journal or on a piece of paper and tell me more about the need to end therapy and to go to the woods in the middle of the night. I think we can find a way out of this conflict and mess for all of you. Does that part have something to say now? I really want to hear him.

Mary: He is not yelling now, but he tells me he is not going to change his mind, and . . . I feel ashamed . . . he is really saying nasty things about you. I am not going to tell you.

Therapist: Well, I am glad this part of you feels free to share with you, and I guess some parts of you must indeed have a lot of feelings about me, not all of them positive. That is OK. I am hopeful that this part of you will find a way to continue to communicate in words with me.

A day or two after the session, the therapist received the following voice message from the father-like part: *You bet I took her to the woods. She does not deserve a safe place; there is no safety, and she better realize she can never get away from me! I like to rape her in the woods—it's plenty of fun, and I don't get disturbed there. I also like to rape her in the house. There is no such thing as a safe place for her; there is nowhere to hide. I told you, don't interfere, because you do not understand anything at all!*

In the next session the therapist thanked the father-like part (again talking through the patient to this part) for the communication. The therapist then asked whether this part knew that the real father was a very old man in a wheelchair who could not hurt them any longer. That suddenly triggered a switch, and the father part came directly forward.

Mary (as father-like part): I knew you were dangerous, telling lies. I am not old; my legs are strong. Do you see a wheelchair here? I am not stupid. You can't trick me with your lies. She *[the patient]* wants to believe I am old, but that is a fantasy. She will never get away from me!

Therapist: No, you are here, and of course, you are not old or in a wheelchair. But can you help me understand who is in that picture Mary brought, that man in the wheelchair she calls her father?

Mary (as father-like part): (Looking momentarily confused) I don't know! Why are you focused on some stupid picture? Who cares who he is? I am here. That is all you need to understand.

Therapist: Well, truthfully, we both need to understand a lot, and that will happen over time. Right now I understand that you are indeed here and I am glad, because you are helping me to understand more about you and the relationships you have with other parts inside.

Working With Perpetrator-Imitating Parts of the Patient   363

Mary (as father-like part): Yeah, I rape them, I beat them, I have a good time.

Therapist: Hmm, what about that makes you feel you are having a good time? And how do you spend your time when you are not raping or beating them? What is it that you enjoy in addition to hurting them? *[Here the therapist begins to challenge the father-like part to broaden his awareness beyond the trauma.]*

Mary (as father-like part): What are you talking about? I hurt them all the time.

Therapist: Well, I am sure it seems that way to you, but everyone needs time off. I am thinking, for example, about how you take the parts to the woods to rape them. Do you ever go the woods alone? Do you like the woods, like walking there, like the feel and sounds of the woods?

Mary (as father-like part): I don't have time for that tiptoeing through the tulips kind of thing. Stupid question! I do like birds sometimes.

Therapist: Yeah, I know that my questions must seem very stupid at times. I apologize for that. Tell me more about what you like about birds.

Mary (as father-like part): Why? So you can humiliate me? No thanks! *[This statement helps the therapist recognizes the deep shame this part defends against.]*

Therapist: No, I am really interested in what you like. Birds are so incredible: their colors, their different sounds, their feathers, the way they make their nests, the way they fly, and even some that don't fly, birds of prey, birds of song. Some of the most amazing creatures on earth, aren't they?

Mary (as father-like part): Yeah, they are pretty cool. I like the sounds. But wait, you are pulling me into your trap. Just shut up about birds. I am going now. *(Patient switches from father-like part to the adult part of Mary.)*

The father-like part is beginning an uneasy alliance with the therapist, who gently alternates challenges to the reality of the part, acceptance of the part's current inner role as torturer in chief, and respectful prodding to enlarge the part's awareness of some type of positive experience.

Over the course of time, the therapist works to further challenge the fixed reality of this part: *Do you realize that you now live in another house, in another town, that Mary has her own family, husband, and children? Do you realize that Mary is 45, and your father is now 79, and that time has passed? And your father is really an old man now, in a wheelchair, and cannot hurt you any longer?*

The therapist also capitalizes on the small window of opportunity that part has offered in liking birds. The therapist might engage this part in more conversations about birds, use metaphors about birds, and eventually have this part develop a calming space with a bird theme. The therapist might ask questions about when this part first began to like birds, which is a kind of orienting-in-time intervention. The therapist can also use imaginal work coupled with somatic work to develop a somatic resource for this part: *I wonder what it would be like to be able to fly? Can you imagine what that might feel like? Just notice that in your body.*

Gradually, the part becomes more confused about whether he is the real father or not. The therapist should not force the issue, but continue respectfully and with good timing to notice differences between this part and the father. *I notice your* [the patient's] *shoes are red today. Did the father have red shoes? I notice you have a smartphone. Those weren't around back then. I notice you do not have a beard, yet your father has one. What do you make of that? If you were a part of Mary, what would that mean to you?*

The therapist encourages other parts also to help orient the part to the present: *Can you allow that part to watch and listen while you take a walk or play with your pet? Would it be all right if that part looked through your adult eyes at your house, to see where he is in the present? Do you know this part likes birds? What if you bought a book about birds as a gift for this part of you?*

Gradually, realization sets in that indeed, this part is a part of Mary, not the father. But still, this part may cling to being the one who hurts rather than the one who is hurt for quite a while. Vulnerability and helplessness are incredibly difficult to accept and realize. The therapist can continue to help broaden the experience of this part for positive experiences. For example, if this part no longer needed to keep other parts in line, or hurt them, what would he want with his life? What does he think of Mary's life and how might he want it to be different?

A Hierarchy of Dissociative Parts

The system of dissociative parts of the patient may be hierarchically organized if there is more than one perpetrator-imitating part. Often the "worst" perpetrator is the most hidden, but also the most powerful. Such parts are often the last ones to decide whether they want to participate in therapy and may sabotage treatment for quite some time. In these patients it is not uncommon for therapists to believe that they now know all the perpetrator-imitating parts, yet self-destructive or sabotaging behaviors continue. Then therapists might consider if there are further hidden parts, often that are very sadistic.

Some very complex patients have whole (sub)systems of parts, with additional groups emerging only as the first group is becoming more resolved and integrated (see Chapter 19). Both therapist and patient may find it disheartening to think treatment is nearly at the end, only to be confronted with more work. But these subsystems can be understood as more concretized versions of the highly complex resistances found in some non-dissociative patients with severe personality disorders, representing defenses against shame, vulnerability, dependency, and so on. Patients may have different groups of parts organized around different perpetrators (one within the family, one at church or otherwise outside the home). Of course, these groups of parts influence each other, as they all remain part of the patient as a whole.

In some cases, patients come to understand that these perpetrator-imitating parts are actually very young child parts of themselves that hold the most traumatic of memories, and much fear, shame, vulnerability, and the pain of having been unwanted. In other cases, there may be child (or other types of) parts that are strongly aligned with a perpetrator-imitating part internally.

Summary

Perpetrator-imitating parts are strong defenses against realization, perhaps the strongest. Their inability to realize they are not the actual perpetrator can create much distress and pain for the patient. The more therapists can accept and include these parts, being genuinely curious and compassionate, the more smoothly therapy can go forward. A major problem is the strong countertransference reactions of therapists to these parts. The therapist should receive regular consultation and supervision if strong feelings emerge, and should receive help in setting appropriate limits as necessary. As these parts gradually accept that they are actually parts of the patient, they can become allies in treatment.

Further Explorations

17.1 We all have negative introjects or internal working models from early caretakers. Would you be able to describe yours? How have they changed over time? Can you use your own work with your negative introjects to better understand perpetrator-imitating parts in your patients?

17.2 What have been your successes and challenges in working with perpetrator-imitating parts in the past? After reading this chapter, would you do anything differently next time?

CHAPTER 18

Resolving Unsafe Behaviors

Clients feel deeply misunderstood when therapists and others fail to distinguish deliberate self-harm from suicidal behavior. . . . Self-harm is intended to terminate an unbearable emotional state, whereas suicidal behavior is intended to bring permanent escape through death.

—Jon G. Allen (2001, p. 218)

For most therapists, working with patients who engage in unsafe behaviors—that is, behaviors that potentially cause harm to the patient and to others—is an enormous challenge. It is important to regard these behaviors as substitute actions, attempts at problem-solving that are less adaptive in the long run than, for example, accepting painful emotions or being able to reflect (Janet, 1945; Van der Hart et al., 2006).

CORE CONCEPT

Unsafe behaviors are coping strategies and attempts to solve problems with substitute behaviors that are not adaptive.

Most patients are highly reluctant and even phobic of disclosing unsafe behaviors to the therapist. They are deeply ashamed of them, at least on some level, and also fear these coping strategies will be "taken away," so they will be left with no way to deal with unbearable experiences. Some patients are even addicted to unsafe behaviors like cutting or dangerous thrill-seeking, which release endorphins, leading to a euphoric feeling that relieves unbearable emotions and is difficult to relinquish.

Dissociation is highly correlated with self-injury and suicidality (Boon & Draijer, 1993a, 1993b; Foote, Smolin, Neft, & Lipschitz, 2008; Low, Jones, MacLeod, Power, & Duggan, 2000), with 60% of dissociative patients reporting amnesia before, during, or after self-injury episodes (Coons & Milstein, 1990). Patients may, for example, wake up with injuries that puzzle them, or "come to" and find themselves in the bathroom after purging. These may be terrifying experiences that feel out of control and shameful. Some parts may not be aware that other parts are engaging in unsafe behavior. Some parts may force other parts to hurt themselves. There is often strong resistance for patients to acknowledge and accept the parts of themselves that engage in unsafe behaviors, much less have compassion.

CORE CONCEPT

Certain dissociative parts are typically involved in unsafe behaviors, and addressing them directly can help eliminate the behaviors.

CASE EXAMPLE OF WORKING WITH SELF-HARM: ELISE

Elise came to session with her left arm swathed in bandages, with blood seeping through in a few places. She did not mention it until the therapist inquired. She merely stated, *Oh, that has been taken care of.* Only after persistent questioning by the therapist and a lot of hesitation did she admit that she "woke up" two days prior and found her arm cut and bleeding profusely. She wrapped it up and took herself to the hospital, where she received stitches. Elise was not curious in the least about what had happened to her arm, a classic symptom of *la belle indifférence*, a severe non-realization displayed by the part of Elise that functioned in daily life.

A major goal in Phase 1—indeed, the first goal—is to establish safety. Yet one of the most difficult challenges is that unsafe behaviors may take quite some time to diminish over the course of therapy. Therapists must know when to have an exclusive focus on unsafe behaviors, and when to deal with the possibility that ongoing unsafe behaviors are serving a major purpose of distracting from other important work. They must find their way with pacing the therapy, knowing when a particular issue is too overwhelming for the patient and likely to increase unsafe behaviors, and when dealing with an issue, although painful and scary, may help the patient reduce unsafe behaviors. These decisions are complex, and therapists are encouraged to get consultation as they are learning how to navigate the stormy waters of unsafe behaviors.

Therapists may feel frustrated when the patient self-injures repeatedly, but must have patience and yet be firm, recognizing that relapses may occur under stress, and that a certain level of safety must exist for treatment to be effective. Sometimes the patient is too ashamed to reveal self-injury until well into therapy, or the part that presents to therapy is amnestic or has severe avoidance and non-realization—that is, *la belle indifférence*, as in the case of Elise above. The therapist may strongly suspect unsafe behavior, but the patient denies it for long periods of time. The more skills the patient learns for adaptive and constructive ways to problem solve inner distress, the more acceptance and compassion among parts, the more stable the therapeutic relationship, the less these behaviors will occur.

Often the first challenge in treating unsafe behaviors is accepting and managing the therapist's countertransference.

Countertransference in Working With Unsafe Behaviors

Patients engage in unsafe behaviors as coping strategies when they are at their most desperate to avoid overwhelming emotions or experiences. Thus, their arousal level is at its highest around the time they engage in these unsafe strategies. Therapists are highly vulnerable to intense countertransference and their own impulsive substitute actions in the face of patients who are engaging in chronic unsafe behaviors. This runs the gamut from near-superhuman efforts to be constantly available and rescue the patient; to fear and anxiety; to profound frustration and punishment of the patient; to feelings of helplessness, incompetence, and shame; to avoiding dealing with unsafe behaviors; to inappropriate termination with the patient. When both patient and therapist become embedded in intense emotions and the urgent need to act, a mutually escalating arousal (Beebe, 2000) can lead to a breakdown of effective therapy.

CORE CONCEPT

- Countertransference with unsafe behaviors, especially self-harm and suicidality, may be intense. Therapists need support and ways to remain grounded, calm, and able to set clear limits with compassion.

Thus, the therapist must find ways to remain calm, curious, and connected with the patient in the face of enormous pressure to act and needs a coherent and relational approach at hand. It is essential to understand that the therapist's own reactions to the patient's ongoing unsafe behaviors play a major role in whether the patient is able to successfully adopt more adaptive coping strategies. The value of ongoing consultation or supervision cannot be overstated.

A Helpful Therapeutic Stance

Therapists must first and foremost understand unsafe behaviors as coping strategies or attempts at problem-solving, often for relational conflicts or loneliness. This allows us to remain curious about how these substitute actions are helping the patient. Only once this is understood do we focus on alternative and more adaptive strategies that the patient can learn.

Second, therapists must recognize the tremendous amount of pain and suffering that leads to unsafe behaviors. This allows them to remain compassionate toward a suffering human being, rather than seeing the behavior as thwarting the therapist's efforts. At all times the patient should be treated with dignity and respect, as a capable adult. A supportive, compassionate, relational stance in which reasonable limits are consistently maintained is the most effective strategy to reduce and eliminate unsafe behaviors. At the same time, both therapist and patient need to understand that therapy cannot progress until these behaviors are contained.

CORE CONCEPT

While therapists can be instrumental in offering help and guidance, it is the patient as a whole who is ultimately responsible for remaining safe. The therapist cannot save the patient, and safety must not become a power struggle between them.

Third, therapists must accept that the patient alone makes the ultimate decision about whether to remain safe or not (Chu, 2011). This is sometimes one of the hardest facts for therapists to accept. It is only natural that our caregiving system is strongly activated when a patient is being hurt. It is not in our nature to stand idly by and watch a disaster unfold. Yet, therapists can no more control what their patients do than they can control any other adult in their lives. Patients make their own choices, for better or worse. The therapist's role is to be a compassionate witness, to point out the pros and cons, to offer more adaptive alternatives, to explore the goals and conflicts of the patient. Sometimes therapists must intervene by hospitalizing the patient when physical harm is severe or self-injury is unremitting. But unsafe behaviors must not become a power struggle between patient and therapist.

Therapists can encourage and support the patient to try different strategies, but are ultimately powerless in this regard. Patients may experience themselves as helpless and desperately try to get the therapist to engage in rescue. But ultimately, we cannot save the patient, nor love the patient into health, nor be available enough to prevent unsafe behavior if the patient continues to choose this road. In fact, too much availability disempowers the patient, giving the implicit message that the patient is incompetent. Being overly available and solicitous may evoke overwhelming dependency needs, which then triggers further unsafe behaviors (see Chapter 13 on dependency).

Therapists must respectfully and compassionately remind the patient time and again that they have agreed on a collaborative treatment contract that includes safety, and that while the therapist will help to the degree possible, patients must do the work and be responsible for their own safety.

Finally, therapists must know when and when not to intervene, and how to intervene in ways that support the patient's competence and autonomy rather than promote dependence on the actions of the therapist. Patients often live in long-term crisis. We do not help the patient by becoming embroiled in a constant emergency atmosphere. Limit setting in terms of how much and when the therapist will respond to the patient between sessions is paramount. The exception is if the therapist is a strict adherent to the dialectical behavior therapy protocol of being available to the patient for skills coaching (Linehan, 1993, 2014). While this may be helpful for many patients, a few may have an adverse reaction, calling even more for coaching (see the section below, "When the Patient Is Unwilling to Take Responsibility for Safety"). Crisis phone calls should be very brief, focused on what the patient has already tried to alleviate the crisis, some grounding, and a safety plan until the next session. Therapy should not be done over the phone in these situations.

Sleep-deprived therapists are not going to be able to make the best decisions and interventions for a patient who calls during the night, or for the rest of their patients the next day. Thus, some limits on after-hours phone calls may be necessary. We strongly recommend that therapists do not give their home numbers to patients, but rather rely on an answering service or voice mail. The therapist can tell patients something like, *I check my voice mail throughout the day and up until about 7 p.m. If you have an urgent crisis between 7 p.m. and 8 a.m., here are the numbers you can call* (crisis services, hotlines, 911, etc.).

Of course, on occasion there may be a reason that the therapist offers more contact than usual to a patient. This should be done, at least for a while, with consultation, as there are many complex reasons why this may or may not be helpful to a given patient. Remember, not all patients are the same, and there may be patients where being slightly more lax is helpful and other patients who need much tighter boundaries.

Below is a list of unsafe behaviors. This is not comprehensive, but it does include most of the major categories of unsafe behaviors.

Unsafe Behaviors

- Self-injury (cutting, burning, head banging, pulling hair or nails, etc.)
- Suicide gestures or attempts (must be distinguished from self-harm)
- Severe alcohol and drug abuse; prescription abuse (addictions have been described as attachment disorders (Flores, 2011), which helps therapists further understand the need for safety, collaboration and careful management of attachment issues in therapy)
- Severe eating problems: restricting, overeating, bingeing and purging
- Prostitution and unsafe sexual behaviors
- Theft or other illegal activities like dealing drugs
- Overspending, gambling
- Thrill-seeking behaviors that include excessive risk taking (e.g., driving too fast, mountain climbing without proper equipment or preparation, hanging out in a dangerous area of the city)
- Physical assault
- Sadism toward self and others
- Masochism in which the patient willingly submits to emotional or physical pain from another
- Seeking unsafe or dangerous relationships
- Ongoing abuse by original perpetrators or others

The Functions of Unsafe Behaviors

Unsafe behaviors are almost always attempts to regulate unbearable emotions and social isolation, self-hatred and shame, feelings of rejection and abandonment, rage, traumatic memories, or profound emptiness and depersonalization (Ferentz, 2014; Klonsky, 2007; Walsh, 2014). In addition, inner conflicts among dissociative parts may further result in unsafe behaviors (Boon et al., 2011). For example, one part of the patient punishes another part with self-injury for feeling pleasure during sexual abuse; or one part engages in prostitution, while another part is highly religious and mortified at any sexual behavior; or one part drinks and uses drugs, while another finds that behavior immature and destructive. Amnesia for and conflict about unsafe behaviors among parts of the patient complicates the treatment of these substitute actions. Unless the therapist can work to resolve conflicts with the parts that are engaging in the behaviors, either by talking through or directly, they are unlikely to abate. Specific approaches to working with dissociative parts that are self-injuring will be discussed below.

Self-Injury and Suicidality

Self-injury and suicidality are probably the most commonly encountered unsafe behaviors in patients with a complex dissociative disorder. They can derail the therapy and paralyze both patient and therapist. The onset of self-injury in patients who have not been hurting themselves requires special attention by the therapist. It is entirely possible that the therapist is not pacing the therapy sufficiently, and the patient is feeling overwhelmed. This is especially true when traumatic memories are the focus of current treatment.

The therapist must make careful inquiries about unsafe behaviors with all parts of the patient. Sometimes while one part is saying the pace of treatment is fine, and even too slow, other parts are overwhelmed. This may involve child parts fixed in trauma-time, or perpetrator-imitating parts that are attempting to stop the patient from remembering because it is perceived as dangerous (see Chapters 14 and 17 for specific approaches to working with these types of parts). If this is the case, the therapist must discuss the issue with the patient and slow down the therapy, stop the focus on memory work with careful explanation, and return to stabilization skills and working with conflicts among dissociative parts that may underlie unsafe behaviors.

Another possibility is some disruption in the therapeutic relationship has preceded self-injury, in which the patient's abandonment fears have been triggered, or shame about dependency needs, or other relational misattunement has occurred. The therapist can say something like, *I wonder if there is something I have done or missed that has caused a painful breach between us, and if you had some pretty overwhelming feelings about that. Could we explore that possibility?*

Of course, unsafe behaviors are not only due to therapy events. They may occur in the wake of any sort of general life distress or trigger that overwhelms a particular patient, such as making a mistake at work, breaking up with a romantic partner, being criticized, feeling unable to manage caring for one's own children, the spontaneous emergence of a dissociative part or traumatic memory, an increase in depression or anxiety, or having a child leave home for school for the first time.

Self-Injury

Self-inflicted pain and injury are attempts at problem-solving. These may be concrete ways to display shame and disgust at a vulnerable body that was unable to protect the patient and had to endure unbearable suffering and humiliation. Often self-harm is an attempt to reduce tension, relieve unbearable emotions, and communicate in a concrete way what patients cannot communicate in words (Physical injury is the only way I can communicate to you the depth of my pain). Some patients injure themselves in ways that cannot easily be seen or known (such as genital or breast mutilation) and rarely reveal it. Other patients may injure themselves where it is likely to be seen, such as on the forearms, as a way to directly show their inner suffering and get help from others; it serves as a relational communication. Some patients engage in self-injury in order to prevent the greater harm of a suicide attempt. Unfortunately, on rare occasions, severe self-injury can result in death even when the patient's intent is not to commit suicide.

Self-injury can take many forms, but cutting, burning, hair pulling, slamming a fist against the wall, and head banging are some of the most common. It can range from superficial scratches to severe injuries that need emergency medical care. Of course, these behaviors can evoke intense feelings of shame in the patient and all kinds of unhelpful reactions in people around the patient, including therapists. For example, emergency medical personnel (and even some crisis psychiatric staff) who must care for self-inflicted wounds or the aftermath of suicide attempts may castigate, shame, and hurt the patient (for example, during the stitching of wounds), showing no compassion or understanding. They may treat the patient roughly, as though the patient deserves poor treatment because of disgusting behavior. This only adds greater shame and propensity to self-injure in patients who actually are much more likely to improve when they are treated with dignity and respect (Christoffersen, Møhl, DePanfilis, & Vammen, 2015).

Some addictive self-injury involves an organized routine or ritual. For example, a patient might intentionally "set the mood" and put on certain music, light candles, lay out specific instruments with which to self-injure, and even prepare bandages and medication to apply afterward. Self-injury or other unsafe behaviors may happen in a specific way or in a particular location (for example, the patient's bedroom or bathroom, in a park at night). Most certainly, self-injury often occurs in private or when the patient is alone. However, it may also impulsively occur in sessions; for example, sudden head banging or punching oneself in the face when intense emotion or frustration arises. A few patients may actually plan to self-injure in session. This is most often due to a rupture in the therapeutic relationship or a blatant attempt to end therapy by parts that want to avoid it.

After the patient is grounded, the therapist should make clear that self-harm in sessions is not acceptable under any circumstances and that all parts must agree to prevent it. Otherwise, the patient may continue, and the therapist will have to intervene time and again. The patient as a whole should be responsible for refraining from self-harm in sessions. This must be done without shaming the patient, in a compassionate but firm way, emphasizing the importance of maintaining a safe space in therapy. Both therapist and patient should examine carefully and thoroughly what triggered the self-harm episode and determine if therapy needs to be adjusted to keep the patient better within a window of tolerance.

Ritualized behavior in self-injury has a trance effect on the patient, increasing the likelihood of unsafe behavior. If the therapist can help the patient change the routine and introduce novelty, trance and automatic behaviors are less likely to occur. For example, the patient can be asked to dispose of a favorite instrument of self-injury, such as a razor blade. This, in itself, will sometimes reduce self-injury.

Suicidality

Chronic suicidal feelings are very much a part of the experience of most patients with dissociative disorders. Patients who self-injure are also highly likely to be suicidal (Paul, Tsypes, Eidlitz, Ernhout, & Whitlock, 2015), and chronic suicidality is common in dissociative patients (Foote et al., 2008). Most patients can distinguish between a chronic wish to die and "get it over with" and a clear intent. However, a major problem in dissociative patients is that they are sometimes unaware of highly suicidal parts and their intentions. Thus, some patients end up hospitalized after making an attempt "out of the blue," for which they have amnesia, with therapist and patient both puzzled about what has happened and why.

CORE CONCEPT

A major problem in dissociative patients is that they are often unaware of and cannot control dissociative parts that engage in unsafe behaviors. Thus, they often cannot explain why they hurt themselves.

Therapists should take care not to become so focused on instituting emergency measures that they fail to explore issues of suicidality with the patient. They should take the time to explore reasons why the patient, or a particular dissociative part, is suicidal, as this may give some insight into interventions that will help. Many suicidal parts are stuck in trauma-time and not well oriented to the present.

CASE EXAMPLE OF SUICIDAL DISSOCIATIVE PART STUCK IN TRAUMA-TIME: KAREN

Karen was a 36-year-old patient with DID who had a 13-year-old part that was intent on suicide. Instead of immediately arranging for hospitalization, the therapist took the time to explore the intent. When he asked about Karen's plan, she said she was going to shoot herself with her uncle's gun. The therapist knew that the uncle was deceased, so he began further inquiry to establish whether this part was oriented in time.

Therapist: So, how do you plan to get your uncle's gun?

Karen (as 13-year-old part): I'll wait until he goes to work and get it from his closet.

Therapist: Where does your uncle live?

Karen (as 13-year-old part): Just down the street from me.

Therapist: Sorry, which city is that?

Karen (as 13-year-old part): San Francisco

Therapist: Do you know where you are now—I mean, which city?

Karen (as 13-year-old part): (Somewhat irritated) Of course, I am in San Francisco.

Therapist: No, actually, you are in Atlanta. You are in my office in Atlanta.

Karen (as 13-year-old part): I don't understand. I just want his gun.

Therapist: Yes, I can see it's very confusing for you. But you see, you no longer live in San Francisco. You live here in Atlanta. You are no longer 13. You are now 36 and an adult who is safe. You left San Francisco a very long time ago. Your uncle died some years ago and does not live in that house anymore. His gun isn't there.

Karen (as 13-year-old part): (Looking extremely confused and anxious) I don't know what you are talking about. I am just going down the street to get the gun.

Therapist: I am sorry that you feel so confused, but it's very important for you to know that your uncle no longer hurts you. That is over now. I can imagine you wanted to kill yourself then, but maybe you need a bit of time to get used to being here, so you can sort it out with me. Let's see if other parts inside can help you right now.

> The adolescent part of Karen believed she was still being abused and felt the only way out was to kill herself. Once she got more oriented to the present, though she still felt suicidal, the suicidal intent to get the uncle's gun drastically decreased.

Parts that are completely stuck in trauma-time live in chronic flashbacks, physical pain, fear, terror, distrust, shame, guilt, hopelessness, anger, and sadness. They do not have any hope for the future and do not participate in actual current life. It is no wonder that they are so suicidal. They tend to have very rigid negative beliefs about themselves and others, including a belief that they do not deserve to live, or that no one cares about them, or that the world is better off without them. Other parts, such as those that function in daily life, may hold different beliefs, though in extremely suicidal patients most parts may share a common suicidal thread. The more that parts functioning in daily life avoid parts stuck in trauma-time, the more the latter can spiral down within their own rigid world of trance-logic solutions. And the more distress these parts cause internally, the more parts in daily life seek a solution to their suffering, often with unsafe behaviors.

Suicidality in parts that function in daily life. Suicidality can also be a problem for parts of the patient that function in daily life. Patients are often constantly on the run to avoid overwhelming inner experiences or realization that traumatic experiences actually happened. In these parts, suicidal feelings or impulses can be caused by:

- gradual exhaustion from constant avoidance, leading to fewer choices, a more narrow life, and a wish to die;
- gradual or sudden realization that something bad really did happen;
- command voices (usually perpetrator-imitating parts) that become stronger, telling them to end their life, especially as they get close to disclosing traumatic events; or
- a realization that they are engaging—in their opinion—in disgusting behaviors (e.g., prostitution, stealing). This activates thoughts like *If I am really like that, I do not want to live*, or *If I really enjoyed sex with my grandfather, I don't deserve to live.*

Interventions to Treat Unsafe Behaviors

There are many approaches to reducing and eliminating unsafe behaviors. The majority of them have emerged from third-generation cognitive behavioral approaches, such as DBT (Ferentz, 2014; Gratz & Gunderson, 2006;

Linehan, 1993, 2014; Walsh, 2014. However, we should always remember that emotion regulation—the essential antidote to unsafe behaviors—first occurs in relationship with another. Our therapeutic relationship with the unsafe patient is, or needs to be, the essential healing factor. To be seen and heard, to be accepted with dignity and compassion, are often new experiences for our patients, and ones which may offer them the support they need to move from substitute actions to adaptive ones. Their unsafe behaviors are a profound outcry against isolation and the terrible, even catastrophic, experience of utter aloneness in their suffering. The therapist's ability to be with patients in these devastating moments often proves to be foundational for these patients to gradually overcome deep shame and learn to accept themselves and their own experiences and emotions.

The Importance of Inquiring About Unsafe Behaviors

First and foremost, therapists should always ask about unsafe behaviors in a nonjudgmental way, being compassionate and rather matter-of-fact. This does not ensure that they will always learn of every unsafe behavior, but at least the subject has been broached, and therapists should continue to ask on occasion as the situation warrants. They should not ever assume that the patient is safe without inquiring first.

The patient may benefit from a shame-reducing approach, which can be accomplished with the therapist's compassionate understanding and with psychoeducation about why people engage in unsafe behaviors. The therapist can explain that these are substitute actions that are attempts at solving problems and to cope with difficult feelings. This approach reduces shame and stigma, and focuses on how the patient can learn new strategies. Then therapist and patient together can explore the purposes of self-harm. Once the meaning of the behavior is understood, appropriate strategies to use other skills can be determined.

Working With Dissociative Parts to Stop Unsafe Behaviors

The patient as a whole or parts that present in therapy must agree that staying alive is a condition for further treatment and that it is their own responsibility, not the therapist's, although the therapist will help. There may be major conflict in the patient, in particular among parts, about whether the patient really wants to live, or even get better. Often perpetrator-imitating parts are vehemently opposed—at least on the surface—to therapy, to improvements of any kind, and to the very idea of safety, which is a foreign concept. Their reasons for such a stance need to be carefully explored over time.

Therapists can consistently talk through (see Chapter 10) to all parts of the patient, reminding them that:

- safety is paramount for therapy to be effective;
- therapy can be paced according to what can be tolerated, and parts are asked to help the therapist recognize when the pace is too fast;
- all parts are responsible for helping the patient as a whole become safer;
- safety is ultimately up to the patient as a whole, not the therapist;
- the therapist will do his or her best to help the patient find other ways that are more effective in coping with unbearable feelings;
- the more patient and therapist can understand and resolve inner conflicts among parts, the quicker the patient will become safe; and
- it is essential for parts to begin to have compassion for each other, as this also promotes safety and harm reduction.

The therapist may serve as a "go-between" or negotiator among parts, explaining the functions of unsafe behavior to parts that are functioning in daily life, and trying to improve inner communication and some compassion among parts. Parts functioning in daily life need to be helped to overcome their phobia for parts fixed in unsafe behaviors and to develop understanding and some compassion for these parts.

Unsafe behaviors may occur when the patient or part of the patient is stuck in trauma-time and not fully oriented to the here and now or triggered by unbearable inner experiences as well as external triggers. Often there is little to no realization in the patient as a whole as to what has triggered these behaviors, because the patient lacks the ability to carefully reflect. Moreover, some unsafe behaviors are addictive, as they may release endorphins and thus act as a kind of self-medication. The patient finds it quite difficult to give up these moments of euphoria.

Suggestions for alternative, more adaptive ways of regulating emotions only make sense if there is a minimal therapeutic alliance with the part of the patient that is engaging in unsafe behavior and with the patient as a whole. If the part feels understood by the therapist and, even more importantly, that part of the patient does not feel rejected by other parts (especially those functioning in daily life), willingness to give up old habits and learn new techniques to deal with emotions will increase. The more acceptance and compassion there is among parts, the more successful interventions will be.

Making a Safety Plan
The patient and therapist together should make a written safety plan for the patient to carry at all times. It may include any of the many emotion-regulation, grounding, mindfulness, and reflective skills that have been shown to decrease and eliminate unsafe behaviors (e.g., Ferentz, 2014; Gratz & Gunderson, 2006; Linehan, 2014; Walsh, 2014).

CORE CONCEPT

A written safety plan is essential. It should include ways for the
patient to engage inner parts in seeking safety and ways to regulate
and soothe.

Interventions for compassionate acceptance of emotion, emotion regulation, distress tolerance and distraction, and others are helpful in reducing the need for unsafe behaviors. A sample safety plan is included in
Appendix C.

When Unsafe Behaviors Occur in Session

The therapist should immediately stop any type of unsafe behavior during
sessions or in the office surroundings, such as head banging, hitting, or
slapping. This behavior not only interferes with the patient's therapy; it is
disruptive to other staff and patients, and it creates an atmosphere of crisis
and lack of safety that is not conducive to a reasonable work environment.

CORE CONCEPT

Self-harm in sessions is not acceptable under any circumstances and
must be immediately stopped.

The therapist first asks, firmly and compassionately, that the patient
immediately stop: *I am asking all parts of you to help you stop hitting yourself
(or pulling your hair, etc.) right now. This behavior is not acceptable in the office.
This must remain a safe place, free of any kind of harm.* After waiting just a
brief moment, if the behavior does not stop, the therapist can say, *I am
going to reach over and hold your wrists firmly so that you cannot continue this
behavior. Let's get you more calm, and then you can try to use some words to
describe what you are feeling.* Or, if the therapist does not use touch: *I am
asking all parts to help you stop hitting yourself immediately. Otherwise, I will
need to stop the session until you can regain control.*

When the Patient Is Unwilling to Take Responsibility for Staying Safe

In the rare case that a patient is unwilling to take basic responsibility for
staying alive or safe, after a reasonable amount of work with unsafe behaviors in traditional ways such as DBT or using addiction models, therapists
may need to change the treatment plan, or even reassess whether they
have the experience and boundary-setting capacity to continue the ther-

apy. For a few patients, the more attention they get for unsafe behaviors, the more they escalate. They end up in repetitive loops of crisis and hospitalization. This often involves an increasing dependency on the therapist. Patients may constantly call, e-mail, or text the therapist, day and night, in the midst of self-injury or when they are about to make a suicide attempt.

- *I am standing on the edge of the bridge about to jump.*
- *I'm driving 90 miles an hour and am going to run off the road.*
- *I have 12 bottles of pills and am going to take them if you haven't called in the next 15 minutes.*
- *I just burned both my arms with an iron and am working on my legs now. I hope you can stop me.*
- *I'm just writing to say goodbye and to thank you for all you have done for me. No need to respond, as I know it is the weekend and you are not available.*
- *Just letting you know I took 30 pills a minute ago. Only 200 more to go.*
- *I am on the street about to get in a car with a man. Don't tell me to have safe sex. That is ridiculous.*

Sometimes these patients also hurt themselves in session or just afterward in the parking lot, or during hospitalization. The therapist may be of two minds. One tendency is to offer more therapy, more sessions, more crisis phone calls, more hospitalizations. For these few patients, however, more is not the answer. Even when hospitalized, they may continue to engage in behaviors that only prolong their hospitalization. The other tendency is for therapists to throw up their hands in disgust and anger, wishing to say, *Go ahead and do whatever you want. I'm done with you.* This also is not the answer. The key is for the therapist not to become overly engaged in rescuing and caretaking on the one hand or too distanced on the other. A compassionate stance focused on process *and* skills and that clearly places the responsibility of the patient's safety on the patient is essential.

CORE CONCEPT

For the rare patient who continues to escalate crisis calls for unsafe behaviors in spite of the patient learning good skills and after the role of dissociative parts has been addressed, a special approach may be needed in which the therapist, after careful consultation, becomes less available except during sessions.

Therapists must have considerable fortitude and experience in treating this type of problem, as they must take some degree of risk to allow the patient to accept their responsibility for safety. However, taking such risk should only be done with consultation and in the context of a unified treatment team, perhaps even with legal consultation. Therapists should never treat such a patient alone and in isolation. For example, the therapist, psychiatrist, group therapist, perhaps a primary care physician, and any other treating professionals should meet and agree on a specific modified plan. Otherwise, the risk of splitting among the team drastically increases, with one wanting to intervene more with the patient and another not.

The therapist insists with the patient that in order to continue treatment, a treatment team is needed and its members must communicate with each other. The therapist reiterates that all parts of the patient are responsible for safety, as usual, and does not fall into a trap of believing that one part is responsible for unsafe behaviors or that patients are completely unable to control their behavior.

CASE EXAMPLE OF HELPING THE PATIENT BE RESPONSIBLE FOR HER OWN SAFETY: REBECCA

Rebecca was a patient with DID who had recently had several weeks of inpatient treatment for bulimarexia. However, she continued to hover at her minimum acceptable weight and engage in restricting and purging to the point of altering her electrolytes. The therapist needed to decide if she could work with Rebecca on an outpatient basis or whether she needed to refer her to a higher level of care.

Therapist: I am very willing to continue therapy with you, but if your weight gets so low again that your life is in danger, I will have to refer you to hospital treatment and will not be able to see you until you are stabilized. I very much would like to continue our treatment, so I hope that you decide this is something you want to do.

Rebecca: But you know I have no control over this behavior. I sometimes can taste that I have vomited, but it happens in a blackout. How can you tell me that it is my responsibility? I have amnesia! I really want this to go away! I thought that you were an expert in dissociation and could help me!

Therapist: I am absolutely willing to help you and try to understand why a part of you withholds food or purges, and to help you as a whole person to make healthy changes. But treatment is a two-way street where we both have responsibilities. I cannot keep you alive; only you can choose to do that. It is impossible to treat you as an outpatient if your physical condition interferes with your ability to engage in treatment. Our agreement is for psychotherapy, which we can only continue when your weight stays out of the danger zone so you are safe. You are near starvation, which affects your thinking and judgment. So, yes, I very much want to continue with you; and yes, it is completely your choice to maintain a physical condition that makes therapy possible, and I do not want to be in a power struggle with you. It is up to you to keep your end of our agreement. I am sure the part of you that does not eat must have a reason, and I hope we can get to that soon. But you are avoiding that part of yourself, which is why you have amnesia. I am glad to help you take small, manageable steps toward becoming more aware, but your weight must remain at or above 120 pounds (54 kg.) and your electrolytes must be within normal limits for us to do that. And you must check in with your medical doctor regularly, and he and I will collaborate with you in this way. I very much hope that you can agree to your end of the treatment contract, as I believe that is what we both want.

As noted above, the therapist makes a very specific safety plan with the patient *in writing*, and then gives it to the patient, with certain parameters outlined below. These may vary to some degree but might look something like the following.

- The therapist defines her role as an outpatient provider who is not an emergency responder.
- The patient is expected to attend therapy as usual and can work on safety issues during sessions.
- The patient has the usual list of many interventions with which he can prevent unsafe behaviors.
- The patient must not engage in self-injury or other unsafe behavior in the office or on the premises, or he will be referred out for treatment elsewhere.
- Instead of calling the therapist, the patient is to call 911 or go to the nearest emergency center if he feels unsafe, as they are most able to respond quickly and effectively.
- The patient should not text or e-mail the therapist about any unsafe behavior, as these are not adequate ways to communicate an emergency.
- The patient is not to call the therapist after hours, but is to call 911 or go to the nearest emergency center.
- Some therapists also specify that these few patients should not call them during business hours with a safety crisis, but rather always call 911 or go to an emergency center. This is not usual, but is a spe-

cific therapeutic intervention that the whole treatment team must agree upon.

- Therapists should get consultation and legal advice about what is appropriate for their particular situation.
- If the patient does call the therapist during business hours to report unsafe behaviors and refuses to disclose his location, the therapist will compassionately tell the patient that he must do what is necessary to get safe and that there is no help the therapist can offer in this situation.
- If a confused or child part calls to report unsafe behaviors and says he does not know where he is, the therapist responds, *There is always a part inside that knows where you are, and that part needs to help you now go to a safe place. I am sorry, but I cannot help when I do not know where you are. Just allow that part of you to come forward and help you, and I will be glad to talk with you about this when we meet in our next session.*

Highly dissociative patients may find it helpful to have a GPS so they can locate themselves and get home, or have their home address and the phone number of a close friend or partner in their wallet or purse.

- If the patient is hospitalized, the therapist will make contact with the staff to coordinate treatment, but will not be directly in contact with the patient until after discharge, and then only in scheduled sessions.
- The patient is not offered additional phone calls, check-ins, or additional sessions in the beginning of this modified treatment plan. As the patient's behavior improves, it might be an option to allow him to leave a voice mail for the therapist to report successful management of unsafe behaviors after the fact. This may reinforce the patient's competence and pride. However, some patients will be unable to tolerate this contact, and their behavior may revert back into self-injury.
- Once the patient has taken reasonable responsibility his safety, the therapy can again focus on particular parts of the patient that are unsafe, with an emphasis on how all parts of the patient can help.

CASE EXAMPLE OF THE COMPLEXITIES OF WORKING WITH PARTS THAT ENGAGE IN UNSAFE BEHAVIORS: MARIA

The following case illustrates the many layers and complexities of the functions of unsafe behaviors, and the system dynamics among parts that maintain these behaviors. Although many patients are not so complex, the interventions of the therapist remain quite similar.

Maria was a 28-year-old woman who had been in treatment for DID for two years and was still in Phase 1. She was a student, and she lived alone. She had previous treatment in an outpatient clinic for severe bulimarexia, a combination of eating disorders that is not unusual in dissociative disorders. During treatment for her eating disorder it had become clear that she was dissociative, and she was then referred for treatment of her dissociative disorder. In the first year of treatment for her DID, therapy continued to focus on her eating disorder, as this remained a severe problem. Maria was afraid that she would end up in an inpatient clinic for eating disorders, as had happened in her adolescence. She felt angry, afraid, and powerless with regard to parts of her that took control and refused to eat, or that were bingeing and purging without her apparent awareness. The therapist tried to engage these parts of Maria in therapy, but they were defensive and kept a distance, refusing to dialogue with the therapist.

The therapist continued with psychoeducation session after session, talking through to these parts of Maria. Once they understood that the therapist wanted to help them and did not intend to hospitalize them, provided that Maria maintain a minimum weight, these parts of Maria finally began to engage in treatment. The therapist introduced many coping skills to Maria, such as grounding, emotion regulation, and working with dissociative parts, and helped her develop a comprehensive safety plan. Nevertheless, many of her eating problems persisted, and Maria continued to have amnesia for significant amounts of time most days.

As the therapist explored the patient's inner world, a 13-year-old part that called herself "Lydia" eventually emerged. She told the therapist she was afraid of getting pregnant and kept her body weight low so she would not menstruate, something that disgusted her. She was convinced that she was in danger all the time, and restricting her eating gave her a sense of control. She seemed unaware of the dangers of a chronic low body weight. Lydia was also ashamed of her body, and hated sex and men. She did not want the therapist to interfere with her eating habits.

Maria herself seemed indifferent to her eating, a sort of *belle indifférence*, as though what she ate was not relevant to her. Maria was generally very passive and depressed in therapy, often not knowing the answers to questions, drifting off to daydream or even to sleep. She reported extensive time loss, but seemed to function at school adequately.

The therapist spent several sessions validating Lydia's reasons for not eating, understanding that of course she did not want to get pregnant, and perhaps not eating seemed the only way Lydia could ensure this. They talked about Lydia's shame of her female body, while Maria was quite indifferent to her body and, indeed, often was physically numb. Gradually, this part of Maria was overcoming her mistrust of the therapist and becoming less hostile and distant.

Lydia began complaining about "Alexa," a part of Maria that stuffed herself with food. Upon exploration, the therapist understood this was a child part that tended to overeat, and even stole food from the store as a reenactment and a way to avoid feelings of loneliness. This behavior bothered Lydia, as she wanted to keep her weight low. Internally, Lydia refused to interact with Alexa but reported "locking her up" inside so she could not eat. Lydia was disgusted by Alexa, and had no curiosity about why she was always wanting to eat. Yet, no matter how often Lydia locked up this child part, Alexa continued to find ways to stuff herself with food. Thus, the therapist understood that at least two parts of Maria were involved in the bulimarexia, and likely for different reasons.

The therapist suggested that Maria could communicate with Alexa with the help of the therapist. The therapist first suggested that they try to understand what sort of problems Alexa was trying to solve with her eating, just as the therapist had tried to understand Lydia.

Alexa appeared frightened and complained of hunger because her mother was always punishing her by locking her in the basement without food. She was always eating because she never knew when her mother would lock her up again without food. Clearly, Alexa was fixed in trauma-time and was not oriented to the present. She seemed to relive her past experiences with her mother each time Lydia was "locking her up again" internally. Maria, who was the main part that functioned in daily life, had not been aware of these inner conflicts and, in fact, she had been unaware of Lydia and Alexa, though she was aware of time loss and felt her eating disorder was out of her control. Maria was very ashamed when she heard that the little girl part of her sometimes stole food, but she was also angry with Lydia for locking up this part. She was also angry that Lydia was worried about getting pregnant, as she vehemently denied she was having sex.

The therapist helped these parts of Maria find a common goal of avoiding further hospitalization. With some explanation from the therapist, Lydia understood that locking up Alexa internally was triggering painful memories and only increased the tendency to eat too much. An imaginary safe space was developed for Alexa, a place with plenty of food and light. Maria became more willing to take care of this young part of herself, making sure she was safe, and inviting her to experience actual meals with her on a regular basis, as well as helping her orient to the present and use anchors in the present as reminders. Lydia agreed to a baseline weight, though she still restricted food. This process took several months of hardwork. Maria reported a greater sense of peace internally, and the intensity of her binge eating and purging dramatically decreased. This was a major success.

However, Lydia was still convinced she was in danger of getting pregnant, while Maria continued to deny she was being sexual. Maria also continued to have significant amnesia in daily life, particularly in the evenings. The therapist wondered what was happening during those times, but neither Maria nor Lydia seemed to know. Yet Lydia reported strange flashes of images of being with men, and insisted this was in the present, not the past. The therapist had no way of knowing if this was indeed happening in the present or not.

One day Maria came to the session extremely upset. She refused to make eye contact with the therapist, finally saying she had found "disgusting stuff" in a drawer at home. It took the entire session to understand that Maria had found sex toys, including handcuffs. Lydia came forward and said, *See, I told you, I saw men! She is a liar. It is dangerous after all; I should never have trusted you!* Immediately following, Maria came forward, upset and crying, *I don't want to live anymore; this is too horrible. This is not me. I cannot live with this.*

The therapist did her best to ground Maria and contain her many emotions, but had to end the session as it was already late in the hour. In order to end the session on time, the therapist said: *Maria, I would like to talk to all parts of you inside. This must be a real shock on some level to you, and perhaps you feel unsafe. But could you agree with me that we need a little more time to fully understand what is going on, just like we needed when we were working with Lydia and Alexa earlier? I agree with you that you need to be safe. I wonder if perhaps some part of you has allowed you to know about this "stuff" so you can now get help with it. In the meantime, let's help all parts of you to put these thoughts and feelings in a safe container, to be opened a few minutes after you come into my office for your next session.*

Maria agreed to keep herself safe. She returned to the next appointment two days later. Maria had locked herself in the house "to stay safe" during that time, but at least had some compassion for Lydia's sense of betrayal, and in return, Lydia had allowed Maria to eat a little. The therapist asked Maria if there might be any part of her mind that knew more about what she had found. Maria said she did not know, but shifted to another part of herself at this point, one that the therapist had never encountered.

Maria (as this part): What do you want? I bet you have never engaged in sadomasochistic sex; you are too dull, just like Maria. She is so stupid! She wonders what happens in the evenings. Does she have any idea who is paying for her school? Her scholarship barely covers anything at all! She doesn't even think about it! That's her way, not to think about things she doesn't want to know.

Therapist: Yes, Maria does indeed have a hard time realizing painful things she doesn't want to talk about, and she is working on that. It seems you are able to know more about this issue than Maria. You are somehow helping her pay for school without her awareness. Does this have something to do with why she doesn't remember her evenings?

Maria (as this part): Yeah. (Laughing) She has no idea how I make money. And that stupid Lydia should know that of course I take precautions. I don't want to get pregnant with a baby. Maria hates men; she should like what I do to them! I make them suffer. Those toys are not for nothing! And you aren't going to take that away from me. Nobody can!

Immediately afterward, Maria returned, but the therapist continued talking through to this part of Maria.

Therapist: I appreciate that you explained a little about what is happening, and I am hoping you are willing to talk with me further. It's curious that that you did not wait for my response. I wonder if perhaps you are worried that I might try to take something away from you. In fact, I would very much like to further understand your position.

This part of Maria came forward again.

Maria (as this part): Lydia knows much more about my work than she told you. *[A common experience with dissociative patients: Amnesia is not always as complete as it seems.]* She is simply pretending that she does not know me because she is ashamed. But she has been with me in the past with men. I have sex with them. I hurt them. I had to take over because she was not tough enough. She didn't really like it, but I do. It's exciting, and at least people see me and pay attention! And now, I can keep the money I make myself; in the past, my mother took everything. She used to sell me to men—did you know that? Now I am the boss!

Therapist: Yes, Maria has shared with me that your mother gave you to men for money. That must has been truly awful. I am glad that I am getting a chance to understand more that you experience a greater sense of control when you are having sex with men and using the money yourself.

Maria (as this part): Yeah, yeah. It's no big deal, this sex stuff. You say nice things, but I know you think I am disgusting, just like Maria. You just want to make me stop. But forget it!

Therapist: Well, I am completely not interested in taking away anything from you; and, in fact, that would be impossible. What you do is completely up to you as a whole person. However, it is clear that there is quite some conflict inside about what is happening; would you agree?

Also, I am surprised that you believe I think you are disgusting. How did you reach that conclusion? *[It is important that the therapist not overly reassure the patient about the therapist's good intentions, as actions will speak louder than words over time. But the therapist should firmly reassure the patient that the locus of control remains completely with her. Finally, the therapist returns the conflict to where it belongs: within the patient, not between the patient and therapist.]*

Maria (as this part): I know people. They are always disgusted. I am sure when Maria realizes who pays for her books, she will be disgusted and never want money from a dominatrix whore! *(Laughing)* But then she will be in real financial hot water. You have really messed things up. She was fine until she started therapy. *(Becoming angry)*

Therapist: I agree that this is a shock for Maria, but I understand that you try to help her, even if it is in a way Maria may not like. Although you may not believe me, I do not judge you. I suspect that you have helped Maria since she was a child. In fact, you told me you had to take over to protect Lydia. So I know that you also tried to help her. But I wonder, do you really believe that everything was fine when Maria came to see me?

Maria (as this part): Yes, my life was perfect! And Maria could do her boring study, just like she wanted! Look what happened these past two days—she didn't even go out of the house. You think that is an improvement? It was far better when she did not know about me.

Therapist: You have a point. But she has told me how depressed and anxious she was, often feeling confused about where she was or what had just happened. Are you aware of that? *(No response.)* How is it that you always managed to hide the sex toys, and now suddenly Maria finds them? I wonder if perhaps somewhere inside there was a hope that maybe this conflict could be resolved if we could work on it together. And also, I wonder if Maria was ready in some way to find them, to accept that you are part of her life, as shameful and painful as that may seem to her. I somehow trust that you are both working together in therapy to make your life better eventually.

Maria (as this part): You are always talking bullshit. I don't know why we come here.

Therapist: I am guessing that you know somewhere within yourself, or else you would not be coming here. Would you be willing to share with Maria what we have talked about?

Maria (as this part): No way! She won't talk to me.

Therapist: OK, what about sharing with Lydia, who can then share it with Maria?

Maria (as this part): Whatever. Lydia is listening anyway. She can tell Maria whatever she wants. I don't care.

Therapist: Good. And I certainly hope that we can continue our conversation, as you are a very important part of Maria.

The therapist quietly sat with Maria as Lydia shared with her internally some selected facts about this other part of herself, which Lydia referred to as "the Tiger." On the one hand, Maria was shocked and dismayed, but on the other, she had been vaguely wondering how she had money to buy books and expensive clothes all the time. She seemed more accepting of the Tiger than that part had feared.

The therapist continued to work for many months with the Tiger, and helped other parts accept this part of Maria. Dynamically, she noted that Maria as the Tiger had major attachment issues such as the need to "get attention from men" and to feel important. Though Maria was hypoaroused and shut down, the Tiger was hyperaroused and often highly dysregulated. She struggled with intense loneliness, boredom, and rage and bitterness about early abuse by her mother. The Tiger had a kind of addiction to the feeling of being powerful and in control, a strong defense against vulnerability and shame. She had a high sex drive that she used aggressively, while any sexual desire was completely missing in Maria. Slowly, over time, the Tiger admitted hearing a female voice that told her she was a whore and this was the only job she was good at. This infuriated, shamed, and frightened her. The therapist suspected this voice might be a perpetrator-imitating part, but was not yet certain.

The therapist was also aware of several child parts stuck in trauma-time that were retraumatized each time the Tiger had sex with a man. The Tiger admitted she was not always in control in her sex work. She reluctantly admitted that sometimes she got hurt because she was unable to use a safe word, because the inner punitive voice would prohibit her from speaking. In this way, the patient as a whole was reenacting her childhood experiences among parts of herself.

A turning point in the therapy came when the Tiger realized child parts were being hurt by her work, as she had a compassionate heart underneath her tough and dismissive exterior. She became more aware that the punitive inner voice controlled her sometimes, when she so prided herself on being completely in control. She told the therapist she had always wanted to protect child parts and take revenge for what had happened to them. She quit her job as a dominatrix shortly after that session.

Eventually, the therapist was able to access the perpetrator-imitating part, who was like Maria's mother. It took another two years, but this mother-like part also gradually developed more compassion and eventually realized she was part of Maria.

Further Explorations

18.1 How do you feel when a patient engages in unsafe behaviors? Angry? Scared? Confused? Disgusted? Helpless? Discuss your feelings with colleagues in order to find ways to help yourself not be overly reactive or withdrawn from patients who self-harm.

18.2 What are your limits regarding unsafe behaviors, and how to you enforce those limits? Discuss with colleagues and learn about the different ways therapists set these limits.

18.3 Make sure your unstable patients have a safety plan that is written and updated.

18.4 What are the parameters of your availability to patients after hours? Have a discussion with your colleagues about the different limits that can be set and the reasons therapists have certain limits.

18.5 Have you ever had a patient attempt or commit suicide? What was that like for you? Did you seek out consultation and support afterward? How do those experiences, if you have had them, affect how you approach suicidality in your patients now?

CHAPTER 19

Selected Issues

*[H]uman beings are immersed in a narrative in which everyone
participates but which can create problems while
simultaneously having the potential for dissolving them.*
—Gianfranco Cecchin, Gerry Lane, & Wendel Ray (1993, p. 128)

This chapter addresses a few topics that are frequently brought up in consultation and supervision and which present significant challenges in treatment. These include how to help patients deal with their current relationships, parenting issues, disclosure, sexuality, and current victimization; and how to deal with conflicts within a treatment team.

Helping the Patient Cope With Current Relationships

The current relationships of the patient are often fraught with conflict. Part of the therapist's role is to help the patient learn to relate differently to others, which will naturally change the dynamics of relationships. Often patients come to therapy with problematic relationships in which lack of boundaries, role confusion, inappropriate caretaking, neglect, and abuse are rampant from one or both sides. The therapist should discuss whether or how patients support others in their life, and are supported by others. Decisions need to be made about whether or how to include partners in therapy, and whether the partner needs to be referred to an individual therapist. Both patient and therapist should consider what to tell a partner or even the patient's friends about the patient's diagnosis, therapy, and history. Sometimes others in the patient's life have begun to interact with dissociative parts and ask the patient about traumatizing events, potentially making the patient even further fragmented and greatly complicating therapy.

CORE CONCEPT

It is essential to take into account the patient's relationships with significant others when planning treatment. Decisions must be made regarding whether or how others might be included in supporting the patient.

The Couple's Relationship

The dynamics between patients and their partners may serve as a guideline for what might and might not be useful for the patient to share (Sachs, 1986). Is the partner likely to become overinvolved, even trying to take on a role of therapist or reparenting with the patient? Or is the partner more likely to withdraw and be unavailable? How much does the patient wish to rely on support from the partner? Is the patient very dependent? How likely is it that the patient might use dissociative parts to get needs met (for example, switching to a scared child part to avoid the anger of a partner or to a dependent part to be cuddled)? How likely is it that the partner may exploit dissociative parts to get his or her own needs met (for example, calling out sexualized parts for sex when the adult part of the patient does not wish to be sexual)? Is the partner likely to pathologize the patient and blame the couple's relational problems on the patient's mental health issues?

Once the therapist understands the dynamics of the couple and the patient's wishes, it can be helpful to have a couples session. This session is for the purpose of psychoeducation, but still should take place only after a discussion with the patient about what might be acceptable to share and what not. The therapist might share general information about dissociation or PTSD, rather than specific details about the patient's experience.

Should the patient wish to reveal the diagnosis of a dissociative disorder, the therapist should carefully explain to the partner that dissociative parts are aspects of the adult patient and should be treated as such. It is important for the partner not to call out parts other than the adult self of the patient, but to learn simple grounding techniques that help the adult part of the patient to stay present and to return should there be a switch. Partners should not interact regularly with child or other parts of the patient, except to help the patient return to an adult and grounded place. This is essential because the more parts are active in daily life, the more autonomous they become, and significant relationship issues may be avoided by both parties by only dealing with more functional adult parts.

In general, it has been our experience that partners and close friends do not understand dissociative behaviors of the patient. They may be quite relieved to receive some education and support. In fact, psychoeducational groups for partners have been shown to be effective to improve relationships and offer support for partners (Tijdink & Cuijpers, 2016). Partners need specific and practical guidelines for how to deal with dissociation. Of course, participation in such a group would first require informed consent from the patient, some understanding of the dynamics in the relationship, and some initial work with the couple.

In some cases, a couple (or family) should be referred to another therapist to receive ongoing couples or family therapy, in addition to the individual therapy of the patient. To avoid conflict of interests with the patient and to prevent inadvertent disclosures from the patient's individual therapy, intensive couples or family therapy should not be undertaken by the patient's individual therapist. However, there should be close collaboration between the couples or family therapist and the individual therapist.

Parenting Issues

Another question for patients is whether and what to explain to their children. Of course, this depends to a large degree on the age of the children and the relationship the patient has with them. It might be helpful for children to understand more if the patient engages in erratic behavior, and some psychoeducation may in fact help them to not blame themselves for the problems of their parent (Benjamin & Benjamin, 1993; ISSTD, 2011). Clearly, children should never be responsible for dealing directly with dissociative parts of a parent. They can be encouraged to go find, if needed, another adult to get their needs met. The patient must be strongly encouraged to gain control over switching and acting out of various parts when they are with their children. They should remain in the role of parent as an adult. They may need help with parenting skills (Benjamin & Benjamin, 1994a, 1994b), and in protecting their children from abuse or other harm (ISSTD, 2011).

Parenting is never easy, and many patients with dissociative disorders may struggle more than usual. In a study of 75 mothers with DID, Kluft (1987d) reported that 38% were competent parents, 16% were abusive, and 45% were compromised or impaired to the extent that they were sometimes emotionally abusive or neglectful. Many reported their dissociative symptoms interfered with their best efforts to be good parents (Benjamin,

Benjamin, & Rind, 1998; Kluft, 1987c). Children whose parents are dissociative seem to be at greater risk of insecure attachment and becoming dissociative themselves (Coons, 1985). Clearly, children of some dissociative parents are at risk and may need therapeutic intervention at some point.

CORE CONCEPT

In some cases, dissociative symptoms can interfere with parenting in spite of the patient's best efforts. The therapist should take care to help the patient with parenting skills and stress management, and ensure that the patient's children are assessed if need be.

Some patients have child parts that want to play with their actual children. The only way this is acceptable is if the adult part of the patient is fully present and co-conscious with the child parts. In this way, child parts can take enjoyment from seeing how the patient is a good parent and how children can enjoy themselves when they feel safe. The adult parts can also learn to be playful and realize that play does not have to be left to children alone. Dissociative child parts of a parent should never be directly in control in the presence of the patient's actual children.

The age of a child may be a trigger for a parent who experienced traumatizing events at the same age. Parents may be triggered by the behavior of their children and switch to angry or frightened dissociative parts. They may feel jealous that the child is receiving more love and care than they did. Some parents find a child disgusting, a projection of disowned shame. These behaviors and feelings can result in frightening or frightened behavior by the parent, the types of experiences that can lead to disorganized attachment in the child if they are persistent (Main & Hesse, 1990). Other parents find healing and redemption in caring for vulnerable children in positive and healthy ways, happy to be able to give what they did not receive. They observe the helplessness and vulnerability their own small children, and the impact of their own parenting successes and failures on them. This can further realization of the parent's true predicament as a child in the past. Often these parents can allow their young dissociative parts to benefit from experiencing their positive parenting abilities with their actual children.

It is important to regularly check with patients about how their children are doing, and how they are managing parenting. It is a serious concern when patients report losing time or switching with their children, as they will be unable to give a clear report on how they are parenting. This may not be an easy topic for patients, as many are terrified that they are not good enough mothers or fathers and that child protective services will be called. In some situations, it is necessary to refer children to a child psychologist or child psychiatrist for assessment, and in a few cases, protective services will need to be called in. The therapist should help the patient to overcome reluctance about talking about parenting, and offer as many skills as possible to them.

Recently there have been initiatives to prevent intergenerational trauma by developing a model for structured psychoeducational groups for dissociative parents (Friberg, 2014; Ruismäki & Mankila, 2013). The focus in these groups is on discussing and sharing fears, doubts, and problems as a parent, and learning effective parenting skills. Most dissociative patients want to become better parents and try hard to do so. Outcome studies have not yet been conducted, but feedback from patients is that they feel greatly supported by these structured groups.

Disclosure to Family and Friends

If the patient has a current family, including a partner and perhaps children, or close friends, the patient needs to decide whether to tell them about a dissociative condition and traumatic background (if that has not yet happened). There are pros and cons to sharing the fact that the patient has been traumatized (not the details) and diagnoses. The therapist might begin to explore with the patient what it might mean to share something of the patient's struggle with a close other. What would the patient expect of the other person? What are the patient's fears about sharing—for example, not feeling safe; worrying others will think the patient is crazy, misuse the information, or share it with other people; worrying they will judge the family of origin? Next, what exactly is important to share with family or friends?

Some patients are averse to sharing anything about their personal experience with others, no matter how close those people may be. However, many patients typically feel isolated in their painful therapy work and wish for someone to understand and share their pain. Most certainly there are usually conflicts among dissociative parts about what and whether to share. Some inner consensus among parts should be gained before disclosure.

Patients may share too much content and need to be helped with staying with a more relational approach. For example, instead of sharing graphic details of abuse or highly vulnerable or revealing information, including specifics about dissociative parts, they can learn to say something like, *I'm really struggling with some painful issues from childhood right now, and I feel sad and depressed.* Or they may switch to child parts yearning for attention and care from their partner or friend. Therapists can help their patients learn to disclose more about how they feel in the present without switching, which ideally makes sharing with family or friends much more safe and effective.

CORE CONCEPT

Prior to patients disclosing information about their history, diagnosis, or therapy, dissociative parts should come to an inner agreement about what can be shared. Otherwise the patients may experience an internal backlash.

One question both therapists and patients ask is whether it is necessary or helpful to share the diagnosis with a partner or a close friend. This depends on the situation of each patient. Not many laypeople fully understand the nature of dissociative disorders, and the patient will most certainly face the possibility of some combination of fascination, fear, and stigma. However, most people can compassionately grasp the concept of post-traumatic stress. Some patients may simply tell others that they are suffering from PTSD or are struggling with issues related to childhood trauma or abuse. They may need to learn which types of questions others may ask, and whether or how they wish to answer. Role-play with the therapist can be helpful. It is important to explore what the patient wishes to gain by sharing the diagnosis and whether it is realistic, and whether all parts of the patient agree that it be disclosed. What kind of support can a partner or friend offer, and what is healthy for the patient and the partner or friend; and what not?

Helping the Patient Cope With Family of Origin

Whether or not to remain in contact with abusive family members is an extremely difficult choice for many patients. The need to maintain ties is strong, yet it competes with the need to be safe and have a more stable and peaceful life. In general, the therapist should not be the one to suggest the patient cut off contact, as this may create an even greater resistance to doing so. The therapist can, however, point out the consequences of being with family. For example, *I notice that each time you visit your family you become suicidal. Let's take a look at what might be happening.* The patient must be helped to struggle with painful and conflicted feelings, even while learning to stay safe.

If the patient is able to mentalize about the family and is able to move forward without getting stuck in anger or bitterness, or completely dismissing feelings, it is more likely to be a healthy move. For example, one patient noted, *I feel sad that I don't have contact with my family. I realize in some ways they did the best they could. But when I am around them, they are so verbally abusive, and I don't handle it well. It's better for me if I don't have contact, even though I have a lot of feelings about it.* Another patient remained angry and was unable to grieve: *Every time I think of them, my blood boils. They hurt me, and they don't deserve anything from me.* A third patient reported, *I don't care about them. I don't have any feelings at all. They are dead to me.*

The first patient is working toward resolution, the second patient is stuck in anger, and the third patient has disowned all the complex feelings associated with abusive parents. Most patients will struggle to find a middle ground involving some limited contact. The therapist should help patients learn to take healthy steps when visiting family of origin; for example, planning shorter stays, taking a friend along for the visit, staying in a hotel instead of in the family home, leaving if things become tense, and taking breaks such as walks or going shopping alone or with someone safe.

Most dissociative patients have always dealt with their families by dissociating inner conflicts about contact. Some dissociative parts may continue contact, unaware or unable to realize the abuse or neglect, often resulting in fierce inner conflicts. Following integration of all parts, a more realistic ability to hold these conflicts and resolve them should occur. Patients should be able to have a more realistic view of "the good" and "the bad" of an abusive family, and to make an accurate appraisal of whether contact is helpful, and if so, what kind of contact.

Coping With Aging and Dying Parents
One dilemma is how to respond to aging, infirm, and dying parents who were (and perhaps still are) abusive (L. Brown, 2012). Many patients care for their parents, regardless of the cost to themselves. Others do not, but feel guilty. For patients who do not have much contact with parents, conflicts arise about reestablishing contact as the parents become infirm, ill, or are dying. Often there is a rekindling of hope in the patient that some resolution can take place and the parent will finally acknowledge the abuse. While this can happen, it is rare. Therapists must support patients in struggling with these hopes and with reality as it is. Most importantly, patients must learn to engage in good self-care and boundaries, regardless of whether they take on some type of caregiving (L. Brown, 2012).

Confrontation
Some patients want to confront their abuser. This is a complex issue, and it should not be approached until the patient is able to gain cooperation

among all parts. While patients may believe confrontation is necessary or helpful, it may well not be. The issue is not whether confrontation takes place, but rather the outcome for which a patient wishes. Thus, the therapist must first and foremost help patients understand their expectations of a confrontation. *What do you hope to have happen? How do you imagine it going? Who do imagine might be there? What do you imagine your father or mother might say? How do you think you might feel if you don't get what you want? What do you imagine it will be like for you if they deny anything happened? What if they ask you to forgive them? What if they acknowledge it, but then say it is now all in the past, to be let go?*

Often patients, or at least some parts of them, desperately wish to have some kind validation from an abusing parent. They want an apology and acknowledgment that the abuse happened. Some want revenge or justice. Some feel it is necessary to their healing for their perpetrator to admit what was done. None of these wishes is attained through confrontation, because the patient has an unrealistic hope that inner change will happen because the perpetrator will somehow be different. Unfortunately, it is relatively rare for childhood trauma survivors to receive much validation during confrontations, and patients must be prepared for all possible reactions by family members. In those cases where acknowledgment does occur, it does not seem to offer major healing beyond a validation of one's reality.

When there is inner agreement by all parts, and when preparations have been made in treatment, a few patients may decide it is important to simply speak their truth to the perpetrator: *I want you to know that I remember what happened. You really hurt me, and it has affected me in ways you would probably find hard to imagine.* They can go into the situation fully prepared for whatever reaction they receive, because the goal has nothing to do with the perpetrator's reaction. In a few cases, a highly trained and sensitive family therapist can work effectively with a family of origin and the survivor to support healing relationships, even when there is denial of abuse by family (M. J. Barrett & Trepper, 2004). This should not be attempted by the individual therapist, and careful choices about which families might be amenable to such therapy is important.

The Issue of Forgiveness

Some patients wonder if they need to forgive their abusers. This is not an easy question to answer, primarily because forgiveness means something different to each person. First, the therapist must not insist the patient forgive. That is up to the patient, and it is not necessary for healing. Second, the therapist should inquire about what forgiveness means to the patient and how it would make a difference in the patient's life in the present.

CORE CONCEPT

Patients may or may not forgive their abusers; this is up to the
individual and should only be brought up in therapy by the patient.
In that case, the therapist should carefully explore what forgiveness
means to the patient and whether it is something the patient desires,
and for what reasons.

Forgiveness should not mean the patient should forget about what happened or believe what happened was acceptable. It should not be done out of guilt, fear, or a sense of religious duty. It can involve mentalizing about an abuser, acknowledging that perhaps the perpetrator did the best he or she could and perhaps had a trauma history as well. This does not mitigate the harm done to the patient, but it does take the blame off the patient and allow the patient to see the abuser as human. It is much harder to resolve trauma when the patient views the abuser as a monster that is larger than life.

Other times, patients may come to the conclusion that their abuser was severely mentally ill or even evil, and continuing to invest emotional energy in being angry takes away from the patient's life. This, too, can be a kind of letting go and moving forward. Patients do not have to forgive, but they truly must reinvest their emotional energy into the present and with people in their current life, however they choose to do that.

Sexual Relationships

Many dissociative patients, especially those who have been sexually abused as children, have problems in their current sexual relationships. Some may avoid sex at all costs, even with their partner. They have sometimes chosen partners who do not mind a relationship without sex for their own reasons. Other patients have a dissociative part that acquiesces to sex with the partner and feels numb. Some only have sex if they initiate it and control their partner. Patients may have highly sexualized parts that enjoy sex, while other parts of the patient are frightened or find it disgusting. This leads to serious inner conflicts. A few have prostitute parts that engage in sex for various reasons. Some partners intentionally seek out sexualized parts, which is a serious relational and treatment problem that maintains dissociation. Sex may involve reenactments of control, dominance, appeasement, freeze, or collapse.

When patients begin to realize more and have less disconnection between dissociative parts over the course of treatment, additional problems in sexual relationships may arise. More parts of the patient may become co-present during sexual activity. Parts that have previously avoided being sexual may now be present and find sex difficult to tolerate. Both patients and their partners may be confused or frustrated by this turn of events.

Sexualized Parts

Sexualized parts of the patient contain disowned sexual impulses and behaviors of the patient as a whole, and are often unable to be emotionally intimate. They may manifest in child, adolescent, and adult forms. Typically, highly sexualized parts develop in reaction to chronic sexual abuse in order to engage in sexual behaviors that were overwhelming or unacceptable. They may use sexual activity as a substitute action—for example, to reduce tension, protect themselves against feeling, or to avoid emotional intimacy. Some confuse sexual intimacy with emotional intimacy.

These parts may play an important role in current relationships, as they take responsibility for whatever sexual activity may exist, if any. This may be quite confusing for the patient's partner—at one moment they may be confronted with a very sexual person, who then inexplicably becomes angry or terrified when approached or touched in a sexual way. For example, a partner described his experience of being in the middle of tender and intimate sex when suddenly his (dissociative) partner jumped out of bed in a rage and began tearing the sheets off the bed and screaming for him to get out.

Therapists who have not encountered sexualized parts before may be shocked at the overt sexual overtures of a few in session. It is helpful to think of these behaviors as reenactments, no different than other behaviors in which patients attempt to engage with therapists. It goes without saying, but must be said again, that therapists should never be sexual with a patient for any reason at any time. However, it is also important not to shame the patient for these parts or related behaviors, and to help them retain their dignity. Therapists should thus be prepared to deal with sexualized parts, should they emerge. Approaching them in a calm, accepting manner while setting limits on sexualized behavior is helpful. The therapist is encouraged to take intense feelings to consultation (or therapy) and to practice working with these parts in role-play with other colleagues.

Sexualized parts are often fixed in trauma and typically have several functions, which may have significant overlap:

- To engage in sex to remain safe. These dissociative parts have learned that giving sexual pleasure to a more powerful adult not only is their role in life but also might appease that person. Then the adult may not hurt them, or at least not hurt them as much as if they were to fight against the inevitable. Sex may also give the illusion of close-ness, but without the emotional vulnerability of true intimacy, so it may protect these parts from feeling too vulnerable in relationships.

- To view themselves as the seducer rather than as the victim. Perhaps the perpetrator told them they caused the abuse, or perhaps they came to this belief on their own. Sex is a means to maintain a sense of control and avoid feeling vulnerable and helpless, both in the past and in the present.
- To hold pleasurable or painful sexual feelings that cause deep shame and revulsion in the patient. Sometimes psychoeducation helps, assuring the patient that sexual feelings are normal in children and may be evoked even if the child does not wish to feel stimulated during abuse. However, shame is rarely resolved by knowledge alone, so there is often much longer and harder work to help the adult accept this type of child or adolescent part (see Chapter 15 for the treatment of shame). Some patients have become hardwired to enjoy pain cou-pled with sexual arousal. Dissociative parts may engage in self-injury, or be injured by a sexual partner. Often during work with traumatic memories, this can be shared with other parts, and some degree of unlinking can occur (see Chapters 20 and 21).
- To form a meaningful relationship in the only way that is available to them. Often these dissociative parts have no idea how to develop a rela-tionship except through sexual behaviors. Some perpetrators give affec-tion along with sexual abuse, making it especially confusing to a child who naturally seeks and enjoys affection. Some sexualized parts may attempt to seduce the therapist as a way to engage in relationship.

Working with sexualized parts of the patient. The therapist can work with sexualized parts in several ways. The adult part of the patient is typi-cally frightened that these parts might act out with the therapist or outside therapy and feels intense shame. On the other hand, the adult part func-tioning in daily life is often dependent on parts to be sexual with a partner and, in order to continue to avoid sex, may not want to further integrate sexualized parts.

Often, the patient may be extremely reluctant to allow these parts to come to the forefront. The part of the patient that presents in therapy may be so phobic of these parts that the therapist may have difficulty accessing them in a therapeutic way. This understandable resistance must be resolved without force and may take a long time. The patient as a whole will likely need ample psychoeducation about the nature and function of these parts, and must be helped to overcome extreme shame.

Considerable time might need to be spent on exploring the reasons such parts developed in a given patient and why they engage in sexual behaviors, and in understanding what the adult part of the patient feels about these dissociative parts. Patients are often unaware that healthy children may have normal sexual feelings, including orgasms. When these normal responses are exploited in abuse, they may become hyper-activated and habituated either as reenactments or as problem-solving strategies, such as efforts to avoid emotion or relieve tension. For example, some dissociative parts masturbate obsessively, even to the point of injury, while others may engage in indiscriminate sex.

CORE CONCEPT

Patients must be helped to feel they have sufficient impulse control to allow the therapist to safely work with sexualized dissociative parts. It may be important to have an observer part of the patient be co-present while the therapist works with these parts.

Patients must have some confidence in their own impulse control during sessions, and sufficient confidence that the therapist will be neither exploitive nor rejecting during work with sexualized parts. Sometimes it is sufficient to obtain an agreement that both therapist and patient agree to sit in separate places and not get up during the session, and to remind patients that part of the therapeutic contract is to never be sexual with each other. It can be helpful to assure the patient that together with the therapist, both will work with this dissociative part, seeking to understand, ground, and heal, just as with every other part. Then the therapist might be able to encourage the adult part of the patient or other dissociative parts to work internally with the sexualized part, with the therapist talking though to the part. Or it may feel safe enough for the patient to allow the sexualized part out to the forefront to work directly with the therapist.

CASE EXAMPLE OF A SEXUALIZED CHILD PART: CASEY

Casey was a 36-year-old patient with DID in treatment with a female therapist. She had a 7-year-old sexualized part she called "Cat," who was perceived internally as wearing "sexy grown-up clothes" and "red lipstick." This part was visualized as a "little whore," with legs spread and a sultry look on her face. Other parts of Casey rejected this sexualized part and were ashamed of her, believing she wanted to be abused and had actually caused it with her seductive behavior. Casey had a long history of promiscuity, in which this dissociative part played a dominant role. For years, Casey would not admit to having this part and kept her well away from therapy. The only evidence of this part in session emerged when Casey would rub her lips with a tissue incessantly in session, as though trying to remove lipstick, or when other parts made vague references to the "whore."

The therapist worked with all parts of Casey to understand and be more accepting of Cat. Eventually Casey was willing to take more risks in therapy to get help with this part of herself, and the more punitive parts of her allowed it. As Cat came to the forefront, the patient began to take on a sexualized posture, very slightly spreading her legs, with a seductive look on her face. The therapist made eye contact and asked Cat to sit up and bring her legs together, and asked for parts inside to help her maintain an appropriate posture. She also handed Cat a blanket to put over her knees and made an agreement that neither patient nor therapist would get up from their chairs for the duration of the session. The therapist recognized how important it was to maintain the dignity and safety of the patient and to contain inappropriate behavior.

Cat made several overt sexual invitations to the therapist, which the therapist firmly but kindly declined, indicating that they would never be sexual, but instead they had another purpose in being together. The purpose was to begin to understand Cat and help her realize she had other options in life. She asked Cat to look around the room and see if she recognized where she was. Cat did not. The therapist asked parts inside, including the adult part, to help orient Cat to the present and to therapy. The sultry look on Cat's face began to change to one of confusion. She began vigorously rubbing her lips as though trying to remove lipstick. The therapist asked if Cat could be more aware of other parts internally, and could these parts notice that she did not want to have lipstick on. Cat said she hated lipstick, and that her perpetrator had put it on her before giving her to other men. This was the first moment when all parts of Casey began to realize that perhaps Cat had been coerced instead of wanting to be abused.

Over time, Cat was able to tell her story of being used in pornographic films and pictures, and Casey could begin to compassionately accept her as part of her own history. The most painful realizations came when Casey could accept that some of the sexual abuse felt good, and that her perpetrator was "extra nice" to her when she performed her role in the films well. She realized she had entirely confused her performance of a scripted sexual role in the films with her own desires. Over the course of several years, Cat evolved from the "little whore" to a thoughtful part that took on the task of growing up and being an adult, and found the compassion of other parts of Casey a great support. She became a central part of

Casey's growing desire to feel genuine connection with other people and to have healthy intimate relationships for the first time.

Working with sadomasochistic sexual parts. Some dissociative parts have become deeply involved in sadomasochistic sex, typically as a way to relieve unbearable feelings. Some patients report that they feel most accepted in a bondage-discipline-submission/dominance/sadomasochism (BDSM) subculture, but there is usually conflict between dissociative parts about it. Although these groups place emphasis on consent, many highly traumatized patients freeze during encounters and are unable to use a safe word to stop. Thus, they become retraumatized. They are caught in a world in which power differentials are role-played, which offers the potential for them to gain mastery. Yet their felt experience—or at least that of some parts—is that the power and control are actual, not scripted. Some patients are unwilling to stop involvement in these behaviors, while others are ashamed and wish to stop.

Clearly, when sexualized or sadomasochistic parts are active in a current relationship with a partner, the therapist should attend to safety issues. First, the therapist should recognize that these parts are retraumatizing the patient each time they repeat their old patterns. Often the part of the patient functioning in daily life may have amnesia for this kind of sex, and may be horrified once he or she discovers it. Some patients repeat their original trauma histories by choosing partners who are addicted to sex, and some parts of the patient may be addicted as well. The case of Nicky below illustrates some of these issues and how they can be resolved.

CASE EXAMPLE OF A SEXUALIZED SADOMASOCHISTIC DISSOCIATIVE PART: NICKY

Nicky was a patient with DID who was heavily involved in the BDSM subculture. Her body was covered with hundreds of piercings, tattoos, and scars from self-harm. A strong and adult part of Nicky, which she called "Fire Walker," found pleasure in the coupling of intense pain with sexual arousal, which she liked to both give and receive. She had substituted this behavior for a previous cocaine addiction. However, there were other parts of Nicky that were terrified and frozen and did not like these behaviors. Nicky was dominant with her partner, who was also a trauma survivor, but she paired with others in the BSDM community so she could be submissive and experience pain. The sexual part of Nicky was unwilling to consider that her sexual self-harm behaviors were not healthy, strongly asserting that this was a lifestyle choice. While she acknowledged that other parts of her found her behavior difficult, she avoided these parts. The therapist suspected that, whether it was a choice or not on the surface, at least on some level parts of Nicky were reenacting her trauma history, in which she had been prostituted by her mother from the age of ten.

The therapist worked to understand Fire Walker, especially what she enjoyed or found meaningful about these behaviors. She also explored other ways Fire Walker found pleasure and enjoyment in life and helped her connect with those more strongly. She discovered that Fire Walker would enter a trancelike state during sexual harm, and only long after the event was over would she feel the pain.

While Nicky was somewhat co-conscious with Fire Walker, she did not exert full control over her behavior when this part was activated. Fire Walker described herself as 14 years old. She reported she had learned BDSM techniques from several men to whom her mother had prostituted her. She learned that she could feel in control in these situations, even though she was being abused. Over time, Fire Walker began to become the dominant in encounters, controlling men who wished to be submissive. This gave her an exhilarating sense of power, a radical departure from the chronic helplessness she had felt as a child. Yet she also liked to receive physical harm during sex, as that also gave her a sense of control. However, this was only one side of the complete story: Other parts experienced the sexual harm as overwhelming and not within their control. Fire Walker rarely used her safe word, as she numbed out and did not feel the pain, while other parts felt it intensely but were unable to use the safe word.

The therapist began to understand just how alluring the world of BDSM was to Fire Walker. It offered a sense of control, power, and acceptance that she never had as a child. The therapist began by simply offering a different type of relationship to Fire Walker, one of collaboration, respect, interest, and care, keeping the relationship as egalitarian as possible. She was careful not to judge Fire Walker, while still insisting that serious self-harm was not acceptable. Nicky was encouraged to communicate with this part and have a better understanding of her functions.

At first this part attempted to offer herself to the therapist for sex. The therapist, with good consultation, was able to stay steadily on course. She helped Fire Walker experience for the first time a truly safe relationship without dominance or submission. The therapist was constantly alert to overt and subtle issues of power and control, enjoyment of pain and suffering, and other related dynamics in the therapeutic relationship, and processed these with the patient as a whole on a regular basis.

Fire Walker gradually was able to eliminate self-injury from sexual activity, and significantly diminished harm during sex. She was helped to learn to feel her body when she was not being sexual and then gradually when she was, so that she could monitor pain more accurately. She was encouraged to pay attention to other parts that did not like what she did and felt pain from it.

As Fire Walker become more connected to Nicky, she also gained more interest in other activities in addition to sex and self-harm, exploring—with the adult part of the patient—her considerable artistic talents. She became willing to talk about some of her painful experiences as a child. The more this part realized her helplessness as a child, the less she needed to engage in dominant or submissive sexual behavior. Although the patient continued to remain in the BDSM community as long as she was with her partner, her self-harm behaviors stopped.

In the seventh year of therapy, Nicky decided to leave her partner. At first she continued to engage in BDSM sex with others, but after a year reported that she was feeling "bored" with these encounters and was interested in a different kind of relationship. By the tenth year of therapy, the patient had completed Phase 2, the integration of traumatic memories; had started her own successful art business; was almost completely integrated; and was partnered with a man with whom she had a much healthier, egalitarian relationship. Her need to pair pain and pleasure had ended. Her sexual behaviors remained in the mild to moderate range of BDSM, within parameters of emotional and physical safety.

The therapist's countertransference with sexualized parts of the patient.

Therapists must be strongly aware of their countertransference to the sexual feelings and behaviors of the patient. Often there is a mutual unspoken rule about not talking about sex, as both therapist and patient may be uncomfortable or even ashamed. The therapist should spend time with colleagues discussing ways to become more comfortable with this important topic.

Therapists who have strong judgments about sadomasochistic sex may have an especially difficult time. In addition, therapists may be unprepared for the intensity of erotic feelings that can be evoked during sessions, both in themselves and in patients. As with other feelings such as anger, shame, or love, the therapist has to gradually learn to accept and tolerate sexual feelings and simply use them as one more avenue to explore what is happening within the patient in the moment rather than acting on them. It is also helpful to understand that profound attachment issues usually underlie erotic transference, and focus on these can be helpful. Consultation with these cases is important to support therapists in working with their own intense reactions.

CORE CONCEPT

The therapist must learn to accept and tolerate sexual feelings like all
other feelings, and use them to explore what is happening with the
patient in the moment.

Treatment Team Conflicts

When patients are being treated by more than one therapist, or by a treatment team in an inpatient unit or in day treatment, it is not uncommon
that inner conflicts of the patient are "taken on" by different members of
the treatment team. This results in parallel process, in which various members of the team are unwittingly enacting parts of the patient's experience.
If not addressed, splitting between team members can result, leading to
impasse and treatment failure. Splitting may result in fierce—but often
unspoken—conflicts among team members, who may see the patient from
different perspectives. For example, one may view the patient as fragile
and needing stabilization and protection, while another views the patient
as needing to take more responsibility for treatment.

CORE CONCEPT

Parallel processes, splitting, and conflicts among treatment team
members may seriously interfere with good treatment. It is essential
that treatment goals are shared by all team members. When there
is a conflict that the team cannot resolve, a consultant should be
called in.

CASE EXAMPLE OF TREATMENT TEAM CONFLICTS: ANGELA

Angela was a 40-year-old woman with DID who was in therapy at an
outpatient trauma clinic. She had an individual psychotherapist, Laura, as
well as an art therapist, Jane, and she participated in a DBT group. She
was in early Phase 1 treatment with a major goal of helping her stabilize
daily life and learn how to accept and tolerate dissociative parts of herself.
Art therapy had been added to help Angela better express herself, as she
often struggled to find words. She also used art to contact her parts. DBT

group was added to help Angela learn more regulatory skills. This team approach went well for about half a year.

Then Angela had a crisis in which she was highly dysregulated. Laura asked her to work on calming child parts by using her DBT skills and other resources. Angela responded, *How do you expect me to soothe these parts? You know nobody ever soothed me! DBT doesn't work! They don't even talk about parts in there. How can you expect me to know what to do? I have talked to these parts and told them it is safe now, but they keep crying. The only time they are calm is when I am with Jane* [the art therapist]. *Jane knows how to calm them, but you refuse to! Jane understands that I cannot do it myself. She takes care of them. Why don't you talk with Jane? She can tell you what to do!*

Because therapy seemed to go well initially, Laura, Jane, and the DBT group cotherapists had not communicated about the therapy process for quite some time and had become split with respect to treatment goals. Subsequently, the therapists became split in the patient's mind, with Jane, the art therapist, becoming the "good" therapist and the others the "bad" therapists. The four therapists set a meeting to talk about how to help Angela. It became clear that Angela was switching to child parts for the art sessions without being present, and that she was not being supported in DBT group to use the skills with her parts. Jane, the art therapist, felt responsible for soothing highly distressed child parts instead of helping Angela stay present and learn how to do so. The DBT therapists were not attending to the challenges of distress being held in different dissociative parts. The adult part of Angela that functioned in daily life was not present during most of the art sessions, and was not allowing child parts to learn DBT skills. The more Jane took care of child parts and interacted with them without the adult part of Angela present, and the more Angela ignored her child parts in DBT, the more the treatment became split.

At first the treatment team felt frustrated and angry with each other. But they realized they had not been communicating well and worked in devising a more integrated plan. Jane realized that she needed to include the adult self of the patient in sessions. The DBT therapists realized they needed to encourage Angela to apply skills with her parts. Laura, the primary therapist, realized she needed to be more attentive to what was happening in Angela's sessions and help her integrate her work more effectively, and coordinate her treatment better. Thereafter, the team agreed to at least check in with each other on a monthly basis and to meet in person as needed. Laura and the art therapist decided to meet with Angela together once a quarter to make sure they aligned. The therapy went much more smoothly, and Angela learned how to work with her child parts more effectively.

Unfortunately, such a good outcome is not always possible. Sometimes one therapist is unwilling to change his or her behavior. Sometimes others in the patient's life may be interfering with therapy. Occasionally a patient will begin to see another therapist and will not tell the primary therapist. Well-meaning people who are highly caretaking may become embroiled in taking care of child parts as though they are actual children, or encouraging patients to share traumatic memories long before they are able to integrate them. These relationships may impede therapy. Such individuals range from other professionals, such as physicians or massage therapists, to clergy, neighbors, and church members. The therapist must, to the degree possible, preserve the treatment frame when these relationships are working against the goals of therapy. It can be a delicate balance to help such individuals set better boundaries with the patient without alienating them or the patient. If there is more than one therapist involved in the treatment of a patient, regular communication and shared treatment goals are essential.

Current Victimization

Unfortunately, retraumatization in both new and old abusive relationships is not uncommon for dissociative patients (Kluft, 1990a, 1990d; Myrick, Brand, & Putnam, 2013). Through a complex combination of dissociation, learned helplessness, absorption, and reenactments, chronically traumatized patients are often unable to heed danger signals in relationships, leading to what Kluft (1990d) has called the "sitting duck syndrome." Many patients become entangled in current relationships in which emotional, physical, or sexual abuse occurs. Some are abused by other professionals, including therapists, in the present. A minority of patients have continued to be abused since childhood. The subject of ongoing victimization is highly complex and is more common than most believe (Boon, 2014; 1997a; Middleton, 2013, 2014; Myrick et al., 2013; Sakheim, 1996; H. L. Schwartz, 2000, 2013; Van der Hart, Boon, Heijtmajer, 1997). It is one thing to treat highly traumatized patients, but it is much more difficult when the trauma continues in the present. Therapists should always inquire about whether patients are being hurt in some way in current relationships, and not assume they are safe.

Typically, reports of ongoing victimization may emerge gradually during the course of therapy, often with subtle hints or clues, but not overt admissions for long periods. When it finally becomes clear in therapy, patients may experience a sudden worsening of symptoms (increasing self-harm or suicidality), as disclosure results in enormous ambivalence, shame, and fear. These patients may (but do not always) differ from other patients in that they may have more amnesia for their past and in current daily life. They may evidence greater conflicts, ambivalence about therapy, and more severe shutdown and switching in sessions. They are often in the category of poorer prognosis. Clusters of severe and unremitting symptoms are common in spite of good treatment, including pseudo-epileptic seizures, severe eating problems, severe forms of self-mutilation and chronic suicidality, extreme and chronic panic and shame, and paranoia. An increase in symptoms typically coincides with reported abuse episodes.

A remarkable phenomenon involves these patients' beliefs about the power and omniscience of their perpetrators. They believe in an almost supernatural power in the perpetrators' ability to control and hurt both the patient and the therapist.

CORE CONCEPT

Ongoing enmeshment with childhood perpetrators or organized criminal networks requires a focus on safety. The therapist must be prepared to deal with these complex issues while remaining grounded and focused on the goals of therapy.

The Veracity of Reports of Ongoing Victimization

The therapist cannot always know whether reported current abuse is actually happening or whether it is an inner reenactment or fantasy that the patient cannot distinguish from reality (ISSTD, 2011). As we have noted, psychic equivalence is a problem for many dissociative patients. For example, a child part of the patient reported telephone and mail threats by a perpetrator that terrified her. After some months it became clear that these were being "sent" to the patient by an internal perpetrator-imitating part. The trance logic of the whole system of the patient created an atmosphere in which she was literally unable to discern that she was listening to her own voice on her voice mail. In another case, a patient reported her brother was harassing her, threatening to kill her. She reported it to police, who investigated and found the threats were credible. In either case, it is not the therapist's role to determine the accuracy of the report, but rather to ensure the patient has taken steps to get safe and stays focused in therapy on treatment goals.

There is a subgroup of adult patients who continue to be abused by and
enmeshed with their original perpetrators in the present (e.g., Middleton,
2013, 2014). They remain both fearful of and intensely loyal to their perpetrators, which creates enormous inner conflict. The part of the patient presenting for therapy may be unaware of ongoing victimization or may be too
ashamed or afraid to tell the therapist. Some report being enmeshed in
some type of ongoing organizational abuse that may involve gangs, religious cults, sex trafficking, drug and arms trade, and other illegal activities
(Boon, 2014; Kluft, 1997a; ISSTD, 2011; Sakheim, 1996; H. L. Schwartz, 2000,
2013; Van der Hart et al., 1997). In some cases, the presenting part of these
patients has no memory of an abuse history (Boon, 2014; Boon & Draijer,
1993a,b; H. L. Schwartz, 2000, 2013; Van der Hart et al., 1997), yet the
patients have severe symptoms of PTSD and a dissociative disorder. Therapists should seek out immediate consultation if a patient reports current
abuse, as these are complex issues and tend to evoke strong countertransference. Therapists may need guidance in how to maintain a sound treatment frame.

Treatment in Cases of Ongoing Victimization

The primary goal of treatment must be to help patients end ongoing abuse
and gain safety. The work is thus similar to that with battered women who
have not yet left their abusers (Dutton, 1992; Walker, 2009). Therapists
must take care not to get derailed by the content of the patient's reports
and by urgency to "save" the patient. This is a major challenge in working
with ongoing victimization. Many patients are extremely reluctant to talk
about what happens, while a few patients want to tell the therapist gruesome details; otherwise they feel unseen, or fear that they will not be not
believed. In a few cases, narcissism leads patients to try to prove that their
abuse is "special" in its severity. Reports of current abuse may be a way to
enlist caretaking from the therapist. Other times, patients cannot sort out
internal fantasies versus what is actually happening, or they focus on fantastical events so the therapist will not believe them, as a defense against
more mundane but no less traumatizing events. In any case, the therapist
should explore with the patient the fear of not being believed and of being
believed, and the dynamic meanings of what they report. The therapist

should declare neither total belief nor total nonbelief, but rather compassionately stay with the inner conflicts within the patient about what (may be) happening in the present. The facts are up to the patient to determine, not the therapist.

The treatment of patients who are being abused in the present can be complex, long, and fraught with conflict. There is a great risk of profound self-destructiveness and undermining of the therapeutic relationship (Boon, 1997, 2014; Kluft, 1997a; Sakheim, 1996; Schwartz, 2000, 2013; Van der Hart et al., 1997). Patients will struggle with rigid beliefs that are often based on very systematic threats, in some cases combined with torture, such as *I am not allowed to tell; if I ever tell, they will kill me. I have to kill myself,* or *My therapist will abandon me when he finds out what I have done.* It may take years to establish a stable working relationship with these highly traumatized patients.

Often particular parts of the patient are loyal to the perpetrators and may exert heavy influence on the patient as a whole to remain involved with them. They may command the patient to hurt herself or undermine the therapeutic relationship. These parts must be worked with steadily by the therapist, who must not be intimidated by them. The therapist must refrain from rescuing or being a detective and stay with a steady focus on how patients can keep themselves safe, and on the inner dynamics that keep the patient in the situation. The phases of treatment should be followed as with other dissociative patients. Typically, Phase 1, with an emphasis on stabilization and safety, is long and arduous.

CORE CONCEPT

A focus on safety and stabilization is a major, long-term, and challenging part of treatment with patients who continue to be abused. Generally, forays into work with traumatic memories should be delayed until the patient is safe.

The dissociative organization of this subgroup of patient may be more complex, conflicted, and layered than in other patients. The therapist must stay organized and focused in order to make sense out of this complexity.

A few patients may report that perpetrators are even threatening the therapist. Whether this is actually happening, whether it is fantasy, or whether it is emanating from parts that wish to destroy the therapy is often impossible to determine. Therapists must make an informed choice about whether they wish to continue work with a patient who reports such threats by others. Above all, therapists must feel safe in order to provide treatment. Too much fear or, conversely, a disregard for threats can result in a derailed therapy.

It may take the patient a long time to disengage from perpetrators, resolve loyalty conflicts, and make a true commitment to healing, as it involves extremely difficult realizations. To relinquish belief in the omnipotence of perpetrators means to become painfully aware of deception, pain, and helplessness. Dissociative parts that are especially loyal to perpetrators often hold the most overwhelming experiences; their loyalty helps them avoid realization. These parts, like all others, need the therapist's steady compassion and consistent focus on growing realization.

Prognosis of Patients Enmeshed in Abusive Relationships

The general prognosis of dissociative patients was addressed in Chapter 6. Clearly, the treatment of patients who continue to be abused in the present is complicated and lengthy, without assurance that it can be successful. Prognosis is determined in part by the extent to which patients are willing and able to separate from perpetrators and stay safe, form a good working alliance with the therapist, confront magical beliefs held by certain parts about the power of perpetrators, and create new meaningful relationships or strengthen existing healthy ties.

Countertransference

While many difficult challenges are inherent in treating patients who continue to be victimized in the present, perhaps the most demanding is to manage intense countertransference. Therapists' reactions may include fascination with (or being overwhelmed by) graphic details of abuse, urgency to save the patient, uncritical belief or disbelief, collusion with a patient in a folie à deux of fear and paranoia, failure to stay with process instead of content, or rejection of and emotional withdrawal from the patient. Therapists may engage with the patient in mutually escalating fear of retribution by perpetrators and uncritical belief of everything the patient says. Content becomes paramount, while process is ignored or minimized. This may lead to breaking the treatment frame and violating boundaries as therapists become increasingly desperate to save the patient, track down perpetrators, and the like. Other therapists may become isolated, unwilling to discuss the case with colleagues for fear of ridicule or disbelief.

Therapists may become so overwhelmed that they develop vicarious traumatization or burnout (Saakvitne & Pearlman, 1996). Other therapists may dismiss everything the patient tells them as a fanciful or histrionic narrative that must be rejected or ignored as much as possible. We find it imperative that therapists seek consultation for support when they have a patient who is reporting or hinting at ongoing victimization.

Patients Who Victimize Others

A few patients may themselves be current perpetrators. Patients may engage in abusive or neglectful parenting, or abuse their partners. They may harass or treat employees badly. Some patients may be acting out violently or sexually in other ways. For example, one female patient would lie in wait in the parking lots of bars at night and would attack men with a knife as they went to their cars. One patient made her child ill repeatedly to gain attention, a disorder known as Munchausen by proxy (Meadow, 1977). Another patient exposed himself to young children and had strong fantasies of raping them. One patient seduced his employees; another provoked verbal and even physical attacks in situations when others were in authority over him. While these behaviors may be understood as reenactments in many cases, the therapist must be vigilant to the fact that they pose a dangerous threat to others, and should not turn a blind eye to the problem. In fact, some behaviors are reportable—for example, to child protective services. Again, therapists are encouraged to seek out consultation for support and management of countertransference and, if needed, legal advice. They should be well versed in the reporting laws of their location.

Further Explorations

19.1 How do you interact—if at all—with your patients' families?

19.2 Do you feel at ease talking about sexuality with your patients? Do you ever check to see if patients have erotic fantasies about you? Have you ever had to deal with an erotic transference, and if so, how did you deal with it?

19.3 Do any of your patients have other professionals involved in their treatment (pastor, art therapist, group or couples therapist, etc.)? Do you have regular treatment team meetings? Have you ever encountered conflicts within a treatment team? If so, how did you handle it, and what might you do differently—if anything—when a conflict arises in the future?

19.4 Do you ever ask whether a patient is actually safe in present-day life? What are your feelings about patients who continue to be victimized? How do you imagine this might affect your ability to be therapeutic?

PART IV

Phase 2 Treatment

CHAPTER 20

Treatment of Traumatic Memory: An Overview

Survivors did not only need to survive so that they could tell their story; they also needed tell their story in order to survive. There is in each survivor an imperative need to tell, and thus to come to know one's story, unimpacted by ghosts from the past, against which one has to protect oneself.

—Dori Laub (1991, p. 78)

Phase-oriented treatment has been embraced as the standard of care for complex trauma and dissociative disorders, as we have noted throughout the book. Phase 2 primarily focuses on the treatment of traumatic memories—that is, the integration of these memories into autobiographical narratives that are no longer relived as present experiences, but rather are remembered as chapters of one's own autobiography (Janet, 1928).

It is essential for the therapist actively to include work with dissociative parts in the treatment of traumatic memories in dissociative patients. One part can recount a traumatic memory in a completely calm but highly depersonalized manner, misleading the therapist to believe the memory is resolved; that is, integrated. However, other parts remain fixed in the traumatic memory and in incomplete actions of defense that continue to repeat. Even after years of therapy, such a patient may continue to remain unintegrated and plagued with flashbacks and reenactments.

CORE CONCEPT

The main goal of the treatment of traumatic memories is not the intense discharge of emotion, but rather realization. While emotion may be intense, it must remain within a window of tolerance for the patient as a whole.

The therapist may be under the mistaken impression that extreme emotional intensity is therapeutic in itself. There is nothing wrong with emotional intensity during work with traumatic memory, but it must be within the overall window of tolerance for the patient. The intense expression of emotion—*abreaction*, in the original meaning of the word (cf. Howell, 2011; Van der Hart & Brown, 1992)—is not the main goal of traumatic memory work. Rather, realization is the goal, including knowing the event has ended and is now a part of one's past. In fact, the therapist needs to understand that remembering per se is not sufficient. Instead, the real key to resolution of traumatic memories is the sometimes long and difficult work of realization after recall. Treatment approaches between therapists who use the terms *synthesis and realization* and *abreaction* are similar, to be sure. However, we believe that the concept of realization more accurately describes the essential healing principle and goal of work with traumatic memory, while the concept of abreaction may overemphasize the discharge of intense emotion (Van der Hart & Brown, 1992; Van der Hart et al., 1993, 2006).

The integration or resolution of traumatic memories in dissociative patients (and in those with complex PTSD) should be part of a more comprehensive relational, phase-oriented psychotherapy that addresses many other issues (e.g., Herman, 1997). It is far too simplistic to explain the complex difficulties of dissociative patients who have serious comorbidity solely by trauma and unresolved traumatic memories. Trauma is almost always deeply embedded in broad developmental deficits and other cognitive, emotional, somatic, relational, and social difficulties in these patients. Typically they grew up in emotionally impoverished homes and were exposed to a wide range of adverse experiences and patterns, such that their everyday milieu contributed as much to their problems as did specific traumatizing events (e.g., Gold, 2000). In fact, for many dissociative patients, traumatizing events were so common that they *were* part of everyday life and cannot be entirely separated from it.

Many dissociative patients are also plagued by temperament and genetic contributions to their suffering, and the transgenerational transmission of trauma, addiction, and serious mental illness. Some have traumatic brain injuries from childhood that can lead to great emotional and functional difficulties that are permanent. Many have enduring personality traits that developed in response to chronic trauma and neglect that are not adaptive under other circumstances.

CORE CONCEPT

There is no single right way to help patients resolve traumatic memories. A variety of methods appear effective. The therapist and patient together should collaborate and determine the best approach based on the patient's integrative capacity and preferences.

There is not a one-size-fits-all approach to the treatment of traumatic memory. When and how to approach traumatic memories are complex issues, given that each patient is relatively unique in her or his needs. Therapists need to assess carefully, in consultation with their patients, which approaches will be most helpful and when, ensuring that the work is within a window of tolerance.

While there are many approaches and techniques available for the treatment of traumatic memories, it is of prime importance that the therapist understand what needs to happen in order for patients to integrate these memories. Work with traumatic memory necessitates both physiological and psychological changes, which cannot be separated. Traumatic memories do not have the same psychobiological correlates as narrative memory. They involve chronically overactivated defense action systems that must be deactivated. Simultaneously, the psychological effects of non-realization must be addressed.

Understanding Traumatic Memory: From Reliving to Realization

By definition, traumatic memories are not integrated into the autobiographical history of the patient (Janet, 1919/1925a, 1928; Van der Hart et al., 1993; Van der Kolk & Fisler, 1995; Van der Kolk & Van der Hart, 1991). Moreover, in patients with complex dissociative disorders, particular dissociative parts contain traumatic memories. Not only are the memories unintegrated, but the patient's personality and self remain unintegrated. This complicates what might otherwise be a relatively straightforward integrative process.

There are quite a few theories that propose neurobiological changes along the shift from non-realization to realization, from a purely somato-

sensory experience to an autobiographical narrative memory, from dissociated to integrated memories. They all suggest that traumatic memories are
experienced differently from narrative memories. We briefly describe
three of these theories below.

Dual Representation System Theory

The dual representation system theory states that there are two types of
memory systems—the nonverbal (situationally accessible memory, or
SAM) and the verbal (verbally accessible memory, or VAM; Brewin, 2001,
2003; Brewin, Dalgleish, & Joseph, 1996). The SAM system is primitive,
amygdala-driven, nonverbal, somatosensory, and highly charged. Somatosensory memories of trauma cannot be realized because of the high level
of activation that accompanies them. They are considered "hot" memories
and include "hot cognitions" that may involve highly charged beliefs, such
as *I am a bad person; It's all my fault; I am in danger right now;* or *I must
never tell or I will die.* Traumatic memories are stuck in the SAM system
without a narrative (Van der Kolk & Fisler, 1995). Thus, these memories
remain unrealized (Van der Hart et al., 1993, 2006).

The VAM system is slower, involving the hippocampus and prefrontal
cortex. These memories are typically more linear, coherent, and complete.
VAM is a central component of autobiographical memory and is known as
"cool" or "cold" memory, without the highly emotional and indelible "punch"
of SAM (Brewin, 2001, 2003; Grey, Young, & Holmes, 2002). VAMs can be
realized, as they are not too overwhelming or ever present in a somatic
way. Not all SAMs are maladaptive, and not all VAMs are adaptive. Traumatic memories are maladaptive SAMs that should actually be VAMs.

Parts stuck in trauma-time primarily have SAMs, or unrealized memories (SAM, maladaptively stored information) that either partially or fully
intrude on parts that function in daily life. The treatment of traumatic
memory is directed to relieving the symptoms of these hot memories and
overcoming them with more fully realized and cool autobiographical memory. In this way, all parts of the patient can put the past in proper context
when they can learn to cooperate, be present in the here and now, and
reflect on the meanings of what happened in ways that support adaptive
functioning as a whole person (see Gonzalez & Mosquera, 2012; Van der
Hart, Groenendijk, Gonzalez, Mosquera, & Solomon, 2014). As the major
phobia of traumatic memories is relieved, the door is opened to further
integration of dissociative parts of the patient.

Adaptive Information Processing

The EMDR Adaptive Information Processing model (AIP; Shapiro, 2001) is
roughly consistent with the dual representation model of traumatic mem-

ory. The AIP model suggests that difficulties or pathology result when "unprocessed"—that is, unrealized—experiences are maladaptively stored in particular neural networks (SAM, hot memories), and patients are unable to link them with "adaptive information" (VAM, cool memories).

The Theory of Structural Dissociation of the Personality

Neither the dual representation theory nor the AIP model specifically addresses the central problem of complex dissociative disorders—that is, the fact that identity and self are also dissociated, in addition to traumatic memory. This adds a layer of complexity to understanding and working with traumatic memory that should not be overlooked. While patients who are dissociative have maladaptive SAM networks, they also have dissociative parts, each of which has its own set of memories, both VAM and SAM. And neither theory explicitly explains why patients with trauma-related disorders do not have sufficient integrative capacity to realize and integrate traumatic memories. To explain this, we need a model specific to dissociation.

As described in Chapter 1, the theory of structural dissociation posits that a lowered integrative capacity leaves the patient unable to synthesize and realize traumatic experiences, including a cohesive sense of self (Van der Hart et al., 2006). Therapy is geared to helping patients develop sufficient integrative capacity prior to work with traumatic memories. Dissociative patients have developed complex and habituated resistances to realizing and integrating traumatic memories. These resistances include trauma-related phobias and must be resolved in Phase 1, prior to most work with traumatic memories. If phobic avoidance is not addressed, attempts at working with traumatic memories can result in therapeutic impasse or decompensation.

We have returned again and again to problems of non-realization in dissociative patients. They have been unable to realize their traumatic memories: that events happened; that they are over; that they belong to all parts, which in turn, belong to a single, whole person. Dissociative parts are stuck in certain actions related to the trauma or to avoidance of the trauma. As Janet noted, they "are continuing the action, or rather the attempt at action, which began when the [trauma] happened; and they exhaust themselves in these everlasting recommencements" (1919/1925a, p. 668). Realization is a key element of integration, and it has three major components that are important to understand, as they guide both patient and therapist in a comprehensive approach to integrating traumatic memories.

Synthesis. The first step toward realization is *synthesis*, which is the linking (binding) and differentiation of experience (Van der Hart et al., 1993;

Van der Hart et al., 2006). The unique step in treating traumatic memories in dissociative patients is the synthesis or *sharing* of the memory among dissociative parts, including those which may have varying degrees of amnesia for what happened (Howell, 2011; Van der Hart et al., 2006). While not all parts may participate at first, eventually every part of the person must become aware of what happened, accept it as the patient's own, and adapt to the present. Various parts share what happened from their perspective (linking), and the story becomes more coherent and less intense.

CORE CONCEPT

Synthesis is the sharing of traumatic memories between dissociative parts and accessing each part's perspective on the memory. It is a unique step in Phase 2 treatment with dissociative patients.

For example, the patient is able to distinguish the memory as a past experience, not something that is happening in the here and now. Indeed, synthesis allows for the differentiation of safety and danger, also on a neural level. This is much more complex than just the extinction of fear as discussed in exposure-based approaches. The deactivation of inappropriate defense systems and the adaptive activation of social engagement in the present through safe connection with the therapist are crucial in the treatment of traumatic memory. Synthesis allows the appropriate linking of daily life action systems among parts, so that they have a more natural and organic flow based on the present. For example, a part frozen in terror can begin to relax and feel safe; a part fixed in attachment cry can feel real connection in the present; a part fixed in collapse can begin to explore the present; and a highly shamed part can experience compassion and competence.

Realization. Synthesis by itself—the awareness that something happened—is not adequate to support integration. Patients must not only be aware of the facts but must *realize* that those facts belong to them, their history. They must realize the present is affected by, but need not be dictated by, the past, nor by the anticipated future. Realization allows for maximum acceptance of reality as it is, not as we wish it to be. When we can accept what is real in the present, we are better able to act adaptively. As described in Chapter 1, the owning of experience (*personification*) and being adaptively present in the here and now based on realization (*presentification*) are two kinds of actions necessary for the complete integration of traumatic memory and of dissociative parts (Van der Hart et al., 1993, 2006).

CORE CONCEPT

Realization involves owning the memory as one's own
(personification) as part of one's autobiography, while being able to
be in the present, accepting reality as it is (presentification).

In short, the treatment of traumatic memory should begin with some type of exposure to traumatic memory, with synthesis (sharing) occurring between some or all parts of the patient, and should be followed by ongoing personification and presentification.

Considerations in Approaching the Treatment of Traumatic Memories

Regardless of the approach, patients generally need an overall ability to integrate traumatic memories, which requires gradually overcoming the general phobia of inner experience first, and then the phobia of dissociative parts.

CORE CONCEPT

Trauma-related phobias must be overcome to a degree before work
on traumatic memories begins. The presence of these phobias
indicates that the patient does not yet have the skills and integrative
capacity to integrate traumatic memories.

Patients need to learn stabilization skills such as overcoming the phobia of inner experience, emotion tolerance and regulation, reflection, and safe connection with others in Phase 1 and beyond (Boon, 1997; Boon et al., 2011; Courtois & Ford, 2013; Kluft, 1993a, 1993b; Korn & Leeds, 2002; Steele & Colrain, 1990; Van der Hart et al., 2006; Van Dijke, 2008). In general, patients need to the capacity to:

- Maintain a significant degree of internal and external safety. This includes the cooperation of perpetrator-imitating parts and others that might strongly resist dealing with traumatic memories.
- Regulate and tolerate intense emotion without engaging in unsafe behaviors.
- Recognize and utilize somatic signals of regulation and dysregulation.
- Stay grounded in the present and maintain dual attention when recalling traumatic memories.

- Have positive experiences and affects in the present that help counterbalance painful memories.
- Have self-compassion instead of prolonged shame, despair, or rage reactions to traumatic material.
- Maintain a positive therapeutic alliance without overwhelming dependence.

Phase 2 may be initiated when integrative capacity has been raised to the extent that major dissociative parts are able to function more or less adequately in the present, maintain a reasonably stable collaborative relationship with the therapist, engage in some degree of mentalizing and other reflective functions, tolerate and regulate arousal to some degree, and exhibit some capacity for inner empathy and cooperation.

There remains some controversy over when and under what conditions traumatic memories can be approached. The majority of therapists caution that ample stabilization must occur first, while a few have proposed that stabilization is not necessary. However, those few who have recently proposed that stabilization is not needed are referring to patients with complex PTSD, not those with dissociative disorders (Bicanic, De Jongh, & Ten Broeke, 2015; Van Minnen, Arntz, & Keijsers, 2006; Van Minnen, Harned, Zoellner, & Mills, 2012). We conclude that there is not sufficient evidence at present to demonstrate that stabilization is unnecessary in dissociative disorders. Thus, therapists must be cautious in using this limited data to alter the phased approach that currently remains the standard of care (ISSTD, 2011).

Collaborative Pacing of the Treatment of Traumatic Memories

Phase 2 work should not be relentless (Kluft, 1989, 2013; Phillips & Frederick, 1995; Van der Hart et al., 1993, 2006), regardless of the approach that is used. Rather, it is paced in small doses so there is ample time to more fully realize all the implications the memories have for the patient in the present. Thus, one or two sessions of direct work with a particular traumatic memory might be interspersed with several to work on realization and inner conflicts, and several more to work on daily life or other concerns (Phillips & Frederick, 1995).

The therapist should take a collaborative approach in deciding when and how to approach a particular traumatic memory, giving the patient full informed consent about the possible benefits and negative effects. The treatment of traumatic memory should be collaborative, not only between the patient and therapist, but among dissociative parts. Even when certain parts temporarily do not participate in a given piece of work, there should be inner agreement that the work can commence.

CORE CONCEPT

It is essential to gain agreement among dissociative parts that traumatic memory work can begin. This is a necessary step in preparation for the work. Otherwise, a backlash can occur that may destabilize the patient.

Table 20.1 includes some specific considerations to help both patient and therapist plan the right timing for the treatment of traumatic memory (Boon, 1997; Boon & Van der Hart, 1997; Kluft, 1996b, 1997b, 2013; Steele & Colrain, 1990; Van der Hart & Steele, 1997; Van der Hart et al., 1993, 2006).

The Therapeutic Relationship

Most publications focus on techniques or theories involved in the treatment of traumatic memory. One aspect that is rarely discussed but is implicit is the need for a strong and stable therapeutic relationship. While techniques abound, the importance of the therapeutic relationship in the successful integration of traumatic memories should not be underestimated (Kluft, 2013; Phelps, 1996). The authentic and compassionate presence of the therapist is the major reason why patients can feel safe in the present with highly threatening traumatic memories. The therapist is the touchstone of social engagement that counters threat responses and overwhelming distress. And the social sharing of terrible events with a compassionate other who can bear witness is a vital healing factor.

CORE CONCEPT

The therapeutic relationship is an essential stabilizing and integrative factor in the treatment of traumatic memories. Therapists should not lose sight of its central significance and overemphasize the use of techniques. Techniques are merely ways to help the patient stay connected with the therapist by helping the patient stay in the window of tolerance.

The therapist is active in supporting, encouraging, guiding, grounding, pacing, and compassionately being with patients during their struggles to integrate traumatic memories. Indeed, for a few patients all that is required for integration is the steady presence of the therapist; no techniques required. Usually these are cases of OSDD, in which the barriers between parts are limited, or sufficient work in therapy has been done to erode the

TABLE 20.1
Considerations in Approaching the Treatment of Traumatic Memories

- Is the patient's life relatively stable and without regular crisis? Periods of crisis or major transitions require energy, so it may not be helpful for the patient to engage in intense memory work during those times. That said, traumatic memories are often evoked by transitions and crisis, so the therapist may need to help the patient contain them until the appropriate time. However, there may be times when it is appropriate to integrate the memory, and even important to do so. For example, if a patient is hurting herself while reenacting the memory, and the patient has a generally high level of integrative capacity, it might be essential to integrate the memory in order to stop the self-harm.

- Can the patient and therapist make a specific collaborative plan about how and when to work on traumatic memories? As noted below in the section on preparation, the first step in the treatment of traumatic memories is not a spontaneous event, but requires careful planning.

- Has the therapist been able to engage perpetrator-imitating parts to the degree that they can agree that some traumatic memory work be undertaken? This work is essential to prevent major backlashes against the revelation of traumatic memories.

- Does the major presenting part of the patient (usually an adult part) have the ability at least to partially realize trauma has occurred? This is often an indication that work may proceed.

- Is there any explicit communication between parts fixed in trauma-time and parts that are functioning in daily life? If so, is there any compassion between parts? The more well-paced and constructive the communication and the greater the inner compassion, the better work goes with traumatic memories, as there can be collaborative efforts to regulate and soothe.

- Does the patient (or do parts involved in working with traumatic memories) have the ability to stay grounded and present to some degree when traumatic memories emerge?

- Is there a strong true/not true conflict among parts about the past? In other words, do some parts insist trauma happened while other parts insist it did not? If so, this may need greater resolution before work begins on traumatic memory. The therapist can help the patient develop some agreement and compassion that all parts are suffering in some way, regardless of what caused the suffering. Or perhaps there can be agreement that some memories happened, while others can still be disputed. The former could then be a focus of treatment. It is imperative that the therapist not take sides in this conflict, which belongs to the patient as a whole.

- How does the traumatic memory present itself? For example, does it suddenly appear in the form of a flashback in reaction to triggers? If so, the patient should be grounded, the flashback contained, and some collaborative agreement made between patient and therapist about the next steps. Does it first appear in the writings, drawings, or other productions of parts? If so, it should be discussed, at least on a cognitive level, in session first. Does some part of the patient share it over e-mail or in letters to the therapist but refuse to talk about it in session? If so, the conflict between telling and not telling must first be addressed.

- Does the patient switch to a part in session that insists on telling the therapist? Hijacking a session does little to help the patient. The therapist can stop the part and have the patient check inside about what is happening with other parts and whether they are aware this part wants to share a memory. Often it is helpful to ask if all parts agree that the memory will be shared, because commonly parts will object. Then the therapist can help the patient focus on the conflicts about remembering among parts, smoothing the way to more direct work on the memory.

- Does a part want to share and insist it is a secret that cannot be shared with other parts? This is a common presentation, and the therapist can become triangulated in a conflict between parts. The therapist can explore why it needs to be a secret rather than listen to the content. The answer is often that the patient or some part of the patient would be overwhelmed. The therapist can then hand the dilemma back to the patient, asking all parts (to the degree possible) to participate in resolving the conflict before preparations for the actual guided synthesis can proceed.

- Is there a strong dependence on the therapist and a tendency to reach out during frequent crises? If so, can the therapist and patient both acknowledge and work with the dependent yearnings and not collude in acting them out? This is essential for the safe and contained integration of traumatic memories. Otherwise, during the treatment of traumatic memories the patient may escalate in the need of the therapist and be unable to tolerate the intensity of dependence, leading to a therapeutic crisis or impasse.

- How strong are amnestic barriers between parts, or how well can they be created temporarily with hypnosis and imaginal techniques to prevent the intrusion of traumatic memory before it is appropriate to share with certain parts of the patient? Amnesia is a double-edged sword. On the one hand, strong amnestic barriers may allow potentially overwhelming work to be done temporarily outside the awareness of some parts. On the other hand, the greater the amnestic barriers, the greater the level of non-realization, meaning that even if work is done with some parts, other parts may be unable to accept that work as their own yet. Finally, there is nothing magical or invincible about dissociative barriers between parts. Even strong dissociative barriers can break down under duress.

continues

- Has the therapist been successful with particular approaches in Phase 1 with the patient (for example, sensorimotor therapy, hypnosis, or EMDR for stabilization and resourcing)? If so, the approach is already familiar to the patient and may work well in Phase 2.
- Is the patient able to remain safe after working on traumatic memories? If self-destructive behaviors or suicidality occur after sessions, these should be immediately explored. The contents of the memory may be beyond the tolerance of the patient, so work should stop until safety can be assured. However, in some instances unsafe behaviors after a synthesis session may indicate that a significant part of the memory was not integrated and needs further attention. Careful exploration of what precipitated the unsafe behavior will help the therapist know whether to slow down or focus more specifically on a memory.
- Is the patient able to be aware of and utilize somatic experiences (sensation, posture, movement) when accessing traumatic memory in each dissociative part, if and when needed? This ability may be important, as traumatic memory is primarily a somatosensory experience, held in some parts and not in others. For example, when the patient can intentionally shift a collapsed posture or make a movement of defense that was inhibited in order to complete it, these somatic interventions facilitate the integration of traumatic memory. Or a fight part can compassionately support a collapsed, shut-down part, giving the latter part a sense of competence, which supports movement from being fixed in despair to realization and integration in the present. The patient's physical experience in both parts then corresponds to a more mindful, present narrative.
- Does a perpetrator-imitating part punish other parts by forcing them to relive what happened? If so, this is a reenactment in itself and needs to be directly addressed. Approaches to these parts of the patient were discussed in Chapter 17.

barriers. All parts might share together with each other and with the therapist simultaneously.

The relational context of flashbacks. The therapist must be alert to the relational and social contexts in which traumatic memories emerge, as they may have unconscious communications that are best approached with a relational process first, before focusing on the content of the memories. Like any symptom, flashbacks may have multiple meanings, including the conveyance of a nonverbal relational communication. For example, uncontained flashbacks serve the function of attachment seeking in some patients. Thus, an upsurge of memories may potentially be the vehicle for an attachment cry to elicit care from the therapist or a partner.

CORE CONCEPT

Flashbacks that creates a crisis may have an additional function in some cases of an attachment-seeking strategy to elicit care from the therapist (or others). Therapists should be aware of the situational and relational context of flashbacks, in addition to the content of the memories.

CASE EXAMPLE OF A RELATIONAL CONTEXT FOR TRAUMATIC MEMORIES: YOLANDA

Yolanda's therapist noticed that her flashbacks always occurred at the end of the sessions. This was not a conscious act on the part of the patient, and was sometimes due to Yolanda's reluctance to deal with painful material until the last minute. However, careful inquiry revealed that Yolanda tended to have more flashbacks when she feared being alone. The flashback partially served to keep the therapist's attention and extend the session. The flashbacks were somewhat contained by helping Yolanda feel more connected as she left session. She was supported in making connections with others during the week, and taking time to support inner parts. She was encouraged to imagine an ideal figure. Yolanda was able to comfort a child part of herself that felt lonely, and this also reduced the flashbacks.

Countertransference in the treatment of traumatic memories. Therapists often have strong emotions and reactions to hearing terrible stories of trauma (Dalenberg, 2000; Figley, 1995; 2015; Pearlman & Saakvitne, 1995; Saakvitne & Pearlman, 1996; Wilson & Thomas, 2004). They may lean toward either of two poles of countertransference (Van der Hart & Steele, 1999; Van der Hart et al., 2006). First, they may develop a morbid fascination with the content of the memories and overly focus on graphic details, asking the patient for gruesome minutiae. While salient aspects of the memory are sometimes contained in the details, the focus of the therapist should be on the patient's process in the present and whether sufficient integration of the memory has taken place rather than on content per se. Details are important only to the degree that allows the patient to realize and integrate the memory.

Fascinated therapists may focus excessively and prematurely on traumatic memories as though that is all the treatment that is needed, neglecting the needs of the patient to have breaks and time to assimilate the memories. We have seen several cases in which therapists worked on traumatic memories in every session for extended times, or had daily sessions for months on end, in the hopes that once all the memories were resolved the patient would get better. None of these patients did well, in part because they were outside their window of tolerance, and in part because a maladaptive dependence developed on the therapists, who did not recognize it as an issue to be resolved.

On the other hand, therapists may overidentify with the patient's avoidance and suffering, and collude to circumvent traumatic memories. While stabilization is important, so is the treatment of traumatic memory. It is understandable that a therapist new to working with traumatic memory would be hesitant, fearful of doing harm. This can be overcome with good consultation and careful small excursions with the patient into the work. In these cases, therapist and patient gain mastery together and can move forward.

Some therapists are overwhelmed by or afraid of the patient's suffering. Perhaps they cannot tolerate hearing the details of horrific abuse. Perhaps they feel too helpless in the face of intense suffering, and their wish to rescue and caretake is overly activated.

Therapists' personal unresolved trauma or other salient issues may be activated. They then may take an overly enmeshed or distanced stance. Good personal therapy, regular consultation or supervision, and maintenance of clear boundaries all help the therapist who feels too close to the intensity or too distant.

Resolution of Major Conflicts About Traumatic Memories

The core of trauma-related disorders is avoidance of traumatic memories. In relational trauma, avoidance is not only due to fear. It can be due to shame, betrayal, pain, loneliness, hopelessness, or helplessness, among others. When patients have dissociated traumatic memories, their avoidance can be extreme. This avoidance manifests in the various trauma-related phobias, and results in resistance. The therapist must take care to ensure that each phobia is addressed sufficiently prior to direct work on traumatic memories. In this way, over the course of Phase 1, the phobias are gradually addressed, allowing the patient to safely approach traumatic memories with mastery. Figure 20.1 depicts the layering of trauma-related phobias and the sequence by which the therapist generally approaches them.

True–not true conflicts. As Judith Herman noted, "To deny horrible events and to proclaim them out loud has been the central preoccupation of traumatized people" (1990, p. 289). Some parts of the patient may deny that anything at all happened, while others are desperately trying to tell the

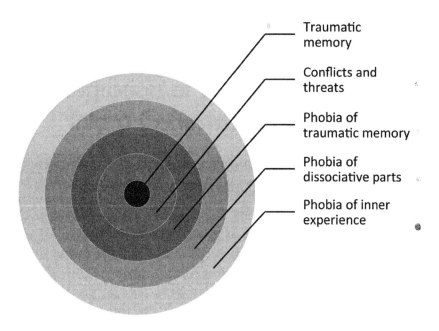

Figure 20.1. Resistances to the Integration of Traumatic Memories

story. In this case, the therapist must not take either side, but should compassionately empathize with the conflict: *On the one hand, part of you seems terrified and wants to tell about what caused that terror. On the other hand, a part of you says that you are lying. It seems to me that regardless of what is true or not, the fact is that you are really suffering. Is that something all parts could agree on?*

Therapists should not be pulled to reflexively tell the patient they believe what happened. This conflict of realization must remain the burden of the patient. However, the therapist can reflect with the patient on what is and is not known (Van der Hart & Nijenhuis, 1999). *Well, we know your father drank heavily and that your mother was depressed and spent a lot of days in bed. We know your father beat your brother and sister. You are questioning this part of you that says he beat you. At the least, you were witnessing some pretty hard things in your house that were terrifying and confusing. Maybe you could just hear what that part has to say without judging yet? I'm sure that over time you and that part can sort it out. But first you need some space to listen to each other.*

There may be times when the story the patient tells is so inconceivable that the therapist does not believe it. There can be many reasons why the patient reports inaccuracies, not the least of which is the imperfect nature of memory and the limited understanding of events by a young child. This does not mean the patient is lying. Misremembered or distorted memories can coexist with accurate ones, and fantasy can become confused with reality. Memory is not like a video recorder; it is a *representation* of what happened, and it may change over time. Sometimes memory distortions serve the purpose of preventing the patient from having to deal with the very real and painful memories of childhood that were more "mundane" but yet too painful to realize. These are called *screen memories*.

However, sometimes a fantastical story turns out to be true. One patient told an implausible story of being kidnapped at age 3 by a strange woman in broad daylight from her living room while her parents were home, used as a human shield during a police chase, and having the kidnapper be shot dead and fall on top of her, tumbling them down a cliff. She said that her parents and siblings denied it happened. However, she was able to find a newspaper account of the story, which exactly fit her description, and was then able to get the police report that included her name. Her parents continued to refuse to acknowledge it happened, for reasons only they might be able to understand.

Threats. A major conflict with many dissociative patients is a chronic terror of being threatened if they "tell." Most commonly, these threats are re-enacted by perpetrator-imitating parts internally (see chapter 17). The patient may hear something like, *Shut up! Don't talk. If you tell you are dead.* The patient feels severely threatened because there is limited realization that the threats are now in the past, not in the present. These inner threats are also protective in that they defend the patient against intolerable memories. Telling is one step closer to realization, and often there is some magical thinking that occurs, such as *If I don't say it out loud, it isn't real.*

Threats are often memories of intimidations by abusers who feared that the patient (as a child) would get them in trouble. Parts that live in trauma-time experience these threats as current and real. However, some threats may not have literally come from the perpetrator but are internally generated coercions to maintain non-realization. Regardless, the patient's sense is that it is dangerous or even life-threatening to talk about what happened. It is important to access threats and resolve the power they have over the patient. Prior to work with traumatic memory, the therapist might work intensively with perpetrator-imitating parts to decrease inner threats and gain cooperation about working on traumatic memories.

CASE EXAMPLE OF INNER THREATS AGAINST TELLING: THOMAS

Thomas told his therapist that he had been sexually abused by his neighbor when he had lived with his grandmother for about six weeks at age 10. In the next session, he reported he had developed a tic: When he was outside his head made an uncontrollable movement of suddenly turning around as far as possible, as though to look behind him. When the therapist explored the tic with Thomas, they found it was a repetitive behavior of a terrified child part stuck in trauma-time, looking behind himself for the perpetrator. This frightened child part reported that the perpetrator had told him, *Don't you dare talk about this to anybody, because whenever you are and wherever you do, I will know about it and will come and kill you.* Once Thomas was able to be aware of the threat and help the child part be more aware of the present and know he was safe, the tic stopped.

Once these inner conflicts have been lessened, and some cooperation and compassion has been established among parts, careful steps to work with traumatic memory can commence. Specific approaches and techniques are discussed in the following chapter.

Further Explorations

20.1 How do you feel about helping patients work through traumatic memories? Do you feel hesitant? If so, why? Discuss your feelings with colleagues.

20.2 Have you ever had the experience of a patient working with a traumatic memory too soon and becoming overwhelmed? Looking back on the experience, what might you have done differently to help contain the memory or keep it within the patient's window of tolerance?

20.3 Do you always believe the traumatic memories of your patients? Are you sometimes skeptical? How do you handle the feeling of not believing your patient, if you have had that experience? How can you be with a patient compassionately even if you are unsure if the memory is accurate?

20.4 What theories do you hold about the nature of traumatic memories, and how do they affect what you do in therapy?

CHAPTER 21

Treatment of Traumatic Memory: Guidelines and Techniques

I suggest that it is not the discharge of tension, the getting it out,
that is helpful, but the communication of emotion and memory
to another person (i.e., a two-person psychology)—and other
parts of self—that is healing.

—Elizabeth Howell (2011, pp. 178–179)

In this chapter we describe practical approaches and techniques that are most commonly used with dissociative patients to resolve traumatic memories in Phase 2. Once the therapist and patient together have determined that it is appropriate to work with traumatic memories, they must spend time preparing for these sessions and making decisions about which approaches will be most effective. Regardless of the approach or techniques employed, therapists should be able to make them their own, so they are organically integrated into the session to the degree possible. The therapist should always explain techniques before they are used and obtain informed consent.

Many of the techniques described below can be used in some form during Phase 1, so both patient and therapist already have a sense of what works best and have both practiced together. We cannot emphasize enough that relational connection is always foremost, followed by a collaborative effort to keep patients within their window of tolerance. Techniques are merely adjuncts to maintain regulation and support integration; they are not magical formulas that create an alchemy of integration. Kluft (2013) has wisely noted that once the therapist understands what makes a technique work, often that knowledge can be used without need of the technique.

CORE CONCEPT

The therapeutic relationship is of prime importance in the treatment of traumatic memories in dissociative patients. Techniques for working with traumatic memories should merely be adjuncts in helping the patient remain within a window of tolerance and present with the therapist.

The treatment of traumatic memory is rarely simple in dissociative patients. While the following approaches and techniques appear straightforward, this work often looks quite messy and unclear in practice. A technique that worked beautifully last week may be completely ineffective this week. Grounding and remaining in the present may be a huge challenge for the patient, and uneven. Parts that agreed to the scope of work may suddenly become too overwhelmed to move forward. Both patient and therapist can get stuck with how to address a memory. The therapist needs to be prepared for the challenges, uncertainties, and imperfections of the work, as with all of the therapy, and maintain realistic expectations and a patient attitude as traumatic memories emerge. Table 21.1 offers an overview of an integrative approach to resolving traumatic memories.

Stabilization skills are described in detail in other publications (e.g., Boon et al., 2011; Chu, 2011; Cloitre et al. 2002, 2006; Courtois & Ford, 2013; Kluft & Fine, 1993). They are a primary focus in Phase 1 and thus will not be discussed here. However, therapists must ensure that patients are ready and able to approach traumatic memories, and must be familiar with contraindications.

Psychoeducation and Informed Consent

Patients need to understand the necessity for approaching traumatic memories. They have avoided them for so long that they need some motivation to integrate what is so very painful. Therapists can help draw links between unintegrated traumatic memories and ongoing nightmares, relational reenactments, fear and shame, and the continued suffering of parts, for example. It is important for the patient to at least cognitively understand the differences between remembering something painful and reliving it. For example, most patients can usually recall a minor emotional experience that they no longer feel acutely.

TABLE 21.1

Treatment Approaches to Traumatic Memory in Dissociative Patients

- A stable therapeutic relationship
- Adequate psychoeducation about traumatic memory work
- Informed consent, including potential benefits and negative consequences, and options regarding various methods
- A preparation time in the first third (or less) of the session (Kluft, 1991, 2013; Van der Hart et al., 1993; Van der Hart et al., 2006)
  - Discussion of what the patient will need after the session for safety, comfort, and support
  - Discussion of how the session will be conducted (e.g., what memory, what kind of fractionation, what parts will be involved)
  - Guided imagery in the beginning of the session, potentially including
    - Meeting space, such as the dissociative table (Fraser, 1991, 2003) for inner agreement about the scope of work and which parts will and will not participate
    - Safe or healing space or other containment imagery for parts that are not participating (Boon et al., 2011; Fraser, 1991, 2003; Hammond, 1990b; Kluft, 1982, 1988a, 1989, 1994b, 2013; Steele & Colrain, 1990; Van der Hart, 2012; Van der Hart et al., 1993, 2006)
    - Ideal, wise figure or advisor for inner support and guidance (Bresler, 1990; Krakauer, 2001; Parnell, 2013; Phillips & Frederick, 1995; Rossman, 1987).
    - Containment imagery for other memories that may emerge, and for the end of the session (Boon et al., 2011; Steele & Colrain, 1990; Van der Hart, 2012)
- Guided synthesis—sharing among dissociative parts, linking and differentiating the past and present in the second third of the session
  - Imaginal exposure
  - Optimal modulation of experience
    - Dual attention between the past and present and ability to stay grounded even when emotion is intense (e.g., Kluft, 1982, 2013; Knipe, 2009b, 2014; Van der Hart et al., 2006)
    - Ability to reground and become present if outside the window of tolerance (Kluft, 2013; Knipe, 2009b, 2014)
    - Use of distancing techniques (e.g., H. Spiegel & Spiegel, 1978)
    - Use of fractionation techniques that involve working with only a small portion of experience at time (e.g., Boon, 1997; Greenwald, 2013; Gonzalez & Mosquera, 2012; Kluft, 1982, 1988a, 1990a, 1990b, 1994b, 2013; D. Johnson & Lubin, 2005; Lazrove & Fine, 1996; Ochberg, 1996;

Paulsen & Lanius, 2014; D. Spiegel, 1981; Twombly, 2000; Van der Hart et al., 2014; Van der Hart et al., 2006; Wolpe, 1982 Wright & Wright, 1987)

- Adequate closure and containment of guided synthesis in the last third of the session
- Guided realization—may take place over time (Van der Hart et al., 1993, 2006)
  - Personification
  - Presentification

CORE CONCEPT

The therapist should describe the differences between reliving and remembering to the patient, using examples from the patient's own experience. The need to stay in the present and connected with the therapist while remembering is emphasized.

Perhaps the most important education is to reassure patients that they are in control and can stop at any time. This might even be practiced in the preparation phase, with the patient saying *Stop!* or indicating with a hand signal to stop. The therapist must indeed stop, but can inquire about why the patient feels that continuing would not be helpful. In this way, a collaborative and trusting partnership is used to support this demanding work.

Psychoeducation involves exploring with the patient what might be needed in order for work on a particular memory to occur and what care might need to be taken after the session. Some patients need much support after sessions, and may want a partner or other support person to drive them home after a session. However, the session should be planned so that the patient has ample time afterward to recuperate and reflect. Thus, generally it should not be conducted in the morning before a patient's workday, for example, or on the first day of a demanding week.

Informed consent is an essential part of every therapy and, of course, should be given before the treatment of dissociative disorders commences. However, the treatment of traumatic memory should have its own informed consent in regard to the techniques and approaches from which the patient and therapist can choose, and the benefits and potential adverse reactions. Again, this gives the patient a sense of choice and control, which is a good foundation with which to begin traumatic memory work.

Preparation

Planned extended sessions of 75 to 90 minutes may be helpful, not to increase intensity and duration of experiences, but rather to more slowly fractionate the traumatic memories for adequate synthesis and realization, and to leave the patient with plenty of time to become regrounded and fully reoriented to the present. Kluft (1991, 2013) has noted that preparation should occur early in the first third or less of the session; synthesis in the second third; and grounding, orientation, and cognitive work in the last third. Work started late in the session is likely to overwhelm the patient at the end, as there is insufficient closure time. It is essential to end synthesis sessions on time, as it gives the patient a sense of containment.

CORE CONCEPT

Sessions dedicated to the treatment of traumatic memory must be paced so that there is plenty of time at the end to help all parts of the patient ground and be calm, to adequately contain any unfinished work, and complete the session on time.

The therapist first prepares the patient for work with traumatic memories by helping the patient stay oriented and grounded in the present, in good contact with the therapist. This grounding and dual attention is carefully maintained (as much as is feasible) throughout work with traumatic memories.

Choosing a traumatic memory. Most patients have many traumatic memories, so which memory is best to choose first? Most simply, it is usually helpful to begin with the least intense and overwhelming memories first, if possible. This way patients learn that they can do the work effectively, and they have ample practice before more overwhelming events are integrated.

Ideally, a cognitive overview of the memory can be obtained from some part of the patient without the risk of reexperiencing, but this is not always possible. Sometimes there are only vague allusions to a trauma, such as *that time in the basement,* or *the time when my brother was mean.* Other times there is no cognitive content at all, but only emotional or sensorimotor symptoms, such as panic, fear, shame, physical pain, or a repetitive movement.

CORE CONCEPT

Guided synthesis should begin with having the patient (and dissociative parts) be present and grounded with the therapist.

Decisions about which parts should participate. Planning also involves decisions about which parts can and should participate. This is a major difference in working with traumatic memories in dissociative patients versus those who are not dissociative. Some, but certainly not most, patients have the integrative capacity for all parts to participate simultaneously. When a patient has DID and a demanding daily life that could potentially crumble—for example, a high-powered job or raising several children—the part or parts that function in daily life may temporarily be left out of the work. They may eventually be able to watch from "a safe distance" when synthesis takes place. This allows more time to build integrative capacity in the adult parts. However, dissociative barriers do not always hold, so work should be fractionated carefully until it is determined what these parts can tolerate. When the time is right, the therapist must be able to help these parts realize that these memories also belong to them.

Managing arousal. It is essential that the patient's level of arousal remain in the window of tolerance, and that both patient and therapist have sufficient control. Panic and switching among parts so that the memory is not accessible to the presenting part of the patient should be prevented.

Beginning and end of a memory. Therapist and patient need to have an idea of the beginning and end of the memory, which offers a time boundary that can be used to help the patient realize the memory had a beginning, a middle, and an end. One difficulty is that often patients had repetitive trauma, so the end of one memory was not the end of being traumatized. Thus, even when they know that one episode ended, they also know more was to come. Therefore, the therapist should also help all parts connect with the present, *after the very last time it happened.*

Pathogenic kernels. It is useful for the therapist to know or at least have a vague notion of the most threatening or overwhelming parts of the traumatic memory, the parts that the patient wants to avoid at all costs, which have been called *pathogenic kernels* (Van der Hart et al., 2006). These can include anything, such as a certain feeling, a bodily sensation, a cognition, a belief (e.g., *I am dying*), or something that was heard, seen, or done. For a traumatic memory to be completely integrated, these pathogenic kernels must be resolved. Of course, it is not always possible to know, so the therapist should be prepared that some unexpected part of the memory may emerge in a synthesis session. For example, one patient was focused on a memory of his father abusing him in bed, and suddenly there emerged the awareness that his younger brother was also in the room. He recalled that his father had made the two of them abuse each other as he watched. This was devastating to him and held tremendous shame, because he felt responsible as the older sibling for abusing his younger brother. The shame needed to be dealt with explicitly during guided synthesis and afterward.

CORE CONCEPT

Traumatic memories contain pathogenic kernels—that is, experiences, emotions, sensations, or beliefs that were the most overwhelming. These must be accessed, realized, and integrated for treatment of traumatic memories to be effective.

The therapist should beware of assuming what might be the most difficult aspect of a traumatizing event. Many patients, for example, report that although being raped was horrible, it was the feeling of being utterly alone afterward or having to pretend like nothing had happened that was the most overwhelming and devastating.

Guided Synthesis

Guided synthesis is a planned, collaborative effort of controlled reactivation and sharing (see Chapter 9). The first step in synthesis with dissociative patients is sharing the memory among dissociative parts, on a cognitive level if at all possible. There is usually some degree of amnesia or other lack of realization for what happened in at least some dissociative parts of the patient. While not all parts may participate at first, eventually the whole person must know and accept that an event happened to her or him.

CORE CONCEPT

Guided synthesis is the planned and intentional sharing of a traumatic memory among dissociative parts, so that there is no longer amnesia for the experience and the long process of realization can begin.

Synthesis is different from reliving or having a flashback. The patient remains grounded in the present and connected with the therapist while intentionally remembering in a paced manner. Fractionation or distancing techniques may be necessary to help the patient in this regard, and some of these are described below.

Synthesis vs. exposure. The term *exposure* is first and foremost a description of the patient coming into awareness of and contact with traumatic memory. It does not necessarily result in integration. All treatment of traumatic memory, by definition, involves at least some degree of exposure. However, the word is currently more commonly used to describe particular approaches. Traditional exposure therapies (including prolonged exposure, flooding, and implosion) emphasize the importance of reexperiencing the memory intensely and in detail, going over and over it until it loses its emotional intensity (e.g., Foa et al., 2009; Foa & Kozak, 1986; Foa & Rothbaum, 1998. The main goal of traditional exposure therapy is to alleviate or reduce fear and anxiety. There should also be a concurrent decrease in the maladaptive thoughts and beliefs that are associated with the fear (Foa & Kozak, 1986). However, many dissociative patients simply cannot tolerate such intense experiences, and thus techniques that do not offer modulation can be destructive.

Furthermore, the core of many memories of relational trauma is not fear, but shame or other intense emotions such as rage, guilt, grief, unbearable loneliness, yearning, or the insoluble conflicts between safety and defense in disorganized attachment. Patients with DID exposed to a memory may perhaps no longer feel fear, but might be left with despair that they had caregivers who were abusive, or that so much of their life has been adversely affected by what happened. Indeed, there is no clear evidence that prolonged exposure approaches alone are helpful with these complicated relational experiences. For example, in one study, intense exposure to shame experiences was rated as unhelpful by patients (Dorahy et al., 2015), whereas the most effective intervention was a focus on how the patient managed shame.

Finally, exposure to a traumatic memory per se does not guarantee that all parts of the patient are aware of the memory, nor does it guarantee synthesis. Patients can be exposed to a memory and continue to experience it as something that happened to someone else.

CORE CONCEPT

Exposure is not synthesis. Exposure is only the beginning of synthesis and does not address the need for dissociative parts to share memories.

Binding and differentiation. Synthesis involves both binding (or linking) and differentiation (Van der Hart et al., 1993, 2006). As parts share what happened from their perspective (linking), the person as a whole can develop a more nuanced and reflective perspective on what happened (differentiation). For example, the patient is able to link or bind somatic sensations and emotions to the memory, and then differentiate the memory as a past experience, not something that is happening in the here and now. One part may help clarify that another part's fear of a dangerous monster who lived in his room was actually a defense against realizing that the patient's brother abused him. Thus, the patient can then differentiate between fantasy and reality, and help the young part of himself accept reality as well. One part stuck in the middle of the memory may link to another part that experienced the end, leading to realization and great relief that the event is over. The part stuck in the middle of the memory can then also distinguish past from present.

Many clinicians use the BASK model of dissociation as a guide for ensuring all aspects of experience are included in synthesis. BASK is an acronym that stands for *behavior, affect, sensation,* and cognitions and beliefs, or *knowledge* (Braun, 1988a, 1988b). The therapist can help the patient know what happened on a cognitive level, what was felt emotionally and bodily (including all the senses), and what were the behaviors and actions of both the perpetrator and the patient. All BASK components should be integrated.

Beginning the synthesis session. All parts that are to participate in working with the memory are gathered, perhaps in a meeting room, or are imagined in the session in the way in which the patient is accustomed. Parts that will not participate, if any, are asked to go to their safe or calm space, to "take a nap," or to otherwise be contained. Any concerns about the upcoming work are briefly discussed, and the therapist ensures again that all parts have agreed to the work. The patient may hold a stone or other anchor as a concrete reminder of the present.

Specific Techniques

There are many approaches to traumatic memories in dissociative patients. While it is not possible to describe each approach in detail, we have tried to give some examples of each. Therapists are strongly encouraged to get appropriate training and supervision on approaches they wish to use. The risk of harm is great with dissociative patients, particularly in working with traumatic memories without sufficient training.

- **Hypnotic approaches, including ego state therapy:** Boon, 1997; D. Brown & Fromm, 1986; Fine, 1993, 1999, 2012; Kluft, 1982, 1988a, 1989, 1990a, 1990b, 1992a, 1992b, 1994b, 1996a, 1996b, 2001, 2013; Phillips & Frederick, 1995; Steele & Colrain, 1990; Van der Hart, 1991; Van der Hart et al., 1993, 2014; J. G. Watkins & Watkins, 1991, 1997
- **EMDR approaches**: Fine & Berkowitz, 2001; Gelinas, 2003; Gonzalez & Mosquera, 2012; Knipe, 2009a, 2009b, 2014; Lazrove & Fine, 1996; O'Shea, 2009; Paulsen & Lanius, 2014; Twombly, 2000; Van der Hart et al., 2014
- **Combinations of hypnosis and EMDR**: Beere, Simon, & Welch, 2001; Fine & Berkowitz, 2001; Forgash & Copeley, 2007; Forgash & Knipe, 2008; Paulsen & Lanius, 2014
- **Somatic approaches:** Fisher, 2011; Levine & Frederick, 1997; Ogden & Minton, 2002; Ogden et al., 2006; Ogden & Fisher, 2015

There are countless entrées into traumatic memory. The most obvious is a cognitive accounting of the memory. Patients can be asked to recall the memory and just notice what happens as they remember. Sometimes a particular part will begin with other parts participating together, or perhaps from a short distance. Any type of body sensation can be used: *As you feel that tightness in your chest, just allow your mind to go back to that time when you felt it so strongly, and notice what happens next.* Sensorimotor approaches utilize somatic entrées (Ogden & Minton, 2002; Ogden et al., 2006; Ogden & Fisher, 2015), as do EMDR approaches (e.g., Gonzalez & Mosquera, 2012; Frewen & Lanius, 2015).

John Watkins (1971) developed a hypnotic technique called the Affect Bridge. With this technique the patient focuses on a particular affect, perhaps fear, and follows the emotion back to the time when it was felt in the past (during the traumatic memory), as though the emotion is a bridge the patient crosses from the present to the past. The EMDR Float Back technique (Shapiro, 1994, 1996) is based on the Affect Bridge technique and may be used in a similar manner.

Optimal Distance From the Memory

Imaginal exposure techniques encourage the patient to experience the full intensity of the memory. However, most dissociative patients quickly go outside their window of tolerance or engage in further dissociation, such as switching between parts, during this type of exposure. Thus, the therapist needs a variety of ways to help the patient approach a memory with slow, careful modulation, building tolerance for the experience and remaining in the present. Distancing techniques primarily involve imagery that helps the patient feel more physical and emotional distance from a traumatic memory.

Screen technique. The traumatic memory can be observed on a small screen by parts of the patient that are participating in the synthesis session. The patient, as the adult part, might imagine a room or theater in which the parts sit far away from the screen. They have a remote control that controls the picture on the screen. They can stop, fast-forward, rewind, or freeze the frame, and change the channel as needed. They can take away colors or sound, or make the picture vague if there is a need to reduce the intensity.

Split screen. The split-screen technique (e.g., Kluft, 2013; D. Spiegel, 1981; H. Spiegel & Spiegel, 1978) involves two screens side by side, one of which has the traumatic memory and the other of which has an image of a safe and serene place. If the patient becomes too dysregulated, the safe image is superimposed upon and blots out the memory image. This provides a kind of pendulation between regulation and dysregulation (Levine & Frederick, 1997).

Other distancing techniques. Parts of the patient can imagine watching the memory as though through the wrong end of binoculars or a telescope, so that it seems at a great distance. Young parts stuck in trauma-time can watch the memory through the eyes of the adult part of the patient, sitting on their lap and being held by the adult part, or through the eyes of an ideal figure.

Dual Attention

The therapist needs to ensure that all parts of the patient that are involved in a synthesis session are anchored in the present (while any other parts are safely contained). This may include fostering mindfulness during the recall of traumatic memories (Walser & Hayes, 2006), or helping the patient engage in what Shapiro (2001) termed dual attention to the past and present simultaneously. This dual focus helps the patient refrain from becoming completely embedded in the memory, which can be retraumatizing.

Dual attention to here and now and then and there helps the patient experience the presence of the therapist. It creates a certain distance from reliving. It helps the patient observe the memory rather than be completely stuck in it. Thus, the patient knows, *I am remembering and I am here, even as I experience the intensity of the memory.* Being in the present supports the patient in staying within the window of tolerance.

The key in using titration is to ensure an optimal distance so that the patient can tolerate the experience, but not so much that salient aspects of the memory continue to be avoided. Indeed, many patients, especially dissociative parts that function in daily life, are masterful at recounting their trauma in detail, but in an entirely depersonalized way, so they continue to be plagued by flashbacks and other symptoms of ongoing integrative failure.

Titration Techniques

There are innumerable techniques to support working with small increments of traumatic memory. A few are listed below.

Connection with the therapist in the present. The therapeutic relationship is the most important grounding and regulating aspect of working with traumatic memories.

Subjective Units of Distress (SUDS). Patients can rate their level of distress on a scale of 1–10. *At what number do you feel calm and present? At what number should we stop? Do parts of you have different experiences of SUDS? If so, let us stop when the part of you least able to tolerate it reaches the limit.*

Rheostat. Patients can imagine a rheostat or a thermometer with which they can turn down particular emotions or sensations. This technique requires some practice before it is used with an intense feeling. It can be paired with relaxation and breathing techniques that help calm the patient.

Pendulation. The patient can be helped to draw attention back and forth between sensations of regulation and dysregulation (Levine & Frederick, 1997). *Just notice a sensation of feeling the safety of here and now and my presence with you. Now notice just one small sensation of the fear. Move your attention back and forth like a pendulum between the feeling of safety and the feeling of fear and notice what happens.* The patient can also imagine tracing a path between the positive and negative sensations in the shape of an infinity symbol (∞), which adds in bilateral stimulation.

Safe, calm, or healing space. During breaks in synthesis, parts can imagine going to their calm space and resting, becoming replenished and full with compassion, safety, calmness, serenity, soothing, and care.

Bracketing. A memory can be bracketed with a positive memory that happened before the event and one that happened afterward (the latter may be in the present), so the patient knows there is a beginning and end, it is over, and it begins and ends with a positive experience.

Time distortions. Time distortions are hypnotic techniques that distort the patient's time sense. Time sense is generally lost during traumatizing events, and traumatic memories feel as though they do not end (Van der

Hart & Steele, 1997). Some techniques can help with linking the patient with the end of an event to know it is over. However, the therapist should be certain that the end of an event does not lead to the beginning of another. For example, a patient told of a time when her father was abusing her. The logical end of the event was when her father left the room. However, in this case, a short while later the patient's mother entered her room and severely beat her for "seducing" her father. The actual "end" was not after she was raped, but after the mother had betrayed her and had beaten her to the point of unconsciousness.

Anchoring the end of the event. The therapist can facilitate the patient's time sense by helping all parts be aware of the end of the event before synthesis begins. For example, the therapist might say something like, *You are here and now, so your mind, some part of your mind knows very well that the event* did *end. There came a certain moment in time, an exact moment in time when you knew in some part of your mind that it was over. That moment in time can be an anchor and when you remember, it will remind you that you are here and now, not then and there. This room, your adult self, and my presence with you allow you, and all parts of you, to know with* absolute certainty *that it* did *end, to know that you, and all parts of you,* did *survive, and that no matter where you find yourself in your memory, those facts accompany you and anchor you. Knowing it ended and being here and now are faithful companions who offer support and confidence in all your remembering. Just take a moment to know and feel that in all corners of your mind and your body, in all parts of yourself.*

Of course, in chronic trauma, the end of one event hardly heralds the end of abuse. The therapist might also add a more definitive link to the present, such as, *And even as you know for certain that event ended, you are also aware of here and now with me, after* all *the times you were hurt have ended. This is the end after the last end, where you are no longer hurt. This is here and now, where it is safe and you are no longer vulnerable or hurt. Let your entire mind, your entire body, all parts of you feel and sense and know for certain that the past, all the past, is over, and you are in the present.*

CASE EXAMPLE OF BEGINNING SYNTHESIS WITH THE END OF AN EVENT: JANNA

Janna, a patient who had DID and a particularly horrible abuse history, needed to integrate a traumatic memory that included the belief that she was going to die (during the trauma). Janna believed a child part of her had died when she passed out during the abuse and was thus adamant in her refusal to proceed with guided synthesis, believing this part would die each time she relived the event. The therapist was able to arrange with other parts that they could first synthesize how this traumatizing event ended, which included, of course, a strong sense that the patient had survived the ordeal. Following a successful synthesis of the end of the experience, work could indeed be done with the "death" experience preceding it.

Time contraction. Speeding up time sense is helpful during synthesis in some cases, especially if the patient is recalling a traumatic event that lasted for a long period; for example, a repeated rape and assault that occurred over the course of several days. The therapist can suggest something like, *As you remember, you will find that the time of the event seems very short, so quick that almost in the blink of an eye, it seems as though a long time has passed. You need only focus on what you have most avoided about the memory, the part that was most difficult for you. It is not necessary to know every detail. Only that which you have avoided. As you remember, you have the ability to control the passage of time, as though the hands of the clock are moving faster and faster, so the hours of what happened seem like mere minutes, and the minutes seem like short seconds, and the seconds so short that you can know and remember all you need of that time in just a few short moments that are hardly noticeable in the passage of time. Remember that you need only know and accept and realize what you have avoided, what was most challenging for you to accept.*

Time expansion. Slowing down time sense may be helpful during breaks when the patient is resting or imaging a safe space. This gives the patient a sense of leisurely recuperation. That therapist can say something like, *And as you take a well-deserved rest for a job well done, as you rest in your beautiful place, just notice how relaxed and replenished you are beginning to feel, taking in the comfort and care, the safety and sustenance that are there for you. Surrounding you, around you, for every part of you, every corner of your mind and body. In the next few moments, you can take all the time you need. The seconds of rest and replenishment will seem like very long minutes, as though the . . . clock . . . has . . . slowed . . . down. The minutes have slowed . . . down . . . like long . . . leisurely . . . hours. Those hours of comfort and care seem like long . . . leisurely . . . days. Days and weeks, months and years, as long as you need and wish, take in rest and replenishment, comfort and care, safety and sustenance.*

Fractionation. Many approaches emphasize the need for small doses of memory in dissociative patients. In addition to maintaining dual attention, some modulation is often needed. This may come in the form of various types of fractionation. Fractionation was first described in the late 19th century by Oskar Vogt. He intended it as a technique to deepen trance through a repeated rapid emergence from and then reinduction of trance

(Kroger, 1977), not as a method for treating traumatic memories. The fractionated abreaction technique for treating traumatic memories in dissociative patients was first described by Kluft (1982, 1990a), who also described a variant called the *slow leak technique* (Kluft, 1982, 2013). It has been further elaborated (Fine, 1991, 1993, 1999; Kluft, 2012, 2013; Paulsen & Lanius, 2014; Van der Hart et al., 1993, 2006). Ever since, it has been used in many variations to help patients integrate traumatic memories in a paced way that prevents them from becoming overwhelmed. However, in line with our emphasis on synthesis and realization, we have called it *fractionated guided synthesis* (Van der Hart et al., 1993, 2006).

Fractionation techniques may include limiting the duration of time that the patient experiences the memory during synthesis, such as 10 or 15 or 30 seconds, and limiting the amount of experience to a small percentage at a given time instead of the full intensity.

Limiting the amount of time the patient experiences the memory may be accomplished by agreeing that synthesis occurs for a certain time period, such as 15 seconds or 30 seconds, followed by rest, and then further rounds as needed. The duration may be increased if needed, and may be started with a very small amount of time, such as 10 seconds or less. This gives the patient a sense of mastery to cope with longer periods.

The therapist can also use various counting methods, which involve the therapist counting out loud to a number previously agreed upon, with the patient visualizing the trauma (Greenwald, 2013; Johnson & Lubin, 2006; Ochberg, 1996; Van der Hart et al., 1993, 2006). Progressive counting (Greenwald, 2013) involves having the patient visualize a series of progressively longer "movies" of trauma while the therapist counts aloud, beginning with 1 to 10, then 1 to 20, then 1 to 30, and so on. However, there must first be a decision about which parts will participate when this method is used with dissociative patients.

There are many variations for fractionating experience:

- A segment of memory; for example, the very beginning or the end and no more. Van der Hart et al. (1993) described a rapid variant of synthesis in which the traumatic experience is divided into several numbered small segments (e.g., 1 to 5, or 1 to 10). This is done in collaboration with the patient, who determines how much each segment should include. The therapist says, *When you are ready, just nod.* Once the patient is ready, the therapist says, *Okay, begin. One. Share this segment of the memory with each other. Two, share the next segment . . .* and so on. The speed of the counting is adjusted to the needs of the patient at that particular moment. The therapist continues the count, encouraging parts of the patient to *share it, make it one whole, bring it together.* After the final count, the therapist says *Stop!* Then suggestions are given for rest and recuperation for several minutes, along with contact with the therapist and grounding in the present. This can be repeated as needed. The therapist can ask after each round, *How much* [of a percentage] *has now been shared?* A SUDS level can also be assessed before and after each round.

- A percentage or small amount of intensity of a segment or the entire memory; for example, just one percent, one drop out of the ocean, a dewdrop, a teaspoonful)
- A specific part or group of parts, while others are safely contained; for example, just the parts of you that were there at the end
- Pathogenic kernels—the worst aspects of the event that are often devastating to the patient and thus have been strongly avoided; for example, *I couldn't breathe while he was choking me. My mother was laughing while he raped me. I couldn't stand the smell and taste. I knew I was going to die. I had to act like I really enjoyed it, but I was dying inside. I couldn't cry out, but I was in so much pain I couldn't stand it. I knew then that it was hopeless and I could not escape. I was weak; I should have fought back. I was a filthy little girl to do those things.*
- Knowledge—this includes what happened; that is, the facts as the patient perceived them and what the patient was thinking at the time
- Emotion—what the patient felt; for example, sad, afraid, ashamed, angry. One specific emotion may be targeted at a time; for example, fear but not rage.
- Sensation—what the patient sensed in his or her body; for example, sexual arousal, pain, heat, cold, frozenness or paralysis. One sensation at a time may be targeted; for example, pain but not sexual arousal. It also includes sensations related to touching and being touched by another, or by something in the environment; for example, the roughness of the blankets, or the pine cone that was sticking in the patient's back. Guided synthesis of extreme pain often needs to be fractionated, for example, one percent at time.
- Sight—what the patient saw; for example, the emotional expression on the face of the perpetrator (*She looked like a wild animal, completely mad and unfocused*); a threat (*I saw a knife in his hand and I froze*); a certain behavior (*I saw him start to unbuckle his belt and I knew then that something terrible was going to happen.*)
- Hearing—what the patient heard is often an important component of synthesis. For example, *I heard him licking and it made me feel so disgusted; I heard him cock the gun and I knew I was dead.* One of the most important aspects of traumatic memory is often what the perpetrator said to the patient during the event. These are essential to

access, particularly any statements that it was the patient's fault, or threats; for example, *You're so pretty, you just make me do it; You're a whore; This is our little secret; Don't you dare say anything or I'll kill you (or your pet or your sister or your mother); If you say anything about this you'll regret it for the rest of your short life. I'll be watching you and I know what you say.*

- Smell—This is an essential sense to work on, as it is directly tied to the emotion of dissmell, a shame and disgust–related feeling that may maintain shame if not integrated
- Taste—Like smell, distaste is closely related to shame and disgust and must be processed to fully integrate the memory
- Behavior—what the patient and the abuser did or did not do

Of course, the entirety of the memory eventually needs to be synthesized and realized, but fractionation allows a manageable and sequenced approach that is tolerable to the patient. The idea is to begin with a very small and relatively minor fractionated episode to give the patient mastery, and move to increasingly difficult material. Most certainly, the therapist needs to collaborate with the patient to determine the ideal balance of fractionation, not too much or too little. And the therapist should beware of being so busy using creative techniques that relational connection or attending to what is happening with the patient is lost in the moment.

Ending the Synthesis Session
Two thirds of the way through the synthesis session, the therapist should help the patient close the work, ground in the present, and contain any unresolved aspects of the memory until another time. The last third of the session is focused on grounding, containing, connecting with the patient, helping parts comfort each other and rest, and some minor guided realization. Sometimes the last part of the session might include a cognitive appraisal of the work, but the therapist must be careful not to reactivate the patient. The therapist should always ask what the patient and all parts need and are experiencing after synthesis in order to ensure a part is not stuck in the memory and that the patient is not spacey or overwhelmed. Some general questions about realization can be asked, such as *Now that you have remembered, what have you learned about yourself? Can you check inside and see how all parts of you are doing? Is there anything that any part would like to say about what you remembered today?*

The patient can be encouraged to engage in good self-care and to make time for reflection as tolerated, and can be reminded of a safety plan that has already been put in place, if needed. The therapist may help the patient find a balance between a need for time alone to further realize the memory and all its meanings and time spent with caring others, which provides relational support and healing. Many patients report they feel very alone while doing memory work, as it is not often appropriate to share the details with others beyond the therapist. It is indeed a lonely journey, and that is part of the realization. However, the therapist can remind patients that meta-sharing can be very effective. For example, they can be encouraged to say something like, *I could use your support as I am going through a tough time right now*; *I am working on some painful issues*; or *I am feeling really alone and sad and would find it helpful if we could spend some time together today*. No details need be given, while the essential message of needing support and connection can be shared.

Containment. In general, any unshared parts of a traumatic memory that remain should be synthesized in future sessions so that the entire memory can be put to rest in the past. The patient can be encouraged to imagine some type of storage or container in which to place the memory or unintegrated aspects of the memory such as emotions, sensations, and so on. If possible, the patient should develop the containment imagery, and this may have already been put in place in order to contain flashbacks (see the section on flashbacks above for examples of containment imagery).

Various parts, as needed, can go to a safe or calm space and even have a deep and restful sleep afterward. Kluft (1982, 1990b, 1994b, 2012, 2013) has described the *slow leak* hypnotic technique in which he suggests that any unintegrated aspects of memory, such as the pain involved, may be leaked as slowly as needed for all parts to be able to tolerate it. This technique can be particularly helpful when there is clearly unintegrated experience at the end of the synthesis session. As helpful as containment can be, it most certainly does not always hold, and this technique anticipates the problem and turns it into a situation of potential mastery (Kluft, 2013).

Guided Realization

Guided realization is the ongoing therapeutic process of helping patients realize their history, grieve the losses, and move forward. Following synthesis sessions, the therapist helps the patient focus on further realization and related integration. What beliefs are changed or challenged? What is different for various parts? How might parts connect more effectively now that the phobia of traumatic memory is resolved? How might the patient cope differently and relate to others in new ways? How will life change when the patient is no longer driven by shame and fear?

Realization of childhood trauma involves an enormous sense of loss;

changing beliefs about self, others and the world; and changing behaviors in the present. Parts that have always been afraid or ashamed will now need to take new risks to be in the present-day world. Parts that have always disowned the trauma must now reflect on how owning what happened might make a difference in the present. Parts that have always defended against remembering now need another focus. The integration of traumatic memory implies that there is less need for parts to remain separate. Parts of the patient may naturally integrate or become much closer. (We will discuss the integration of dissociative parts in Chapter 22.)

Grieving

Successful navigation through grief is essential, a major task not only in Phase 2 but also in Phase 3 (see Chapter 23). Patients grieve what happened as well as the loss of idealized fantasies of their families. Some parts may have had truly unrealistic versions of childhood and may feel devastated, while other parts are better able to accept the way it was. Some parts are relieved to finally know the trauma is over, while other parts are in shock, only now realizing it happened at all, or that it happened to them. The therapist can encourage all parts to be together with compassion and talk about the meaning of what happened and how the present can be different now that the memory has been accepted and gradually integrated.

In their grieving, patients must be able to remain connected with what is good about their lives in the present, even if it is only enjoyment of small pleasures or gratitude for being alive. This linking of positive emotions and experiences while still grieving is a major step in moving forward, with more energy directed to the present than to the past.

Examples of Guided Synthesis

Many patients are overwhelmed by the slightest attempts to deal directly with traumatic memories, while others do well with repeated short periods of stabilization followed by limited forays into memory work. Some patients seem to do best when the therapist is able to work with specific parts behind dissociative barriers, so that adult parts may continue to function relatively well in daily life. Only later, when integrative capacity is greater in adult parts, and the parts fixed in trauma-time are stabilized, are the memories shared across all parts of the patient.

CORE CONCEPT

There is no single right way to help dissociative patients integrate traumatic memories, as each patient may need different approaches. The therapist must collaborate with patients to find what works for them rather than trying to treat traumatic memories with a single technique or approach in every case.

Some patients do well when groups of parts work on traumatic memories initially before sharing the memories with other parts. (Nonetheless, traumatic memories belong to the person as a whole and eventually must be realized and integrated by all parts.)

Others need a gradual erosion of barriers between dissociative parts, so that memories are shared among all parts slowly and over time. As one patient put it, *I am realizing slowly, like a soft spring rain that gradually sinks into the ground.* She would more and more often say to herself, *My father raped me*, while refraining from acknowledging the details. Over a long period of time, she could gradually tell a specific story and remain present, with all parts participating. In that way, she integrated the overall meaning of the trauma before she dealt with the details. In other words, she made progress in realization before she was able to completely accept and know the emotional, cognitive, and sensorimotor components of some memories. For other patients it is the opposite.

Synthesis outside of sessions. A few patients work on their traumatic memories mostly by themselves and only bring them in to therapy if they feel stuck or after they have been integrated. Quite a few individuals are able to work more and more on their own with memories as Phase 2 progresses and they feel more confident of their ability to handle memories.

Additional approaches. Some patients have found standard EMDR helpful, while others do not like bilateral stimulation or decompensate unless much more titrated approaches are used, such as the *tip of the finger* (Gonzalez & Mosqera, 2012). Hypnotic techniques are very helpful for most patients, and in fact, most titrated approaches draw upon these techniques, whether they are recognized as such or not.

Creative therapies. Some patients need to talk about their memories, but others better integrate them through some type of art, which does not require the patient to be so verbal. This should be done in conjunction with a trained art therapist in order to help the patient remain contained.

Additional Issues in Synthesis

While therapists are strongly urged to help patients remain in the present while attending to traumatic memories, in reality there are a few patients who are unable to fully do so, yet are still able to integrate their memories with support. Some patients never retrieve clear memories and must learn to be satisfied with a more general realization and narrative—*Something bad happened to me and it scared and hurt me*—without ever knowing the details of what happened. Some patients are never able to deal with traumatic memories, or not all of them: They may lack the necessary integrative capacity, or are too conflicted or remain too avoidant to be able to do Phase 2 work.

Case Examples of Realizing the Trauma Is Over Without Processing Details

One of the authors (Kathy) has treated three cases, two DID and one OSDD, in which major dissociative child parts were able to integrate by being helped to be present and realize the trauma was over and that they now had decent adult lives, without ever going into the details of what happened. Each of these three patients achieved full integration and were doing well 10 to 14 years following completion of therapy. On the other hand, some patients need to go into great detail to integrate traumatic memories.

CASE EXAMPLE OF ALL PARTS PARTICIPATING IN A SYNTHESIS SESSION: EDDIE

Eddie, a high-functioning patient with OSDD, had established excellent cooperation and communication among the majority of his dissociative parts, using his own spiritual concept of wholeness and unity as a paradigm for empathically restructuring his inner world. After 18 months of stabilization, he felt ready to approach a very painful and shameful memory of sexual abuse by an aunt, during which they were discovered and he was blamed. He imagined all parts of himself sitting in the therapy room. In this image, he gave each part a stone to hold, as a reminder of being in the present, and then each part shared its portion of the memory with all the others.

A Subjective Units of Distress Scale (SUDS) of 0–10 was utilized throughout the session so that Eddie could rate his level of distress from the perspective of any part of himself, allowing therapist and patient to collaboratively maintain his arousal level within an acceptable window of tolerance among all parts. During the synthesis the patient had intense feelings and sensations, but not beyond what any part of him could tolerate. At the end of the session all parts had come to recognize, *It happened to me, and it wasn't my fault, despite being blamed!*

CASE EXAMPLE OF TREATING TRAUMATIC MEMORY IN DISSOCIATIVE PSYCHOSIS: CELIA

Celia, a patient with OSDD, had episodes of dissociative psychosis that would last for several weeks at a time (cf. Van der Hart & Witztum, 2008), even though otherwise she had a very high integrative capacity. During these times she was not oriented to current reality, had auditory and visual hallucinations of people stabbing her, spoke in word salad, made sucking sounds like a baby, and wandered around moaning and clutching her stomach as though in severe pain. Celia became completely relaxed and lucid and easily entered deep trance when she was directed to go to her "safe space" internally. Finger signals were used to determine if there was a particular part active in the "psychosis." There was, and that part was also invited to relax and be in deep trance. The therapist had the adult part imagine looking out through the child's eyes to see what happened, while using her adult mind. Usually the child part is asked to look through the adult's eyes, but this patient could not respond to that suggestion.

The therapist then used a counting method. *As I count from 1 to 5, you can allow yourself to simply know and remember that there was a beginning, a middle, and an end to what happened.* The focus was on realizing there was an end, not yet on the content. During this the child part made young sucking and moaning noises. The adult part of Celia was instructed to stay with the child part and another round of counting began, this time focused on what happened. *As I count from 1 to 5, you can move from the beginning to the middle to the end, knowing just as much as you need and are able to know about what happened.* As the therapist counted, the child part screamed and cried and the therapist was unable to engage the adult part. The counting was done twice more, and the child part became more and more quieted. The patient's breathing regulated and she seemed much calmer. Finally an adult part could be accessed and told the therapist some of what she had remembered. The psychotic symptoms abated. Celia eventually achieved full symptom reduction, and she chose not to continue therapy after an additional year following the final psychotic episode. On follow-up 9 years later, she is retired from a successful career, enjoys her family and activities in her community and church, and continues to do well with no signs of dissociation or psychosis.

CASE EXAMPLE OF GUIDED SYNTHESIS: SHARON

Sharon, a 32-year-old woman with OSDD, was referred for therapy after her boyfriend left her with a small baby. This had been a breaking point for Sharon: She decompensated and was flooded with memories of abuse. She had been working as nurse on the night shift and was unable to continue work. Sharon needed approximately four years of stabilization work before she was ready to continue with Phase 2. In these four years, she had to start a completely new life, adjusting to being a new parent, finding a different apartment, organizing her finances, getting another job, and finding daycare for her child. As the main part functioning in daily life, Sharon had to overcome the phobia of other parts and learn to cooperate internally. In the beginning she insisted that she knew all about the abuse and did not need to work on her traumatic memories. However, after several years she realized that even though she was much better able to regulate her emotions and was not losing time or being self-destructive any longer, traumatic memories kept returning, especially at night. She gradually overcame her phobia of the traumatic memories, realizing that the younger parts of herself continued to suffer as long as they remained unintegrated. She was very motivated to become a " better mom than my own" and wanted to own her trauma in order to be fully present for her child.

Sharon herself was able to describe several episodes of abuse starting at age 4 and lasting until age 15. As a young child she was abused by an uncle while she and her mother lived with the mother's parents. She also had very threatening memories of her mother, who had extreme anger outbursts when Sharon was very young. Her mother found a new boyfriend when Sharon was 5 and left her with her grandparents for several years. At age 8 she joined the new family of her mother and had to care for two younger stepbrothers. She was abused by her stepfather as soon as she moved in with them. At 15 she ran away, and afterward she was placed in a good foster home through child protection services. As a first attempt at synthesis, Sharon and her therapist chose a less intense memory of having her tonsils removed, an experience that had been frightening and painful. She remembered having to stay several days in the hospital, when she knew other children went home the same day after surgery, but no one explained why she could not come home. Her mother had not been there to reassure her.

Sharon first wrote about the fragments of the memory that she could recall. She received help from a cognitive "helper" part inside, a wise older woman part that reported she held all of Sharon's memories. With the help of this part she identified the dissociative parts that had been present: One kept pain and a fear of dying as she was vomiting blood; one kept feelings of intense longing for her absent mother; one part held anger because her mother had not come to comfort her; and a perpetrator-imitating part like the mother held feelings of powerlessness, negative sense of self, anger, and shame. Sharon was able to cognitively identify several pathogenic kernels from experiences that were part of her chronic flashbacks: (a) panic, being left alone in the hospital with strange people and not knowing or understanding what was going to happen; (b) the experience of tasting blood and having blood in her throat; (c) the fear she was going to die; (d) being left alone at the hospital after other children's parents took them home at the end of the day; and (e) shame and humiliation, with the idea that she must be a horrible girl and deserved what happened.

With her therapist, Sharon was able to divide this "story" in eight smaller steps. For example, the first step involved being taken to the hospital without any explanation, and the second step was in being held down to get blood drawn. All parts of Sharon were given psychoeducation about synthesis. Sharon and the wise old woman part felt it would be too much to be shared across all parts just yet, so some parts went to their safe space. Sharon had organized a friend to bring her to session and take her home, and for someone to care for her daughter that day after school so she could rest if needed. As this was the first synthesis session for Sharon, her therapist had made a phone appointment the day after the session to check in and see how she was doing.

During the 90-minute synthesis session, Sharon and her parts were able to synthesize this experience step-by-step. The most difficult aspect was the feelings of abandonment by her mother, which also strongly linked to other experiences throughout her life. The therapist had to help her to go back to these feelings several times, asking for a SUDS rating after each time to evaluate the remaining intensity of the feeling. Sharon's SUD did not reach zero, but it was quite low and Sharon felt that it was enough. During synthesis an important moment came when she suddenly recalled that there had been a nice nurse who had given her ice cream, talked to her, and comforted her in the hospital. This was an important moment in her life that she had not remembered, and it offered her hope and comfort. She realized this event had influenced her own decision to become a nurse.

Sharon's feedback the next day and a week later were positive; she felt calm and reported that she had been able to comfort her younger parts. She had not had any flashbacks of the traumatic experience: It was now "just a memory." She was willing to make a plan, together with the wise old woman part, for further synthesis sessions of other traumatic experiences. She came up with several themes in the following order: early sexual abuse by her uncle; later sexual abuse by her stepfather; and, finally, the fear and pain related to her mother's violence toward her. Over the course of the following three years she was gradually able to integrate these experiences. Most of the time the therapist could work simultaneously with Sharon, the helper part, and the parts that were holding certain pathogenic kernels belonging to these traumatic experiences. The focus was always on *what is bothering you now, as you (and all parts of you) think about this experience?* Thus, not every single detail had to be focused on.

In one synthesis session, the therapist decided to work temporarily with a single part without Sharon or the helper part. This was decided because Sharon was so phobic of this part, who kept a very shameful bodily sensation of an orgasm. Sharon's uncle had told her (as this adolescent part of herself) how much she enjoyed sex, in fact almost asked for it, that she was his little whore, and he had proof because she had orgasms. The adolescent part felt very bad about herself but was also reviled by other parts, who believed she had intentionally asked for the abuse. She felt that her body had betrayed her, and she was extremely ashamed and sometimes suicidal. The therapist worked first with this part to help her reduce the intensity of her bodily sensations and feelings of shame and humiliation. As this experience was hidden internally and never discussed, the therapist also offered psychoeducation to all other parts to achieve more understanding of this part and of the normal physiological reactions of sexual arousal.

Summary

There are many different ways to help patients integrate traumatic memories. Therapist and patient together need to make informed decisions about which approaches will likely give the most effective results and are best suited to the needs of the patient. An important indicator of successful treatment is the elimination of PTSD symptoms related to memories that have been integrated. Often the most difficult part of the integration of traumatic memories is the gradual realization that these events have happened and have so profoundly influenced patients' lives across time. This increasing personification and presentification is achieved throughout Phase 3, which is described in Chapters 22 and 23. Many patients must mourn what they have lost.

Further Explorations

21.1 Which techniques are you most familiar with, and which would you like more experience using?

21.2 What are your hesitations, if any, in working with a patient on traumatic memories? What would help you take small steps with your patient?

21.3 What have your experiences been in working with traumatic memories? What has gone well? What might have gone wrong?

21.4 Discuss with colleagues how to know when a particular patient is ready for work with traumatic memories.

PART V

Phase 3 Treatment

CHAPTER 22

Integration of Dissociative Parts Into a Cohesive Personality

The struggle in the post-traumatic experience is to reconstitute the self into the single self, reintegrate itself.
—Robert Lifton (in Lifton & Caruth, 2015, p. 12)

Phase 3 includes a major goal of integrating dissociative parts of the patient into a cohesive personality and sense of self. Treatment is focused on reducing and eliminating the reasons for dissociation over time, particularly trauma-related phobias, so that the patient has no need for dissociative parts. Over the course of therapy, each part should become more flexible, more open to learning, more cooperative with other parts, and better able to share with them their respective experiences. Some parts are quite minor, mere fragments, and need nothing more than to merge spontaneously in the background with the patient as a whole as the patient engages in overcoming inner phobias. This may occur in the first two phases from time to time. Others are more elaborated and autonomous and need more direct work to integrate with other parts.

Some patients with poor prognoses will never integrate and cannot resolve their traumatic memories, that is, move to Phase 2. These patients may be able to achieve some degree of stability, but they remain highly prone to crisis and decompensation. Not all patients achieve a complete integration of all parts, but many are at least able to create enough cooperation among parts to achieve good functioning. There remains debate in the field about whether complete integration of dissociative parts is necessary, or whether it is sufficient for parts to have awareness of each other and work together in harmony, as is the case for normal ego states. This semantic debate has mostly to do with the idea that we all have ego states, and thus, dissociative parts should be able to coexist effectively while still somewhat separate (H. H. Watkins & Watkins, 1993; J. G. Watkins & Watkins, 1997). However, as noted in Chapter 1, there are significant differences between ego states and dissociative parts, primarily in terms of a sense of self, degree of separateness and elaboration, and whether dissociative symptoms are present or not. It may be that dissociative parts in some patients revert to normal ego states, relegated to a background cooperative functioning under the umbrella of the whole person. If this is the case, a cooperative "inner group" is likely adaptive. Other patients find no evidence of dissociative parts after integration, merely feeling like "me, myself, and I." Regardless, our clinical experience is that if any significant reasons for dissociation of the personality remain, the patient is at great risk of further distress (cf. Brand, Loewenstein, & Spiegel, 2014; Kluft, 1988a, 1993a, 1993b).

The Road to Integration of Dissociative Parts

Integration is an overarching and ongoing series of actions that goes far beyond the coming together of dissociative parts into one whole. It is the overall focus of all psychotherapy. We are all engaged in integration all the time, as discussed in Chapter 1. Since integration is ongoing, it is, by definition, always imperfect and somewhat incomplete. However, it should be sufficient to help us adapt effectively to our world and accept our past and learn from it. It should be enough for us to experience ourselves as unitary across time and situations.

Even when all dissociative parts are integrated into a cohesive personality and sense of self, patients continue to change and grow. As we have noted, personality and self are neither entities nor static. One's self and personality are representations of who that person is and continually grow, change, adapt, and reorganize (Damasio, 1999; Janet, 1929; Schore, 1994). The problem for dissociative patients is that parts of their personality have become too rigid and separate, unable to change and adapt to the present. From the beginning, treatment supports each dissociative part of the patient toward more flexible functioning as part of a whole human being, as well as the acceptance of the patient of all parts as belonging to a cohesive and adaptable self.

Patients who no longer have symptoms of dissociation or evidence of parts should have a consistent sense of who they are across situations, realizing they can grow and change yet remain the same person. They experience themselves as "me, myself, and I" regardless of what they are thinking, feeling, or doing; regardless of whether they are remembering the past, experiencing the present, or imagining the future. They do not have dissociative flashbacks, though of course, the past does arise—as it does for all people—sometimes in minor ways, and sometimes in intense ways.

CORE CONCEPT

The integration of dissociative parts allows for a cohesive sense of
self that is consistent and adaptable across time and situations.
Patients should no longer experience dissociative symptoms such as
amnesia, switching, auditory voices, or passive influence.

The complete integration of all dissociative parts of the patient into a cohesive whole has been called *unification* (e.g., Kluft, 1982, 1993b). Unification is achieved over time through the successive integration of two or more parts at a time, a process called *fusion* (Braun, 1986). Temporary fusion between two or more parts is called *blending* (Boon et al., 2011; Fine, 1991, 1993; Fine & Comstock, 1989; Kluft, 1982, 1993b). Each of these will be discussed below.

Addressing Resistances to Integration of Dissociative Parts
The therapist should never try to force the integration of parts (e.g., ISSTD, 2011). While some patients are not invested in parts remaining separate in order to maintain separate identities per se, all patients are rather phobic of integrating the experiences of parts in the beginning because integration requires them to accept the painful realizations that parts may hold for them. Most dissociative patients are phobic of the idea of parts coming together in some way and become highly distressed when the therapist tries to discuss it. Thus, while it may be a major goal of treating dissociative disorders, the way in which the therapist first talks about it will make a difference.

Psychoeducation. The therapist must be cautious about bringing up the idea of integration of parts prematurely. While some patients, often with OSDD, have a shared goal of integration from early in treatment, others may be fearful. Some believe parts will die; others are fearful of not having their major coping strategy available. This does not mean that the therapist agrees with the patient that unification is not necessary. It is simply a matter of pacing and timing. For example, patients can be assured that it is a choice, and it is completely within their control (which it is). They will not be forced to integrate, and in fact, forcing it will not be effective anyway.

CORE CONCEPT

Patients may resist integration of parts because they are afraid of these parts and related inner experiences, are afraid of change, are afraid they will become different, or are strongly attached to parts as separate entities to which they relate. These resistances must be resolved prior to integration of parts.

The therapist might say something like, *I know it's hard for you to imagine, but many people have found that it feels quite natural and right for all parts to be together when the time is right for them. They experience it as something quite positive and helpful. Parts are fine with it. You can take your time and just be where you are right now, without needing to worry about it. If and when you are ready, we will deal with it together, just like we do with whatever is in front of us right now. We are a team, and you have choices. But for right now, we have agreed to focus on helping parts of you feel better and work together more effectively so that every part of you is getting more of what you need in life.*

There are several reasons why patients may be resistant to unification of parts. These include (a) phobic avoidance of dissociative parts and their experiences; (b) fear of loss—that is, of losing one's identity, losing specific parts, or losing functions relegated to parts; and (c) intense investment in remaining separate as an identity and lifestyle. Thus, one patient reacted to the idea of unification, mentioned prematurely, by shouting at the therapist, *I'm quitting therapy. I don't want to work with somebody who is going to murder my inner people!* Another patient said, *These are not parts. They don't belong to me. They are souls. Every soul has its place in the universe. They can't come together. It's just not possible. You don't understand at all!* Fortunately, both patients had quite different experiences a number of years later and noted that integration was natural and not something to be concerned about. The therapist did not push the idea, but allowed the patient's resistance and focused on other integrative actions that provided a natural pathway to unification over time.

Phobic avoidance. The phobia of dissociative parts is the main and most common reason patients are fearful of fusion and unification. They are ashamed or fearful of parts or despise them. Thus, with good reason, they do not want to integrate a perpetrator-imitating part that has terrifying anger, or a part that is sexually acting out in ways that disgust the patient, or a child part that holds dependency yearnings that the adult part of the patient finds shameful. Therapy must address these issues gradually, helping the patient to own—that is, to personify—them along with the dissociative parts that hold them.

If the therapist is rather insistent on the integration of parts, some patients may report a false integration as a way to avoid further painful work. Other patients may have a particularly strong controlling-caregiving relational strategy that may intertwine with even the subtlest pressure from the therapist, leading to apparent success in treatment, with avoidance remaining underneath. As the treatment guidelines of dissociative disorders note, "Premature attempts at fusion may cause . . . a superficial compliance wherein the alternate identities in question attempt to please the therapist by seeming to disappear" (ISSTD, 2011, p. 144).

Integrative work with dissociative parts begins already in Phase 1, when the therapist supports the patient in accepting and understanding dissociative parts. One step toward the fusion of two parts is for the patient to realize, *Yes, of course that part is angry. I can understand why she is so very angry.* A next step might involve personification, *Yes that part is angry, and that is my anger, too*, or *That angry part is a part of me.* Further steps involve resolving the anger, often as part of Phase 2 work.

CORE CONCEPT

Over the course of therapy, the therapist should continue to check in with the patient about why parts need to remain separate. A focus on the need for ongoing dissociation can target specific problems that maintain dissociative parts, such as phobia of anger or lack of realization that one was sexually abused.

Once therapy has progressed to the point that parts are working well together for the most part and at least some traumatic memories have been integrated, the therapist can begin to pique the patient's curiosity about fusion in an indirect way. The therapist should regularly ask in a curious way, *I wonder what keeps those parts of you separate from you?* or *Have you ever thought about why those parts still need to be separate from each other? Have you ever thought about why that part of you has never grown up? I'm curious about what might it be like for you if those parts were closer together?* This approach keeps the focus of treatment on reasons that dissociation still exists—that is, trauma-related phobias and lack of sufficient integrative capacity—so that they can be addressed and resolved in a consistent manner (Kluft, 1993b). Otherwise, it is far too easy for both therapist and patient to continue work without considering whether the need for having dissociative parts is decreasing.

Unresolved trauma and hidden dissociative parts. Two main reasons for avoidance of fusion or unification are the presence of unresolved trauma or dissociative parts that are not yet known to the therapist (and often to the patient), both indicating strong phobias.

CASE EXAMPLE OF THE EMERGENCE OF HIDDEN PARTS: RENEE

Renee, as the adult part of the patient that functions in daily life, did a tremendous amount of work on accepting a very angry, obstinate child part, and the child part gradually became more cooperative over a long period of therapy. Renee and her child part could sometimes come together in a unified way (blending) in therapy, during which her usually tense body visibly relaxed, but she could not hold the integration outside of session. On careful exploration, the patient became aware of "black holes in a wall" internally, in which previously unknown parts resided with their fragments of traumatic memories. The patient began to describe these fragments as "little pieces" of the child part that held memories that were too shameful or horrific to be shared. These "little pieces" held several pathogenic kernels of memory that were synthesized and realized at one at a time. The "little pieces" (fragmentary parts) spontaneously integrated upon successful completion of the memory work, and shortly thereafter the patient and her child part integrated permanently.

Fear of loss. Dissociative patients actually have a very fragile sense of themselves because of their extreme dissociative fragmentation. For example, one patient was fearful of any change in therapy, because she believed it would irrevocably alter who she was, "and then I won't be myself." This patient had many dissociative parts, each of which was equally rigid in sense of self and equally fearful of any changes in perspective or ways of being. While parts may be adamant about who they are (and are not), patients as a whole may feel quite unsure and have a rather brittle sense of who they are. The more fragile patients' overall sense of self, the more they are fearful of changing, believing they may lose themselves.

Some patients are afraid fusion and unification will be experienced as a loss or death. The therapist should not rush to reassure. Patients with dissociative disorders have had a dissociative inner organization since childhood. They may have become strongly attached to particular parts of themselves, especially once they learn to be more compassionate. Thus, some may mourn the loss of the "little girl" or the "feisty adolescent," as though they are actual people. Others do not feel loss, but a sense of gratitude for such parts, which is expressed as they integrate.

Some patients acutely feel the loss of some type of function when parts integrate. This is especially true with some creative capacities that involve intense concentration. Such losses most likely occur because the ability to exclude everything from awareness while concentrating on one thing lessens as the patient gains more presence in the moment. For example, prior to unification, one patient was able, in one part of herself, to write for 16 hours at a time with nothing more than quick bathroom breaks. Once she integrated all parts, she complained that she could not concentrate for more than a few hours at a time and then needed a break to eat and rest, which she did not yet realize was normal. Another patient lost some abilities to paint. While she was still an accomplished artist, she was no longer able to paint the main theme for which she had gained popularity. Often, these losses are temporary, and may return in some form over time. Overall, however, most patients generally feel much better with unification, once they are adjusted, and they agree with its benefits and do not want or feel the need for dissociative parts. As one patient put it, *I am me, just me, completely me, always me, and that is OK with me!* However, there may be a brief period of disorientation and sensorial changes following unification. Braun noted that patients "will often report changes in vision, hearing, and other sensations as well as periods of confusion. These will normalize over time (usually completed by three months)" (1986, p. 16).

Investment in DID as a lifestyle. A few DID patients are extremely invested in keeping their parts, with whom they have developed relationships that they are unwilling to relinquish. They may also be unwilling to take responsibility for their actions, keeping them sequestered in various parts. One patient referred to her parts as her "best friends." Another described the inner lives of parts, noting that each part had its own separate rich, busy life, completely distinct from what was happening externally. This fantasy world was so fulfilling that she was unwilling to consider the real world and her actual life, which included painful feelings. Her fantasy world was a way to avoid inner pain. Thus, some patients have substituted interactions with their inner parts, or inner fantasy worlds, for real relationships with people, who may be much more unpredictable and challenging. This builds on the idea of imaginary playmates, a normal developmental experience. These patients have tried to solve the conflict between fundamental distrust of others and unbearable loneliness with the creation of specific inner relationships with parts, which maintains non-realization.

A few patients have developed a strong identity around being DID, and thus cling to parts as a way of defining themselves to others. They are strongly focused on the different preferences and needs and dramatic conflicts among parts. Some have more flamboyant presentations, with different clothes, hairstyles, and mannerisms. They are unwilling and uninterested in integration because they would lose their primary identity. However, the majority of dissociative patients are phobic of their parts, which is the main reason patients are fearful of integration.

Blending

Blending is typically an intentional therapeutic intervention to improve the patient's functioning or ability to cope through the cooperative temporary merging of two or more parts, for example, for better functioning at work or to deal with a difficult medical procedure that might otherwise be triggering. It can also be used as a trial for the patient to experience what integration between parts might be like (Boon et al., 2011; Fine, 1991; Fine & Comstock, 1989; Kluft, 1993b).

CORE CONCEPT

Blending, the temporary integration of two or more parts, can be a powerful first step in achieving permanent integration of these parts. Patients can practice integration in this way and are able to experience what it is like before they decide it is ultimately helpful.

Blending can occur incrementally when two or more parts have achieved awareness of each other and a good degree of cooperation. At first compassion between them may not even be necessary; rather, the focus is on working together to accomplish something that serves both parts. For example, two worker parts might be quite avoidant of feelings, including compassion, but they can agree to work together to get a project completed on time at work. Or a worker part might agree to temporarily join with a part that is a parent in order to help organize things at home more effectively. The payoff for the worker part is that there is less intrusive anxiety at work about things that have not been done at home, and the loving but disorganized parent part of the patient gets inner help at home so things run more smoothly.

Blending or fusion should never be attempted among parts that hold intense negative emotion or engage in self-harm. For example, suicidal parts or child parts that hold intense dependency yearnings should not be blended together. The idea of blending is to *increase* the patient's integrative capacity. Blending parts with negative affects and beliefs may overwhelm the patient.

Blending as successive approximation to fusion. Most dissociative patients need help breaking down large goals into much smaller and successive steps. Movement toward blending can occur in the same way. For example, the adult part of the patient can practice small steps toward blending simply as a series of experiments to notice what happens. For example, the adult part of the patient can be invited to ask another part to "come a little bit closer" inside. The patient is encouraged simply to stop and notice what happens. The patient might say, *It feels OK*; *It actually feels good! It's not what I expected*; *It feels warm*; or *I don't like it!*

If the reaction is negative, the therapist simply stops and says, *That's fine, we are just noticing and no more. You did really well.* The therapist asks the parts to step back from each other, and works on the resistance: *Can you tell me more about what you don't like? I hear that you don't like it. I wonder, how is it for that other part of you?* It may simply be that the adult part of the patient is reluctant because the experience is unfamiliar, and not for a particular reason. If that is the case, the patient can be encouraged to try again, just for the purpose of getting used to being closer to the part. Or the patient can be helped to use a distancing technique to still be in contact with the part, but from a perceived distance or through a protective glass. For example, the therapist might say, *That's just fine. Take a step back, exactly the space you need to be comfortable. I'm wondering what it might be like if you imagined looking at that part from a distance, like looking through the wrong end of binoculars?* If the patient agrees, the therapist instructs the patient just to notice what happens. A further suggestion might be to look with eyes of compassion and just to notice what that it might be like. The therapist can ask, *I am curious—aren't you—about what that part might be feeling while he is looking at you?* These are small steps that promote reflection and a growing comfort level between parts that has not existed before.

If the patient's response is positive when parts are asked to be close, the therapist asks if it is all right to take another small step, reminding the patient that she or he can stop at any time. Perhaps the two parts could reach out and touch index fingers and see what that is like. Then they might shake hands or embrace or simply stand face-to-face or side-by-side and notice that experience. If it is a positive experience, the therapist might encourage them to try coming together just a few seconds and no more. These parts can then *look out of one set of eyes and hear with one set of ears, two heartbeats blending into one, so naturally, so easily.* The therapist should seek out the right imagery and words for each patient. And then the therapist might say, *Now take a small step away from each other. Breathe deeply and relax, and just notice what that was like.* If the experience is positive, the therapist can encourage it for a longer time, gradually to extend over sessions. The patient can be instructed to practice blending in the privacy of home, when things are quiet and there is space to notice and reflect. Usually over a short period of several sessions the blending feels so natural that fusion occurs between the parts.

Fusion

Fusion is the integration of two or more parts of the patient and may occur spontaneously or intentionally (Kluft, 1993b).

Spontaneous fusions. Some patients report spontaneous fusions over the course of Phase 1 and Phase 2: *There seem to be a lot fewer voices inside; I had 15 parts, and now I only have 8. I wonder what happened?* This is a natural occurrence and is a sign that therapy is going well and is addressing the reasons that dissociation continues to exist. The therapist can reassure patients that it is normal and listen to any concerns they might have. Most patients take it in stride.

Fusion is usually most successful in parts that are most alike (such as a group of child parts) or between an adult part that is very compassionate and a child part. In cases of OSDD, fusion or unification may occur more easily than in DID. For example, one patient with OSDD "adopted" all her young parts when she was at home—that is, integrated them—and reported it to the therapist. In spite of ongoing daily-life stressors, the patient remains integrated. The greater the differences and the greater the conflicts between parts, the more challenges there will be to fusion.

Gradual fusions. Fusion may occur very gradually. Patients might report that a particular part is less active, more quiet, less interactive internally. They might say things like, *That part seems kind of transparent, almost like I can see through her, like she's becoming a shadow, a bit like a memory; He's a bit like a ghost, but a friendly ghost; She's sleeping most of the time. Not like she's avoiding, but like she is done with what she needed to do; I know he's still there, but he's just there, quiet, and no more; It's almost more of an image now than a presence, if that makes any sense.*

One patient noted that gradual fusion of parts seemed rather natural and that it now required less effort to manage the needs of conflicting parts:

> I am more and more together without having to think about who inside needs this or that. It just flows a lot of the day. We—I—am starting to feel a certain peace that runs through all parts of me. We are less afraid to be together. It is becoming pleasant and safe to be me.

Parts that disappear. Occasionally a part will "disappear" instead of integrating after sharing its experiences with other parts. One patient realized that once parts had shared with all the others, it was time to "depart." This occurred during a leave-taking ritual, during which a part whose time had ended had the privilege of choosing what to eat for dinner, with other parts applauding this one for all the contributions to the person as a whole. Once dinner was complete and parts had appreciated each other, this part simply disappeared.

Other times, the disappearance of a part is intensely distressing and does not involve integration at all. One patient "lost" a part that was an important soothing figure inside. She was convinced the part did not integrate, because it vanished during an intense crisis in which the patient was suicidal. The therapist could only empathize with the loss and help the patient grieve and try to find other ways to soothe herself. The part never reappeared over the course of treatment.

Another patient reported that the main adult part that functioned in daily life had disappeared because "she just couldn't take it anymore." The patient severely decompensated, as she did not have other parts that were able or willing to function well in daily life. In both of these cases, overwhelming life events and the inability to cope led to what might be considered the disintegration of parts, rather than fusion. The therapist must be able to tell the difference and intervene when patients are overwhelmed.

Unification

The integration of all parts into a cohesive whole is called unification (Kluft, 1986b, 1993b). This usually occurs toward the latter part of therapy, at some point in Phase 3, though not always. A few patients may become nearly unified prior to the treatment of traumatic memory. In these cases, parts are already quite compassionate and cooperative, which makes work on traumatic memories more simple and straightforward, and they may become one (integrate) during or shortly after that work is done. But most patients have a much longer road to integration, well into Phase 3. Most commonly, parts gradually merge over time in a naturalistic way.

Like fusions, unification may occur spontaneously or be more gradual in various patients (Kluft, 1993b). Some patients see it as an important milestone; others take it in stride as though it is expected; and a few avoid it even when they are ready, due to a phobia of fusion. Some patients recognize the time has come for unification; others are surprised by it. Some experience it as a loss or death or sad leave-taking. Others see it as a joyful celebration, a sign of success and mastery. Each patient will approach unification differently, and the therapist must understand and help the patient through in the patient's unique way.

In general, it is best if the idea of unification comes from the patient, but as noted above, the therapist should be gently persistent in questioning the ongoing need for separation between parts. Whether or not the patient needs or wants suggestions or imagery for unification will depend on the individual. Sometimes the therapist can merely be present while all parts "come together." Some patients will suggest their own imagery, some of which is described above.

Fusion imagery and unification rituals. For some patients, images or rituals are an important part of fusion or unification (Braun, 1986; ISSTD, 2011; Kluft, 1986b, 1993b; C. A. Ross, 1997; Putnam, 1989; Van der Hart et al., 2006). For example, in one patient, the adult part imagined taking her child parts to a park. Sitting in a quiet, peaceful place, the four child parts sat close to her. When she felt the time was right, she embraced all of them, and then brought her arms together, hugging herself. At that moment, the fusion took place.

Common integrative imagery includes coming together in a beautiful white light, coming together in a healing body of water, stepping into each other, hugging, standing in a circle and holding hands, streams flowing together into a beautiful sea, different colors blending to make the most beautiful color in the world, threads being woven into a rich tapestry, turning a kaleidoscope until it become a whole image with many beautiful colors, and so on.

One metaphor of integration that may be shared with patients is the image of a beautiful source of water high in the mountains (Kluft 1990b). The water source becomes a powerful river. However, over time, storms, earthquakes, and other terrible events cause the earth to change and the river to become clogged with trees, debris, and mud. This causes the river to divide into many smaller streams. Years later the river is cleaned up, and the barriers that kept the water from flowing freely along its original course are removed. Each small stream is able to flow back into the river, without any water being lost. The river grows stronger and clearer as the all the streams flow back to their home.

The patient may request to perform a particular ritual, actual or imaginary. The former might include bringing objects that represents the best of each part and putting them in a beautiful box, or making a collage with pictures representing each part. As an example of the latter, one patient imagined each part coming up on a stage in which they each received a special thank-you for their role from the adult part of the patient and the therapist. Each part received an acknowledgment, faced the audience and curtsied or bowed, then turned and merged with the adult part of the patient in a hug. The imagined audience consisted of millions of survivors who could learn that healing was possible, and their applause was thunderous.

> This feeling, that I am somebody with a whole life and a history and that is me: I didn't know it. And I am very happy with how

that life looks now with all the good things and the bad. I am very happy with it and I feel enriched by it. Funny, I feel rich for the first time in my life and I can look back on much that was mine. A lot.

Signs of Unification

Once the patient has integrated all parts, signs and symptoms of dissociation should remit (Kluft, 1986b; 1993b). The patient no longer hears voices or experiences the influence of dissociative parts. There is no sense of separate parts. Conflicts are generally able to be held in mind and tolerated. Some patients, especially those who have been severely dissociative, may struggle with living in and managing a sequential sense of time. They comment, for example, on how long the days seem, as they are present more of the time instead of checked out for prolonged periods. They no longer have other parts to share the burden of both mundane and stressful components of life, and they need time to adjust to a different experience of energy management. Some patients have unusual sensory experiences right after unification, reporting being able to see or hear more clearly, that colors are more vibrant, that touch is more sensitive, and so on. They may feel more present in their bodies, which may feel uncomfortable or pleasurable. Their posture may straighten and their movements become more fluid—their somatic experience is integrating as well.

Relapse Prevention

The therapist should help the patient anticipate situations that might evoke the separation of unified parts, both before and after unification. This is good relapse prevention, and it helps the patient prepare for the fact that life does not magically become easy after unification. Life is still life, and patients need all of their coping strategies to be successful. After decades of relegating coping to other parts and, in some cases, using inner contact between parts to cope with loneliness, the patient is vulnerable after unification and requires some time to adjust.

It can be instructive to ask the patient, *What could you imagine, if anything, that might make integration fall apart?* The patient may identify general life events, such as "When my father dies," or "If I ever got divorced." If difficult but not unusual life events are predicted to overwhelm the patient, then most certainly more work in therapy needs to be done to increase the patient's general coping strategies. The therapist could then explore, *So, when your father dies, what would be intolerable about that for you? How would parts help you in ways that you could not help yourself?* or *If you were to get divorced, how do you imagine you could cope with it? Can you think of a friend who has coped with divorce and talk a little about how she got through it?*

Sometimes patients might say nothing would ever make them re-dissoci-ate, while some might name traumatic events: *Well, I could imagine I would need my parts if I was raped again.* While such events are possible, they are certainly not likely. The therapist should ensure that general life events are within the range of the patient's coping skills. Then further exploration can be done regarding how the patient might cope differently in the future with potentially traumatic experiences; for example, reminding her of the fact that here and now she could protect herself more effectively, or would have people to whom she could go for support immediately.

In spite of relapse prevention, unification does not hold in some patients. Unification is not magic and is truly a process, not an event. It is just one step, albeit a major step, in the patient's lifelong journey of integration. That it may wax and wane a bit should not be surprising, particularly given that patients have lived most of their lives with a dissociative organization. There are a number of reasons for these integrative failures (Kluft, 1986b, 1993b), which in most cases turn out to be temporary.

CORE CONCEPT

The therapist should take ample time to help the patient explore reasons why integration of parts might not hold, and learn to recognize triggers and be proactive in maintaining integrative gains.

The major reason for a lapsed unification of parts is that there remain unresolved issues that maintain dissociation among parts (Kluft, 1988a, 1993b). Perhaps an issue was successfully resolved in some parts, but not in others. A previously unknown traumatic memory may emerge. Some parts might hold back and be in opposition to unification, but not say so. Some parts may emerge that were previously unknown. This is not unusual, and it follows the general uncovering patterns of any psychotherapy, where new memories and conflicts emerge as the patient is better able to reflect. For a few patients, lapsed unification may be due to unresolved attachment issues. The patient may believe that unification heralds the end of therapy and thus wishes to remain dissociative in order not to lose the relationship with the therapist.

Some patients take a flight into health, suddenly announcing all their parts are gone, even though there remain major issues that have not been addressed. One patient was suddenly unable to visualize parts, saying it was "empty inside, with nothing but fog." He insisted he was fine and left treatment a few weeks later. This raises a high index of suspicion in the therapist that the patient is avoiding, not integrating. Indeed, six months later he returned to therapy after a relapse with drugs; parts of himself were viciously fighting internally, with more conflict than ever.

Some patients report they are integrated in order to please the therapist, if the therapist has strongly emphasized that integration is an expected outcome of therapy or pushed for it prematurely. The therapist must be on the alert for appeasing and caretaking behaviors in patients along the way in therapy.

Summary

The integration of parts is a long journey and is the main goal in the treatment of complex dissociative disorders. Integration may be gradual or quick, spontaneous or planned, temporary and eventually permanent. Many patients achieve full integration of their parts—that is, unification—while some do not. There are many pathways to unification, and each therapist and patient must find the ways that work best for them.

Further integration of the patient's personality does not stop with unification. As noted, ongoing reorganization continues across the lifespan. The patient needs time to establish new patterns, from simple ones to more complex. Living in less divided ways requires new ways of thinking, feeling, and being, and relating. Therapy can continue with the issues of Phase 3, which are discussed in the following chapter.

Further Explorations

22.1 What are your thoughts on whether patients should integrate their dissociative parts or have them remain as a cohesive functioning "group"? What do you see as the pros and cons of not completely integrating parts?

22.2 What have been your experiences with patients who do not want to integrate parts?

22.3 What have been your experiences with patients who have blended or fused with at least some parts of themselves?

22.4 Some patients experience physiological changes with integration of parts; for example, seeing or hearing more clearly. What do you think causes these changes?

22.5 Integration is something we are doing all the time. Do you think of integration of dissociative parts as a unique kind of integration? Why or why not?

CHAPTER 23

Phase 3 and Beyond

This work ain't for sissies. But I've gotten here and I'm alive and kicking. I'm all right. Was it worth it? I got myself back from hell. Yeah, it was worth it.

—Anonymous patient upon completion of therapy

Phase 3 work is recursive throughout therapy, as it involves so much focus on the patient's daily life and relationships. In addition to the ongoing unification of dissociative parts, this phase involves grief work, solidification of a healthy sense of self, improvement of relationships, and many other issues. Excursions into the treatment of traumatic memory will continue from time to time, and there may even be the occasional return to stabilization.

In this stage of therapy patients generally have much greater integrative capacity than before, so their ability to realize grows, with a sense of ownership of more of their lives and the ability to be present more of the time. In general, patients focus more on experiencing the present and improving their quality of life, with less energy invested in their past. Hopefully, they are increasingly able to face challenges in life. Patients generally find life much better in Phase 3, as one noted:

> I never believed that I could get to the "other side," could not even imagine there was a better place for me before I die. I'm not exactly sure how I got here. It is only in looking back that I can notice I am no longer in a black hole, not knowing who I was. It is not what I expected. It's good, but it's not always easy. There are

still some struggles. But I think they are more like the struggles that everyone has, not so different. Maybe I expected a fairy tale, where I would "live happily ever after." But the point is now I have a decent life, better ways to cope, some people to share with. I'm glad I'm here, and it seems that "here" is just another step in a journey that continues.

Learning to Cope With Normal Life

Dissociative patients have longstanding patterns of avoidance and constriction of everyday life. Some DID patients have had specific parts of themselves that engaged in working, raising children, bill paying, and so on. It can be daunting for them to realize all these tasks. More and more of their lives must be personally owned and completed without avoidance, both external and internal (e.g., ISSTD, 2011; Kluft, 1993b; Van der Hart et al., 2006). Many severely dissociative patients find it a struggle to cope with a newly developed continuous time sense following unification, accustomed to "checking out" for long periods.

Work does not stop at unification. The integration of parts is only one step along the way of living a more integrative life. The patient may need further support to continue to develop more flexible ways of living, and learn to own more fully those skills, behaviors, emotions, sensations, and so on that have previously been dissociated from awareness (Braun, 1986; ISSTD, 2011). The patient's history continues to be examined and placed in context in the present and with regard to the future.

CORE CONCEPT

As patients integrate dissociative parts, they must adjust to living life without dissociation, owning more and more of their daily lives, and focusing less on the past.

Trauma-related phobias are triggered less often and are gradually resolved. Patients need time to grieve the past, as well as what has subsequently been lost and remains lost in the future; to develop a more comfortable relationship with their bodies; and to solidify new coping skills and more social skills, learning to sustain authentic, intimate relationships. All of this work implies that patients suffer fewer catastrophic predictions and are more willing to take healthy risks and tolerate change.

Many patients have had a lifelong struggle to integrate a balance between work, play, rest, and relationships. Phase 3 is a time for more concentrated work on developing and maintaining balance and extending the gains made in therapy. Often patients have been oblivious to signals that they were overextended or were not attending to necessary aspects of life, such as self-care, including energy regulation and maintaining healthy boundaries, managing a household, or being social. As they become more grounded and parts are less active or integrated, they must attend to cues that are unfamiliar but essential. They may complain that it is hard work to maintain balance, as though they expect it to be effortless—which, of course, it is not. Therapists must continually encourage them to make ongoing efforts to maintain a better equilibrium, which will pay off in the long run.

As dysregulation becomes less of a chronic problem, patients must learn how to make meaning out of leading a more regulated life. Many patients who have been chronically hyperaroused find it rather boring not to have chaos in their lives. They have become addicted to chaos as a way of avoiding. These patients need time and patience to overcome this addiction and learn to live a "normal" life without unnecessary tumultuous interludes, and to have that life be meaningful and fulfilling to the degree possible.

Grieving

Effective grieving is an integral part of realization. In fact, we think of the failure to grieve as a particular form of non-realization. Grieving is essential because it is a process of acknowledging loss, letting go of the need to change what cannot be changed, and moving forward (Herman, 1997; Van der Hart et al., 2006). This is not an even or quick process.

CORE CONCEPT

The failure to grieve what was and what cannot be is a major non-realization that must be overcome in treatment.

Some patients avoid acknowledging loss and grief, while others are overly focused on loss and cannot seem to move forward. These patients tend to be unable to work successfully in Phase 2 with traumatic memories, as they continue to phobically avoid them or be stuck in them. Helping patients work through resistances to grieving is an essential part of therapy that begins in Phases 1 and 2, where forays into grieving will already naturally occur.

Patients may have grieved along the way. In fact, every integrative accomplishment may be followed by a grief response. Each new step toward healing, each new positive experience in life, may be coupled with grief about missing out for so long. Both joy and sadness are part of the realization of the present and should be expected. The therapist should not try to talk the patient out of the sadness, but should be with both the positive and the negative as two sides of a coin of realization and acceptance. In Phase 3 the full weight of their suffering sometimes comes to bear, as patients really begin to engage in life and realize exactly what they have missed. By now most patients are aware of their autobiography and have begun to realize what could have been, and what never was nor ever shall be.

Albeit painful, this grieving leads to greater *personification* and *presentification*. The more patients can own and accept their lives, the more they can take charge and act in the present to improve what they can.

Life after trauma is not a fairy tale that involves living happily ever after. While at times life can be wonderful and fulfilling, it has its rough and painful moments with which patients must still cope, as everyone must, becoming sadder but wiser. Some consequences of being seriously abused or neglected will remain and must be accepted in the same way that healing and positive change must be accepted. Some patients suffer terrible consequences of their traumatization and avoidance. Perhaps they have remained extremely lonely their whole lives without partner or friends due to relational avoidance and shame, have no children despite their strong wishes because they did not trust their parenting abilities, or were unable to fulfill their intellectual or professional potential out of a phobia of risk and change. They may be living in poverty and lack sufficient skills to change their circumstances. And some may be suffering from serious medical conditions caused or exacerbated by chronic stress.

Patients also begin to realize that life will always hold new losses, new pain, new disappointments. It is now *how* the patient deals with these that makes the difference between ongoing suffering and the ability to balance pain and joy. Instead of avoiding, the patient can embrace all of life with some degree of acceptance and adaptation.

Grieving often involves periods of anger and rage. It is important for the patient to feel anger at injustices done, but the patient must also be able to move beyond it into a quieter and more resolved acceptance of what has been. Often angry dissociative parts have avoided grief, and once they realize their anger is a defense, they are better able to move toward integration with other parts and acceptance of what has happened to them.

Resolving Relationships With Perpetrators

In Phase 3, many patients must grapple with more effective ways to cope with an abusive family of origin. Perpetrators often never acknowledge what has happened, and patients must come to terms with not having their reality validated. Some patients decide to cut off contact with parents; some try to have modified relationships; some find a degree of repair is possible. What is important is that each patient has been able to relinquish unrealistic hopes for acceptance and love, grieve this loss appropriately, and accept the family of origin as it is. Sometimes patients either cut off or continue contact in order to avoid grieving, and the therapist must be alert to this ongoing non-realization.

Leave-Taking Rituals

Some patients find leave-taking rituals powerful, in which they symbolically let go of a loss (Van der Hart, 1983, 1986; Vesper, 1991). Therapists can ask patients if they have considered rituals and whether they feel one would be helpful. For example, one patient who had already integrated all her dissociative parts brought to session a beautiful wooden box in which she had placed photographs of her abusive parents when they were young. She spent the session talking about how they had behaved toward her, and who she had wanted them to be. After session, she went home and burned the box as a symbol of letting go of the past and her need for her parents to be people they never could be. Another patient with DID, not fully integrated, wrote leave-taking letters to her parents, who were already dead. She subsequently went to their graves and buried the letters there. If there are still some parts not yet integrated, it is important to check with all of them about any conflicting attitudes regarding these types of leave-taking rituals.

Overcoming the Phobia of Change

Patients come to therapy because they are reluctant to make changes that they also want. Resolving this conflict begins in Phase 1. Many trauma patients are afraid that change will be out of their control and worse than what they experience currently (Boon et al., 2011; Van der Hart et al., 2006). In other words, they believe change itself will be traumatizing, which is a projection of the past onto the future. When therapists have helped patients take one small step at a time from the beginning of therapy, this phobia gradually diminishes. However, it may reemerge in Phase 3 as patients begin to function more as unified individuals. They may be quite apprehensive about trying new things for the first time.

CORE CONCEPT

Therapists can help patients make adaptive change by
compassionately exploring the conflicts and fears about it and
encouraging them to take small steps at a time.

Indeed, change involves a certain amount of anxiety and uncertainty.
The sensations of these feelings in the body can serve as subconscious
reminders of traumatic experiences, leading to avoidance and fear. Patients
may also be fearful of failure when making changes, evoking shame, which
also inhibits their ability to move forward. The therapist should help the
patient explore beliefs about change that may impede progress in Phase 3.
The fear of being ashamed of failure needs careful attention and compassion, as shame will emerge over the course of this last stage of treatment
(see Chapter 15).

CASE EXAMPLE OF OVERCOMING THE PHOBIA OF CHANGE: DONNA

Donna was a patient who was just beginning to become more social. She
wanted to take an art class for the first time, but she had many fears:
*What if I can't do it? What if people think I am weird? What if I don't like
it?* Donna discussed her fears with the therapist, who helped her realize
she could withdraw from the class if she did not like it or felt too overwhelmed. They decided she would ask to sit in and observe a class before
she signed up. The art teacher allowed her, and Donna found she enjoyed
it. This small step gave her the freedom to try the course. Donna had a
wonderful time, and she signed up for the next course, eventually developing lasting relationships with the art teacher and another class participant.

Overcoming the Phobia of the Body

Most dissociative patients have a sustained phobia of body sensations and
even of movement. Hopefully over the course of therapy this phobia has
lessened. In Phase 3, growing realization leads to more bodily awareness
and a greater sense of responsibility in caring for physical needs (Ogden et
al., 2006; Van der Hart et al., 2006). Many traumatized patients feel betrayed
by their bodies, which have been vessels of physical and emotional suffering and the locus of unmet needs. Sometimes their bodies have responded

with unwanted arousal during sexual abuse. It is as though they experience their bodies as separate from themselves, as an enemy, a container of shame, disgust, and weakness. For example, one patient said, *I want to crawl out of my skin and leave this ugly body behind. I hate it! It is so disgusting and useless.*

These individuals must come to accept embodiment with both its joys and discomforts. They must learn to tolerate and interpret physical sensations as signals that help guide them toward dealing with physical needs, such as hunger or pain, or with emotional needs. They must grieve the sense of betrayal they experience from their bodies, and learn to accept them as part of being a whole human being. Some must deal with the long-term physical sequelae of chronic trauma, including disease and physical disability. Aging also brings an additional sense of loss and perhaps even triggers new and old feelings of vulnerability and fear. One aging patient lamented that she no longer felt able to physically protect herself, which had been an important part of her healing in her early therapy.

Nevertheless, many patients become friendlier with their bodies, inhabiting their physical space more often and more fully, as one patient described:

> I begin to feel ever more in my body, also during the day. I still remember that some years ago I completely separated head and body, and that, basically, I could hardly perceive my body. I floated above the ground, as it were.

In Phase 1 patients have often struggled, without much success, to accept their bodies compassionately and with care. Once the majority of traumatic memories and shame are resolved, it becomes easier for them to experience more pleasurable physical sensations. Therapists can encourage them to notice more often what is happening in their bodies and to experience more pleasurable and comforting physical sensations and accompanying positive affect, and to use their bodies as resources (Ogden & Fisher, 2015). For example, the therapist can suggest simple exercises such as noticing sensations while taking a warm bath or shower, applying lotion, receiving a massage, being in the sauna, and exercising. Sometimes the patient needs to learn to be more physically active, as the patient may have previously avoided movement because it could evoke traumatic memories.

Sexual Intimacy and the Body

Patients who have issues with their bodies, particularly those who were sexually abused, often have problems with sexual intimacy. Perhaps they avoid being sexual or are hypersexual, even engaging in sexual addictions in which meaningful relationships and emotional intimacy are absent. Regardless of the form of sexual struggles, most patients remain significantly disembodied and avoidant of certain sensations. Sex may have become associated with control and dominance. Some dissociative parts became submissive, while others—parts that imitate the perpetrator or, for example, aggressive sexual parts—became dominant. These power conflicts must be resolved between parts before fusion, and the patient as a whole needs to learn that sexual intimacy is about mutuality and care.

While couples work may be appropriate anytime during treatment, in Phase 3 it can support the patient and partner in gently exploring both nonsexual and sexual touch with emotional intimacy. The patient should be encouraged to experiment and take control of stopping and starting as much as possible, with a focus on relational connection rather than specifically on sexual touch. Gradually, as emotional safety is developed, more sexual intimacy may occur.

One patient began laughing in session and told her therapist, *You will never believe what I did! Sam [patient's partner] and I made out on the sofa last night! We haven't done that in ten years, and it was fun. We didn't have sex, but I could feel my body going "Wow!" That's something new, and it surprised both of us. I didn't get triggered at all!* Another patient, who had been single since a painful divorce 15 years earlier, began talking in therapy for the first time about missing both emotional and sexual intimacy, and indicated that she felt she could take small steps in being more present in everyday conversations with men. Others are simply not interested in being sexual, finding fulfillment in other aspects of life.

Patients who have integrated sexual parts of themselves may begin feeling sexual sensations for the first time they can remember. While pleasurable, this can also be frightening and feel out of control. Some psychoeducation, normalizing, and general acceptance of the feelings by the therapist are usually sufficient to help patients accept their sexuality more fully.

The Fear of Getting Well

Many patients harbor a secret fear of getting better (Van der Hart et al., 2006). This is not because they wish to continue suffering, but because they are afraid of what it might mean. They often have very unrealistic beliefs about "getting well." Some believe it means other people will no longer help them and they must then figure out how to do everything on their own. Some are fearful they will not like being better and then cannot change back to something more familiar—something that they leaned on their whole lives. Some are afraid it will change who they are.

Most importantly, patients in Phase 3 are beginning to realize that therapy will eventually draw to a close, so the idea of getting better can be coupled with a fear of losing the therapist. This fear is very important to address without promises that the therapist will always be there. In long-term treatments, the therapeutic relationship has generally become extremely important to both the patient and the therapist. For some patients it may have been the first relationship that was healthy; for others it may have been their only healthy relationship. Intense transference (and countertransference) may have transpired and is not always completely resolved as treatment nears its end. Ideally, resolution of transference should occur. Patients need to be helped to somehow envision what it might be like to manage without regular contact with the therapist. Therapists, too, can be very attached to their patients and find it painful to let them go. It is not only the patient who may need to grieve the end of therapy.

Termination of Treatment

Therapists have an ethical responsibility to end treatment when it is no longer needed or possible, or when it is unhelpful (Barnett, MacGlashan, & Clarke, 2000; Vasquez, Bingham, & Barnett, 2008). Edelson (1963) has noted that the most important issue in termination is how to end so that the patient continues to grow and develop after treatment. The way in which therapy ends can either facilitate this ongoing change or stymie it. Often, dissociative patients have had very long-term treatments, so termination is especially challenging, with the potential to evoke abandonment fears and great loss. Nevertheless, the therapist has an ethical responsibility to end therapy in the best way possible (Davis & Younggren, 2009; Vasquez et al., 2008). Ideally, the patient has been able to integrate a positive and realistic mental representation of the therapist that serves as a continuing guide to healing after therapy (Arnold, Farber, & Geller, 2004).

CORE CONCEPT

Termination is not merely the end of therapy. It is a major intervention that in itself can help the patient continue to grow and develop over a lifetime.

How the therapist brings up termination is important; too prematurely and the patient can become panicked; too late and the therapy can become stale (Quintana, 1993). In long-term therapies with patients working on abandonment issues, it is not appropriate to explicitly remind them that the relationship will end. They cannot yet imagine an ending that does not involve abandonment and rejection. Yet knowledge that therapy will eventually end is implicit in setting and achieving goals. Over time, the patient may fearfully bring up the idea of ending. The therapist can reassure the patient that when the time comes, the patient will know and be ready, and the time is not yet here.

Termination will be more challenging when the therapy relationship and transference (and countertransference) are intense, and when the pathology of the patient is greater (Vasquez et al., 2008). This is typical in patients with complex dissociative disorders. Those patients who have unresolved dependency and hostility issues will have a particularly negative reaction to termination (Werbart, 1997). If termination does not help the patient resolve the loss of a meaningful relationship with the therapist, the consequences can be negative and long-lasting (Roe, Dekel, Harel, Fennig, & Fennig, 2006).

In addition to potential challenges in ending well, both therapist and patient must consider whether or not dissociative parts have integrated or will do so in the future. If not, they must determine whether resolving issues that maintain separateness is a reasonable and shared goal of treatment, or whether there is sufficient cooperation and cohesion among remaining dissociative parts to maintain good function in daily life. The process of termination should include ample work on how patients can prevent further avoidance and dissociation.

Is the Patient Ready to End Therapy?
The end of therapy is not the end of change and growth. It should be a catalyst for further healthy development. How do therapist and patient determine when enough therapy has been done, in spite of some ongoing issues with which the patient struggles? First, there must be open and honest conversations about what is possible, what goals remain, and how reasonable those goals are. Second, both therapist and patient need a relatively realistic perspective about the potential capabilities of the patient. Based on the reasonable capacities of the patient, the following guidelines in Table 23.1 can be helpful.

Setting the Stage for Termination
Consideration of termination begins when the therapist sets the treatment frame and contract. The therapy contract guides the work of patient and therapist, and either it must be revised with new goals when old ones are met, or the time has come to end the therapy. When the time comes for termination in Phase 3, the goals for ending therapy need to be clearly out-

> ### TABLE 23.1
> ### Factors in Determining Termination
>
> - Are all parts integrated and a dissociative disorder no longer exists? If the patient is determined to maintain separate parts, the therapist should thoroughly discuss options and caveats, including the possibility to return to therapy for further work.
> - Is the patient functioning at his or her best for the current situation?
> - Has the patient been able to develop and maintain at least some relationships and use some relational skills?
> - Is the patient able to mentalize?
> - Is the patient able to regulate normal emotions in daily life?
> - Does the patient have some significant self-compassion?
> - Are major traumatic memories integrated?
> - Is the patient able to self-soothe and ask for support when needed?
> - Is the patient able to be present enough to function relatively well in daily life?
> - Is the patient able to have and enjoy positive experiences and emotions at least some of the time?

lined and understood by both patient and therapist. The treatment frame should include an agreement that at least several sessions be dedicated to the termination process, so the patient does not leave without talking about ending. The therapist should regularly review treatment goals and gains with the patient, help the patient identify relapse risks and how to manage them, anticipate problems that might arise in the future, and help the patient determine when therapy might again be helpful (Vasquez et al., 2008). The therapist should help the patient feel competent and confident, yet also open to knowing when help might be needed.

In long-term therapies of dissociative patients, much work over time needs to be done to prepare patients for eventual separation. For example, the therapist's vacations or other absences can be opportunities to talk about loss and the need of the therapist, and how the patient can manage more effectively. Some of the deepest grief and loss can be evoked by thinking about termination, and the therapist must be prepared to compassionately deal with occasional regressions due to fear.

Talking about termination. The way in which the therapist helps the patient handle termination is essential, as leave-taking is a fundamental skill needed for most relationships. It is the responsibility of therapists to bring up the possibility of termination if they believe that the major goals of therapy have been met. Patients can be reassured that when the time comes they will be ready, and it will be a joint decision made with the therapist. Therapists can explore the patient's fears and concerns, resolving conflicts and attachment issues along the way. Taking a thorough history of the patient's leave-taking experiences can be helpful in crafting a good termination. For example, many patients have never had the opportunity to actually talk about an ending or about what a relationship has meant to them. Taking the time to discuss what went well, what did not, what might have been more helpful from the therapist are all part of wrapping up. Sometimes the therapist can offer a perspective on how the patient has changed over time that is helpful.

Winding down. Often therapy winds down gradually. The intensity of sessions decreases and topics are more focused on the present. Transference with the therapist should be resolved to a large degree, so the patient has energy to put into other relationships. Some patients may find they have less to talk about in therapy. Many patients may shift from weekly to biweekly sessions, and sometimes to an "as-needed" basis. In fact, some clinicians have suggested a different model in which an ending of therapy is merely considered a temporary interruption in treatment that can continue periodically over the life of the patient, as needed (Cummings, 2001). Each patient has a different need in this regard.

Premature Termination

Some endings occur before major issues in therapy are resolved. The patient or therapist moves, the therapist retires or changes jobs, the patient abruptly ends therapy, insurance and finances become insurmountable issues, and so on. Sometimes patients end therapy prematurely because they feel hurt or angry with the therapist, and sometimes because they cannot face painful issues. If the patient ends without explanation, the therapist should contact the patient by phone and with a follow-up letter, asking the patient to come for at least one termination session to determine what when wrong. If the patient does not respond, an additional letter should be sent, noting the patient is considered terminated, but can return if the patient chooses at a later time. This way, therapist and patient are both clear that the patient is no longer in treatment and the therapist no longer has ethical or legal obligations for the patient.

Occasionally a therapist must terminate with a patient who is unwilling or unable to maintain sufficient functioning to be treated on an outpatient basis, or who chronically violates the treatment frame in serious ways, such as being violent, refusing to pay, or being unwilling to accept the boundaries of therapy. Sometimes a therapist has health problems that necessitate premature termination, or the therapist's own trauma has been triggered to the degree that a traumatic countertransference is developed, and termination may be the best solution. In such cases, a consultant can be brought in to help the therapist and patient with their leave-taking and separation, while the therapist can enter therapy for trauma-related issues (Kluft, 1988b).

Contact After Termination

Patients are often fearful of completely losing contact with their therapist, with whom they have had a long-term and intense relationship. Most ethics guidelines strongly recommend that friendships and certainly sexual relationships with former patients should not occur after termination, and we concur. However, most therapists are open to having occasional contact from patients who have completed therapy. For example, patients may call the therapist annually or send holiday cards giving an update on how they are doing. This can be rewarding follow-up for both, sharing the fruits of good treatment. The therapist should be clear about whether there is a possibility for future consultation or additional therapy, should the patient need it.

A Professional Will

As part of their ethical obligations to patients, therapists are increasingly encouraged to prepare a professional will. A will offers directions in how to contact and care for patients in the event of the therapist's unexpected incapacitation or death (Ragusea, 2013; Pope & Vasquez, 2005, 2011). For purposes of confidentiality, patients should sign an informed consent agreeing to be contacted by a designated person in the event the therapist becomes unavailable. A copy of the will should be accessible to the person who is designated to deal with the therapist's professional affairs. It should include at least the following (Pope & Vasquez, 2005, 2011):

- the name and contact information of the designated person who will contact patients;
- names of therapists who can serve as temporary backup for patients, and therapists to whom patients will be permanently referred;
- contact information for current patients, which should be periodically updated;
- access to your calendar or appointment book and computer, including passwords;
- instructions for how the designated person will gain access to the office and to patient records, including keys, access codes, and passwords for any online records; and
- access to billing records.

Further Explorations

23.1 What have your own experiences with grief been like for you? What helped you move forward? How does your own grieving affect your ability to be with a grieving patient?

23.2 What are your experiences with termination with your patients? What would you do differently in the future, if anything?

23.3 What are your policies about contact with patients after termination? Why did you set these particular policies? Discuss them with a group of your colleagues.

23.4 Do you have a professional will? If not, please consider making one.

Screening Self-Report Questionnaires

Dissociative Experiences Scale II (DES)

(Carlson & Putnam, 1993)

A 28-item self-report questionnaire that identifies three symptom categories: *amnesia, absorption/imaginative involvement,* and *depersonalization/derealization.* It is a screening rather than a diagnostic instrument.

- Available at no charge online (various websites), including
  http://www.neurotransmitter.net/dissociationscales.html

Dissociative Experiences Scale-Taxon (DES-T)

(Waller et al., 1996)

A subset of 8 items from the DES (see above) that are likely to more accurately distinguish pathological dissociation from absorption and imaginative involvement (alterations in consciousness)

- Available at no charge from http://www.isst-d.org/default.
  asp?contentID=66

Multidimensional Inventory of Dissociation (MID)

(Dell, 2006b)

A 218-item multi-scale instrument that distinguishes DID, OSDD, and PTSD. The MID measures 14 major facets of pathological dissociation. It has a validity scale and reports severity of dissociation, critical items such as suicidality or psychosis, cognitive dissociation, full and partial intrusions, and has a borderline personality index.

- Available at no charge from the author. Also reprinted in *Rebuilding Shattered Lives: Treating Complex PTSD and Dissociative Disorders,* by J. A. Chu, 2011, New York, NY: Wiley.

Multi-Scale Dissociation Inventory (MDI)

(Briere, 2002)

The MDI is a 30-item self-report test of dissociative symptomatology. It includes six different types of dissociative response: disengagement, depersonalization, derealization, emotional constriction/numbing, memory disturbance, and identity dissociation. It also has a total dissociation score.

- Available at no charge from http://www.johnbriere.com/multiscale. htm

Somatoform Dissociation Questionnaire (SDQ-20)

(Nijenhuis, Spinhoven, Van Dyck, Van der Hart, & Vanderlinden, 1997)

A 20-item questionnaire that examines symptoms of somatoform dissociation. A short 5-item version (SDQ-5) is also available.

- Available at no charge from http://www.enijenhuis.nl/sdq.html

Diagnostic Interviews

Office Mental Status Exam for Dissociation

(Loewenstein, 1991a)

Assesses symptoms of dissociation, PTSD, hypnotic trance, and traumatic transference.

- May be purchased from *Psychiatric Clinics of North America* or available from the author

Structured Clinical Interview for DSM-IV Dissociative Disorders, Revised (SCID-D-R)

(Steinberg, 1994, 1995, 2004)

A semistructured interview for all the dissociative disorders based on the *Diagnostic and Statistical Manual for Mental Disorders*. It inquires about five dissociative symptom clusters: amnesia, depersonalization, derealization, identity confusion, and identity alteration.

- May be purchased from http://www.appi.org/ or online bookstore

Dissociative Disorders Interview Schedule (DDIS)

(C. A. Ross, Heber, Norton, Anderson, Anderson, & Barchet, 1989)

A structured interview that assesses *DSM-5* diagnoses of somatization disorder, borderline personality disorder, and major depressive disorder, as well as all the dissociative disorders. It inquires about positive symptoms of schizophrenia, secondary features of DID, extrasensory experiences, substance abuse, and other items relevant to the dissociative disorders.

- Available at no charge from the author at
  http://www.rossinst.com/ddis.html

Trauma and Dissociation Symptoms Interview (TADS-I)
(Boon & Matthess, 2016)
The TADS-I is a new clinician-administered semistructured interview to assess dissociative symptoms and disorders and other trauma-related symptoms. Based on the symptom profiles, clinicians can make *DSM-5* and *ICD-10* diagnoses of dissociative disorders and Complex PTSD (as formulated in *ICD-11* draft). The interview is currently being validated.

- Available at no charge from the author at
  http://www.suzetteboon.com/

Add the numbers in a column to get a subtotal for Part 1, and then for Part 2. Add the two subtotals together for a total score. The total score ranges from 0 to 256. The *higher* the score, the poorer the prognosis or treatment progress over time. When treatment is progressing, the score should decrease over time as symptoms abate and patients learn more effective skills. Please note the scoring in Part 2 is reversed from that in Part 1.

Scoring for Part 1
0 = Absent
1 = Rare (a few times a year)
2 = Seldom (a few times a month)
3 = Often (a few times a week)
4 = Almost all the time (daily)
N/A = Not applicable or unknown

Part 1

	Baseline Score Date:	Time 2 Score Date:	Time 3 Score Date:	Time 4 Score Date:	Time 5 Score Date:
Dissociation					
Amnesia for the present					
Amnesia for trauma (in the past)					
Chronic derealization or depersonalization					
Somatoform dissociation					

Passive influence (e.g., voices, made feelings or behaviors)					
Severe conflicts among parts					
Frequent switching between parts					
Highly invested in DID diagnosis					
Comorbidity					
Significant post-traumatic stress disorder					
Significant mood disorder					
Significant personality disorder					
Significant psychotic disorder					
Developmental disorder (e.g., mental retardation, autism spectrum)					
Persistent substance abuse disorder					
Persistent eating disorder					
Trauma History					
Reports of multiple perpetrators					
Reports of sadistic abuse					
Reports of multiple types of abuse					
Abuse or neglect as an infant or young child					
Ongoing Victimization					
Reports of current victimization					

Patient is currently abusing others					
Crisis Proneness					
Requires regular, ongoing crisis intervention					
Needs frequent hospitalization					
Unsafe Behaviors					
Self-injury (e.g., cutting, burning)					
Multiple suicide attempts					
Persistent compulsive behaviors					
Other unsafe behaviors					
Part 1 Subtotal Score:					

Part 2

In this section, the scoring is reversed.

0 = Almost all the time (daily)
1 = Often (a few times a week)
2 = Seldom (a few times a month)
3 = Rare (a few times a year)
4 = Absent
N/A = Not applicable or unknown

Functioning in Daily Life					
Functions adequately in daily life (work, school, parenting, daily tasks)					
Consistently able to provide financially for basic needs, even if via assistance					
Tolerates the stress of every-day life					

Manages leisure time adaptively (hobbies, exercise, recreation, alone time)					
Other Significant Relationships					
Able to parent own children appropriately					
Has a social support system, even if only one other person in addition to the therapist					
Able to maintain at least one close friendship					
Works well with others at school or work					
Able to maintain relatively healthy relationship with a partner					
Participates in group activities (social, religious, charitable, volunteer)					
Coping with Dissociative Disorder					
Parts able to be oriented to the present					
Has communication and cooperation among dissociative parts at least regarding daily life					
Willing to allow therapist to access or work with parts					
Sadistic, punishing, or other acting-out parts willing to engage with therapist					
Has an adult part willing to be responsible and engage in therapy					

Participation in Therapy					
Attends sessions regularly and on time					
Able to set reasonable treatment goals					
Abides by treatment frame and boundaries					
Follows reasonable treatment recommendations (e.g., medication, adjunctive group therapy, hospitalization)					
Shares private thoughts and feelings and Is honest with the therapist					
Skills Development					
Has capacities to mentalize, reflect, and take perspective					
Able to manage and contain flashbacks and other PTSD symptoms					
Has at least some self-compassion					
Accepts and regulates intense emotions					
Uses positive emotions and experiences as resources					
Has some capacity to be mindful and present					
Able to synthesize, realize, and integrate traumatic memories					
Realizes and integrates experiences of loss, pain, distress, and rejection over time					

Insight and Motivation					
Motivated to change					
Takes reasonable responsibility for the work of therapy					
Has at least some insight					
Uses insight to make adaptive changes					
Therapeutic Relationship					
Willing and able to engage with the therapist					
Has a (relatively) positive response to the therapeutic relationship					
Able to accept the therapist's attempts to repair the relationship when a rupture occurs					
Able and willing to talk about and work through transference					
Part 2 Subtotal Score =					
+ Part 1 Subtotal Score =					
TOTAL SCORE =					

From "The Treatment of Traumatic Memories in DID: Indications and Contra-Indications," by S. Boon, 1997, *Dissociation, 10*, pp. 65–80. Adapted with permission.

My Warning Signs and Triggers

What signs should I be aware of that alert me to the need to increase safety?

What do I think might have triggered me?

What was happening just before I felt the urge to engage in unsafe behaviors?

How have I successfully coped in the past with these urges?

What am I thinking?

Feeling?

Sensing?

Doing?

How do I think that unsafe behavior will help me right now?

What else could I do that achieves the same goal?

Ways I Can Help Myself

Ways I can check inside and help parts of myself and ask parts to help each other:

Ways I can accept my experiences and emotions with compassion:

Ways I can ground myself in the present:

Ways I can distract myself:

Ways I can support and reassure myself:

Substitute Behaviors

If I still feel the urge to hurt myself, I may:

Making a Call to Get Support From Someone Else

If I still feel the urge to hurt myself, I may call the following friends, family, or lastly my therapist (include phone numbers):

Emergency numbers (for example, crisis hotlines, hospitals):

REFERENCES

Aderibigbe, Y. A., Bloch, R. M., & Walker, W. R. (2001). Prevalence of depersonalization and derealization experiences in a rural population. *Social Psychiatry & Psychiatric Epidemiology, 36*, 63–69.

Ainsworth, M., Blehar, M., Waters, E., & Wall, S. (1978). *Patterns of attachment.* Hillsdale, NJ: Erlbaum.

Allen, J. G. (2001). *Traumatic relationships and serious mental disorders.* Chichester, NY: Wiley.

Allen, J. G. (2012). *Restoring mentalizing in attachment relationship: Treating trauma with plain old psychotherapy.* Arlington, VA: American Psychiatric Publishing.

Allen, J. G., & Coyne, L. (1995). Dissociation and vulnerability to psychotic experience: The Dissociative Experiences Scale and the MMPI-2. *Journal of Nervous and Mental Disease, 183*, 615–622.

Allen, J. G., Coyne, L., & Huntoon, J. (1998). Trauma pervasively elevates Brief Symptom Inventory profiles in inpatient women. *Psychological Reports, 83*, 499–513.

Allen, J. G., Coyne, L., & Console, D. A. (1996). Dissociation contributes to anxiety and psychoticism on the Brief Symptom Inventory. *Journal of Nervous and Mental Disease, 184*, 639–641.

Andrews, B., Brewin, C. R., Rose, S., & Kirk, M. (2000). Predicting PTSD symptoms in victims of violent crime: The role of shame, anger, and childhood abuse. *Journal of Abnormal Psychology, 109*, 69–73.

Arnold, E. G., Farber, B. A., & Geller, J. D. (2004). Termination, posttermination, and internalization of therapy and the therapist: Internal representation and psychotherapy outcome. In D. P. Charman (Ed.), *Core processes in brief psychodynamic psychotherapy: Advancing effective practice* (pp. 289–308). Mahwah, NJ: Erlbaum.

Balcom, D., Call, E., & Pearlman, D. N. (2000). Eye movement desensitization and reprocessing treatment of internalized shame. *Traumatology, 6*(2), 69–83.

Barach, P. B. (1991). Multiple personality disorder as an attachment disorder. *Dissociation, 4*(3), 117–123.

Barnett, J. E., MacGlashan, S., & Clarke, A. J. (2000). Risk management and ethical issues regarding termination and abandonment. In L. VandeCreek & T. Jackson (Eds.), *Innovations in clinical practice* (pp. 231–246). Sarasota, FL: Professional Resources Press.

Barrett, M. J., & Trepper, T. S. (2004). Treatment of denial in families where there is child sex abuse. In C. W. Lecroy & J. M. Daley (Eds.), *Case studies in child, adolescent and family treatment* (1st ed., pp. 229–241). Belmont, CA: Brooks Cole.

Barrett, M. S., & Berman, J. S. (2001). Is psychotherapy more effective when therapists disclose information about themselves? *Journal of Consulting and Clinical Psychology, 69*, 597–603.

Beebe, B. (2000). Co-constructing mother-infant distress. *Psychoanalytic Inquiry, 20*, 421–440.

Beere, D. B., Simon, M. J., & Welch, K. (2001). Recommendations and illustrations for combining hypnosis and EMDR in the treatment of psychological trauma. *American Journal of Clinical Hypnosis, 43*(3–4), 217–231.

Bender, L. (Producer), & Van Sant, G. (Director). (1977). *Good Will Hunting* [Motion picture]. USA: Miramax Home Entertainment.

Benjamin, L. R., & Benjamin, R. (1993). Interventions with children in dissociative families: A family treatment model. *Dissociation, 6*(1), 54–65.

Benjamin, L. R., & Benjamin, R. (1994a). Utilizing parenting as a clinical focus in the treatment of dissociative disorders. *Dissociation, 7*(4), 239–245.

Benjamin, L. R., & Benjamin, R. (1994b). Various perspectives on parenting and their implications for the treatment of dissociative disorders. *Dissociation, 7*(4), 246–260.

Benjamin, L. R., Benjamin, R., & Rind, B. (1998). The parenting experiences of mothers with dissociative disorders. *Journal of Marital Family Therapy, 24*(3), 337–354.

Bernstein, E. M., & Putnam, F. W. (1986). Development, reliability, and validity of a dissociation scale. *Journal of Nervous and Mental Disease, 174,* 727–735.

Beutler, L. E., Harwood, T. M., Michelson, A., Song, X., & Holman, J. (2010). Resistance/Reactance level. *Journal of Clinical Psychology, 67,* 133–142.

Beutler, L. E., Rocco, F., Moleiro, C. M., & Talebi, H. (2001). Resistance. *Psychotherapy, 38,* 431–436.

Bicanic, I., De Jongh, A., & Ten Broeke, E. (2015). Stabilisatie in traumabehandeling bij complexe PTSS: Noodzaak of mythe? [Stabilization in trauma treatment for complex PTSD: Necessity or myth?]. *Tijdschrift voor Psychiatrie, 57,* 332–339.

Black, R. S. A., Curran, D., & Dyer, K. F. W. (2013). The impact of shame on the therapeutic alliance and intimate relationships. *Journal of Clinical Psychology, 69,* 646–654.

Blizard, R. (1997). Therapeutic alliance with abuser alters in dissociative identity disorder: The paradox of attachment to the abuser. *Dissociation, 10,* 246–254.

Blizard, R. (2003). Disorganized attachment, development of dissociated self states, and a relational approach to treatment. *Journal of Trauma and Dissociation, 4*(3), 27–50.

Boehm, C. (2012). *Moral origins: The evolution of virtue, altruism, and shame.* New York, NY: Basic Books.

Boesky, D. (1990). The psychoanalytic process and its components. *Psychoanalytic Quarterly, 59,* 550–584.

Book, H. E. (1998). *How to practice brief psychodynamic psychotherapy: The core conflictual relationship theme method* (2nd ed.). Washington, DC: American Psychological Association.

Boon, S. (1997). The treatment of traumatic memories in DID: Indications and contra-indications. *Dissociation, 10,* 65–80.

Boon, S. (2014). The treatment of clients reporting (ritual) abuse by organized perpetrator networks: A reflection on nearly 30 years experience. *ESTD Newsletter, 3*(6), 4-13.

Boon, S., & Draijer, N. (1993a). *Multiple personality disorder in the Netherlands.* Lisse, the Netherlands: Swets & Zeitlinger.

Boon, S., & Draijer, N. (1993b). Multiple personality disorder in the Netherlands: A clinical investigation of 71 patients. *American Journal of Psychiatry, 150,* 489–463.

Boon, S., & Draijer, N. (1995). *Screening en diagnostiek van dissociatieve stoornissen* [Screening and diagnostics of dissociative disorders]. Lisse, the Netherlands: Swets & Zeitlinger.

Boon, S., & Draijer, N. (2007). Diagnostiek van dissociatieve stoornissen met de SCID-D: Mogelijkheden en beperkingen [Diagnosis of dissociative disorders with the SCID-D: Possibilities and limitations]. *Psychopraxis, 9,* 27–32.

Boon, S., & Matthess, H. (April 14, 2016). *The trauma and dissociation symptoms interview.* Workshop presented at the Fifth Biennial Conference of the European Society for the Study of Trauma and Dissociation, Amsterdam, the Netherlands.

Boon, S., Steele, K., & Van der Hart, O. (2011). *Coping with trauma-related dissociation: Skills training for patients and therapists.* New York, NY: Norton.

Boon, S., & Van der Hart, O. (2003). De behandeling van de dissociatieve identiteitsstoornis [Treatment of dissociative identity disorder]. In O. van der Hart (Ed.), *Trauma, dissociatie en hypnose* [Trauma, dissociation and hypnosis] (4th ed., pp. 193–238). Lisse, the Netherlands: Swets & Zeitlinger.

Bowlby, J. (1969). *Attachment and loss* (Vol. 1: Attachment). New York, NY: Basic Books.

Bowlby, J. (1988). *A secure base: Parent-child attachment and healthy human development.* New York, NY: Basic Books.

Bowman, E. (2006). Why conversion seizures should be classified as a dissociative disorder. *Psychiatric Clinics of North America, 29*(1), 185–211.

Brach, T. (2003). *Radical acceptance: Embracing your life with the heart of a Buddha.* New York, NY: Bantam.

Brady, K. T. (1997). Posttraumatic stress disorder and comorbidity: Recognizing the many faces of PTSD. *Journal of Clinical Psychiatry, 58*(Suppl. 9), 12–15.

Brady, K. T., Killeen, T. K., Brewerton, T., & Lucerini, S. (2000). Comorbidity of psychiatric disorders and posttraumatic stress disorder. *Journal of Clinical Psychiatry, 61*(Suppl. 7), 22–32.

Brand, B. L., Armstrong, J. G., & Loewenstein, R. J. (2006). Psychological assessment of patients with dissociative identity disorder. *Psychiatric Clinics of North America, 29*(1), 145–168.

Brand, B. L., Armstrong, J. G., Loewenstein, R. J., & McNary, S. W. (2009). Personality differences on the Rorschach of dissociative identity disorder, borderline personality disorder, and psychotic inpatients. *Psychological Trauma: Theory, Research, Practice, and Policy, 1*(3), 188–205.

Brand, B. L., & Chasson, G. S. (2015). Distinguishing simulated from genuine dissociative identity disorder on the MMPI-2. *Psychological Trauma: Theory, Research, Practice, and Policy, 7*(1), 93–101.

Brand, B. L., Classen, C. C., Lanius, R., Loewenstein, R. J., McNary, S. W., Pain, C., & Putnam, F. W. (2009). A naturalistic study of dissociative identity disorder and dissociative disorder not otherwise specified patients treated by community clinicians. *Psychological Trauma: Theory, Research, Practice, & Policy, 1*(2), 153–171.

Brand, B. L., Classen, C. C., McNary, S. W., & Zaveri, P. (2010). A review of dissociative disorders treatment studies. *Journal of Nervous and Mental Disease, 197*, 646-654.

Brand, B. L., & Loewenstein, R. J. (2010). Dissociative disorders: Assessment, phenomenology and treatment. *Psychiatric Times*, 62–69. Retrieved from www.psychiatrictimes.com

Brand, B. L., & Loewenstein, R. J. (2014). Does phasic trauma treatment make patients with dissociative identity disorder treatment more dissociative? *Journal of Trauma & Dissociation, 15*(1), 52–65.

Brand, B. L., Loewenstein, R. J., & Spiegel, D. (2014). Dispelling myths about dissociative identity disorder treatment: An empirically based approach. *Psychiatry, 77*, 169–189.

Brand, B. L., McNary, S. W., Loewenstein, R. J., Kolos, A. C., & Barr, S. R. (2006). Assessment of genuine and simulated dissociative identity disorder on the structured interview of reported symptoms. *Journal of Trauma & Dissociation, 7*(1), 63–85.

Brand, B. L., McNary, S. W., Myrick, A. C., Loewenstein, R. J., Classen, C. C., Lanius, R. A., Pain, C., & Putnam, F. W. (2013). A longitudinal, naturalistic study of dissociative disorder patients treated by community clinicians. *Psychological Trauma: Theory, Research, Practice, & Policy.* doi:10.1037/a0027654

Brand, B. L., Myrick, A. C., Loewenstein, R. J., Classen, C. C., Lanius, R., McNary, S. W., Pain, C., & Putnam, F. W. (2011). A survey of practices and recommended treatment interventions among expert therapists treating patients with dissociative identity disorder and dissociative disorder not otherwise specified. *Psychological Trauma: Theory, Research, Practice, & Policy, 4*, 490–500.

Bratton, K. L. (2010). *Shame, guilt, anger, and seeking psychological treatment among a trauma exposed population.* Available from ProQuest Dissertations and Theses database. (UMI No. 3423674).

Braun, B. G. (1986). Issues in the psychotherapy of multiple personality disorder. In B. G. Braun (Ed.), *Treatment of multiple personality disorder* (pp. 3–28). Washington, DC: American Psychiatric Association.

Braun, B. G. (1988a). The BASK model of dissociation, Part I. *Dissociation, 1*(1), 4–23.

Braun, B. G. (1988b). The BASK model of dissociation, Part II. *Dissociation, 1*(2), 16–23.

Bresler, D. E. (1990). Meeting an inner advisor. In D. C. Hammond (Ed.), *Handbook of hypnotic suggestions and metaphors* (pp. 318–320). New York, NY: Norton.

Bretherton, I., & Mulholland, K. A. (1999). Internal working models in attachment relationships: A construct revisited. In J. Cassidy & P. R. Shaver (Eds.), *Handbook of attachment: Theory, research, and clinical applications* (pp. 89–111). New York, NY: Guilford.

Brewin, C. R. (2001). A cognitive neuroscience account of posttraumatic stress disorder and its treatment. *Behaviour Research and Therapy, 39*, 373–393.

Brewin, C. R. (2003). *Posttraumatic stress disorder: Malady or myth?* New Haven, CT: Yale University Press.

Brewin, C. R., Dalgleish, T., & Joseph, S. (1996). A dual representation theory of post-traumatic stress disorder. *Psychological Review, 103*, 670–686.

Briere, J. (2002). *Multiscale Dissociation Inventory.* Odessa, FL: Psychological Assessment Resources.

Briere, J., & Scott, C. (2012). *Principles of trauma therapy: A guide to symptoms, evaluation, and treatment* (2nd ed.). Thousand Oaks, CA: Sage Publications.

Britner, P. A., Marvin, R. S., & Pianta, R. C. (2005). Development and preliminary validation of the caregiving behavior system: Association with child attachment classification in the preschool Strange Situation. *Attachment & Human Development, 7*, 83–102.

Bromberg, P. M. (1993). Shadow and substance: A relational perspective on clinical process. *Psychoanalytic Dialogues, 10*, 147–168.

Bromberg, P. M. (1998). *Standing in the spaces: Essays on clinical process and trauma and dissociation.* Hillsdale, NJ: Analytic Press.

Bromberg, P. M. (2003). On being one's dream: Some reflections on Robert Bosnak's "embodied imagination." *Contemporary Psychoanalysis, 39*, 697–710.

Bromberg, P. M. (2006). *Awakening the dreamer: Clinical journeys.* Mahwah, NJ: Analytic Press.

Bromberg, P. M. (2011). *The shadow of the tsunami and the growth of the relational mind.* New York, NY: Routledge.

Brown, B. (2009). *Connections: A 12 session psycho-educational shame resilience curriculum.* Center City, MN: Hazelden.

Brown, B. (2012). *Brené Brown: Listening to Shame.* TED Talk [Video file]. Retrieved from http://www.ted.com/talks/brene_brown_listening_to_shame?language=en

Brown, B. (2015). *Daring greatly: How the courage to be vulnerable transforms the way we live, love, parent, and lead.* New York, NY: Avery.

Brown, D. P., & Fromm, E. (1986). *Hypnotherapy and hypnoanalysis.* Hillsdale, NJ: Erlbaum.

Brown, D. P., Scheflin, A. W., & Hammond, D. C. (1998). *Memory, trauma treatment, and the law.* New York, NY: Norton.

Brown. L. (2012). *Your turn for care: Surviving the aging and death of the adults who harmed you.* Publisher: Author.

Butler, L. D. (2006). Normative dissociation. *Psychiatric Clinics of North America, 29*, 45–62.

Cardeña, E. (1994). The domain of dissociation. In S. J. Lynn & J. W. Rhue (Eds.), *Dissociation: Clinical and theoretical perspectives* (pp. 15–31). New York, NY: Guilford.

Carlson, E. B., & Armstrong, J. (1994). The diagnosis and assessment of dissociative disorders. In & J. W. Rhue (Eds.), *Dissociation: Clinical and theoretical perspectives* (pp. 159–174). New York, NY: Guilford.

Carlson, E. B., & Putnam, F. W. (1993). An update on the Dissociative Experiences Scale. *Dissociation, 6*(1),16–27.

Carlson, E. B., Smith, S. R., Palmieri, P. A., Dalenberg, C. J., Ruzek, J. I., Kimerling, R., Burling, T. A., & Spain, D. A. (2011). Development and validation of a brief self-report measure of trauma exposure: The Trauma History Screen. *Psychological Assessment, 23*, 463–477.

Case Management Society of America (2008). What is a case manager? Retrieved December 20, 2015, from http://www.cmsa.org/Home/CMSA/WhatisaCaseManager/tabid/224/Default.aspx

Cecchin, G., Lane, G., & Ray, W. A. (1993). From strategizing to nonintervention: Toward irreverence in systemic practice. *Journal of Marital and Family Therapy, 19*(2), 125-136.

Cheek, D. B., & LeCron, L. M. (1968). *Clinical hypnotherapy*, New York, NY: Grune & Stratton.

Cheek, D. B, & Rossi, E. L. (1994). *Mind-body therapy: Methods of ideodynamic healing in hypnosis*. New York, NY: Norton.

Chefetz, R. A. (2015). *Intensive psychotherapy for persistent dissociative processes: The fear of feeling real*. New York, NY: Norton.

Christoffersen, M. N., Møhl, B., DePanfilis, D., & Vammen, K. S. (2015). Non-suicidal self-injury—Does social support make a difference? An epidemiological investigation of a Danish national sample.

Chu, J. A. (2011). *Rebuilding shattered lives: Treating complex PTSD and dissociative disorders* (2nd ed.). New York, NY: Wiley.

Cloitre, M., Cohen, L. R., & Koenen, K. C. (2006). *Treating survivors of child abuse: Psychotherapy for the interrupted life*. New York, NY: Guilford.

Cloitre, M., Koenen, K. C., Cohen, L. R., & Han, H. (2002). Skills training in affective and interpersonal regulation followed by exposure: A phase-based treatment for PTSD related to child abuse. *Journal of Consulting and Clinical Psychology, 70*, 1067–1074.

Coons, P. M. (1985). Children of parents with multiple personality disorder. In R. P. Kluft (Ed.), *Childhood antecedents of multiple personality* (pp. 151–165). Washington, DC: American Psychiatric Press.

Coons, P. M. (1991). Iatrogenesis and malingering of multiple personality disorder in the forensic evaluation of homicide defendants. *Psychiatric Clinics of North America, 14*(3), 757–768.

Coons, P. M., & Milstein, V. (1990). Self-mutilation associated with dissociative disorders. *Dissociation, 3*(2), 81–87.

Coons, P. M., & Milstein, V. (1994). Factitious or malingered multiple personality disorder: Eleven cases. *Dissociation, 7*, 81–85.

Cortina, M., & Liotti, G. (2007). Implicit unconscious processes, intersubjective abilities and evolutionary models of mind: New approaches to understand human nature. *Fromm Forum* (English ed.),. *11*, 40–51.

Cortina, M., & Liotti, G. (2010). Attachment is about safety and protection, intersubjectivity is about sharing and social understanding: The relationships between attachment and intersubjectivity. *Psychoanalytic Psychology, 27*, 410–441.

Cortina, M., & Liotti, G. (2014). An evolutionary outlook on motivation: Implications for the clinical dialogue. *Psychoanalytic Inquiry, 34*, 864-899.

Courtois, C. A. (1999). *Recollections of sexual abuse: Treatment principles and guidelines*. New York, NY:Norton.

Courtois, C. A. (2008). Complex trauma, complex reactions: Assessment and treatment. *Psychological Trauma: Theory, Research, Practice, and Policy, S*(1), 86-100.

Courtois, C. A. (2010). *Healing the incest wound: Adult survivors in therapy* (2nd ed.). New York, NY:Norton.

Courtois, C. A., & Ford, J. D. (2012). *Treating Complex PTSD: A relational, sequenced approach*. New York, NY: Guilford.

Courtois, C. A., & Ford, J. D. (Eds.). (2013). *Treatment of Complex PTSD: Scientific foundations and therapeutic models* (2nd printing). New York, NY: Guilford.

Cozolino, L. (2004). *The making of a therapist: A practical guide for the inner journey*. New York, NY: Norton.

Cozolino, L. (2010). *The neuroscience of psychotherapy: Healing the social brain* (2nd ed.). New York, NY:Norton.

Crittenden, P. M. (2006). A dynamic-maturational model of attachment. *Australian and New Zealand Journal of Family Therapy, 27*, 105–115.

Crittenden, P. M., & Landini, A. (2011). *Assessing adult attachment: A dynamic maturational approach to discourse analysis.* New York, NY: Norton.

Cronin, E., Brand, B., & Mattanah, J. (2014). The impact of the therapeutic alliance on treatment outcome in patients with dissociative disorders. *European Journal Of Psychotraumatology, 5.* doi:http://dx.doi.org/10.3402/ejpt.v5.22676.

Cummings, N. A. (2001). Interruption, not termination: The model from focused, intermittent psychotherapy throughout the life cycle. *Journal of Psychotherapy in Independent Practice, 2*(3), 3-18.

Curtis, J. M. (1985). Elements of prognosis in psychotherapy. *Psychological Reports, 56*(1), 11–18.

Cusack, K. J., Grubaugh, A. L., Knapp, R. G., & Frueh, B. C. (2006). Unrecognized trauma and PTSD among public mental health consumers with chronic and severe mental illness. *Community Mental Health Journal, 42,* 487–500.

Dale, K. Y., Berg, R., Elden, À., Ødegård, A., & Holte, A. (2009). Testing the diagnosis of dissociative identity disorder through measures of dissociation, absorption, hypnotizability and PTSD: A Norwegian pilot study. *Journal of Trauma & Dissociation, 10*(1), 102–112.

Dalenberg, C. J. (2000). *Countertransference and the treatment of trauma.* Washington, DC: American Psychological Association.

Dalenberg, C. J., & Paulson, K. (2009). The case for the study of "normal" dissociation processes. In P. F. Dell, & J. A. O'Neil (Eds.), *Dissociation and the dissociative disorders: DSM-V and beyond* (pp. 145–154). New York, NY: Routledge.

Damasio, A. (1999). *The feeling of what happens: Body and emotion in the making of consciousness.* Boston, MA: Houghton Mifflin Harcourt.

Damasio, A. (2012). *Self comes to mind: Constructing the conscious brain.* New York, NY: Vintage.

Davidson, J., & Smith, R. (1990). Traumatic experiences in psychiatric outpatients. *Journal of Traumatic Stress, 3,* 459–475.

Davies, J. M. (1997). Dissociation, therapeutic enactment, and transference-countertransference processes: A discussion of papers on childhood sexual abuse by S. Grand and J. Sarnat. *Gender and Psychoanalysis, 2,* 241–257.

Davies, J. M., & Frawley, M. G. (1994). *Treating the adult survivor of sexual abuse: A psychoanalytic perspective.* New York, NY: Basic Books.

Davis, D. D., & Younggren, J. N. (2009). Ethical competence in psychotherapy termination. *Professional Psychology: Research and Practice, 40,* 572–578.

Dell, P. F. (1998). Axis II pathology in outpatients with dissociative identity disorder. *Journal of Nervous and Mental Disease, 186*(6), 352–356.

Dell, P. F. (2002). Dissociative phenomenology of dissociative identity disorder. *Journal of Nervous and Mental Disease, 190*(1), 10–15.

Dell, P. F. (2006a). A new model of dissociative identity disorder. *Psychiatric Clinics of North America, 29*(1), 1–26.

Dell, P. F. (2006b). The Multidimensional Inventory of Dissociation (MID): A comprehensive measure of pathological dissociation. *Journal of Trauma & Dissociation, 7*(2), 77–106.

Dell, P. F. (2009a). The long struggle to diagnose multiple personality disorder (MPD): MPD. In P. F. Dell & J. A. O'Neil (Eds.), *Dissociation and the dissociative disorders: DSM-V and beyond* (pp. 383–402). New York, NY: Routledge.

Dell, P. F. (2009b). The long struggle to diagnose multiple personality disorder (MPD): Partial MPD. In P. F. Dell & J. A. O'Neil (Eds.), *Dissociation and the dissociative disorders: DSM-V and beyond* (pp. 403–428). New York, NY: Routledge.

Demos, V. (1995). (Ed.). *Exploring affect: The selected writings of Sylvan Tomkins.* New York, NY: Cambridge University Press.

DeYoung, P. A. (2015). *Understanding and treating chronic shame: A relational/neurobiological approach.* New York, NY: Routledge.

Dickerson, S. S., & Kemeny, M .E. (2004). Acute stressors and cortisol responses: A theoretical integration and synthesis of laboratory research. *Psychological Bulletin, 130*, 355–391.

Dominguez, D. V., Cohen, M., & Brom, D. (2004). Trauma and dissociation in psychiatric outpatients. *Israel Journal of Psychiatry and Related Sciences, 41*, 98–110.

Dorahy, M. J. (2010). The impact of dissociation, shame, and guilt on interpersonal relationships in chronically traumatized individuals: A pilot study. *Journal of Traumatic Stress, 23*(5), 653–656.

Dorahy, M. J., Corry, M., Shannon, M., Webb, K., McDermott, B., Ryan, M., & Dyer, K. (2013). Complex trauma and intimate relationships: The impact of shame, guilt and dissociation. *Journal of Affective Disorders, 147*(1-3), 72–79.

Dorahy, M. J., Gorgas, J., Hanna, D., & Wiingaard, S. U. (2015). Perceptions of therapist responses to shame disclosures by clients: A quasi-experimental investigation with non-clinical participants. *Counselling and Psychotherapy Research, 15*, 58–66.

Dorahy, M. J., Shannon, C., Seagar, L., Corr, M., Stewart, K., Hanna, D., Mulholland, C., & Middleton, W. (2009). Auditory hallucinations in dissociative identity disorder and schizophrenia with and without a childhood trauma history: Similarities and differences. *Journal of Nervous and Mental Disease, 197*, 892–898.

Draijer, N., & Boon, S. (1999). The imitation of dissociative identity disorder: Patients at risk, therapists at risk. *Journal of Psychiatry & Law, 11*, 301–322.

Drapeau, M., & Perry, J. C. (2004). Childhood trauma and adult interpersonal functioning: A study using the Core Conflictual Relationship Theme Method (CCRT). *Child Abuse & Neglect, 28*, 1049–1066.

Dutton, M. (1992). *Empowering and healing the battered woman: A model for assessment and intervention*. New York, NY: Springer.

Edelson, M. (1963). *The termination of intensive psychotherapy*. Springfield, IL: Thomas.

Eels, T. D. (Ed.). (2010). *Handbook of psychotherapy case formulation* (2nd ed.). New York, NY: Guilford.

Eels, T. D. (2015). *Psychotherapy case formulation*. Washington, DC: American Psychological Association.

Ellason, J. W., Ross, C. A., & Fuchs, D. L. (1995). Assessment of dissociative identity disorder with the Millon Clinical Multiaxial Inventory-II. *Psychological Reports, 76*(3, Pt. 1), 895–905.

Epstein, R. S. (1994). *Keeping boundaries: Maintaining safety and integrity in the psychotherapeutic process*. Washington, DC: American Psychiatric Press.

Ewin, D. M., & Eimer, B. N. (2006). *Ideomotor signals for rapid hypnoanalysis: A how-to manual*. Springfield, IL: Charles C. Thomas.

Felitti, V. J., Anda, R. F., Nordenberg, D., Williamson, D. F., Spitz, A. M., Edwards, V., Koss, M. P., & Marks, J. S. (1998). Relationship of childhood abuse and household dysfunction to many of the leading causes of death in adults: The Adverse Childhood Experiences (ACE) Study. *American Journal of Preventive Medicine, 14*, 245–258.

Ferentz, L. (2014). *Treating self-destructive behaviors in trauma survivors: A clinician's guide*. New York, NY: Routledge.

Figley, C. R. (1995). *Compassion fatigue: Coping with secondary traumatic stress disorder in those who treat the traumatized*. New York, NY: Brunner/Mazel.

Figley, C. R. (2015). *Treating compassion fatigue*. New York, NY: Routledge.

Fine, C. G. (1991). Treatment stabilization and crisis prevention: Pacing the therapy of the multiple personality disorder patient. *Psychiatric Clinic of North America, 14*, 661–675.

Fine, C. G. (1993). A tactical integrationalist perspective on the treatment of multiple personality disorder. In R. P. Kluft & C. G. Fine (Eds.), *Clinical perspectives on multiple personality disorder* (pp. 135–153). Washington, DC: American Psychiatric Press.

Fine, C. G. (1999). A tactical-integration model for the treatment of dissociative identity disorder and allied dissociative disorders, *American Journal of Psychotherapy, 53*, 361–376.

Fine, C. G. (2012). Cognitive behavioral hypnotherapy for dissociative disorders. *American Journal of Clinical Hypnosis, 54*, 331–352.

Fine, C. G., & Berkowitz, A. (2001). The wreathing protocol: The imbrication of EMDR and hypnosis in the treatment of Dissociative Identity Disorder and other dissociative responses. *American Journal of Hypnosis, 43*, 275–290.

Fine, C. G., & Comstock, C. (1989). Completion of cognitive schemata and affective realms through temporary blending of personalities. In B. G. Braun (Ed.), *Dissociative Disorders 1989—Proceedings of the 6th International Conference on Multiple Personality Dissociative States* (p. 17). Chicago, IL: Rush University.

Fisher, J. (2011). Sensorimotor approaches to trauma treatment. *Advances in Psychiatric Treatment, 17*, 171–177.

Fisher, P. A., & Gunnar, M. (2010). Early life stresses as a risk factor for adult disease. In R. A. Lanius, E. Vermetten, & C. Pain (Eds.), *The impact of early life trauma on health and disease: The hidden epidemic* (pp. 133–141). New York, NY: Cambridge University Press.

Flores, P. J. (2011). *Addiction as an attachment disorder*. New York, NY: Jason Aronson.

Foa, E. B., Keane, T. M., Friedman, M. J., & Cohen, J. A. (Eds.). (2009). *Effective treatment for PTSD: Practice guidelines from the International Society for Traumatic Stress Studies*. New York, NY: Guilford.

Foa, E., & Kozak, M. (1986). Emotional processing of fear: Exposure to corrective information. *Psychological Bulletin, 99*, 20–35.

Foa, E., & Rothbaum, B. (1998). *Treating the trauma of rape: Cognitive-behavioral therapy for PTSD*. New York, NY: Guilford.

Fogel, A., & Garvey, A. (2007). Alive communication. *Infant Behavior & Development, 30*, 251–257.

Fonagy, P. M., Gergely, G., Jurist, E. L., & Target, M. (2005). *Affect regulation, mentalization, and the development of the self*. New York, NY: Other Press.

Foote, B., Smolin, Y., Neft, D., & Lipschitz, D. (2008). Dissociative disorders and suicidality in psychiatric outpatients. *Journal of Nervous and Mental Disease, 196*, 29–36.

Ford, J., Courtois, C., Steele, K., Van der Hart, O., & Nijenhuis, E. (2005). Treatment of complex posttraumatic self-dysregulation. *Journal of Traumatic Stress, 18*, 437–447.

Forgash, C., & Copeley, M. (Eds.). (2007). *Healing the heart of trauma and dissociation with EMDR and ego state therapy*. New York, NY: Springer.

Forgash, C., & Knipe, J. (2007). Integrating EMDR and ego state treatments for clients with trauma disorders. In C. Forgash & M. Copeley (Eds.), *Healing the heart of trauma and dissociation with EMDR and ego state therapy* (pp. 1–60). New York, NY: Springer.

Frank, K. A. (2002). The ""ins and outs"" of enactment: A relational bridge for psychotherapy integration. *Journal of Psychotherapy Integration, 12*, 267–286.

Frankel, A. S. (2009). Dissociation and dissociative disorders: Clinical and forensic assessment with adults. In P. F. Dell & J. A. O'Neil (Eds.), *Dissociation and the dissociative disorders: DSM-V and beyond* (pp. 571–583). New York, NY: Routledge.

Frankel, A. S., & Dalenberg, C. (2006). The forensic evaluation of dissociation and persons diagnosed with dissociative identity disorder: Searching for convergence. *Psychiatric Clinics of North America, 29*(1), 169–184.

Fraser, G. (1991). The dissociative table technique: A strategy for working with ego states in dissociative disorders and ego state therapy. *Dissociation, 4*, 205–213.

Fraser, G. (2003). Fraser's' "Dissociative table technique" revisited, revised: A strategy for working with ego states in Dissociative Disorders and Ego-State Therapy. *Journal of Trauma and Dissociation, 4*, 5–28.

Frawley-O'Dea, M. G. (1997). Who's doing what to whom? *Contemporary Psychoanalysis, 33*, 5–18.

Frewen, P., & Lanius, R. (2015). *Healing the traumatized self: Consciousness, neuroscience, and treatment*. New York, NY:Norton.

Freyd, J. J. (1996). *Betrayal trauma: The logic of forgetting child abuse.* Cambridge, MA: Harvard University Press.

Freyd, J. J. & Birrel, R. (2013). *Blind to betrayal: Why we fool ourselves that we aren't being fooled.* New York, NY: Wiley.

Friberg, L. (June 2014). *Preliminary experiences from a pilot group treatment for dissociative parents.* Paper presented at the World Association for Infant Mental Health 14th World Congress. Edinburgh, Scotland..

Gabbard, G. O. (1989). Two subtypes of narcissistic personality disorder. *Bulletin of the Menninger Clinics, 53,* 527–532.

Gallagher, S. (2000). Philosophical conceptions of the self: Implications for cognitive science. *Trends in Cognitive Sciences, 4,* 14–21.

Gelinas, D. (2003). Integrating EMDR into phase-oriented treatment of trauma. *Journal of Trauma and Dissociation, 4*(3), 91–135.

Gentile, J. P., Dillon, K. S., & Gillig, P. M. (2013). Psychotherapy and pharmacotherapy for patients with dissociative identity disorder. *Innovations in Clinical Neuroscience, 10*(2), 22–29.

George, C., Kaplan, N., & Main, M. (1996). *Adult Attachment Interview Protocol* (3rd ed.). Unpublished manuscript. University of California, Berkeley.

George, C., & Solomon, J. (1999). Attachment and caregiving: The caregiving behavioral system. In J. Cassidy & P. R. Shaver (Eds.), *Handbook of attachment: Theory, research, and clinical applications* (pp. 649–670). New York, NY: Guilford.

Giang, V. (2013, November 15). The 14 most stressful jobs in America. *Business Insider.* Retrieved from http://finance.yahoo.com/news/the-14-most-stressful-jobs-in-america-171029957.html

Gilbert, P. (1989). *Human nature and suffering.* Hove, UK: Erlbaum.

Gilbert, P. (1997). The evolution of social attractiveness and its role in shame, humiliation, guilt and therapy. *British Journal of Medical Psychology, 70* (Pt. 2), 113–147.

Gilbert, P. (2009). Introducing compassion focused therapy. *Advances in Psychiatric Treatment, 15,* 199–208.

Gilbert, P. (2011). Shame in psychotherapy and the role of compassion focused therapy. In R. L. Dearing & J. P. Tangney (Eds.), *Shame in the therapy hour* (pp. 325–354). Washington, DC: American Psychological Association.

Gold, S. (2000). *Not trauma alone: Therapy for child abuse survivors in family and social context.* New York, NY: Routledge.

Gonzalez, A., & Mosquera, D. (2012). *EMDR and dissociation: The progressive approach* [English ed.]. Charleston, SC: Amazon Imprint.

Gratz, K. L., & Gunderson, J. G. (2006). Preliminary data on an acceptance-based emotion regulation group intervention for deliberate self-harm among women with Borderline Personality Disorder. *Behavior Therapy, 37,* 25–35.

Greenwald, R. (2013). *Progressive counting within a phase model of trauma-informed treatment.* New York, NY: Routledge.

Grey, N., Young, K., & Holmes, E. (2002). Hotspots in emotional memory and the treatment of posttraumatic stress disorder. *Behavioural and Cognitive Psychotherapy, 30,* 37–56.

Groth-Marnat, G., Gottheil, E., Liu, W., Clinton, D. A., & Beutler, L. E. (2008). Personality and treatment planning for psychotherapy: The systematic treatment selection model. In G. J. Boyle, G. Matthews, & D. H. Saklofske (Eds.), *The SAGE handbook of personality theory and assessment, Vol 1: Personality theories and models* (pp. 620–634). Thousand Oaks, CA: Sage.

Gutheil, T. G., & Brodsky, A. (2011). *Preventing boundary violations in clinical practice.* New York, NY: Guilford.

Gutheil, T. G., & Gabbard, G. O. (1993). The concept of boundaries in clinical practice: Theoretical and risk-management dimensions. *American Journal of Psychiatry, 150,* 188.

Gutheil, T. G., & Gabbard, G. O. (1998). Misuses and misunderstandings of boundary theory in clinical and regulatory settings. *American Journal of Psychiatry, 155,* 409–414.

Hammond, D. C. (Ed.). (1990a). *Handbook of hypnotic suggestions and metaphors.* New York, NY: Norton.

Hammond, D. C. (1990b). The serenity place. In D. C. Hammond (Ed.), *Handbook of hypnotic suggestions and metaphors* (pp. 130–131). New York, NY: Norton.

Hammond, D. C., & Cheek, D. B. (1988). Ideomotor signaling: A method for rapid unconscious exploration. In D. C. Hammond (Ed.), *Hypnotic induction and suggestion: An introductory manual* (pp. 90–97). New York, NY: Norton.

Harper, K., & Steadman, J. (2003). Therapeutic boundary issues in working with childhood sexual-abuse survivors. *American Journal of Psychotherapy, 57,* 64–79.

Hayes, S. C., Strosahl, K. D., & Wilson, K. G. (2011). *Acceptance and Commitment Therapy: The process and practice of mindful change* (2nd ed.). New York, NY: Guilford.

Herman, J. L. (1990). Discussion. In R. P. Kluft (Ed.), *Incest-related syndromes of adult psychopathology* (pp. 289–293). Washington, DC: American Psychiatric Press.

Herman, J. L. (1997). *Trauma and recovery: The aftermath of violence—From domestic abuse to political terror* (2nd ed.). New York, NY: Basic Books.

Herman, J. L. (2011). Shattered shame states and their repair. In J. Yellin & K. White (Eds.), *Shattered states: Disorganized attachment and its repair* (pp. 157–170). London, UK: Karnac Books.

Hesse, E., Main, M., Abrams, K. Y., & Rifkin, A. (2003). Unresolved states regarding loss or abuse can have "second-generation" effects: Disorganized, role-inversion and frightening ideation in the offspring of traumatized non-maltreating parents. In D. J. Siegel & M. F. Solomon (Eds.), *Healing trauma: Attachment, mind, body and brain* (pp. 57–106). New York, NY: Norton.

Hill, D. (2015). *Affect regulation theory: A clinical model.* New York, NY: Norton.

Hill, E. L., Gold, S. N., & Bornstein, R. F. (2000). Interpersonal dependency among adult survivors of childhood sexual abuse in therapy. *Journal of Child Sexual Abuse, 9,* 71–86.

Hood, B. (2013). *The self illusion: How the social brain creates identity.* London: Oxford University Press.

Horevitz, R., & Loewenstein, R. J. (1994). The rational treatment of multiple personality disorder. In S. J. Lynn & J. W. Rhue (Eds.), *Dissociation: Clinical and theoretical perspectives* (pp. 289–316). New York, NY: Guilford.

Horowitz, M. J. (1997). *Formulation as a basis for planning psychotherapy treatment.* Arlington, VA: American Psychiatric Association.

Howell, E. F. (2005). *The dissociative mind.* Hillsdale, NJ: The Analytic Press.

Howell, E. F. (2011). *Understanding and treating Dissociative Identity Disorder: A relational approach.* New York, NY: Routledge.

Huber, M. (2003). *Wege der Traumabehandlung: Trauma und Traumabehandlung* [Ways of trauma treatment: Trauma and trauma treatment]. Paderborn, Germany: Junferman.

Huber, M. (2013). *Der Feind im Innern: Psychotherapie mit Täterintrojekten* [The enemy inside: Psychotherapy with perpetrator introjects]. Paderborn, Germany: Junferman.

Hultberg, P. (1988). Shame—a hidden emotion. *Journal of Analytic Psychology, 33,* 109–126.

Ingram, B. L. (2011). *Clinical case formulations: Matching the integrative treatment plan to the client.* New York, NY: Wiley.

International Society for the Study of Trauma and Dissociation (2011). Guidelines for treating dissociative identity disorder in adults, third revision. *Journal of Trauma & Dissociation, 12,* 115–187.

Irwin, H. J. (1998). Affective predictors of dissociation. II Shame and guilt. *Journal of Clinical Psychology, 54,* 237–245.

Jallema, A. (2000). Insecure attachment states: Their relationship to borderline and narcissistic personality disorders and treatment process in cognitive analytic therapy. *Clinical Psychology & Psychotherapy, 7,* 138–154.

Janet, P. (1898). Le traitement psychologique de l'hystérie [The psychological treatment of hysteria]. In A. Robin (Ed.), *Traité de thérapeutique appliqué* (pp. 140–216). Paris, France:

Rueff. Also in P. Janet (1911), *L'état mental des hystériques* (2nd ed., pp. 619–688). Paris, France: Félix Alcan.

Janet, P. (1904). L'amnésie et la dissociation des souvenirs par l'émotion. *Journal de Psychologie, 1*, 417–453. Also in P. Janet, *L'état mental des hystériques* (2nd ed., pp. 506–544). Paris, France: Félix Alcan.

Janet, P. (1907). *The major symptoms of hysteria*. New York: Macmillan.

Janet, P. (1925a). *Psychological healing*. New York, NY: Macmillan.

Janet, P. (1925b). Memories which are too real. In C. MacFie et al. (Eds.), *Problems of personality: Studies presented to Dr. Morton Prince* (pp. 141–150). New York, NY: Harcourt, Brace.

Janet, P. (1928). *L'évolution de la mémoire et de la notion du temps*. Paris, France: A. Chahine.

Janet, P. (1929). *L'évolution de la personnalité*. Paris, France: A. Chahine.

Janet, P. (1935). Réalisation et interprétation. *Annales Médico-Psychologiques, 93*, 329–366.

Janet, P. (1945). La croyance délirante. *Schweizerische Zeitschrift für Psychologie, 4*, 173–187.

Janoff-Bulman, R. (1992). *Shattered Assumptions: Towards a new psychology of trauma*. New York, NY: Free Press.

Johnson, D., & Lubin, H. (2006). The Counting Method: Applying the rule of parsimony to the treatment of posttraumatic stress disorder. *Traumatology, 12*, 83-99.

Johnson, J. G., Cohen, P., Kasen, S., & Brook, J. (2006). Dissociative disorders among adults in the community, impaired functioning, and axis I and II comorbidity. *Journal of Psychiatric Research, 40*, 131–140.

Johnson, S. M. (1985). *Characterological transformation: The hard work miracle*. New York, NY: Norton.

Johnson, S. M. (1987). *Humanizing the narcissistic style*. New York, NY: Norton.

Karan, E., Niesten, I. J. M., Frankenburg, F. R., Fitzmaurice, G. M., & Zanarini, M. C. (2014). The 16-year course of shame and its risk factors in patients with borderline personality disorder. *Personality and Mental Health, 8*, 169-177.

Kaufman, G. (1989). *The psychology of shame: Theory and treatment of shame-based syndromes* (2nd ed.). New York, NY: Springer.

Kaufman, J. (Ed.). (2014). *Loss of the assumptive world: A theory of traumatic loss*. New York, NY: Routledge.

Kihlstrom, J. F. (1992). Dissociation and conversion disorders. In D. J. Stein & J. E. Young (Eds.), *Cognitive science and clinical disorders* (pp. 247–270). San Diego, CA: Academic Press.

Klonsky, E. D. (2007). The functions of deliberate self-injury: A review of the evidence. *Clinical Psychology Review, 27*, 226–239.

Kluft, R. P. (1982). Varieties of hypnotic interventions in the treatment of multiple personality. *American Journal of Clinical Hypnosis, 24*(4), 230–240.

Kluft, R. P. (1983). Hypnotherapeutic crisis intervention in multiple personality. *American Journal of Clinical Hypnosis, 26*(2), 73–83.

Kluft, R. P. (1985a). The natural history of multiple personality disorder. In R. P. Kluft (Ed.), *Childhood antecedents of multiple personality* (pp. 197–238). Washington, DC: American Psychiatric Press.

Kluft, R. P. (1985b). Using hypnotic inquiry protocols to monitor treatment progress and stability in multiple personality disorder. *American Journal of Clinical Hypnosis, 28*(2), 63–75.

Kluft, R. P. (1986a). High-functioning multiple personality patients: Three cases. *Journal of Nervous and Mental Disease, 174*, 722–726.

Kluft, R. P. (1986b). Personality unification in multiple personality disorder: A follow-up study. In B. G. Braun (Ed.), *Treatment of multiple personality disorder* (pp. 29–60). Washington, DC: American Psychiatric Press.

Kluft, R. P. (1987a). The simulation and dissimulation of multiple personality disorder. *American Journal of Clinical Hypnosis, 30*(2), 104–118.

Kluft, R. P. (1987b). First-rank symptoms as a diagnostic clue to multiple personality disorder. *American Journal of Psychiatry, 144*(3), 293–298.

Kluft, R. P. (1987c). The parental fitness of mothers with multiple personality disorder: A preliminary study. *International Journal of Child Abuse and Neglect, 11,* 271–280.

Kluft, R. P. (1988a). The postunification treatment of multiple personality disorder: First findings. *American Journal of Psychotherapy, 42,* 212–228.

Kluft, R. P. (1988b). On giving consultation for therapists treating multiple personality disorder: Fifteen years' experience. *Dissociation, 1*(3), 23–29.

Kluft, R. P. (1989). Playing for time: Temporizing techniques in the treatment of multiple personality disorder. *American Journal of Clinical Hypnosis, 32*(2), 90–98.

Kluft, R. P. (1990a). Dissociation and subsequent vulnerability: A preliminary study. *Dissociation, 3,* 167–173.

Kluft, R. P. (1990b). Another fusion ritual. In D. C. Hammond (Ed.), *Hypnotic suggestions and metaphors* (pp. 341–342). New York, NY: Norton.

Kluft, R. P. (1990c). The fractionated abreaction technique. In D. C. Hammond (Ed.), *Hypnotic suggestions and metaphors* (pp. 527–528). New York, NY: Norton.

Kluft, R. P. (1990d). Incest and subsequent revictimization: The case of therapist-patient sexual exploitation, with a description of the sitting duck syndrome. In R. P. Kluft (Ed.), *Incest-related syndromes of adult psychopathology* (pp. 263–288). Washington, DC: American Psychiatric Press.

Kluft, R. P. (1991). Multiple personality disorder. In A. Tasman and S. M. Goldfinger (Eds.), *The American Psychiatric Press Annual Review, 10,* (pp. 161–188). Washington, DC: American Psychiatric Press.

Kluft, R. P. (1992a). The use of hypnosis with dissociative disorders. *Psychiatric Medicine, 10*(4), 31–46.

Kluft, R. P. (1992b). Hypnosis with multiple personality disorder. *American Journal of Preventive Psychiatry and Neurology, 3,* 19–27.

Kluft, R. P. (1993a). Basic principles in conducting the psychotherapy of multiple personality disorder. In R. P. Kluft & C. G. Fine (Eds.), *Clinical perspectives on multiple personality disorder* (pp. 19–50). Washington, DC: American Psychiatric Press.

Kluft, R. P. (1993b). Clinical approaches to the integration of personalities. In R. P. Kluft & C. G. Fine (Eds.), *Clinical perspectives on multiple personality disorder* (pp. 101–133). Washington, DC: American Psychiatric Press.

Kluft, R. P. (1994a). Countertransference in the treatment of MPD. In J. P. Wilson & J. D. Lindy (Eds.), *Countertransference in the treatment of PTSD* (pp. 122–150). New York, NY: Guilford Press.

Kluft, R. P. (1994b). Applications of hypnotic intervention. *HYPNOS, 21,* 205–223.

Kluft, R. P. (1994c). Treatment trajectories in multiple personality disorder. *Dissociation, 7*(1), 63–76.

Kluft, R. P. (1994d). Clinical observations on the use of the CSDS Dimensions of Therapeutic Movement Instrument (DTMI). *Dissociation, 7,* 272–283.

Kluft, R. P. (1995). Psychodynamic psychotherapy of multiple personality disorder and allied forms of dissociative disorders not otherwise specified. In J. P. Barber & P. Crits-Cristoph (Eds.), *Dynamic therapies for psychiatric disorders* (Axis I) (pp. 332–385). New York, NY: Basic Books.

Kluft, R. P. (1996a). The diagnosis and treatment of dissociative identity disorder. *The Hatherleigh guide to psychiatric disorders* (pp. 49–96). New York, NY: Hatherleigh Press.

Kluft, R. P. (1996b). Treating the traumatic memories of patients with dissociative identity disorder. *American Journal of Psychiatry, 153*(Suppl.), 103–110.

Kluft, R. P. (1997a). Overview of the treatment of patients alleging that they have suffered ritualized or sadistic abuse. In G. A. Fraser (Ed.), *The dilemma of ritual abuse: Cautions and guides for therapists* (pp. 31–63). Washington, DC: American Psychiatric Press.

Kluft, R. P. (1997b). On the treatment of traumatic memories of DID patients: Always? Never? Sometimes? Now? Later? *Dissociation, 10,* 80–91.

Kluft, R. P. (1998). Reflections on the treatment of traumatic memories in dissociative identity disorder patients. In S. Lynn & K. McConkey (Eds.), *Truth in memory* (pp. 304–322). New York, NY: Guilford.

Kluft, R. P. (2001). Dissociative disorders. In G. D. Burrows, R. O. Stanley, & P. B. Bloom (Eds.), *International handbook of clinical hypnosis* (pp. 187–205). New York, NY: Wiley.

Kluft, R. P. (2006). Dealing with alters: A pragmatic clinical perspective. *Psychiatric Clinics of North America, 29,* 281–304.

Kluft, R. P. (2007). Applications of innate affect theory to the understanding and treatment of dissociative identity disorder. In E. Vermetten, M. J. Dorahy, & D. Spiegel (Eds.), *Traumatic dissociation: Neurobiology and treatment* (pp. 301–316). Washington, DC: American Psychiatric Publishing.

Kluft, R. P. (2012). Hypnosis in the treatment of Dissociative Disorders and allied states: An overview and case study. *South African Journal of Psychology, 42,* 146–155.

Kluft, R. P. (2013). *Shelter from the storm: Processing the traumatic memories of DID/DDNOS patients with the fractionated abreaction technique.* North Charleston, SC: Author.

Kluft, R. P. & Fine, C. G. (Eds.). (1993). *Clinical perspectives on multiple personality disorder.* Washington, DC: American Psychiatric Press.

Kluft, R. P., & Foote, B. (1999). Dissociative identity disorder: Recent developments. *American Journal of Psychotherapy, 53,* 283–288.

Knipe, J. (2009a). "Shame is my safe place": Adaptive information processing methods of resolving chronic shame-based depression. In R. Shapiro (Ed.), *EMDR solutions II: For depression, eating disorders, performance, and more* (pp. 49–89). New York, NY: Norton.

Knipe, J. (2009b). The method of constant installation of present orientation and safety (CIPOS). In M. Luber (Ed.), *Eye movement desensitization (EMDR) scripted protocols: Special populations* (pp. 235–241). New York, NY: Springer.

Knipe, J. (2014). *EMDR toolbox: Theory and treatment of complex PTSD and dissociation.* New York, NY: Springer.

Koerner, K., Tsai, M., & Simpson, E. (2011). Treating shame: A functional analytic approach. In R. L. Dearing & J. P. Tangney (Eds.), *Shame in the therapy hour* (pp. 91–113). Washington, DC: American Psychological Association.

Kohlenberg, R. J., & Tsai, M. (2012). *Functional analytic psychotherapy: Creating intense and curative therapeutic relationships.* New York, NY: Springer.

Kohut, H. (1971). *The analysis of the self: A systematic approach to the psychoanalytic treatment of Narcissistic Personality Disorder.* Chicago, IL: University of Chicago.

Korn, D. L., & Leeds, A. M. (2002). Preliminary evidence of efficacy for EMDR resource development and installation in the stabilization phase of treatment of complex posttraumatic stress disorder. *Journal of Clinical Psychology, 58,* 1465–1487.

Krakauer, S. Y. (2001). *Treating dissociative identity disorder: The power of the collective heart.* Philadelphia, PA: Brunner-Routledge.

Kramer, S. (1983). Object coercive doubting: A pathological defense response to maternal incest. *Journal of the Psychoanalytic Association, 31*(Suppl.), 325–351.

Kroger. W. S. (1977). *Clinical and experimental hypnosis* (2nd ed.). New York, NY: J. B. Lippincott.

Lanius, R. A., Brand, B., Vermetten, E., Frewen, P. A., & Spiegel, D. (2012). The dissociative subtype of posttraumatic stress disorder: Rationale, clinical and neurobiological evidence, and implications. *Depression and Anxiety, 29*(8), 701–708.

Lanius, R. A., Wolf, E. J., Miller, M. W., Frewen, P. A., Vermetten, E., Brand, B., & Spiegel, D. (2014). The dissociative subtype of PTSD. In M. J. Friedman, T. M. Keane, & P. A. Resick (Eds.), *Handbook of PTSD: Science and practice* (2nd ed., pp. 234–250). New York, NY: Guilford.

Laska, K. M., Gurman, A. S., & Wampold, B. E. (2014). Expanding the lens of evidence-based practice in psychotherapy: A common factors perspective. *Psychotherapy: Theory, Research, Practice, Training, 51,* 461–481.

Laub, D. (1991). An event without a witness. In S. Felman & D. Laub (Eds.), *Testimony: Crises of witnessing in literature, psychoanalysis, and history* (pp. 75–92). New York, NY: Routledge.

Laub, D., & Auerhahn, N. C. (1993). Knowing and not knowing massive psychic trauma: Forms of traumatic memory. *International Journal of Psycho-Analysis, 74,* 287–302.

Lazrove, S., & Fine, C. G. (1996). The use of EMDR in patients with dissociative identity disorder. *Dissociation, 9,* 289–299.

Leeds, A. M. (1998). Lifting the burden of shame: Using EMDR resource installation to resolve a therapeutic impasse. In P. Manfield (Ed.), *Extending EMDR: A casebook of innovative applications* (pp. 256–282). New York, NY: Norton.

LeRoy, M. (Producer), & Fleming, V. (Director). (1939). *The wizard of Oz* [Motion picture]. USA: Metro-Goldwyn-Mayer.

Leskela, J., Dieperink, M., & Thuras, P. (2002). Shame and posttraumatic stress disorder. *Journal of Traumatic Stress, 15,* 223–226.

Levine, P. (2008). *Healing trauma: A pioneering program for restoring the wisdom of your body.* Louisville, CO: Sounds True Inc.

Levine, P., & Frederick, A. (1997). *Waking the tiger: Healing trauma.* Berkeley, CA: North Atlantic Books.

Levine, P., & Mate, G. (2010). *In an unspoken voice: How the body releases trauma and restores goodness.* Berkeley, CA: North Atlantic Books.

Lewis, M. (1992). *Shame: The exposed self.* New York, NY: Free Press.

Lichtenberg, J. D. (1989). *Psychoanalysis and motivation.* Hillsdale, NJ: The Analytic Press.

Lichtenberg, J. D., & Kindler, A. R. (1994). A motivational systems approach to the clinical experience. *Journal of the American Psychoanalytic Association, 42,* 405–420.

Lifton, R. J., & Caruth, C. (2015). Giving death its due: An interview with Robert Jay Lifton. In C. Caruth, *Listening to trauma: Conversations with leaders in the theory and treatment of catastrophic experience* (pp. 3–22). Baltimore, MD: Johns Hopkins University Press.

Linden, M., Rotter, M., & Baumann, K. (2007). *Posttraumatic embitterment disorder.* Boston, MA: Hogrefe & Huber Publishing.

Linehan, M. M. (1993). *Cognitive behavioral treatment of Borderline Personality Disorder.* New York, NY: Guilford.

Linehan, M. M. (2014). *DBT skills training manual* (2nd ed.). New York, NY: Guilford.

Liotti, G. (1992). Disorganized/disoriented attachment in the etiology of dissociative disorders. *Dissociation, 5,* 196–204.

Liotti, G. (1999). Disorganization of attachment as a model for understanding dissociative psychopathology. In J. Solomon & C. George (Eds.), *Attachment disorganization* (pp. 297–317). New York, NY: Guilford.

Liotti, G. (2009). Attachment and dissociation. In P. F. Dell & J. A. O'Neil (Eds.), *Dissociation and the dissociative disorders: DSM-V and beyond* (pp. 53–65). New York, NY: Routledge.

Liotti, G. (2011). Attachment disorganization and the controlling strategies: An illustration of the contributions of attachment theory to developmental psychopathology and to psychotherapy. *Journal of Psychotherapy Integration, 21,* 232–252.

Lipschitz, D. S., Kaplan, M. L., Sorkenn, J. B., Faedda, G. L., Chorney, P., & Asnis, G. M. (1996). Prevalence and characteristics of physical and sexual abuse among psychiatric outpatients. *Psychiatric Services, 47,* 189–191.

Loewenstein, R. J. (1991a). An office mental status examination for complex chronic dissociative symptoms and multiple personality disorder. *Psychiatric Clinics of North America, 14*(3), 567–604.

Loewenstein, R. J. (1991b). Psychogenic amnesia and psychogenic fugue: A comprehensive review. In S. M. G. Allan Tasman (Ed.), *American Psychiatric Press review of psychiatry* (Vol. 10, pp. 189–222). Washington, DC: American Psychiatric Press.

Loewenstein, R. J., & Goodwin, J. (1999). Assessment and management of somatoform symptoms in traumatized patients: Conceptual overview and pragmatic guide. In J. Goodwin, & R. Attias (Eds.), *Splintered reflections: Images of the body in trauma* (pp. 67–88). New York, NY: Basic Books.

Loewenstein, R. J., & Welzant, V. (2010). Pragmatic approaches to stage-oriented treatment for early life trauma-related complex post-traumatic stress and dissociative disorders. In R. A. Lanius, E. Vermetten, & C. Pain (Eds.), *The impact of early life trauma on health and disease* (pp. 257–267). New York, NY: Cambridge University Press.

Low, G., Jones, D., MacLeod, A., Power, M., & Duggan, C. (2000). Childhood trauma, dissociation and self-harming behaviour: A pilot study. *British Journal of Medical Psychology, 73* (Pt. 2), 269–278.

Luborsky, L., & Crits-Cristoph, P. (1998). *Understanding transference: The core conflictual relationship themes method* (2nd ed.). Washington, DC: American Psychological Association.

Luoma, J. B., & Platt, M. G. (2015). Shame, self-criticism, self-stigma, and compassion in Acceptance and Commitment Therapy. *Current Opinion in Psychology, 2*, 97–101.

Lyons-Ruth, K. (2007). The interface between attachment and intersubjectivity: Perspective from the longitudinal study of disorganized attachment. *Psychoanalytic Inquiry, 26*, 596–616.

Lyons-Ruth, K., Dutra, L., Schuder, M. R., & Bianchi, I., (2006). From infant attachment disorganization to adult dissociation: Relational adaptations or traumatic experiences? *Psychiatric Clinics of North America, 29*, 63–86.

Lyons-Ruth, K., & Jacobvitz, D. (1999). Attachment disorganization: Unresolved loss, relational violence, and lapses in behavioral and attentional strategies. In J. Cassidy & P. Shaver (Eds.), *Handbook of attachment: Theory, research, and clinical implications* (pp. 520–554). New York, NY: Guilford.

Main, M., & Cassidy, J. (1988). Categories of response to reunion with the parent at age 6: Predictable from infant attachment classification and stable over a 1-month period. *Developmental Psychology, 24*, 415–426.

Main, M., & Goldwyn, R. (1984). *Adult attachment scoring and classification system*. Unpublished manuscript. University of California, Berkeley.

Main, M., & Hesse, E. (1990). Parents' unresolved traumatic experiences are related to infant disorganized/disoriented attachment status: Is frightened and/or frightening behavior the linking mechanism? In M. T. Greenberg, D. Cicchetti, & E. M. Cummings (Eds.), *Attachment in the preschool years* (pp. 161–182). Chicago, IL: University of Chicago Press.

Malatesta, C., Culver, C., Tesman, J., & Shepard, B. (1989). The development of emotion expression during the first two years of life. *Monograph of the Social Research in Child Development, 54*(1-2), 1–103.

Matos, M., & Pinto-Gouveia, J. (2010). Shame as a traumatic memory. *Clinical Psychology and Psychotherapy, 17*, 299–312.

McCann, I. L., & Pearlman, L. S. (1990). *Psychological trauma and the adult survivor*. New York, NY: Brunner/Mazel.

McClellan, J., Adams, J., Douglas, D., McCurry, C., & Storck, M. (1995). Clinical characteristics related to severity of sexual abuse: A study of seriously mentally ill youth. *Child Abuse and Neglect, 19*, 1245–1254.

McDougall, W. (1926). *An outline of abnormal psychology*. London, UK: Methuen.

McDowell, D. M., Levin, F. R., & Nunes, E. V. (1999). Dissociative identity disorder and substance abuse: The forgotten relationship. *Journal of Psychoactive Drugs, 31*, 71–83.

McWilliams, N. (1999). *Psychoanalytic case formulation*. New York, NY: Guilford.

Meadow, R. (1977). Munchausen syndrome by proxy: The hinterlands of child abuse. *The Lancet 310*, 343–345.

Messer, S. B. (2002). A psychodynamic perspective on resistance in psychotherapy: *Vive la Résistance. Journal of Clinical Psychology, 58*, 157–163.

Middleton, W. (2013). Ongoing incestuous abuse during adulthood. *Journal of Trauma and Dissociation, 14*, 251–272.

Middleton, W. (2014). Parent-child incest that extends into adulthood: A survey of international press reports, 2007–2012. In V. Şar, W. Middleton, & M. Dorahy (Eds.), *Global perspectives on Dissociative Disorders: Individual and societal oppression* (pp. 45–64). London, UK: Routledge.

Middleton, W., Seager, L., McGurrin, P., Williams, M., & Chambers, R. (2015). Dissociation, shame, complex PTSD, child maltreatment and intimate relationship self-concept in dissociative disorder, chronic PTSD and mixed psychiatric groups. *Journal of Affective Disorders, 172,* 195–203.

Miller, W. R., & Rollnick, S. (2012). *Motivational interviewing: Helping people change* (3rd ed.). New York, NY: Guilford.

Miller-Karas, E. (2015). *Building resilience to trauma: The Trauma and Community Resiliency Models.* New York, NY: Routledge.

Mitmansgruber, H., Beck, T. N., Höfer, S., & Schüßler, G. (2009). When you don't like what you feel: Experiential avoidance, mindfulness and meta-emotion in emotion regulation. *Personality and Individual Differences, 46,* 448–453.

Moskowitz, A., Schäfer, I., & Dorahy, M. (Eds.) (2008). *Psychosis, trauma and dissociation: Emerging perspectives on severe psychopathology.* New York, NY: Wiley.

Mueller-Pfeiffer, C., Rufibach, K., Perron, N., Wyss, D., Kuenzler, C., Prezewowsky, C., Pitman, R. K., & Rufer, M. (2012). Global functioning and disability in dissociative disorders. *Psychiatry Research. 200,* 475-481.

Muenzenmaier, K., Struening, E., Ferber, J., & Meyer, I. (1993). Childhood abuse and neglect among women outpatients with chronic mental illness. *Hospital and Community Psychiatry, 44,* 666–670.

Muller, R. T. (2010). *Trauma and the avoidant client: Attachment based strategies for healing.* New York, NY: Norton.

Myers, D., & Hayes, J. A. (2006). Effects of therapist general self-disclosure and countertransference disclosure on ratings of the therapist and sessions. *Psychotherapy: Theory, Research, Practice, and Training, 43,* 173–185.

Myrick, A. C., Brand, B. L., & Putnam, F. W. (2013). For better or worse: The role of revictimization and stress in the course of treatment for dissociative disorders. *Journal of Trauma & Dissociation, 14,* 375–389.

Myrick, A. C., Chasson, G. S., Lanius, R. A., Leventhal, B., & Brand, B. L. (2015). Treatment of complex dissociative disorders: A comparison of interventions reported by community therapists versus those recommended by experts. *Journal of Trauma and Dissociation, 16,* 51–67.

Nathanson, D. L. (Ed.). (1987). *The many faces of shame.* New York, NY: Guilford.

Nathanson, D. L. (1989). Understanding what is hidden: Shame in sexual abuse. *Psychiatric Clinics of North America, 12,* 381–388.

Nathanson, D. L. (1992). *Shame and pride: Affect, sex, and the birth of the self.* New York, NY: Norton.

Nathanson, D. L. (1997). Affect theory and the compass of shame. In M. R. Lansky & A. P. Morrison (Eds.), *The widening scope of shame* (pp. 339–354). Mahwah, NJ: Analytic Press.

Nemiah, J. C. (1991). Dissociation, conversion, and somatization. *American Psychiatric Press Review of Psychiatry, 10,* 248–260.

Nijenhuis, E. R. S. (2000). Somatoform dissociation: Major symptoms of dissociative disorders. *Journal of Trauma & Dissociation, 1*(4), 7–32.

Nijenhuis, E. R. S. (2004). *Somatoform dissociation: Phenomena, measurement, and theoretical issues.* New York, NY: Norton.

Nijenhuis, E. R. S. (2010). The scoring and interpretation of the SDQ-20 and SDQ-5. *Activitas Nervosa Superior, 52*(1), 24–28.

Nijenhuis, E. R. S. (2015). *The trinity of trauma: Ignorance, fragility, and control: The evolving concept of trauma/The concept and facts of dissociation in trauma.* Göttingen, Germany: Vandenhoeck & Ruprecht.

Nijenhuis, E. R. S., Spinhoven, P., Van Dyck, R., Van der Hart, O., & Vanderlinden, J. (1996). The development and the psychometric characteristics of the Somatoform Dissociation Questionnaire (SDQ-20). *Journal of Nervous and Mental Disease, 184,* 688–694.

Nijenhuis, E. R. S., Spinhoven, P., Van Dyck, R., Van der Hart, O., & Vanderlinden, J. (1997). The development of the somatoform dissociation questionnaire (SDQ-5) as a screening instrument for dissociative disorders. *Acta Psychiatrica Scandinavia, 96*(5), 311–318.

Nijenhuis, E. R. S., & Van der Hart, O. (2011). Defining dissociation in trauma. *Journal of Trauma & Dissociation, 12,* 469–473.

Nijenhuis, E. R. S., Van der Hart, O., & Kruger, K. (2002). The psychometric characteristics of the traumatic experiences checklist (TEC): First findings among psychiatric outpatients. *Clinical Psychology and Psychotherapy, 9,* 200–210.

Nijenhuis, E. R. S., Van der Hart, O. & Steele, K. (2002). The emerging psychobiology of trauma-related dissociation and dissociative disorders. In H. D'haenen, J. A. den Boer, & P. Willner (Eds.), *Biological Psychiatry* (pp. 1079–1098). Chicester, NY: Wiley.

Norcross, J. C., & Lambert, M. J. (2011). Psychotherapy relationships that work II. *Psychotherapy, 48*(1), 4–8.

Norcross, J. C., & Wampold, B. E. (2011). Evidence-based therapy relationships: Research conclusions and clinical practices. *Psychotherapy, 48*(1), 98–102.

Nouri, N. (2013). *Psychologists' knowledge of the impact of shame on psychopathology and treatment* (Doctoral dissertation, Alliant International University). Retrieved from ProQuest Dissertations and Theses database. (UMI No. 3567605)

Ochberg, F. (1996). The counting method for ameliorating traumatic memories. *Journal of Traumatic Stress, 9,* 873–880.

Ogawa, J. R., Sroufe, L. A., Weinfield, N. S., Carlson, E. A., & Egeland, B. (1997). Development and the fragmented self: Longitudinal study of dissociative symptomatology in a nonclinical sample. *Development and Psychopathology, 9,* 855–879.

Ogden, P., & Fisher, J. (2015). *Sensorimotor psychotherapy: Interventions for trauma and attachment.* New York, NY: Norton.

Ogden, P., & Minton, K. (2002). Sensorimotor approach to processing traumatic memory. In C. R. Figley (Ed.), *Brief treatments for the traumatized: A project of the Green Cross Foundation* (pp. 125–147). Westport, CT: Greenwood Press/Greenwood Publishing Group.

Ogden, P., Minton, K., & Pain, C. (2006). *Trauma and the body: A sensorimotor approach to psychotherapy.* New York, NY: Norton.

Ogden, T. H. (1992). *The primitive edge of experience.* Oxford, UK: Jason Aronson.

Orne, M. T. (1959). The nature of hypnosis: Artifact and essence. *Journal of Abnormal and Social Psychology, 58,* 277–299.

Orne, M. T., Dinges, D. F., & Orne, E. C. (1984). On the differential diagnosis of multiple personality in the forensic context. *International Journal of Clinical and Experimental Hypnosis, 32*(2), 118–169.

O'Shea, K. (2009). The EMDR early trauma protocol. In R. Shapiro (Ed.), *EMDR solutions II: For depression, eating disorders, performance, and more* (pp. 313–334). New York, NY: Norton.

Panksepp, J. (1998). *Affective neuroscience: The foundations of human and animal emotions.* New York, NY: Oxford University Press.

Panksepp, J. (2012). *The archaeology of mind: Neuroevolutionary origins of human emotions.* New York, NY: Norton.

Parnell, L. (2013). *Attachment-focused EMDR: Healing relational trauma.* New York, NY: Norton.

Paul, E., Tsypes, A., Eidlitz, L., Ernhout, C., & Whitlock, J. (2015). Frequency and functions of non-suicidal self-injury: Associations with suicidal thoughts and behaviors. *Psychiatry Research, 225,* 276–282.

Paulsen, S., & Lanius, U. (2014). Fractionating trauma processing: TOTEMSPOTS and other attenuating tactics. In U. F. Lanius, S. L. Paulsen, & F. M. Coringan (Eds.), *Neurobiology and treatment of traumatic dissociation* (pp. 367–382). New York, NY: Springer.

PDM Task Force. (2006). *Psychodynamic diagnostic manual*. Silver Springs, MD: Alliance of Psychoanalytic Organizations.

Pearlman, L., & Saakvitne, K. (1995). *Trauma and the therapist: Countertransference and vicarious traumatization in psychotherapy with incest survivors*. New York, NY: Norton.

Phelps, A. K. (1996). The influence of the therapeutic relationship on the process of retrieving traumatic memories of childhood sexual abuse: A qualitative study from the client's perspective. *Dissertation Abstracts International, 56*, 5779.

Phillips, M., & Frederick, C. (1995). *Healing the divided self: Clinical and Ericksonian hypnotherapy for dissociative conditions*. New York, NY: Norton.

Pinto-Gouveia, J., & Matos, M. (2011).Can shame memories become a key to identity? The centrality of shame memories predicts psychopathology. *Applied Cognitive Psychology, 25*, 281–290.

Plakun, E. M. (1998). Enactment and the treatment of abuse survivors. *Harvard Review of Psychiatry, 5*, 318–325.

Pope, K. S. (1994). *Sexual involvement with therapists: Patient assessment, subsequent therapy, forensics*. Washington, DC: American Psychological Association.

Pope, K. S., & Feldman-Summers, S. (1992). National survey of psychologists' sexual and physical abuse history and their evaluation of training and competence in these areas. *Professional Psychology: Research and Practice, 23*, 353–361.

Pope, K. S., & Vasquez, M. J. T. (2005). *How to survive and thrive as a therapist: Information, ideas, and resources for psychologists in practice*. Washington, DC: American Psychological Association.

Pope, K. S., & Vasquez, M. J. T. (2011). *Ethics in psychotherapy and counseling: A practical guide* (4th ed.). New York, NY: Wiley.

Porges, S. W. (1995). Orienting in a defensive world: Mammalian modifications of our evolutionary heritage: A polyvagal theory. *Psychophysiology, 32*, 301–318.

Porges, S. W. (2001). The Polyvagal Theory: Phylogenetic substrates of a social nervous system. *International Journal of Psychophysiology, 42*, 123–146.

Porges, S. W. (2003). Social engagement and attachment: A phylogenetic perspective; roots of mental illness in children. *Annals of the New York Academy of Sciences, 1008*, 31–47.

Porges, S. W. (2004). Neuroception: A subconscious system for detecting threat and safety. *Zero to Three: Bulletin of the National Center for Clinical Infant Programs, 24*, 9–24.

Porges, S. W. (2011). *The Polyvagal Theory: Neurophysiological foundations of emotions, attachment, communication, and self-regulation*. New York, NY: Norton.

Putnam, F. W. (1989). *Diagnosis and treatment of multiple personality disorder*. New York, NY: Guilford.

Putnam, F. W. (1997). *Dissociation in children and adolescents: A developmental perspective*. New York, NY: Guilford.

Quintana, S. M. (1993). Toward an expanded and updated conceptualization of termination: Implications for short-term, individual psychotherapy. *Professional Psychology: Research and Practice, 24*, 426–432.

Ragusea, S. A. (2013). Creating a professional living will for psychologists. In G. P. Koocher, J. C. Norcross, & B. A. Greene (Eds.), *Psychologists' desk reference* (3rd ed., pp. 677–681). New York, NY: Oxford University Press.

Rizvi, S. L., & Linehan, M. M. (2005). The treatment of maladaptive shame in Borderline Personality Disorder: A pilot study of "opposite action." *Cognitive and Behavioral Practice, 12*(4), 437–447.

Rodewald, F., Dell, P. F., Wilhelm-Gößling, C., & Gast, U. (2011). Are major dissociative disorders characterized by a qualitatively different kind of dissociation? *Journal of Trauma & Dissociation, 12*, 9–24.

Rodewald, F., Wilhelm-Gößling, C., Emrich, H. M., Reddemann, L., & Gast, U. (2011). Axis-I comorbidity in female patients with dissociative identity disorder and dissociative identity disorder not otherwise specified. *Journal of Nervous and Mental Disease, 199*, 122–131.

Roe, D., Dekel, R., Harel, G., Fennig, S., & Fennig, S. (2006). Clients' feelings during termination of psychodynamically oriented psychotherapy. *Bulletin of the Menninger Clinic, 70*(1), 68–81.

Rose, S. M., Peabody, C. G., & Stratigeas, B. (1991). Undetected abuse among intensive case management clients. *Hospital and Community Psychiatry, 42*, 499–503.

Ross, C. A. (1995). Diagnosis of dissociative identity disorder. In L. M. Cohen, J. N. Berzoff, & M. R. Elin (Eds.), *Dissociative identity disorder: Theoretical and treatment controversies* (pp. 261–284). Lanham, MD: Jason Aronson.

Ross, C. A. (1997). *Dissociative identity disorder: Diagnosis, clinical features, and treatment of multiple personality*. New York, NY: Wiley.

Ross, C. A., Heber, S., Norton, G. R., & Anderson, G. (1989). Somatic symptoms in multiple personality disorder. *Psychosomatics, 30*(2), 154–160.

Ross, C. A., Heber, S., Norton, G. R., Anderson, B., Anderson, G., & Barchet, P. (1989). The dissociative disorders interview schedule: A structured interview. *Dissociation, 2*, 169–189.

Ross, C. A., Miller, S. D., Reagor, P., Bjornson, L., Fraser, G. A., & Anderson, G. (1990). Schneiderian symptoms in multiple personality disorder and schizophrenia. *Comprehensive Psychiatry, 31*, 111–118.

Ross, T. A. (1941). *Lectures on war neuroses*. Baltimore, MD: Williams & Wilkins.

Rossman, M. L. (1987). *Healing yourself: A step-by-step program for better health through imagery*. New York, NY: Walker.

Rothschild, B. (2000). *The body remembers: The psychophysiology of trauma and trauma treatment*. New York, NY: Norton.

Rothschild, B. (2006). *Help for the helper: The psychophysiology of compassion fatigue and vicarious trauma*. New York, NY: Norton.

Ruismäki, M., & Mankila, P. (2013, November). *Stabilization group for dissociative parents*. Paper presented at the 30th Annual Conference of the International Society for the Study of Trauma and Dissociation, Baltimore, MD.

Saakvitne, K .W., & Pearlman, L. A. (1996). *Transforming the pain: A workbook on vicarious traumatization*. New York, NY: Norton.

Sachs, R. G. (1986). The adjunctive role of social support systems in the treatment of multiple personality disorder. In B. G. Braun (Ed.), *Treatment of multiple personality disorder* (pp. 157–174). Washington, DC: American Psychiatric Press.

Sakheim, D. (1996). Clinical aspects of sadistic ritual abuse. In L. K. Michelson & W. J. Ray (Eds.), *Handbook of dissociation: Theoretical, empirical, and clinical perspectives* (pp. 569–594). New York, NY: Plenum Press.

Şar, V. (2011). Epidemiology of dissociative disorders: An overview. *Epidemiology Research International, 2011*, 1-8; doi: 404538.

Sar, V., Tutkun, H., Alyanak, B., Bakim, B., & Baral, I. (2000). Frequency of dissociative disorders among psychiatric outpatients in Turkey. *Comprehensive Psychiatry, 41*, 216-222.

Schoenewolf, G. (1993). *Counterresistance: The therapist's interference with the therapeutic progress*. Northvale, NJ: Jason Aronson.

Schore, A. N. (1991). Early superego development: The emergence of shame and narcissistic affect regulation in the practicing period. *Psychoanalysis and Contemporary Thought, 14*, 187–250.

Schore, A.N. (1994). *Affect regulation and the origin of the self*. Hillsdale, NJ: Erlbaum.

Schore, A. N. (2003). *Affect regulation and the development of the self*. New York, NY: Norton.

Schore, A. N. (2009). Right-brain affect regulation: An essential mechanism of development, trauma, dissociation, and psychotherapy. In D. Fosha, D. Siegel, & M. Solomon (Eds.), *The healing power of emotion: Affective neuroscience, development and clinical practice* (pp. 112–144). New York, NY: Norton.

Schore, A. N. (2012). *The science of the art of psychotherapy*. New York, NY: Norton.

Schwartz, H. L. (2000). *Dialogues with forgotten voices: Relational perspectives on child abuse trauma and treatment of dissociative disorders*. New York, NY: Basic Books.

Schwartz, H. L. (2013). *The alchemy of wolves and sheep: A relational approach to internalized perpetration for complex trauma survivors*. New York, NY: Routledge.

Schwartz, R. (1997). *Internal family systems therapy*. New York, NY: Guilford.

Serban, G. (1992). Multiple personality: An issue for forensic psychiatry. *American Journal of Psychotherapy, 46*(2), 269–280.

Shapiro, F. (1994). *Eye Movement Desensitization and Reprocessing Level I Training Manual*. Watsonville, CA: EMDR Institute.

Shapiro, F. (1996). *Eye Movement Desensitization and Reprocessing Level II Training Manual*. Watsonville, CA: EMDR Institute.

Shapiro, F. (2001). *Eye movement desensitization and reprocessing (EMDR): Basic principles, protocols, and procedures* (2nd ed.). New York, NY: Guilford.

Shaw, D. (2013). *Traumatic narcissism: Relational systems of subjugation*. New York, NY: Routledge.

Siegel, D. J. (2010a). *Mindsight: The new science of personal transformation*. New York, NY: Bantam Books.

Siegel, D. J. (2010b). *The mindful therapist: A clinician's guide to mindsight and neural integration*. New York, NY: Norton.

Siegel, D. J. (2015). *The developing mind: How relationships and the brain interact to shape who we are* (2nd ed.). New York, NY: Norton.

Solomon, J., & George, C. (1996). Defining the caregiving system: Toward a theory of caregiving. *Infant Mental Health Journal, 17*, 183–197.

Solomon, J., & George, C. (2011). The disorganized attachment-caregiving system: Dysregulation of adaptive processes at multiple levels. In J. Solomon & C. George (Eds.), *Disorganized attachment and caregiving* (pp. 3–24). New York, NY: Guilford.

Somer, E. (2002). Maladaptive daydreaming: A qualitative inquiry. *Journal of Contemporary Psychotherapy, 32*, 197–212.

Spiegel, D. (1981). Vietnam grief work using hypnosis. *American Journal of Clinical Hypnosis, 12*, 33–40.

Spiegel, D. (1990). Trauma, dissociation, and hypnosis. In R. P. Kluft (Ed.), *Incest-related syndromes of adult psychopathology* (pp. 247–261). Arlington, VA: American Psychiatric Association.

Spiegel, H., & Spiegel, D. (1978). *Trance and treatment: Clinical uses of hypnosis*. New York, NY: Basic Books.

Spitzer, C., Liss, H., Dudeck, M., Orlob, S., Gillner, M., Hamm, A., & Freyberger, H. J. (2003). Dissociative experiences and disorders in forensic inpatients. *International Journal of Law and Psychiatry, 26*(3), 281–288.

Sroufe, A. L. (1977). Attachment as an organizational construct. *Child Development, 48*, 1184–1199.

Sroufe, L. A. (1990). An organizational perspective on the self. In D. Cicchetti & M. Beeghly (Eds.), *The self in transition: Infancy to childhood* (pp. 281-307). Chicago, IL: University of Chicago Press.

Sroufe, A. L., Fox, N. E., & Pancake, V. R. (1983). Attachment and dependency in developmental perspective. *Child Development, 54*, 1615–1627.

Stark, M. (2000). *Modes of therapeutic action*. New York, NY: Jason Aronson.

Stark, M. (2002). *Working with resistance* (2nd ed.). London, UK: Rowman & Littlefield.

Stark, M. (2006). Transformation of relentless hope: A relational approach to sadomasochism. Retrieved from http://www.lifespanlearn.org/documents/STARKtranform.pdf

Steele, K. (1989). Sitting with the shattered soul. *Pilgrimage: Journal of Psychotherapy and Personal Exploration, 15*, 19–25.

Steele, K. (2009). The road is made by walking: A quarter century of being with dissociation. *Voices: Journal of the American Academy of Psychotherapists, 45*(2), 6–12.

Steele, K. (2014, September 21). *Alternative relational models for trauma-informed psychotherapy: Beyond the parent-child attachment paradigm.* Lecture presented at the Congress on Attachment and Trauma, Rome, Italy.

Steele, K., & Colrain, J. (1990). Abreactive work with sexual abuse survivors: Concepts and techniques. In M. A. Hunter (Ed.), *The sexually abused male* (Vol. II, pp. 1–55). Lexington, MA: Lexington Press.

Steele, K., Dorahy, M. J., Van der Hart, O., & Nijenhuis, E. R. S. (2009). Dissociation versus alterations in consciousness: Related but different concepts. In P. F. Dell & J. A. O'Neil (Eds.), *Dissociation and the dissociative disorders: DSM-V and beyond* (pp. 155–169). New York, NY: Routledge.

Steele, K., & Van der Hart, O. (2013). Understanding attachment, trauma and dissociation in complex developmental trauma disorders. In A. Danquah & K. Berry (Eds.), *Using attachment theory in adult mental health: A practical guide* (pp. 78–94). Abingdon, UK: Routledge.

Steele, K., Van der Hart, O., & Nijenhuis, E. R. S. (2001). Dependency in the treatment of complex posttraumatic stress disorder and dissociative disorders. *Journal of Trauma and Dissociation, 2*(4), 79–116.

Steele, K., Van der Hart, O., & Nijenhuis, E. R. S. (2005). Phase-oriented treatment of structural dissociation in complex traumatization: Overcoming trauma-related phobias. *Journal of Trauma and Dissociation, 6*(3), 11–53.

Steinberg, M. (1994). *Therapist's guide to the Structured Clinical Interview for DSM-IV Dissociative Disorders (SCID-D).* Washington, DC: American Psychiatric Press.

Steinberg, M. (1995). *Handbook for assessment of dissociation: A clinical guide.* Washington, DC: American Psychiatric Press.

Steinberg, M. (2004). Systematic assessment of posttraumatic dissociation: The Structured Clinical Interview for DSM-IV Dissociative Disorders. In J. P. Wilson & T. M. Keane (Eds.), *Assessing psychological trauma and PTSD* (2nd ed., pp. 122–143). New York, NY: Guilford.

Steinberg, M., Cicchetti, D., Buchanan, J., & Hall, P. (1993). Clinical assessment of dissociative symptoms and disorders: The Structured Clinical Interview for DSM-IV Dissociative Disorders (SCID-D). *Dissociation: Progress in the Dissociative Disorders, 6*(1), 3–15.

Steinberg, M., & Spiegel, H. D. (2008). Advances in assessment: The differential diagnosis of dissociative identity disorder and schizophrenia. In A. Moskowitz, I. Schäfer, & M. J. Dorahy (Eds.), *Psychosis, trauma and dissociation: Emerging perspectives on severe psychopathology* (pp. 177–189). New York, NY: Wiley-Blackwell.

Stern, D. N. (2004). *The present moment in psychotherapy and everyday life.* New York, NY: Norton.

Stern, D. N., (2010). *Partners in thought: Working with unformulated experience, dissociation and enactment.* New York, NY: Routledge.

Stoler, D. R., & Hill, B. A. (2013). *Coping with concussion and mild traumatic brain injury: A guide to living with the challenges associated with post concussion syndrome and brain trauma.* New York, NY: Avery.

Strean, H. S. (1993). *Resolving counterresistances in psychotherapy.* New York, NY: Routledge.

Swett, C., Jr., Surrey, J., & Cohen, C. (1990). Sexual and physical abuse histories and psychiatric symptoms among male psychiatric outpatients. *American Journal of Psychiatry, 147,* 632–636.

Talbot, J. A., Talbot, N. L., & Tu, X. (2005). Shame-proneness as a diathesis for dissociation in women with histories of childhood sexual abuse. *Journal of Traumatic Stress, 17,* 445–448.

Talbot, N. L. (1996). Women sexually abused as children: The centrality of shame issues and treatment implications. *Psychotherapy: Theory, Research, Practice, Training, 33*(1), 11–18.

Tangney, J. P., & Fischer, K. W. (Eds.). (1995). *Self-conscious emotions: The psychology of shame, guilt, embarrassment, and pride.* New York, NY: Guilford.

Target, M., & Fonagy, P. (1996). Playing with reality, II: The development of psychic reality from a theoretical perspective. *International Journal of Psycho-analysis, 77,* 459–479.

Teachman, B. A., & Clerkin, E. M. (2010). A case formulation approach to resolve treatment complications. In M. W. Otto & S. G. Hofmann (Eds.), *Avoiding treatment failures in the anxiety disorders* (pp. 7–30). New York, NY: Springer.

Thomas, A. (2001). Factitious and malingered Dissociative Identity Disorder: Clinical features observed in 18 cases. *Journal of Trauma and Dissociation, 2,* 59–77.

Tijdink, D., & Cuijpers, D. (2016). Group program for partners of patients with dissociative disorders. *Proceedings of the 5th Bi-Annual Conference of the European Society for Trauma and Dissociation,* 135 Amsterdam, the Netherlands.

Tomkins, S. S. (1963). *Affect imagery consciousness* (Vol. II: The negative affects). New York, NY: Springer.

Trevarthen, C. (1980). The foundations of intersubjectivity. In D. R. Olsen (Ed.), *The social foundations of language and thought* (pp. 216–242). New York, NY: Norton.

Trevarthen, C., & Aitken, K. J. (1994). Brain development, infant communication, and empathy disorders: Intrinsic factors in child mental health. *Development and Psychopathology, 6,* 597–633.

Tronick, E., & Cohn, J. (1989). Infant-mother face-to-face interaction: Age and gender differences in coordination and miscoordination. *Child Development, 59,* 85–92.

Tsai, M., & Kohlenberg. R. J. (2009). *A guide to functional analytic psychotherapy: Awareness, courage, love and behaviorism.* New York, NY: Springer.

Twombly, J. (2000). Incorporating EMDR and EMDR adaptations in the treatment of Dissociative Identity Disorder. *Journal of Trauma and Dissociation, 1*(2), 61–81.

Van Denburg, T. F., & Kiesler, D. J. (2002). An interpersonal communication perspective on resistance in psychotherapy. *Journal of Clinical Psychology, 58,* 195–205.

Van Derbur, M. (2003). *Miss America by day: Lessons learned from ultimate betrayals and unconditional love.* Denver, CO: Oak Hill Ridge Press.

Van der Hart, O. (1983). *Rituals in psychotherapy: Transition and continuity.* New York, NY: Irvington.

Van der Hart, O. (Ed.). (1986). *Coping with loss.* New York, NY: Irvington.

Van der Hart, O. (Ed.). (1991). *Trauma, dissociatie en hypnose* [Trauma, dissociation and hypnosis]. Lisse, the Netherlands: Swets & Zeitlinger.

Van der Hart, O. (2012). The use of imagery in Phase 1 treatment of clients with complex dissociative disorders. *European Journal of Psychotraumatology, 3,* 1-8. doi:10.3402/ejpt.v3i0.8458

Van der Hart, O. & Boon, S. (1997). Treatment strategies for complex dissociative disorders: Two Dutch case examples. *Dissociation, 9*(3), 157-165.

Van der Hart, O., Boon, S., & Heijtmajer, J. O. (1997). Ritual abuse in European countries: A clinician's perspective. In G. A. Fraser (Ed.), *The dilemma of ritual abuse: Cautions and guides for therapists* (pp. 137–166). Washington: American Psychiatric Press.

Van der Hart, O. & Brown, P. (1992). Abreaction re-evaluated. *Dissociation, 5*(3), 127–140.

Van der Hart, O., Brown, P., & Van der Kolk, B. A. (1989). Pierre Janet's treatment of post-traumatic stress. *Journal of Traumatic Stress, 2,* 379–396.

Van der Hart, O., & Dorahy, M. (2009). Dissociation: History of a concept. In P. F. Dell & J. A. O'Neill (Eds.), *Dissociative disorders: DSM-V and beyond* (pp. 3–26). New York, NY: Routledge.

Van der Hart, O., Groenendijk, M., Gonzalez, A., Mosquera, D., & Solomon, R. (2014). Dissociation of the personality and EMDR therapy in complex trauma-related disorders: Applications in Phase 2 and 3. *Journal of EMDR Practice and Research, 8*(1), 33–48.

Van der Hart, O., & Nijenhuis, E. R. S. (1999). Bearing witness to uncorroborated trauma: The clinician's development of reflective belief. *Professional Psychology: Research and Practice, 30,* 37-44.

Van der Hart, O., Nijenhuis, E. R. S., & Steele, K. (2006). *The haunted self: Structural dissociation of the personality and treatment of chronic traumatization.* New York, NY: Norton.

Van der Hart, O., & Steele, K. (1997). Time distortions in dissociative identity disorder: Janetian concepts and treatment. *Dissociation, 10*(2), 93-105.

Van der Hart, O., & Steele, K. (1999). Relieving or reliving childhood trauma: A commentary on Miltenburg and Singer (1997). *Theory and Psychology, 9*, 533-540.

Van der Hart, O., Steele, K., Boon, S., & Brown, P. (1993). The treatment of traumatic memories: Synthesis, realization and integration. *Dissociation, 6*, 162–180.

Van der Hart, O., & Witztum, E. (2008). Dissociative psychosis: Clinical and theoretical aspects. In A. Moskowitz, I. Schäfer, & M. Dorahy (Eds.), *Dissociation and psychosis: Multiple perspectives on a complex relationship* (pp. 257–269). London, UK: Wiley.

Van der Kloet, D., Giesbrecht, T., Franck, E., Van Gastel, A., De Volder, I., Van Den Eede, F.,Verschuere, B., & Merckelbach, H. (2013). Dissociative symptoms and sleep parameters: An all-night polysomnography study in patients with insomnia. *Comprehensive Psychiatry, 54*, 658–664.

Van der Kolk, B. A. (1987). The separation cry and the trauma response: Developmental issues in the psychobiology of attachment and separation. In B. A. van der Kolk (Ed.), *Psychological trauma* (pp. 31–62). Washington, DC: American Psychiatric Press.

Van der Kolk, B. A. (1994) The body keeps the score: Memory and the evolving psychobiology of posttraumatic stress. *Harvard Review of Psychiatry, 1*, 253–265.

Van der Kolk, B. A. (2014). *The body keeps the score: Brain, mind and body in the healing of trauma.* New York, NY: Viking.

Van der Kolk, B. A., & Fisler, R. (1995). Dissociation and the fragmentary nature of traumatic memories: Overview and exploratory study. *Journal of Traumatic Stress, 8,* 505–525.

Van der Kolk, B. A., & Van der Hart, O. (1991). The intrusive past: The flexibility of memory and the engraving of trauma. *American Imago, 48,* 425–545.

Van Dijke, A. (2008). The clinical assessment and treatment of trauma-related self- and affect dysregulation. In A. Vingerhoets, & J. Denollet (Eds.), *Emotion regulation: Conceptual and clinical issues.* New York, NY: Springer.

Van Dijke, A., Ford, J. D., Van der Hart, O., Van Son, M., Van der Heijden, P., & Bühring, M. (2010). Affect dysregulation in borderline personality disorder and somatoform disorder: Differentiating under- and over-regulation. *Journal of Personality Disorders, 24* (3), 296–311.

Van Dijke, A., Van der Hart, O., Ford, J. D., Van Son, M., Van der Heijden, P., & Bühring, M. (2010). Affect dysregulation and dissociation in borderline personality disorder and somatoform disorder: Differentiating inhibitory and excitatory experiencing states. *Journal of Trauma and Dissociation, 11*, 424–443.

Vanderlinden, J. (1993). *Dissociative experiences, trauma, and hypnosis: Research findings and applications in eating disorders.* Delft, the Netherlands: Eburon.

Vanderlinden, J., Spinhoven, P., Vandereycken, W., & van Dyck, R. (1995). Dissociative and hypnotic experiences in eating disorder patients: An exploratory study. *American Journal of Clinical Hypnosis, 38*, 97–108.

Van Minnen, A., Arntz, A., & Keijsers, G. P. (2006). Prolonged exposure in patients with chronic PTSD: Predictors of treatment outcome and dropout. *Behaviour Research and Therapy, 40*, 439–457.

Van Minnen, A., Harned, M. S., Zoellner, L., & Mills, K. (2012). Examining potential contraindications for prolonged exposure therapy for PTSD. *European Journal of Psychotraumatology, 3.* doi:10.3402/ejpt.v3i0.18805

Vasquez, M. J. T., Bingham, R. P., & Barnett, J. E. (2008). Psychotherapy termination: Clinical and ethical responsibilities. *Journal of Clinical Psychology, 64*, 653–665.

Vasterling, J. J., Bryant, R. A., & Keane, T. M. (Eds.). (2012). *PTSD and mild traumatic brain injury.* New York, NY: Guilford.

Vesper, J. G. (1991). The use of healing ceremonies in the treatment of multiple personality disorder. *Dissociation, 4*(2), 109-114.

Walker, L. E. (2009). *The battered woman syndrome* (3rd ed.). New York, NY: Springer.

Waller, G., Ohanian, V., Meyer, C., Everill, J., & Rouse, H. (2001). The utility of dimensional and categorical approaches to understanding dissociation in the eating disorders. *British Journal of Clinical Psychology, 40*, 387–397.

Waller, N. G., Putnam, F. W., & Carlson, E. B. (1996). Types of dissociation and dissociative types. *Psychological Methods, 1*, 300–321.

Wallin, D. J. (2007). *Attachment in psychotherapy.* New York, NY: Guilford.

Walser, R. D., & Hayes, S. (2006). Acceptance and Commitment Therapy in the treatment of posttraumatic stress disorder. In V. M. Follette & J. I. Ruzek (Eds.), *Cognitive behavioral therapies for trauma* (2nd ed.) (pp. 146–172). New York, NY: Guilford.

Walsh, B. W. (2014) *Treating self-injury: A practical guide* (2nd ed.). New York, NY: Guilford.

Wampold, B. E. (2001). *The great psychotherapy debate: Models, methods, and findings.* Mahwah, NJ: Erlbaum.

Wampold, B. E., Imel, Z. E., Bhati, K. S., & Johnson-Jennings, M. D. (2007). Insight as a common factor. In L. G. Castonguay & C. Hill (Eds.), *Insight in psychotherapy* (pp. 119–139). Washington, DC: American Psychological Association.

Watkins, H. H., & Watkins, J. G. (1993). Ego-state therapy in the treatment of dissociative disorders. In R. P. Kluft & C. G. Fine (Eds.), *Clinical perspectives on multiple personality disorder* (pp. 277–299). Washington, DC: American Psychiatric Press.

Watkins, J. G. (1971). The affect bridge: A hypnoanalytic technique. *International Journal of Clinical and Experimental Hypnosis, 19*, 21-27.

Watkins, J. G., & Watkins, H. H. (1991). Hypnosis and ego-state therapy. In P. Keller, S. Heyman (Eds.), *Clinical practice: A source book*, Vol. 10 (pp. 23-37). Sarasota, FL: Professional Resource Exchange.

Watkins, J. G., & Watkins, H. H. (1997). *Ego states: Theory and therapy.* New York, NY: Norton.

Werbart, A. (1997). Separation, termination process and long-term outcome in psychotherapy with severely disturbed patients. *Bulletin of the Menninger Clinic, 61*(1), 16–43.

Westen, D. (1998). Case formulation and personality disorders: Two processes or one? In J. W. Barron (Ed.), *Making diagnosis meaningful: Enhancing evaluation and treatment of psychological disorders* (pp. 111–137). Washington, DC: American Psychological Association.

Wilson, J. P., & Lindy, J. D. (Eds.). (1994). *Countertransference in the treatment of PTSD.* New York, NY: Guilford.

Wilson, J. P., & Thomas, R. B. (2004). *Empathy in the treatment of trauma and PTSD.* New York, NY: Routledge.

Winnicott, D. W. (1968). *The child, the family, and the outside world.* Harmondsworth, UK: Penguin Books.

Wolpe, J. (1982). *Practice of behavior therapy* (3rd ed.). New York, NY: Pergamon Press.

Woody, S. R., Detweiler-Bedell, J., Teachman, B. A., & O'Hearn, T. (2003). *Treatment planning in psychotherapy: Taking the guesswork out of clinical care.* New York, NY: Guilford.

Wright, M. E., & Wright, B. A. (1987). *Clinical practice of hypnotherapy.* New York, NY: Guilford.

Wurmser, L. (1987). Shame, the veiled companion of narcissism. In D. L. Nathanson (Ed.), *The many faces of shame* (pp. 64–92). New York, NY: Guilford.

Yalom, I. D. (1980). *Existential psychotherapy.* New York, NY: Basic Books.

Young, J., & Brown, G. (2001). *Young Schema Questionnaire: Special edition.* New York, NY: Cognitive Therapy Center of New York.

Young, J., Klosko, J. S., Weishaar, M. E. (2003). *Schema therapy: A practitioner's guide.* New York, NY: Guilford.

Zur, O. (2007). *Boundaries in psychotherapy: Ethical and clinical explorations.* Washington, DC: American Psychological Association.

INDEX

In this index, *f* denotes figure and *t* denotes table.

Boon, S., xi, 18, 95-97, 99-100, 103-4, 109, 111, 117, 119, 127, 129, 140, 154, 157, 180-81, 184, 193, 201, 204-5, 279, 345-46, 356, 368, 372, 410, 412-13, 425, 427, 437-38, 445, 467, 472, 484, 497, 504
boundaries
 abusive behavior management and, 340, 342, 350
 appropriate communication and, 149–150
 dependency and repair of, 282–87
 importance of, 146–47, 173–74
 setting and maintaining, 40–41, 42t, 43
 sexualized parts and, 401, 403, 404
 in treatment planning, 146–47, 152–53
 unsafe behaviors and, 371
Bowlby, J., 14, 256, 266
Brach, T., 124
bracketing, 447
Brady, K., 108
Brand, B., x-xi, xv, 95, 97, 103, 106, 109, 136, 141, 179, 202, 210, 410, 466
Bratton, K., 304
Braun, B., 444, 467, 471, 476
breaking points, 16–17
Bresler, D., 438t
Bretherton, I., 131
Brewin, C., 6, 422
Briere, J., 18, 163, 496
Britner, P.,
Brodsky, A., 43
Bromberg, P., 37, 40, 59, 77, 212, 308
Brown, B., 318, 326, 328
Brown, D., 30, 163, 174-75, 179, 180, 184, 445
Brown, L., 398
burnout, 48, 414
Butler, L., 398

calm spaces. *See* safe or calm spaces
Cardeña, E., 96
caregiving, collaboration versus, 13, 70–74, 73t
 See also controlling-caregiving strategies
Carlson, E., 96, 103-4, 135, 495
case formulation, 141–43, 156
case management, psychotherapy versus, 196–97
CBT. *See* cognitive behavior therapy (CBT)
CCRT (core conflictual relational themes), 124
change, phobia of, 484–85
check ins, 150
Checklist for Evaluation of DID Treatment, 140–41
Cheek, D., 219, 250
child parts. *See* dissociative child parts
Christoffersen, M., 374
chronic crises, 271–72
Chu, J., xii, 20, 23, 47, 52, 163, 173, 176, 179-80, 184, 201, 211, 289, 370, 437
Cloitre, M., 181, 437
cognitive approaches to shame, 319–323
cognitive behavior therapy (CBT), 138, 170
cognitive resistance, 238–240
cognitive resources and deficits, 122–24
 See also insight

collaborative model of attachment, 69–72, 76–89, 84t, 90t–91t
Colrain, J., 445
common factors theory, x
communication, 173, 217–19
 See also between-session contact; emails and texts; implicit communication; language; somatic experiences
comorbidity, 101, 103, 104, 108, 138
compassion, 40, 55, 60, 62, 64, 69, 72, 76, 78, 85, 86, 110, 125, 140, 155, 157, 162, 176, 229, 249, 251, 266, 279, 309, 317, 319, 320 321-23, 325, 326, 328, 335, 360, 369, 378, 414, 424, 435, 447, 454, 472, 485
 See also self-compassion
compassion-focused therapy, 321–23
competence, 325–26
confidentiality, 149
confrontation, family of origin and, 398–99
consultation
 abusive behavior management and, 340
 anxious-avoidant dyads and, 276, 277, 278
 counterresistance, 232–33
 countertransference, 407, 414, 432
 disclosures and, 88
 emails, 219
 false-positive diagnosis, 109, 110
 ongoing victimization, 412
 reenactments and, 59–60
 therapist tolerance, 169
 unsafe behaviors, 370, 372, 382
containment strategies, 184–88, 186t–87t, 453
controlling-caregiving strategies, 54, 233, 333
 See also caregiving, collaboration versus
controlling-punitive strategies, 54, 80, 244, 333
Coons, P., 109, 110, 368, 395
Copeley, M., 445
coping skills, 477–78
 See also stabilization skills
core beliefs, 124
core conflictual relational themes (CCRT), 124
Cortina, M., 11, 13, 58, 67, 69–70
counterresistance, 230–32, 231t–32t, 235, 244
countertransference
 awareness of, 177
 boundary differences and, 173–74
 in collaborative models, 87–89, 90t–91t
 dependency and, 275–78
 goal ownership and, 154
 non-realization in therapists and, 22–24
 ongoing victimization and, 414
 with perpetrator-imitating parts, 347–350
 sexualized parts and, 407
 traumatic memory integration and, 431–32
 unsafe behaviors and, 369–372
 See also reenactments
couple relationships, 393–94
 See also sexual relationships
Courtois, C., 23, 30, 157, 163, 173, 179, 180-81, 425, 437
Cozolino, L., x, 35, 36, 63
creative therapies, 455

perpetrators
  confrontation and forgiveness of, 399
  distinguishing between internal and external, 354–55
  inner experience of rage of, 333–34
  patients as, 415
  relationship resolution with, 483–84
  treatment of insecure attachment to, 193
  See also enmeshment; victimization, ongoing
personality, 203, 216
personality organization. *See* dissociative personality organization
personification, 25, 483
phase-oriented treatment
  about, 29–30, 179–180
  Phase 1, 180–89, 182*t*, 183*t*, 186*t*–87*t*, 191
  Phase 2, 190, 192–94, 192*t*, 456, 465
  Phase 3, 190, 194–96, 195*t*, 480–81, 482
Phelps, A., 427
Phillips, M., 30, 174, 175, 202, 426, 438, 445
phobias of change, 484–85
phobias of inner experience, 155–56, 189, 190, 267–271, 306
  See also trauma-related phobias
phobia of the body, 485–87
phobic avoidance, 226–260, 231*t*–32*t*, 236*t*–37*t*, 241*t*–42*t*, 468–69
phone calls, 152, 271
physiological empathy, 62, 63, 64*t*–65*t*
Pinto-Gouveia, J., 317
PITQ (Progress in Treatment Questionnaire), 141
Plakun, E., 37
playful dissociative child parts, 298–99
Pope, K., 47, 131, 492
Porges, S., 12, 14, 77, 97
positive experiences, 168, 169, 172, 250, 280
power struggles in therapy, 244
premature termination, 491–92
presentification, 25, 168–69, 483
privacy. *See* confidentiality
process versus content, 164–66, 172, 412–13
professional will, 492
prognosis, 124, 136–140, 414
Prognosis and Treatment Progress Rating Scale for Dissociative Disorders, 499–504
progress. *See* treatment progress
Progress in Treatment Questionnaire (PITQ), 141
protection. *See* resistance
psychic equivalence, 10–11, 174
Psychodyamic Diagnostic Manual (PDM) Task Force, 119
psychoeducation
  anger and, 335
  dissociative parts, 212–13, 352–54, 402–3
  integration, 467–68
  for parents, 396
  for partners, 393–94
  shame resolution and, 318–19, 328
  traumatic memories, 439
psychological defenses, 129–130
psychological resources, 250, 325–26
  See also self-regulation

psychosis, 22, 100, 107, 108, 182, 457, 495
psychotherapy, case management versus, 196–97
PTSD, 111, 138, 180, 304, 426Putnam, F., 30, 163, 201, 476

Ragusea, S., 492
ranking or competition system, 12, 16, 307
realization
  about, 4, 420, 424
  nature of, 24–28, 28*t*–29*t*
  phase-oriented treatment and, 29–30
  somatic experiences in, 6, 7
  true-not true conflicts, 432–34
  See also guided realization; insight
reassessment, 255–56, 272, 489–490
reenactments
  case examples, 38, 61
  dependency as, 273
  internal, 356
  relational, 58–62, 59*f*, 60*t*
  sexualized parts and, 401
  therapists' experience of, 37–40
  See also countertransference
relapse prevention, 477–79
relational dysregulation, 62–63, 64*t*–65*t*
relational models in psychotherapy, 72–73, 73*t*
  See also collaborative model
relational regulation, 13, 62, 73*t*, 77, 78–83, 84*t*, 238
relationships, 52–53, 392–97, 400–407
  See also enmeshment; family of origin; parenting issues; therapeutic relationships
resistance
  assessment of, 248
  as co-creation of patient and therapist, 230–32, 231*t*–32*t*
  dependency as, 243
  in dissociative child parts, 300–301
  insight without change and, 125
  to integration, 467–472
  as phobic avoidance, 226–260, 231*t*–32*t*, 236*t*–37*t*, 241*t*–42*t*
  problems with the term of, 227–28
  as protection, 177–78
  temporary versus enduring, 234–240, 236*t*–37*t*, 258
  trauma-related phobias and, 189
  traumatic memory realization and, 423
  treatment principles for, 236*t*–37*t*, 248–260
  types and sources of, 126–27, 129, 133, 241*t*–42*t*
resource management. *See* case management, psychotherapy versus; support people
resources and needs assessments, 120–136
retraumatization, 446
  See also victimization, ongoing
rheostat, 447
rituals, 374–75, 474–75, 476–77, 484
Rizvi, S., 320
Rodewald, F., 97, 104, 119
Roe, D., 489
Rorschach, 109
Rose, S., 46

Steele, K., ii, 9, 14, 18-20, 23, 30, 49, 50, 57, 58, 68, 69, 87, 96, 97, 132, 163, 179, 181, 182, 193, 226, 228, 229, 263, 344, 425, 427, 431, 438, 445
Steinberg, M., 96, 103, 106, 496
Stern, D., 37, 69
Stoler, D., 123
Strean, H., 226, 227, 230
Structured Clinical Interview for DSM-IV Dissociative Disorders, Revised (SCID-D-R), 496
Subjective Units of Distress (SUDS), 327, 447
substitute actions, 20, 138, 367, 369-70, 373, 378
substitute beliefs, 10
suffering, as resistance, 245-47
suicidality, 206, 375-77
    See also unsafe behaviors
supervision. *See* consultation
support people, 85, 131, 453
switching
    child parts and, 296-97
    perpetrator-imitating parts and, 358
    precipitants and management of, 133-34, 221-24, 223t
    resistance and, 258-59
Swett, C., 46
symptoms
    about, 98, 100, 102, 103-4, 105t-8t
    dissociative personality organization and, 112
synthesis, 423-24
    See also guided synthesis

TADS-I. *See* Trauma and Dissociation Symptoms Interview (TADS-I)
Talbot, J., 260
Talbot, N., 304
talking through, 217-19, 224, 353, 360
talk therapies, 6
    See also cognitive behavior therapy (CBT)
Tangney, J., 309
Target, M., 10
TBI (traumatic brain injury), 122-23
Teachman, B., 119
team conflicts. *See* treatment team conflicts
TEC (Traumatic Experiences Checklist), 135
termination. *See* treatment termination
texts. *See* emails and texts
theory of structural dissociation of the personality, 423
therapeutic relationships
    anxious-avoidant dyads within, 276-78
    attachment and defense within, 53
    collaboration within, 69-72, 76-77
    D-attachment strategies within, 54, 58
    dependency needs within, 278-282
    dissociation within, 43-45, 336, 401
    distress as relational strategy within, 272-73
    enduring phobic avoidance and, 235
    fear of getting well and, 488
    importance of, 212, 263, 266
    process, not content, in, 164-66, 172

reenactments within, 37-40, 58-62, 59f, 60t
relational dysregulation and impact on, 62-63, 64t-65t
repair within, 177
safety within, 166-170
secure attachment versus dependency within, 268
shame within, 317
traumatic memories and, 427, 430, 447
unsafe behaviors and, 373, 378
    See also countertransference; relational regulation
therapist availability, 68, 79, 83, 85
    See also between-session contact; boundaries
therapists
    collaborative characteristics of, 76
    counterresistance in, 227-28, 230-32, 231t-32t, 235, 244
    disclosures by, 87-89, 90t-91t
    needs of, 45-47, 169
    over- versus under-involved, 74, 75t
    professional will for, 492
    shame in, 314-15
    toll of trauma work on, 47-50, 49t
    as trauma survivors, 47
    See also countertransference; good enough therapists; therapeutic relationships
therapist self-care, 50, 63, 64t-65t
    See also boundaries
therapist training and experience, 98-99, 110, 175
Thomas, A., 109
Thomas, R., 62-63
threats, 13-14, 434-35
    See also dependency-threat cycle
THS (Trauma History Screen), 135
Tijdink, D., 394
time distortions, 447-49
titration
    about, 191, 194
    dependency and, 274
    resistance as phobic avoidance and, 260
    traumatic memories and, 446-49
    working with angry dissociative parts and, 337-38
    See also fractionation
Tomkins, S., 303, 305, 306, 324
training. *See* therapist training and experience
trance and trance logic, 10, 174-75, 338, 411
Trauma and Dissociation Symptoms Interview (TADS-I), 115, 497
trauma history, 135-36, 420-21
Trauma History Screen (THS), 135
trauma-related phobias
    about, 19-20, 433f
    assessment of, 129
    general approaches to resolution of, 190-91
    in phase-oriented treatment, 189, 190, 193-94
    See also phobias of inner experience; phobic avoidances